TRANSLATIONS OF EARLY DOCUMENTS

SERIES I

PALESTINIAN JEWISH TEXTS

(PRE-RABBINIC)

D1457969

THE BIBLICAL

ANTIQUITIES OF PHILO

THE LIBRARY

OF

BIBLICAL STUDIES

Edited by

Harry M. Orlinsky

THE BIBLICAL ANTIQUITIES OF PHILO

NOW FIRST
TRANSLATED FROM THE OLD LATIN VERSION

BY

M. R. JAMES, LITT.D., F.B.A.

HON. LITT.D. DUBLIN, HON. LL.D. ST. ANDREWS,
PROVOST OF KING'S COLLEGE, CAMBRIDGE

Prolegomenon by
LOUIS H. FELDMAN

KTAV PUBLISHING HOUSE, Inc.
NEW YORK
1971

FIRST PUBLISHED 1917
REPRINTED BY PERMISSION OF S.P.C.K.
HOLY TRINITY CHURCH, MARYLEBONE
ROAD, LONDON N.W. 1.

NEW MATTER
COPYRIGHT © 1971

KTAV PUBLISHING HOUSE, INC.

SBN 87068-069-2

LIBRARY OF CONGRESS CATALOG CARD NUMBER: 69-13579
MANUFACTURED IN THE UNITED STATES OF AMERICA

CONTENTS

PROLEGOMENON: TABLE OF CONTENTS

PROLEGOMENON

CHAPTER I

IMPORTANCE
(*James, p.* 7)

Pseudo-Philo's *Liber Antiquitatum Biblicarum* (hereafter to be be abbreviated LAB) has at last, and deservedly, become fashionable in scholarly circles. Whereas during the three hundred years from its last reprinting in the sixteenth century until its rediscovery by Cohn at the end of the nineteenth century it was mentioned only by Conybeare, Fabricius, Furst, Pitra (*Analecta Sacra Spicilegio Solesmensi Parata*, 2 [Paris, 1884], who already, p. 321, realized its importance and argued that it deserved a place among the Pseudepigrapha), Schürer, and Steinschneider, it has, as the appended bibliography (which endeavors to be complete) shows, since the publication of James' translation in 1917 and especially since the publication of Kisch's edition in 1949 (before Kisch's publication the Latin text was rare and very difficult to obtain), become the subject of considerable study. There is good reason for this, since LAB, as Ginzberg, Bloch, and Vermès have seen, is one of the most significant links between early haggadah and rabbinic midrash. Even so, though obviously an important example of Pseudepigrapha, it is completely overlooked in the collections and commentaries of Charles, Kautzsch, Pfeiffer, and Strack-Billerbeck. And yet, if the dating arrived at by Cohn, James, and Kisch, the three scholars who have done must with LAB, is correct, LAB is, with the exception of the somewhat earlier Genesis Apocryphon, our oldest substantive midrashic work. Because the work has apparently not been tampered with by Christians, it is one of our most important sources of information for Jewish ideas and beliefs of the early Talmudic period, to be studied side by side with the somewhat earlier Dead Sea Scrolls and the rabbinic writings themselves.

In a number of cases LAB has preserved motifs or legends that are found in no other extant source: e.g., the connection of the motif of the Tower of Babel (6.4 ff.) with the story of Abram and the furnace; the appearance of the Golden Rule in the framework of the Decalogue (11.12); the reason for God's refusal (19.7) to allow Moses to enter Palestine, namely, lest he see graven images; Moses' rod as a symbol of a covenant (19.11); details concerning the con-

struction of an altar by the two and a half tribes (22.1); the credal
heresy of the Benjamites (25.13); many proper names, e.g., the father
of Hannah, Bethuel (51.6); many prayers and psalms (47.1 ff., 59.4,
60.2-3); and the selfish motive for Saul's expulsion of the sorcerers
(64.1). Of course, the fact that LAB presents a unique extant tradition
in the above cases does not mean that it is unique, since we know that
many midrashim were lost and can be reconstructed only from references in the Apocrypha and Pseudepigrapha, writings of the Church
Fathers, etc.; but even where, as is usually the case, LAB is paralleled,
often closely, by rabbinic midrashim, it often represents the oldest
extant source containing the tradition: e.g., that Job married Dinah,
Jacob's daughter (8.8), important in spreading the author's universalistic point of view, since Job was not Jewish; that Moses was born
circumcised (9.13); and that Elijah is to be identified with Phinehas
(48.1). Finally, because it is contemporary—if the usual dating is
correct—with the Gospels, it may be expected to show close parallels
in thought and language with the New Testament.

CHAPTER II
INFLUENCE
(*James, pp. 9–12; Kisch, pp. 18–22*)

One of the great puzzles about LAB is why, if—as most critics argue—it was composed in the first century in Hebrew, then translated into Greek, and later, in the fourth century, translated into Latin, it is not mentioned by the Church Fathers. A check of the indices to Migne's collection of the Church Fathers, as well as the indices to individual works, has proven fruitless for the present editor.

a. Clement of Alexandria

To be sure, there are some tantalizing references. The second-century Clement of Alexandria (*Stromateis,* 1.23.1) mentions Melchi as a name of Moses, a name very close to Moses' name Melchiel in LAB (9.16). Clement also (*Paedagogus,* 3.11.68.3) draws the same unfavorable comparison of Samson with Joseph that is found in LAB, 43.5; but the most likely explanation is that Clement knew some of the traditions that Pseudo-Philo knew; in any case, Clement never mentions LAB by name.

b. Origen

James (pp. 11-12) finds what looks to him like an allusion to LAB in Origen (*Comment. in Johannem, P.G.* 14.226), namely, the identification of Phinehas and Elijah, which is found in LAB, 48.1. Similarly Origen (*Enarrationes in Librum Job,* f. 2 r–3 v) supports LAB in the view that Job (8.8) lived in the days of the Patriarchs. But both of these accounts are found in rabbinic literature, to be sure later than LAB but undoubtedly dependent upon ancient traditions; and since Origen knew rabbis and rabbinic midrashim well, it seems more likely that both drew upon similar traditions. Again, in a postscript (p. 73), James cites a passage in Origen concerning the angel sent to Esther which he says parallels the passage in LAB concerned with angels sent to Kenaz and David, and suggests that this may indicate that the story of Esther was found in the original Pseudo-Philo. But in the Talmud, Megillah 15b, we find an account very similar to that which Origen quotes: "Three ministering angels were appointed to help her [Esther] at that moment [when Esther went to see the king: Esther 5.2]: one to make her head [lit. neck] erect, a second to endow her with charm [lit. to draw a thread of grace over her = Origen's angel of grace], and a third to stretch the golden sceptre."

c. Aphraates

We may ask whether Aphraates in the fourth century knew Pseudo-Philo since he, too, shares certain traditions with him. Thus he (272) regards Eli as the immediate successor of Phinehas (LAB 52.2); but this he more probably derived from Origen's commentary on John, which has the same tradition. Again, like LAB (19.10-13), he finds in Deuteronomy 34.1–4 a revelation of the future history of Israel, but this is also a rabbinic tradition (see L. Ginzberg, *Legends of the Jews*, 6.151, n. 902); and Aphraates, who wrote in Syriac, which is closely akin to the language of the Talmud, may have known it from the rabbis. Finally, Aphraates (*Patrologia Syriaca*, ed. Griffin, vol. 1, 14.27, pp. 641–642) agrees with LAB's statement (48.1) that Phinehas surpassed the age of 120, since he says that he attained the age of 365; but while there is no parallel in rabbinic literature, Aphraates or his source most likely saw the obvious parallel between Phinehas-Elijah's translation into heaven and that of Enoch, who reached the same age of 365 at the time of his translation.

d. Ephraem Syrus

Ephraem Syrus (1.202A), Aphraates' contemporary, agrees with LAB 9.3 in resolving the problem of the apparent contradiction between Genesis 15.13 (400 years) and Exodus 12.40 (430 years) as to the number of years that the Israelites spent in bondage. Similarly, Ephraem shares with LAB (10.7) the tradition of the well that followed the Israelites in the desert. But in both these cases the tradition is also found widely in midrashic literature; and Ephraem, whose language was Syriac, could easily have derived the information from Aramaic-speaking Jews.

e. Ambrose

The fact that in the fourth century Ambrose knew and used the Latin translation of Philo's *Quaestiones in Genesin*, as P. Wilpert, "Philon bei Nikolaus von Kues," in his edition of *Miscellanea Mediaevalia*, vol. 1: *Antike und Orient im Mittelalter* (Berlin, 1962), pp. 69–79, has shown, may be of value, if we could be sure, as is Wilpert, that LAB was already at that date in the same roll and hence must have been translated before that time; but the fact that Ambrose apparently nowhere cites or alludes to LAB leaves the matter in doubt.

f. Theodoret

The fifth-century Theodoret (*Quaest.* 22) agrees with LAB
(43.8) in increasing the number slain by Samson when he brought
the temple down upon the Philistines. The Bible (Judges 16.27) says
that the temple was full of men and women (no precise number is
given) and that on the roof there were about 3000 men and women;
LAB brings the total to 40,000, and Theodoret says that there were
3000 men and many times more women. But the Biblical text itself
leaves room for speculation, so that the Midrash (Genesis Rabbah
98.14) can state that there were 3000 on the edge of the roof, but
no one knows how many were behind them. In any case, Theodoret
does not give the number that is given by LAB, and so influence is far
from proven.

g. The Middle Ages

We are left with the fact that there is no undoubted reference to
our work before Peter Comestor's twelfth-century *Historia Scholastica,*
the summary of Biblical history which soon became the most popular
book in the Middle Ages; and since the earliest MSS. of LAB date from
the eleventh century, we must account for the strange fact that a book
full of legends and speculations that should have fascinated the
medieval mind, being based on the Bible and written in Latin suppos-
edly in the fourth century, was not quoted until eight centuries had
elapsed. It is clear, as L. Cohn, "Pseudo-Philo und Jerachmeel,"
Festschrift zum siebzigsten Geburtstage Jakob Guttmanns (Leipzig,
1915), pp. 173–185, has conclusively shown, that Jerahmeel is derived from LAB, but this does not push the date of LAB's composition
back any further, since Jerahmeel was probably not composed before
the twelfth century. Of course, it is not unknown for works that should
have been of interest to Christians to disappear from circulation for
many centuries only to reappear much later: one may cite as an
example the *Odes of Solomon,* from which Lactantius (*Inst.* 4.12.3)
quotes a brief passage and from which the Gnostic writing *Pistis Sophia*
(preserved in Coptic) includes five odes, only to disappear thereafter
until rediscovered in 1909 by J. Rendell Harris (see E. Hennecke and
W. Schneemelcher, *New Testament Apocrypha,* 2 [Philadelphia,
1965], pp. 808–810, and bibliography there cited).

h. Book of Cethel

Perhaps we may obtain a clue from a study of the medieval
lapidaries which are derived from the mysterious Book of Cethel

(Cheel, Cehel, Thethel, Thetel, Techel, Theel, Zethel, Zahel, Zachel, Zael, Eethel, Ethel, Gethiel, Rechel), whom Ginzberg, 6.181, n. 1, has identified with Kenaz, whose twelve stones are described at length by Pseudo-Philo, 26.9 ff. For this investigation the list of lapidaries in M. Steinschneider, "Lapidarien," in G. A. Kohut, ed., *Semitic Studies in Memory of Rev. Dr. Alexander Kohut* (Berlin, 1897), pp. 42–72, especially his list of works in Latin, pp. 54–61, 64–66, should be carefully studied.

The Book of Cethel itself is a very brief work, of about two or three pages in manuscript, which has been transcribed *in extenso* in Book 14 of the still unpublished (except for excerpts) *De naturis [natura] rerum* of the thirteenth-century Thomas de Cantimpré (Cantinpratanus), who asserts that he translated it into Latin, though he does not tell us from which language. Quite clearly, however the Book of Cethel differs from LAB 26.9 ff. since it describes 67, not 12, stones, and, in any case, associates the seals with the planets (see the text as published by Joan Evans, *Magical Jewels of the Middle Ages and the Renaissance particularly in England* [Oxford, 1922], pp. 104–108)—an association totally absent in LAB. The texts in the various MSS. apparently differ, and Cethel also appears in separate and divergent form as a treatise on *Seals* as early as the twelfth century. Thomas calls the author a "Jewish philosopher" and cautions his readers that Cethel's views are not to be trusted on every point. That the treatise was popular is clear from the fact, noted by Lynn Thorndike, *A History of Magic and Experimental Science,* vol. 2 (New York, 1923), p. 390, that its prefaces note spurious imitations of it.

Thorndike, pp. 389–390 and 399–400, and George Sarton, *An Introduction to the History of Science,* vol. 2.2 (Baltimore, 1931) p. 593, both identify Cethel with the ninth-century Jewish astrologer Sahl ibn Bishr (Bisr) ben Habib, whose other treatises are coupled with it in MSS., and several of whose works are listed in Albertus Magnus' *Speculum Astronomiae.* Thorndike, p. 390, notes that he was highly regarded by the Byzantines, who called him Sechel or Sachel, the wisest Jew, the son of Pesr.

i. Nicholas of Cusa

The only significant study of LAB's *fortleben* that has appeared to date is Paul Wilpert's "Philon bei Nikolaus von Kues," in his *Miscellanea Mediaevalia,* vol. 1: *Antike und Orient im Mittelalter* (Berlin, 1962), pp. 69–79, which surveys LAB's influence in the Middle Ages, especially on the thirteenth-century Albertus Magnus and the fifteenth-century Nicholas of Cusa (*Coniectura de ultimis diebus*, 14.98. 5–10), who cites Philo's *Historiae* as the source of his statement that the flood occurred in the thirty-fourth jubilee after creation, and that (16.99.3–6) the end of the world will come in 1732–1750. Wilpert argues, because of errors that are made in citations, that LAB was known to the Middle Ages only in combination with Philo's *Quaestiones in Genesin* and *De Vita Contemplativa*. It may be well to suggest, therefore, that one should check patristic and medieval literature for references to these two works as well.

j.   Juan Luis Vives

The famous Spanish humanist and philosopher Johannes Ludovicus (Juan Luis) Vives (1492-1540), the friend of Erasmus, in his important work on educational theory, *De Tradendis Disciplinis seu de institutione christiana*, Book 5, chapter 2, as pointed out by Guido Kisch (*per litt.*), in his survey of historical writers about the Biblical period, states that Philo of Alexandria summarizes the history from Adam to the death of King Saul (cited by Friedrich Kayser, *Ausgewählte pädagogische Schriften des Desiderius Erasmus. Johannes Ludovicus Vives' pädagogische Schriften* in *Bibliothek der katholischen Pädagogik*, 8 [Freiburg im Breisgau, 1896], p. 319). This is quite obviously a reference to Pseudo-Philo. Because the work in the same century attracted the attention of two other famous philologists, Sichardus (the editor of the *editio princeps*) and Budé(see Kisch, p. 31), and especially since there was a lively dispute about its authorship, in which Budé became involved, one would expect that a further search of the works of humanists of this period would yield further allusions.

k.   Azariah dei Rossi

So far as the present editor knows, the work was unknown to Jewish scholars prior to Steinschneider in the nineteenth century, with the exception of the sixteenth-century Azariah dei Rossi, who regarded it (*Meor Einayim*, 4.104) as "'full of mistakes because it was copied of old from a manuscript missing words and lines." A careful search ought to be made of the writings of Azariah's Italian friends and followers for further references.

CHAPTER III
MANUSCRIPTS
(*James, pp.* 12–26; *Kisch, pp.* 22–31, 53–93)   *

a.   MSS. known to James

James' translation is based primarily upon the *editio princeps,* which, in turn, is based upon two manuscripts, one from Fulda, still extant, and the other from Lorsch, now lost, though he used three other MSS. containing the complete work and three others containing excerpts. In particular, James profited greatly from use of the Vatican MS., whose readings he often prefers to those of the *editio princeps* apd for good reason (e.g., 58.3: "they shall preserve"). Though James did not consult the Admont MS., the fact that he had collated the Vatican, which is derived from the Admont (or from a common ancestor) means that he had before him most of the changes of the Admont.

b.   Kisch's list

Kisch, in his edition which he termed a *Schulausgabe,* follows the Admont MS., which James was unable to consult, almost without exception, and notes in his apparatus the readings of the Melk MS., of whose existence James was unaware, as well as of all the MSS. consulted by James. James knew of eleven MSS. containing LAB *in toto* (plus the lost Lorsch MS.) and three containing excerpts, plus the Hebrew adaptation of Jerahmeel. Kisch, pp. 23–28, adds the Berlin, Budapest, Coblenz, and Melk MSS., making a total of twenty; but the Berlin Görres 132 and Coblenz G 132 are one and the same MS., as Professor Irmscher has now verified for me. (It is now in the Staatsbibliothek der Stiftung Preussischer Kulturbesitz in West Berlin.)

c.   Three additional MSS.

To these may now be added three others, whose existence has been verified for me by Prof. Julian G. Plante, curator of the Monastic Manuscript Microfilm Library, St. John's University, Collegeville, Minnesota:

1.   *SALZBURG. Erzabtei Sankt Peter*

Codex S. Petri Salisburgensis a. VII. 17. Saec. 13. f. 2^r–78^r. Parchment.

(Tit. [in a later hand]) Hieronymus in Catalogo Scriptorum Ecclesiasticorum. (Inc. prol.) Philo Iudeus natione alexandrinus de genere sacerdotum. (Expl. prol.) sensuum et eloquii. (Inc. text.) Adam genuit tres filios et unam filiam. (Expl. text.) neque iniusticie mee.

No colophon. The microfilm of this codex in MMML bears the identifying project no. 10,140.

2. *REIN. Stiftsbibliothek*

Codex Runensis 55. Saec. 13. f. 113ʳ–162ᵛ. Parchment.

(Tit.) Ieronimus de philone in cathalogo uirorum illustrium. (Inc. prol.) Philo iudeus natione alexandrinus de genere sacerdotum. (Expl. prol.) sensuum et eloquii. (Inc. tit. text.) Incipit Genesis. (Inc. text.) Initium mundi; Adam genuit tres filios et unam filiam. (Expl. text.) neque iniusticie mee.

No colophon. The microfilm of this codex in MMML bears the identifying project no. 7,454.

3. *GÖTTWEIG. Stiftsbibliothek*

Codex Gottwicensis 246 (254). Saec. 15. [b] f. 1ʳ–43ᵛ. Parchment.

(Inc. prol.) Philo judeus natione alexandrinus de genere sacerdotum. (Expl. prol.) sensuum et eloquii. (Inc. text.) Initium mundi adam genuit tres filios et unam filiam. (Expl. text.) neque iniusticie mee.

No titulus; no colophon. This codex is composed of several parts, each of which has its own enumeration. This Pseudo-Philo text is in the second part, hence the designation above: [b]. The microfilm of this codex in MMML bears the identifying project no. 3,511.

I have checked these three hitherto unknown MSS. and have found that they contain the same major lacunae found in the *editio princeps* and in the other MSS. Father Harrington, who has collated them fully, reports that Salzburg and Rein are close to Admont, while Göttweig, like Cusa, is related to Melk. In any case, a closer study of them is not likely to improve the text very much.

d. Munich and Budapest MSS.

Cohn, "Pseudo-Philo und Jerachmeel," p. 174, states that he had collated the Admont, Munich, and Budapest MSS.; but he died shortly after writing this article, and his collations have never been published. He had, however, already noted the importance of these MSS., which, he was convinced (*ibid.*), would correct many of the errors of the *editio princeps* and would fill in many of its lacunae. None of these were used by James, and only the Admont was used by Kisch. I have secured copies of the Munich and Budapest MSS. (which almost always agree with one another) and have found that they side sometimes with the *editio princeps* (e.g., in 11.12 they have *falsum testimonium ne,* omitted by Admont; and in 14.1 they have *quadraginta . . . Egipti,* omitted by Admont) and sometimes with Admont (e.g., in 12.4 they have merely *relinquam,* whereas the *editio princeps* has *et nunc quoque relinquam*; and in 13.8 they, like Admont, omit *et tunc . . . hominum*); but I have generally been disappointed in the contribution that they make to the establishment of the text.

e.   Kisch's edition

Every scholar must be grateful to Kisch for his edition, as was unanimously acknowledged by scholarly criticism; and the fact that so much work on LAB has appeared during the past two decades is due chiefly to the stimulus of his edition. But A. E. Housman has put it well, if strongly, when in his edition of Manilius (London, 1903), p. xxxi, he criticizes the practice of many an editor in calling one of the MSS. "the best MS." and resigning his editorial functions. "He adopts its readings when they are better than its fellow's, adopts them when they are no better, adopts them when they are worse: only when they are impossible, or rather when he perceives their impossibility, is he dislodged from his refuge and drawn by stress of weather to the other port." Again, in the introduction to his edition of Lucan (Oxford, 1926), Housman laments the "weakness of the present age" in its "indulgence of love for one MS. and dislike for another."

While it is true that Kisch expressly states (p. 93) that his is a mere *Schulausgabe,* that is, a textbook-like edition, and that he regarded it as merely a step in the direction of a critical edition, the fact is that Kisch did, of course, have the *editio princeps* at his disposal, as well as, in James' appendix, the significant readings from the various MSS. consulted by James. But Kisch, in almost every case, chose to place them in his critical appendix, so that the student of LAB will often find inferior and even impossible readings in the text and superior readings in the apparatus. Thus, for example, as Dietzfelbinger (*per litt.*) has pointed out, it is surely preferable to read *posui* (F) for *posuit* (3.2), *servis* (A) for *domus* (9.1), *in occultis* (AP) for *de occultis* (21.9), *relucebat* (MAP) for *relucebant* (25.11), *malus facta est* (A) for *malum factum est* (37.3), *preciosi* [emend to *pretiosis*] (PPhT) for *Moysi* (40.6), *fronivit,* "enjoyed" (APPhT) for *fronduit,* "put forth leaves" (40.6), *voluisti* (A) for *noluisti* (47.1), *iurassem* (A) for *iurasses* (47.3), *commisit* (A) for *dimisit*

(47.7), and *linguam* (A) for *ligna* (63.4). (On the other hand we cannot accept McCracken's objection, in his review of Kisch [*Crozer Quarterly*, 27 (1950), p. 175], that Kisch on 33.6 has printed the meaningless *sepem*, while relegating *septem* to the apparatus; James, in his translation, has rightly preferred *sepem* [=*saepem*, "fence"], which is the reading of Phillipps 461 and the Vatican MSS., since "seven" would make no sense in the context.) Moreover, since the *editio princeps* reflects two MSS., those of Fulda-Cassel and Lorsch, the latter of which is lost, as well as the editor's own emendations, it is important to note, as Kisch was unable to do, which readings are to be found in Fulda-Cassel and which are not. Thus, for example, in Kisch's list of places (pp. 64–65) where the Admont MS. is superior to the *editio princeps,* it may be noted that *iuxta* (5.8) is to be found only in the *editio princeps* and not in the Fulda-Cassel MS., and *conflictus* (20.5) appears in the *editio princeps* as against *flictus* in Fulda-Cassel. One cannot complain if, in view of the conditions prevailing immediately after World War II, when his edition appeared, Kisch was unable to consult other MSS.; but his own apparatus gave him enough material to present a considerably superior text, since, as he himself was forced to admit (pp. 91–92), the Admont MS. contains some deficiencies. The Melk MS., which is the only other MS. which Kisch was able to consult, almost always follows the Admont MS., though in a few places (e.g., 18.6 [*uocaui*] and 47.1 [*Zambri*]) it has superior readings. We must note, finally, that the original Admont and Melk MSS., which were in the possession of Howard L. Goodhart of New York, were not available to Kisch, and he had to use photostats only.

f. Relative merits of the Admont MS. and the editio princeps

Even if Kisch had decided to ignore the basic principle of printing the best text available, a good argument might be made for preferring the *editio princeps* to the Admont MS. James, p. 21, says that he prefers it to any of the complete MSS. that he had seen; and Kisch, p. 157, n. 11, is surprised at this in view of the fact that James so often prefers the readings of the Vatican MS.; but James follows the *editio princeps* more often; and a number of modern scholars, even after the publication of Kisch's edition, still prefer the *editio princeps,* notably B. Botte, in *Recherches de Théologie Ancienne et Médiévale,* 18 (1951), p. 163; A. Spiro, *Manners of Rewriting Biblical History from Chronicles to Pseudo-Philo* (Columbia University diss., 1953), p. 192, n. 129; R. Bloch, "Note Méthodologique pour l'Étude de la

Littérature rabbinique," *Recherches de Science Religieuse*, 43 (1955), p. 206, n. 13; G. Vermès, *Scripture and Tradition in Judaism: Haggadic Studies* (Leiden, 1961), p. 9; R. Le Déaut, *La Nuit Pascale* (Rome, 1963), p. 188, n. 143; and C. Perrot, "Les Récits d'Enfance dans la Haggada antérieure au IIᵉ Siècle de Notre Ère," *Recherches de Science Religieuse*, 55 (1967), p. 485, n. 7. It is true that Admont and Melk often have better readings (e.g., see my notes on 8.10, 18.5, 30.3, 42.9, and 54.5); but Harrington, in his forthcoming thesis, has been able to eliminate a large number of them as late corrections rather than as original readings; and as noted above, as well as in my commentary (see especially on 28.8, 30.1, 40.8, 47.1, 51.2, 51.6, 59.4, and 63.3), there are a number of places where the *editio princeps* definitely has the superior reading.

g. Stemma of MSS.

A preliminary report which I have received from Father Harrington and from his thesis advisor Professor Strugnell indicates that he has reduced the MSS., including the three unknown to Kisch, to a rigid stemma, with two rather than three branches: A (the *editio princeps*, based on K [Fulda-Cassel] and the lost L [Lorsch]), P (Cheltenham Phillipps 461, now in the hands of Martin Bodmer in Geneva), the fragmentary Ph (Phillipps 391), and the fragmentary T (Trèves), as against all the rest, the latter being divided into three groups: 1) X, Y, Z (Munich 18481, 17133, and 4569), R (Vatican), W (Würzburg 276), H (Budapest), and F (the fragmentary Fitzwilliam); 2) Ad (Admont), D (Salzburg), and E (Rein); and 3) V (Vienna), M (Melk), G (Göttweig), B (Berlin), and C (Cusa). S (Würzburg 210) cannot be classified in any one of these three particular groups since it has errors common to all of them. That Harrington's classification is valid may be seen by noting that of the 21 passages listed by Kisch (pp. 64–65) where the Admont MS. is superior to the *editio princeps*, there are only two places where the division is not clear-cut (13.7, where all the MSS., except for Admont, Rein, and Salzburg, agree with the *editio princeps*, and 52.4, where the reading of the *editio princeps* is found in Fulda-Cassel, Melk, Vienna, Berlin, Cusa, and Göttweig). Similarly, in the list of 11 passages where the *editio princeps* has phrases missing from the Admont and Melk MSS., there are only two cases where Admont and Melk are not joined by all the other MSS., namely, 11.12 and 14.1, where (in both cases) Admont and Melk are joined by Salzburg, Rein, Vienna, Berlin, Cusa, and Göttweig.

Professor Strugnell is attempting to get a computer to make a concordance of LAB which would be able to show the kind of Latinity which the translator prefers. One point which Kisch neglected and which Wilpert, p. 77, has called to our attention is that the combination of LAB with the other genuine Philonic treatises (portions of *Quaestiones in Genesin* and *De Vita Contemplativa*) is very ancient and perhaps goes back as far as the fourth century; if so, a study of Cohn's edition of *De Vita Contemplativa* (pp. l–liii) and F. C. Conybeare, *Philo about the Contemplative Life* (Oxford, 1895), pp. 139–145, should prove enlightening for the classification of MSS.

We may expect that most of the improvements in the text resulting from a full collation of the MSS. will be minor, and that real improvements will have to come through emendation. Several fine suggestions have already been made by Ginzberg and Strugnell; and since, in many cases, these have resulted from a reconstruction of the Greek from which the Latin was translated and especially from a reconstruction of the Hebrew from which the Greek was translated, it would be most helpful to attempt a retranslation of the work into these languages (the translation into Hebrew has now been made by Hartom, but unfortunately his knowledge of Latin is limited).

CHAPTER IV
TITLE
(*James, pp.* 26–27)

James (p. 27) notes that the title *Liber Antiquitatum Biblicarum* is due to Sichardus, the editor of the *editio princeps.* It is to be found in not a single manuscript. The only MSS. which have a title are the twelfth-century Munich MS. 4569, which has *Hystoria ab inicio mundi usque ad David regem,* which seems more descriptive than a title, and the Phillipps MS. 461, which has *De successione generationum veteris testamenti,* which is written in a fifteenth-century hand. A number of MSS. begin with *Genesis* or *In Genesim* and/or *Initium Mundi.* The Budapest, Munich 18481, Vatican, and Würzburg 276 MSS. end with "Explicit Hystoria Philonis ab initio mundi usque ad David regem." The title *Antiquitates* undoubtedly derives, as James, p. 27, remarks, from the analogy which Sichardus rightly saw to Josephus' *Antiquities* (which, strangely, neither James nor Kisch exploited), since the book has little to do with antiquities as we understand the term. On the title page of the 1527 edition and the 1538 reprint the title is given merely as *Antiquitates,* without the adjective *Biblicae.* The title *Genesis* perhaps became identified with our work because it was included in the same manuscripts with Philo's *Quaestiones in Genesin.* In fact, the twelfth-century Petrus Comestor and the thirteenth-century Albertus Magnus refer to LAB as *Quaestiones,* presumably for this reason and because LAB stood without a title. It is of significance that the fifteenth-century Nicholas of Cusa (*Coniectura de ultimis diebus,* 14.98.5–10) refers to it as *Historiae* even though the MS. at Cusa which we know he used has the title *In Genesim.* From this and from the *explicit*'s in the MSS. listed above we may conclude that the work was known as the *Historia* or *Historiae* of Philo.

CHAPTER V
AUTHORSHIP
(*James, p.* 27)

Though Sichardus, the editor of the *editio princeps* (1527), was convinced that LAB was written by Philo, there was already then doubt about the attribution, for he explicitly disassociates himself from the view of the great humanist Guillaume Budé that the work was not by Philo of Alexandria but by another Philo. In his *Bibliotheca Sancta* (Venice, 1566), p. 314, Sixtus Senensis (Sisto da Siena), a Dominican monk of Jewish descent, noted that the language of LAB was everywhere redolent of Hebraisms and that the narrative abounded in apocryphal materials, and hence concluded that either it was not by Philo of Alexandria or, if by chance it was, it had been composed not in Greek but in Hebrew. A Jewish contemporary, the learned Azariah dei Rossi, *Meor Einayim,* 4.104, likewise notes that there are scholars who deny the Philonic authorship. He himself (p. 107) then proceeds to offer three proofs that Philo is the author. Firstly, he notes that LAB places the prohibition of adultery before that of murder in the Ten Commandments (11.10–11) as does Philo (see my comment *ad loc.*); but we may note that the reversal in the order is quite ancient, being found in the Nash Papyrus; and moreover, LAB, 44.6–7, as well as Jeremiah 7.9, gives the order of the traditional Hebrew (Masoretic) Text. Secondly, in 9.12, LAB uses the same word *thibin* that Philo uses, but all that this shows is that LAB and Philo both used the LXX at this point; by such an argument one could prove that Augustine is the author of LAB since he too (*Locut. in Hept.* 2.5) uses the word *tibin,* which, as he notes, both the LXX and Itala kept without translating. Finally, LAB 9.8 and Philo, *De Gigantibus,* 55, both connect the 120-year age limit for man with that of Moses. But aside from the fact that the connection might easily be made by anyone who recalled Genesis 6.3, the connection is also found in rabbinic tradition (see my comment on 9.8), and LAB could have derived it from there.

On the other hand, though several scholars have commented in general terms on the difference in style and literary character between LAB and Philo, particularly the latter's general lack of legendary accretions, and on the fact that LAB goes back to a Hebrew original, no one has hitherto really attempted to answer Azariah and to prove

the contrary. However, we may note that there are definite contra-
dictions between Philo and LAB: 1) LAB (3.6), following the
Hebrew text, gives 1652 (1656) as the number of years that had
elapsed from Adam to the Flood, whereas Philo, following the LXX,
adds up to 2242; 2) In a number of other places (e.g., 3.2, *diudicabit*,
see my note), LAB agrees with the Hebrew text against the LXX and
Philo; 3) In 15.1 (see my note) LAB says that it was on God's
initiative that the spies were sent, whereas Philo and Josephus say that
it was on Moses' initiative; 4) In 18.2 ff. (see my note) there is a
major contrast between LAB's generally favorable portrait of Balaam
and Philo's pejorative description; 5) According to LAB (19.16: see
my note) God Himself buried Moses, whereas Philo asserts that he
was buried by celestial beings. We conclude that just as the Fourth
Book of Maccabees is generally found together with the works of
Josephus though it is obviously by another author, so LAB is by an
author other than Philo.

CHAPTER VI
ORIGINAL LANGUAGE
(*James, p. 28; Kisch, pp. 15–16*)

Ever since 1566, when Sixtus Senensis concluded, on the basis of Hebraisms and apocryphal style, that LAB had been composed originally in Hebrew, scholars, with the exception of his contemporary, Azariah dei Rossi, have been unanimous in agreeing with him. The list of modern scholars who have reached this conclusion includes Cohn, "An Apocryphal Work Ascribed to Philo of Alexandria," *Jewish Quarterly Review,* Old Series, 10 (1898), pp. 306–313; James, p. 28; Kisch, pp. 15–16; J. Klausner, *The Messianic Idea in Israel from Its Beginning to the Completion of the Mishnah* (trans. from Hebrew by W. F. Stinespring [New York, 1955]),p. 366; O. Eissfeldt, "Zur Kompositionstechnik des Pseudo-Philonischen Liber Antiquitatum Biblicarum," in N. A. Dahl and A. S. Kapelrud, eds., *S. Mowinckel Festschrift* (Oslo, 1955), p. 53; M. Philonenko, "Remarques sur un hymne essénien de caractère gnostique," *Semitica,* 11 (1961), p. 44; and C. Dietzfelbinger, *Pseudo-Philo, Liber Antiquitatum Biblicarum* (Theol. diss., Göttingen, 1964), p. 167. Cohn, pp. 312–313, for example, points to names with a Hebrew sound invented by the author, sentences connected by "and," the peculiar Hebrew expression לאמר, doubling of the verb (e.g., 6.14, 6.15), the Hebrew הסיף with the infinitive, the frequent use of הנה (*ecce*), and the frequent use of ויהי (*et factum est*). James, p. 28, has cited additional Hebraisms. To them may be added such Hebraisms as *plasmatio iniqua* (33.3) (=יצר הרע, "evil inclination"), *Stelac* (40.4) (=a combination of Hebrew שלג and Aramaic תלג, "snow"), and *die bono paschae* (50.2) (=יום טוב של פסח, lit., "the good day [i.e. holiday] of Passover). James, p. 28, n. 1, cites one mistranslation, though since Genesis 46.16 does not have the name of Isui, his conjecture that it is a misreading is far from proven. Ginzberg has, however, cited several cases where the translator misread or misunderstood the Hebrew original: 12.10, 26.12, 52.1, 53.10, and (less likely) 62.5 (see my notes). In addition, the suggestions of Riessler and Spiro that Noaba (1.1) be read backwards as Awan, that Nidiazec (4.2) be read backwards as Chezaidin, i.e., Chassidim, and that Danaben (48.1) be read backwards as Na Venad, if significant, indicate that the author knew Hebrew; but these suggestions are too fanciful to admit of serious refutation. Finally,

M. Delcor, "Philon (Pseudo-), "Supplément 7 in *Dictionnaire de la Bible* (Paris, 1966), p. 1369, has called attention to Hebraic-like parallelism in such non-Biblical passages as 9.1 and 9.2, though he admits that this may be simply an imitation of Biblical style. The same question, we may note, as to the original language of the book is found in a number of apocryphal books, such as I Esdras, Tobit, Judith, Baruch, and Wisdom of Solomon. In the last case, a number of attempts have been made (see, e.g., E. A. Speiser, "The Hebrew Origin of the First Part of the Book of Wisdom," *Jewish Quarterly Review*, 14 [1923–24], pp. 455–482) to prove a Hebrew original on various grounds, including numerous Hebraisms and mistranslations from the Hebrew; and yet most scholars still believe that the original was in Greek. Hebraisms are, after all, part of Hellenistic Greek and need not come from a Hebrew original. The strongest arguments for a Hebrew original are the fact that LAB often uses the Hebrew text rather than the Septuagint (see below) and—a point unmentioned by James, Kisch, or most other commentators—that he has close affinities to the Targumic tradition. But even these do not necessarily prove a Hebrew original, since the same can be said for Josephus' *Antiquities,* which was certainly originally written in Greek (see H. St. J. Thackeray, *Josephus the Man and the Historian* [New York, 1929; reissued, Ktav, 1967] 81 ff.). The analogy with Josephus may be instructive, especially in view of the numerous parallels with Josephus noted below. Pseudo-Philo may have known an author such as Josephus or his Greek sources (for the theory of an Alexandrian midrashic source behind Josephus see G. Hölscher, "Josephus," Pauly-Wissowa, *Real-Encyclopädie,* 9 [1916], pp. 1934–2000), and still not have known Hebrew; or, alternatively, like Josephus, he may have known Hebrew (see, e.g., my notes on 18.2 and 25.8) but may have chosen to write in Greek. Even if he were a Palestinian (and perhaps, despite all the critics, he was not, if his use of the expression *terra sancta* [19.10] has the significance claimed by Zeitlin; see my note *ad loc.*) there is no reason to doubt that he, like Josephus, might have been able to write in Greek; there is abundant literary and archaeological evidence that Greek was well known to the Jews of Palestine (see now J. N. Sevenster, *Do You Know Greek?: How Much Greek Could the First Jewish Christians Have Known?* [*Supplements to Novum Testamentum,* vol. 19, Leiden, 1968]). In any case, we must make closer studies of the language and style of the other apocryphal and pseudepigraphical books before we can conclude with Cohn, *JQR,* p. 312, that among these there is none in which the Biblical style is so faithfully reproduced as in LAB.

Even the theory (Cohn, p. 307; James, p. 28; Kisch, pp. 15–16) that our Latin translation is a translation from Greek, though supported by the occurrence of Greek words, is not necessarily proven, since Greek words, particularly in matters of religion, had made their way into the Latin vocabulary. In this connection a study should be made of LAB's Latin translation as compared with the Latinity of others of his time (presumed to be the fourth century). A. Souter's *Glossary of Later Latin to 600 A.D.* (Oxford, 1964), which should be used for this purpose, incorporates many words from LAB, but these are all drawn second-hand from James' Appendix II, and he even misses many that James has. Pitra's hypothesis, accepted by Kisch, p. 19, that the translator of LAB was also the translator of the fragmentary *Quaestiones in Genesin* and *De Vita Contemplativa* with which LAB is generally combined in MSS., has been, with good reason, questioned by B. Botte, in *Recherches de Théologie Ancienne et Médiévale*, 18 (1951), p. 163.

CHAPTER VII
DATE
(*James, pp.* 32–33; *Kisch, p.* 17)

a. Terminus a quo: *after* 70

In 22.8, a passage hitherto unnoticed in this connection, LAB states that Joshua appointed in the new sanctuary at Gilgal the sacrifices that were offered annually "even unto this day" (*usque in hodiernum diem*). From this it is clear that Pseudo-Philo himself sought to have his readers believe that his work had been ·composed while the Temple still stood. But the most systematic attempt to date LAB, that by C. Dietzfelbinger, *Pseudo-Philo, Liber Antiquitatum Biblicarum* (Theol. diss., Göttingen, 1964), pp. 191–193, finds a *terminus a quo* after 70 on the basis of its relationship to the *Assumptio Mosis,* the lack of mention of the Passover sacrifice and the de-emphasis on sacrifices generally, the polemic against priests, LAB's understanding of history, and the connection of Pentecost (23.2) with the giving of the Torah; but these are either very general factors (e.g., understanding of history) or, as in the case of the connection of Pentecost with the giving of the Torah, they may very well represent more ancient traditions, as is generally true for rabbinic materials.

An attempt to date LAB on the basis of his method of writing has been made most recently by P. Bogaert, *Apocalypse de Baruch,* 1 (Paris, 1969), p. 246, who contends that, thus considered, it lies between Eupolemus (c. 160 B.C.E.) and Josephus' *Antiquities* (93 C.E.), and he would consequently prefer to date LAB before 70. But Eupolemus most probably is an Alexandrian-Jewish writer, and LAB is a Palestinian writer; secondly, the purposes of the works are different; and finally, not enough of undoubted authenticity of Eupolemus' work has survived to form a judgment.

b. Terminus ante quem: 132

Dietzfelbinger, pp. 193–194, offers 132 as a *terminus ante quem* since LAB makes no mention of the Bar Kochba rebellion and gives little attention to circumcision, which became such a problem under Hadrian shortly before 132; but the *argumentum ex silentio* is particularly dangerous in an apocalyptic type of work such as LAB seems to be. James, p. 33, n. 1, suggests that the vagueness of the author's hopes and aspirations may point to a period after Bar Kochba, but that the fact of its acceptance by the Church and the absence of anti-Christian polemic forbid it to be dated in the second century. First of all, however, while it is true that the book was preserved by Christians, it is strangely, as noted above, never quoted nor referred to by the Church Fathers nor in fact by medieval writers before the twelfth century. Again, while it is true that the Bar Kochba rebellion marked the final split between Judaism and Christianity, Jewish writers of this period never engage in anti-Christian polemic: it is not until they are forced to do so by disputations with Christians that they engage in such writings.

Attempts to date LAB (see James, pp. 29–33) have centered on 19.7, which speaks of "the place where the people shall serve me 740 [Cohn, 850] years," and states that the destruction of the Temple took place on the same day as the one when Moses broke the tablets, the seventeenth of Tammuz. This, says Cohn, can refer only to the capture of Jerusalem by Titus, since the capture of Jerusalem by Nebuchadnezzar took place on the ninth of Tammuz, though there is also a tradition in the Palestinian Talmud (see James, p. 31) that the first occasion on which the city was broken into occurred on the seventeenth of Tammuz. We must stress, however, that LAB 19.7 speaks of the utter destruction (*demolientur*) of the city, and not merely the breach of the walls; and hence P. Bogaert, *Apocalypse de Baruch*, vol. 1 (Paris, 1969), pp. 256–257, argues, plausibly enough, that the reference is to the breach of the wall in 587 by Nebuchadnezzar. Cohn's interpretation requires his emendation together with the assumption that LAB is following the chronology of the Seder Olam. And yet, as Harrington (*per litt.*) has pointed out, if Cohn is basing his view on the chronology of the Seder Olam, "place" is the land of Israel and not Jerusalem, since he cannot say that the Jebusites worshiped the true God in Jerusalem.

Cohn's dating is accepted by E. Schürer, *Geschichte des jüdischen Volkes im Zeitalter Jesu Christi*, vol. 3[4] (Leipzig, 1909), p. 385; Kisch, p. 17; and Delcor, p. 1371. J. Klausner, *The Messianic Idea in Israel from Its Beginning to the Completion of the Mishnah*, trans. by W. F. Stinespring (New York, 1955), p. 366, has attempted to reinforce this hypothesis by noting the peculiar coincidence that the number of those slain from the army of Sisera (31.2; see my note) is 90 times 97,000, whereas 97,000 is, according to Josephus (*Bellum Judaicum*, 6.420), the number of those taken captive throughout the entire war leading to the destruction of the Temple.

c. Shortly after 70

Cohn, p. 325, attempts to support his dating of LAB as shortly after 70 by stressing that little attention is given in LAB to sacrifices and the service of the Temple. But the Qumran texts and archaeological evidence, in conjunction with Josephus, *Antiquitates Judaicae,* 18.19 (see the note in my Loeb Library edition), indicate that the Qumran community, if LAB originated there, did offer sacrifices, though they disapproved of the procedures of the priests in the Temple; and this may explain the paucity of references to the Temple sacrifices. James, pp. 32–33, without adducing any specific evidence, suggests that a considerable interval must have elapsed after the destruction of the Temple before the composition of the book; but Delcor, p. 1371, argues that if any considerable lapse of time had passed the book would hardly have been translated or adopted by the Church.

d. 101–102, 110–130

Gry's theory ("La date de la fin des temps, selon les révélations et les calculs du Pseudo-Philon et de Baruch," *Revue Biblique,* 48 [1939], pp. 337–356) dating LAB in 101–102 is based on his peculiar interpretation of 19.15 (see my note). Klausner (pp. 366–367) attempts to date it from about 110 to about 130 on the basis of the fact that LAB is not overcome with grief at the destruction of the Temple as are II Baruch and IV Esdras asd hence must have been written after those books. Even more nebulous than this argument is the suggestion that the extreme cruelty shown in this book toward Jewish transgressors and toward Gentiles argues for a date during the revolts under Trajan and Hadrian (c. 110–130). The fact that LAB does not stress political success and material prosperity is accounted for by the failure of the revolts.

e. Quotations from the Bible as a criterion

Strugnell, in his article on Pseudo-Philo in the forthcoming *Encyclopaedia Judaica,* suggests another approach which may prove more useful, namely, a systematic examination of the Biblical text of LAB. A few Septuagintal, Proto-Lucianic, and Palestinian readings have been noted, he remarks, but their number is far greater. A comparison, we may add, with Philo's Bible (see P. Katz, *Philo's Bible: The Aberrant Text of Bible Quotation in Some Philonic Writings and Its Place in the Textual History of the Greek Bible* [Cambridge, 1950]) and with Josephus' Bible (see A. Mez, *Die Bibel des Josephus* [Basel, 1895] and H. St. J. Thackeray, *Josephus the Man and the Historian* [New York, 1929; reprinted by Ktav, 1967], pp. 75–99) would prove useful in dating all three works and in determining their relationship to one another. Strugnell states that it is very improbable that the translator, influenced by some form of the Greek Bible, substituted its text for LAB's, but this is precisely what has happened in some MSS., at least, of Philo and Josephus. Rather, it is the fact that so many readings counter to the Septuagint and agreeing with the Hebrew text or with the Targum are still found in LAB that leads one to conclude that LAB, like Josephus, had both a LXX and a Hebrew text before him, as well as a Targum.

f. Targumic traditions as a criterion

Perhaps the question of the date of LAB should be viewed from still a different point of view. In the case of rabbinic midrashim we consider not merely the date when they were reduced to writing but also the antiquity, which is much greater, of the traditions embodied in them. G. Vermès, *Scripture and Tradition in Judaism: Haggadic Studies* (Leiden, 1961), p. 6, realizes this distinction and suggests that the exegetical traditions in LAB certainly are more ancient than the first century if, as is likely, the Targumic traditions which it so often parallels are as old as the Septuagint. The studies of the late lamented Renée Bloch ("Midrash," Supplément 5 in *Dictionnaire de la Bible*, pp. 1263–1268) have shown how ancient is the midrashic method exemplified in LAB, since its roots are to be found in the Bible itself; and from this point of view, at any rate, the sources of LAB may be very ancient. Thackeray (*The Relation of St. Paul to Contemporary Jewish Thought* [London, 1900], pp. 243–244), finds a remarkable parallel between Paul's combination of phrases in 1 Corinthians 2.6 and LAB's similar combination in 26.13, and concludes that since Paul cannot have cited LAB, which was posterior to him, both Paul and LAB were dependent upon a common Jewish source; but it may be that LAB, or at any rate the tradition behind it, should be dated earlier than the traditional first century dating. Spiro ("Samaritans, Tobiads, and Judahites in Pseudo-Philo, Use and Abuse of the Bible by Polemicists and Doctrinaires," *Proceedings of the American Academy of Jewish Research,* vol. 20 [1951], p. 282) argues that LAB is a polemic against the Samaritans and says that it may be dated perhaps as early as the Jewish historian Eupolemus, c. 150 B.C.E. Philonenko, in his various articles, contends that it is related to the Dead Sea Scrolls; if it is, it may be dated perhaps as early as the Damascus Document, c. 63–48 B.C.E. (so dated by A. Dupont-Sommer, *Les écrits esséniens découverts près de la mer Morte*[3] [Paris, 1964], p. 136), though it does not exclude, as Philonenko is careful to point out (*per litt.*) the possibility that LAB is to be dated at the end of the first century C.E.

CHAPTER VIII
FORM: THE BOOK OF CHRONICLES
(*James, p. 33; Kisch, p.* 17)

Cohn, p. 315, had already commented on the parallel between
LAB and the Biblical Book of Chronicles in its tendency to amplify
Biblical genealogies. We may add that in the narrative portions there
is the same tendency in both works to amplify certain passages while
omitting or glossing over others (so as, for example, to present a more
saintly picture of David and Solomon in Chronicles than is found in
the Books of Kings). Riessler (*Altjüdisches Schrifttum ausserhalb der
Bibel, übersetzt und erläutert* [Augsburg, 1928], p. 1315) has noted
the interesting fact, furthermore, that 1 Chronicles in its narrative
portion, which starts in Chapter 10, begins at the very point where
LAB ends, namely, with Saul's death. Hence the hypothesis has been
presented by Spiro (*PAAJR,* vol. 20 [1951], pp. 304–308) and
Le Déaut (*La Nuit Pascale* [Rome, 1963], p. 188) that LAB is
merely an anterior supplement to Chronicles. James contradicts himself on page 33 when, on the one hand, he notes that both LAB and
Chronicles devote much space to prayers, while, on the other hand, he
notes that LAB lacks the liturgical interest of Chronicles. The fact is
that LAB, like Chronicles, does have a number of prayers, hymns, and
psalms, such as those of Moses (12.8–9, 19.8–9, 19.14), Joshua
(21.2–6), Kenaz (25.6, 27.7, 28.5), Jael (31.5, 31.7), Deborah
(32.1–17), Jephthah (39.7), Eluma the mother of Samson (42.2),
Samson (43.7), Phinehas (46.4–47.2), the Israelites in the time of
Elkanah (49.6, 49.8), Hannah (50.4–5, 51.3–6), and David (59.4,
60.2–3). But a real clue has escaped the commentators, namely the
references to the Midrash of the Prophet Iddo (2 Chronicles 13.22)
and the Midrash of the Book of Kings (2 Chronicles 24.27); there is
an obvious contrast between these midrashim, which were presumably
expanded commentaries and explanations, and, for example, the
presumably straightforward Chronicles of King David (1 Chronicles
27.24). LAB may perhaps be classified as a midrashic type of work
rather than as a type of work resembling Chronicles, which restricts
itself to an intensive account of David and Solomon, instead of the
selective history of the Israelites, and which has much less legendary
and apocalyptic material.

A better parallel to LAB, so far as form is concerned, is that with
Josephus' *Antiquities* and with Targumim (see below).

CHAPTER IX
PURPOSE
(*James, pp. 33–34; Kisch, pp. 17–18*)

In his original article rediscovering LAB, Cohn (p. 322) emphatically asserted that the author had no other end than to interest and to edify the reader and to strengthen his religious beliefs. In this appraisal he was joined by James (p. 59), who specifically denies that the author is a speculative theologian or a polemicist, and by Kisch (p. 17). But how then do we explain the extraordinary additions, notably the special interest in genealogies and numbers, the inordinate length of certain episodes, notably that of Kenaz, and the reduction or omission of others? Hence theories have been presented that the work is a pamphlet or tract, as Spiro (*Manners of Rewriting Biblical History from Chronicles to Pseudo-Philo* [Columbia University diss., 1953], p. 2), for example, argues, such as the Book of Chronicles, Ecclesiasticus, Eupolemus, Jubilees, and pseudo-Clementines (add Josephus' *Antiquities*), revising the Biblical record with a particular purpose in mind. Specifically it has been argued that LAB was written to reinforce the Deuteronomic conception of Israel's history, to defend the Samaritans (M. Gaster), to attack the Samaritans (Spiro, *passim*), to attack the Tobiads (Spiro, "Samaritans, Tobiads, and Judahites in Pseudo-Philo," *PAAJR*, 20 [1951], pp. 335–337), to attack the worshippers of Mithra (so Dietzfelbinger, pp. 61–62, 187–188), to attack intermarriage, or that it is a sectarian pamphlet somehow connected with the Essenes or the Dead Sea Sect or with some mystical, perhaps Gnostic, movement (so Philonenko, *passim*), or that it is an apologetic work intended to answer critics of Judaism and heretics.

a. Deuteronomic conception of Israel's history

The theory that there exists a pattern of Deuteronomic conception of Israel's history which had a profound and enduring influence upon subsequent books of the Bible, as well as on late Judaic literature, including especially LAB, has been presented by O. H. Steck (*Israel und das gewaltsame Geschick der Propheten* [Neukirchen, 1967]), pp. 173–176. LAB's emphasis upon Israel's sin and the admonition of Israel to repent fits into this pattern: thus, for example, in 12.4 LAB goes beyond Exodus 32.7 ff., which he is there paraphrasing, and mentions not merely the sin of the golden calf but also the sins which the Israelites will commit after entering the land and the destruction

of the Temple in 586 as a punishment therefor. Other examples in a
similar vein that may be cited are 3.9–10, 13.10, and 19.2–5. Steck,
p. 176, finds the prophetic prediction of Deuteronomy in such passages
as 23.7 and 30.5. But, we may object, if LAB were really so deeply
imbued with the Deuteronomistic outlook, we would expect the
humanitarian interest, with its concern for the needy, which runs so
deeply in Deuteronomy, to be more prominent in LAB.

b. Anti-Samaritan polemic

James (p. 151, note on 25.10) had already raised the possibility
of anti-Samaritan bias in the treatise. If indeed, as indicated above,
Pseudo-Philo is imitating the Book of Chronicles he may also have
been influenced by the anti-Samaritan bias that several scholars have
claimed to detect there. Spiro's argument, in his several articles and in
his doctoral thesis, adopted by Delcor, pp. 1360–1361, rests largely
on the omission of certain episodes which the Samaritans had used
to cast legitimacy upon themselves. In particular, says Spiro (p. 318),
though the Bible (Genesis 12.6–7) mentions that Abram stopped at
Shechem, where God revealed Himself to him and where he built an
altar, LAB is silent. There is similar silence about Abram's next stop-
ping place, Bethel (Genesis 12.8), which is similarly in Samaritan
territory, and about Abram's meeting with Melchizedek, king of
Salem, because, according to Spiro's argument, the Samaritans had
maintained that Salem was adjacent to the Samaritan capital of
Shechem (cf. LXX on Genesis 33.18, which introduces the name of
Salem as a city of Shechem, whereas the Hebrew text states merely
that Jacob went to Shechem). Likewise, in his account of the sacrifice
of Isaac, LAB (18.5, 32.1–4) omits the fact that the sacrifice took
place in the land of Moriah because the Samaritan text of Genesis 22.2
reads המוראה, which could have been an allusion to מורה, a place
near Shechem. Conversely LAB (Spiro, "Samaritans, etc.", p. 352)
omits that the sinner Achan (LAB 21.3, 25.7,) came from the tribe
of Judah, the great opponents of the Samaritans. Again (Spiro,
"Samaritans, etc.", pp. 339–340), though the Bible states that half
the Jews stood in front of Mt. Gerizim and the other half stood in
front of Mt. Ebel, while Joshua read the Torah to them, LAB
(21.7–9) omits mention of Gerizim, the sacred mountain of the
Samaritans, and says nothing of the altar that was built there. Moreover (Spiro, p. 338) LAB is silent about the cities of refuge, since one
of them was Shechem (Joshua 20.7), as well as about the fact that
Joseph was buried in Shechem (Joshua 24.32). Again, Spiro (pp.

308–309) argues that there is no lacuna, as James would have it, between 37.1 and 37.2; LAB, he says, has deliberately omitted the beginning of the parable of Jotham in order not to mention the fact that Jotham ascended Mount Gerizim to pronounce the parable (Judges 9.6–9); we consequently have not a parable but an actual historical fact. Similarly, Spiro (pp. 309–310) argues that there is no lacuna after 37.5; the omission of the judgeship of Tola son of Puah is due to the fact that the Bible (Judges 10.2) reports that he was buried in Shamir—which the Codex Alexandrinus of the LXX renders as Samaria—and according to Samaritan tradition on Mt. Gerizim. Spiro, who regards Pseudo-Philo as a supreme master of the black art of character-assassination, also cites more direct attacks on the Samaritans ("Pseudo-Philo's Saul and the Rabbis' Messiah ben Ephraim," *Proceedings of the American Academy for Jewish Research,* 21 [1952], p. 120). Thus he explains ("Samaritans, etc.", p. 350) that Pseudo-Philo has told the story of Kenaz at such length because it gives him an opportunity to attack the Samaritans, since the images were buried on Mt. Shechem (25.10) and God's lightning came down (26.3, 26.8) to burn the Samaritan books at Shiloh. Again (Spiro, "The Ascension of Phinehas," *Proceedings of the American Academy for Jewish Research,* 22 [1953],p. 114), whereas the Samaritans maintained that Phinehas had pontificated on Gerizim, LAB 48.2 says that it was at Shiloh, and whereas they denied his immortality, LAB (48.2) identifies him with Elijah.

The *argumentum ex silentio* is always a dangerous one, especially in a treatise as short as ours. One might ask, for example, with Dietzfelbinger, p. 292, n. 405, why in telling the story of Micah the idol-worshipper (44.2 ff.) Pseudo-Philo omitted that he came from the hills of Ephraim (Judges 17.1), at least part of which belonged to Samaria. Again, the LXX likewise (Genesis 22.2) omits the fact that the binding of Isaac took place on Moriah by translating המוריה as ὑψηλήν , "lofty"; does this show that the LXX here also is engaging in an anti-Samaritan polemic? Again, the Vulgate renders *in terram visionis* (as if המוריה were derived from ראה); is the Vulgate here engaging in anti-Samaritan polemic? There can be no doubt that there is some anti-Samaritanism in LAB, but that LAB is a systematic polemic against the Samaritans is highly questionable, as Vermès ("La Figure de Moïse au tournant des deux Testaments," in H. Cazelles et al., *Moïse l'Homme de l'Alliance* [Paris, 1955], p. 89), Dietzfelbinger (pp. 153–166), and Strugnell ("Philo [Pseudo-],

Liber Antiquitatum Biblicarum," forthcoming in *Encyclopaedia Ju-daica*) all point out.

c. Anti-Tobiad polemic

Another theory proposed by Spiro ("Samaritans, etc.", pp. 335–337) is that the treatise has contemporary overtones, being directed against the Hellenizing Tobiads with their easy morals; thus, as Spiro (pp. 336–337) would have it, the veiled reference (7.3) to scattered people of a divided tongue is to the multi-lingual colony of Tobias. Again, the description (18.13) of the opulence of the Midianites beyond the Jordan is said (Spiro, pp. 335–336) to be an attack on contemporary looseness of living, as seen, for example, in the Zenon Papyri of the third century B.C.E. On this basis, Spiro (p. 337, n. 122) keeps *Egipti* in 19.12 as a vague and secretive hint of the Ptolemaic colony of the Tobiads. Finally, in 22.1 LAB, according to Spiro (p. 343), avoids saying that the western Israelites gave their consent to an altar in Trans-Jordan by asserting that the two and a half tribes dwelt around (*circa*) the Jordan rather than across from the Jordan. But the theory rests on little evidence; thus in 7.3, as Dietzfelbinger, p. 250, n. 34, remarks, there is no specific reference to Trans-Jordan, but the passage rather applies to the race of mankind in general. Again, as Winter (*per litt.*) and Dietzfelbinger (p. 268, n. 183) have noted, it may be that LAB's charge rests upon a simple error in transcription, since the Greek word for "across" is πέραν and that for "around" is the very similar περί . But, in any case, why would Pseudo-Philo, writing, according to the usual date assigned to him, so long after the Tobiads had disappeared, choose to attack them?

d. Anti-Mithraic polemic

James (p. 200, note on 44.4, 5) had already noted that one of the extra-Biblical additions in LAB, a description of the images carved by Micah, is reminiscent of the carvings in a Mithraic sanctuary; perhaps, we may add, the very name Michas found here in LAB was suggested by Mithra. In addition, Dietzfelbinger, p. 188, has noted the stress on human sacrifice (4.16, 25.9) so important in Mithraism; the idea of the creation of Abraham from a stone (23.4), reminiscent of the birth of Mithra from a stone; and the fact that the number of Amorite stones is seven (26.8), a number which plays a prominent role also in Mithraism. To this we may add that the number three prominent in 44.5 is also of key significance in Mithraism, which had something like a trinity. Elsewhere (pp. 61–62) Dietzfelbinger notes the sharp attack in LAB (34.1) against the worship of the sun, an

object that was so prominent in Mithraism; moreover, the name of the
second son of Dedila, Heliu, may be an allusion to the god Helios,
whose very name means "sun." Again, Dietzfelbinger, p. 92, notes the
fact that Doeg (63.4) not only is not granted a share in the world to
come but is presented as a Syrian, reinforcing his thesis that Pseudo-
Philo is struggling against the Mithra religion brought from Syria.
Since, as Dietzfelbinger, pp. 61–62, has remarked, the Mithra cult had
a special center in Cilicia and Syria, it is quite natural that the Palestinian author of LAB should regard it as a threat.

That the major purpose of LAB is to combat Mithraism is unlikely
since we have no evidence of the serious penetration of Mithraism into
Palestine. While it is true that the images of three male figures
(LAB 44.5) are quite Mithraic, in the representations of this trinity
Mithra is more prominent than the other two figures, whereas there is
no such differentiation in LAB. The mention here of a calf and more
than one at that, and also the lack of reference to a slaughter create
doubts, though perhaps we should equate LAB's calves and the
Mithraic bull, in which case the slaughter of the bull as generating all
forms of life is somewhat comparable to the calves who grant male
and female offspring in LAB 44.5 (see L. A. Campbell, *Mithraic
Iconography and Ideology* [Leiden, 1968], pp. 248–249, 260–268).
Again, the main Mithraic bird was the raven-crow-falcon (Campbell,
pp. 22–25), which took the place of the hawk in Mithraic iconography
(so Campbell, p. 20); the eagle does appear in the syncretistic
Mithra-Jupiter Dolichenus relief (Campbell, p. 22), but apparently
is hardly found in a purely Mithraic context; and, in any case, the
eagle, when it does appear, represents the power of the ruler and not
the bestower of riches as in LAB. The dove would suit the cult of
Juno Regina better than the cult of Mithra. It is true that the lion,
which is mentioned here, is the most constant companion of Mithra
and is the embodiment of strength (so LAB 44.5); but in Mithraism
the lion is even more the maximum embodiment of the Mithraic fire
of life (Campbell, pp. 68, 309–310). Similarly the dragon or snake
(δράκων) is prominent enough in Mithraism (Campbell, pp. 15–
22); yet it represented not length of days, as in LAB 44.5, but the
pneumatic *psyche* in transition into and out of the body (Campbell,
p. 351). But we miss references to the dog and the scorpion, so
prominent in Mithraic iconography (Campbell, pp. 12–14, 25–28).

Again, Dietzfelbinger is hardly correct in regarding LAB 4.16,
with its reference to sons and daughters passing through fire, as an
attack upon Mithraism, since females were generally excluded from

the Mithraic cult. If there is any contemporary reference here, it is perhaps, as Campbell, *per litt.,* suggests, to the cult of El-Kronos-Saturnus of Phoenicia-Carthage, in which sacrifice to a Moloch or MLK in times of stress was practiced down to Roman Imperial times, even secretly against Imperial decree.

As to creation from a stone, this is a common motif in Judaism (cf. Isaiah 51.1–2 and rabbinic developments) and, in any case, hardly unique with Mithraism, since rock cults were prominent in all of Anatolia, as well as in northern and western Syria from remote antiquity. Again, the fact that the Amorite stones are seven in number is hardly in itself significant, since the number seven very often represents the seven planets in the astrological cults so common in the Hellenistic period. Finally, LAB is not alone in presenting Doeg as a Syrian; Josephus, *AJ* 6.244, and the Septuagint itself, which both are following, do likewise, and no one has yet argued that the Septuagint and Josephus are anti-Mithraic polemics. In conclusion, inasmuch as LAB never mentions Mithra by name and in the key passage in 44.4–5 does not refer to such central features as the sun and the slaying of a bull, we must assert that while it is possible that LAB has elements of an anti-Mithraic polemic the evidence is hardly convincing.

e. An Essene pamphlet

When Cohn rediscovered LAB he raised the possibility (p. 326) that the book might have originated with the Essenes, but immediately dismissed this by noting that apart from the scantiness of references to sacrifices and ceremonial observances, there was nothing in the book itself to support such a view. James, who likewise notes the lack of interest in the Temple services and ceremonial law (p. 32), does not ascribe it to Essene authorship. It was Riessler (first in his review of James in *Theologische Quartalschrift,* 102 [1921], pp. 219–221, and later in the notes to his translation of LAB, p. 1315) who argued for an Essene origin on the very grounds that seemed insignificant to Cohn, namely, that there was little attention given to the Book of Leviticus and to the laws of the priests, adding that LAB actually shows aversion to the special claims of the priests (53.9) and a special concern with precious stones (26.10 ff.), which was characteristic of the Essenes (Josephus, *Bellum Judaicum,* 2.136). To this Philonenko, in his various articles, has added, the Messianic phraseology, universal outlook, the fervor of the hymns, and the stress on silence. Dietzfelbinger (p. 302, n. 534) has added as a possible Essene outlook the view (53.6) that the right side has greater dignity than the left. In his unpublished essay, "Pseudo-Philo, an Essene Work," K. R. Stow (pp. 21–22) has added that the insertion of the long excursus on Kenaz fits into an Essene history of salvation; and indeed, we may note that Kenaz parallels Moses in that the secret of the number of years of the world's existence is revealed to both of them (19.15, 28.8). To this we may add such Essene characteristics as stress on angelology and on particular reverence for Moses (Josephus, *Bellum Judaicum*, 2.145; LAB 19.3).

The theory has found few followers, though it has been propounded in recent years by J. Schmitt ("L'Organisation de l'Église primitive et Qumran," in J. van der Ploeg, et al., *La Secte de Qumran et les Origines du Christianisme* [Louvain, 1959], pp. 225–226), Philonenko in his various articles, A. Strobel (*Untersuchungen zum eschatologischen Verzögerungsproblem auf Grund der Spätjüdischchristlichen Geschichte von Habakuk 2.2 ff.* [Leiden, 1961], p. 74), Le Déaut (*La Nuit Pascale* [Rome, 1963], p. 189, n. 147), ascribing the curious absence of all allusions to the Paschal lamb to the Essene origin of the work, and Stow, in his unpublished paper.

In the first place, however, it is not quite correct to speak of LAB's lack of interest in the Temple and priests, since the author does speak (11.15, 13.4–8, 13.13, 14.4), as Spiro ("Samaritans, etc.", p. 332) has noted, of the laws regarding the tabernacle, its furnishings, the priests and their garments, the sacrifices and their number, tithes, and festivals. Again, LAB shows his concern and respect for the priests when he has Kenaz declare (28.3): "Shall any other speak before the priest which keepeth the commandments of the Lord our God, and that, seeing that truth proceedeth out of his mouth, and out of his heart a shining light?" We may note in particular that, contrary to Riessler and his followers, LAB does show a deep concern for the priests in his account (52.1) of the improper conduct of Eli's sons; instead of focusing on their improprieties with the women who came into the sanctuary, LAB's concern is with their misconduct in connection with the sacrifices themselves. Delcor (p. 1373) acknowledges the relative lack of emphasis on sacrifices and the Temple but explains this as due to the fact that the book was composed after the destruction of the Temple, when sacrifices had ceased; but it is a mistake to regard the cessation of the sacrifices as an indication of lessened interest in the Temple, as a perusal of the Talmudic corpus will show. As to LAB's interest in precious stones, we must also note that the heathen Amorites (25.12) use them to recover their eyesight, as Dietzfelbinger (p. 182) has commented; and an Essene author would hardly have mentioned this fact. The alleged Messianic interpretation of 51.3 is also found in documents—the Targum on 1 Samuel 2.20, the Midrash Shemuel 5.17 (ed. Buber), and Batte Midrashoth (4.9)—which are hardly Essene in origin. The universal outlook is stressed in Amos, hardly an Essene prophet. Again, the pious fervor displayed in LAB's hymns is a characteristic not only of the Essenes but of the Psalms themselves. The view that the right side has greater dignity than the left is a commonplace (cf. Catullus, 45, and commentaries thereon, and A. S. Pease, in *Classical Philology*, 6 [1911], pp. 429–443); and, in any case, LAB is speaking of the right ear as against the left ear, whereas the Essenes (Josephus, *Bellum Judaicum*, 2.147) were careful not to spit to the right; as a matter of fact the Palestinian Talmud (Berakhoth 3.5) has a similar prohibition in connection with prayers, and no one will accuse the Talmud of being an Essene document. The notion (Philonenko, "Remarques sur un hymne essénien de caractère gnostique," *Semitica*, 11 [1961], p. 48) that the discipline of silence observed in Essene communities (Josephus, *Bellum Judaicum*, 2. 133) could have favored the speculation of an initial silence before creation (60.2) fails to take into account the widespread praise of silence in the Talmud; thus Rabbi Simeon ben Gamaliel (Aboth 1.17) is quoted as saying that he had found nothing better for a person than silence, and Rabbi Akiba (Aboth 3.13) similarly remarks that silence is a fence to wisdom. Moreover, if the reading of the MSS. (in contrast to the Epitome and the Latin version) of Josephus' *Antiquities*, 18.19, is correct (see the note *ad loc.* in my Loeb Library translation), the Essenes did send votive offerings to the Temple, but performed their sacrifices employing a different ritual of purification. Again, as Dietzfelbinger (p. 181) has noted, if LAB is really an Essene work, it is strange that it is silent about such characteristic features of that sect as community of property, ablutions, hierarchical ordinances, holy banquets, maintenance of their character as a particular group, forbidding of oaths, preservation of sectarian books, and strictness of Sabbath-observance, to which we may add their strict rules of dress, deportment, dining, the nature of the novice's probationary period, expulsion from the order, rules in trying cases, and varying views and practices with regard to marriage. Granted that we would not expect to find all of these features in an Essene work, but that so many of them should be lacking is surely significant. Finally, if the book was composed after 70, as is almost universally agreed, it is unlikely that it would be Essene, since this sect came to an end apparently after the destruction of the Temple.

f. Connection with the Dead Sea Scrolls

With the discovery of the Dead Sea Scrolls it was inevitable that an attempt would be made to connect LAB with the Dead Sea Sect, whether or not this sect is identical with the Essenes. In particular, Philonenko ("Essénisme et gnose chez le Pseudo-Philon. Le symbolisme de la lumière dans le Liber Antiquitatum Biblicarum," *Studies in the History of Religions,* 12 [Leiden, 1967], pp. 406–407) has stressed the mysticism in such passages as 9.8 and 28.3 which he says is typical of the Qumran scrolls. Stow, in his unpublished paper, has made a systematic attempt to connect LAB with the Dead Sea Sect. In particular, he lists (pp. 3 ff.) a number of major ideological themes which LAB has in common with the scrolls: 1) dualism, i.e., the opposition of the forces of good and evil (LAB 32.10, 51.5); 2) predestination and election of grace (3.10, 4.11, 26.13, 56.6, 59.4); 3) *civitas Dei,* i.e. the formation of the sectaries into a special congregation having a unique rule and standard of purity (19.12–13); 4) the new, or special, covenant (14.1–2); 5) baptism (27.12); 6) the consciousness of the elect that he is in possession of a unique spirit (12.1, 19.15, 61.8–9); 7) the dualism of flesh and spirit (3.1–4). In addition he claims to find in LAB a number of motifs which are found in the Dead Sea literature: 1) descriptions of the Teacher of Righteousness, especially the concept that he is the guardian of the divine garden (23.12), and even a direct reference to the Teacher (19.3); 2) punishment by fire (6.17, 20.7, 26.1 ff., 32.11, 37.12, 38.3–4); 3) the last judgment (3.9–10, 19.14–15, 28.8); 4) the major role of the priests (17.1, 28.3, 46.1, 53.9, 63.1); 5) the holy war (27.12–14, 61.3 ff.); 6) the stress on the notion that sin leads to expulsion (11.2); and 7) the stress on study rather than on impure sacrifices (22.5). To this list Philonenko ("Une paraphrase du cantique d'Anne," *Revue d'Histoire et de Philosophie Religieuses,* 42 [1962], p. 166) adds the idealization of poverty and chastity (51.4; *contra* Dietzfelbinger, p. 299, n. 498). Finally, Stow, as well as Schmitt (pp. 225–226), cite a number of parallels in phraseology between LAB and the scrolls, notably such expressions as visitation (for punishment, 1.20), enlightenment (11.2, 51.3; see also Philonenko, "Une paraphrase," p. 164 and "Essénisme et gnose," pp. 405–406, who adds 18.4, 20.3, 23.7, and 23.10), justification (51.2), prince (25.2), and friend of God (25.3). This last expression, says Stow, is unique to the Dead Sea literature (Damascus Document, 3.2–4, where Abraham is termed the friend of God and is said to have transmitted this status to Isaac and Jacob). Philonenko adds such verbal parallels as *qui possident plurima*=מקני הון, "those who possess goods" (51.4); *spiritus sanctus*=רוח הקודש (60.1), which is not, it should be noted, found in the *editio princeps*); *multi*=הרבים, as used in the Dead Sea Scrolls to denote the adherents of the sect (60.3: but *multi* seems to be used in a general rather than in a technical sense in LAB; in any case, the equivalent term, πλῆθος , is used in the New Testament in reference to the masses rather than to a special group [e.g., Acts 2.6, 6.2, 6.5, 15.12, 15.30], and is likewise found in Talmudic literature with reference to members of a synagogue [Palestinian Talmud, Megillah 3.73d]), and "new womb" (60.3: to which, however, there is no exact parallel in the Dead Sea Scrolls, though 1 QH 3.9–10 speaks of new life coming to birth amid throes of death).

ᐟ Many of the allegedly parallel themes are, however, common in rabbinic literature. Thus, for example, the allegedly new or special covenant of 14.1–2 is based upon LAB's statement that only one-fiftieth of the Israelites went out of Egypt; but this is found in the Midrash (Mekilta Beshallaḥ, 1.24a, and Mekilta di R. Shimon, 38). Some of these, for example *civitas Dei,* are not at all specifically mentioned in LAB; and in some cases it should be noted that LAB's doctrine is in opposition to that of the Scrolls, as for example 60.2, which speaks of the light created from darkness and regards them as complementary, whereas the Manual of Discipline (1 QS 3.13–4.26) speaks of light and darkness as antithetical. As to phraseology, it is hardly unique to LAB and the Scrolls (thus the term "visitation" in the sense of punishment is found in Isaiah 10.3), or, as in 51.4, the parallels are not sufficiently close. Again, a closer parallel to the naming of Abraham in the Dead Sea Scrolls as "friend of God" is to be found in Isaiah 41.8, where God speaks of "Abraham, my friend" (similarly 2 Chronicles 20.7); LAB speaks of Moses, "the friend of the Lord." A closer parallel may be found in the Epistle of James (2.23) in the New Testament, where Abraham is called "the friend of God." Certain other comparisons between LAB and the Scrolls are not sufficiently unique to indicate a relationship. Thus in 12.5, as Vermès (*Scripture and Tradition,* pp. 56–57) notes, Moses is compared to a woman giving birth to her first-born, and in the Dead Sea Scrolls (*Hodayoth* 3.7–10) the poet compares himself to a woman in labor giving birth to her first-born, but the comparison is a commonplace one and is already found in Jeremiah 4.31; the actual comparison between Moses and a woman giving birth, which would have been striking, is not made in the Scroll. Again, a comparison of the language of the hymn in LAB 59.4 with that of Psalm 151 of

Grotto 11 of Qumran shows no common quality, as Delcor (pp. 1366–1367) has rightly concluded. The two verbal parallels which do seem striking are the phrase *sanctus christus* (59.2), which, as Winter has remarked ("The Holy Messiah," *Zeitschrift für die neutestamentliche Wissenschaft*, 50 [1959], p. 275), is paralleled by two passages in the Qumran literature and by no other passages in the Bible or rabbinic writings, and *minimus inter fratres meos* (62.5), which even Delcor (p. 1367) and Strugnell ("More Psalms of David," *Catholic Biblical Quarterly*, 27 [1965], p. 215, n. 6), who are generally skeptical of the theory of a connection between LAB and Qumran, regard as quite possibly connected with the opening phrase of Dead Sea Psalm 151 A.

g. *Mysticism*

Goodenough (*By Light, Light* [New Haven, 1935], pp. 265–266) notes thirteen passages (9.10, 12.1, 12.7, 12.9, 19.16, 20.2–3, 22.3, 23.6, 37.3, 51.3, 51.5, 53.2, 64.6; to this list add the following occurrences of the terminology of light: 9.8, 11.1, 11.2, 12.2, 18.4, 19.6, 20.3, 23.7, 23.10, 28.3, 33.3, 51.4, 51.6, 51.7, 53.8, 60.2) in which he finds evidence of LAB's acquaintance with mystic Judaism, especially as seen in reference to illumination. (On the symbolism of light see G. Vermès, "The Torah Is a Light," *Vetus Testamentum*, 8 [1958], pp. 436–438, who cites the aphorism "Light is the Law" [Megillah 16b] and notes Targumic parallels; also, most recently, M. Philonenko, "Éssénisme et gnose chez le Pseudo-Philon: Le symbolisme de la lumière dans le Liber Antiquitatum Biblicarum," *Studies in the History of Religions*, 12 [1967], pp. 401–410.) In particular, the description of God as invisible light and the reference to the illumination of the Patriarchs leads him to the conclusion that though the author of LAB was himself a Jew of the normative type, he could not avoid being influenced by the mystical group of Jews. Goodenough, p. 266, furthermore remarks that it is "very tempting" to interpret the vision of Samuel clothed in a white robe with two attendant angels (64.6) as a vision of the Logos and the two Powers. By the time, just before his death in 1965, that Goodenough had written the Corrigenda for his monumental work, *Jewish Symbols in the Greco-Roman Period* (vol. 13, Princeton, 1968, p. 228), he regarded this as a fact. But some of the passages cited by Goodenough have no significance because they are part of the mainstream of Jewish tradition (e.g., 9.10, the prophecy by a man in linen garments is quite clearly drawn from Ezekiel 10.2); but the fact that Clement of Alexandria asserts that initiates (μύσται) believed that Moses had the power to kill the Egyptian by a mere name, and then adds ʳhat with his new name, Melchi (Melchiel in LAB, 9.16), he ascended to heaven would indicate a special association of this name with a mystic cult. The fact that there are allusions to thaumaturgy, especially in the one major addition of the story, that of Kenaz, might suggest an affinity with such a personage as Apollonius of Tyana or Neoplatonism; but, of course, such motifs, as M. Hadas (*Review of Religion,* 16 [1951], p. 44) has acknowledged, are common in the Apocrypha and Pseudepigrapha, as well as in midrashic literature.

Even in the case of Philo himself, whose language is much closer to that of the mystery religions, we are hardly justified, as Goodenough himself recognized (*Journal of Biblical Literature,* 58 [1939], pp. 57–58) in accepting his thesis in *By Light, Light* that Philo was a mystic to whom Judaism was secondary; nor are we justified, as H. Chadwick (*Bulletin of the John Rylands Library,* 48 [1966], p. 304, n. 5) has properly observed, in concluding that Philo's Hellenistic Judaism actually possessed a concrete ritual imbedded in the mystery religions, since the metaphorical use of the language of the mysteries is common both to Greek philosophy starting with Plato's *Symposium* and to much of rabbinic literature. Indeed, as G. Scholem remarks (*Jewish Gnosticism, Merkabah Mysticism, and Talmudic Tradition* [New York, 1960], p. 5), the rabbinc mystics, far from constituting themselves a separate scct, wcrc highly conscious of their attachment to rabbinic Judaism. It seems hardly likely, then, that LAB, which has much less of the language of the mysteries than Philo, represents a work produced by mystics. Similarly, as P. Bogaert, *Apocalypse de Baruch,* vol. 1 (Paris, 1969), p. 246, has most recently recognized, there is nothing in LAB which authorizes its being classified as a kind of apocalypse of a historical type.

h. Gnosticism

Though Philonenko regards LAB as, properly speaking, an Essene work, he dates it later than the Qumran texts in that it contains notions that we may call "Gnostic." If we define Gnosticism with Scholem (*op. cit.,* p. 1) as "a mystical esotericism for the elect based on illumination and the acquisition of a higher knowledge of things heavenly and divine," it is perhaps tempting to join Philonenko, who argues that the conception of the illumination of the heart (9.8, 28.3) is found also in a Gnostic milieu in the Odes of Solomon (10.1). As a result of his study of David's psalm (60.2–4), Philonenko ("Remarques sur un hymne essénien de caractère gnostique," *Semitica,* 11 [1961], p. 48) not only calls Pseudo-Philo one of the creators of Jewish mysticism, stating that he is completely centered on what the rabbis called מעשה בראשית, "the work of creation," but also claims to find certain traits that are peculiar to Gnosticism, especially of the Valentinian type ("Essénisme et gnose chez le Pseudo-Philon. Le symbolisme de la lumière dans le Liber Antiquitatum Biblicarum," *Studies in the History of Religions,* 12 [Leiden, 1967], p. 409). In particular, he and E. Stauffer (*New Testament Theology* [trans. J. Marsh, London, 1955], p. 267, n. 125) claim that the primordial syzygy of Darkness and Silence (60.2) is typically Gnostic (Pseudo-Clementine, *Homilies,* 2.15–16; Irenaeus, *Adversus Haereses,* 1.1.1.). Likewise the distinction between the Echo and the Logos (60.3) is said (Philonenko, "Remarques," p. 52) to be typically Gnostic. The phrase "the silence spoke" is related, according to Philonenko (pp. 49–50) and R. M. Wilson (*The Gnostic Problem* [London, 1958], pp. 43–44, n. 122), to the notions that Christ is the Logos coming from Silence (Ignatius of Antioch, *Magnesians,* 8.2), that it is the intellect which utters the unique word in the silent grace (*Evangelium Veritatis,* attributed by some to Valentinus, 37.10–12), and that Man is the mouth of the silent Silence (Mark the Magician, *ap.* Irenaeus, *Adversus Haereses,* 1.14.3)—all of which help to place LAB in a typically Gnostic atmosphere. But the theory of LAB's relation to Gnosticism loses force when we realize that there is no indication that the work is intended for a specially elected group, nor is there the dualism of body and soul or the speculations on cosmology, which are central to the movement.

i. Dura Europus

   That there is a possible connection between LAB's mysticism and that displayed in the frescoes at Dura Europus has been suggested by Philonenko ("Une paraphrase du cantique d'Anne," *Revue d'Histoire et de Philosophie Religieuses,* 42 [1962], pp. 162–163), who points out a parallel between the milk streaming forth from Hannah's breasts (51.2) as a fountain for the twelve tribes and the well of Miriam portrayed at Dura from which come forth a dozen streams, destined for the twelve tribes of Israel. Again, Goodenough (*Jewish Symbols in the Greco-Roman Period,* vol. 9, pp. 190–191), has indicated the parallel between 59.4, referring to David in the care of angels and guardians, and the painting of Dura depicting the six brothers of David in a hieratic pose. Finally, Goodenough (*Jewish Symbols,* vol.

9, p. 170) finds a connection between LAB's depiction of Samuel in a white robe (64.6) and the painting of Samuel in such garb at Dura. But none of these is sufficiently distinctive to prove the connection; thus in the first instance, we have Hannah vs. Miriam, breasts vs. a well, milk vs. water; in the second, the whole point of LAB is that David required angelic guardians because his brothers envied him, whereas in Dura the brothers are aligned with him; and the depiction of Samuel in a white robe may have no further significance than that it indicates that he is dead and is dressed in the usual white shroud (see my note *ad loc.*).

j. LAB as apologetic

Another theory, propounded by Winter ("Philo, Biblical Antiquities of," in the *Interpreter's Dictionary of the Bible,* vol. 3 [New York, 1962], p. 796), among others, is that LAB is an apologetic work, comparable, we may suggest, to Philo's *Hypothetica* and to Josephus' *Contra Apionem* and the early books of the *Antiquities* (see below, Chapter XI f.), and intended to correct certain misconceptions about Judaism. We know that there is a long history of *aporiai* ("difficulties") literature (cf., e.g., Philo's *Quaestiones et Solutiones in Genesin et Exodum*), noting difficulties and embarrassing details in the Bible. For example, the statement that Job married Dinah, Jacob's daughter (8.8) shows the universalistic strain in Judaism, since Job was not even a Hebrew (Baba Bathra, 15b). Again, if we adopt the reading *omnes* of the *editio princeps* in 51.4, this would support Philonenko's universalistic understanding of the hymn. Likewise, heretics were constantly pointing to lacunae in Scriptural accounts, particularly in the names of women. The Talmud (Baba Bathra, 91a), well aware of this practice, justifies supplying such information by asking the following: "In what [respect] do [these names, i.e., of the mothers of Abraham, Haman, David, and Samson] matter?" It answers that these names matter in respect to a reply to *minim*, presumably sectarians, heretics, Gnostics, or Christians.

k. Polemic against intermarriage

One way to determine the purpose of LAB is by noting those passages that have no parallels in other extant midrashic writings. Such a passage is LAB 9.5, in which we read that Tamar's intent in having relations with Judah was to prevent her being joined with Gentiles. The incident of the Midianite women who lead the Israelites astray (18.13–14), though, of course, based on Scripture, is stressed. Similarly, the elaboration of the incident of Micah and of the idol which he made culminates in the statement (44.7) that as a result the Israelites "lusted after strange women." Similarly LAB (45.3) adds the unique detail that the Levite's concubine of Judges 19.25 had transgressed against her husband by having relations with foreigners, the Amalekites, and thus attempts to justify the abuse that she suffered.

CHAPTER X
TEACHINGS
(*James, pp. 34–42*)

There is little in LAB which is in direct conflict with rabbinic Judaism. Even the one exceptional passage (33.5) cited by Cohn (p. 324, n. 4), expressing the view that the prayers of the dead have no efficacy, is hardly in conflict with the prevalent rabbinic view opposing the intrusion of any, even the most pious, dead between God and Israel. The notion that a husband (LAB 42.1) asks a wife to set him free to marry another is consonant with Mark 10.2, but opposed to rabbinic law. However, LAB is completely consonant with rabbinic practice in its avoidance of any indication of knowledge of classical Greek and Latin literature and science, though there are a number of passages where it might have displayed such knowledge.

That LAB has nothing to do with the Sadducees is clear from its strong belief in resurrection of the dead (3.10, 19.12, etc.), the implied acceptance, and, at any rate, lack of denunciation of the Oral Law, and belief in angels (15.5, 19.16, etc.).

Two areas of doctrine which are of particular interest to Pseudo-Philo are eschatology and angelology. The relevant passages connected with the former have been collected by James, pp. 34 ff.; to these should be added 15.5, 25.7, 44.4, and 60.3, cited by Klausner (*The Messianic Idea in Israel from Its Beginning to the Completion of the Mishnah,* trans. by W. F. Stinespring [New York, 1955], p. 367).

a. Angelology

James (pp. 38–39) had already noted the importance of the role played by angels in LAB, an importance which in itself would make a tie between LAB and the Dead Sea Scrolls not unlikely. Interest centers on four angels mentioned by name by LAB, Gethel or Ingethel (27.10), Zeruel or Cervihel (27.10, 61.5), Nathaniel 38.3), and Phadahel (42.10), whose names, to be sure, are apparently found in rabbinic and magical literature, but without the association with the incidents cited in LAB. What seems rather remarkable (though hitherto unnoticed) is that there is some reason for thinking that the angel in question in all of these cases is Gabriel, who is preeminently the angel of war, as Origen (*De Princip.* 1.8.1) had already noted, and as the rabbis similarly observe (it was Gabriel, for example, who destroyed Sodom, annihilated Sennacherib's camp, and set fire to the

Temple in Jerusalem: see Ginzberg, 5.71, n. 13). Thus in 9.10, the man clothed in linen who appears to Miriam is, according to rabbinic tradition (Tanḥuma [Buber] 3.84), identical with Gabriel. In 27.10 Jerahmeel says that it was Gabriel who aided Kenaz; in 38.3 the angel appointed over fire is Gabriel in rabbinic angelology; in Luke 1.19, which parallels LAB in 42.10, the angel corresponding to Phadahel who appears to Zechariah, the father of John, is Gabriel, who plays a role as guide of war in the Scroll of the War of the Sons of Light and the Sons of Darkness (9.16): If, indeed, Gabriel is here meant, the chances of a connection between LAB and the Scrolls are increased because of the role of Gabriel in the war against the Sons of Darkness, though the men of the first human tower carry the legend Michael, whereas the name of Gabriel appears only on the second tower. The fact that LAB has apparently given special significance to Gabriel rather than to Michael, who holds a higher rank in Jewish angelology (Ḥagigah 12b and Ḥullin 40a) and in the Dead Sea Scroll cited above, may be a clue as to the circle of the author. Ginzberg, 5.71, n. 13, notes that among the Babylonian Jews Gabriel's prestige almost equaled that of his rival Michael, but there is no direct indication that the author of LAB lived in Babylonia, though perhaps the possible connection of LAB and the mysticism in the paintings at Dura may be so interpreted. Gabriel has a special role in Christianity as the angel who announced the births of John (Luke 1.19) and of Jesus (Luke 1.26), but there is no direct indication that the work is of Christian origin. Gabriel does play a special role explaining the apocalyptic vision of Daniel concerning the ram and the he-goat (Daniel 8.16 ff.) and in the eschatological prediction of the Seventy Weeks (Daniel 9.21 ff.); and this may be a clue as to the provenance of LAB, which may reflect the rivalry in Jewish tradition between Michael and Gabriel (see Ginzberg, 5.4–5, n. 8). But the matter is very much in doubt.

b. Messiah

It would be surprising in a work showing eschatological interest that there should be no reference to the Messiah. And yet, as James (pp. 41–42) has indicated, there are no direct references to the Messiah in the work, though Winter ("Philo, Biblical Antiquities of," *Interpreter's Dictionary of the Bible,* vol. 3 [New York, 1962], p. 795) has noted the occurrence of the striking expression *sanctus christus,* "the holy one, the anointed" (59.2), which has a parallel only in the Dead Sea Scrolls and which may be of messianic significance, even though the passage clearly refers to David.

Philonenko's claim ("Une paraphrase du cantique d'Anne") that Hannah's prayer (51.3 ff.) is important for the history of messianic doctrine rests on regarding as messianic passages "The light shall come forth out of which wisdom shall be born" (51.4), and "And so shall all judgment endure until he be revealed which holdeth it" (51.5), to which we may add the sense of anticipation found in 51.6.

Delcor (p. 1373) raises the possibility (cf. A. Jaubert, "La notion d'alliance dans le Judaisme aux abords de l'ère chrétienne," in *Patristica Sorbonensia,* 6 [Paris, 1963], p. 286) that the reason why LAB ends with the death of Saul is to mark the expectation of the Davidic Messiah; and we may add that the prediction in David's psalm (60.3) that from his loins will be born after a time "he that shall subdue you" [Saul's evil spirit] perhaps supports this conjecture. In any case, even A. Strobel (*Untersuchungen zum Eschatologischen Verzögerungsproblem auf Grund der Spätjüdischurchristlichen Geschichte von Habakuk 2.2 ff.* [Leiden, 1961], p. 75), who is skeptical of all other references to the Messiah in our work, regards this passage as an allusion to the Messiah rather than to Solomon.

Still, as Klausner (p. 367) must concede, the number of even indirect messianic references in LAB are not numerous, presumably because it is primarily a historical account. Dietzfelbinger (p. 153) concludes that LAB is a quite unmessianic book and stresses that if it were messianic, we should expect a reference to the Messiah in 48.1 in connection with the identification of Phinehas and Elijah, since Elijah is traditionally regarded as a precursor of the Messiah; but this very passage has definite eschatological and perhaps messianic expectations.

Chapter XI
RELATION TO OTHER BOOKS
(*James, pp.* 42–60)

a. The Septuagint

The citation of several Biblical passages in LAB exactly reproduces the LXX: we may give as examples 1.16 (*placuit . . . Deus*),
1.20 (*Hic requiem dabit*), 2.9 (Tubal rather than Tubal-Cain), 9.12
(*thibin*), 11.10–11 (the reversal [in some MSS. of the LXX] in the
order of murder and adultery in the Ten Commandments), 23.1
(Shiloh), 56.4 (Baam), and 63.2 (Doeg the Syrian). Yet in many
other places his text is in agreement with the Hebrew text: we may
cite 2.1 (LAB translates the Hebrew Nod as *tremens,* "trembling"),
2.5 (Matusael, a close transliteration of the Hebrew vs. the LXX's
Μαθουσαλά), 3.1 ("sons of God" vs. LXX's angels), 3.2 ("shall
not judge" vs. LXX's "shall not remain"), 3.3 ("it repenteth me" vs.
LXX's "was angry"), 3.4 ("of cedar wood" vs. LXX's "square"), 3.6
("for man's sake" vs. LXX's "because of the works of man"), 3.9
("hath left off" vs. LXX's "is bent upon"), 4.9 (omission of the
two Cainans), 8.3 (Sarai vs. LXX's Sara), 12.4 ("is corrupted" vs.
LXX's "has transgressed"), 17.2 ("almonds" vs. LXX's "nuts," especially "walnuts"), 18.2 ("interpreter of dreams" vs. LXX's Phathoura), 19.16 ("according to the mouth of the Lord" vs. LXX's "by
the word of the Lord"), 19.16 ("he buried" vs. LXX's "they buried"),
and 50.6 (Eli himself speaks to Hannah vs. LXX, where the words are
spoken by his serving lad). Hence Cohn concluded that the book was
originally written in Hebrew and that all traces of the influence of the
Septuagint and of other Greek versions are to be ascribed to the
person who translated the book from Hebrew into Greek. But, as in
the case of Philo's and Josephus' quotations, which do not always
agree with our LXX, so LAB's quotations may reflect a text of the
LXX which differs from the majority of our MSS. (as in 3.1: "sons of
God"; 3.3: "it repenteth Me" and 11.10–11: the reversal of the order
of murder and adultery in the Ten Commandments), since, as is well
known, many versions of the Greek translation are no longer extant.
In some cases, as in 2.1, we have reason to suspect that the text of LAB
or the LXX on which it was based had been corrected in accordance
with Aquila (e.g., 51.1, *fortis*), Symmachus and/or Theodotion.

A complicating factor is that LAB has a number of passages which agree neither with the Hebrew text nor with the LXX. Thus, in the chronology of the Patriarchs (1.2 ff.) there are three such instances in the ages at the birth of their sons and two such instances in the years that they lived after the birth of their sons. Again, despite Azariah dei Rossi's and Cohn's emendation, the text of 3.6 giving the date of the Flood is in accord with neither the Hebrew text nor the LXX. The reading of 3.8 ("a savor of rest," a play on the name of Noah) is found in neither the Hebrew text nor the LXX and apparently indicates a slightly different text of the Bible (הנוח for הניחח) or a different interpretation. In the order of the twelve stones (26.10 ff.) LAB is sometimes in agreement with the Hebrew text, sometimes with the LXX, and sometimes with neither. Finally, in 63.3, in giving the number of priests slain, LAB agrees with neither. G. Hölscher ("Josephus," Pauly-Wissowa, *Real-Encyclopädie*, 9 [1916], pp. 1955–1960), confronted with a similar problem in Josephus, argued that Josephus used neither the Hebrew nor the Greek Bible but made use of histories or paraphrases of the Bible written by Jewish Hellenists. The same possibility exists for Pseudo-Philo, though if he lived in Palestine and was as pious as he appears to be, it seems unlikely that he would not consult the Bible directly—and generally in Hebrew.

b. Jubilees

James (pp. 45–46) argues that Pseudo-Philo had not only read Jubilees, but to a certain degree deliberately supplements it. To the evidence cited by James we may add the following: 1) Though Pseudo-Philo states (1.2) that Adam begat twelve sons he proceeds to enumerate (1.3) only nine, precisely the number specified by Jubilees (4.10); 2) There is a possible analogy between 3.10 and Jubilees 23 ("They will all complete their days in peace and joy and live without Satan or other corrupter") and Jubilees 50 ("No Satan nor any evil one shall oppose Israel, and the earth shall be pure from thenceforth forever," cited by Thackeray, *The Relation of St. Paul to Contemporary Jewish Thought* [London, 1900], p. 124, together with *Assumptio Mosis* 10.1: "And then His kingdom will appear throughout all His creation, and then Satan will be no more and sorrow will depart with him"); 3) As in Jubilees 19.29, LAB 18.5 also calls Jacob God's first-born son, though such a statement is also found in rabbinic literature; 4) Perhaps the date of Pentecost (23.2), the sixteenth or seventeenth of the third month, which is only one day away from the reckoning of the Book of Jubilees (1.1, 15.1, 44.1–4), which asserts that it must be kept on the fifteenth day of the third month. But LAB also apparently deliberately corrects Jubilees. In addition to the one instance cited by James (p. 45), we may take note of the following: 1) In 3.2 LAB departs from the LXX, Jubilees, and Philo (*De Gigantibus* 5.19) and follows the Hebrew text in reading "judge" rather than "remain"; 2) In 3.8 LAB disagrees with the LXX of Genesis 8.19 and with Jubilees in the order of the victims mentioned; 3) In 4.11 Ragau's wife is Melcha, in Jubilees 11.7 she is Ora; 4) In 6.4 ff. Abram refuses to lie and thus declines to join in Joctan's plot, whereas in Jubilees 12.28 Abram deceives his father in telling him that he merely desires to see the land of Canaan and in promising that he will thereafter return home; 5) According to Jubilees 2.2, the spirits were created on the first day, whereas according to LAB 60.3, they were created on the second day. We conclude, as does Steck (*Israel und das gewaltsame Geschick der Propheten* [Neukirchen, 1967], p. 174, n. 6), that James' contention (p. 45) that LAB is primarily dependent upon Jubilees is doubtful. Moreover, we see that Pseudo-Philo is a more responsible theologian, as may be discerned from the fact that whereas Jubilees 4.9–11 says that Cain and Seth married sisters, LAB 1.1 states merely that Adam's second child was a daughter. On the whole, however, the theological viewpoint of Jubilees, particularly with regard to the problem of evil and of fallen angels and demons, is close to that of LAB.

c. The Genesis Apocryphon

In particular it is tempting to investigate the non-committal suggestion of Winter ("Der gegenwärtige Stand der Erforschung der in Palästina neu gefundenen hebräischen Handschiften," *Theologische Literaturzeitung,* 82 [1957], p. 260), that an investigation of the parallels between LAB and the Genesis Apocryphon should prove fruitful. This is particularly so, as Delcor (p. 1364) has rightly remarked, because the midrashic method of LAB is similar to that of the Apocryphon in that both often present their discussions in connection with specific Biblical texts. Philonenko ("Une paraphrase du cantique d'Anne," *Revue d'Histoire et de Philosophie Religieuses,* 42 [1962], p. 158) goes so far as to couple Pseudo-Philo with the authors of the Book of Jubilees and the Genesis Apocryphon as masters of Essene Midrash. Unfortunately, most of the Apocryphon is in such a poor state of preservation that, when unrolled, it cannot be read. In the part, however, that has been published we may perhaps note three indications of a possible relationship with LAB: 1) Genesis Apocryphon 22.13–17 reads "Salem, that is Jerusalem," an explanation that is not to be found in Genesis 14.18, though it is found several times in Josephus (*Bellum Judaicum*, 6.438; *Antiquitates Judaicae*, 1.180, 7.67; and *Contra Apionem*, 1.172–173). It is not, to be sure, found in LAB, but one detects in the explanation a refutation of the Samaritan contention that Melchizedek had worshipped God in a region around Shechem in Samaritan territory. If we grant (as I do not), with Spiro, that LAB is an anti-Samaritan polemic, this would tie together the Apocryphon and LAB. But we may, first of all, note that if LAB were interested in combating the claims of the Samaritans, he does not take advantage of the opportunity, for he omits all mention of Melchizedek and Salem; and secondly, as Winter ("Note on Salem-Jerusalem," *Novum Testamentum*, 2 [1957], pp. 151–152) has rightly noted, the phrase "that is Jerusalem" is a gloss which may have come from the hand of the author of the Apocryphon but which may also be due to a later copyist. 2) In 60.1 David appears as an exorcist of Saul's evil spirit; similarly, as Philonenko ("Remarques sur un hymne essénien de caractère gnostique," *Semitica*, 11 [1961], p. 47) has noted, in the Genesis Apocryphon, 20.16–19, when Pharaoh is smitten by an evil spirit, Abraham is sent for to lay his hands upon him and to chase the demon. 3) M. R. Lehmann, "I Q Genesis Apocryphon in the Light of the Targumim and Midrashim," *Revue de Qumran*, 1 (1958–59), pp. 249–263, notes a number of instances of complete agreement between the Apocryphon and Targum Onkelos and Targum pseudo-Jonathan; LAB quite probably has affinities with these Targumim, and we may perhaps conjecture that it has a relationship with the Apocryphon as well. But too little of the Apocryphon is legible for a definitive judgment; and, moreover, in the one case where LAB does parallel it, it differs from it in giving the names of the two wives of Lamech: LAB, 2.6, following the Hebrew text, gives the names of the wives as Ada and Sella, whereas the Apocryphon 2, gives the names of one of them as Bet Enosh, in agreement with Jubilees 4.28 (Betenos) and the Damascus MS. (published by Harkavy in *Ha-Pisgah*, 1.58; see Ginzberg, 5.146, n. 42); that this is indeed her name may be seen from the fact that in the Damascus MS. the word שמה, "her name" is added.

d. IV Esdras and Syriac Apocalypse of Baruch

James (pp. 46–58) points out at length what he considers the very marked resemblances between IV Esdras and Baruch on the one hand, and LAB on the other. He even states that the Latin of

IV Esdras is so similar to that of LAB that "one is tempted to say that they are by the same hand; but it is safer to regard them as products of the same school and age" (p. 54). None of the critics has thus far challenged James' conclusion, which is supported by numerous parallels in ideas and phraseology among the three works. [After these words were written, P. Bogaert, *Apocalypse de Baruch,* vol. 1 (Paris, 1969), p. 243, appeared, challenging James' and Violet's view that LAB is a sister of the apocalypses of Baruch and Esdras. However, the fact that Baruch is concerned primarily with the capture of Jerusalem and the destruction of the Temple sets it far apart from LAB, where, as noted above, the Temple is hardly of central interest.] B. Violet, *Die Apokalypsen des Esra und des Baruch in deutscher Gestalt* (Leipzig, 1924), p. xlviii, accepts James' statement that IV Esdras used LAB, though he adds that until we have a critical edition of the Latin text of LAB we must wait for a final judgment. He likewise concludes (p. lxxxi) that LAB must be looked upon as one of the most important sources of Baruch, and conjectures that if the sequel should be discovered, the parallels with Baruch will be even stronger. O. Eissfeldt, *Einleitung in das Alte Testament*[3] (Tübingen, 1964), p. 853, accepts the dependence of IV Esdras and Baruch upon LAB or upon one of its sources and uses this to provide a *terminus a quo* for determining the date of LAB. Delcor (p. 1370), in the latest comprehensive survey of LAB, accepts the relationship as certain. But, as James himself (p. 54) realizes, not all the parallels are equally strong, and some, probably most, as G. F. Moore contends (*Judaism in the First Centuries of the Christian Era,* vol. 2 [Cambridge, Mass., 1927], p. 285), for example, LAB 25.10 ff. and Baruch 60.1, pertaining to the ways of the Amorites, may more likely be explained as due to LAB's indebtedness to rabbinic tradition, while others, e.g., the primordial silence mentioned in 60.2 and IV Esdras 6.39 and Baruch 3.7, may be due to a common tradition which eventually finds its way into Gnostic literature. Moreover, as P. Bogaert, *Apocalypse de Baruch,* vol. 1 (1969), p. 246, has remarked, the revelations made to Moses and other personages in LAB are neither central nor essential, unlike the situation in the Apocalypse of Baruch and, for that matter, in the *Assumptio Mosis.* Finally, the verbal similarities between IV Esdras and Baruch and LAB may be due to the usage of the translator rather than to the usage of the original author. In any case, the question of LAB's relation to IV Esdras and Baruch deserves to be reexamined, especially in their quotation and exegesis of the Bible.

e. New Testament

In his article announcing the rediscovery of LAB, Cohn (p. 313), makes the strong and unequivocal statement that Christian elements are entirely absent, and that there is not even the faintest allusion to Christianity, nor is there any Christian addition to the narrative. James (p. 59) is not quite so sure. He says that there are not many direct resemblances and that he doubts whether the author allowed his consciousness of Christianity to find expression in his book, though he does note (pp. 59–60) a number of coincidences of language. In his extended treatment of LAB, Dietzfelbinger (pp. 196–245) comes to a very different conclusion, for he finds numerous analogies between LAB and the New Testament both in language and in the ideas of God, creation, sin, birth stories, eschatology, and the treatment of such Biblical figures as Abel, Abraham, Sarah, Isaac, Jacob, Moses, Balaam, Phinehas, and Samuel. The truth is that one can indeed cite a number of verbal parallels which James missed: 1) 6.11 ("Thy blood be upon thy head": cf. Matthew 23.34–35, 27.25, Acts 5.28, especially 18.6, and 20.26); 2) 9.8 ("a perpetual light": cf. John 1.9); 3) 9.10 ("that which shall be born of you": cited by James, p. 60, but without the interesting notation made by Winter, "Jewish Folklore in the Matthaean Birth Story," *Hibbert Journal,* 53 [1954–55], p. 39, that the use of the neuter may have been unconsciously influenced by its use in Luke 1.35); 4) 11.1 ("I will give light unto the world": cf. John 1.5); 5) 11.2 (the use of the phrase "on the third day" as equivalent to "after three days": so also Matthew 27.63, Mark 8.31, 9.31, 10.34, Luke 24.7, Acts 10.41, and 1 Corinthians 15.4, noted by Dietzfelbinger, pp. 236–237; 6) 22.3 ("with him light abideth": cf. John 1.4); 7) 25.3 ("Moses the friend of the Lord": cf. the Epistle of James 2.23: "He [Abraham] was called the friend of God"); 8) 25.7 and 26.1 (handing over a sinner to death in order to save him: cf. 1 Cor. 5.5 and 1 Tim. 1.20); 9) 26.13 ("When the sins of my people are filled up": cf. Matthew 23.32, cited by O. H. Steck, *Israel und das gewaltsame Geschick der Propheten* [Neukirchen, 1967], pp. 174–175); 10) 26.13 ("The light of the precious stones shall be their light": cf. Revelation 21.23, where, as Thackeray [*The Relation of St. Paul to Contemporary Jewish Thought,* p. 244] notes, the making of the twelve stones has likewise preceded); 11) 27.9 ("the spirit of the Lord clothed him": cf. Romans 13.14 and Galatians 3.27); 12) 28.9 ("they shall be changed": cf. 1 Corinthians 15.51); 13) 29.4 ("let not your heart be like unto the waves of the sea": cf.

James 1.6); 14) 30.7 ("God is life: cf. John 1.4, "In him was
life"); 15) 40.6 ("let the moth eat it": cf. Matthew 6.19–20, Epistle
of James 5.2); 16) 42.2, 42.5 (the upper chamber as a place for
prayer: cf. Acts 1.13, 9.39–40, 20.8); 17) 44.10 (the punishment
fits the crime: cf. Matthew 7.2–3, Mark 4.24, Acts 7.41–43, Romans
1.22–32, 2.1); 18) 52.3 ("if ye . . . persist in your iniquities I shall
be guiltless": cf. Acts 18.6); 19) 53.6 ("with thy right ear attend
and with thy left refrain": cf. Luke 22.50, John 18.10).

In addition there are certain ideas which are common to LAB
and the New Testament: 1) Klausner (p. 367) regards the end of
21.6 as possibly a Christian interpolation, since it speaks of the
Israelites as fighting "against the salvation that shall be born unto
them." Klausner (*ibid.*) regards as probably a Christian interpolation
LAB 60.3, which speaks of the forthcoming birth from the loins of
David of one who will subdue demons; 2) Winter ("The Proto-
Source of Luke I," *Novum Testamentum,* 1 [1956], p. 186) has noted
a number of parallels between the narrative of the birth of Samson
(42.1 ff.) and the account of the birth of John in Luke 1. We may
add that Gabriel, who, under other names, plays a key role in LAB, is
the angel who announces the birth of John (Luke 1.19) and of Jesus
(Luke 1.26). Similarly there are correspondences, as noted by Winter
(*op. cit.,* p. 193), between the story of Samuel's birth (LAB 49.1 ff.)
and those of John and Jesus in Luke 1, to the point where Winter
(p. 199) claims that he can partly reconstruct the form of the Baptist
Document from LAB. Philonenko ("Une paraphrase du cantique
d'Anne," *Revue d'Histoire et de Philosophie Religieuses,* 42 [1962],
p. 163) even goes so far as to suggest that it is not unlikely that the
author of the Protoevangel of James 6.3 gave the name of the mother
of Samuel to the mother of Mary, so much was he influenced by LAB's
version of Hannah's prayer. 3) The idea that a husband (LAB 42.1)
asks a wife to set him free to marry another is contrary to rabbinic
interpretation of the Torah but is found in Mark 10.12.

A close examination of these parallels, however, will show that
in some cases there are parallels with rabbinic literature as close as
those with the New Testament (e.g., 9.8: cf. Debarim Rabbah 4.4
["The soul and the Torah are compared to a lamp"]); 25.7: cf. Yoma
8.8; 30.7: cf. Aboth 6.7, Sifre Debarim 32.2, Mekilta on Exodus
17.18, cited by Winter, "Monogenēs Para Patros," *Zeitschrift für
Religions- und Geistesgeschichte,* 5 [1953], p. 364; 44.10: cf. Ta'anith
21a, Aboth 5.11, Shabbath 2.6). In others there are closer parallels

with other Apocryphal and Pseudepigraphical books, notably IV Esdras
and Baruch (e.g., 11.1: cf. IV Esdras 9.31, Baruch 59.2; 28.9: cf. IV
Esdras 6.1, Baruch 49.3, 51.1–10); in some cases the very idea is
opposed to Christianity (e.g., 11.2, 11.5: the idea of the eternity of
the Law is overthrown by the Christian zealots); in some cases there
are considerable discrepancies in outlook between LAB and the New
Testament (2 Peter 2.15, Jude 1.11, and Revelation 2.14 are all
derogatory in condemning Balaam as an evil teacher and in stressing
his lust for money, whereas the picture of Balaam in LAB [18.2 ff.] is,
on the whole, much more favorable); and in some cases the motifs
(e.g. 52.6, 53.6) may be too common to be distinctive. But enough
parallels remain so that we may say that both LAB and the New
Testament go back to common traditions.

f. Josephus
      Aside from James' remarks (p. 27) that the title of LAB is
probably due to a recollection of Josephus' *Antiquities* and that (p.
146, n. on 25.1) the best text of Josephus substitutes the name of
Kenaz for that of Othniel, thus providing some slight parallel for the
extensive treatment of Kenaz in LAB, James makes no attempt to
describe any parallels between the two works. And yet that there is a
relationship seems indicated both by their general method and outlook
and a number of specific details; and in fact we may with justice
conclude that one of the closest counterparts to LAB is indeed
Josephus' homiletic exposition of the Scriptures in the early books of
the *Antiquities,* though, to be sure, it is presumed that Josephus'
readers have never read the Bible, whereas the author of LAB assumes
that they have (cf., e.g., 35.7, 56.7, 63.5). Moreover, in addition to a
number of differences of detail, LAB has much more legendary material, as Schürer, 3[4], p. 385 notes, and has nothing of the Hellenism
which is evident in Josephus. To be sure, Spiro, particularly in "Samaritans, Tobiads, and Judahites in Pseudo-Philo," *PAAJR,* 20 (1951),
p. 282, and in his doctoral thesis, *Manners of Rewriting Biblical History from Chronicles to Pseudo-Philo* (Columbia University diss.,
1953), and Bogaert (*Apocalypse de Baruch,* vol. 1 [Paris, 1969], p.
246) have remarked that LAB is a half-way point between the Jewish
historians Eupolemus and Josephus (see above Chapter VIIa).
      First we may note parallels with Josephus which are to be found
in no other work: 1) In both 3.9 and *Antiquitates Judaicae* (=*AJ*)
1.70, Adam predicts a destruction of the universe in one case by a
violent fire and in another by a mighty deluge of water. In the Talmud

(Zebaḥim 116a) there is no prediction or vow as in LAB and Josephus; 2) Both LAB 6.18 and *AJ* 1.160 know the tradition of a place named after Abram; 3) 9.1 and *AJ* (1.157, 160) both omit Abram's stay at Shechem and Bethel (Gen. 12.6–8), which the Samaritans equated with their sacred Mount Gerizim, perhaps out of anti-Samaritan motives; 4) 10.1 and Josephus (*AJ* 2.294 ff.), in enumerating the ten plagues, mention only nine, though each omits a different plague, boils (the sixth plague) in the case of LAB, and the murrain on cattle (the fifth plague) in the case of Josephus; 5) Both LAB (14.3) and Josephus (3.196, 3.288) differ from the Hebrew text and LXX in their count of the Israelites, though the actual numbers vary somewhat; 6) 18.10 and *AJ* 4.113 indicate that it was Balaam who offered the sacrifice, whereas according to the LXX and Philo (*De Vita Mosis* 1.277) it was Balak who did so, and, according to the Targumim, following the Hebrew text, both Balaam and Balak sacrificed together; 7) Both LAB 18.10 ff., and *AJ* 9.199 ff. combine the four prophecies of Balaam in Numbers 23.7 ff.; 8) The very language of *AJ* 4.129 ("Take of your daughters those who are comeliest") is similar to 18.13 ("Choose out the most comely women that are among you"); 9) 19.15 and *AJ* 4.303 both speak of God's predictions to Moses of future events; 10) In the one place where LAB's list of Kenaz's twelve stones (26.9 ff.) does not agree with the LXX, namely, in the identity of stones 8 and 9, it agrees with Josephus (*AJ* 3.168); 11) 31.2 says that of the army of Sisera there were slain 90 times 97,000 men, and similarly Josephus (*Bellum Judaicum* 6.420) mentions 97,000 as the number of Jews who were taken captive during the war against the Romans; 12) Isaac's implication (32.3) that he ought never to have been born at all if he were to reject the decision of God and of Abraham to sacrifice him is also found in *AJ* 1.232; 13) In Jotham's parable (37.2–3) LAB departs from the order in Judges 9.7 and follows the order of Josephus (5.235–239) in placing the fig tree and vine first, though, to be sure, at the end of the parable (37.3) LAB returns to the order of Judges in putting the fig tree and vine second and third; 14) The statement of Jephthah's daughter (40.2) that she cannot be sorrowful in her death because she sees her people delivered is paralleled by a similar statement in *AJ* 5.265; 15) Both LAB 42.1 and *AJ* 5.276 stress Samson's noble origin, whereas the rabbis, in their criticism of Samson, omit all references to his ancestry; 16) LAB 42.7 is closer to Josephus (5.281) than to Scripture in asserting that Manoah had lingering doubts about the angel's promise; 17) LAB 42.8 and Josephus 5.282 avoid mentioning Manoah's ignorance, stressed by the Midrash, of the fact that this was an angel whom he had invited to eat; 18) Both 42.9 and Josephus 5.284 add the statement (taken from an earlier passage in Judges 6.21) that the angel put forth his hand and touched Manoah's sacrifice with the end of his sceptre and that fire came forth out of the rock; 19) Both LAB 43.6 and Josephus 5.309 indicate that Samson violated the Nazirite prohibition against drinking; 20) Both 43.7 (in the only reading which is stemmatically possible) and Josephus 5.314 state that the Philistines called for Samson in order that they might mock him, whereas the Hebrew text and LXX (Judges 16.25) state that they summoned him that *he* might make sport before them; 21) Both LAB 55.5 and Josephus 6.8–10 present a dispute among the Philistine wise men as to what to do with the ark which they have captured; 22) LAB 55.7 and Josephus 6.11 speak of the cattle being set by the Philistines at the head of three ways; 23) In 56.3 and Josephus 6.37–40 it is during the night rather than during the day, as in 1 Samuel 9.15, that God appears to Samuel to reveal the forthcoming visit of Saul; 24) In 57.2 and Josephus 4.46–50 we find the same connection between the false accusation by Korah of Moses' corruptibility and the punishment of Korah and his followers by being swallowed up by the earth; 25) After Samuel anoints David as king he begins to sing a psalm (59.4) in Pseudo-Philo and to prophesy in Josephus (6.166); 26) Both LAB 63.2 and *AJ* 6.244, following the LXX, read "Doeg the Syrian"; 27) The three oldest MSS. of Josephus (6.260) agree with LAB (63.3) in giving the number of the priests slain at Nob as 385; 28) Two MSS. and the Latin version of Josephus (6.370–371) agree with LAB 65.3 in using successively two different words for the sword, ῥομφαία (*romphea*) and μάχαιρα (*machera*), in the account of Saul's death, whereas the LXX on 1 Samuel 31.4 uses only the former.

In addition there are a number of cases where Josephus is not alone in agreeing with LAB, but both may reflect a common tradition: 1) LAB 1.1–2 and Josephus 1.52 both note that Adam and Eve had daughters, a point in which they agree with Jubilees 4.1, 8; 2) LAB 6.14, Josephus, *AJ* 1.113–114, and Pirke di R. Eliezer 24 all connect Nimrod with the Tower of Babel; 3) LAB 10.1 calls the fourth plague *panmixia,* that is, a mixture (of wild beasts), in contrast to the LXX on Exodus 8.17 (21), and Philo *De Vita Mosis* 1.23, where it is called κυνόμυια (dog-fly). Josephus, *AJ* 2.303, and the prevailing view of the rabbis agree with LAB; 4) Balaam's prediction that Israel will be spread over the entire world is found in LAB 18.11, Josephus, *AJ* 4.115–117, and Targum Onkelos on Numbers 23.9; 5) The view that Moses' death took place in public and that God buried him is found in LAB 19.16. Josephus, *AJ* 4.326, and *Assumptio Mosis* 1.15, thus combatting the view that Moses did not die at all; 6) That Joshua used free speech in addressing God is clear from the tone of LAB 21.3, as well as from Josephus, *AJ* 5.38, and rabbinic literature (Sanhedrin 43b, etc.); 7) In identifying Sarah with Iscah LAB 23.4 agrees with Josephus 1.151, as well as with the rabbis (Sanhedrin 69b, etc.); 8) The description of the elements of nature joining in the battle between Barak and Sisera found in LAB 31.1 is paralleled both by Josephus, *AJ* 5.205, and rabbinic literature (Vayikra Rabbah 7 [end], etc.); 9) LAB 40.2 and Josephus, *AJ* 1.225–236, agree with the Targumic tradition (Pseudo-Jonathan on Genesis 22.1) in presenting the episode of the sacrifice of Isaac as a test of Isaac's faith (cf. also IV Maccabees 13.12); 10) The statement (LAB, 53.1) that Samuel was only eight years old when he began to prophesy is paralleled by Josephus, *AJ* 5.348, and midrashic literature (Midrash Tehillim 25, 212 and Midrash Shemuel 1.46), which give the age as twelve; 11) The tradition that a descendant of Agag will cause great harm to the Jews is found in LAB 58.3, as well as in Josephus 11.211 and in rabbinic literature (Megillah 13a, etc.), where he is identified with Haman; 12) In his anti-Samaritanism (as seen, for example, in 25.10), LAB is paralleled by *BJ* 6.438 and *AJ* 1.180 and 7.67, as well as by the Genesis Apocryphon 22.13–17, all of which identify Salem, Melchizedek's city, as Jerusalem, and decline to place it in Samaritan territory.

On the other hand, there are a number of instances where Pseudo-Philo and Josephus disagree: 1) According to LAB 9.2 and 9.4 Amram objected to the edict of the Israelites' leaders that the people should refrain from sexual relations so as not to give birth to children in such dire times, whereas there is no council of Israelite leaders in Josephus *AJ* 2.210, and Amram's wife is already pregnant when he becomes anxious on his own account and in great perplexity because of Pharaoh's decree that male children are to be drowned; 2) LAB 9.5 mentions the incident of Judah and Tamar (Gen. 38) but Josephus (*AJ* 2.39) omits it; 3) The birth of Moses is predicted in Miriam's dream in 9.10, but in a prediction of an Egyptian sacred scribe in Josephus 2.205, and in a dream of Amram in 2.215, though in both cases there is a similar miraculous and providential framework, as Vermès ("La Figure de Moïse au tournant des deux testaments," in

H. Cazelles et al., *Moise l'Homme de l'Alliance* [Paris, 1955], p. 89)
has noted; 4) According to LAB 9.15 Pharaoh's daughter, directed
by a dream, goes down to the river to bathe, whereas according to
Josephus 2.224 there is no dream and she plays by the river bank in a
scene reminiscent of Nausicaa in Homer's *Odyssey* 6.100 ff.; 5) LAB
11.10–11, following certain MSS. of the LXX, the Nash Papyrus,
Philo (*De Decalogo* 121 ff., etc.) and most occurrences in the New
Testament, inverts the order of the prohibitions of murder and adultery
in the Decalogue, whereas Josephus 3.92 follows the order of the
Hebrew text, though it should be noted that in 44.6–7, LAB reverts to
the order of the Hebrew text; 6) LAB, which is, in general, much
more highly selective than Josephus, narrates at some length (12.2
ff.) the incident of the Golden Calf (Exodus 32), whereas Josephus
3.201 omits it; 7) LAB 14.3 gives the number of Levites above 50 as
47,300, and those below 20 as 850,850, and a very large (hopelessly
corrupt) number as a total, but Josephus (3.290) gives 22,880
(23,880, according to some MSS.) as the total, though both disagree
with the Hebrew text and LXX (Numbers 3.39), which give 22,000;
8) LAB 15.1 says that it was on God's initiative that Moses sent spies
into Palestine, whereas Philo, *De Vita Mosis* 1.40.221 and Josephus,
AJ 3.302, say that he did so on his own initiative; 9) LAB 16.1 gives
us the motive of Korah's rebellion as the inability to observe the
commandment concerning the fringes, whereas in Josephus 4.14 the
motive is Korah's envy of Moses and Aaron; 10) LAB 16.1 gives he
number of those who revolted with Korah as 200, whereas Josephus
4.22, in accordance with both the Hebrew text and the LXX, gives the
number as 250; 11) LAB 17.3 mentions the incident of Jacob's
cunning in connection with Laban's flock (Genesis 30.37 ff.), but
Josephus 1.309 omits it; 12) Neither Joshua 22 nor Josephus 5.114
knows of the destruction of the altar beyond the Jordan by Joshua and
the people (LAB 22.7); 13) Kenaz ruled 57 years according to LAB
(27.16), 40 years according to Josephus 5.184; 14) According to
LAB 41.1 Addo [=Abdon] fought against the enemy, whereas according to Josephus (5.273) Abdon ruled during a very peaceful time;
15) Pseudo-Philo (42.1–2), as well as the Midrash, indicates that the
tension between Manoah and his wife was due to their dispute as to
who was responsible for their childless marriage, whereas Josephus
(5.277) stresses the erotic, jealous suspicion of Manoah; 16) In
Josephus 5.280 it is Manoah's wife who entreats God to send the
angel again that her husband might see him, whereas in LAB 42.5, as
in the Bible, Judges 13.8, and in the Midrash, it is Manoah who does

so; 17) LAB 42.8 differs from the Bible (Judges 13.16) and from
Josephus (*AJ* 5.282) in omitting Manoah's invitation to the angel to
eat; 18) Josephus 5.286 ff. elaborates on the erotic aspects of the
episode at Timnah (Judges 14.1 ff.), whereas LAB 43.1 abbreviates it
in two brief sentences; 19) In the episode of Samson's escape from the
Philistine ambush at Gaza, LAB (43.2) has Samson show utter
contempt for the enemy and militant faith in God, whereas Samson's
contempt in Josephus 5.305 is not as extreme; 20) Whereas Judges
16.1 and LAB 43.5 describe Delilah as a harlot or prostitute, Josephus
5.306 speaks of her as a courtesan; 21) In his development of
Samson's prayer (43.7), stressing that it is God who had given him
the eyes that the Philistines had taken from him, with the clear
implication that it is for God to obtain revenge for the affront to Him,
LAB is paralleled by Midrashim, but Josephus 5.314 ff. omits the
prayer completely; 22) LAB 43.8 gives the total slain by Samson
when he brought down the pillars at the Philistine banquet as 40,000,
whereas Josephus 5.316 gives the total as 3000; 23) LAB 44.2 ff.
dates Micah's activity and the crime of the Benjamites toward the end
of the period of the Judges, but the rabbis and Josephus 5.136 ff.,
who omits the story of Micah altogether, place these events at the
beginning of the period; 24) LAB 46.3 gives the number of Israelites
slain by the Benjamites as 46,000 whereas Josephus 5.158 follows the
Bible (Judges 20.25) in giving the number as 18,000; 25) LAB 47.1
gives the number of Israelites who died by the plague after commit-
ting harlotry with the Moabite women as 24,000 in accordance with
the Bible (Numbers 25.9), but Josephus 4.155 gives the number as
"no less than 14,000," though to be sure one MS. does read 24,000;
26) When Samuel begins to prophesy he is eight years old according
to LAB 53.1, but according to Josephus 5.348 he had completed his
twelfth year; 27) In presenting the motive for Samuel's sparing of
Agag, LAB 58.2–3 maintains that it was hidden treasures that Agag
had promised him, but Josephus 6.137 says that it was admiration for
Agag's beauty and stature; 28) LAB 58.4 asserts that Samuel killed
Agag, thus indicating that he did not regard Samuel as a Nazirite,
since a Nazirite is forbidden to touch a corpse, whereas Josephus 6.155,
apparently aware of the tradition that Samuel was a Nazirite, says that
Samuel gave orders to slay him; 29) It is at Bethel (though this may
be a scribal error for Bethlehem), according to LAB 59.2, that Samuel
anoints David, whereas, according to Josephus 6.157, following the
Bible (1 Samuel 16.4), this takes place at Bethlehem; 30) According
to LAB 63.3 (so the LXX on 1 Samuel 31.1), the Israelites and their

king are to fall down wounded because of their silence when the priests of Nob were slain, whereas according to Josephus 6.369, following the Hebrew text, they are slain; 31) LAB 64.8 and rabbinic literature depict Saul's motive in encountering death as repentance for his sins, but Josephus 6.349 gives Saul's motive in seeking death as a quest for glory and renown after death; 32) Unlike Josephus, who, apart from the much-disputed *Testimonium Flavianum* (*AJ* 18.63–64) has nothing to say about messianic belief, LAB does, as suggested above, have some possible references to messianic anticipations, notably in 60.3.

From this list it is not clear on what principle either LAB or Josephus chose to expand on or to omit certain Biblical passages. We may, however, note that the rabbis list certain passages to be read in the synagogue but not translated, and others to be both read and translated. It may be instructive to present in tabular form whether Josephus and LAB have these passages; it must, of course, be noted that LAB ends with the death of Saul (2 Samuel 1). We must also note that LAB is much briefer than Josephus' account, and it is therefore all the more significant that it agrees even more with the rabbinic position than does Josephus.

Narrative passages to be read but not translated (Megillah 25a–b)

	LAB	JOSEPHUS
1. Reuben's intercourse with his father's concubine Bilhah (Gen. 35.22)	omits	omits
2. The second account of the Golden Calf (Ex. 32.21–24)	omits	omits
3. The blessing of the priests (Num. 6.24–27)	omits	omits
4. The incident of David and Bathsheba (2 Sam. 11.2–17)	——	7.130 ff.
5. (Disputed in Talmud) The beginning of the incident of Amnon son of David and Tamar (2 Sam. 13.1–4)	——	7.162 ff.

Passages to be read and translated

1. The story of Judah and Tamar (Gen. 38)	9.5	omits
2. The first account of the Golden Calf (Ex. 32.1–20)	12.2 ff.	omits
3. Account of creation (Gen. 1)	15.6, 60.2	1.27 ff.
4. The story of Lot and his daughters (Gen. 19.31–38)	omits	1.205
5. The curses and blessings (Lev. 26 and Deut. 27)	13.10	4.305 ff. (but does not actually enumerate the blessings and curses)
6. The story of the concubine in Gibeah (Jud. 19, 20)	45–46	5.136 ff.

The purposes of LAB and Josephus are different in that the major goal of Josephus' apologetic in the *Antiquities* is to answer non-Jewish criticisms of the Jews (see my "Abraham the Greek Philosopher in Josephus," *Transactions of the American Philological Association,* 99 [1968], pp. 143–144), whereas Pseudo-Philo is clearly addressing a Jewish audience. Josephus (*AJ* 1.5) asks whether there is a basis in Jewish tradition for imparting knowledge of Judaism to non-Jews, and, secondly, whether Greeks were indeed curious to learn about Jewish history; LAB has no such problem.

Though it would be a mistake to regard Josephus as Pseudo-Philo's source or vice versa, there are enough coincidences to regard it as likely that both Josephus and the author of LAB have common sources. Both used both the Hebrew text as well as the Septuagint (and in the latter case, the text of the LXX employed by both shows affinities with that of proto-Lucian); or perhaps—though this is less likely, as G. Hölscher, "Josephus," *Real-Encyclopädie* (1916), pp. 1955–60, argues for Josephus' *AJ*—he used a Targum (for Josephus, see H. St. J. Thackeray, *Josephus the Man and the Historian* [New York, 1929, reprinted 1967], pp. 81–82) and/or a secondary source which embodied both, as well as haggadic materials. But LAB's approach, as seen particularly in his treatment of the Samson narrative, places him between Josephus and the rabbinic Midrashim: thus Manoah's suspicion and the mysterious nature of the angel's errand are increased in Josephus (5.281), where the angel refuses to repeat what he had revealed to Manoah's wife, whereas in the Bible (Judges 13.13–14) the angel repeats substantially what he had told Manoah's wife; LAB (42.7) occupies something of a midway position between Josephus and the Midrash, for while, as in the Midrash, the angel does give directions to Manoah, he does so in a very much briefer form. Or, alternatively, we may regard Josephus as a bridge between LAB and the Midrashim, as in the story of the priests of Nob, whom LAB 63.1 regards unfavorably and the rabbis favorably, while Josephus, AJ 6.260, bridges the gap by noting God's prediction that by reason of the sins of Eli's two sons his descendants would be destroyed.

g. Targumim

It is surprising that Cohn, James, and Kisch failed to comment on the relationship of LAB and the Aramaic paraphrases of the Bible known as Targumim. Vermès ("La Figure de Moïse au tournant des deux Testaments," in H. Cazelles et al., Moïse l'Homme de l'Alliance [Paris, 1955], p. 89) conjectures that in his desire to reply to some objections which the Biblical text would be able to suggest to a pious Jew, LAB does not attack heresies directly but adopts an apologetic view in line with the Targumim.

The following parallels between LAB and Targumim may be cited as typical (the list is hardly exhaustive): 1) LAB's translation (3.4) of the Hebrew gopher by cedrinis ("cedar") is duplicated by the Palestinian Targum on Genesis 6.14 and by several midrashic sources (so M. McNamara, The New Testament and the Palestinian Targum to the Pentateuch [Rome, 1966], pp. 51–52); 2) Vermès (Scripture and Tradition, p. 77) conjectures that "our name" in 6.2 refers to idols, as seen in the Palestinian Targum and in Bereshith Rabbah 38.8; similarly, as Wadsworth (per litt.) indicates, in 44.2 Micah is led by his mother to make himself a name—a statement followed immediately by the injunction to make idols; 3) The picture (6.14) of Nimrod as a persecutor of Abram and of the other opponents of polytheism is similar to that in the Palestinian Targum and Bereshith Rabbah 37.2, which interprets "hunter" as sinner or as one who ensnared people by words; 4) The tradition of a well following the Israelites in the desert is found not only in LAB (10.7) but also in Targum Onkelos on Numbers 21.16–20, 1 Corinthians 10.4, Shabbath 35a, and a number of midrashic sources; 5) The proviso that God will visit the sins of fathers upon their children only if they walk in their fathers' ways is also found in Targum Onkelos on Exodus 34.7 and Sanhedrin 27b; 6) The statement that Moses' face became glorious (LAB 12.1), as noted by McNamara (*op. cit.*, pp. 171–172), is also found in the LXX and all the Targumim of Exodus 34.29; 7) The phrase "I bowed the heavens" is paralleled by the Palestinian Targum and IV Esdras 3.18; 8) The description of Balaam as an interpreter of dreams (18.2) is likewise found in 2 TJ; 9) The mention of Abraham in God's answer to Balaam (18.5–6) has a basis likewise in 1 TJ (see Vermès, p. 132); 10) The promise of Israel's eternity and supremacy over the nations is found in LAB 18.11, Josephus AJ 4.115–117, and Targum Onkelos on Numbers 23.9 (see Vermès, pp. 146–147); 11) The prophecies of Eldad and Medad (20.5) are mentioned in the Palestinian Targum on Numbers 11.26, as well as in Midrashic sources (Bereshith Rabbah 15.10, etc.); 12) Ginzberg, 6.199, n. 90, has noted that a parallel to 32.1 ff. may be found in the shorter paraphrase of the history of the Israelites after Abraham which is found in the Targumim on Judges 5.1 ff.; 13) Vermès (p. 199) and R. Le Déaut (*La Nuit Pascale* [Rome, 1963], pp. 191–194) have noted a number of respects in which the Palestinian Targum on Genesis 22 and LAB 32.1–4 and 40.2–3 (cf. also Josephus, AJ 1.225–236) coincide, namely, the joy of Abraham, the voluntary acceptance of the sacrifice on the part of Isaac, and the influence of this act on the destiny of Abraham's descendants. In seeking to stress the contrast between Abraham's sacrifice and that of Jephthah, LAB thus follows the Targumic tradition; 14) The identification of Elijah and Phinehas found in LAB 48.1 appears in 1 TJ on Numbers 25.12, as well as in a number of midrashic sources (Pirke di R. Eliezer, 47, etc.); 15) Tosefta-Targum 1 Samuel 4.12, as well as midrashic sources (Midrash Shemuel 11.78–79, Midrash Tehillim 7.63), join LAB 54.4 in identifying the speedy messenger as Saul.

In almost every case, as noted above, the Targum is not alone in presenting the point of view found in LAB; and, in any case, that LAB's source is not the Targum is seen, for example, in the fact that in 18.10 Balaam performs the sacrifice, whereas in Targum Onkelos and Targum Pseudo-Jonathan, Balaam and Balak sacrifice together. It is better to speak of a Palestinian tradition dating back to at least the first century which is often reflected in Josephus, Pseudo-Philo, and the Targumim. In style, however, LAB is closer to Midrashim than to Targumim. But with the crucial discovery in 1956 of Codex Neofiti I by A. Diez-Macho (see "The Recently Discovered Palestinian Tar-

gum: Its Antiquity and Relationship with the Other Targums,"
Supplements to Vetus Testamentum, 7 [1960], pp. 222–245; and
Targum Palestinense, vol. 1: *Genesis* [Madrid-Barcelona, 1968]), the
question deserves to be further examined.

h. Midrashim

Azariah dei Rossi (*Meor Einayim,* 104 ff.) in the sixteenth
century had already given a generous sampling of the parallels of
LAB and rabbinic midrashim; and Cohn (pp. 314–32) adds slightly
to the list; but, as James himself (p. 65) admits, his references to
rabbinic literature are very incomplete; and, as Moore (*Judaism,*
2.285) and R. Bloch ("Note méthodologique pour l'Étude de la
Littérature rabbinique," *Recherches de Science religieuse,* 43 [1955],
p. 206) correctly remark, many of the parallels which have been
drawn to Apocrypha and Pseudepigrapha are actually midrashic
commonplaces. A glance at the index to Ginzberg's *Legends,* 7.537–
539, and subsequent references to the notes in Ginzberg, volumes 5
and 6, will reveal the extent of this relationship, even to the point of
including use of similar rules of exegesis, as in 48.3 (cf. Ginzberg,
6.213, n. 135), as well as in using foreshadowing and retrospection as
stylistic devices by mentioning Biblical stories out of their chronological
context. (On this technique of composition see O. Eissfeldt, "Zur
Kompositionstechnik des pseudo-philonischen Liber Antiquitatum
Biblicarum," in N. A. Dahl and A. S. Kapelrud, eds., *S. Mowinckel
Festschrift* [Oslo, 1955], pp. 53–71; reprinted in his *Kleine Schriften,*
vol. 3 [Berlin, 1966], pp. 34–353.) LAB's similarity to midrashic
technique is seen particularly in its predilection for naming everything
and fixing everything numerically. Indeed, one of the reasons for
asserting that the work is not Philo's is that both in style and content
it is considerably closer to the haggadic literature than is Philo. While,
to be sure, some of the traditions found in LAB are not found in
extant midrashim, so many are found that it is safe to conclude that if
the many lost midrashim should reappear we would be able to find
parallels with practically all the traditions embodied in LAB. To be
sure, there are some instances where LAB differs with existing midrashim, as in 19.16, where Moses' face is said to have changed, whereas
in Lekah Deuteronomy 34.7 we read that Moses' face retained its
brightness, or again in 60.2, where darkness is said to have given birth
to light, whereas in Shemoth Rabbah 15.22 darkness is created from
water and light from fire, or again in 63.1, where LAB gives an
unfavorable opinion of the priests of Nob, whereas the targumic

(1 Samuel 22.18) and midrashic (Tanhuma [Buber] 3.45, etc.) traditions speak of them as worthy to be high priests. But, as is well known, there are frequent cases where the midrashim present contradictory traditions, and this freedom of elaboration is itself an integral part of the midrashic tradition. The fact that LAB has parallels to all kinds of literature from the period of the Second Temple may indicate also that haggadic midrash was still in a very fluid and largely oral state and circulated among all kinds of groups, sometimes even among groups that were antithetical and antipathetic to one another. As it is, LAB is certainly, together with Josephus' *Antiquities,* among the very oldest examples of historical haggadah, as Kisch (p. 18) rightly concludes.

Among extant midrashic works, taken as a whole, LAB bears the closest relationship to Sefer Ha-Zikhronoth (Jerahmeel) and Sefer Ha-Jashar, though there are numerous parallels, most of which have not yet been noticed, with the Hebrew paraphrase of Josephus' *Bellum Judaicum* known as Josippon and the midrashic compilation known as Yalkut Shimoni. While the dates of all these works are disputed, none of them probably dates before the eleventh century, though D. Flusser ("The Author of the Book of Josippon: His Personality and His Age" [in Hebrew], *Zion,* 18 [1953], pp. 109–126) has argued for a tenth-century date for Josippon. The inevitable conclusion is that they were influenced by LAB.

Unfortunately we lack a critical edition of the Sefer Ha-Jashar, let alone a critical study comparing it with LAB, Josephus' *Antiquities,* Josippon, Jerahmeel, and Yalkut Shimoni; but in form this work is certainly similar to LAB in that it presents a haggadically embellished history from Adam to the time of the Judges.

Jacob Reiner, in his doctoral dissertation at Yeshiva University (*The Book of the Hasmonean Kings from the Chronicles of Jerahmel,* 2 vols., 1966) has finally given us a critical text of Sefer Ha-Zikhronoth (Jerahmeel) for the portion dealing with the Second Jewish Commonwealth, but we still lack a critical text for the earlier portion of the work, which is our concern here. Gaster, we may note, had not only not edited the text (he does not even give us the Hebrew) but had not even described the manuscript properly, in addition to which his translation is faulty, as Bloch (*op. cit.,* p. 218) has said. Reiner is not concerned except in passing (vol. 1, p. 62, n. 36) with the relationship of Jerahmeel and LAB, and is much more concerned with the close relationship of Jerahmeel and Josippon; and yet, as

Ginzberg (5.197) has already noted, a careful study of Jerahmeel will be rewarding since the text of LAB which he had before him differs from those of the extant MSS. (It is closer to the Admont, Munich, and Budapest MSS. than to the *editio princeps,* according to Cohn, "Pseudo-Philo und Jerachmeel," *Festschrift zum siebzigsten Geburtstage Jakob Guttmanns* [Leipzig, 1915], p. 180, on the basis of his collations of these MSS.)

i. Unique features of LAB

No one has yet attempted to list those passages in LAB which, so far as we can tell, contain information or motifs which are not to be found in any other extant work and are indeed unique with the author of LAB. Such a list may help us to determine the purpose of the work and the extent to which it is the product of the thought of one man (though he speaks of himself in the first person singular only once, in 10.5 [end]), rather than of any midrashic or targumic writing. Of course, many of these apparently unique features would undoubtedly not be unique if we had all the midrashic and other literature which has been lost.

Perhaps the most striking recurrent feature is the introduction of names and numbers that are missing from the Biblical text. This would reinforce the view, expressed above (LAB as apologetic), that LAB accords with the Talmudic statement (Baba Bathra 91a) that justifies such information in order to answer the sectarians. Another result of the compilation of such a list is that it leads us to conclude that LAB is much more individual in nature than has hitherto been recognized, and is not merely an example of midrashic and targumic writing.

The following is a preliminary list of the unique features of this work:

1.1: Noaba the name of Adam's daughter.

1.3–4: The names of Adam's additional 12 sons and 8 daughters.

1.6: The number and names of Seth's 3 sons and 2 daughters.

1.7: Enosh was 180 (Hebrew 90, LXX 190) at the birth of his son.

1.8: The number and names of Enosh's two sons and one daughter.

1.9: Kenan was 520 (Hebrew 70, LXX 170) at the birth of his son.

1.10: The number and names of Kenan's 3 sons and 2 daughters.

1:12: The number and names of Mahalalel's 7 sons and 5 daughters.

1.13: Jared was 172 (both Hebrew and LXX 162) at the birth of his son.

1.14: The number and names of Jared's 4 sons and 2 daughters.

1.17: The number and names of Enoch's 5 sons and 3 daughters.

1.19: The number and names of Methuselah's 2 sons and 2 daughters.

2.1: Themech, the name of Cain's wife (vs. Awan in Jubilees 4.8).

2.3: Cain built seven cities (one in Jubilees 4.9), including names.

2.4: The number and names of Cain's 3 sons and 2 daughters.

2.5: The names of Enoch's 3 children.

3.6: The Flood occurred in the 1652nd year of Creation (1656th, according to the Hebrew text).

3.7: The Flood continued for 140 days (*ed. pr.;* 150 days according to Gen. 7.24 and Admont).

3.8: For "in the second month, on the twenty-seventh day of the month" (Gen. 8.14) LAB reads "on the 90th day," i.e., *after* two months and 27 days.

3.10: Noah's apocalypse of the end of days and of the resurrection.

4.2 ff.: Numerous names of the descendants of Noah.

4.13: Serug was 29 (Hebrew 30, LXX 130) at the birth of his son.

4.14: Nahor was 34 (30) years old (Hebrew 29, LXX 79 [179]) at the birth of his son.

4.16: The origin of divination.

4.16: Serug and his sons were God-fearing.

5.4 ff.: The numbers of the various families descended from Noah.

6.3: Names of the twelve men who refused to write their names on bricks (Tower of Babel incident).

6.4 ff.: Connection of the building of the Tower of Babel with the casting of Abram into the furnace. Also certain details of the rescue of Abram from the furnace.

6.18: Deli (=God), place named after Abram.

8.8: The names of Job's children.

8.11: Dinah gave birth to 14 sons and 6 daughters.

8.12–14: The names of some of the sons of Naphtali, Gad, and Benjamin.

9.3: Amram (Moses' father) objects to the edict of the Israelite leaders that husbands and wives not live together.

9.5: Tamar's intent in having relations with Judah was that she might avoid being joined with Gentiles.

9.10: It is in a dream that Miriam prophesies the birth of Moses.

9.10: The connection between Moses being cast into the water and his later drying up of the waters of the Red Sea.

9.15: The reason Pharaoh's daughter went down to the river to bathe was that she was directed to do so in a dream.

10.1: LAB enumerates only 9 plagues, omitting the 6th plague, boils.

10.6: The Egyptians, pursuing the Israelites, did not know that they were entering the sea.

11.12: The Golden Rule appears within the framework of the Decalogue.

12.1: The Israelites saw Moses when he came down from Mount Sinai and did not recognize him.

12.7: The peculiar signs by which the sinners of the Golden Calf were recognized.

12.10: Moses, rather than God, writes upon the second tablets.

13.7–10: Apocalypse of Moses, including "the year of the life of Noe" and the vision of Paradise, presented in connection with God's precepts concerning the ceremonial law and the festivals.

14.3: The number of Israelites counted by Moses is 604,550 (both Hebrew and LXX 603,550).

14.3: The number of Levites over 50, under 20, and in total.

14.4: The total number of Israelites in Egypt and of those who were left after God put 49/50 to death.

15.2: Moses' spies are accompanied by lightning and thunder.

16.1: 200 (not 250) men revolted with Korah.

17.4: As Jacob's cattle brought forth according to the almond rods, so was the priesthood established by means of the almond rods.

18.3 ff.: LAB presents a more favorable picture of Balaam.

18.6: Jacob as the third son of Abraham.

19.7: The reason God does not allow Moses to enter the Promised Land is to keep him from seeing the idols by which the Israelites will be led astray.

19.10 ff.: The apocalypse of Moses.

19.11: The rod of Moses is to be a witness between God and the Israelites.

19.15: God reveals to Moses when the world will end (in 2500 years).

20.2: Joshua assumes the garments of Moses' wisdom.

2.1: The Reubenites, Gadites, and the half-tribe of Manasseh did offer sacrifices on their altars (contradicts Joshua 22.23, 26, 28, 29).

22.1: The other Israelites meet the Reubenites, Gadites, and the half-tribe of Manasseh at Shiloh (rather than at Gilead, as in Joshua 22.13–15).

22.7: Joshua and the Israelites offer 1000 rams as a sin-offering for the schismatic altar built by the Reubenites, Gadites, and the half-tribe of Manasseh.

22.8: Joshua establishes the Urim and Thummim at Shiloh.

23.2: Joshua gathers the Israelites on the 16th day of Sivan.

25–28: The long excursus on Kenaz, especially his election (25.1–2), the number of sinners in each tribe (25.4), the use of the Urim and Thummim (25.5), the confessions of the various tribes (25.6 ff.), including the hiding by Asher of the seven Amorite images of the nymphs with precious stones on Mount Shechem (25.10–11), the credal heresy of the Benjamites (25.13), the destruction of the idols and books and stones by fire and water (26.1 ff.), the description of the twelve precious stones (26.10 ff.), Kenaz's victory over the Amorites (27.1 ff.), the names of the 37 men who rise against Kenaz (27.3–4), and the apocalypse of Kenaz (28.6–10).

27.10: Ingethel (Gethel), the angel set over hidden things, aids Kenaz.

27.10: Zeruel, the angel set over strength, aids Kenaz.

29: The achievements of Zebul.

29.2: Zebul gives inheritances to Kenaz's daughters.

30.5 ff.: Deborah's speech to the Israelites.

32.5: Rebekah gave birth to Jacob and Esau in the third year of her marriage to Isaac (not, as in Genesis 25.20, 26, after 20 years of marriage).

32.5: No woman after Rebekah will give birth to twins after three years of childless marriage.

32.16–17: Apocalypse of Deborah.

33.3: The evil "creation" [i.e. inclination] ceases immediately after death and not merely in the Messianic Era.

34.1 ff.: Aod the wizard.

38.1: Evil deeds of Jair.

38.1: Names of the seven who refused to sacrifice to Baal when ordered by Jair.

38.3: Nathaniel, the angel set over fire, burns some of the servants of Jair but saves seven men.

39.5: God has "time and place to repose Himself of His long-suffering."

39.9: LAB confuses the Ammonites and Amorites (cf. 25.9 ff.).

39.9: Jephthah denies that the *gods* have given possessions to the Ammonites, whereas the Bible (Judges 11.24) speaks of only one god, Chemosh.

40.1: The name of Jephthah's daughter, Seila.

40.5 ff.: The lamentation of Jephthah's daughter.

41.1–2: LAB reverses the order of the judges in Judges 12.11–13, which has Elon *before* Abdon.

41.1: The number of Israelites in Abdon's army and the number of Moabites slain by them.

41.2: Elon was judge for 20 years (not 10, as in Judges 12.11).

42.1: Manoah asks his wife to set him free to marry another.

42.3: Samson himself, rather than Samson's mother (Judges 13.4), is told to avoid drinking wine.

42.8: LAB differs from the Bible (Judges 13.16) in omitting the invitation by Samson's father to the angel to eat.

42.10: LAB gives the name, Phadahel, of the angel that came to Samson's father.

44.5: Description of the images fashioned by Micah and of the manner by which requests were made of them.

44.9–10: The punishment of Micah and of his followers.

44.10: The *ius talionis* in connection with Micah: The Israelites will be punished in a manner appropriate to their sin.

45.1: The crime of the Benjamites is transferred from Gibeah to Nob.

45.2: LAB gives the name of the Levite, Beel (Behel), whose concubine is seized by the Benjamites and likewise gives the name of the Levite, Bethac, who offers shelter to him.

45.3: The Levite's concubine had transgressed against her husband by having relations with foreigners.

45.5: The Israelites gather at Shiloh to discuss the case of the Benjamites (according to Judges 20.1 there was an assembly at Mizpah; according to Judges 20.18 there was an assembly at Bethel).

46.3: The number of Israelites slain by the Benjamites is 46,000; in Judges 20.25 the number is 18,000.

46.4: The complaint of Phinehas to God.

47.1 ff.: Phinehas' prayer.

47.4–6: The fable of the lion which is quiet when other beasts attack his wards but roars when one of the animals of his own forest attacks the young of another evil beast, told by God to contrast the indifference of the Israelites to those who had sinned in following Micah with their anger against the Benjamites in the case of the concubine.

47.11: Names of the Benjamite chiefs.

48.1: Phinehas lived 120 years.

48.1: Mount Danaben as the place where Phinehas is to dwell.

48.3: The festival on which the Benjamites went up to Shiloh was Passover.

49.4–5: Casting of lots to determine wherefrom a savior will come to Israel; the lot falls on Ramah and on Elkanah.

50.2: It is on Passover that Peninah reviles Hannah (the mother of Samuel).

50.3: Elkanah addresses Hannah though he is in Shiloh and she has not yet come there.

51.1: The etymology of Samuel's name: "Mighty."

51.6: The name of Hannah's father, Bathuel.

53.1: Samuel begins to prophesy at the age of eight.

53.10: Connection of the sin of Eli's sons with the sin of taking the mother bird with the young.

55.9: The Philistines bring the ark to Shiloh (not to Beth-shemesh, as in 1 Samuel 6.12).

55.10: The number of Philistines who died in the plague caused by their retention of the ark.

56.7: Silence about the anointing of Saul as king.

58.2: Saul's motive in sparing Agag is Amalekite booty.

58.2: Agag is brought to Ramah (Arimatha), not to Gilgal, as in 1 Samuel 15.12, 21, 33.

59.2: Samuel anoints David at Bethel, not Bethlehem (though this may be a scribal error).

59.2: Samuel calls David *sanctus christus,* "the holy one, the anointed" (משיח הקדוש).

59.4: A non-canonical psalm of David.

59.4: David is under the care of angels and watchers.

60.2–3: A non-canonical psalm of David centered on the work of creation.

61.1: David's encounter with the Midianites.

61.2: Goliath's direct challenge to Saul (James' emendation).

61.2: If the Israelites lose to Goliath they are to serve the Philistine gods, and not merely the Philistines (as in 1 Samuel 17.9).

61.5: There were seven stones (not five, as in 1 Samuel 17.40) on which David wrote before meeting Goliath.

61.5: Cervihel (=Zeruel), the angel set over strength, aids David against Goliath.

62.2: The content of Saul's prophecy, including his forthcoming death and the end of his kingdom.

62.5: If Saul kills David, Saul will die too (*ius talionis*).

63.1: An unfavorable opinion of the priests of Nob.

63.2: Saul himself, rather than Doeg, slays Ahimelech and his kin.

64.1: Saul's motive in expelling the sorcerers is to win renown.

64.3: The name of the witch of Endor, Sedecla.

64.5: LAB combines the Hebrew and LXX (certain MSS.) in reading that the witch of Endor saw Samuel and Saul.

64.6: When Samuel appears to the witch of Endor he is clad in a white robe, and two angels accompany him.

CHAPTER XII
INCOMPLETENESS OF LAB
(*James, pp. 60–65*)

That a book which starts "Initium mundi" should end with the death of Saul had already led Sixtus Senensis (*Bibliotheca Sancta*, p. 314) in the sixteenth century to regard it as incomplete. James (pp. 60–65) presents a number of specific points which he thinks were included in the original work but which are now lost; and Kisch (p. 29) concludes, "How much further the narration of the lost conclusion went is an enigma." That the work is incomplete is likewise the conclusion of Dietzfelbinger (pp. 170 ff.) and Strugnell (in his forthcoming article on LAB in the *Encyclopaedia Judaica*). James himself initially (p. 65), and most recently Dietzfelbinger (p. 171) and O. H. Steck (*Israel und das gewaltsame Geschick der Propheten* [Neukirchen, 1967], p. 173), have conjectured that the work ended with the Babylonian captivity, with some anticipation of the return from exile; but before he had laid down his pen James went further (p. 73) and suggested that the story of Esther found a place in the original work—a suggestion which, as already noted, is based upon the questionable view that Origen derived from LAB the tradition of an angel of grace sent to Esther.

There is no direct reference in LAB to any promised treatments, as there is, for example, in Josephus' *Antiquities* (see my edition, note *d* on 20.267); and even if there were, it is quite conceivable that the sequel was never written. Riessler (p. 1315), however, noted the significant point that LAB and the Book of Chronicles seem to supplement each other, since the latter begins its full-fledged treatment with the death of Saul; and this point is reiterated by Spiro ("Samaritans, etc.," *PAAJR*, 20 [1951], p. 280, n. 8 and pp. 303–308). It is also possible, as Delcor (p. 1373) has suggested, that the book deliberately ended with the beginning of David's reign to mark the expectation of the Davidic Messiah; but if so, we should have expected the author to call attention to this at the end of his work instead of trailing off inconclusively with details about the death of Saul. However, no one has demonstrated that the Book of Jashar, which has chronological limits similar to those of LAB, is incomplete; and it is similarly far from demonstrated that LAB is in an unfinished state.

CHAPTER XIII
DESIDERATA

1. Serious scholarly work on LAB did not begin until Cohn's article in 1898 but what hampered work more than anything else was the lack of a readily accessible Latin text. This was not remedied until the appearance of Kisch's edition half a century later in 1949. But this edition, as noted above, depends almost exclusively upon one MS., the Admont, which may very well be inferior to those upon which the *editio princeps* was based; and, in any case, what is needed is a critical edition based upon all our MSS., a work which we are now awaiting from Father Daniel J. Harrington, who is preparing this for his doctoral dissertation at Harvard under Professor John Strugnell, and who is scheduled to publish it in the *Sources chrétiennes* series. We also await the publication of Harrington's stemma of the transmission of the work.

2. No truly definitive work on the language and date of LAB and its relation to other works can be done until it has been retranslated into Greek and into Hebrew (the translation into Hebrew by Hartom is often unsatisfactory), as James did for the passages he published in *Apocrypha Anecdota*, Second Series (Cambridge, 1897) and as Strugnell did for David's Psalm in LAB 59 in the *Catholic Biblical Quarterly*, 27 (1965), pp. 207–216, though, of course, great caution must be used when modern retranslations are used as criteria in the textual criticism of an ancient document. A number of likely emendations have already been made by Ginzberg and Strugnell on the basis of a retranslation into Greek and Hebrew, and we can expect more if the task is accomplished systematically.

3. We need concordances (including variant readings) of the works in question: LAB in Hebrew, Greek, and Latin (Strugnell is currently attempting to get a computer to make a concordance of the Latin text: such a concordance will enable us to improve on the retranslations into Greek and Hebrew), Jubilees, Baruch, IV Esdras, Philo (J. Leisegang's *index verborum* in volume 7 [Berlin, 1926] of the Cohn-Wendland-Reiter edition is selective and quite inadequate), the first half of Josephus' *Antiquities* (where he paraphrases the Bible), the Latin Josephus, Josippon, Sefer Ha-Jashar, Yalkut Shimoni, Sefer Ha-Zikhronoth (Jerahmeel), the Targumim, the Itala, the Vulgate, Aquila, Symmachus, Theodotion; and the existing concordances of the Septuagint, the New Testament, and the Dead Sea Scrolls

(especially the *Genesis Apocryphon,* which, however, except for a small portion, is so damaged that it has turned out to be illegible) should likewise be used toward this end. This should enable us to answer more definitely the question as to whether, from the point of view of language, LAB could have been composed by Philo. We also need a concordance and systematic analysis of the other Latin treatises which are found in many MSS. together with LAB, namely, a portion of Philo's *Quaestiones et Solutiones in Genesin* and a fragment of *De Vita Contemplativa* to determine whether the translation is contemporaneous. This should enable us, among other things, better to establish the date of the translation of LAB into Latin.

4. We should also be able to establish which recension of the LXX LAB used, and the extent to which LAB's Greek Biblical text is a modification of the LXX based on an attempt to harmonize it with the Hebrew text. We need for LAB a work like Peter Katz's essay in *Theologische Zeitschrift,* 5 (1949), pp. 1–24, and his book, *Philo's Bible* (Cambridge, 1950), or like Thackeray's chapter on Josephus' Biblical text in his *Josephus the Man and the Historian* (pp. 75–99), which will examine the quotations from the Greek Bible in LAB. The retranslation into Hebrew will enable us to see the nature of the Hebrew text of the Bible used by LAB, its relationship to the Masoretic Text, the Nash Papyrus, fragments from the Hebrew Bible found in the Dead Sea Scrolls, the Samaritan text of the Pentateuch, the Septuagint, the Targumim (including the newly discovered Neofiti I), etc. In determining the language of the original of LAB, much that is useful may be learned from an examination of the criteria that have been used in solving a similar problem found in connection with other books of the Apocrypha and Pseudepigrapha, such as the Book of Wisdom (Wisdom of Solomon), Tobit, Judith, IV Esdras, and Baruch.

5. In particular, the form of the various hymns, prayers, and psalms in LAB should be studied and compared with other prayers in the Apocrypha, Pseudepigrapha, the Dead Sea Scrolls, Josephus, Philo, the New Testament, Targumim, and Midrashim. It is quite conceivable that we shall find that some of them will end up as alphabetical acrostics such as are found in the Book of Psalms.

6. Many problems in LAB arise from corruptions in the text where proper names appear, especially in the early chapters. James, Riessler, and Strugnell have done much to restore the text in such cases, but more can be done through a systematic study of the names of persons; and it will prove fruitful to make a comparison with the

proper names as spelled in the various MSS. of the Latin Josephus, for which we now have an excellent critical edition for *Antiquities,* Books 1–5 by F. Blatt (Aarhus and Copenhagen, 1958). It will prove profitable to note how many errors have been introduced into the MSS. due to the influence of the Vulgate on copyists.

7. One of the most striking features of the early chapters of LAB is the existence of precise numbers, notably in the list of the descendants of Noah. These numbers should be compared with numbers found in the Apocrypha, Pseudepigrapha (especially Jubilees), the Dead Sea Scrolls, Philo, Josephus, and the rabbinic writings (especially such works as Pirke di R. Eliezer) to see whether there may be a clue as to the relationship of LAB with one or more of these.

8. Though Ginzberg has noted many parallels between LAB and the Targumim and Midrashim, corners of the field still remain to be worked. Ginzberg himself apparently did further work, still unpublished, on LAB, according to a statement (now misplaced) of an inventory of his unpublished MSS. which the current librarian of the Jewish Theological Seminary, Dr. Menachem Schmelzer, recalls having seen; but a search by the present editor of Ginzberg's unpublished papers in the library of the Seminary has proved unavailing. In any case, we need a systematic comparison of LAB, the Sefer Ha-Jashar (for which we need a critical edition), Jerahmeeel, Josippon, and the Yalkut Shimoni.

9. Michael Wadsworth, a graduate student of Geza Vermès of Oxford, is writing a thesis on Apocalypse and Haggadah in Pseudo-Philo, which he hopes to complete in 1970. In addition, it should prove fruitful—even if will be difficult—to compare the vocabulary and ideas of LAB with those of the Merkabah mystics, who likewise had a great many secret names, some of which have meaning when evaluated in terms of their numerical summations. A similar comparison should be made with Gnosticism. It may also be useful to study the Jewish art in Goodenough's collection, *Jewish Symbols in the Greco-Roman Period,* especially the frescoes of Dura, to determine the relationship, if any, to mystical themes in LAB.

10. It may be worthwhile to study the fragments of Philo in the collections of J. R. Harris, P. Wendland, K. Praechter, and H. Levy, especially those which have not yet been assigned to any particular treatise of Philo and those which are assigned to the *Quaestiones in Genesin* and *De Vita Contemplativa* to see whether any of these fragments are from LAB or possibly from lost parts of LAB.

11. A systematic study of the *fortleben* of LAB would be of value. In particular, a thorough perusal of the Greek and Latin Church Fathers may yield some clues as to the date and use made of LAB. One should check also for references to Philo's *Quaestiones in Genesin* and *De Vita Contemplativa* since these were, in the late Middle Ages and perhaps much earlier, in the same manuscript with LAB, and citations of the three works are confused in the later Middle Ages at any rate. We need a critical edition of the thirteenth-century Thomas of Cantimpré's *De Naturis Rerum* (see G. J. J. Walstra, "Thomas de Cantimpré, *De Naturis Rerum*: État de la question," *Vivarium*, 5 [1967], pp. 146–171; 6 [1968], pp. 46–61, which lists 144 MSS. and gives a complete bibliography), and, in any case, of Book 14 on precious stones, which purports to contain the treatise of Cethel, as well as of separate MSS. containing the Book of Cethel itself. A study should then be made of the medieval Book of Cethel (and its *fortleben*) dealing with the twelve stones on the breastplate of the high priest (and of the lapidary literature generally, notably Epiphanius' *De XII Lapidibus*) as a clue to the relationship with the account in LAB (26.10 ff.). Thomas of Cantimpré's work should be compared with similar encyclopedic works of Alexander Neckam, Michael Scot, Bartholomaeus Anglicus, and Vincent of Beauvais. Moreover, the scholia (see Kisch, pp. 20–21) on Petrus Riga's *Aurora* (twelfth century) and on other such Biblical paraphrases should be examined for further quotations from LAB (James, p. 18, discovered one such set of scholia), which may help to determine the *fortleben* of LAB, as well as to establish the text in some places where our MSS. seem to be faulty, and perhaps even to find missing portions of LAB. Finally, since Azariah dei Rossi was involved in a great deal of controversy because of his use of such extra-Talmudic sources as Philo and LAB, a considerable literature attacking and defending him arose in the sixteenth century; a search should be made for references to LAB in this literature.

Chapter XIV

COMMENTARY

(Including Corrections of James)

Page 8, line 8: For *in* read *to*.

P. 13, line 8: In his copy James has noted that the Lorsch MS. is not in the tenth Cassel printed catalogue.

P. 28, line 27: For למנצח read לנצח.

P. 34, note 1, line 3: The font of the word *fact* should be corrected. A period should then be added.

P. 36, after line 15: Add 25.7, 44.4, 60.3.

P. 36, after last line: Add 15.5.

P. 38, after line 6: Add 18.10.

P. 41, line 34: For LIX.1,4 read LIX.2,4.

P. 45, after line 2: Add Enoch 51.1.

P. 51 (col. 2), XXXIV.2: For *are* read *over*.

P. 51 (col. 2), XI.5: For *bared* read *bowed*.

P. 54 (col. 2), four lines from bottom: For *et* read *ei*.

P. 73, line 5 of Additional Note: For *Ananchel* read *Ananeel*.

P. 75 (margin) on LAB 1.1: Add Gen. 4[1,2,25], 5[3].

P. 75, LAB 1.1: Delete "The beginning of the world," which, according to Daniel Harrington, is stemmatically impossible. Harrington's stemma is based on a reading of all the MSS. His text is to appear in the *Sources chrétiènnes* series, and I am indebted to him and to the editors of the series for permission to note this and other cases which are here labeled "stemmatically impossible."

P. 75, LAB 1.1 ff.: J. Bowker, *The Targums and Rabbinic Literature* (Cambridge, 1969), Appendix I, pp. 301-314 has translated and briefly commented upon those portions of LAB related to Genesis.

P. 75, LAB 1.1: A. Spiro, *Manners of Rewriting Biblical History from Chronicles to Pseudo-Philo* (Columbia Univ., diss., microfilm, 1953), p. 183, notes that in Jubilees 4.1 Adam is said to have had a daughter, and that by reading one of the names (Awan) backward and changing *w* to *b* we get the same name (Noaba) that is found in LAB.

P. 75, LAB 1.1-4: Josephus, AJ 1.52, also mentions that Adam and Eve had daughters but does not give their names. According to rabbinic tradition, twin sisters were born at the time that Eve gave birth to Cain and Abel (see Sanhedrin 38b and 58b, etc., cited by Ginzberg, 5.134, n. 4 and 5.137, n. 17).

P. 75, LAB 1.2 ff.: The following table shows the relationship of LAB to the Hebrew text, the Septuagint, and Josephus with regard to the chronology of the patriarchs until the Flood:

	Age at birth of son			Years of life after this birth		
	Hebrew	LXX, Josephus[a]	LAB	Hebrew	LXX, Josephus	LAB
Adam	130	230	230[b]	800	700	700
Seth	105	205	105[c]	807	707	707
Enosh (Enos)	90	190	180[c]	815	715	715
Kenan (Cainan)	70	170	520[c]	840	740	730 (830)
Mehalalel (Malalech)	65	165	165	830	730	730
Jared (Jareth)	162	162	172[c]	800	800	800
Enoch	65.	165	165	300	200	200
Methusaleh (Methusalam)	187	187	187	782	782	782
Lamech	182	188[d]	182	595	565	585[e]
Noah (Noe)	600[f]	600	600	350	350	350
Totals	1656	2262	2506			

NOTES: a) See Thackeray in Loeb Classical Library, translation of AJ 1.82.
   b) Not actually stated.
   c) Emended by Cohn (p. 281) to conform with LXX.
   d) 182 according to some MSS. of Josephus.
   e) Cohn (p. 281) says that Lamech's years after the Flood should be changed to 595, to accord with the Hebrew text.
   f) Age at time of the Flood.
   g) In 3.6 LAB says 1652 (emended to 1656 by Cohn to make it agree with the Hebrew text) years elapsed until the Flood.

That LAB is eclectic in chronology is clear from the fact that in the ages at the birth of the sons, he agrees specifically with the Hebrew text twice, with the LXX three times, with both twice, and with neither three times. In the years after the birth he never agrees specifically with the Hebrew text, with the LXX five times, with both three, times, and with neither twice.

P. 76, LAB 1.3: After stating in 1.2 that Adam had twelve sons, LAB here enumerates only nine. But cf. Jubilees 4.10, which actually specifies nine sons.

P. 76, LAB 1.4: Ginzberg, 5.146, n. 42, notes that the name of Adam's oldest daughter has been transmitted to us in no less than 22 forms.

P. 76 (margin) on LAB 1.5: For Gen. 5^7 read Gen. $5^{6,7}$.

P. 76, LAB 1.5: The reading "*two* daughters" is stemmatically impossible, according to Harrington. The reading *three* of the *editio princeps* should be adopted.

P. 76, LAB 1.9: For Malalech the Hebrew text of Genesis 5.12-17 has Mahalalel, but the LXX is close to our reading, with its Maleleel, and Jubilees 4.14, with its Malalel.

P. 76, LAB 1.10: For Athach, stemmatically impossible, read Athac.

P. 76 (margin) on LAB 1.15: For $5^{22,23}$ read $5^{21,22}$.

P. 76, LAB 1.15: Dietzfelbinger, in his forthcoming translation and commentary on LAB, notes the interesting coincidence that the Vulgate also repeats "and lived," whereas, we may note, neither the Hebrew text nor the LXX has this.

P. 77, LAB 1.20: The meaning of Noah's name, "to give rest," is that which is found in the Latin translators before Jerome, "requiescere nos faciet"; cf. Jerome, *Quaestiones Hebraicae in Genesin,* p. 11 (Lagarde). The Vulgate gives *consolabitur,* "he will console." Bereshith Rabbah gives both "rest" and "comfort." So Cohn (p. 308, n. 2).

P. 77 (margin) on LAB 1.22: Omit 6^{20}.

P. 77 (margin) on LAB 2.1: For Cf. Gen. 4^{14} read Gen. 4^{16} (cf. $4^{12,14}$).

P. 77, LAB 2.1: That LAB did not rely exclusively upon the LXX is seen in *terra tremens* ("trembling land," translating Hebrew *Nod*), whereas the LXX has "in the land of Naid." But perhaps a later editor corrected LAB in accordance with Symmachus and Theodotion, who have a similar version; the Vulgate has *profugus,* "exile."

P. 77, LAB 2.1 (end): Jubilees 4.8 gives the name of Cain's wife as Awan. Cain's wife must have been a daughter of Adam: LAB 1.2 says that Adam had eight daughters, yet enumerates only seven in 1.4. Perhaps, as Spiro (*Manners,* p. 184, n. 126) suggests, LAB did not want to state explicitly that Adam's sons had committed incest, and hence refrained from listing her.

P. 77, LAB 2.3: Ginzberg, 5.136, n. 11, cites the Book of Adam, 77 (end), which likewise states that Cain was fifteen at the time that he brought his sacrifice. According to Jubilees 4.9 Cain built only one city. For "cities" our text reads *civitates,* which usually implies states.

P. 77, line 31 (margin), on LAB 2.3: 4^{17} should be on the line above.

P. 77, LAB 2.3: For Leeth, stemmatically impossible, read Leed.

P. 78, line 12 (margin), on LAB 2.5: Add Gen. 4^{18}.

P. 78, LAB 2.6: In the names of the wives of Lamech, LAB disagrees with Jubilees 4.28, which gives Betenos, and the Genesis Apocryphon, which similarly gives Bat-Enosh.

P. 78 (margin) on LAB 2.7: Add 4^{20}.

P. 78, LAB 2.7: Kisch, following L. Cohn, "Pseudo-Philo und Jerachmeel," *Festschrift . . . Jakob Guttmanns* (Leipzig, 1915), pp. 182-183, reads, "And began to play upon the lute and the harp and on every instrument of sweet psalmody" (2.8), since this statement can apply only to Iobal, at the end of 2.7 (after "playing of instruments"). He likewise places "and to corrupt the earth" before "God was angry."

P. 78 (margin) on LAB 2.10: Add $4^{23,24}$.

P. 79, LAB 2.10: For "seventy times seven" read "seventy-seven times."

P. 79 (margin) on LAB 3.1: For Gen. 6^1 read Gen. $6^{1,2}$.

P. 79, LAB 3.1: LAB, reading *filii dei,* "sons of God," agrees with some MSS. of the LXX on Genesis 6.3; but the best MSS. of the LXX, as well as Philo (*De Gigantibus,* 2.6) and Josephus (*AJ* 1.73), read *angeloi,* "angels."

P. 79 (margin) on LAB 3.2: Add 6[3].

P. 79, LAB 3.2: In reading *diiudicabit,* "judge," LAB disagrees with the LXX on 6.3, Philo (*De Gigantibus,* 5.19), Jubilees, and the Vulgate, which read "remain," to agree with the Hebrew text and Symmachus.

P. 79, LAB 3.2: Perhaps we should translate *terminos seculi* as "the limits of life."

P. 79 (margin) on LAB 3.3: For 6[5] (which should be one line lower) read 6[5,7].

P. 79 on LAB 3.3: For "it repenteth" the oldest MSS. of the LXX (Gen. 6.7), as well as Philo and the Itala, have "was angry": some MSS. of the LXX have "pondered," but LAB agrees with the Hebrew text, Aquila, and the Vulgate.

P. 79 (margin) on LAB 3.4: Add 6[8,9].

P. 80 (margin) on LAB 3.4: For Gen. 6[13] read 6[13-15].

P. 80, line 6, LAB 3.4: The word *gopher,* here translated "cedar," is a *hapax legomenon* in the Hebrew Bible. The LXX has *tetragōnōn,* "square," and the Vulgate has *laevigatis,* "smooth." M. McNamara, *The New Testament and the Palestinian Targum to the Pentateuch* (Rome, 1966), pp. 51-52, has noted that *kadrinon,* "cedar," is the word used to explain *gopher* in the Palestinian Targum on Genesis 6.14, as well as in Bereshith Rabbah 31 and Symmachus, hence reinforcing his thesis of the connection between LAB and the Targumic tradition, which consequently must go back to at least the first century.

P. 80, LAB 3.5: The speculation of J. van Goudoever, *Biblical Calendars,* 2nd ed. (Leiden, 1961), pp. 122-123, that LAB starts the flood on the first of Nisan, the first month of the civil year, is based not upon any statement in LAB but on the conjecture that LAB would want the flood, having lasted 287 days (in disagreement with the Hebrew), to end on a significant day, namely, the seventeenth day of Tammuz, the day that the tablets were broken and Jerusalem was captured by Nebuchadnezzar and Titus.

P. 80, line 25 (margin), on LAB 3.5: Add 7[12].

P. 80, LAB 3.6: Azariah dei Rossi (*Meor Einayim,* 4.107-108, Cassel ed.) already in the sixteenth century notes that whereas Philo everywhere follows the LXX, LAB here follows the Hebrew (Azariah has anticipated Cohn's emendation to 1656). It is Cohn's contention that Pseudo-Philo took his chronological data here from the Hebrew text, but that the individual figures for the various patriarchs were altered, as is sometimes true in connection with the text of Josephus, in accordance with the LXX.

P. 80 (margin) on LAB 3.7: Add 7[24,23], 8[1].

P. 80, LAB 3.7: 140 is the reading of the *editio princeps*; the Admont reads 150.

P. 80 (margin) on LAB 3.8: For 8[16] read 8[14-20].

P. 80, LAB 3.8: Apparently, as Dietzfelbinger remarks in a note in his forthcoming translation, LAB understood Genesis 8.14 as meaning *after* two months and 27 days, i.e., approximately on the 90th day.

P. 81, LAB 3.8, "And all the beasts": LAB disagrees with the LXX and Jubilees, as noted by Cohn, p. 309, in the order of creatures mentioned.

P. 81, LAB 3.8, "A savour of rest": Cohn, p. 309, remarks that LAB here disagrees with both the LXX and the Hebrew of Genesis 8.21 (and, we may add, with Philo, *De Congressu,* 115); but he is merely presenting a midrashic interpretation of *niḥoaḥ,* "pleasantness," as in Bereshith Rabbah 25: "He named Noah with reference to his sacrifice (*niḥoaḥ*)."

P. 81, LAB 3.9: Cohn, p. 310, plausibly suggests *desipit,* "is foolish," for *desiit,* "hath left off," since quite clearly LAB is very closely following the Hebrew, as the phrase "the guise of man's heart" indicates.

P. 81, LAB 3.9: On the statement that God will judge mankind by fire cf. Josephus, *AJ* 1.70, where Adam predicts not only a flood but also a destruction by fire. See my article, "Hellenizations in Josephus' Portrayal of Man's Decline," *Studies in the History of Religions,* 14 (1968), pp. 351-352.

P. 81, LAB 3.9: "day and night": The Admont and Melk MSS. agree with the LXX in reading "by day and night."

P. 81, LAB 3.9: "until the times are fulfilled": Cf. Luke 21.24: "Until the times of the Gentiles are fulfilled" (Philonenko, *per litt.*).

P. 81, LAB 3.10: H. St. J. Thackeray, *The Relation of St. Paul to Contemporary Jewish Thought* (London, 1900), p. 124, aptly compares Assumptio Mosis 10.1, Jubilees 23 and 50. To this add Enoch 51.1. For a commentary on LAB 3.10 see M. Delcor, "Philon (Pseudo-)," Supplément 7 in *Dictionnaire de la Bible* (Paris, 1966), p. 1357.

Pp. 81-82, LAB 3.10: "And Hell shall pay his debt and destruction give back that which was committed unto him": James has adopted the reading of the *editio princeps* (*paratecen* = παραθήκην), lit., "deposit." That this is the likely reading seems indicated by the close parallel with II Baruch 21.23 and IV Esdras 4.41-42. Cf. LAB 33.3: "Hell, which receiveth that is committed to it will not restore it unless it be demanded by him that committed it."

P. 82, LAB 3.10: "the world shall rest": Dietzfelbinger, in a note in his forthcoming translation, rightly understands *requiescet* here in the same sense as in 3.9 ("day and night shall not cease") and translates "the world shall cease."

P. 82, LAB 3.10: "and death shall be quenched": Cf. 1 Corinthians 15.26: "The last enemy to be destroyed is death" (Philonenko, *per litt.*).

P. 82, LAB 3.10: "And there shall be another earth and another heaven": Cf. 2 Peter 3.13: "We wait for new heavens and a new earth" (cited by Dietzfelbinger, note in his forthcoming translation).

P. 82 (margin) on LAB 3.11: For Gen. 9^8 read Gen. $9^{8,9,11}$.

P. 82, line 15 (margin), on LAB 3.11: For 9^2 read $9^{3,4,6,1}$.

P. 82, LAB 3.11: "And all . . . meat": The Admont and Melk MSS. omit this sentence.

P. 82, LAB 3.11: "his blood shall be shed": The Admont and Melk MSS. add "by the hand of God," whereas the Hebrew reads "by man shall his blood be shed."

P. 82 (margin) on LAB 3.11: For 9^{12} read $9^{12,14,16}$.

P. 82, LAB 3.11: Kisch, following the division in the Admont MS., starts a section 3.12 after "in the waters."

P. 82, LAB 4.2-8: Riessler, pp. 1315-1317, who otherwise has a very brief commentary, has explanations of all these proper names, noting the peoples and countries that they represent.

P. 82 (margin) on LAB 4.2: For 10^2 read 10^{2-4}.

P. 82, LAB 4.2: Riessler, p. 1315, suggests that the puzzling Nidiazech, which here stands in place of Javan, when read backwards (cf. note on 1.1, Noaba), gives Chezaidin, which sounds like Chasidim; and this is another indication of violent polemic of religious parties, in this case against the Pharisees, who rose from the Chasidim. Dietzfelbinger, p. 249, n. 23, rightly finds this untenable. Delcor, p. 1359, however, rightly stresses that when we shall be able to explain LAB's substitution of Nidiazech for Javan of the Bible we shall probably have a clue to the date of the work.

P. 82, LAB 4.2: Cenez and Cethin should be italicized. Tudant is presumably Dodanim.

P. 83, LAB 4.2: "And the sons of Gomer" should be italicized.

P. 83, LAB 4.2: The Admont MS., followed by Kisch, adds "Deber" after "Lud," but this is stemmatically impossible.

P. 83 (margin) on LAB 4.3: Add Gen. 10[5].

P. 83, LAB 4.3: The last clause does not seem to be connected with the context; Dietzfelbinger, p. 228, conjectures that the meaning is that a third of the earth which had been destroyed by the flood was resettled. He compares Revelation 8.7-12, 9.15, 18, which similarly speak of the destruction of a third of the earth or of mankind.

P. 83, LAB 4.4: For the lacuna which James filled with Rōō read Iesca, found in the Admont and Melk MSS.

P. 84 (margin) on LAB 4.6: For Gen. 10[6] read Gen. 10[6,7].

P. 84, LAB 4.6: James himself (p. 245) plausibly suggests that after Saba a line has fallen out by homoeoteleuton and that the text should consequently be corrected thus: "Saba, Hevila, Sabatha, Regma, Sabatacha. And the sons of Regma: Saba [=Sheba] and Tudan."

P. 84 (margin) on LAB 4.7: For 10[8] read 10[8,9].

P. 84, LAB 4.7: Megimin is James' conjecture. The *editio princeps* has Iuenugin, the Admont MS. has Niemigin.

P. 84, LAB 4.7: Labin and Petrosonoin should be italicized.

P. 84, LAB 4.7: If the reading of the Admont MS., Philistiim, is correct, we have an instance where the Hebrew original of our treatise has been retained.

P. 84, line 30 (margin), on LAB 4.8: Add Gen. 10[19].

P. 84 (margin) on LAB 4.9: For 10[22] read 10[22-25].

P. 84, LAB 4.9: For *Gedrum Ese* read *Gedru Mese.*

P. 85 (margin) on LAB 4.10: Add 10[26-29].

P. 85, line 6 (margin), on LAB 4.10: For Cf. Gen. 11[18] read Cf. Gen. 11[18,19].

P. 85 (margin) on LAB 4.11: Add Cf. Gen. 11[29].

P. 85, LAB 4.11: In Jubilees 11.7 Ragau's wife is named Ora.

P. 85, LAB 4.12: The chronology of the Noahides (see Thackeray in Loeb Library on Josephus, AJ 1.148), according to the Hebrew text, the Septuagint, Josephus, and LAB, may be seen in the following table:

	Age at birth of son				Years of life after this birth			
	Hebrew	LXX	Josephus	LAB	Hebrew	LXX	Josephus	LAB
Reu (Ragau)	32	132	130	—	207	207	——	119
Serug (Seruch)	30	130	132	29	200	200	——	67
Nahor (Nachor)	29	79	120	34	119	129	——	200
		(179)		(30)		(125)		
Terah (Thara)	70	70	70	70	135	135	135	——

Here, unlike the chronology of the early patriarchs, there is no relation between LAB and either the Hebrew or the LXX or Josephus.

P. 85 (margin) on LAB 4.13: Add 11[22,23].

P. 85 (margin) on LAB 4.14: Add 11[24,25].

P. 86 (margin) on LAB 4.15: Add 11[26,27].

P. 86, LAB 4.16: "to prognosticate by them": Dietzfelbinger, in his forthcoming translation, renders *imaginari* "to make images."

P. 86, LAB 4.16: Delcor, p. 1359, notes that LAB significantly places the origin of divination after his enumeration of the descendants of Thara, who was from Ur of Chaldaea, the place noted for astrology.

P. 86 (margin), on LAB 4.17: Add Gen. 10[31,32,5].

P. 86, LAB 5.1 ff.: On the role of this chapter in the Middle Ages see Cohn, "Pseudo-Philo und Jerachmeel," p. 176.

P. 86, LAB 5.1: Cf. Pirke di R. Eliezer 24, which cites Rabbi Akiba's statement that the children of Ham appointed Nimrod as their king, "a slave, the son of a slave." This work, like LAB, then proceeds to presuppose a similar division between the sons of Ham and the sons of Japheth, since it records an incident in which King Nimrod routs the descendants of Japheth.

P. 87 (margin) on LAB 5.4: Add Cf. Gen. 10^{2,3}.

P. 87, LAB 5.4: "And first Phenech the son of Japheth looked upon them. The sons of Gomer . . .": The Admont and Melk MSS. read: "And they looked upon the sons of Japheth and the sons of Gomer."

P. 87, line 26, LAB 5.4: For Thogorma, which is stemmatically impossible, read Torgoma, the reading of the *editio princeps*.

P. 88, lines 7-8, LAB 5.4: "besides women and children": Exactly the same expression is found in LAB 5.7 and Matthew 14.21 and 15.38, as noted by Dietzfelbinger, p. 209.

P. 88, LAB 5.4 (end): The total of Japheth's descendants actually comes to 132,900.

P. 88 (margin) on LAB 5.5: Add Cf. Gen. 10$^{6-8}$.

P. 89, LAB 5.5 (end): The total of Cham's descendants actually comes to 214,200

P. 89 (margin) on LAB 5.6: Add Cf. Gen. 10^{22}.

P. 89, LAB 5.6: For "The number of the sons of Cham was 73,000," which is clearly intrusive, the Admont and Melk MSS. read: "And this is the number of the sons of Sem."

P. 89, LAB 5.6 (end): The total of Shem's descendants actually comes to 351,900.

P. 89, LAB 5.7: The number ix is omitted by the Admont and Melk MSS., thus confirming James' comment (p. 246) that the number is corrupt.

P. 89, LAB 5.8: The total of Noah's descendants actually comes to 734,500.

P. 89, LAB 5.8: James, translating the *editio princeps' iuxta*, has "in the presence of." The Admont and Melk MSS. read *vixit*, "And Noe *lived* 350 years after the flood"—which makes much better sense and is in accord with Genesis 9.28.

P. 89, line 30 (margin), on LAB 5.8: Add Gen. 9^{28,29}.

P. 89, LAB 5.8: Italicize "Noe 350 years . . . and he died."

P. 90 (margin) on LAB 6.1: For Gen. 11^{2} read Gen. 11$^{2-4}$.

P. 90, LAB 6.1: "we shall be fighting one against another": Cf. Matthew 10.35: "For I have come to set a man against his father, and a daughter against her mother. . . ." (Philonenko, *per litt.*).

P. 90 (margin) on LAB 6.2: Add Gen. 11^{3}.

P. 90, LAB 6.2: "Let us take bricks [lit., stones]": J. Bowker, *The Targums and Rabbinic Literature,* p. 306, n. d, remarks that in view of what they did with them, *bricks* must be meant. So also Pirke di R. Eliezer 24: "Since there were no stones . . . they baked bricks." Jubilees 10.20 says that "the bricks served them for stone." Bowker cites Sanhedrin 107b (uncensored), where Jesus is accused of having set up a brick and worshipped it, and argues convincingly, on the basis of our passage, against the theory of H. J. Zimmels that the word intended was "fish" not "brick."

P. 90, LAB 6.2: Vermès, *Scripture and Tradition,* p. 77, asserts that "our names" means "our gods," an interpretation found in the Palestinian Targum and in Bereshith Rabbah 38.8. Wadsworth (*per litt.*) aptly compares LAB 44.2, which likewise speaks of a name which Micah is to make by fashioning idols.

P. 90, LAB 6.3: The names of the twelve men correspond to the names given in Genesis 10.26-29. As Ginzberg, 5.197, n. 76, notes, Esar = Ḥazar in Ḥazarmavet, Tenute and Zaba are Latin corruptions for Evila (= Ḥavilah) and Uzal respectively.

P. 90, LAB 6.4 ff.: R. H. Charles, *The Apocrypha and Pseudepigrapha in English,* vol. 2 (Oxford, 1913), p. 30, has questioned the antiquity of the tradition of Abraham in the furnace because Jubilees is silent about it; but, as Vermès,

p. 86, notes, he had overlooked Pseudo-Philo's account, which is the only one extant that connects the building of the Tower of Babel with the casting of Abraham into the furnace. Other accounts are to be found in Baba Bathra 91a, Bereshith Rabbah 38, Midrash Tehillim on Psalm 118.5, and (cited by Philonenko, *per litt.*) Koran 2.68 and 37.95-96. The whole tradition is undoubtedly influenced by the story in the Book of Daniel, chapter 3.

P. 92, LAB 6.11: "the will of God be done": Cf. Matthew 6.10 (Lord's prayer): "Thy will be done" (Philonenko, *per litt.*).

P. 93, LAB 6.11: For the clause "thy blood be upon thy head," Dietzfelbinger, pp. 227-228, compares Matthew 23.35-36, 27.25, Acts 5.28, 18.6, 20.26. Add Testament of Levi 16.3: "taking innocent blood through wickedness upon your heads." Cf. Philonenko, *Les interpolations chrétiennes des Testaments des Douze Patriarches et les manuscrits de Qoumrân* (Paris, 1960), p. 15.

P. 93, LAB 6.14: Where the Bible (Genesis 10.9) says merely that Nimrod was a hunter, the Palestinian Targum, in line with LAB, interprets hunter as a rebel or sinner, as does Bereshith Rabbah 37.2. Josephus, AJ 1.113-114, who like LAB and Pirke di R. Eliezer 24, connects Nimrod with the Tower of Babel, portrays him as being insolently contemptuous of God.

P. 94 (margin) on LAB 6.17: For Dan. 3^{22} read cf. Dan. 3^{22}.

P. 94 (margin) on 6.17: For 3^{27} read cf. 3^{27}.

P. 94, LAB 6.18: Ginzberg, 5.198, n. 76, suggests that Deli is a haggadic interpretation of Ur (read Uri for Deli) and compares Eupolemus, 418 d, where for Ur Uria ("light of God") is given. Eusebius, *Praeparatio Evangelica,* 9.18.2, quotes a lost work of Alexander Polyhistor that Belus settled in Babylon, and lived in a tower which he had built [cf. Nimrod's Tower of Babel] and which was named after him. Josephus, *AJ* 1.160, also knows the tradition of a place in the region of Damascus named after Abram.

P. 94, LAB 6.18: "which is being interpreted": The same phrase is found in LAB 51.1 and, as Dietzfelbinger, p. 205, notes, in Matthew 1.23, Mark 5.41, 15.22, 15.34, John 1.38, 1.41, and Acts 4.36.

P. 94 (margin) on 7.1: Add Gen. 11⁴.

P. 94, LAB 7.1: "Build us a city and a tower" should be italicized.

P. 94 (margin) on 7.2: Add 11⁵.

P. 94, LAB 7.2: "God saw the city and the tower which the children of men were building" should be italicized.

P. 95 (margin) on 7.3: Add 11⁷.

P. 95, line 10 (margin), on LAB 7.3: Add Cf. Isa. 40¹⁵.

P. 95, LAB 7.4: "The land which mine eye hath looked upon": Cf. 1 Corinthians 2.9: "What no eye has seen. . . ." (Philonenko, *per litt.*).

P. 95, LAB 7.4: That it did not rain in the land of Israel in the time of the Flood is stated in Zebaḥim 113a and Shir Hashirim Rabbah 1.15.

P. 95 (margin) on 7.5: Add 11⁷⁻⁹.

P. 95, LAB 7.5: "Changed their likeness" refers to the differentiation into the various races, and not to the transformation into monsters, according to Ginzberg, 5.203, n. 46; but the fact that Baruch, with which, according to James, LAB is closely related, understands it in the latter sense argues for such an interpretation in LAB also.

P. 96, LAB 7.5: "they ceased building the city: and" should be italicized.

P. 96 (margin) on LAB 8.1: For Gen. 12⁵ read Gen. 12⁴,⁵, 13¹².

P. 96, LAB 8.1: Remove italics from "thence and dwelt in the land of Chanaan."

P. 96, line 15 (margin), on LAB 8.1: For 16¹ read 16¹,¹⁵.

P. 96, line 17 (margin), on LAB 8.1: For 25¹² read 25¹²,¹⁶.

P. 96, LAB 8.2: For Cam read Cham.

P. 96, note on 8.2: For Cam (last and next to last line) read Cham.

P. 96 (margin) on LAB 8.3: for 13[14], 17[3] read 13[15], 17[5].

P. 96, LAB 8.3: Italicize "Unto thy seed . . . shall be called Sara."

P. 96, line 26 (margin), on LAB 8.3: Add 17[8,7].

P. 96 (margin) on LAB 8.4: For 25[20 sqq.] read 25[20-26].

P. 97 (margin) on LAB 8.5: For Gen. 26[3], 36 read 26[34], 28[9], 36[2,4,5].

P. 97, LAB 8.5: For "and the sons of Adelifan were" (the reading of the *editio princeps*), the Admont and Melk MSS. read "and a daughter Danelitan and a daughter Elifan."

P. 97, LAB 8.5: For Ieruebemas, the reading of the *editio princeps* and of Phillipps 461, the Admont, Melk, Vatican, and Cambridge MSS. read Isier Vebemas.

P. 97, line 9 (margin), on LAB 8.5: Omit Gen. 36[12].

P. 97 (margin) on LAB 8.5: After I Chron. 1[37] add Gen. 36[13,14].

P. 97 (margin) on LAB 8.6: For Gen. 35[22 sqq.] read Gen. 29[31-35], 30[1-24], 35[18,23,26].

P. 97 (margin) on LAB 8.7: For 34 read 37[1], 34[1,2,25,26].

P. 97, LAB 8.7: Italicize "with the edge of the sword, and took Dina" and "and went out thence."

P. 97, LAB 8.8: The basis of LAB's introduction of Job is apparently the identification of Jobab (Gen. 36.33) with Job, as seen also in the postscript to the Septuagint of Job 42.17d. Eusebius, *Praeparatio Evangelica* 9.25, cites a fragment of Aristeas (c. 100 B.C.E.), *On the Jews,* which makes this identification. That Dinah married Job is found in Baba Bathra 15b, Bereshith Rabbah 19, and Targum on Job 2.9. Though the Testament of Job 1.6 and LAB agree in making Dinah the wife of Job, they disagree on the names of their children: see M. Delcor, "Le Testament de Job, la prière de Nabonide et les traditions targoumiques," *Bibel und Qumran* (*Festschrift Hans Bardtke*) (Leipzig, 1968), p. 65; and M. Philonenko, *"Le Testament de Job,* Introduction, traduction et notes," *Semitica,* 18 (1968), p. 25.

P. 97, line 28 (margin), on LAB 8.8: Add Cf. Job 42[13,14].

P. 98 (margin) on LAB 8.9: For Gen. 37 read Gen. 37[1,11,36], 39[1].

P. 98, LAB 8.9: LAB is in accord with the LXX (Gen. 37.36, 39.1), Philo (*Leg. All.* 3.236, *De Jos.* 27), Josephus (*AJ* 2.39, 2.78), and Jubilees (34.11) in calling Petephres (Potiphar) the chief of the cooks of Pharaoh, whereas the meaning of Hebrew *sar ha-tabahim* is "captain of the guard" or "chief of the executioners." (The Vulgate in 37.36 reads *magistro militum,* "master of the soldiers" and in 39.1 *princeps exercitus,* "chief of the army.").

P. 98, line 12 (margin), on LAB 8.10: Add Gen. 41[41,56].

P. 98, LAB 8.10: "had foreseen": lit., had judged, determined, discerned (*diiudicaverat*).

P. 98, line 14 (margin), on LAB 8.10: For 41, 42, etc., read 42[3,5,1].

P. 98, line 16 (margin), on LAB 8.10: Add 42[8].

P. 98, LAB 8.10: Italicize "And Joseph knew . . . known to them."

P. 98, LAB 8.10: The Admont MS. has "was *not* made known to them"; and O. Eissfeldt, "Zur Kompositionstechnik des Pseudo-Philonischen Liber Antiquitatum Biblicarum," in N. A. Dahl and A. S. Kapelrud, eds., *S. Mowinckel Festschrift* (Oslo, 1955), p. 70, notes that a comparison of the scene of Exodus 34.29-35 with Genesis 42.7 makes it clear that Admont has the right reading. Perhaps the *non* before *malignatus est* ("dealt evilly, maligned") should be omitted in view of Gen. 42.7 and in effect transferred to precede *est agnitus.* A confusion between *agnitus* and *malignatus* is not difficult to imagine.

P. 98 (margin) on LAB 8.11: For 46[8 sqq.] read 46[8].

P. 98, LAB 8.11 (end): "Of Lia" is James' insertion. The MSS. read: "These are the generations of sons which Jacob bore." That this should be kept is indicated by the sentence following which speaks of the number of all of Jacob's sons and not merely of Leah's.

P. 98, line 34 (margin), on LAB 8.11: Add 46[27].

P. 99, LAB 8.12: Some MSS., because of the plural *filii* read *Us Imam* (which defies Gen. 46.23 with its mention of only one son of Dan and which brings the total of Bilhah's descendants to nine. But the plural seems due to the desire to make Dan parallel to the other tribes. Jubilees 44.28, as P. Winter, *"Monogenēs Para Patros," Zeitschrift für Religions- und Geistesgeschichte*, 5 (1953), p. 342, n. 21, remarks, explains the plural by stating that Dan was the father of five sons, four of whom died shortly after arriving in Egypt.

P. 99 (margin) on LAB 8.13: For 46[16,17] read 46[16-18].

P. 99, LAB 8.13: The Admont, Melk, and Vatican MSS. read: "Sariel, Sua, Visui, Mofar, and Sar, their sister. Now the sons of Aser: Iebel and Melchiel." To speak of Melchiel as a female, as James does in his text, following the *editio princeps* and Phillipps 461, violates Genesis 46.17, which speaks of him as a son of Beriah.

P. 99 (margin) on LAB 8.14: For 46[20,21] read 46[20-22].

P. 99 (margin) on LAB 9.1: For Ex. 1[6 7] read 1[6,7].

P. 99, line 22 (margin), on LAB 9.1: Add Ex. 1[10].

P. 99, LAB 9.1: "to our bondmen": The reading of Admont (*domus*) printed in Kisch's edition makes no sense, whereas the reading of the *editio princeps, servis*, which is translated by James, does make sense. The error, as Dietzfelbinger (*per litt.*) has suggested, arose at the stage when LAB existed in a Greek translation and οἰκείοις or οἰκέταις , "bondsmen," was read, perhaps in its abbreviated form, as οῖκος .

P. 100, LAB 9.2: "an untimely birth": Evidence for a Greek *Vorlage* for our text is to be seen in the fact that the reading here, ὠμοτοκείαν in the *editio princeps* and *Ometoceam* in the Admont MS., retains the accusative singular ending of the Greek.

P. 100, LAB 9.2: "and now we are cut off. Yet": The Admont MS. reads "And now let us cease and. . . ."

P. 100, LAB 9.2: "an ordinance" [*terminos*]: As in 3.2 the meaning is "appointed times."

P. 100, LAB 9.2: In rabbinic tradition (Sotah 12a, Mekhilta di R. Shimon ben Yoḥai 3, Shemoth Rabbah 1.13, Pesikta Rabbati 43, 180 a-b, Bamidbar Rabbah 13.20, Koheleth Rabbah 9.17, Midrash Hagagdol 11.12-13, Dibre Ha-Yamim 2 [cited by Ginzberg 5.394, n. 27]), Amram advises that husbands and wives not live together. (Similar advice not to marry because the observance of the Torah was forbidden is found in Baba Bathra 60b and Tosefta Sotah 15.10). In LAB Amram *objects* to the edict of the leaders. In Josephus, *AJ* 2.210, Amram's wife is already pregnant when he becomes anxious for the child.

P. 100, LAB 9.3: "utterly [*in victoria*]": Cf. Luke 18.5, "continual" (εἰς τέλος), and perhaps John 13.1, "to the end" (εἰς τέλος), cited by Dietzfelbinger, p. 215.

P. 100, line 36, note on LAB 9.3: For לְמַנצֵחַ read לנצח.

P. 100, line 20 (margin), on LAB 9.3: Add Gen. 15[13].

P. 100, LAB 9.3: LAB is here attempting to reconcile the apparent contradiction between Genesis 15.13, which prophesies that the Israelites will be slaves in Egypt for 400 years, with the statement in Exodus 12.40 that the Israelites lived in Egypt for 430 years. The difference is accounted for by the fact that God spoke to Abraham thirty years before Isaac's birth: so also Mekhilta Bo 14, 15b; Mekhilta R. Shimon 27, Seder Olam 3, Pirke di R. Eliezer 48, Palestinian Targum Exodus 12.40, Ephraem Syrus 1.202 A (cited by Ginzberg, 5.420, n. 126; add Bamidbar Rabbah 13, cited by Azariah dei Rossi, 4.104).

P. 100, LAB 9.3: "was passed" (*inventus est*, lit., "was found"): Strugnell (*per litt.*) plausibly suggests that this is the Latin translation of εὑρέθη , "was found," a misreading for ἐρρέθη , "was spoken."

P. 101, LAB 9.5: Shemoth Rabbah 1.20, Mekhilta di R. Shimon 3, and Sotah 12b (cited by Ginzberg, 5.397, n. 44) all mention that Jochebed had been pregnant for three months when she separated herself from Amram; Bereshith Rabbah 85.10 remarks that a woman does not become noticeably pregnant until the end of the third month.

P. 101, LAB 9.5: Thamar: The detail that Tamar's intent in having relations with Judah was that she might avoid being joined with Gentiles is found only in LAB. On the special role in LAB played by the polemic against mingling with foreigners, see also 18.13-14, 21.1, 44.7, 45.3, and 47.1, cited by G. Delling, *Jüdische Lehre und Frömmigkeit in den Paralipomena Jeremiae* (Berlin, 1967), p. 51. The incident of Judah and Tamar, though it is, to be sure, told here only in retrospect, is entirely omitted in Josephus' *Antiquities*. In this respect, LAB is in accord with the rabbis, who declare (Megillah 25a) that this incident should be both read and translated in the synagogue.

P. 101, line 5 (margin), on LAB 9.5: Add Gen. 38.

P. 101, LAB 9.5: "goatskin": The Latin *melotes* is a transliteration of the Greek μηλωτή , "sheepskin" or any rough woolly skin. LAB thus differs from both the Hebrew in Gen. 38.18 and 28.25, which has *pethilim*, "threads" or "cords," and the LXX, which has ὁρμίσκος , "small necklace," and the Vulgate, which has *armilla*, "bracelet."

P. 101, LAB 9.8: P. Winter, *"Monogenēs Para Patros," Zeitschrift für Religions- und Geistesgeschichte*, 5 (1953), p. 364, compares John 1.9, "The true light that enlightens every man was coming into the world," and Debarim Rabbah 4.4, in which the soul and the Torah are compared to a lamp.

P. 102, line 4 (margin), on LAB 9.8: Add Gen. 6[3].

P. 102, LAB 9.8: For the connection of the 120-year age limit for men and for Moses see Bereshith Rabbah 26.6, Midrash Tannaim (ed. Hoffmann), p. 226. Philo also connects the two in *De Gigantibus* 55.

P. 102 (margin) on LAB 9.9: Add Ex. 2[1], 6[20].

P. 102, LAB 9.9: Italicize "And . . . of the tribe of Levi went forth and took a wife of his tribe." The Admont, Melk, Vatican, and Vienna MSS. add: "Jacobe [Jocobe, i.e., Jochabeth of 9.12 — Jochebed] by name."

P. 102, LAB 9.10: Cf. Megillah 14a, Sotah 12b, Shemoth Rabbah 1.22, Mekhilta Beshalah 10, Mekhilta di R. Shimon 15, Midrash Mishle 14.1, 31.17, Midrash Vayosha (Jellinek, p. 41), Sefer Hayashar, p. 242, cited by S. Rappaport, *Agada und Exegese bei Flavius Josephus* (Frankfort, 1930), p. 114, n. 129. P. Winter, "Jewish Folklore in the Matthaean Birth Story," *Hibbert Journal*, 53 (1954-1955), pp. 38-39, compares Joseph's dream foretelling Jesus' birth in Matthew 1.21. In Josephus Moses' birth is twice foretold, once by one of the Egyptian sacred scribes (*AJ* 2.205) and once by God in Amram's dream (*AJ* 2.215). E. R. Goodenough, *By Light, Light* (New Haven, 1935), p. 266, in commenting on the man in a linen garment, notes that in the Egyptian religion the appearance of Isis and Osiris in dreams to give prophetic messages or warnings was a constant feature, and that the linen garb of Osiris was a distinctive feature (see, we may add, Lucan, 9.153-161). But the man in a linen garment is taken from Ezekiel 10.2; he is Gabriel, as we see from Tanḥuma (Buber) 3.84; cf. Zohar, 2.19a (cited by Ginzberg, 5.396, n. 40).

P. 102, line 16 (margin), on LAB 9.10: Add Cf. Ezek. 10[2].

P. 102, LAB 9.10: "Behold that which": Winter, *Hibbert Journal*, 53 (1954-55), p. 39, suggests that the neuter (*quod*) was perhaps unconsciously influenced by the neuter τὸ γεννώμενον of Luke 1.35 with reference to the impending birth of Jesus.

P. 102, LAB 9.10: The connection of Moses' being cast into the water with his later effecting the drying up of the water of the Red Sea is unique with LAB.

P. 102, James' note on LAB 9.10: For *Megillah* read *Megillah* 14a.

P. 102 (margin) on LAB 9.12: Add 2^{2,3}.

P. 102, LAB 9.12: "hid the child in her womb 3 months": Shemoth Rabbah 1.20, Mekhilta di R. Shimon 3, and Sotah 12a (cited by Ginzberg, 5.397, n. 44) all likewise note that Jochebed had been pregnant for three months at the time of her separation from Amram, but that the Egyptians had been unable to perceive her condition. After *per tres menses* ("for three months") there seems to be a lacuna, probably due to homoeoteleuton, unnoticed by James or Kisch or other commentators, to the effect that after she gave birth she hid the child for three months (Exodus 2.2). Ginzberg, *op. cit.*, suggests that the text of LAB here be emended.

P. 102, LAB 9.12: Unmistakable evidence of LAB's use of the LXX is to be seen in his word (including even the accusative case ending) for "ark," *thibin*, which is the LXX's spelling in Exodus 2.3 of the Hebrew word *tebah*. Philo, in the two passages referring to Exodus 2.3, *De Confusione Linguarum* 106 and *De Vita Mosis* 1.10, does not mention the ark at all.

P. 102, LAB 9.12: "edge" [*os*]: In using the word *os*, lit., "mouth," in the unusual sense of "edge," LAB has clearly been influenced by the Hebrew original, *sephath*, lit., "lip," "edge," as noted by Dietzfelbinger in his commentary. The LXX has merely "beside [παρά] the river."

P. 103, LAB 9.13: That Moses was born already circumcised is seen in Sotah 12a and Shemoth Rabbah 1.24 on Exodus 2.2. This is the only mention of circumcision in LAB.

P. 103, LAB 9.14: For "our fruit" read "fruit of our womb," adding *ventris* after *fructus* in accordance with the stemmatically more probable reading of the *editio princeps*.

P. 103 (margin) on LAB 9.15: Add 2^{5,6}.

P. 103, LAB 9.15: Italicize "But the daughter of Pharao came down to wash in the river" and "He is of the children of the Hebrews."

P. 103, LAB 9.15: "according as she had seen in a dream": This detail is unique in LAB.

P. 103 (margin) on LAB 9.16: Add 2^{10}.

P. 103, LAB 9.16: S. Krauss, "The Names of Moses," *Jewish Quarterly Review*, O.S., 10 (1898), p. 726, notes that the name Melchi occurs twice in Epiphanius, *De Vita Sanctissimae Deiparae Liber* (Rome, 1774), p. 14, in the apocryphal genealogies of Mary and of Joseph, and that Epiphanius also has the name Ioakeim, another name which Clement of Alexandria, who has Melchi (*Stromateis* 1.23.1), gives to Moses. Goodenough, *Jewish Symbols in the Greco-Roman Period*, vol. 12, pp. 4-5, citing Clement's statement that initiates (*mustai*) had an elaborately spiritualized account of Moses, who, with his name Melchi exercised some permanent function in heaven, conjectures that his function was as a priestly mediator and that his name had some relation to Melchizedek.

P. 103 (margin) on LAB 10.1: Add Ex. 2^{23,24}.

P. 103, line 27 (margin), on LAB 10:1: Add Cf. Ex. 7^{14}-12^{36}.

P. 104, LAB 10.1: LAB strangely enumerates only nine plagues, omitting the sixth plague, boils. Josephus, though he specifically states (*AJ* 2.293) that he will enumerate all of them, actually proceeds, like LAB, to enumerate nine, though in his case it is the fifth, the murrain on cattle, that he omits. One may further note that LAB enumerates the plagues in the order 1, 2, 4, 7, 5, 8, 3, 9, 10. Josephus maintains the order of the Hebrew and LXX. But Philo, *De Vita Mosis* 1.98 ff., has the order thus: 1, 2, 3, 7, 8, 9, 6, 4, 5, 10.

P. 104, LAB 10.1: *Panmixia* is not "all manner of flies" but all manner of animals, as the rabbinic parallels (cited by Ginzberg, 5.430, n. 188) make clear. Here

LAB parallels Josephus (*AJ* 2.303: θηρίων καὶ παντοίων καὶ πολυτρόπων —"wild beasts of every species and kind") and disagrees with the LXX on Exodus 8.17 (21), Artapanus (*ap.* Eusebius, *Praeparatio Evangelica* 9.27), Ezekiel the tragedian 138 (ed. Wienecke), and Philo, *De Vita Mosis* 1.130, which render this plague as κυνόμυια ("dog-fly"). Aquila (*ap.* Jerome, *Ep.* 106.85) uses almost exactly the same word as LAB, πάνμικτον .

P. 104, line 4 (margin), on LAB 10.1: Add Ex. 10²¹.

P. 104, LAB 10.2: For "unto their God" read with the *editio princeps*, "unto their Lord," which is stemmatically more probable.

P. 104, line 16 (margin), on LAB 10.2: Add Gen. 12⁷.

P. 104 (margin) on LAB 10.3: Add Cf. Jud. 5¹⁴⁻¹⁸.

P. 104, LAB 10.3: The threefold division of the tribes is found in Mekhilta Beshalaḥ, Pirke Rabbenu Hakadosh (ed. Grünhut), 43, and Midrash Vayosha (ed. Jellinek), 51-52. Ginzberg, 6.4, n. 23, who cites the last two passages, contends that the midrashic statement of a threefold division is derived from Psalms 68.28 (27) and not from Judges 5.15, as stated by James in his note on this passage, but the passage in Psalms couples Zebulun and Naphtali with Benjamin and Judah, whereas here they are of three different opinions. James is right in noting the parallel with the Song of Deborah so far as a division of opinion among the tribes when it came to the prospect of fighting. The fact that the rabbis established the Song of Deborah as the Haphtarah portion for the Sabbath when the Song of Moses is read shows that they regarded the two as parallel.

P. 104, line 26 (margin), on LAB 10.3: Add Cf. Ex. 14¹².

P. 104, line 32 (margin), on LAB 10.4: Add Ex. 3¹³,¹⁴.

P. 105, LAB 10.4: Lia (MSS. Lie): Is this not a misreading for an abbreviation for Israel? The Melk MS. indeed reads Israhel.

P. 105 (margin) on LAB 10.5: Add Ex. 14¹⁵,¹⁶.

P. 105, line 9 (margin), on LAB 10.5: Add Ex. 15⁸.

P. 105 (margin) on LAB 10.6: Add Ex. 14²².

P. 105, LAB 10.6: Italicize "And Israel passed over on dry land in the midst of the sea."

P. 105 (margin) on LAB 10.7: For Ps. 78⁵² read Ps. 78²⁴.

P. 105, LAB 10.7: In addition to appearing in Targum Onkelos on Numbers 21.16-20, the tradition of the well is also found in Shabbath 35a, Vayikra Rabbah 22.4, Bamidbar Rabbah 18.22, Midrash Tehillim 24.206, and Ephraem Syrus 1.263 (cited by Ginzberg, 6.15, n. 82, and 6.21, n. 129).

P. 106, line 1 (margin), on LAB 10.7: Add Ex. 13²¹, cf. Neh. 9¹².

P. 106, LAB 11.1: For "word" read "words."

P. 106, LAB 11.1: On light cf. John 1.5, IV Esdras 9.31, and Baruch 59.2 (cited by Winter, *Zeitschrift für Religions- und Geistesgeschichte*, 5 [1953], p. 364).

P. 106, line 15 (margin), on LAB 11.2: Add Ex. 19¹⁵.

P. 106, LAB 11.2: The equivalency of "after three days" and "on the third day" is seen here and in 11.3. Dietzfelbinger, pp. 236-237, compares Matthew 27.63, Mark 8.31, 9.31, 10.34, Luke 24.7, Acts 10.41, and 1 Corinthians 15.4.

P. 106, LAB 11.2: "come near": James translates *ascendat* ("let him ascend") as if it were *accedat*, to which perhaps it should be emended, as Strugnell (*per litt.*), suggests, to accord with the Hebrew and LXX on Exodus 19.15.

P. 106, LAB 11.2: Another possible reading, as Dietzfelbinger in the notes to his translation suggests, is "Thou shalt enlighten my people with this which I have given into thy hands, the everlasting law. . . ."

P. 106, 11.2: Cf. Abodah Zarah 2b, which indicates that since God offered the Torah to all nations they can have no excuses. Ginzberg, 6.39, n. 212, wrongly emends to "because they have known My laws." He is also wrong in stating that this passage is given by LAB as a comment on the first commandment of the Decalogue, which does not begin in LAB until 11.6.

P. 107 (margin) on LAB 11.3: For Ex. 19[14] read Ex. 19[14,15].

P. 107 (margin) on LAB 11.4: For 19[16] read 19[16,17].

P. 107, LAB 11.5: For "an eternal commandment" read "eternal commandments." Philonenko (*per litt.*) compares Matthew 5.18: "For truly I say to you, till heaven and earth pass away, not an iota, not a dot, will pass from the law until all is accomplished."

P. 107 (margin) on LAB 11.6: For 20[1] read 20[1,2].

P. 107, line 28 (margin), on LAB 11.6: For 20[4] read 20[4-6].

P. 108, LAB 11.6: "if they walk in the ways of their fathers:" A similar proviso, as Azariah dei Rossi, 4.105, notes, is found in Targum Onkelos on Exodus 34.7 and Sanhedrin 27b.

P. 108, LAB 11.7: Ginzberg, 6.40-41, n. 219, cites Shabbath 33a: "For the crime of vain oaths . . . the roads become desolate," and brilliantly suggests that the text of LAB is a mistranslation of the Hebrew, which read "that My roads [i.e., the roads of My land] become not desolate."

P. 108 (margin) on LAB 11.8: For 20[8] read 20[8-10].

P. 108, line 16 (margin), on LAB 11.8: Add Ex. 20[11].

P. 109 (margin) on LAB 11.10: For Ex. 20[14] read Ex. 20[13 (14)].

P. 109, line 3 (margin), on LAB 11.10:. Add Ex. 14[8].

P. 109, LAB 11.10-11: Azariah dei Rossi, pp. 107-108, cites the reversal in the order of the prohibitions of murder and adultery, which is likewise found in Philo (*De Decalogo,* 121 ff., *De Specialibus Legibus,* 3.8, *Quis rerum divinarum haeres,* 173) as evidence for Philonic authorship of our treatise, since this inversion is unknown to him in any other writer except Paul (Romans 13.9: to this add Luke 18.20, Epistle of James 2.11 and some MSS. of the LXX [Ex. 20.13-14] and of Mark 10.19, and, most important, the Hebrew Nash Papyrus, dating from about 100 B.C.E.). Josephus *AJ* 3.92, Matthew 19.18, and LAB in 44.6-7, as well as Jeremiah 7.9, give the order of the Hebrew text. D. Flusser, " 'Do Not Commit Adultery,' 'Do Not Murder,' " *Textus* 4 (1964), p. 223, who notes the above, concludes that the author of LAB probably used a Hebrew MS. of the Nash type; but if so, why did he not do so in 44.6 and again in 44.7? On the reversal of the order see F. Hauck in G. Kittel and G. Friedrich, *Theologische Wörter-buch zum Neuen Testament* (Stuttgart, 1933), 4.738 A 2. See also H. M. Orlinsky, "Prolegomenon: The Masoretic Text: A Critical Evaluation," in reissue of Christian D. Ginsburg, *Introduction to the Massoretico-Critical Edition of the Hebrew Bible* (New York, Ktav, 1966), p. xl, n. 12, who suggests that there was an Alexandrian order of the Ten Commandments as well as a Judaean order. But the fact that the Hebrew Nash Papyrus has the same inversion found in Philo and in most of the texts of the New Testament would indicate that the two versions are both ultimately Palestinian in origin.

P. 109, LAB 11.11: The *editio princeps,* as well as the Berlin and Cusa MSS., omitting *non,* reads: "because thine enemies got the mastery." This should be noted in James, Appendix I, p. 250. The readings with and without *non* make sense, but that of the *editio princeps* is preferable as the *lectio difficilior.*

P. 109 (margin) on LAB 11.12: For 20[16] read 20[13 (16)].

P. 109, LAB 11.12: Here, as Dietzfelbinger, p. 227, has correctly noted, is the foundation of the Golden Rule, which is found in many formulations throughout this period. But what is peculiar and without analogy is the appearance of the Golden Rule within the framework of the Decalogue.

P. 109 (margin) on LAB 11.13: For 20[17] read 20[14 (17)].

P. 109 (margin) on LAB 11.14: For 20[18] read 20[15-17 (18-20)].

P. 109, line 17 (margin), on LAB 11.14: Add Num. 12[8].

P. 109, LAB 11.14: Italicize "Fear not . . . sin not)."

P. 109 (margin) on LAB 11.15: For 20[21] read 20[18 (21)].

P. 109, line 29 (margin), on LAB 11.15: Add Ex. 24[18].

P. 109, LAB 11.15: James' note mentioning as peculiar to LAB the notions that the tree of life sweetened the waters of Marah and that these were the waters that followed Israel is challenged by Ginzberg, 6.14, n. 82, who cites Mekhilta Vayassa 1.45b and Mekhilta di R. Shimon 72-73, stating that the tree is the Torah. Aboth di R. Nathan 157 (ed. Schechter) says that Moses' rod was taken from the tree of life. Ginzberg, 6.15, n. 82, further suggests that since LAB in 10.7 speaks of the well of Miriam, he may here have confused the well of Miriam (מרים) with the well of Marah (מרה). Dietzfelbinger, pp. 237-238 and 340, n. 149, suggests that 11.15 better belongs after 10.7.

P. 110, line 2, LAB 11.15: "and followed them": The Admont MS. adds *Dominus,* "and the Lord followed them." The *editio princeps,* here followed by James, omits it, leaving the water of Mara as subject, and is thus in accord with Tosefta Sukkah 3.11 ff., as Dietzfelbinger notes in his forthcoming commentary.

P. 110, line 4 (margin), on LAB 11.15: Add Ex. 25-31.

P. 110, line 5, LAB 11.15: After "commanded him" the Admont MS. has *in faciem,* "with regard to the appearance."

P. 110, line 8, LAB 11.15: "Base" (Latin *base*) is James' emendation, presumably on the basis of Exodus 30.18. The MSS. read *vase* (*vasis*), "vessel(s)."

P. 110, line 9, LAB 11.15: "shoulder-piece and the breastplate": LAB uses the LXX's word for the ephod (Ex. 28.6), ἐπωμίς , and for the breastplate (Ex. 28.15), λογεῖον . The Vulgate translates these terms into Latin as *superhumerale* and *rationale* respectively.

P. 110, line 11 (margin), on LAB 11.15: Add Ex. 25[9,8].

P. 110, line 13, LAB 11.15: Insert *he* before *said.*

P. 110 (margin) on LAB 12.1: For Ex. 34[29], etc., read Ex. 34[29-35] and raise to beginning of 12.1.

P. 110, LAB 12.1: The rays sent forth from Moses' face came from the Shekhinah of God (the place of light mentioned here), according to the Zohar, 2.58a (Ginzberg, 6.50, n. 260). M. McNamara, *The New Testament and the Palestinian Targum to the Pentateuch* (Rome, 1966), pp. 171-172, remarks that the statement that Moses' face became glorious is found in the LXX and in all the Targumim of this passage (Exodus 34.29). According to Biblical and Midrashic tradition, the scene of Moses covered with invisible light belongs after, not before, the episode of the Golden Calf (LAB 12.2 ff.), as Dietzfelbinger, in his forthcoming commentary, remarks. The notion that the Israelites saw Moses and did not recognize him is unique with LAB, as Dietzfelbinger there notes, though we may now add that the Targum Neofiti on Exodus 16.15, in an obvious pun in connection with the manna, similarly states: "The children of Israel saw and said to one another, 'What [man] is he?', for they did not know Moses." See G. Vermès, "He Is the Bread: Targum Neofiti 16.15," *Neotestamentica et Semitica: Studies in Honour of Matthew Black* (Edinburgh, 1969), pp. 256-263.

P. 110 (margin) on LAB 12.2: For Ex. 32 read Ex. 32[1,2].

P. 110, LAB 12.2 ff.: Though LAB is generally much more highly selective than Josephus, he chooses to narrate the incident of the Golden Calf at some length, whereas Josephus omits it. It is interesting that in this LAB is in accord with the rabbis (Megillah 25a), who expressly declare that this account is to be both read and translated in the synagogue.

P. 111, lines 2-3, LAB 12.2: "bring judgement near to [*appropiabit, apportabit*]": Dietzfelbinger, in his forthcoming commentary, suggests that perhaps this should be emended to *appropriabit,* "will make his own." This would then allude to the tradition that Moses himself assumed the blame for the golden calf (see Ginzberg, 3.126-127, n. 131).

P. 111 (margin) on LAB 12.4: For 32[7] read 32[7,8].

P. 111, LAB 12.4: Italicize "And the Lord . . . which I commanded them."

P. 111, line 22 (margin), on LAB 12.4: Add Gen. 12[7].

P. 111, LAB 12.4: For "make peace" (*concordabor*), which is stemmatically impossible, read "be reconciled" (*reconciliabor*).

P. 112, LAB 12.5: For a fuller list of the Midrashim having this account see Ginzberg, 6.54, n. 279. Vermès, *Scripture and Tradition*, pp. 56-67, compares the passage in the Dead Sea Scrolls (Hodayoth 3.7-10) where the poet compares himself to a woman in labor bringing forth the first-born, but this picture is drawn from Jeremiah 4.31, and none of the peculiar features of LAB is to be found in the Scroll.

P. 112, LAB 12.7: The rabbis also (Abodah Zarah 44a, Palestinian Talmud Sotah 3, 19a, Palestinian Targum on Exodus 32.30 and other passages cited by Ginzberg, 6.54, n. 281) tell of the drinking of the waters as a means of differentiating gradations of sinners, a punishment reminiscent of the water drunk by adulterous women; but none of the rabbinic passages has LAB's peculiar signs.

P. 112, LAB 12.8: Dietzfelbinger, p. 256, n. 80, compares Ezekiel 31 (note especially 31.4: "The waters nourished it, the deep made it grow tall"). Philonenko (*per litt.*) notes a similar image in John 15.6: "If a man does not abide in me, he is cast forth as a branch and withers; and the branches are gathered, thrown into the fire and burned." A similar description of Israel as a tree whose branches tower to heaven and whose roots sink down to the abyss is found in the Dead Sea Scrolls (1 QH 6.15).

P. 113, LAB 12.9: "For thou art he that art all light": cf. John 1.4 ff.

P. 113, line 21 (margin), on LAB 12.10: Add Ex. 34[1].

P. 113, LAB 12.10: Italicize "Hew thee . . . stone."

P. 113, LAB 12.10: "write upon them": LAB plainly contradicts Exodus 34.1 and Deuteronomy 10.4, which in the Hebrew text and in all the versions state that God Himself wrote upon the second tablets. Ginzberg, 6.59, n. 305, conjectures that the original Hebrew of LAB had *vekatavti*, "I will write," which he misread as *vekatavta*, "you will write." But the Codex Vaticanus and many other MSS. of the LXX on Deuteronomy disagree with the Hebrew in having God tell Moses, "*Thou* shalt write." And, in any case, Exodus 34.27 and 28 clearly indicate that God told Moses to write on the second tablets and that Moses did so. S. Lieberman, *Hellenism in Jewish Palestine* (New York, 1950), pp. 80-81, notes that the rabbis are divided on the question as to who wrote on the second tablets. The majority (Tosefta Baba Kamma 7.358.1 ff. and Debarim Rabbah 3.17) declare that it was God who did so. Pseudo-Philo is in accord with the minority (Shemoth Rabbah 47.9), who state that it was Moses who wrote upon them. Hence Ginzberg's conjecture is unnecessary. The credal heresy of the Benjamites noted in LAB 25.13 is due to their being in doubt as to whether God or Moses had written on the tablets.

P. 113 (margin) on LAB 13.1: For Ex. 34 read Ex. 34-40.

P. 113, LAB 13.1: "and the tabernacle": Spiro, "Samaritans," *PAAJR*, 20 (1951), p. 345, n. 135, discusses this emendation by James at length and upholds it.

P. 113, lines 32-33, LAB 13.1: Remove italics from *rest*.

P. 113, LAB 13.1: Kisch joins "and the holy crown" with the sentence that follows.

P. 114, line 2 (margin), on LAB 13.1: Add Ex. 40[33,34].

P. 114 (margin) on LAB 13.2: Add Lev. 1[1].

P. 114, line 8 (margin), on LAB 13.2: Add Lev. 1[10,14].

P. 114 (margin) on LAB 13.3: Lev. 14 should be on line 9, not on line 10. For Lev. 14 read Lev. 14[2-6].

P. 114 (margin) on LAB 13.4: 23 should be on line 16, not on line 19. For 23 read 23[4-8].

P. 114, line 26, note on LAB 13.4-7: For Talmud read Palestinian Talmud.

P. 114, LAB 13.4: James is surely right in keeping the reading of the *editio princeps,* *memorialem.* Kisch's *inmemoriale* (in Admont, Vatican MSS.) would mean "indescribably large, indescribable, unmentionable, unworthy to be mentioned."

P. 114 (margin) on LAB 13.5: Add Lev. 23[15-21].

P. 115, LAB 13.5: The connection of the bread and the fruits on Pentecost is also found, as Azariah dei Rossi, 4.105, has noted, in Rosh Hashanah 16a: "Bring before Me two loaves on Pentecost so that the fruit of your trees may be blessed."

P. 115 (margin) on LAB 13.6: Add Lev. 23[24-32].

P. 115, LAB 13.6: "offering for your watchers": Sacrifice to watchers [i.e., angels] is attacked in 34.2 as pagan. Perhaps, as Dietzfelbinger in his forthcoming commentary suggests, the meaning is that on the New Year, Israel is brought to judgment by God's angels.

P. 115, LAB 13.6: That the New Year is the anniversary of creation is seen also in Rosh Hashanah 11a.

P. 115, LAB 13.6: "ye shall fast": The allusion is to the Day of Atonement.

P. 115 (margin) on LAB 13.7: Add Lev. 23[33-40].

P. 115, LAB 13.7: The word for Tabernacles, *scenophegie,* is also found (σκηνο-πηγία) in the LXX (Deut. 16.16, 31.10, Zechariah 14.16, 18, 19, I Esdras 5.51, I Macc. 10.21, II Macc. 1.9, 18, John 7.2, Josephus *BJ* 2.515, *AJ* 4.209, 8.100, 8.225, 11.77, 11.154, 13.46, 13.241, 13.372, 15.50, as well as in a second century C.E. papyrus (*Corpus Papyrorum Judaicarum,* eds. Tcherikover, Fuks, Stern, vol. 3, no. 452a, line 16), and in an inscription from Egypt (*CIG* 5361). Philo, however (*De Migratione Abrahami* 202, *De Fuga et Inventione* 186, *De Specialibus Legibus* 1.189, 2.204) calls the holiday σκηναί ("Tents"). Plutarch (*Quaestiones Conviviales* 4.6.2.) calls it σκηνή ("Tent"). That the people are judged for water on Tabernacles is seen also in Rosh Hashanah 16a.

P. 115, LAB 13.7: For "pleasant boughs," "willows," and "cedars," read "beautiful branch," "willow," and "cedar."

Pp. 116-117, LAB 13.8-10: Ginzberg, 6.151, n. 902, notes that whereas in haggadic literature there are many references to the cosmic revelations made to Moses the occasion when they took place is not given. Cf. LAB 19.10-13.

P. 116, LAB 13.8: "The first man [*protoplastum*]":The term *protoplastum* first occurs in the Book of Wisdom 7.1 and 10.1 (second–first centuries B.C.E.) and in Philo, fragment 61 (Harris). It is frequent in the Greek and Latin Church Fathers.

P. 116, line 11 (margin), on LAB 13.8: Add Cf. Gen. 1[28,29].

P. 116, line 13 (margin), on LAB 13.8: Add Cf. Gen. 3[12,13,3].

P. 116, LAB 13.8: The last sentence, "And then . . . men," is found in the *editio princeps* but not in the Admont, Melk, Budapest, or the two Munich MSS. The authenticity is doubtful.

P. 116, LAB 13.9 (note): It is not certain that it is to Moses that God here shows Paradise; perhaps Noah is meant.

P. 116 (margin) on LAB 13.10: Add Lev. 26[2-5].

P. 117 (margin) on LAB 14.1: For Num. 1[2] read Num. 1[1-3].

P. 117, line 13 (margin), on LAB 14.1: Add Cf. Ex. 13[18].

P. 117, LAB 14.1: Mekhilta Beshallaḥ 1.24a and Mekhilta di R. Shimon (cited by Ginzberg, 6.138, n. 806) also state that forty-nine fiftieths (the midrashic explanation of וחמשים, Ex. 13.18) died in Egypt during the three days of darkness.

P. 117, LAB 14.2: After "in their own land" the Admont, Melk, and Vatican MSS. add: *et non in corde suo,* "and not in their own heart," the meaning of which is unclear; presumably, as Dietzfelbinger in his forthcoming commentary indicates, the contrast is between God's reliability and man's unreliability.

P. 117, LAB 14.2: For "I will not diminish" (*minueram*), which is stemmatically impossible, read "they have not diminished" (*minuerunt*).

P. 117, line 22 (margin), on LAB 14.2: Add Gen. 22[17].

P. 117, line 23 (margin), on LAB 14.2: Add Dt. 28[62].

P. 117, LAB 14.2: "By number [*in numero*]": That is, in finite number.

P. 117, line 27 (margin), on LAB 14.3: For 1[46] read 1[46,47,49], 2[33].

P. 117, LAB 14.3: For 604,550 both the Hebrew text and the LXX have 603,550. Josephus, curiously enough, also differs from the Hebrew and the LXX, giving the number as 605,550 in one place (*AJ* 3.196) and as 603,650 in another place (*AJ* 3.288). The number of Levites in Josephus (*AJ* 3.290) is 22,880 (23,880 in some MSS.), which likewise disagrees with the Hebrew and the LXX (Numbers 3.39), both of which give 22,000.

P. 118, line 16 (margin), on LAB 14.5: Add Cf. Num. 9[1].

P. 118 (margin) on LAB 15.1: For Num. 13 read Num. 13[1-3,25-29,32-33].

P. 118, LAB 15.1: Whereas Philo (*De Vita Mosis* 1.40.221) and Josephus (*AJ* 3.302), following Deuteronomy 1.22-23, speak of the spies as due to Moses' initiative, LAB, following Numbers 13.2, declares it to have been due to God's command.

P. 118, LAB 15.2: James, following the *editio princeps*, omits "not" (found in the Admont MS.) before "overcome," "conquer," and "resist." The sense requires the reading of the Admont MS.

P. 118, LAB 15.2: "fowls of the air": This is James' emendation. The text reads *a volatilibus hominum*, "by fleeting men."

P. 118, LAB 15.2: "these men": The Admont MS. reads *hec*, "these things," referring presumably to the stars, lightning, and thunder.

P. 118, LAB 15.2: There is no rabbinic parallel for this particular miracle which accompanied the spies, but Mekhilta Shirah 9.43a says that if anybody wanted to betray them, he was rendered as still as a stone (Ginzberg, 6.94, n. 515).

P. 119, line 10 (margin), on LAB 15.4: Add Ex. 3[8].

P. 119, line 12 (margin), on LAB 15.4: Add Num. 14[3].

P. 119 (margin) on LAB 15.5: Add Num. 14[10].

P. 119, LAB 15.5: "unto which [*cui*]": The Admont MS. reads *quod*, "about which."

P. 119, LAB 15.5: "shall come[*adveniet*]": Strugnell (*per litt.*) plausibly suggests emending to *advena erit*, "will be a stranger" to accord with Genesis 15.13.

P. 119, LAB 15.5: "and subjected angels under their feet": Cf. LAB 30.5 and Matthew 4.6 [quoting Psalm 91.11]: "He will give his angels charge of you (Philonenko, *per litt.*).

P. 119, LAB 15.6: "word": Or "event," taking *verbo* as equivalent to Hebrew דָּבָר.

P. 119, line 34 (margin), on LAB 15.6: Add Gen. 1[9].

P. 119, LAB 15.6: Italicize "Let . . . place."

P. 120, LAB 15.6: "I bowed the heavens": Exactly the same phrase, *inclinavi coelos*, is found in IV Esdras 3.18. A very similar phrase is found in the Palestinian Targum (see McNamara, pp. 75-76).

P. 120, line 8 (margin), on LAB 15.6: Add Num. 14[32].

P. 120 (margin) on LAB 15.7: Add Cf. Num. 14[13-19].

P. 120, LAB 15.7: After "days" the Admont, Melk, and Vatican MSS. add: "since unless thou hast pity, who will be begotten?"

P. 120 (margin) on LAB 16.1: For Num. 16 read Num. 15[37-41], 16[1-3].

P. 120, LAB 16.1: The motive for Korah's rebellion is different from that of envy of Moses and Aaron stated in Josephus, *AJ* 4.14.

P. 120, LAB 16.1: LAB, in stating that 200 men revolted with Korah, differs from the Hebrew (Num. 16.2), LXX, Josephus *AJ* 4.21, and the Vulgate, all of which give the number as 250.

P. 120 (margin) on LAB 16.2: Add Cf. Gen. 41[1-16].

P. 120, LAB 16.2: Similarly Sanhedrin 37b notes that from the time it swallowed Abel's blood until the time that it swallowed up Korah, the earth did not open its mouth. Ginzberg, 6.103, n. 581, suggests that Sion [found in the *editio princeps* but not in the Admont MS.] is an error for *zayon*, "dry land," a rare word. This would seem to be another indication that our text is ultimately a translation from Hebrew.

P. 120, last line, LAB 16.2: Kisch starts 16.3 with "And now" and then adds the word *quia*, "because," from the Admont MS., continuing the sentence with "lo, I will command."

P. 121, line 15 (margin), on LAB 16.3: Add Num. 16^{30}.

P. 121, LAB 16.3: "and I will not do any more unto them": If we adopt the reading of the Vatican, Admont, and Melk MSS., the translation would be "and I will not add any more about them."

P. 121, LAB 16.3: The Mishnah in Sanhedrin 109b records a dispute between R. Akiba, who says that the assembly of Korah have no portion in the world to come, and R. Eliezer, who denies this. Aboth di R. Nathan 26.107 says that they will never be resurrected.

P. 121, line 18, LAB 16.4: Remove comma after "Choreb."

P. 121, LAB 16.5: After "therein" add "lawfully" or "befittingly [*legitime*]."

P. 122, line 4 (margin), on LAB 16.6: Add Num. 16^{32}.

P. 122, LAB 16.6: "company": Latin *sinagoga*. Similarly the word used by the LXX throughout Numbers 16 is συναγωγή .

P. 122, last line, note 1, on LAB 16.7: For *Sina* read *Syna.*

P. 122, line 18 (margin), on LAB 17.1: Add Num. 17^{17,19,20}.

P. 122 (margin) on LAB 17.2: Add Num. 17^{22,23}.

P. 122, LAB 17.3: The connection of Aaron's rod with Jacob's is also found in Tanhuma (Buber) 3.66-67 (see Ginzberg, 6.106, n. 600).

P. 122, line 26 (margin), on LAB 17.3: Add Gen. 30$^{37-39}$.

P. 122, LAB 17.3: "parti-coloured": The Vatican MS. has *cenarios*, which occurs nowhere else in Latin. James, p. 253, suggests the possibility of emending to *cinerarios*, but an easier emendation is *cenereos*, "ash-coloured."

P. 123, LAB 18.1: "unto his people": Instead of this reading of the *editio princeps* the Admont has "and their people."

P. 123, LAB 18.2 ff.: LAB's portrait of Balaam is unique, according to Vermès, *Scripture and Tradition*, p. 174, in that it is favorable, in contrast to rabbinic tradition. Yet it is fair to say that the Biblical account which LAB is here paraphrasing (Numbers 22-24) is itself not so unfavorable and that it is other Biblical passages, notably Deuteronomy 23.6, Joshua 24.10, and Nehemiah 13.2, which reveal his baser side. Moreover, LAB 18.13 has brought his paraphrase of Numbers 31.16, which is highly unfavorable to Balaam, into juxtaposition with his paraphrase of the main account of Balaam, though the Bible separates the two accounts. It is therefore an exaggeration for Vermès to say that Balaam's only desire is to do the will of God. Vermès' statement ("Deux traditions sur Balaam: Nombres XXII.2-21 et ses interpretations midrashiques," *Cahiers Sioniens*, 9 [1955], pp. 299-300) that aside from LAB the entire Jewish tradition about Balaam is pejorative is likewise an exaggeration in view of Aggadath Bereshith 65.130, which represents him as obeying God's will, and Eliyahu Rabbah (ed. Friedmann), 28, p. 141, which regards him as a prophet comparable to Moses. There is, however, a great contrast between the attitude of LAB and that of Philo, *De Vita Mosis*, 1.286, who says that Balaam proved himself to be even worse than King Balak. On the whole LAB's point of view is paralleled by that of Origen, *In Numeros Homilia* (Migne, *Patrologia Graeca*, 12.683 d), who likewise notes both the praiseworthy and blameworthy aspects of his character. Jerome, *Quaestiones in Genesin*, 22.20 (Migne, *Patrologia Latina*

23.971) has a point of view toward Balaam which is as favorable as that of LAB, for he stresses that he was at first a deeply pious man, indeed a true prophet who became corrupt through his greed.

P. 123 (margin) on LAB 18.2: For 22 read 22[2,3,5].

P. 123, LAB 18.2: "that lived": The Latin requires that "that" refer to Balac and not to Moab.

P. 123, LAB 18.2: "interpreter of dreams": Here LAB departs from the LXX, which keeps the place-name *Phathoura* of Numbers 22.5, and shows his knowledge of Hebrew, since the root *pathar* means to interpret, and his connection with the Targumic tradition, since 2 TJ likewise translates "interpreter of dreams." The fact that Josephus (*AJ* 4.104), in the passage which obviously corresponds to Numbers 22.5, since it speaks of Balaam as hailing from the Euphrates, calls him μάντις, "diviner, seer, prophet," that Philo, *De Vita Mosis*, 1.264, similarly calls him far-famed in soothsaying (μαντεία), and that the Vulgate on Numbers 22.5 translates as *hariolus*, "soothsayer, prophet," shows a similar tradition.

P. 123, LAB 18.2: "in the reign of my father": Cf. Bamidbar Rabbah 19.30, 20.7.

P. 123, line 16 (margin), on LAB 18.2: For 22[6] read 22[6,17].

P. 123, LAB 18.2: "many, more": Omit the comma.

P. 123 (margin) on 18.3: For 22[17] read 22[18].

P. 123, line 23 (margin) on 18.3: For 22[8,9] read 22[8].

P. 123 (margin) on 18.4: Add 22[9].

P. 123, LAB 18.4: That LAB presents a picture more favorable to Balaam than is found in the Bible may be seen in Balaam's reply here to God. LAB has Balaam give the reply which, according to Bamidbar Rabbah, 20.6, he *ought* to have given. So Ginzberg, 6.125, n. 730 and Vermès, 131-132.

P. 123, LAB 18.5: The mention of Abraham in God's reply to Balaam is also found in the Targumic tradition; cf. Vermès, *Scripture and Tradition*, p. 132. The fact that the chief features of the Jewish theology built around the binding of Isaac are found in Philo, Josephus, Pseudo-Philo, the Targumim, and the Mekhilta leads Vermès, pp. 193-227, and R. Le Déaut, "La présentation targumique du sacrifice d'Isaac et la sotériologie paulinienne," in *Studiorum Paulinorum Congressus Internationalis Catholicus*, 1961 (Rome, 1963), 2. 563-574, to conclude that this theology is mainly pre-Christian.

P. 123, LAB 18.5: "I raised him above the firmament": Cf. Bereshith Rabbah 45, cited by Azariah dei Rossi, 4.104.

P. 124, LAB 18.5: "the blood of him": According to Yoma 5a there can be no atonement without the shedding of blood. The Mekhilta di R. Shimon, 4, likewise speaks of Isaac's blood as a sacrifice; so Ginzberg, 5.254, n. 255.

P. 124, LAB 18.5: "And then I said unto the angels that work subtilly": James says that this clause, though it is not in the *editio princeps,* must be genuine; his intuition is confirmed by the presence of this clause in the Admont and Melk MSS.

P. 124, line 6 (margin) on LAB 18.5: For Gen. 18[15] read Gen. 18[17].

P. 124, James' note on LAB 18.5: The clause "and unto Jacob his son's son [literally, "his third son"—a peculiar expression] whom he (I) called (my) first-born" should be included in the text: it is found in the Admont and Melk MSS. James' suggested emendation, *vocavi,* "I called," is found in the Melk MSS., though not in the Admont, and should be adopted. Jubilees 19.29 likewise calls Jacob God's first-born son and hence confirms the preference for *vocavi.*

P. 124 (margin) on LAB 18.6: Add Gen. 32[25-27].

P. 124, LAB 18.6: On the angel whose name is not given but who is either Michael or Gabriel, see Bereshith Rabbah 78.2 and Pirke di R. Eliezer 27, cited by Ginzberg, 5.306, n. 249. According to the latter passage, the angel had to chant his hymn [cf. LAB's *angelo qui stabat super ymnos*] on earth; and when the other angels heard him sing they realized that Jacob had prevented his returning to heaven.

P. 124, line 12 (margin), on LAB 18.6: Add Num. 22^{12}.

P. 124, LAB 18.7 (end): "Thy [*tuas*] offerings" is stemmatically impossible; read with Admont and *editio princeps,* "his [*suas*] offerings."

P. 124, line 26 (margin), on LAB 18.8: For 22^{19} read 22^{19-21}.

P. 124, LAB 18.18: Cf. Bamidbar Rabbah 20.9, 12, 15; Tanḥuma (Buber) 4.136-137, Tanḥuma Balak 5, 15, cited by Ginzberg, 6.126, n. 736, and Vermès, *Scripture and Tradition,* pp. 134 and 140.

P. 125, LAB 18.8: "thy journey shall be an offence [*in scandalum*]": The same phrase, *in scandalum,* is found in LAB 43.5, 44.8, and 58.4, as well as in Romans 11.9 (quoting Psalm 69.22) (so Dietzfelbinger, p. 211).

P. 125 (margin) on LAB 18.9: Add Num. $22^{27,31,32}$.

P. 125, LAB 18.9: "he opened": The "he" refers to the angel, whereas in Numbers 22.3 it is God.

P. 125 (margin) on LAB 18.10: For Num. 23, 24 read 22^{41}, $23^{2,6,7}$.

P. 125, LAB 18.10: Targum Onkelos, Targum Pseudo-Jonathan, and the Vulgate follow the Hebrew text (Numbers 23.2) in asserting that Balaam and Balak sacrificed together. The LXX and Philo (*De Vita Mosis* 1.277) make Balak alone the celebrant; LAB and Josephus (*AJ* 4.113) make Balaam the celebrant. (To be sure, it is not clear in LAB that Balaam is the subject; but, as Dietzfelbinger, p. 261, n. 136, remarks, a sudden change of subject to Balak would disturb the unity of the passage.)

P. 125, LAB 18.10 ff.: In both Josephus (*AJ* 4.119 ff.) and LAB, Balaam's four prophecies of Numbers 23.7 ff. are combined into one. Vermès, *Scripture and Tradition,* p. 145, remarks that LAB stresses Balaam's great discouragement rather than his prophecies, following the exegesis also found in Bamidbar Rabbah 20.19.

P. 125, LAB 18.10: "the spirit of God abode not in him": Cf. Romans 8.9: "If the Spirit of God really dwells in you" (Philonenko, *per litt.*).

P. 125, LAB 18.10: "run into the fire": Ginzberg, 6.130, n. 764, suggests that LAB is here contrasting *arah,* "curse," with *or,* "fire."

P. 125, LAB 18.10: "all the topmost part of them": For *eorum,* "their," Ginzberg, 6.130, n. 764, plausibly suggests reading *terrae,* "the earth's." The contractions for *eorum* and *terrae* in Latin MSS. are, we may add, sometimes confused.

P. 125, LAB 18.10: "And Balac himself": The text reads "And he himself," and most likely refers to Balaam.

P. 125, LAB 18.11: "overshadowing [*obumbrans*]": The sense, as Dietzfelbinger, in his forthcoming commentary suggests, requires "overshadowed," i.e., protected.

P. 126, LAB 18.11: That Israel will never be condemned to destruction is the thought in Targum Onkelos on Numbers 23.9, as well as here and in Josephus, *AJ* 4.115-117; so Vermès, *Scripture and Tradition,* pp. 146-147.

P. 126, LAB 18.11: "I have lost [*perdidi*]": This is the reading of the *editio princeps.* The Admont MS. reads "he has destroyed [*perdidit*]."

P. 126, LAB 18.12: The Admont, Melk, and Vatican MSS. start this section with an added sentence: "And behold my hour, which [still] remains."

P. 126, LAB 18.12: "the heritage of the abode": Dietzfelbinger, in his forthcoming translation, follows the Admont, Melk, and Vatican MSS. in rendering it "the heritage and the diffusion," but admits that the meaning "diffusion" for *dissolutio,* though perhaps warranted by the literal meaning of the word, is unique here; and the context, all of which is disposed positively toward the Israelites, favors James' interpretation (note on p. 126).

P. 126, LAB 18.12: Cham: James' conjecture "Chemosh" is very appealing, because in Numbers 21.29 Chemosh is mentioned as the national god of Moab, and in our passage he appears likewise in juxtaposition with Moab.

P. 126 (margin) on LAB 18.13: Add 25.1 ff.

P. 126, LAB 18.13: Targum Jonathan has a similar statement of Balaam's advice to use seductive women. Josephus, *AJ* 4.129, has an even more similar statement: "Take of your daughters and those who are comeliest and most capable of constraining and conquering the chastity of their beholders by reason of their beauty, deck out their charms to add to their comeliness. . . ." Spiro, "Samaritans," *PAAJR*, 20 (1951), pp. 335-336, attempts to see in this description in LAB a contemporary reference to the opulence, finery, and easy morals in Trans-Jordan as reflected in the Zenon Papyri; but the similarity is much too general.

P. 127 (margin) on LAB 18.14: Add Num. 24^{25}.

P. 127 (margin) on LAB 19.1: Add Num. 31^{27}.

P. 127 (margin) on LAB 19.2: For Dt. 31^{27} etc. read Dt. 31^{16} etc.

P. 127 (margin), on LAB 19.3: For Asc. Mos. read Ass. Mos.

P. 127, LAB 19.3: The language of LAB does not sufficiently parallel that of the Dead Sea Scrolls to justify the assumption of K. R. Stow, "Pseudo-Philo, an Essene Work" (unpublished essay, Columbia Univ., 1968), p. 11, that this is a direct reference to the Teacher of Righteousness. The fact that there is a parallel in the *Assumptio Mosis*, which may well have originated in Essene circles, is in itself insufficient evidence, since this may merely indicate a common tradition.

P. 127, LAB 19.3: "a [*unum*] shepherd": The use of *unus* as an indefinite article is rare, and Strugnell (*per litt.*) suggests that *unum* may go back to אחד in the original Hebrew text, which was easily misread as אחד. But *unus* as an indefinite article is found in Plautus and Terence and may reflect the colloquial usage which was resurrected in Christian literature and in the Romance language vernaculars.

P. 127 (margin) on LAB 19.4: Dt. 4^{26}, etc. should be on line 24, not on line 23.

P. 127 n. 4 should read 7.

P. 127, line 25 (margin), on LAB 19.4: Add Dt. 32^1.

P. 127, LAB 19.4: For *hath revealed* read *will reveal*, since all the MSS. have the future, *revelabit*. But Dietzfelbinger, p. 262, n. 141, suggests reading *revelavit*, "hath revealed," and *finem*, "end," in the sense of *telos*, "goal."

P. 128, line 4 (margin) on LAB 19.4: Add 5^{27}.

P. 128, line 5, LAB 19.4: For *we will hear and do* read *we will do and hear*.

P. 128, line 8 (margin), on LAB 19.5: Add Cf. Ps. 78^{25}.

P. 128, LAB 19.5: "the bread of angels": That manna is the food of the angels is the interpretation of the LXX on Psalms 78.25 (correct Ginzberg's note, 5.236, n. 143) and of Rabbi Akiba (Yoma 75b: correct Ginzberg's note, 6.17, n. 95).

P. 128 (margin) on LAB 19.6: Add Dt. 31^{16}.

P. 128, LAB 19.7: LAB is unique in stating that the reason why God did not allow Moses to enter the Promised Land was to keep him from seeing the idols by which the Israelites would be led astray, though such a statement may be inferred from Deuteronomy 31.16.

P. 128, LAB 19.7: "it shall be delivered": The Admont and Melk MSS. read *populus hic* ("this people") after "thereafter" as subject of "shall be delivered." These same words are found in 19.7 two sentences before this; and, as P. Bogaert, *Apocalypse de Baruch*, vol. 1 (Paris, 1969), pp. 253-254, remarks, the repetition is probably a mechanical repetition by a scribe.

P. 128, line 27 (margin), on LAB 19.7: Add Cf. Ex. 32^{19}.

P. 128, LAB 19.7: "which I made with": "Which" refers to the tables; for "made with" a better rendering would be "drew up for."

P. 128, LAB 19.7: Moses ascended the mountain forty days before 17 Tammuz, i.e., on the eighth of Sivan, two days after the Feast of Weeks. Cf. Seder Olam 6 and J. van Goudoever, *Biblical Calendars,* 2nd ed. (Leiden, 1961), p. 119. The fact that 17 Tammuz commemorates the breach of the walls of Jerusalem before the destruction of the Temple in 70 C.E. (the breach of the walls by Nebuchadnezzar took place on 9 Tammuz, and hence 17 Tammuz was chosen to commemorate both) provides James, pp. 29 ff., a *terminus post quem* for LAB. On the significance of 17 Tammuz see Jerome, *Commentary on Zechariah,* 8.19, who, interestingly enough, like LAB, couples the breaking of the tablets and the downfall of Jerusalem as the two events which took place on 17 Tammuz; the Mishnah, Ta'anith 4.6, mentions five sad events that occurred on that date, and since so much of Jerome shows a knowledge of rabbinic tradition it seems reasonable to suppose that this too derives therefrom.

P. 128 (margin) on LAB 19.8: Add Dt. 32⁴⁹.

P. 128, LAB 19.8: Oreb: The Admont, Melk, and Vatican MSS. read Abarim. So also Josephus, *AJ* 4.325, in accordance with Numbers 27.12 and Deuteronomy 32.49.

P. 129 (margin) on LAB 19.9: Add Ex. 31⁻⁶.

P. 129, LAB 19.9: "thou gavest a law and judgements whereby they should live": Philonenko (*per litt.*) suggests a possible parallel in Romans 7.10: "The very commandment which promised life proved to be death to me."

P. 129, LAB 19.9: After "they should live" the Admont, Melk, and Vatican MSS. add "and might enter as the sons of men," but the meaning is unclear.

P. 129, LAB 19.9: "For what man . . . against thee" should not be italicized, since it is not a quotation from 1 Kings 8.46.

P. 129, line 17 (margin), on LAB 19.10: For Dt. 34 read 34¹,⁴.

P. 129, LAB 19.10-13: Ginzberg, 6.151, n. 902, remarks that among the Church Fathers it is Aphraates, 420, who, like the rabbis and Pseudo-Philo, finds in Deuteronomy 34.1-4 an allusion to the future history of Israel.

P. 129, LAB 19.10: "the holy land": S. Zeitlin, in his edition (with S. Tedesche) of *The Second Book of Maccabees* (New York, 1954), p. 102, comments that the expression "*The Holy Land* . . . is an indication that this letter [with which the book starts] was not written by the Jews of Judaea," since Josephus and the Tannaitic rabbis do not employ this term. If so, we must either revise the usual theory that LAB was composed in Palestine, or we must revise Zeitlin's theory about this expression. But the expression is found in Zechariah 2.12, in II Baruch 63.10 (which is most probably Palestinian in origin: see P. Bogaert, *Apocalypse de Baruch,* vol. 1 [Paris, 1969], pp. 331-334), and in IV Esdras 13.48 (which is likewise most probably Palestinian in origin).

P. 129, LAB 19.10: For "the sign [*sic*] whereby men shall interpret" read "the signs whereby men begin to interpret." *Incipient,* James' and Kisch's reading, is stemmatically impossible; read *incipiant* with the *editio princeps.* The signs may be a reference to the zodiac.

P. 129, LAB 19.10: "they sinned [lit., for themselves]": Strugnell (*per litt.*) suggests that the awkward *sibi,* "for themselves," may have resulted from a misreading of the Hebrew original, which was לי (= to me, against me), and was read as לו (though grammatical syntax would demand להם).

P. 130, line 3, LAB 19.11: For "my [*mee*]," which is stemmatically impossible, read "thy [*tue*]" with the *editio princeps.*

P. 130, line 6 (margin), on LAB 19.11: Add Gen. 9¹³,¹⁵.

P. 130, line 14 (margin), on LAB 19.12: Add Dt. 34⁶.

P. 130, LAB 19.12: The notion that not even angels shall know where Moses is to be buried contradicts Philo, *De Vita Mosis* 2.291, which states that he was buried by "immortal powers," i.e., angels (cf. LAB 19.16). Ginzberg, 6.162-163, n.

952, cites a Falasha legend, partly found also in Mohammedan literature, that indicates that three angels dug his grave.

P. 130, LAB 19.12: All the MSS. have "of Egypt." The reference is to the resurrection of those of the Israelites who died in Egypt. Spiro, "Samaritans," *PAAJR*, 20 (1951), p. 337, n. 122, makes the fantastic suggestion that we have here a secretive hint about the colony of Ptolemaic Tobiads.

P. 130, LAB 19.13: "they shall be shortened": Cf. Mark 13.20: "For the sake of the elect, whom he [God] chose, he shortened the days." (Cited by Dietzfelbinger in his forthcoming commentary.)

P. 131, LAB 19.15: L. Gry, "La date de la fin des temps, selon les révélations et les calculs du Pseudo-Philon et de Baruch," *Revue Biblique*, 48 (1939), pp. 339-340, proposes a far-fetched correction for *istic mel apex magnus*, which involves too many unexplained changes. He suggests (pp. 342-345) that $4\frac{1}{2}$ and $2\frac{1}{2}$ be each multiplied by seven, giving $31\frac{1}{2}$ and $17\frac{1}{2}$, a total of 49 years, since from 19.7 it may be seen that we must reckon from the destruction of the Temple by Titus. The world, it is thus predicted, will end in 49 years. Of these 49 years, $31\frac{1}{2}$ have already passed; hence the treatise was written $31\frac{1}{2}$ years after 70, i.e., in 101/102. The obvious answer to Gry is that Moses could hardly have understood that he was to reckon $4\frac{1}{2}$ and $2\frac{1}{2}$ from the date of the destruction of the Temple by Titus. We, in turn, should like to suggest another solution, namely, that *quatuor* (IV) and *duo* (II) were interchanged, so that the correct reading should be: "For $2\frac{1}{2}$ have passed by, and $4\frac{1}{2}$ remain." This would put LAB in exact accordance with the *Assumptio Mosis* 1.2, which places Moses' death in the year 2500, and close to Jubilees, which puts his death a jubilee earler in 2450, and Josephus, *AJ* 8.61-62, who puts his death a jubilee later at 2550 (3102, date of Solomon's temple, minus 592 years from Exodus to the Temple, plus 40 years in the desert: a similar date is implicit in *AJ* 7.68), and *AJ* 20.230 and *Contra Apionem* 2.19, which put his death at 2530. With the statement of the time that has passed by and the time that remains (presumably until the coming of the Messiah), cf. Josephus, *AJ* 4.303, who states that Moses bequeathed a book which was preserved in the Temple, "containing a prediction of future events, in accordance with which all has come and is coming to pass."

P. 132 (margin) on LAB 19.16: For Dt. 34[6] read Dt. 34[5,6].

P. 132, LAB 19.16: "his likeness was changed gloriously": McNamara, pp. 173-175, suggests that 2 Corinthians 3.12-13 also implies that Moses put a veil over his face so as to hide from the Israelites the passing character of the glory with which his face shone, and that since this idea of Moses' transient glory is not to be found in Exodus 34.29-35, he may have derived it from LAB (or from LAB's source), inasmuch as other Jewish sources (e.g., Lekah Deut. 34.7), in speaking of the glory of Moses' face, imply that it was lasting. But, unlike 2 Corinthians 3.12-13, neither LAB 12.1 nor 19.16 implies that Moses' glory was transient; LAB merely indicates that Moses' face was *changed* in that it became illuminated.

P. 132, LAB 19.16: "he buried him": LAB here follows the Hebrew text (so also the Vulgate), and not the LXX, which has "they buried." He also differs with Philo *De Vita Mosis* 2.291, which, presumably under the influence of the plural subject in the LXX, asserts that he was buried by "immortal powers." The prevalent rabbinic interpretation of Deuteronomy 34.6 (Sanhedrin 39a, Sotah 14a) is that God Himself buried Moses, though, according to others (Sifre Bamidbar 52, Bamidbar Rabbah 10.17), Moses buried himself; see Ginzberg, 6.162, n. 952, as amended in the present note).

P. 132, LAB 19.16: "the hymn of the hosts" (lit., "the hymn of the soldiers"): The reference is to the song of the angels; cf. H. Bientenhard, *Die himmlische Welt im Urchristentum und Spätjudentum* (Tübingen, 1951), p. 138, cited by Dietzfelbinger in his commentary.

P. 132, LAB 19.16: "because of a man": On the angels' mourning for Moses see Aboth di R. Nathan 25.51. The angels did cease their song on the occasion of the Flood, the drowning of the Egyptians, and the destruction of the Temple; see Ginzberg, 6.397, n. 32.

P. 132, LAB 19.16: "in the light of the whole world": Ginzberg, 6.151-152, n. 904, notes a similar statement in *Assumptio Mosis* 1.15: "I am now going in the presence of all the people to meet with my fathers." Josephus, *AJ* 4.326, also sought to combat the notion that Moses had not died but had gone back to the Deity.

P. 133 (margin) on LAB 20.1: Add Cf. Dt. 31^{23}.

P. 133 (margin) on LAB 20.2: Add Jos. 1$^{1-3}$.

P. 133, LAB 20.2: On Joshua's mourning for Moses see Midrash Tannaim 225, Aboth di R. Nathan, 12.51, 57 and Sifre Debarim 305, cited by Ginzberg, 6.165, n. 957.

P. 133, line 13 (margin), on LAB 20.2: Add Cf. 1 Sam. 10^6.

P. 133, line 22 (margin), on LAB 20.3: Add Cf. Num. 14^{35}.

P. 133, LAB 20.4: For "he hath chosen" read "he hath not chosen." The *editio princeps* omits *non*, but all other MSS. do have it. It would be contrary to the whole approach of LAB to conceive of the election of any nation other than Israel.

P. 134, LAB 20.5: The prophecy of Eldad and Medad is recorded in Bamidbar Rabbah 15.19, Tanhuma (Buber) 4.57, Tanhuma Beha'alothekha 12, Palestinian Targum Numbers 11.26 (see McNamara, p. 235), Ephraem Syrus 1.257 E, cited by Ginzberg, 6.88-89, n. 482.

P. 134, LAB 20.5: "if there be conflict" (*etiamsi fuerit conflictus*): The Admont and Melk MSS. read *etiamsi fueris fluctuatus*, "even if you will waver." As to the tradition of Joshua's wavering see *Assumptio Mosis* 11.9-19, 12.3.

P. 134, line 13 (margin), on LAB 20.5: Add Jos. 1^{6,9}.

P. 134 (margin) on LAB 20.6: For Jos. 2 read Jos. 2^1.

P. 134, LAB 20.6: Seenamias: Either Mesha (מֵישַׁע), son of Caleb, or Shema (שֶׁמַע), great-grandson of Caleb; cf. 1 Chronicles 2.42-43, cited by Ginzberg, 6.171, n. 10.

P. 134, line 29 (margin), on LAB 20.7: Add Jos. 6^{24}.

P. 135, LAB 20.8: On the well of water for the sake of Miriam see Tanhuma (Buber) 189, Mekhilta Sifra 129a, Seder Olam 10, Shir Hashirim Rabbah 4.13, Vayikra Rabbah 27.6, Sifre Debarim 305, Aphraates 452.

P. 135, LAB 20.8: Ginzberg, 6.19-20, n. 113, notes that LAB agrees, even in phraseology, with the midrashic tradition: Mekhilta Vayassa 5, 51b; Sifre Debarim 304; Seder Olam 9, 10; Tosefta Sotah 11.10; Ta'anith 9a; Tanhuma (Buber) 4.2-3; Tanhuma Bamidbar 2; Midrash Mishle 14.74; Bamidbar Rabbah 1.2, 14.20; Midrash Shir Hashirim 4.5; Midrash Hashkem 193; Yelamedenu in Yalkut 2.15, 554, 578; Pirke di R. Eliezer 34b, cited by Ginzberg, *ibid.* LAB also recalls a parallel in Philo, *De Vita Mosis*, 1.198, that one of God's motives in sending the manna was to honor Moses.

P. 135, James' note on LAB 20.8 (last line): For Taanith 1 read Ta'anith 9a.

P. 135 (margin) on LAB 20.9: Add Jos. 12$^{7-24}$, 13^1 sqq..

P. 135, LAB 20.9: 39 kings: This is the reading of the Fulda-Cassel MS. embodied in the *editio princeps*. The Hebrew has 31, LXX 29, all other MSS. 38. The fact that Joshua defeated 39 kings refutes Spiro's theory ("Samaritans," *PAAJR*, 20 [1951], pp. 347, 352) that Joshua was an utterly peaceful leader.

P. 135, line 19 (margin), on LAB 20.10: Add Jos. 14^{13}.

P. 135, LAB 21.1-6: Dietzfelbinger, p. 23, suggests that 21.1-6 is out of place and belongs better at the beginning of chapter 24 or after 24.3.

P. 135 (margin) on LAB 21.1: For 23 read 13^1 (23^1).

P. 135, line 26 (margin), on LAB 21.1: Add Dt. 31[16].

P. 136, line 3 (margin), on LAB 21.2: Add Cf. 1 Kings 3[9].

P. 136 (margin) on LAB 21.3: Add Jos. 7[1].

P. 136, line 9 (margin), on LAB 21.3: Add Jos. 7[11].

P. 136, LAB 21.3: In Joshua 7.1 the name is Achan, in 1 Chronicles 2.7 the name is Achar. Here James has adopted the reading of the Vatican MS., Achar; Kisch adopts the reading of the Melk MS., Achan; the *editio princeps* has the meaningless Achiras, the Admont the impossible Achab. Spiro, "Samaritans," p. 352, attaches significance to the fact that LAB omits giving the name of Achar's tribe, Judah, since he was biased for Judah and against Samaria.

P. 136, LAB 21.3: Josephus, *AJ* 5.38, says that Joshua used free speech (παρρησίαν) toward God. So also Sanhedrin 43b, Palestinian Talmud Sanhedrin 6.23b, Eliyahu Rabbah 18.102, and LAB here.

P. 136, LAB 21.3: "shall befall us": The reading of the Admont MS., "shall befall you" (plural), adopted by Kisch, makes no sense; to whom can "you" (plural) refer?

P. 136, LAB 21.4: "whereas . . . another": Dietzfelbinger, p. 266, n. 173, suggests translating "whenever man cannot imagine that God redeems one generation through the others. . . ."

P. 136, line 28 (margin), on LAB 21.5: Gen. 49[10] should be one line above.

P. 136, LAB 21.6: "fight against": Dietzfelbinger, in his commentary, argues that the meaning of *expugnabunt* is the very opposite of that assigned here by James, since the text speaks of the faithfulness of Israel, and suggests "win," "gain by fighting." But *expugno* means to take by storm or capture by assault, and denotes violence.

P. 137, LAB 21.6: J. Klausner, *The Messianic Idea in Israel from Its Beginning to the Completion of the Mishnah* (trans. by W. F. Stinespring; New York, 1955), p. 367, suggests that the idea that the Jews will fight against the salvation that will be born to them may be a Christian interpolation. But the whole point of LAB, as seen in the career of Kenaz especially, is that the Jews fight against the salvation that is born to them.

P. 137 (margin) on LAB 21.7: For Jos. 8[30] read Jos. 8[30-35].

P. 137, LAB 21.7-9: Spiro, "Samaritans," pp. 339-340, cites this passage in support of his theory that LAB was written to combat the Samaritans. He notes that whereas the Bible (Joshua 8.30) says that the Jews stood in front of Mt. Gerizim and Mt. Ebal, LAB omits mention of Mt. Gerizim, and mentions no altar as having been constructed on Mt. Gabal (=Ebal: Joshua 8[30]=9[3], LXX).

P. 137, line 6, LAB 21.7: For *from* read *to*.

P. 137, line 14 (margin), on LAB 21.8: Add Jos. 8[31].

P. 137, line 17 (margin), on LAB 21.8: Add Cf. Ps. 150[3-5].

P. 137, LAB 21.9: "psalms": The Admont, Melk, Vatican, and Vienna MSS. read "trumpets."

P. 137, line 22 (margin), on LAB 21.9: Add Jos. 8[31].

P. 137, LAB 21.9: "Behold, our Lord hath fulfilled that which he spake with our fathers": Cf. Luke 1.55: "as he spoke to our fathers" (Philonenko, *per litt.*)

P. 137, line 25 (margin), on LAB 21.9: Add Dt. 11[9].

P. 138 (margin) on LAB 22.1: For Jos. 22 read Jos. 22[10-12].

P. 138, LAB 22.1: Spiro, "Samaritans," p. 343, makes much of the fact that LAB says that the tribes lived not in Transjordan but around the Jordan. It may be, as Winter (*per litt.*) and Dietzfelbinger, p. 268, n. 183, have pointed out, that *circa* is the translation for περί , whereas the original Greek word here was the similar πέραν , "across," though we may note that Josephus, *AJ* 5.100-101, uses the same word πέραν in his description of the incident.

P. 138, LAB 22.1: "did offer sacrifices thereon": This statement is in direct contradiction to the statement repeated four times in Joshua 22.23, 26, 28, 29 that the
Reubenites, Gadites, and the half-tribe of Manasseh did not offer sacrifices on
their altars.

P. 138, LAB 22.1: Silon: In Joshua 22.13-15 the meeting takes place in the land of
Gilead. But just prior to this the Israelites had gathered at Shiloh to make war
against the deviant tribes.

P. 138 (margin) on LAB 22.2: Add 22[15] sqq..

P. 138, LAB 22.2: "spoil": Lit., "exterminate," "root out," in the sense of root out
your good deeds, as Dietzfelbinger in his forthcoming commentary suggests.

P. 138, LAB 22.3: "enlarged": James has emended the reading of the MSS., *ampu-
tavit*, "cut off," to *ampliavit·*

P. 138, line 32 (margin), on LAB 22.3: Add Dan. 2[22].

P. 139, LAB 22.5: "a sanctuary made with hands": Cf. Mark 14.58: "I will destroy
this temple that is made with hands"; Acts 7.48: "Yet the Most High does not
dwell in houses made with hands" (Philonenko, *per litt.*).

P. 139, LAB 22.6: "sanctuaries": In 22.7 we hear of only one sanctuary; but, as
Dietzfelbinger in his commentary remarks, the use of the plural in 42.9 in the
sense of "holy place" shows that the singular and plural of this word are
interchangeable.

P. 139, line 30 (margin), on LAB 22.6: Add Jos. 1[8].

P. 140, line 10 (margin), on LAB 22.7: For Acts 1[24] read cf. Acts 1[24].

P. 140, LAB 22.8: Spiro, "Samaritans," p. 350, n. 144, says that Galgala is probably
a scribal error; and Dietzfelbinger, *op. cit.*, pp. 268-269, n. 180, agrees, noting
that in 21.7 Joshua has already constructed an altar at Galgala, which can hardly
be termed new, as it is here. But an emendation such as Silo, which transcriptionally is most improbable, is unnecessary; in 21.7 the altar was set up at the
foot of the mountain, as indicated by the verb *descendit*; in 22.8 the tabernacle
was set up on the mountain, as indicated by the verb *ascendit*.

P. 140, LAB 22.8: "even unto this day": None of the commentators has seized upon
this phrase, which would indicate that the author of LAB sought to have his
work regarded as having been written while offerings were still brought in the
Temple.

P. 140, LAB 22.9: What significance, if any, should be attached to the fact that this
is the only mention of Jerusalem in LAB remains a question.

P. 141, line 6 (margin), on LAB 23.1: Add Jos. 23[2].

P. 141, LAB 23.1: "the ark of the covenant": Lit., "the ark and the covenant," but
James' translation is justified by regarding this as an example of hendiadys.

P. 141, LAB 23.1: Spiro, "Samaritans," p. 354, and Delcor, "Pentecôte," Supplément
7 in *Dictionnaire de la Bible* (Paris, 1966), pp. 868-869, explain as an indication of anti-Samaritan bias the fact that LAB transfers from Shechem (Joshua
24.1) to Shiloh the site of this assembly, but the explanation may simply be
that LAB is here following the LXX.

P. 141 (margin) on LAB 23.2: Add Jos. 24[1,2].

P. 141, LAB 23.2: J. van Goudoever, *Biblical Calendars*, 2nd ed. (Leiden, 1961),
pp. 116-117, has called attention to the fact that according to the calendar of the
Book of Jubilees (1.1), the festival of Pentecost must be kept on the fifteenth
day of the third month and suggests that there may consequently be a relationship between LAB and Jubilees. But the assembly is gathered on the sixteenth
(seventeenth, according to the Melk MS.). The covenant (to be sure, Pentecost
is not named, but there is a clear allusion in 23.2 to the covenant at Horeb,
whose anniversary this presumably celebrates) here takes place on the following
day, the seventeenth of Sivan (LAB 23.4). To be sure, Goudoever says that the
small discrepancy between Jubilees and LAB may have come about because the

author of LAB did not know how to reckon the fifty days between Passover and Pentecost, but this is unlikely in view of the fact that this was a subject of crucial debate between the Pharisees and Sadducees (Mishnah Hagigah 17a) ; and even if we say that LAB followed the Sadducean point of view, the date of Pentecost would be flexible and not on a given day of Sivan. Moreover, LAB, even according to Goudoever, knew a second date for the Feast of Weeks, one in accord with the Pharisaic calendar, for in 29.7, which mentions the seventeenth of Tammuz, we may see that Moses ascended the mountain forty days earlier, namely, on the eighth of Sivan, two days after the Feast of Weeks. Among sectaries a difference of two days is a major one. I should like to suggest that the reading in 23.2 was originally "sixth," a difference of only one letter in the writing of either Greek or Latin numerals, and that we may have an allusion to the disagreement in Shabbath 86b as to whether the Torah was given on the sixth or seventh of the month. LAB reflects the viewpoint of R. Jose, as against the majority of the rabbis (and our present-day calendar), who declare that it was given on the seventh.

P. 141, line 14 (margin), on LAB 23.2: Add Dt. 6⁴.

P. 141, LAB 23.3: "vision": Pseudo-Philo here retains the Greek word *oramate* (= δραμα), indicating, in all probability, that he was translating from a Greek version.

P. 141 (margin), LAB 23.4: For Isa. 51^{1,2} read Cf. Isa. 51^{1,2}.

P. 141, LAB 23.4: "One rock": The Talmud also (Yebamoth 64a-b) likewise cites the passage from Isaiah 51.1-2, but it cites it in order to show that Abraham and Sarah were originally of doubtful sex.

P. 141, line 27 (margin), on LAB 23.4: Add Gen. 11^{27,29}.

P. 141, LAB 23.4: The identification of Sarah with Iscah (Gen. 11.29) is one found in Josephus, *AJ* 1.151. Sanhedrin 69b, Megillah 14a, Seder Olam 221, Targum Pseudo-Jonathan on Gen. 11.29, 20.12, Midrash Tehillim 118.11, Midrash Hallel (ed. Jellinek) 5.107.

P. 141, line 29 (margin), on LAB 23.4: Add Jos. 24^2.

P. 141, line 37 (margin), on LAB 23.5: Add Gen. 12^7.

P. 142, line 1 (margin), on LAB 23.5: For Gen. 15 read Gen. 15$^{2-5}$.

P. 142, line 3, LAB 23.5: James puts "seed" in italics to indicate that it is his own supplement. The word *semen*, though omitted in the *editio princeps*, is found in both the Admont and Melk MSS.

P. 142, LAB 23.5: "womb [*metra*]": This is the reading of Phillipps 461, the *editio princeps*, and Admont; several other MSS. have *petra*, "rock," presumably an allusion to 23.4, where Abraham, Nachor, Sarah, and Melcha are said to have been born of one rock. *Petra* is the more difficult reading, but it is supported by Isaiah 51.1-2. The confusion between *metra* and *petra* might easily have occurred because of a similar phrase in the opening sentence of 23.7, where the Vatican MS. has *metra* after *de conclusa*.

P. 142, line 7 (margin), on LAB 23.6: Add Gen. 15^{10}.

P. 142, LAB 23.7: Symbolic explanations for the five animals mentioned in Genesis 15.9 are likewise offered by Bereshith Rabbah 44.

P. 142, LAB 23.7: The Admont and Melk MSS. omit "thee" and liken the city to a dove. Dietzfelbinger, p. 270, n. 197, favors this reading because the other four animals symbolize episodes from the history of Israel; but Abraham is part of that history, and in any case the other four animals are compared to people. Dietzfelbinger, *ibid.*, compares Baruch 4.4, where God shows Abraham Jerusalem during the night between sacrifices.

P. 142, lines 28-29, LAB 23.7: "these things shall be": The Vatican, Admont, and Melk MSS. read: "And the prophets themselves and this night shall be. . . ."

P. 142 (margin) on LAB 23.8: Add Jos. 24^3.

P. 142, LAB 23.8: Rosh Hashanah 11a also states that Isaac was born in the seventh month. Ginzberg, 6.217, n. 13, also notes that according to Midrash Hagadol 2.13, all prophets were seven-months children. The notion that children born after seven months of pregnancy live is found in Bereshith Rabbah 14.2.127, cited by S. Lieberman, *Hellenism in Jewish Palestine* (New York, 1950, pp. 76-77, where the fourth-century Rabbi Abbahu puns in Greek, ζῇ τὰ ἑπτὰ ἢ τὰ ὀκτώ , i.e., infants born after seven months of pregnancy are more likely to survive than those born after eight months. Lieberman, p. 76, n. 240, also notes that according to two MSS. and the Armenian version of *Protoevangelium Jacobi* 5.2, Anna gave birth to Mary after seven months of pregnancy. Lieberman also reports a tradition cited by Rabbi Simeon Duran in the fifteenth century that the reason, according to the Gentiles (Lieberman traces it to Moslem sources), why a child born after eight months cannot survive is that Jesus, who was born after eight months of pregnancy, ordained that thereafter no child thus born should survive.

P. 143, LAB 23.8: "and showed forth the new age": This is added in the *editio princeps* and presumably comes from the lost Lorsch MS. (Kisch, pp. 91-92).

P. 143 (margin) on LAB 23.9: Add Jos. 24⁴ (+LXX).

P. 143, LAB 23.9: Italicize "And I gave . . . into Egypt."

P. 143, LAB 23.10: Ginzberg, 6.38, n. 210, cites as parallels Erubin 55a, Tosefta Arakhin 1.10, Asereth Ha-Dibroth, Sifre Debarim 313, Mekhilta Beshalah 2,63b, and 9,71b.

P. 143, line 15 (margin), on LAB 23.10: For Ps. 18⁹ read Ps. 18¹⁰⁽⁹⁾.

P. 143 (margin) on LAB 23.11: Add Jos. 24¹³.

P. 143, LAB 23.11: "Ye dwell in cities" is the addition of the *editio princeps* and is in accord with Joshua 24.13.

P. 143, LAB 23.12: "fight [*expugnare*]": Better, "prevail."

P. 144, line 12 (margin), on LAB 23.13: Add Cf. Mal. 3²⁴ (4⁶).

P. 144, line 17 (margin), on LAB 23.14: Add Jos. 24¹⁷,¹⁸.

P. 144, LAB 24.2: For "Lord," stemmatically impossible, read "God" with the *editio princeps*.

P. 145, line 8 (margin), on LAB 24.3: Add Jos. 24²⁸ (LXX).

P. 145 (margin) on LAB 24.5: Place comma between 49³³ and 46⁴.

P. 145, line 35 (margin), on LAB 24.6: Add Jud. 1¹.

P. 145, LAB 25.1: Kisch, following the Admont MS., starts chapter 25 with the last sentence of 24.6 ("And after the death of Jesus . . ."), a more logical division.

P. 146, lines 40-41, James' note on LAB 25.1: For Ant. V. 33 read Ant. V. 3.3.

P. 146, LAB 25.1 ff.: Azariah dei Rossi, 4.105, cites as a parallel to the long excursus on Kenaz Temurah 16a, which, to be sure, contains an extensive account of Othniel, the son of Kenaz and of Achsah his wife; but there is almost no point in common between the two accounts. J. B. Pitra, *Specilegium Solesmense Complectens Sanctorum Patrum Scriptorumque Ecclesiasticorum Anecdota Hactenus Opera*, vol. 2 (Paris, 1855), p. 334, mentions a manuscript (Paris 2454) containing the great and secret book of the seals of Gethel which the children of Israel made in the desert. Thomas of Cantimpré, who says that he has translated it into Latin, calls it the Book of Cethel, and Pitra expresses the belief that this book was derived from Pseudo-Philo. Steinschneider ("Literarische Beilage: Lapidarien," *Hebräische Bibliographie,* 16 [1876], pp. 104-106; and *Die Hebräische Uebersetzungen des Mittelalters und die Juden also Dolmetscher* [Berlin, 1893], pp. 237, n. 922, 603, n. 53, and 963, n. 105) and Ginzberg, 6.181, n. 1, note the many medieval references to Cenec or Zenec or Cethel or Cetel or Cenel or Cheel or Cehel or Cethes or Theel or Thetel or Tetel or Techel (to these add Rechel and Eethel), who was noted for his knowledge of precious stones. Ginzberg concludes that this is obviously the Kenaz or Cenez of

LAB; but, as noted in the Introduction above (IIh), this is highly unlikely. The grave of the holy Getha (still another spelling presumably), described by a medieval traveler in Palestine, is that of Kenaz according to Ginzberg, 6.181, n. 1. Dietzfelbinger, p. 30, cites J. Jeremias, *Heiligengräber*, pp. 89-90, who notes that a Kenaz, according to Genesis 36.11, 15, 42, and 1 Chronicles 1.36, 53, was the ancestor of the Edomite race of Kenites. The glorification of Kenaz, including a grave for him, he suggests, points to an Idumaean tradition; but if so, why is Idumaea not mentioned?

P. 148, line 2 (margin), on LAB 25.2: Add Cf. Jos. 19^1.

P. 148, LAB 25.3: Moses is similarly termed my [i.e., God's] friend in 23.9. K. R. Stow, "Pseudo-Philo, an Essene Work" (unpublished), p. 16, points to a parallel between "Moses the friend of the Lord" and "Abraham the friend of God" in the Damascus Document 3.2-4; but the phrase "friend of God" with reference to Abraham is also found in the Epistle of James 2.23, and thus the parallel with the Dead Sea Scrolls is hardly unique.

P. 148, line 8 (margin), on LAB 25.3: Add Cf. Dt. 28^{14}, Jos. 1^7.

P. 148, LAB 25.4: The MSS., including the Budapest and the two Munich MSS., which I have myself checked, all have Isachar before Zabulon; and the order should consequently be changed in James' translation. The number for Isachar in the Melk MS. is 645. The number for Zabulon in all the MSS. is 545, rather than 655 (or 645). The number for Manasse is 480 in the *editio princeps*, Budapest, and the two Munich MSS., but 490 in Admont; and Harrington, in his forthcoming edition of the text, reports that the reading of Admont is stemmatically impossible. The number for Effraim in all MSS. is 448 rather than 468 as in James. In his note James says that Dan has dropped out; so, we may add, has Naphtali. The separate numbers in the text add up to 5280 in the *editio princeps*, with 5260 and 5290 being other possible totals if variants are taken into account. This leaves 830 (820, 850) as the number to be assigned to Dan and Naphtali in order to make up the total of 6110 given by LAB. Ginzberg, 6.181, n. 3, gives the total as 5480, but the figures which he cites (from the *editio princeps*) add up to 5280. The fact that Simeon has the largest number of sinners and Levi the smallest is in accord with Jewish tradition; see Ginzberg, 6.155, n. 924, who cites Sifre Debarim 349-352, Midrash Tannaim 214-215, and Ephraem Syrus 1.191 A-C.

P. 149, line 2 (margin), on LAB 25.5: For Dt. 29^{18} read Dt. 29$^{17(18)}$.

P. 149, LAB 25.7: James adopts the reading of the *editio princeps*, Achiar. Kisch rightly adopts the reading of the Admont MS., Achar (the Melk MS. reads Achan), thus identifying him with the Achar of 21.3. Ginzberg, 6.176, n. 31, quotes Aboth di R. Nathan 45, 126: "Three men, by their confessions, lost this world and gained the world to come: the gatherer of wood on the Sabbath, the blasphemer, Achan." Cf. also Soṭah 7b: "Judah confessed and was not ashamed; what was his end? He inherited the life of the world to come." For the concept of handing over a sinner to death in order to save him cf. 1 Corinthians 5.5 and 1 Timothy 1.20, cited by Dietzfelbinger, p. 245.

P. 149, LAB 25.8: That our author knew Hebrew is indicated by the name Elas, in whose tent the foreign gods were hidden. The name *elah* means "terebinth" (turpentine-tree) and is found in Genesis 35.4 as the place where Jacob also hid the foreign gods.

P. 150, line 14, LAB 25.9: After *hid* add: "under the mountain of Abraham and are deposited under a mass of earth. Send therefore and thou shalt find them. And Cenez sent and found them. And he asked those who were left over of the tribe of Neptali, and they said: We have desired to do what the Amorites did, and behold these things are hid." This passage, found in the Admont and Melk MSS. and in Jerahmeel, is omitted by homoeoteleuton in the *editio princeps*. Dietzfelbinger, p. 271, n. 205, aptly remarks that since the tribe of Judah is not mentioned in this enumeration of tribes, we may see that Kenaz was of that tribe.

P. 150, LAB 25.9: The mountain of Abraham (found in Vatican, Admont, and Melk MSS.) presumably refers to Mount Moriah.

P. 150, LAB 25.10 ff.: On the wicked ways of the Amorites see also Apocalypse of Baruch 60.1.

P. 151, LAB 25.10: On the burial of images under an oak at Shechem see Genesis 35.4.

P. 151, LAB 25.11: James adds Cham to make up the required seven; but Jerahmeel shows that the last name is Suah (שוח). Perhaps Desuath is a corruption of Dedan, Suah. Cf. Genesis 10.7.

P. 151, line 15 (margin), on LAB 25.11: Add Cf. Gen. 2¹¹.

P. 151, LAB 25.11: Euilath=Havilah (Genesis 2.11), land of gold and precious stones.

P. 151, LAB 25.11: Why LAB, after indicating that there are seven stones, describes here only four of them is unclear.

P. 152, line 29, James' note on 25.12: Place a period after *Solesm*.

P. 152, LAB 25.13: Dietzfelbinger's commentary suggests that the reason for the omission of Simeon here is that this tribe had, for practical purposes, joined the tribe of Judah (to Josephus 5.120 and 128 add Judges 1.1 ff.). On the manner by which idols must be destroyed see Abodah Zarah 42a ff. The Mishnah (42b) prescribes that idols are to be cast into the Dead Sea, that is, they are to be destroyed in such a manner that no benefit may possibly, even indirectly, be derived from them. Rabbi Jose (43b) expresses the minority point of view that the idol may be ground to powder and scattered to the wind or thrown into the sea.

P. 153, line 2 (margin), on LAB 26.1: Add Cf. Gen. 2¹¹.

P. 153, LAB 26.1: Dietzfelbinger, in his edition, notes that there is no river by this name in Palestine and says that the emendation *Kison* is a mere conjecture. He likewise dismisses his other suggestion, that the river Pishon, which in the LXX has precisely the spelling Phison, of Genesis 2.11 is meant. Geographically this is impossible, since the Bible says that the Pishon encompasses the land of Havilah; and Josephus (*AJ* 1.38) specifically states that it runs toward India and is called the Ganges by Greeks. And yet it is precisely the precious stones of this land that the Bible (Gen. 2.12) singles out, and here too it is in juxtaposition with the fanciful account of the precious stones (26.2).

P. 153, LAB 26.3: For "when the fire hath consumed those men," which is stemmatically impossible, read "when you will have consumed those men with fire."

P. 153, LAB 26.3: "the new altar": Dietzfelbinger, in his forthcoming edition, notes that according to 25.10 the stones were hidden under the top of the Mount Shechem, and according to Jubilees 31.1-2, Jacob burned and buried the idols at the oak of Shechem. But he rightly prefers Shiloh as the site, since 26.7 speaks of the new altar (*novum sacrarium*), precisely the phrase which is used in 22.8 of the altar set up at Shiloh by Joshua.

P. 154, lines 10-11, LAB 26.4: James, following the *editio princeps*, reads: *nomen tribus secundum nomen lapidis et*, "the name of the tribe answering unto the name of the stone, and. . . ." The Admont and Melk MSS. read *nomen tribus, et secundum nomen tribus nomen lapidis*, "the name of the tribe and the name of the stone answering to the name of the tribe."

P. 154, LAB 26.6: "Blessed . . . men": The form of this blessing for miracles is not paralleled in rabbinic sources (Berakhoth 54a ff.).

P. 155, LAB 26.10 ff.: One hitherto unexplored way to discern the relationship of LAB to the Hebrew text, LXX, Josephus, New Testament, and the Midrash is to compare the names and order of the twelve stones here listed. The names of the stones follow:

Hebrew text (Ex. 28.17-20)	LXX and Philo, Leg. Alleg. 1.81 (first five stones)	Josephus (BJ) 5.234)	Josephus (AJ) 3.168)	NT (Rev. 21.19)	Midrash Shemoth Rabbah 38.8	LAB 26.10-11
1. אדם (sardius, aurelian)	σάρδιον (sardius)	σάρδιον (sardius)	σαρδόνυξ (sardonyx = sardius)	ἴασπις (jasper)	שדרגנין (=שרדגנין) (=σαρδονύχιον) (sardonyx)	sardinus (sardine)
2. פטדה (topaz)	τοπάζιον (topaz)	τόπαζος (topaz)	τόπαζος (topaz)	σάπφιρος (sapphire)	שומפוזין (=טומפוזין) (=τοπάζιον) (topaz)	topazion (topaz)
3. ברקת (smaragd, emerald)	σμάραγδος (smaragd)	σμάραγδος (smaragd)	σμάραγδος (‹smaragd)	χαλκηδών (agate)	דייקינתין (=ὑάκινθος) (jacinth)	smaragdinus (smaragd, emerald)
4. נפך (carbuncle)	ἄνθραξ (carbuncle)	ἄνθραξ (carbuncle)	ἄνθραξ (carbuncle)	σμάραγδος (smaragd)	כרכרינין (=כרכדינין) (=καρχηδόνιος) (carbuncle)	christallus (crystal), carbunculus (carbuncle)
5. ספיר (sapphire)	σάπφειρος (sapphire)	ἴασπις (jasper)	ἴασπις (jasper)	σαρδόνυξ (sardonyx, onyx)	סנפירינון (=σαπφείρινον) (sapphire)	saphirus (sapphire)
6. יהלם (emerald, diamond)	ἴασπις (jasper)	σάπφειρος (sapphire)	σάπφειρος (sapphire)	σάρδιον (sardius)	אזמרגדין (=σμάραγδος) (smaragd)	chrysoprassus (chrysoprase) (other MSS.: caraxdtus [meaning unknown]), iaspis (jasper)
7. לשם (jacinth)	λιγύριον (ligure, jacinth[?])	ἀχάτης (agate)	λίγυρος (ligure, jacinth[?])	χρυσόλιθος (chrysolite)	כוחלין (=בירולין) (=βηρύλλιον) (beryl)	ligurius (ligure, jacinth[?])
8. שבו (agate)	ἀχάτης (agate)	ἀμέθυστος (amethyst)	ἀμέθυστος (amethyst)	βήρυλλος (beryl)	אבא סיס (=אכאטיס) (=ἀχάτης) (agate)	ametistus (amethyst)
9. אחלמה (amethyst)	ἀμέθυστος (amethyst)	λιγύριον (ligure)	ἀχάτης (agate)	τοπάζιον (topaz)	הימיסיון (=אמטיסטון) (=ἀμέθυστος) (amethyst)	achates (agate)
10. תרשיש (beryl)	χρυσόλιθος (chrysolite)	ὄνυξ (onyx)	χρυσόλιθος (chrysolite)	χρυσόπρασος (chryso prase)	קרומססין (=כרומסק[ל]סין) (=? כרוסליתין) (=χρῶμα θαλάσσιον) (=χρυσόλιθος?) (chrysolite)	chrisolitus (chrysolite)
11. שהם (onyx)	βηρύλλιον (beryl)	βήρυλλος (beryl)	ὄνυξ (onyx)	ὑάκινθος (jacinth)	פראלוקין (=παράλευκος or περιλεύκιος) (partly white stone)	berillus (beryl)
12. ישפה (jasper)	ὀνύχιον (onyx)	χρυσόλιθος (chrysolite)	βήρυλλος (beryl)	ἀμέθυστος (amethyst)	מרגליטוס (=μαργαρίτης) (pearl)	onichrinus (onyx)

It will be seen that LAB agrees in the names with the Hebrew text eleven times, with the Septuagint twelve times, with Josephus' *Bellum Judaicum* twelve times, with Josephus' *Antiquitates Judaicae* eleven or twelve times, with the Book of Revelation in the New Testament eleven or twelve times (with chrysoprase and jasper separated), and with the Midrash nine times. In the key matter of order LAB agrees with the Hebrew text six times, LXX ten times, Josephus' *BJ* six times, Josephus' *AJ* eight times, Revelation no times, and the Midrash four or five times. It is interesting that in the one place where LAB does not agree with the LXX, namely, in the identity of stones 8 and 9, it is in agreement with Josephus' *AJ*, which is a later version and obviously, to judge from the wording of the passages, a correction of *BJ*. On the identity and order of the stones see W. Bacher, "Une Ancienne Liste des Noms Grecs des Pierres Précieuses relatées dans Exode, XXVIII, 17-20: Fragment du Midrasch de l'École d'Ismael sur le Lévitique," *Revue de Études Juives*, 29 (1894), pp. 79-90, as corrected by S. Lieberman, *Greek in Jewish Palestine* (New York, 1942), pp. 56-59; and S. von Gliszczynski, "Versuch einer Identifizierung der Edelsteine im Amtsschild des jüdischen Hohenpriesters auf Grund kritischer und ästhetischer Vergleichs-momente," *Forschungen und Fortschritte*, 21-23 (1947), pp. 234-238. None of these treatments, however, mentions LAB or explains the inconsistencies between *BJ* and *AJ*.

P. 157, LAB 26.12: Ginzberg, 6.183, n. 13, solves the problem of the identity of Jahel by retranslating the passage into Hebrew, עַד אֲשֶׁר יָקוּם אֲתִיאֵל, "until Ithiel will arise," Ithiel being one of Solomon's ten names. To say with Dietz-felbinger, p. 276, n. 237, that Jahel may be a name of God (*Apocalypsis Mosis* 29.33, *Apocalypsis Abraham* 17.11) does not account for the awkwardness of having God speak of Himself in both the third and first persons in the same sentence. A better possibility is that Jahel is an angel; cf. Jaoel in *Apocalypsis Abraham* 10.4, 9.

P. 157, LAB 26.13: Dietzfelbinger, p. 276, n. 238, compares the burial of the vessels of the Temple by Jeremiah (Rest of the Words of Baruch, 3.7-14) or, more aptly, by an angel (Syr. Baruch 6.4-10).

P. 157, LAB 26.13: "and lay them up in the place whence they were brought forth in the beginning": Cf. *Assumptio Mosis* 1.17: "lay up in vessels of earthenware in the place which God made from the beginning of the creation of the world" (Philonenko, *per litt.*).

P. 157, LAB 26.13: "and visit the dwellers upon earth": Cf. *Assumptio Mosis* 1.18: "in the visitation wherewith the Lord will visit them in the consummation of the end of the days" (Philonenko, *per litt.*).

P. 157, line 21 (margin), on LAB 26.13: For Isa. 64[4, etc.] read 64[3(4)], 65[17].

P. 158, LAB 26.13: "for the light of the precious stones shall be their light": II. St. J. Thackeray, *The Relation of St. Paul to Contemporary Jewish Thought*, p. 244, also notes the striking resemblance of this clause to Revelation 21.23, where also, most remarkably, the list of the twelve stones has just preceded.

P. 159, LAB 27.4: Though LAB in 27.3 speaks of 37 men, there are only 36 enum-erated, according to James' text, and 35, according to Kisch, who does not accept the division of *Leetuz* into *Le et Uz*. Other differences between the two lists are: Anaph: Anas; Gethel: Getel; Cehec: Cehceh (this reading of Kisch is stem-matically impossible: the correct reading, stemmatically at any rate, seems to be Cehech); Iabal: Labat; Ezeth: Ecenc (stemmatically the correct reading is Ecent); Desaph: Dephap; Moab: Moach; Azath: Azat; Phelac: Felat; Igat: Igath; Zophal: Zefal; Eliesor: Helieser; Ecar: Echar; Sebath: Sebeth; Zere: Cere.

P. 159, LAB 27.5 ff.: Dietzfelbinger, pp. 34-35, has noted several parallels between this account and that of Gideon in Judges 7.8 ff., notably the 300 men.

P. 159, line 13 (margin), on LAB 27.5: Add Cf. Jud. 7[8].

P. 159 (margin) on LAB 27.6: Add Cf. Jud. 7[9-18].

P. 160, LAB 27.9: "for the spirit of the Lord clothed him" (also 36.2): Cf. the similar metaphor in Romans 13.14 and Galatians 3.27.

P. 161, LAB 27.10: "he was clothed with the spirit of might": Cf. Luke 24.49: "until you are clothed with power from on high" (Philonenko, *per litt.*).

P. 161, LAB 27.10: Ginzberg, 6.183, n. 17, suggests that Gethel is a transliteration of עֲטִיאֵל or עֲטֵהאֵל from עָטָה, "covered," "hid," and hence appropriate for one set over hidden things, i.e., the secrets of nature. There is in the midrashic tradition an angel גמטיאל, though there is no similarity in function in that he is there not set over hidden things; see R. Margaliouth, *Malakhe Elyon*[2] (Jerusalem, 1964), p. 47. There is an angel, Satarel, whose name likewise signifies that he is the angel of hidden things; see Ginzberg, 5.153, n. 57. Zeruel, in accordance with the etymology from זרוע, "strength," arm," holds up the arms of Cenez. Cervihel (61.5) is probably identical with Zeruel since, like Zeruel, he too is said to be the angel set over strength. According to Jerahmeel, it is the angel Gabriel, the prince of strength (see Ginzberg, 6.246, n. 12), rather than Ingethel and Zeruel, that is sent to aid Kenaz.

P. 161, lines 15-16, LAB 27.10: For "lest they should perceive him" (*considerent*, from *considero*, which would involve the wrong sequence of tenses and be meaningless) read "lest they should sink down" (from *consido*, third conjugation).

P. 161, line 20 (margin), on LAB 27.11: Add Cf. 2 Sam. 23[10].

P. 161, LAB 27.11: For a similar story of how Joab freed his hand from the gory weapon stuck to it see Ginzberg, 4.100 and 6.258, n. 77.

P. 163, LAB 27.16: According to Josephus, *AJ* 5.184, Kenaz ruled for forty years.

P. 164, LAB 28.1: Jerahmeel also speaks here of a prophet Phineas and a priest Phineas; but, as Ginzberg, 6.184, n. 19, remarks, they are identical, as seen by the fact that Phineas the priest is in 48.1 identified with the prophet Elijah. James' theory that there was but one prophet has been energetically challenged by Spiro, "The Ascension of Phinehas," *PAAJR,* 22 (1953), pp. 113-114, and *Manners of Rewriting Biblical History from Chronicles to Pseudo-Philo* (diss., Columbia Univ., 1953), pp. 246-247.

Pp. 165-167, LAB 28.6-10: M. Wadsworth (*per litt.*) suggests that Kenaz's vision may be compared with the description of the four men who entered paradise (Hagigah 14b). The springs of water without foundation may be parallel to the water mentioned in Hagigah.

P. 165 (margin) on LAB 28.6: Add Ezek. 20[1].

P. 165, LAB 28.6: "the holy spirit that dwelt in Cenez": Cf. Romans 8.9: "if the Spirit of God really dwells in you" (Philonenko, *per litt.*).

P. 166, LAB 28.8: For "came up" (*ascendit*) the Admont MS. reads "came down" (*descendit*).

P. 166, LAB 28.8: "behold a voice saying": The same phrase is found in Matthew 3.17 and 17.5, Luke 9.35, and Acts 21.3 (cited by Dietzfelbinger, p. 215).

P. 166, LAB 28.8: The forms of men are those of angels. Dietzfelbinger, p. 278, n. 256, compares *Apocalypsis Abraham* 15.6.

P. 166, LAB 28.8: For 7000 (*editio princeps*) the Admont MS. has 4000. The former reading is supported by 19.15. The view that the millennium will occur after 7000 years is also found in II Enoch 33.

P. 166, LAB 28.8-9: None of the commentators has noticed that there is one passage in the Talmud, Temurah 16a, which bears a definite relation to LAB's excursus on Kenaz; in it Caleb says to the wife of Othniel (the son of Kenaz), "One to whom all the secrets of the upper and nether worlds are revealed, need one ask food from him?"

P. 167, second line of James' note on LAB 28.9: This is also the reading of the Admont MS.

P. 167, LAB 28.9: For "they shall be changed" Dietzfelbinger, p. 279, n. 261, cites IV Esdras 6.16, Syr. Baruch 49.3, 51.1-10, and 1 Cor. 15.51.

P. 167 (margin) on LAB 29.1: Add Jud. 9[28-41].

P. 167, LAB 29.1: Zebul (Iebul in 30.5, *editio princeps*) is Iehud or Ehud, the second judge (see Judges 3.15). For the interchange of I and Z see Jambri 47.1) = Zambri; for the interchange of D and L see Dedila (44.2) = Delila: so Ginzberg, 6.184, n. 21.

P. 168, line 9 (margin), on LAB 29.2: Add Jos. 15[46].

P. 168 (margin) on LAB 29.3: For Cf. 2 Chr. 24[8] read Cf. 2 Chr. 24[8] sqq·, 2 Kings 14[4] sqq·.

P. 168, LAB 29.3: "the synagogue of the Lord": Cf. ἐκκλησία τοῦ Χριστοῦ in Romans 16.16, and ἐκκλησία τοῦ θεοῦ. in Acts 20.28, etc. (cited by Dietzfelbinger, p. 212).

P. 168, LAB 29.4: Cf. Epistle of James 1.6: "He who doubts is like a wave of the sea that is driven and tossed by the wind." Apparently LAB here starts with this negative comparison to the sea and then proceeds to a positive comparison.

P. 169, line 7 (margin), on LAB 30.1: Add Cf. Jud. 2[17].

P. 169, line 9 (margin), on LAB 30.1: Add Cf. Num. 25[1,2].

P. 169, LAB 30.1: "daughters" (*editio princeps, filias*): Kisch, following the Admont MS., reads *filios*, "sons." But the references in 18.13-14 and 44.7 argue for the reading of the *editio princeps*; the Admont is, moreover, as Harrington in his forthcoming edition notes, stemmatically impossible.

P. 169, line 11 (margin), on LAB 30.2: For Jud. 2[1] read Jud. 2[1-3].

P. 169, LAB 30.2: "Yet shall a woman rule over them which shall give them light 40 years": James has apparently emended *principabatur* ["ruled"] . . . *illuminavit* ["gave light"] to *principabitur . . . illuminabit*. If we wish to retain the text we must remove this sentence from God's speech; but this leaves the awkward "after these things" (30.3) which *begins* the story of Deborah.

P. 169, line 24 (margin), on LAB 30.3: For 4 read 42[,3].

P. 169, LAB 30.3: 8000: James here follows the *editio princeps*. The Admont MS. has 9000, which is more likely, since Judges 4.3 and 4.13 speak of 900 chariots.

P. 170, line 3 (margin), on LAB 30.4: Add Jer. 2[8].

P. 170, line 4 (margin), on LAB 30.4: Add Cf. 1 Sam. 15[3], 22[14].

P. 170, line 12 (margin), on LAB 30.5 Add Cf. Isa. 53[7].

P. 170, line 18, LAB 30.5: For "subdued" read "subjected," since the same verb (*subicio*) in the same phrase is found here and in LAB 15.5, where James renders it "subjected."

P. 170, line 21 (margin), on LAB 30.5: Add Cf. Jos. 10[12,13,11].

P. 171, LAB 30.7: "will have compassion": This is the reading of the *editio princeps* and Phillipps 461. The other MSS. read *inviscerabitur*, "will be put into the entrails," which is here meaningless, though, as Dietzfelbinger in his commentary has indicated, it is a very literal rendering of σπλαγχνίζεσθαι , which does have the meaning of "to feel pity." Here again we have probable evidence of a Greek text behind our Latin version.

P. 171, LAB 30.7: "for his covenant's sake which he made with your fathers and for his oath's sake": Cf. Luke 1.72-73: "to remember his holy covenant, the oath which he swore. . . ." (Philonenko· *per litt.*).

P. 171 (margin) on LAB 31.1: Add Jud. 4[6].

P. 171, LAB 31.1: "gird up thy loins as a man": Philonenko, "Le Testament de Job," *Semitica*, 18 (1968), p. 56, compares Job 38.3 and Testament of Job 47.5, as well as LAB 20.2-3, 35.5, and 51.6 (these last three passages, to be sure, lack the phrase "as a man").

P. 171, James' note on LAB 31.1: For *The stars fighting* read *The constellations fighting*. Josephus, *AJ* 5.205, has a similar description: "Amidst the clash of arms there came up a great tempest with torrents of rain and hail." Rabbinic tradition (Pesaḥim 118b) tells how the stars heated the iron staves with which Sisera advanced to fight the Israelites. Cf. also Vayikra Rabbah 7 (end), Abba Gorion 27, Aguddath Aggadoth 77, Neveh Shalom 47, Aggadath Bereshith 1.2, Tosefta Soṭah 3.14, cited by Ginzberg, 6.197, n. 81, and Alpha-Beta of Ben Sira (*Blau Festchrift*, p. 269), cited by S. Rappaport, *Agada und Exegese bei Flavius Josephus* (Frankfort, 1930), p. 128, n. 197.

P. 171, line 19 (margin), on LAB 31.1: Add Cf. Ex. 14^{25}.

P. 171, line 31 (margin), on LAB 31.2: Add Cf. Jud. 5^{20}.

P. 171, LAB 31.2: "spake unto them": The gender of them (*eos*) and the phrase "for our (*or* your) enemies fall upon you" indicates that it refers to Deborah and the people and Barak, and not to the stars.

P. 172, LAB 31.2: J. Klausner, *The Messianic Idea in Israel*, p. 366, cites this passage to date LAB after the destruction of the Temple and to prove LAB's acquaintance with Josephus, since the latter (*BJ* 6.420) says that the same figure, 97,000, were taken captive throughout the war leading to the destruction of the Temple. But Josephus is speaking of the number of prisoners, whereas LAB is speaking of the number slain. Moreover, the fact that LAB says that the number was 90 times 97,000 instead of giving the total, 8,730,000, indicates that this is merely a large number. On ninety as a large number cf. the ninety ass-loads of Egyptian goods said to have been carried away by each Israelite at the time of the Exodus (see Ginzberg, 4.411).

P. 172 (margin) on LAB 31.3: For Jud. 4^{17} read Jud. 4^{15,17}.

P. 172, line 11 (margin), on LAB 31.3: Add Judith 12^{15}.

P. 172, line 12 (margin), on LAB 31.3: Add Jud. 4^{18}.

P. 172, LAB 31.3: On the influence which Jael's beauty exercised upon Sisera see also Vayikra Rabbah 23.10, Midrash Hagadol 1.336, Yebamoth 103a-b, Nazir 23b, and Horayyoth 10b, cited by Ginzberg, 6.198, n. 85.

P. 172, line 20 (margin), on LAB 31.3: Add Cf. Jud. 5^{28}.

P. 172 (margin) on LAB 31.4: Add Jud. 4^{19}.

P. 173, line 5 (margin), on LAB 31.5: Add Jud. 4^{19}.

P. 173, LAB 31.6: That Jael managed to get Sisera drunk is also stated in Midrash Hagadol 1.336.

P. 173 (margin) on LAB 31.7: Add Jud. 5^{26}.

P. 173, line 15 (margin), on LAB 31.7: Add Cf. Judith 13^7.

P. 173, line 32 (margin), on LAB 31.7: Add Jud. 4^9, Judith 13^{15}.

P. 173, LAB 31.7: That Deborah's statement (Judges 4.9) that the Lord will deliver Sisera into the hands of a woman refers in fact to Jael is confirmed by Bamidbar Rabbah 10.

P. 174, LAB 32.1 ff.: LAB, in his history of the Israelites, parallels the Targumim on Judges 5.1 ff. The Targum Jonathan, as Vermès, *Scripture and Tradition*, pp. 199-201, stresses, like LAB, underlines two aspects of the Akedah, Abraham's obedience as justifying his election by God, and Isaac's self-sacrifice as justifying God's choice of mankind generally. See further R. Le Déaut, *La Nuit Pascale* (Rome, 1963), pp. 189-191. There is also a parallel to the elaboration of Josephus, *AJ* 1.222-236, in the attitudes of the participants and in the fidelity to ritual, as in the apologetic attitude of the author, as Le Déaut, p. 190, remarks. Above all, there is a parallel, which none of the commentators has noticed, between LAB 32.3, where Isaac asks, "What if I had not been born in the world to be offered a sacrifice unto Him that made me?" and Josephus, *AJ* 1.232, "He [Isaac] exclaimed that he deserved never to have been born at all, were he to reject the decision of God and of his father." H. Riesenfeld, *Jésus Transfiguré* (Copenhagen, 1947), p. 87, n. 30, cites the passages in LAB and Josephus, as well as Jubilees 17.15-18.19, 1 Macc. 2.52 and 4 Macc. 13.12, 16.20, as evidence that the importance of the sacrifice of Isaac in Jewish Aggadah is not due to rabbinic reaction to the Christian dogma of the redemption but dates from pre-Christian times.

P. 174, LAB 32.1: On the jealousy of the angels see Bereshith Rabbah 55.4, where the angels, rather than Satan, accuse Abraham before God.

P. 174, line 21 (margin), on LAB 32.1: Add Gen. 11^7.

P. 174, LAB 32.1: "orderers": This is James' emendation, *custodes*, for *cultores*, "cultivators," "worshippers," on the basis of 11.12, where the guardian angels are thus called.

P. 174, line 32 (margin), on LAB 32.2: Add Gen. 22² sqq·.

P. 175, LAB 32.3: Bowker, p. 313, note c, remarks that the phrase *in odorem suavitatis* ("for an odour of sweetness") is the phrase used by the Vulgate to describe the sacrifice of Noah (Gen. 8.21).

P. 175, LAB 32.3: "inherit a life secure": Cf. Mark 10.17: "What must I do to inherit eternal life?" (Philonenko, *per litt.*).

P. 175, line 13, LAB 32.3: For "What and if" read "What if."

P. 175, LAB 32.3: "And it . . . all men": Another possible translation is "Moreover, my blessedness shall be upon all men," i.e. Isaac's sacrifice will bring blessing to all mankind.

P. 175, LAB 32.3: "be instructed" [*adnuntiabuntur*]: Or, with Admont, "announce" [*annuntiabunt*].

P. 175, LAB 32.3: As to the availability of Isaac's merit to the Gentiles, A. Jambert, *La Notion d'Alliance dans le Judaïsme aux abords de l'Ère Chrétienne* (*Patristica Sorbonensia*, vol. 6; Paris, 1963), p. 271, n. 77, suggests that this text of LAB is perhaps Christianized, but the fact that this theme is found in Vayikra Rabbah 2.11 argues against this.

P. 175, LAB 32.4: For "body" read "womb" (*ventris*).

P. 175, line 28 (margin), on LAB 32.4: Add Cf. Gen. 22¹⁷,¹⁸.

P. 175 (margin) on LAB 32.5: Add 25²¹.

P. 175, LAB 32.5: "third year of her marriage": According to Genesis 25.20, Isaac was forty when he married, and according to Genesis 25.26 he was sixty when Rebekah gave birth to Jacob and Esau. LAB is unique in indicating, contrary to Scripture itself, that Rebekah was in only the third year of her marriage when she gave birth. The Targum Yerushalmi on Genesis 25.21 (cited by Ginzberg, 5.270, n. 7) states that Rebekah was barren for twenty-two years, i.e. she gave birth in the twenty-third year of her marriage. There is, to be sure, a tradition (see Ginzberg, 5.270, n. 4) that Rebekah was three years old when she married.

P. 176, line 10 (margin), on LAB 32.7: Add Cf. Ex. 19.

P. 176, LAB 32.7: "the foundation was moved, the hosts": Kisch and Dietzfelbinger put the comma after "hosts" and read "the foundation of the hosts was moved."

P. 176, LAB 32.7: "the earth was stirred from her foundation": Lit., "from her firmament."

P. 176, LAB 32.8: The spread of a heavenly fragrance over Israel at the time of the revelation is also found in Shabbath 88b, Midrash Shir Hashirim 7a, 38b, 44b, and the Zohar 2, 84b, cited by Ginzberg, 6.39, n. 210, who conjectures that the purpose of this fragrance was to restore life to the dead.

P. 176, LAB 32.9: In a marginal note in his own copy, James suggests *disposuit ei testamentum per firmamentum*, "appointed unto him a testament through the firmament," in place of *disposuit ei firmamentum*, "appointed unto him the firmament."

P. 177, line 9 (margin), on LAB 32.10: Add Jos. 10¹².

P. 177, LAB 32.10: "And they did so": In the margin of the *editio princeps* at this point are the words "Something appears to be missing." The Admont and Melk MSS. add: *sicut praeceptum erat eis*, "just as it had been ordered them."

P. 177, line 27 (margin), on LAB 32.12: Add Jud. 5²⁴.

P. 177, LAB 32.13: For "Many wonders will I perform for your sons" the Admont, Melk, and Vatican MSS. read: "For, saying the least things to you he hath done many things for your sons."

P. 178, LAB 32.14: For "let him call upon" or Kisch's "you will call upon," both of which are stemmatically impossible, read "he will call upon" (*invocabit*).

P. 178, LAB 32.15: "knowledge": James reads *conscientia* (*editio princeps*). Kisch, following the Admont MS., reads *concio*, "assembly," which makes more sense if *thurificat* is given its original meaning of "burneth incense" and is not emended to the otherwise non-existent *turrificat* on the basis of 32.1, where the *editio princeps'* *turrificationis* is required by the sense. Hence translate this: "for the assembly of the Lord is present which burneth incense unto thee."

P. 178, line 23 (margin), on LAB 32.15: Add Cf. Gen. 2^{21,22}.

P. 178, line 31 (margin), on LAB 32.16: Add Ex. 12^{29} sqq.

P. 178, LAB 32.16: The connection of the struggle against Sisera and Passover night is also commemorated near the end of the Passover Haggadah in Jannai's hymn "Uvechen Vayehi Bahazi Halailah," recited on the first Seder night. Cf. also Bamidbar Rabbah 20.12.

P. 178, LAB 32.17: "as in the renewing": There is no basis for "as" in the text.

P. 179, line 1 (margin), on LAB 32.17: Add Cf. Ex. 14-15.

P. 179, LAB 32.17: "camp [*castra*]": The Vatican MS. has *astra*, "stars." The mention of the Red Sea in the earliest part of this sentence would seem to require a reference to the heavens in the latter part. Again there is a reference to the stars in 32.18; but in 31.1 the constellations fight for, not against, the Israelites.

P. 179, LAB 32.18: Ginzberg, 6.199, n. 92, cites a text, no longer extant but often referred to by medieval authors, from the Palestinian Talmud which connects the hundred cries of Sisera's mother with the hundred sounds of the shofar sounded on Rosh Hashanah.

P. 179, James' note on LAB 32.18: For *on* read *upon*.

P. 179, line 14 (margin), on LAB 33.1: Add Jud. 5^{31}.

P. 179, LAB 33.1: Kisch, following the division in the Admont MS., includes "and Debbora . . . 40 years" with 32.18, as is more logical.

P. 179 (margin) on LAB 33.2: Add Jos. 23^{14}.

P. 179, LAB 33.2: The rabbis also (Shabbath 153a) stress that one should repent one day before one's death. Cf. Midrash Koheleth 1.15, where a parable is told illustrating the impossibility of repenting after death.

P. 179, LAB 33.3: The unique feature in LAB's views of the "evil creation" (i.e., the evil inclination) is that it ceases immediately after death and not merely in the Messianic era. See further Dietzfelbinger, p. 283, n. 307.

P. 180, LAB 33.3: "unless it be demanded": Kisch, following Admont and all the MSS. other than the *editio princeps*, reads *reposcat* ("unless he demand"), but the context demands the reading of the *editio princeps*.

P. 180, LAB 33.5: Cohn, p. 324, n. 4, cites this, with its notion that the prayers of the dead are ineffective, as the only case where LAB is in conflict with an accepted Jewish opinion. But, as Ginzberg, 5.160-161, n. 60, 5.419, n. 118, and 6.199, n. 91, remarks, this notion is soundly based in rabbinic sources, and the rabbis were careful not to make the dead, however great, intercessors between God and Israel.

P. 180, LAB 33.5: After "any man" there is in the margin of the *editio princeps* the words: "There is no intercession of the holy dead for us"; but that this is a gloss added by the editor is clear from the fact that above these words is the word *Adverte*, as noted by P. Bogaert, *Apocalypse de Baruch*, vol. 1 (Paris, 1969), p. 252, n. 1.

P. 180, LAB 33.6: J. Jeremias, "Das spätjüdische Deboragrab," *Zeitschrift des deutschen Palästina-Vereins*, 82 (1966), pp. 136-138, asks whether LAB's statement that Deborah was buried in her ancestral city is a mere phrase or a fact, and concludes that it is a fact, since in rabbinic times honoring graves was deeply ingrained.

P. 180, LAB 33.6: "lamentation": The fact that the text has transliterated the Greek word θρῆνος and has even retained, in the Vatican MS., the Greek accusative singular ending is a further indication of the likelihood that the author was translating from a Greek text.

P. 180, line 24 (margin), on LAB 33.6: Add Jud. 5[7].

P. 180, LAB 33.6: "which made fast the fence about her generation": Cf. Isaiah 58.12, which in the Vulgate, as H. L. Ginsberg (*ap.* G. Kisch, *Historia Judaica,* 12 [1950], p. 156) points out, similarly has the words *fundamenta generationis suscitabis, et vocaberis aedificatio sepium* (i.e., of fences).

P. 180, line 28 (margin), on LAB 33.6: Add Jud. 5[31].

P. 180, LAB 34.1 ff.: The episode of Aod the wizard is unique with LAB.

P. 180 (margin) on LAB 34.1: Add Cf. Jud. 6[1-6].

P. 180, LAB 34.1: Dietzfelbinger, p. 285, n. 321, disagrees with James' note on this passage and argues that Aod is not like the Antichrist but rather is one who leads people astray to a strange religion and ungodly cult. As to seeing the sun at night, he aptly compares Apuleius, *Metamorphoses,* 11.23: "I saw the sun gleaming with a bright light in the middle of the night." This phenomenon also plays a role in Mithraism; and Dietzfelbinger, pp. 61-62, suggests that LAB may be particularly directed against the sun-worship so prominent in this cult. In 34.1, however, LAB's attack is not on sun-worship but on wizardry. Ginzberg, 6.199, n. 93, compares Sifre Deut. 84, which states that God will test Israel's faith by permitting the false prophet to cause the sun and moon to stand still.

P. 180, LAB 34.1: "priests": The meaning of *sacris* is not "priests" but "sanctuary."

P. 181, LAB 34.3: "For this . . . by the angels": Lit., "For at this time it [magic] was pointed out [to Aod] by the angels."

P. 181, LAB 34.3: Dietzfelbinger, p. 285, n. 318, rightly understands *immensurabile seculum* ("the unmeasurable world") as "the coming age," just as *immensurabile tempus* in 32.7.

P. 181, line 22, LAB 34.4: For "by art magic" read "by art of magic."

P. 181, line 23 (margin), on LAB 34.4: Add Cf. Jud. 6[7-10].

P. 182, line 1 (margin), on LAB 34.5: Add Jud. 6[1].

P. 182, LAB 35.1: For Joath (*editio princeps*) and Ioza (Kisch, following Admont), both of which are stemmatically impossible, read Ioaz.

P. 182, line 7 (margin), on LAB 35.1: For Jud. 6[11] read Jud. 6[11,12].

P. 182, line 10 (margin), on LAB 35.1: Add Jud. 19[17].

P. 182, line 15 (margin), on LAB 35.2: Add Jud. 6[13].

P. 182, line 27 (margin), on LAB 35.3: Add Jud. 6[13] (LXX).

P. 182, LAB 35.3 (end): The notion that God will have mercy upon Israel because of those who have died is found in II Maccabees 8.15.

P. 182 (margin) on LAB 35.4: Add Jud. 6[14].

P. 183 (margin) on LAB 35.5: For Jud. 6[15] read Jud. 6[15,16].

P. 183 (margin) on LAB 35.6: Add Jud. 6[17].

P. 183, line 23 (margin), on LAB 35.6: Add Jud. 6[20].

P. 183, line 27 (margin), on LAB 35.7: For Jud. 6[21] read Jud. 6[20,21] (raise to line 26).

P. 183, line 36, LAB 35.7: "did . . . consume": All the MSS. read *excussit,* "shook off," "drove out." Apparently James has emended this to *exussit,* which indeed makes better sense.

P. 184 (margin) on LAB 36.1: Add Jud. 7[19].

P. 184, line 8 (margin), on LAB 36.1: For Jud. 7[11] read Jud. 7[14].

P. 184 (margin) on LAB 36.2: Add Jud. 7[15], 6[34].

P. 184 (margin) on LAB 36.3: 8[24] should be on line 29, not line 28. For 8[24] read 8[24-27].

P. 185, line 2 (margin), on LAB 36.4: Add Cf. Jud. 6[25].

P. 185, LAB 36.4: "that they may not have whereof to speak": The *editio princeps,* which James is here translating, does not have "not," but apparently, since Sichardus has indicated in the margin that something is missing, James inserted the word "not." His conjecture is now confirmed by the Admont and Melk MSS.

P. 185, line 11 (margin), on LAB 36.4: Add Jud. 8[32].

P. 185 (margin) on 37.1: Add Jud. 9[18].

P. 185 (margin) on 37.1: Place Jud. 9[5] one line above.

P. 185, LAB 37.1-2: Spiro, "Samaritans," *PAAJR*, 20 (1951), pp. 308-309, cites this passage as an arch-example to support his theory that LAB is an anti-Samaritan tract. He asserts that there is no lacuna here but that Pseudo-Philo has deliberately mutilated the beginning of the parable so as not to mention that Jotham ascended Mount Gerizim, sacred to the Samaritans, to pronounce it (Judges 9.6-9): in fact Jotham the "Samaritan" is not mentioned at all in the parable, and the story is presented not as a parable but as an actual event. But Spiro forgets that the readers of LAB would know the Biblical account and would realize that it was a parable, and that unless we ascribe no sense of style to LAB, it is presented as a parable. There is, however, not much of a lacuna, since Abimelech is mentioned in 37.1 and again in 37.2. Cf. Dietzfelbinger, p. 286, n. 331.

P. 185, LAB 37.2-3: In Jotham's parable in Judges 9.7 the olive-tree is approached first, then the fig-tree, then the vine. In Josephus, *AJ* 5.235-239, the order is fig-tree, vine, olive-tree. LAB follows Josephus' order—fig-tree, vine, and apple (myrtle), though at the end of the parable the order is apple, fig, vine. LAB is, moreover, a combination of the approach of Judges, in which the bramble is presented with praise, and Josephus, where it is presented with blame.

P. 185, James' note on 37.2 seq.: For 84 (85)[12] read 84[11] (85[12]). The parallel to Psalm 84.12 is not apt, since there is no mention there of a thornbush.

P. 186, line 4 (margin), on LAB 37.2: Add Cf. Ezek. 3[18].

P. 186, LAB 37.2: "apple": This is the reading of the *editio princeps* and Phillipps 461, but the fact that the fruit is described as one "of sweet savour" indicates that it is most likely a myrtle.

P. 186 (margin) on LAB 37.3: Add Jud. 9[14].

P. 186, line 13 (margin), on LAB 37.3: Add Gen. 3[19,18].

P. 186, line 19 (margin), on LAB 37.3: Add Jud. 9[15].

P. 186, LAB 37.3: "was made for": An alternate translation, as Dietzfelbinger in his commentary indicates, is "signifies."

P. 186, line 33 (margin), on LAB 37.4: Add Jud. 9[15].

P. 186 (margin) on LAB 37.5: Add Jud. 9[22].

P. 187, line 1 (margin), on LAB 37.5: For Jud. 9[10 sqq.] read Jud. 9[53].

P. 187, LAB 37.5: Spiro, "Samaritans," *PAAJR*, 20 (1951), pp. 309-310, denies that there is a lacuna after this chapter. The fact that LAB jumps from the judgeship of Abimelech to that of Jair, while omitting that of Tola the son of Puah (Judges 10.1-2) is deliberate anti-Samaritan bias, he asserts, because Tola was buried in Samaria, according to Codex A of the LXX, and indeed Samaritans report that Tola was buried on Mt. Gerizim. But LAB omits two other judges, Shamgar (Judges 3.31, 5.6) and Ibzan (Judges 12.8-10), and there is no possible anti-Samaritan bias in these cases. Indeed, the only reason for the omission may be simply that these three judges were unimportant.

P. 187, LAB 38.1: Ginzberg, 4.42 (cf. 6.202, n. 104), basing himself upon Jerahmeel, gives the names of the seven as Deuel, Abi Yisreel, Jekuthiel, Shalom, Ashur, Jehonadab, and Shemiel.

P. 187, last line, note on LAB 38.1: After Maccabaean martyrs add: (II Macc. 7). Another—and more likely analogy—is to be found in the story of the rescue of Abraham from the furnace (LAB 6.3-18).

P. 187, line 14 (margin), on LAB 38.2: Add Dt. 5[29(32)], Jos. 1[7,8].

P. 187, line 16 (margin), on LAB 38.2: Add Cf. 1 Kings 18[24].

P. 187, LAB 38.3: The name of Nathaniel is found in the Fulda-Cassel MS. (embodied in the *editio princeps*), but is omitted in all the other MSS. K. Kohler,

"Angelology," *Jewish Encyclopedia,* 1.593, suggests that the name may be Nuriel (= Fire of God). Ginzberg, 6.202, n. 105, suggests that perhaps the name should be Atuniel, from אתונא, "furnace." The angel in charge of fire in rabbinic literature is Gabriel, who apparently thus had additional theophoric names in accordance with his mission, and it is perhaps of significance to note that in 27.10, at least according to Jerahmeel, it is Gabriel, rather than Ingethel and Zeruel, who is sent to help Kenaz. An angel named Nathaniel (נתנאל, נתנאל) does appear in popular and rabbinic tradition, but he is nowhere mentioned as being in charge of fire: cf. M. Schwab, "Vocabulaire de l'Angélologie d'après les Manuscrits Hébreux de la Bibliothèque Nationale," *Mémoires présentés par divers savants à l'Académie des Inscriptions et Belles-Lettres de l'Institut de France,* vol. 10, part 2 (Paris, 1897), p. 304; R. Margaliouth, *Malakhe Elyon*[2] (Jerusalem, 1964), p. 23; M. Margalioth, *Sefer Harazim* (Jerusalem, 1966), 1.22, 68.

P. 188 (margin) on LAB 39.1: Jud. 10[17,18] should be on line 13, not line 14.

P. 188, line 16 (margin), on LAB 39.1: Add Jud. 10[9].

P. 188, line 25 (margin), on LAB 39.2: Add 11[2].

P. 188, LAB 39.2: Strugnell (*per litt.*) convincingly suggests reading *vani* ("empty") for *vagi* ("vagrant") in accordance with the Hebrew text and LXX of Judges 11.3.

P. 188 (margin) on LAB 39.3: For 11[5] read 11[5,6].

P. 188 (margin) on LAB 39.4: Add Jud. 11[7].

P. 189, LAB 39.5: The notion that God has time and place to repose Himself of His long-suffering is unique with LAB within the Jewish tradition, as Dietzfelbinger points out in his commentary.

P. 189, LAB 39.5: The dove is cited as Israel's symbol in IV Esdras 5.26, Berakhoth 53b, Shir Hashirim Rabbah 2.14 and 4.1 (cited by Ginzberg, 6.228, n. 110).

P. 189 (margin) on LAB 39.6: Add Jud. 11[11].

P. 189, line 28 (margin), on LAB 39.6: Add Cf. Jud. 10[13].

P. 189, LAB 39.6: "For although our sins do overabound, nevertheless his mercy filleth all the earth": Cf. Romans 5.20: "Where sin increased, grace abounded all the more" (cited by Dietzfelbinger, *ad loc.,* in his forthcoming commentary).

P. 190 (margin) on LAB 39.8: Cf. Jud. 11[29].

P. 190, line 12 (margin), on LAB 39.8: For Jud. 11[14] read Jud. 11[12].

P. 190, LAB 39.9 (beg.): "Did . . Amorites": The Admont MS. reads: "Did Israel think that it would possess the land of the Amorites, so far as it had taken it?" For "it would possess it" the stemmatically more probable reading is "it would be possessed."

P. 190, line 31 (margin), on LAB 39.9: Add Jud. 11[14].

P. 190, last line (margin), on LAB 39.9: Add Cf. Jud. 11[24].

P. 190, LAB 39.9: "they are not . . . gods which have given you the inheritance": LAB here contradicts Judges 11.24, which speaks of only one god, Chemosh.

P. 191, LAB 39.9: "because ye have been led astray after stones": LAB has confused the Ammonites and Amorites (cf. 25.9 ff.).

P. 191 (margin) on LAB 39.10: Add Jud. 11[28].

P. 191, line 7 (margin), on LAB 39.10: For Jud. 11[31] read Jud. 11[30,31].

P. 191, LAB 39.11: "if a dog": Cf. the similar thought in Ta'anith 4a: "It [the creature that might meet Jephthah after his vow] might have been an unclean thing. He, however, was fortunate in that it so happened that his own daughter came to meet him."

P. 191, LAB 39.11: P. Winter, "*Monogenēs Para Patros*," *Zeitschrift für Religions- und Geistesgeschichte,* 5 (1953), p. 341, cites this passage in noting the basic identity of meaning of *bekhor* (*prōtotokos,* "first-born") and *yahid* (*monogenēs,* "only-begotten").

P. 191, LAB 40.1: For "threescore" (*sexaginta*), which is the reading of the *editio princeps*, Kisch, following the Admont MS., has the stemmatically impossible "forty" (*quadraginta*).

P. 191, line 24 (margin), on LAB 40.1: For 11^{34} read 11^{32} sqq..

P. 191, LAB 40.1: The name of Jephthah's daughter, Seila, is found only in LAB within the Jewish tradition.

P. 191, LAB 40.1: "rejoicing" (*epulatio*): Literally, "feasting."

P. 192 (margin) on LAB 40.2: Add Jud. 11^{36}.

P. 192, LAB 40.2: "When they see the people delivered": So also Josephus, *AJ* 5.265: "She without displeasure learned her destiny, to wit that she must die in return for her father's victory and the liberation of her fellow-citizens."

P. 192, line 4 (margin), on LAB 40.2: Add Gen. 22^2 sqq-.

P. 192, LAB 40.2: Vermès, *Scripture and Tradition*, p. 199, and Le Déaut, p. 191, note that the same presentation of the episode as a test of Isaac's as well as of Abraham's fidelity is found in Josephus, *AJ* 1.225-236, and in the Targum of Pseudo-Jonathan on Genesis 22.1.

P. 192, LAB 40.3: The rabbinic position is that Jephthah's vow was entirely invalid. See Bereshith Rabbah 60.

P. 192, line 11 (margin), on LAB 40.3: For Jud. 11^{37} read Jud. $11^{37,38}$.

P. 192 (margin) on LAB 40.4: 11^{38} should be on line 26, not line 30.

P. 192, LAB 40.4: "Now that I have shut up the tongue of the wise": The rabbis believed (see Vayikra Rabbah 37.4, Bereshith Rabbah 60.3, cited by Ginzberg, 6.203, n. 109) that it was the fact that the scholars had forgotten the Halakhah that such a vow as Jehthah's was entirely invalid that led to the sacrifice of his daughter.

P. 192, LAB 40.4: M. Gaster, *The Chronicles of Jerahmeel* (London, 1899), p. xcix, says that Telag (or Selac or Thelac) is the local Aramaic name for Hermon. Telag combines the Hebrew *sheleg*, "snow," with the Aramaic *thelac*, also meaning "snow," as noted by Ginzberg, 6.203, n. 108. The Targum Onkelos on Deuteronomy 3.9 explains Hermon as Tur Talga, the snow-capped mountain.

P. 193, LAB 40.4: "She is more wise than [*prae*] her father": Dietzfelbinger, p. 290, n. 380, rightly translates "she is wise in contrast to her father," and explains that nowhere in LAB does *prae* have the comparative sense.

P. 193, LAB 40.4: "her death shall be precious in my sight": Cf. Psalms 116.15: "Precious in the sight of the Lord is the death of his saints" (cited by Dietzfelbinger, *ad loc.*).

P. 193, LAB 40.4 (end): The note at the bottom of p. 192 belongs at the bottom of p. 193.

P. 193, LAB 40.5 ff.: On the alleged parallel between this lament of Jephthah's daughter and the lament of Baruch for Jerusalem (*Apocalypse of Baruch* 10.6-12.4), see P. Bogaert, *Apocalypse de Baruch*, vol. 1 (Paris, 1969), p. 247, who concludes that there is a stylistic resemblance and notes the similar appeal to nature, but who says that the resemblance ends there.

P. 193, LAB 40.5: At the beginning of this section Kisch, following the Admont MS., adds: "The lament of Seila the daughter of Iepta," but this obvious gloss is stemmatically impossible.

P. 193, LAB 40.6: "sitting in my maidenhood": This is the reading of Phillipps 461. The Admont, Melk, Vatican, and Vienna MSS. read "according to my nobility."

P. 193, LAB 40.6: For "my precious ointment" Kisch, following the Admont, Melk, Vienna, and Vatican MSS. and the *editio princeps*, has "the odor of my Moses," which seems corrupt, as Dietzfelbinger, in his forthcoming translation, notes.

P. 193, LAB 40.6: "enjoyed": Lit., "become leafy."

P. 193, LAB 40.6: Dietzfelbinger, p. 226, notes that the rare picture of the moth is found also in Matthew 6.19-20 and Epistle of James 5.2.

P. 193, LAB 40.6: "aforetime": Better "with time," omitting comma thereafter.

P. 193, LAB 40.6: "she wove of violet and purple for my virginity": Translate: "my talent has woven of violet and purple."

P. 194, LAB 40.7: "my virginity (*virginitatem meam*)". This reading of the *editio princeps* is in accord with Judges 11.37-38. Kisch, following the Admont MS., reads the much more difficult and less likely *virgines meas*, "my maidens."

P. 194, LAB 40.8: The Admont MS. reads: "He offered her as burnt offerings"; but the plural *holocaustomata* ("offerings") argues for the correctness of the *editio princeps* adopted by James.

P. 194, LAB 40.9: According to Judges 12.7, as well as Josephus, *AJ* 5.270, Jephthah was judge for six years.

P. 194, LAB 41.1: James errs in citing Judges 12.12, which refers to Elon the Zebulunite. The facts that the rule was for eight years and that the name of the place from which the judge came was Praton (Phraathon in the LXX, Pharathon in Josephus *AJ* 5.273) indicate that the reference is to Abdon. Elech, the name of Addo's (Abdon's) father is a MS. variant for Elel (Hillel in MT, Ellel in LXX [variant reading], Elōn in Josephus). Ephrata, where, according to LAB, Addo was buried is Praton in the Hebrew text, LXX, and Josephus *AJ* 5.274. Quite obviously the Elon of 41.2 is different from Addo of 41.1; LAB has reversed the order of the judges in Judges 12.11-13, which has Elon *before* Abdon. The portrait of Abdon is in contradiction to Josephus (5.273), who states that "thanks to the prevailing peace and security of the state, he did no brilliant deed."

P. 194, line 36 (margin), on LAB 41.1: Add Jud. 12^15.

P. 195, LAB 41.2: According to Judges 12.11, Elon was judge for ten years.

P. 195, line 5 (margin), on LAB 41.2: Add Jud. 12^12.

P. 195 (margin) on LAB 41.3: Add 13^1.

P. 195 (margin) on LAB 42.1: For 13^9 read 13^2.

P. 195, LAB 42.1 ff.: Winter, "The Proto-Source of Luke I," *Novum Testamentum,* 1 (1956), p. 186, noting that of the many motifs in LAB that are absent from the account in Judges 13, virtually all are to be found in the account of the birth of John the Baptist in Luke 1 concludes that the author of Luke used LAB as his model. S. Muñoz Iglesias, "El Evangelio de la Infancia en S. Lucas," *Estudios Bíblicos,* 16 (1957), pp. 329-382, on the other hand, suggests that the reverse may be the case, and that LAB is dependent on Luke, a verdict with which C. Perrot, "Les Récits d'Enfance dans la Haggada antérieure au IIe Siècle de Notre Ère," *Recherches de Science Religieuse,* 55 (1967), p. 495, disagrees. A comparison of LAB and Luke, however, will show that the parallels are fewer and less striking than noted by Winter.

P. 195, LAB 42.1: LAB, with typically midrashic concern for giving names (the name of Samson's mother, Eluma, is nowhere else to be found in Jewish literature), stresses Samson's noble origin. Similarly Josephus, *AJ* 5.276, adds that Manoah, Samson's father, was one of the foremost among the Danites. The rabbis, in line with their general criticism of Samson, omit all references to his ancestry and indeed condemn Manoah as an ignorant man—almost the most severe criticism that can be given by the rabbis. See Bamidbar Rabbah 10.5, Midrash Hagadol Genesis 1.357, Berakhoth 61a, Erubin 18b, Yalkut 2.68, cited by Ginzberg, 6.205, n. 111.

P. 195, LAB 42.1: Manoah's request to his wife to set him free to marry another is contrary to the Jewish law whereby it is the husband who takes the initiative in divorcing his wife. But cf. Mark 10.12: "If she divorces her husband. . . ."

P. 195, LAB 42.1-2: Whereas LAB and the Midrash (Bamidbar Rabbah 10.5 and 11.88c, Vayikra Rabbah 9.9, Derekh Erez, Perek Hashalom) stress the strife between Manoah and his wife as to who is responsible for their childlessness, Josephus, *AJ* 5.277, stresses rather the erotic, jealous suspicion of Manoah.

P. 195, LAB 42.2: "upper chamber [*solarium*]," i.e., a terrace, balcony, or part of the house exposed to the sun: Cf. Acts 1.13, 9.39-40, 20.8.

P. 196, line 2 (margin), on LAB 42.3: Add Jud. 13[3].

P. 196, line 6 (margin), on LAB 42.3: Omit Jud. 13[4,7].

P. 196, line 7 (margin), on LAB 42.3: Add Cf. Jud. 13[24].

P. 196, LAB 42.3: "Call his name Samson": Ginzberg, 6.205, n. 161, finds LAB's etymology rather obscure, since there is no Hebrew word "holy" which can in any way be connected with the word Samson. But LAB may have had in mind a derivative from *shimesh*, to minister or serve, in allusion to Samson's Nazirite status. Ginzberg himself suggests that "holy unto the Lord" may be an inaccurate rendering of "anointed to the Lord" in allusion to *shemen*, "oil." Perhaps, we may add, this reflects the rabbinic midrash that Samson was shown to Jacob as the future Messiah who would be an anointed king (see Bereshith Rabbah 98.14, 99.11, and other passages cited by Ginzberg, 5.368, n. 392). Cf. *sanctus christus* (=משיח הקדוש), LAB 59.2.

P. 196, line 9 (margin), on LAB 42.3: Add Jud. 13[4,14,5].

P. 196, LAB 42.3: "Take heed . . ." Winter, *Novum Testamentum*, 1 (1956), pp. 189-190, comments that the Admont MS. inserted *tibi* to bring LAB into agreement with Judges 13.4, but the Admont MS. failed to replace *comedat* by *comedas* and *gustet* by *gustes*. But if he were following the LXX, the author would have found no του there (similarly the Vulgate has no *tibi*). Pseudo-Philo may well have had a different (or supplemental) tradition that the angel told Samson's mother to take heed so far as she could so that her son would not drink wine.

P. 196, LAB 42.3: In Judges 13.4, it is Samson's mother, rather than Samson himself, who is told to avoid drinking wine.

P. 196 (margin) on LAB 42.4: Add Jud. 13[6].

P. 196, line 19 (margin), on LAB 42.4: Add Jud. 13[7].

P. 196, line 21 (margin), on LAB 42.4: Add Jud. 13[3].

P. 196, LAB 42.5: Josephus, *AJ* 5.280, has Manoah's wife entreat God to send the angel again, whereas in the Bible (Judges 13.8), Midrash, and LAB it is Manoah and not his wife who does so.

P. 196, line 24 (margin), on LAB 42.5: Add Jud. 13[8].

P. 196 (margin) on LAB 42.6: Add 13[9,10].

P. 196, line 30 (margin), on LAB 42.6: Omit 13[2].

P. 196 (margin) on LAB 42.7: Add Jud. 13[10-12].

P. 196, LAB 42.7: Manoah's suspicion and the mysterious nature of the angel's errand are increased in Josephus (*AJ* 5.281) when the angel refuses to repeat what he had revealed to Manoah's wife, whereas in the Bible (Judges 13.13-14) the angel repeats substantially what he had told Manoah's wife. Here LAB occupies something of a midway position between Josephus and the Midrash, for while, as in the Midrash, the angel does give directions to Manoah, he does so in a very much briefer form: "Go in unto thy wife and do quickly all these things." But LAB is closer to Josephus (*AJ* 5.281) than to Scripture in implying that Manoah, in seeking to be reassured that the angel's word would be accomplished, had lingering doubts.

P. 197 (margin) on LAB 42.8: For Jud. 13[15] read Jud. 13[15,16].

P. 197, LAB 42.8: LAB differs from the Bible (Judges 13.16) and Josephus (*AJ* 5.282) in omitting the invitation to the angel to eat. The Midrash (Bamidbar Rabbah 10.5) stresses Manoah's ignorance of the fact that this was an angel, noting that it was because of this ignorance that he invited the angel to eat.

P. 197, LAB 42.8: "that which is not thine": A better rendering for *aliena* here would be "strange" or "foreign."

P. 197 (margin) on LAB 42.9: Add Jud. 13[23].

P. 197, line 14 (margin), on LAB 42.9: Omit 13[19].

P. 197, line 16 (margin), on LAB 42.9: Add Cf. Jud. 6²¹.

P. 197, LAB 42.9: "put forth his hand": James' insertion of *his hand* is confirmed by the readings of the Admont and Melk MSS., *manum suam*. The statement that the angel put forth his hand and touched the flesh with the end of his scepter and that there came forth a fire out of the rock is taken from Judges 6.21. So also Josephus, *AJ* 5.284: "That done, he with the rod which he held touched the meat."

P. 197, LAB 42.10: Ginzberg, 6.205, n. 111, suggests that Phadahel is very likely פחדיאל and not פדיאל; but M. Schwab, "Vocabulaire de l'Angélologie d'après les Manuscrits Hébreux de la Bibliothèque Nationale," *Mémoires présentés par divers savants à l'Académie des Inscriptions et Belles-Lettres de l'Institut de France,* vol. 10, part 2 (Paris, 1897), p. 330, knows of an angel פדאל at the gates of heaven and chief of the fourth region of the earth. R. Margaliouth, *Malakhe Elyon*² (Jerusalem, 1964), p. 165, and M. Margalioth (Margulies), *Sefer Harazim* (Jerusalem, 1966), pp. 88, 98 (2.129, 4.21) know of a פדיאל or פדאל or פדהאל in the seventh heaven, as well as a פחדיאל (Margaliouth, p. 166). Hartom in his commentary notes that a similar name, פדהאל, occurs in Numbers 34.28, as the leader of the tribe of Naphtali. In the account of John's birth in Luke 1, which in several respects parallels LAB, the angel (Luke 1.19) who appears to Zechariah, the father of John, is Gabriel. Note that there is reason for identifying the other angels in LAB—Ingethel and Zeruel (27.10) and Nathaniel (38.3) with Gabriel also; see my notes on these passages.

P. 197, line 24 (margin), on LAB 42.10: Add 13¹⁷,¹⁸.

P. 197, line 25 (margin), on LAB 42.10: Add Jud. 13¹⁶.

P. 197, line 26 (margin), on LAB 42.10: Add Jud. 13⁸.

P. 197, LAB 43.1: Whereas LAB is only mildly interested in the erotic episodes in Samson's career, here abbreviating chapter 14 of Judges in two brief sentences, Josephus (*AJ* 5.286 ff.) retells the episode at Timnah in such a way as to highlight its erotic aspect.

P. 197, line 29 (margin), on LAB 43.1: Add Cf. Isa. 7¹⁴.

P. 197, line 31 (margin), on LAB 43.1: Add 14¹ sqq.

P. 197, line 32 (margin), on LAB 43.1: The citation 15⁶ should be in the margin on line 33.

P. 197 (margin) on LAB 43.2: For 16¹ read 16¹⁻³.

P. 197, LAB 43.2: "Azotus": This is the reading of the *editio princeps*. The Admont MS. is in accord with the Hebrew text, LXX, and Josephus, *AJ* 5.304, in reading Gaza.

P. 197, LAB 43.2: "Entered into (*or* was enraged against)": There is no basis for the translation "entered into."

Pp. 197-198, LAB 43.2-3: Josephus (*AJ* 5.305) avoids the extreme contempt for the enemy found in LAB's account of Samson's escape from the Philistine ambuscade at Gaza, for LAB has put into Samson a speech un-Josephan both in its utter contempt for the enemy and in its militant faith in God. Josephus adds fury to Samson, but in LAB he is almost a kind of superman.

P. 198 (margin) on LAB 43.3: Add Jud. 16³.

P. 198 (margin) on LAB 43.4: For Jud. 15 read Jud. 14⁵,⁶, 15¹⁵,⁹⁻¹⁴,⁴⁻⁵.

P. 198 (margin) on LAB 43.5: Add Jud. 16¹.

P. 198, LAB 43.5: Josephus is more romantic than Judges 16.1 or LAB in describing Delilah as a courtesan (*AJ* 5.306).

P. 198, line 32 (margin), on LAB 43.5: Add Cf. Gen. 39.

P. 198, LAB 43.5: The same unfavorable comparison of Samson with Joseph is found in Clement of Alexandria's *Paedagogus*, 3.11.68.3: "But another woman did not beguile Joseph." Did Clement know LAB or, more probably, the traditions which LAB knew, or did he quite independently compare Samson and Joseph, as any student of the Bible might well do?

Pp. 198-199, LAB 43.5: "they shall blind him": Cf. Mishnah Sotah 1.8: "He who went astray after his eyes lost his eyes."

P. 199, line 2 (margin), on LAB 43.5: Add Jud. 16^{28}.

P. 199, line 7 (margin), on LAB 43.6: Add 16^{15,16}.

P. 199, line 10 (margin), on LAB 43.6: For 16^{16} read 16^{19}, and remove 16^{19} from the margin of line 14.

P. 199, LAB 43.6: In Josephus (AJ 5.309) also, in an extra-Biblical addition, Samson violates the Nazirite prohibition against drinking (certain of the Greek MSS. of Josephus here read καθεύδοντα , and the Latin version similarly reads *dormientem*, "asleep," but μεθύοντα , "being drunk," is doubtless correct, as Schalit, in his commentary on this passage notes, because it is in accord with AJ 5.306, which states that Samson debased his own rule of life by foreign ways).

P. 199 (margin) on LAB 43.7: For 16^{23} read 16^{23,25}.

P. 199, LAB 43.7: "that they might mock him": This is the reading of the *editio princeps* and agrees with the wording of Josephus, AJ 5.314: "that they might mock him [ἐνυβρίσωσιν] over their cups." The Admont MS., adopted by Kisch, reads "that he might make sport for them" and is in agreement with the Hebrew text and LXX of Judges 16^{25}, but is stemmatically impossible.

P. 199, line 20 (margin), on LAB 43.7: For 16^{26} read 16^{28,30}.

P. 199, LAB 43.7: In his elaboration of Samson's prayer and its theological implications LAB is once again closer to the Midrash (Bereshith Rabbah 66.3) than to Josephus, who has no such prayer (AJ 5.314 ff.).

P. 199 (margin) on LAB 43.8: For 16^{29} read 16^{29,30}.

P. 199, LAB 43.8: The Bible (Judges 16.27) says that there were 3000 men and women upon the roof, with an undetermined number elsewhere in the building. The LXX rationalistically reduces the number to 700. Josephus (AJ 5.316) brings the total slain to 3000. The Midrash (Bereshith Rabbah, 98.14) says that the number far exceeded 3000, while LAB increases the number to 40,000. G. F. Moore, *A Critical and Exegetical Commentary on Judges* (New York, 1895), p. 362, notes that Theodoret, *Quaest.* 22, exaggerates the number to 3000 men and many times more women, but there is no reason to think that he knew LAB or even the tradition of LAB, since his statement might well be inferred from the original text.

P. 199, line 31 (margin), on LAB 43.8: For 16^{13} read 16^{31}.

P. 200 (margin) on LAB 44.2: For Jud. 17^2 read Jud. 17$^{1-4}$.

P. 200, LAB 44.2: "wedges": The meaning of the *editio princeps'* reading, *tegulas*, is "tiles," that of the Admont's *ligulas* is "little tongues" or "spoons."

P. 200, line 4 (margin), on LAB 44.2: Omit Jos. 7^{21}.

P. 200, LAB 44.2: The story of the idol which Micah made from the money which Delilah received from the Philistines is paralleled by Tosefta-Targum Judges 17.2, as well as by a quotation from an unknown midrash in Rashi and Kimhi *ad loc.* (cited by Ginzberg, 6.209, n. 125). LAB apparently assigns the stories of Micah and of the Benjamites to the end of the period of Judges, whereas the rabbis and Josephus (AJ 5.136 ff.), who omits the story of Micah altogether, assign these events to the beginning of that period (cf. Ginzberg, 6.43, n. 136).

P. 200, LAB 44.3: "they shall come [*venient*]": This is the reading of the *editio princeps*; Kisch, following the Admont MS., has the stemmatically impossible *veniet*, "he shall come."

P. 200, James' note on LAB 44.4-5: Dietzfelbinger, pp. 61-62, expands at length on this note in discussing the parallel between LAB and Mithraism. Since the cult of Mithra had a special center in Cilicia and Syria, so close to Palestine, it is reasonable to suppose, in his opinion, that the Palestinian Pseudo-Philo regarded it as a danger to Israel. One wonders also whether the very name Michas may not in Pseudo-Philo's mind be connected with Mithraism. But see my remarks on Mithraism and LAB in my introduction.

P. 200 (margin) on LAB 44.5: Add Cf. Jud. 17[5].

P. 200, LAB 44.5: The Admont MS. has *tres,* "three," with calves also. It also has *leones,* "lions," where the *editio princeps,* as in 45.6, has the singular.

P. 201, line 13 (margin), on LAB 44.6: Add. Ex. 20.

P. 201, LAB 44.6: "sanctify themselves": Strugnell, *per litt.,* suggests that the *se* of *ut sanctificarent se* may be a mistranslation of *αὐτό* or *αὐτά* [=Sabbath].

P. 201, line 24 (margin), on LAB 44.6: Add Cf. Jer. 7[9].

P. 201, LAB 44.7: Cf. Wisdom of Solomon 13.10 ff.

P. 201, LAB 44.7: "They have made": this is the reading of the *editio princeps* and Phillipps 461. The other MSS. read "nor."

P. 202, line 13, LAB 44.7: For *when* read *whom.*

P. 202, LAB 44.7: "And where they did choose not": To make this parallel with the preceding statements we would have to understand it as follows: Because they chose not to bear false witness and yet did not keep to their promise, they have received false witness, etc.

P. 202, LAB 44.8: James assumes a lacuna here presumably because of the sudden mention of the tribe of Benjamin; but, as Dietzfelbinger, p. 293, n. 421, remarks, Benjamin is integral to this chapter.

P. 202, LAB 44.9: The notion that great sinners are eaten alive by worms is found in II Macc. 9.9, Sotah 35a, Acts 12.23, cited by Ginzberg, 6.213, n. 136, and 6.98-99, n. 552.

P. 202, LAB 44.9: "shall speak," "shall say," "shall answer": James has here interpreted the perfect tenses as prophetic perfects and hence has translated as futures.

P. 203, LAB 44.10: On the punishment suiting the sin see also Matthew 7.2-3, Mark 4.24, Acts 7.41-43, Romans 1.22-32, 2.1, cited by Dietzfelbinger, p. 227. For the sins that keep back the rain see Ta'anith 7b, Midrash Mishle 25.97-98, and Yelammedenu in Yalkut 1.771, cited by Ginzberg, 6.269, n. 112.

P. 203, line 17 (margin), on LAB 44.10: Add Ex. 20[14] ([17]), Dt. 5[8].

P. 203, line 19 (margin), on LAB 44.10: Add Ex. 20[7], Dt. 5[11].

P. 203, line 34, James' note on LAB 44.10: For *notewortny* read *noteworthy.*

P. 203, line 27 (margin), on LAB 45.1: Add Jud. 19[15].

P. 204, line 2 (margin), on LAB 45.1: Add Jud. 19[13].

P. 204 (margin) on LAB 45.2: Add 19[16-20].

P. 204, LAB 45.2: LAB is unique in giving the name of the Levite, Beel (Behel), whose concubine is seized by the Benjamites, and likewise in giving the name of the Levite, Bethac, who offers shelter to him.

P. 204, line 15 (margin), on LAB 45.2: Add Cf. Gen. 19[10,11].

P. 204, LAB 45.2: Kisch here, in 45.3 and 52.1 has Betahc, which is stemmatically impossible; read Bethac.

P. 204, line 19 (margin), on LAB 45.3: Add Cf. Gen. 19[5].

P. 204, line 21 (margin), on LAB 45.3: Add Jud. 19[23].

P. 204, line 29 (margin), on LAB 45.3: Add Cf. Jud. 19[2].

P. 205, line 2 (margin), on LAB 45.4: Add Jud. 19[28].

P. 205 (margin) on LAB 45.5: Add Jud. 20[6].

P. 205, LAB 45.5: Silo: According to Judges 20.1 the assembly took place at Mizpah; in Judges 20.18 there is an assembly at Bethel.

P. 205, LAB 45.6: "Adversary" [*anteciminum*]: The same word (αντικείμενος) is used in reference to Satan (as seen in the next verse) in 1 Timothy 5.14.

P. 205, LAB 45.6: "hour when": This is James' emendation [*in hora in qua*] for the MSS.' "land where [*in terra in qua*]."

P. 205 (margin) on LAB 46.1: Add 20[3].

P. 205, line 30 (margin), on LAB 46.1: Add Jud. 20[13].

P. 205, line 32 (margin), on LAB 46.1: Add 20[27,28].

P. 206 (margin) on LAB 46.2: For Jud. 20[13] read Jud. 20[12,13].

P. 206, LAB 46.2: 45,000: in the Bible (Jud. 20.21) and Josephus (*AJ* 5.157) the number is 22,000.

P. 206, line 20 (margin), on LAB 46.3: Add Jud. 20[26].

P. 206, line 23 (margin), on LAB 46.3: Add Jud. 20[23,28].

P. 206, line 28 (margin), on LAB 46.3: For 20[24] read 20[24,25].

P. 206, LAB 46.3: 46,000: In the Bible (Jud. 20.25) and Josephus (*AJ* 5.158) the number is 18,000.

P. 206, line 35 (margin), on LAB 46.4: For 20[26,28] read 20[26-28].

P. 207, LAB 46.4: The complaint of Phinehas to God is an elaboration of Judges 20.28 which is peculiar to LAB.

P. 207, LAB 47.1: "thou wouldest [*voluisti*] destroy their evil [*malefacta*]": This is the reading of the *editio princeps*. The Admont MS. has "thou wouldest not [*noluisti*] destroy their evil-doer [*malefactôrem*]." The word *forte* ("peradventure") gives some basis to the otherwise illogical reading of the Admont MS.

Pp. 208-209, LAB 47.7-8: The rabbis also (Seder Olam 12 and Esther Rabbah 37.7, cited by Ginzberg, 6.211, n. 134) likewise connect the sin of Micah and the crime of the Benjamites, noting that Micah's image was set up on the day when the war against the Benjamites began.

P. 208, LAB 47.7: "committed [*commisit*]": This is the reading of the *editio princeps*; less likely is the reading of the Admont MS., "gave up [*dimisit*]."

P. 209 (margin) on LAB 47.9: For Jud. 20[30] read Jud. 20[30,31].

P. 209, line 19 (margin), on LAB 47.9: Add Jud. 20[34].

P. 209, line 21 (margin), on LAB 47.9: For 20[32,36] read 20[32,33,36,37].

P. 209 (margin) on LAB 47.10: For 20[33] read 20[41,42].

P. 209, line 27 (margin), on LAB 47.10: 20[48] should be on line 29.

P. 209, line 30 (margin), on LAB 47.10: Add 20[47].

P. 209 (margin) on LAB 47.11: Add Cf. 1 Chron. 8.

P. 210, LAB 47.11: "of ten families": The word for family, *patria*, is used in the sense of the Greek πατριά , as found in the LXX on Exodus 12.3 and elsewhere. The fact that it is used in this Greek sense would seem to indicate a Greek text behind our Latin version.

P. 210, LAB 47.11: For *Nethac* read *Netach*, the reading of the *editio princeps*.

P. 210, line 23 (margin), on LAB 48.1: Add Cf. Gen. 6[3].

P. 210, LAB 48.1: "120 years": Aphraates (*Patrologia Syriaca*, ed. Griffin, vol. 1, 14.27, pp. 641-642) asserts that Phinehas lived 365 years, but this is obviously taken from Genesis 5.23-24, where it is stated that Enoch, who likewise was translated into heaven, lived 365 years.

P. 210, LAB 48.1: Danaben: Ginzberg, 6.214, n. 140, suggests that this may be a corruption of Lebanon or Abarim. Spiro, "The Ascension of Phinehas," *PAAJR,* 22 (1953), pp. 100-101, n. 22, suggests reading Danaben backwards, thus yielding נֶבָדָן‬ ‪ : "a fugitive and a wanderer" (Gen. 4.12, 14): this would suit Elijah's career both prior and subsequent to his ascension. But this would parallel Phinehas with Cain, which hardly seems the intention of the author.

Pp. 210-211, James' note on LAB 48.1-2: other passages noting the identification of Elijah and Phinehas are found in Palestinian Targum on Exodus 6.18, Numbers 25.12, and Deuteronomy 30.4, Bamidbar Rabbah 21.3, and Tanhuma Pinehas, 1, cited by Ginzberg, 6.136, n. 3. Ginzberg incorrectly cites PRE 44.

P. 211, LAB 48.1: "eagle": Cf. *Assumptio Mosis* 10.8: "Thou, O Israel, . . . shalt mount on the neck and wings of the eagle."

P. 211, James' note on LAB 48.1: The *Quaestiones Hebraicae* is ascribed to Jerome.

P. 211, LAB 48.1: "ye shall taste what is death": Cf. Matthew 16.28: "There are some standing here who will not taste death" (Philonenko, *per litt.*). Add Mark 9.1, Luke 9.27, John 8.52. Only Hebrews 2.9, as Dietzfelbinger, p. 204, notes, has, like LAB here, the positive form.

P. 211, LAB 48.2: Spiro, *Manners of Rewriting Biblical History,* p. 238, construes the identification of Phinehas and Elijah as part of a polemic against the Samaritans. The Samaritans maintained that Phinehas had been priest on Mount Gerizim, their sacred mount, but LAB here, in a passage significantly out of context, says that he was anointed by the Lord at Shiloh. The Samaritans emphatically denied the immortality of Phinehas [in the eleventh-century Kitāb al-Tabākh by Abu-l-Ḥasan al-Ṣūr; see A. S. Halkin, "Samaritan Polemics against the Jews," *PAAJR,* 7 (1935), pp. 13-59, esp. 28-30]. The Samaritans contended (see Spiro, *Manners,* pp. 226 ff.) that the house of Phinehas had continued its legitimate line on Gerizim; but LAB 50.3 and 52.2 report that Eli, who pontificated at Shiloh, was Phinehas' immediate successor; hence perhaps for *eum,* "him," in 48.2 read *Heli,* "Eli," as suggested by Ginzberg, 6.220, n. 25. For a long excursus on Phinehas see Dietzfelbinger, pp. 68-70, who especially dwells on the relationship of LAB's Phinehas and the Phinehas of later Judaism.

P. 211, LAB 48.3: The statement that the festival on which the Benjaminites went up to Shiloh (Judges 21.19) was Passover is an addition by LAB. Ginzberg, 6.213, n. 135, comments that LAB has arrived at this by the hermeneutic rule of analogy known as *gezerah shavah,* according to which מימים ימימה in Judges 21.19 has the same meaning as in Exodus 13.10, where it refers to Passover. Cf. LAB 50.2.

P. 211, LAB 49.1 ff.: Winter, *Novum Testamentum,* 1 (1956), pp. 193, 198, notes that the story of the nativity in Luke bears a strong affinity with the account of Samuel's birth, just as it does with the story of Samson's birth (see my note on 42.1 ff.). Winter, p. 199, then suggests that the primitive form of the Baptist Document can be partly reconstructed on the basis of LAB.

P. 212, LAB 49.3: Ginzberg, 6.218, n. 17, conjectures that the name Nethez is related either to נתזה (Nithza, Sanhedrin 74a) or to Aramaic נבזין, "lots."

P. 212, LAB 49.4: "And the people said": The Admont MS., followed by Kisch, has the stemmatically impossible "And he said to the people."

P. 212, LAB 49.4: For *before [super]* read *over.*

P. 213, LAB 49.5: Ginzberg, 6.218, n. 17, regards "leapt out [*supervolavit*]," as a Hebraism; but הגורל נפל would not have the connotation of flying out.

P. 213, line 25 (margin), on LAB 49.6: Add Gen. 16.10.

P. 214, line 14 (margin), on LAB 49.8: Add 1 Sam. 1.8.

P. 214, LAB 50.1: Italicize "had two wives . . . the other Phenenna." Italicize also "Phenenna had sons, and Anna had none."

P. 214, LAB 50.1: On Phenenna's (Peninnah's) reproaches see parallel passages in Pesikta Rabbati 43,181b, and Midrash Shemuel 1,45-46, cited by Ginzberg, 6.216, n. 7.

P. 214 (margin) on LAB 50.2: Add 1 Sam. 1.8.

P. 214, LAB 50.2: "the good day of the Passover": This, as Ginzberg, 6.216, n. 9, has noted, is a Hebraism, יום טוב של פסח. The identification of the day (1 Samuel 1.4) as Passover rests on the fact that the preceding verse speaks of מימים ימימה, which, in accordance with the principle of *gezerah shavah* with Exodus 13.10, is interpreted to mean Passover (see my note on 48.3). Midrash Shemuel 1.46, on the other hand, identifies it as the Feast of Weeks.

P. 215, line 1 (margin), on LAB 50.2: Add 1 Sam. 1.3.

P. 215, line 4 (margin), on LAB 50.2: Add 1 Sam. 2.10 (LXX).

P. 215, line 13 (margin), on LAB 50.2: Add 1 Sam. 1.10.

P. 215, LAB 50.3: In 1 Samuel 1.4 ff., as Dietzfelbinger (*ad loc.*) notes, the entire scene takes place in Shiloh; in LAB Elkanah addresses Hannah though he is in Shiloh and she has not yet come there.

P. 215, LAB 50.3: On Eli as a disciple of Phinehas see LAB 52.2 and Aboth di Rabbi Nathan B, chap. 1, p. 1b, Eliyahu Rabbah 11,57, Origen on John (6.14), and Aphraates 272.

P. 215 (margin) on LAB 50.5: Add 1[13].

P. 215, line 34 (margin), on LAB 50.5: Add Cf. Ps. 42.3, 13.

P. 216 (margin) on LAB 50.6: Add 1 Sam. 1[12-15].

P. 216, line 8 (margin), on LAB 50.6: Omit 1 Sam. 1[13].

P. 216, LAB 50.6: LAB here follows the Hebrew text (1 Samuel 1.14), according to which Eli himself speaks to Hannah, whereas the LXX and Philo (De Ebrietate 146) put the words into the mouth of his lad.

P. 216, LAB 51.1 ff.: M. Philonenko, "Une paraphrase du cantique d'Anne," Revue d'Histoire et de Philosophie Religieuses, 42 (1962), pp. 157-168, gives the Latin text of this chapter, Kisch's apparatus, a French translation, dividing it into strophes, and a commentary. He concludes that Pseudo-Philo here reveals himself as a master of Essene midrash with close relations with the Dead Sea sect.

P. 216, LAB 51.1: Ginzberg, 6.218, n. 17, cites Rimze Haftaroth, Rosh Hashanah 1, which explains his name as שמו של קאל עליון, i.e., "his name is given to him by the Most High God." A similar explanation, which also accounts for LAB's explanation of the meaning of the name as "mighty," is to read his name as שמו אל, i.e., "his name is strength [power]."

P. 216, line 33 (margin), on LAB 51.1: For 1[23] read 1[23,24].

P. 216 (margin) on LAB 51.2: For 1[26] read 1[25,26].

P. 216, LAB 51.1: "The child was very fair": Cf. a similar description of Moses in Acts 7.20 and Hebrews 11.23.

P. 216, LAB 51.2: For "Heli" Kisch, following the Admont MS., has the stemmatically impossible Domini ("Lord"). Perhaps the error reveals a Hebrew Vorlage and came about through someone's misconstruing Heli as the Hebrew word "my God."

P. 217, line 6 (margin), on LAB 51.2: Add cf. 1 Sam. 3[20].

P. 217, LAB 51.2: "prophecy": Kisch follows the Admont and Vatican MSS. in reading proficuum, "beneficial," "advantageous." But, as Philonenko, p. 162, remarks, there is an allusion to 1 Samuel 3.20, which states that Samuel was established as a prophet.

P. 217, LAB 51.2: "before the people": Philonenko, p. 162, interprets populis as referring to the nations of the world and thus finds here an indication of LAB's universalism. Dietzfelbinger, p. 298, n. 491, objects that populus in the plural often means "people" and that it may refer to Israel. But the plural is probably a translation of גויים, "nations," "gentiles," which must refer to the nations of the world and not to Israel.

P. 217, LAB 51.2: "milk of thy breasts": Philonenko, pp. 162-163, compares the frescoes of the synagogue at Dura Europus, depicting the well of Miriam from which come forth a dozen streams (of water, rather than milk, to be sure) destined for the twelve tribes of Israel. Philonenko also compares the Testament of Joseph, 19.5, which speaks of a dozen oxen, representing the twelve tribes, being suckled by a cow which produces a sea of milk. Protoevangel of James 6.3 reads: "Who will answer to the children of Reuben that Anna is suckling a child? Inform, inform the twelve tribes of Israel that Anna is suckling a child." Philonenko, p. 163, suggests that this is so close to LAB that one may with justice suppose that its author was acquainted with the traditions which LAB here attests. But a comparison of the texts shows that the points of comparison are hardly distinctive.

P. 217, LAB 51.3 ff.: Parallels to LAB's version of Hannah's prayer of thanks will be found in Targum 1 Samuel 2.1-11, Midrash Shemuel 4-6, 55-65, Batte Midrashoth 4.6-9, cited by Ginzberg, 6.219, n. 20. These texts, it should be noted, like ours, have a Messianic motif. Philonenko, p. 163, finds a Gnostic motif in the importance attached to the rite of suckling, since Samuel will drink a milk which is not only a physical drink but also the initiatory drink of Gnosis. In the portrait of Samuel the hierophant and illuminator Philonenko sees a parallel to the master of justice in the Dead Sea Hymns (1 QH 4.27): "Through me hast Thou illumined the faces of full many." It is true that, as Goodenough, *By Light, Light* (New Haven, 1935), pp. 265-266, and Steck, *Israel und das gewaltsame Geschick der Propheten* (Neukirchen, 1967), p. 176, have noted, there are many expressions in LAB embodying the terminology of illumination, but these are hardly distinctive, and surely prove no immediate tie with the Dead Sea Scrolls.

P. 217, LAB 51.3: "at my voice [*in voce mea*]": This is the reading of the *editio princeps.* The Admont MS. reads "with loud voice (*in voce magna*)."

P. 217, LAB 51.3: "boundaries" (*terminos*): Philonenko, p. 164, suggests that the Hebrew original for this was קצים, "times," "utmost limits," often found in the Dead Sea Scrolls in an eschatological sense.

P. 217, LAB 51.3: "horn": In Essene circles the horn symbolized the Messiah; cf. Syriac Psalms of David, 2.33-37.

P. 217, line 20 (margin), on LAB 51.4: Add cf. Isaiah 51.4.

P. 217, LAB 51.4: "Out of me shall arise the ordinance of the Lord": It is possible, though hardly necessary, to interpret this, as does Philonenko, p. 165, as an indication that Samuel was regarded as the incarnation of the Law; if it is so interpreted, compare the view of the Moreh Hazedek of the Dead Sea Scrolls as the Law incarnate.

P. 217, LAB 51.4: "all men": This is the reading of the *editio princeps*. The Admont and the other MSS. omit *omnes*, "all," but Philonenko, p. 165, restores it, since it is in accord with what he finds to be universalistic outlook of the hymn and parallels the Book of Hymns of the Dead Sea Scrolls (1 Q 6.12): "That all nations may know Thy truth." To this parallel Philonenko (*per litt.*) adds 11 Q Psᵃ 155.10: "That many may hear of your works and that the peoples may celebrate your glory." Some support for the reading *omnes* here, and consequently for LAB's universalism, may be fund in LAB 32.3, where all the MSS. agree: "Erit autem mea beautitudo super omnes homines."

P. 217, LAB 51.4: "The light shall come forth": Light is here the anticipated prophet. For the personification of wisdom, see Proverbs 8.30 and Wisdom of Solomon 9.4. Philonenko suggests that "out of which wisdom shall be born" may be a gloss.

P. 217, LAB 51.4: "which have most possessions": Perhaps parallel to Dead Sea Scrolls' (1 QS 11.2) מקני הון, "those who possess goods." Philonenko, p. 166, is on doubtful ground in implying a connection between an ideal of poverty here and in the Dead Sea Scrolls.

P. 217, line 28 (margin), on LAB 51.4: Add 1 Sam. 2⁵.

P. 217, line 30 (margin), on LAB 51.4: Add 1 Sam. 2⁶.

P. 217, line 33 (margin), on LAB 51.5: Add 1 Sam. 2⁹.

P. 218, LAB 51.5: "which holdeth" (*qui tenet*): Klausner, *The Messianic Idea in Israel*, p. 367, compares this clause to "until Shiloh come" (Genesis 49.10), with Shiloh being taken as *shello*, the one to whom shall be the obedience of the peoples. Hence *qui tenet* means "he who grasps," i.e., he who takes over the rulership and the one to whom shall be the obedience of the peoples. A. Strobel, "Eine Katechon-Parallele in Pseudo-Philo? Zur Interpretation von Cp. 51, 5," in *Untersuchungen zum Eschatologischen Verzögerungsproblem auf Grund der*

Spätjüdischurchristlichen Geschichte von Habakuk 2.2 ff. (Leiden, 1961), pp. 75-76, and Philonenko, p. 166, say that *qui tenet* refers to God Himself; but there is a sense of anticipation in the word *quousque,* "until," and it would make more sense to say that God reveals than that He is revealed.

P. 218, LAB 51.6: Only Pseudo-Philo among our authorities mentions the name of Hannah's father Batuel (Bethuel).

P. 218, line 8 (margin), on LAB 51.6: Add Isa. 51⁴.

P. 218, LAB 51.6: "bring forth a light": Philonenko, p. 167, aptly compares the pseudepigraphic *Joseph and Asenath,* 6: "What sort of belly will give birth to such a light?"

P. 218, line 9 (margin), on LAB 51.6: Add Cf. Jer. 1¹⁷, Job 38³.

P. 218, LAB 51.6: The connection of Asaph and Elkanah is also rabbinic: cf. Pesikta Rabbati, p. 43, 182a, noting that Asaph is identical with Tohu, the great-grand-father of Elkanah (cited by Ginzberg, 6.215, n. 1).

P. 218, line 15 (margin), on LAB 51.6: Add Cf. 1 Sam. 2¹⁰.

P. 218, LAB 51.6: "anointed": James, p. 42, asserts that the anointed (*christus*) of 51.6 refers to Saul, but if this were so we should have expected *det,* "until he [Samuel] give."

P. 218, line 18 (margin), on LAB 51.6: Add Isa. 51⁴.

P. 218, LAB 51.6: "until there arise a light unto this people (*lumen genti huic*)": The Admont MS. reads: "until he become a light unto the nations" (*lumen gentibus hic*). That the *editio princeps* is preferable, despite Philonenko, p. 167, is clear from the end of the next section (51.7), "let him be a light unto this nation (*lumen genti huic*)," where the MSS. do not disagree. Moreover, it would not make sense to say that Samuel should minister to God until he should become a light unto the nations, since no one anticipated that Samuel would be the Messiah.

P. 218 (margin) on LAB 51.7: Add 1 Sam. 2¹¹.

P. 218, LAB 52.1: Bethac: This name, otherwise unknown, is explained by Ginzberg, 6.221, n. 26, as a misreading for ק"א בית (*Beth Ak,* "House of God"), where Ak is an abbreviation for Elokim. Kisch's spelling, Betahc, is stemmatically impossible.

P. 219, line 1 (margin), on LAB 52.1: Add 1 Sam. 2³⁴.

P. 219, line 11, LAB 52.2: For "us," Kisch, following Admont, reads "you (*vos*)," which is stemmatically impossible.

P. 219, LAB 52.4: "their father": This insertion by James is found in the Admont MS., though omitted by the Melk MS.

P. 219, LAB 52.4: Ginzberg, 6.222, n. 27, cites an apt parallel (Yoma 85b): "If one says, 'I shall continue to sin and later repent,' the opportunity to repent is not granted to him."

P. 220, LAB 53.1: Josephus, *AJ* 5.348, says that Samuel had completed his twelfth year when he began to prophesy. We may deduce that the rabbis had a similar view from the fact that Midrash Tehillim 25, 212, states that Samuel ruled for forty years and that Midrash Shemuel 1.46 states that he died at the age of 52. It is possible that in our text XII was misread as VIII, though all our surviving MSS. read *octo,* "eight."

P. 220, line 10 (margin), on LAB 53.2: Add 1 Sam. 3⁷,³.

P. 220, LAB 53.2: For "would reveal" read "wished to reveal."

P. 220, LAB 53.3: Dietzfelbinger, p. 301, n. 523, objects that "And Heli said unto him . . . therefore ran I unto thee" have their rightful place after "thou didst never call me in the night." But the shift is unnecessary if we suppose that Eli's words "Woe is me, can it be that an unclean spirit hath deceived my son Samuel?" are spoken to himself.

P. 221, LAB 53.4: Ginzberg, 6.226, n. 40, emends "In thee do I behold" to "and now behold . . ." and "noonday" to "midnight."

P. 221 (margin) on LAB 53.5: For 1 Sam. 3⁸ read 1 Sam. 3⁶.

P. 221, LAB 53.5: After "a voice from heaven," Dietzfelbinger in his translation inserts "and when he perceived that the speech of his father had come down unto him" from 53.7, where he asserts that it is inappropriate (since God is speaking for the third time in His own person). But this is unnecessary since in 53.7 God is speaking in a manner similar to the way that He spoke the first two times, namely in the voice of Samuel's father; and it is only the fact that it is the third time that He is speaking out that verifies that it is indeed God who is speaking.

P. 221, line 10 (margin), on LAB 53.5: Add 1 Sam. 3⁸,⁹.

P. 221 (margin) on LAB 53.6: Add Cf. 1 Sam. 3¹¹.

P. 221, LAB 53.6: Dietzfelbinger, p. 243, understands Luke 22.50 and John 18.10, where the right ear of a slave of the high priest is cut off, in the light of this passage, stating that the right ear represents the ability to hear God. He also (p. 302, n. 534) cites as a parallel Josephus, *BJ* 2.147, in which the Essenes are said to be careful not to spit to the right. But there is a parallel to a later prohibition in rabbinic literature (Palestinian Talmud, Berakhoth 3.5); and the notion that the right side is favorable is widespread in Greek and Roman lore as well (cf., e.g, Catullus 45.9 and the commentary by C. J. Fordyce [Oxford, 1961], pp. 205-206).

P. 221 (margin) on LAB 53.7: For 3¹⁰ read 3⁸.

P. 221, LAB 53.7: "hast formed me": This is James' emendation to make this passage parallel with the same phrase in 53.6, but there is nothing wrong with the text, "knowest well [lit. more] concerning me," which is the unanimous reading of the MSS.

P. 221, LAB 53.8: "Verily I enlightened": Kisch, following the Admont MS., has the stemmatically impossible *illuminavi, illuminavi* ("I enlightened, I enlightened") instead of the Hebraic construction indicated in *illuminans illuminavi*.

P. 222 (margin) on LAB 53.9: Add Cf. Num. 16³.

P. 222, line 18 (margin), on LAB 53.10: For Deut. 22²⁶ read Dt. 22⁶.

P. 222, LAB 53.10: The connection of the sin of the sons of Eli with the sin of taking the mother bird with the young is unique with LAB. Ginzberg, 6.227, n. 40, suggests that the Hebrew original spoke of the commandment of קִנִּים (as the Talmud calls it in reference to Lev. 12.6), in the sense of an offering of purification for a woman after childbirth. LAB (52.1) speaks earlier of oblations which Eli's sons had seized, and it is these that are meant. The translator or glossator understood קִנִּים, however, in the sense of קַן צִפּוֹר, "bird's nest." But the whole point of 53.10 is that the parent (Eli in this case) is to perish with his sons; and this is the penalty, "measure for measure," for violating the commandment of removing the mother bird with its young, but not for seizing the offerings after childbirth.

P. 222 (margin) on LAB 53.12: Add 1 Sam. 3¹⁵.

P. 223 (margin) on LAB 53.13: Add 1 Sam. 3¹⁵.

P. 223, LAB 53.13: "which hath prophesied" (*prophetavit*): Kisch, following the Admont MS., has the stemmatically impossible *prophetabit*, "which will prophesy."

P. 223 (margin) on LAB 54.2: For 4⁵,⁶ read 4⁵.

P. 223, LAB 54.2: Cf. Eliyahu Rabbah 12.57.

P. 223, LAB 54.2: For *befel* read *befell*.

P. 223 (margin) on LAB 54.3: For 4¹⁰ read 4¹⁰,¹¹.

P. 224, LAB 54.4: In identifying as Saul the nameless man of Benjamin (1 Samuel 4.12) who ran to Shiloh with the news of the Israelite loss LAB agrees with rabbinic tradition. Cf. Midrash Shemuel 11.78-79, Midrash Tehillim 7,63, Tosefta-Targum 1 Sam. 4.12, cited by Ginzberg, 6.231, n. 48.

P. 224, line 5 (margin), on LAB 54.4: Put 1 Sam. 4[12] two lines above.

P. 224 (margin) on LAB 54.5: For 4[18] read 4[18,19].

P. 224, LAB 54.5: "from the truth [a veritate]": The Admont MS. has a vertice, "utterly," which makes better sense.

P. 224, line 19 (margin), on LAB 54.5: Add 1 Sam. 4[18].

P. 224, LAB 54.6: "Where is the glory?": In 1 Samuel 4.21 the name is Ichabod, i.e., "no glory." Similarly in Josephus, AJ 5.360, the name is said to signify πατριά, "no glory," "ingloriousness." Perhaps the Latin translator had before him אי כבוד of the Hebrew text and read it as איה כבוד, "where is glory?"

P. 224, line 35 (margin), on LAB 55.1: Add 7[17].

P. 225, LAB 55.1: "destruction": All MSS. read exercitum, "army." James apparently understands it (and presumably emended it with good reason) as exitium, "destruction."

P. 225, line 16 (margin), on LAB 55.2: Add Cf. 1 Sam. 6[4(5)].

P. 225, LAB 55.3: "going forth [exitu]": Perhaps we should translate "end."

P. 225 (margin) on LAB 55.4: For 5[6] read 5[10].

P. 226, line 1 (margin), on LAB 55.4: Omit 1 Sam. 5[11].

P. 226, line 5 (margin), on LAB 55.4: Add 1 Sam. 5[7].

P. 226, line 7 (margin), on LAB 55.4: Add 1 Sam. 5[3,4].

P. 226, LAB 55.5: Josephus, AJ 6.8-10, likewise presents a dispute among the priests and diviners as to what to do; the fact that it is also found in LAB argues against Thackeray's theory (Loeb Library, ap. AJ 6.8) that Josephus' version is the invention of his "Sophoclean" assistant.

P. 226, LAB 55.5: "affliction": Lit., "dominion," "despotism."

P. 226, line 34, note on LAB 55.5: For 1 Sam. 6[7] read 1 Sam. 6[9].

P. 226, LAB 55.7: "assay [temptemus]": Stemmatically the reading to be preferred is tempus ("time"), which makes no sense.

P. 226, LAB 55.7: "at the head of three ways": Josephus, AJ 6.11, very similarly remarks: "Then having driven them, drawing the ark, out to a place where three roads met, thy should leave them. . . ."

P. 226, LAB 55.7: "For the middle way leadeth": The editio princeps reads dirigite, hence "lead along the middle way," which is stemmatically more probable.

P. 227, LAB 55.7 (end): James follows the editio princeps, which makes the best sense. Kisch, following the Admont, Vatican, and Vienna MSS., reads: "And now therefore we shall deny our gods."

P. 227 (margin) on LAB 55.9: Add 1 Sam. 6[21].

P. 227, LAB 55.9: Ginzberg, 6.224, n. 34, notes that LAB's statement that the Philistines brought the ark to Shiloh contradicts 1 Samuel 6.12, as well as LAB 55.7, and suggests that for Allophili, "Philistines," we should read Israel or populi.

P. 227 (margin) on LAB 56.2: Add 1 Sam. 8[6].

P. 228, LAB 56.2: Mekhilta Debarim 5.6 likewise believes that the first national duty was building the Temple and that the appointment of a king was secondary. LAB apparently is in accord with Rabbi Nehorai (Nehemiah in the Munich MS. of the Talmud) that the statement about appointment of a king is not a command but a prediction of the Israelites' future murmurings, and thus disagrees with Rabbis Jose and Judah (Sanhedrin 20b), who believe that the Israelites, upon entering the land of Israel, are commanded to appoint a king, wipe out the Amalekites, and build the Temple, in that order. Ginzberg, 6.230, n. 47, also notes that the expression petentibus regem ante tempus, "inasmuch as these desire a king before the time," is practically identical with the language of Sifre Debarim 156.

P. 228 (margin) on LAB 56.3: Add 1 Sam. 8[9].

P. 228, line 10 (margin), on LAB 56.3: For 1 Sam. 9^{15} read 9^{15}.

P. 228, LAB 56.3: In 1 Samuel 9.15 it is during the day that God reveals to Samuel the forthcoming visit of Saul, whereas here and in Josephus, *AJ* 6.37-40, God appears during the night.

P. 228, LAB 56.4 ff.: Spiro, "Pseudo-Philo's Saul and the Rabbis' Messiah ben Ephraim," *PAAJR*, 22 (1953), pp. 119 ff., discusses a number of un-Biblical features in LAB's portrait of Saul: he is an Ephraimite rather than a Benjaminite, he is not called "the anointed," he is not brave, and the burden of his selection rests on Samuel, with God's role diminished. For a reply to Spiro see now Dietzfelbinger, pp. 82-85.

P. 228, LAB 56.4: Baam: LAB is here following the LXX, which renders *bamah* (1 Samuel 9.14) as a proper name Βαμᾶ instead of "high place."

P. 228, line 19 (margin), on LAB 56.4: For 9^9 read $9^{18,9}$.

P. 228, line 21 (margin), on LAB 56.4: For 9^{16} read 9^{19}.

P. 228, line 28 (margin), on LAB 56.5: Add 1 Sam. 9^{24}.

P. 228, line 31 (margin), on LAB 56.5: Add 1 Sam. 10^1.

P. 228, line 36 (margin), on LAB 56.6: Add Cf. Jer. 1^6.

P. 229, line 1, LAB 56.6: "Who will grant . . .": This is a Hebraism which is equivalent to "Would that. . . ."

P. 229, line 7 (margin), on LAB 56.7: Add 1 Sam. 8^5.

P. 229, line 10 (margin), on LAB 56.7: Add 1 Sam. 10^9.

P. 229, LAB 56.7: LAB is perhaps significantly silent about the anointing of Saul as king (1 Samuel 10.1).

P. 229, LAB 56.7: "the book of the kings": In referring thus to the Book of Samuel, LAB follows the arrangement of the LXX.

P. 229 (margin) on LAB 57.1 :For 1 Sam. 12^{1-4} read 1 Sam. 12^{1-3}.

P. 229, LAB 57.1: For Lord (*Dominus*), which is stemmatically impossible, read God (*Deus*).

P. 229, LAB 57.2: On the comparison of Samuel with Moses see Midrash Shemuel 9.74-75 and other passages cited by Ginzberg, 6.229, n. 43. According to rabbinic tradition (Midrash Tehillim 99.424 and Seder Olam 20, cited by Ginzberg, 6.99, n. 561 and 6.215, n. 1) Samuel was a descendant of Korah; hence the aptness of Samuel's reference to that episode. On Samuel's incorruptibility see Makkoth 23b, Bereshith Rabbah 85.1, and Midrash Shemuel 14.90-91, cited by Ginzberg, 6.228, n. 43. The connection of Moses' statement in Numbers 16.15 and Samuel's in 1 Samuel 12.3, namely that both deny having taken anyone's ass, is found also in Nedarim 38a. The connection of the punishment of Korah and his followers with the false accusation of Moses on grounds of corruptibility is likewise found in Josephus, *AJ* 4.46-50.

P. 229, line 20 (margin), on LAB 57.2: Add Num. 16^{15}.

P. 229, line 27 (margin), on LAB 57.3: Add 12^5.

P. 229, LAB 57.3: Dietzfelbinger, p. 305, n. 569, speculates that "my father's house" may refer to the Temple; but that "my father" does not refer to God seems indicated by the use of the same expression in 56.6, though perhaps the fact that earlier (53.5) God likens Himself to Samuel's father is evidence for Dietzfelbinger's conjecture. Spiro, "Pseudo-Philo's Saul," p. 130, n. 22, speculating on LAB's motive in omitting specifically the Biblical injunction (1 Samuel 15.3) to wipe out Amalek's oxen, sheep, camels, and asses, suggests that perhaps he was prompted by more mundane considerations, namely, that since the Hasmonean armies (who are contemporary with the author, according to Spiro's dating of LAB) were heavily dependent on booty, they could not afford the luxury of such destruction. But even if Spiro's dating is correct, the Bible does not prohibit plundering in general, but rather in this specific case, and since the Hasmoneans did not fight the Amalekites they needed no justification for their policy.

P. 229, line 33 (margin), on LAB 57.4: Add 1 Sam. 8[5].

P. 230, line 3 (margin), on LAB 57.4: Add 1 Sam. 13[9].

P. 230, LAB 57.4: "And when the king was appointed [*et constituto rege*]": This is the reading of Phillipps 461; the Admont and Melk MSS., reading "while the king exists [*consistente rege*]," connect this phrase with the previous sentence.

P. 230, line 10 (margin), on LAB 58.1: Add Dt. 25[19].

P. 230 (margin) on LAB 58.2: Add 1 Sam. 15[7].

P. 230, line 15 (margin), on LAB 58.2: For 15[8] read 1 Sam. 15[8,9].

P. 230, LAB 58.2: LAB, as Ginzberg, 6.233, n. 62, points out, is here in disagreement with rabbinic tradition (Yoma 22b, Midrash Shemuel 18.99, Targum 1 Samuel 16.4), according to which Saul was so wealthy that he had no interest in the Amalekite booty. Josephus, *AJ* 6.137, like LAB, gives a reason for Saul's sparing of Agag. But in Josephus the reason is aesthetic, namely, admiration for Agag's beauty and stature.

P. 230, LAB 58.2: "Armathem": According to 1 Samuel 15.12, 21, and 33, Agag is brought to Gilgal.

P. 230, LAB 58.3: The un-Scriptural notion that a descendant of Agag will cause ruin to the Jews is connected with the tradition that Haman was a descendant of the Amalekites and sought vengeance on the Jews for this reason. In this LAB parallels Josephus, *AJ* 11.211. Megillah 13a, and Targum on Esther 3.6.

P. 230, LAB 58.3: "they shall preserve": This is the reading of the Vatican MS. Both the *editio princeps* and the Admont MS. read *consuluerunt*, "they have concerned themselves with."

P. 230 (margin) on LAB 58.4: 15[13] (read 15[12,13]) should be on line 29, not line 30.

P. 231, line 5 (margin), on LAB 58.4: For 1 Sam. 15[3] read 1 Sam. 15[33,34].

P. 231, LAB 58.4: LAB here follows the Hebrew text and LXX in stating that Samuel slew Agag. Josephus, *AJ* 6.155, apparently because he regarded Samuel as a Nazirite, who consequently would be forbidden to touch a corpse, says that he merely ordered him to be put to death.

P. 231 (margin) on LAB 59.1: Add 16[1-3].

P. 231 (margin) on LAB 59.2: 16[4-7] should be on line 11, not on line 12.

P. 231, LAB 59.2: Cf. Sifre Debarim 17, Midrash Tannaim 10, Tanḥuma Vayera 6, Midrash Shemuel 14,88, cited by Ginzberg, 6.248, n. 19.

P. 231, LAB 59.2: "Bethel": The Hebrew text (1 Sam. 16.4), LXX, and Josephus (*AJ* 6.157) all read Bethlehem. Bethel is an error, easily explained, for Bethlehem (see James, p. 276, s.v. Bethel).

P. 231, LAB 59.2: "the holy one, the anointed" (*sanctus christus*): This corresponds to משיח הקדוש, which is a phrase not found in the Bible or in rabbinic writings but which does appear in two places in the Dead Sea Scrolls (CD 6.1 and Barthelémy and Milik, 1.132, no. 30), cited by P. Winter, "The Holy Messiah," *Zeitschrift für die Neutestamentliche Wissenschaft*, 50 (1959), p. 275.

P. 231, line 18 (margin), on LAB 59.2: Add 1 Sam. 9[10].

P. 231, line 20 (margin), on LAB 59.2: Add 1 Sam. 16[11,12].

P. 231 (margin) on LAB 59.3: For 16[11] on line 22 read 16[11-13] on line 21.

P. 231, LAB 59.4: In the Dead Sea Scrolls (11 Q Ps[a]) the total number of psalms composed by David is said to be 4050. Josephus, *AJ* 7.6, mentions songs of David (laments and eulogies for the funeral of Saul and Jonathan), which survived until his own day but which presumably were not to be found in the Bible. Josephus also (*AJ* 6.166) mentions, in an extra-Biblical addition, that at this point David began to prophesy, though Josephus does not give the contents of this psalm. The Hebraic character of the psalm is clearly recognizable, as shown in the attempt to reconstruct the Hebrew original by J. Strugnell, "More Psalms of David," *Catholic Biblical Quarterly*, 27 (1965), pp. 207-216. Psalm 151 of Grotto 11 of Qumran (see J. A. Sanders, in *Discoveries in the*

Judaean Desert of Jordan, vol. 4 [Oxford, 1965], pp. 54-55) resembles this hymn in that it, too, is by David and mentions the anointing of David by Samuel. But, as Delcor, pp. 1366-1367, comments, our psalm is very far in spirit and language from the Essenes and Qumran.

P. 231, LAB 59.4: One of the paintings found at Dura shows the six brothers of David in a hieratic pose that is nowhere else to be found. Goodenough, *Jewish Symbols,* vol. 9, 190-191, suggests that this passage in LAB referring to David as being in the care of angels and guardians is the only passage by a Jew that might explain David's standing with the mystical holy seven.

P. 231, line 36 (margin), on LAB 59.4: Add Cf. Ps. 27^{10}.

P. 232, LAB 59.4: "they called [*clamaverunt*]": Strugnell, p. 213, comments that the use of *clamo* in the sense of "summon" is unusual, and that the difference from Old Latin in choice of vocabulary is significant; but *clamo,* used to mean "invoke," "call upon," with the accusative of the person as here, is frequently found from the time of Plautus (see Harper's Latin Dictionary, s.v. *clamo,* II) ; and DuCange's dictionary, s.v. *clamare,* 1, likewise shows the frequency of its use in the sense of "call" or "summon."

P. 232, line 2, LAB 59.4: For *forgat* read *forgot.*

P. 232, LAB 59.4: "all the days": James has adopted the reading of the *editio princeps—omnes dies.* Kisch, following the Admont MS., reads *dies istos,* "those days," which, as Strugnell, p. 214, remarks, is certainly the more difficult reading. But, as he notes, the phrase כל ימי חיי is such a stereotyped phrase in Hebrew.

P. 232 (margin) on LAB 59.5: For 1 Sam. 17^{34} ,read 1 Sam. 17$^{34-37}$.

P. 232, LAB 59.5: Ginzberg, 6.248, n. 15, notes that the fact that the bear was a female reflects the belief, also found in Bereshith Rabbah 87, that the female is more fierce than the male. He also conjectures that *bulls* may be a misreading of שׂה (sheep, as in 1 Samuel 17.34 and Josephus, *AJ* 6.282) as שׁר "bull." But שׁוֹר is usually spelled with a *vav.*

P. 232, LAB 59.5: "And this shall be a sign unto thee": Similarly, as Ginzberg, 6.248, n. 15, remarks, Mekilta Amalek 2,56a says, with reference to David's slaughter of the wild beast, that a sign was given to him.

P. 232 (margin) on LAB 60.1: For 16^{14} read 16^{14} sqq·.

P. 232, line 22 (margin), on LAB 60.1: Add 16^{23}.

P. 232, LAB 60.1 ff.: M. Philonenko, "Remarques sur un hymne essénien de caractère gnostique," *Semitica,* 11 (1961), pp. 43 ff., has an extensive commentary on this psalm, which he calls an Essene hymn of Gnostic character. This psalm, like 59.4, is another of the non-canonical psalms of David. The Genesis Apocryphon (20.16-24) and the Prayer of Nabonides make of Abraham and David types of Essene exorcists. For variant readings of this psalm see James, pp. 22 ff.

P. 232, LAB 60.1: "spirit of the Lord": This, the reading of the *editio princeps,* is in accord with the Hebrew text, LXX, and Vulgate, the Admont MS. reading "holy spirit," is the *lectio difficilior.*

P. 232, line 20 (margin), on LAB 60.1: Add 1 Sam. 16^{19}.

P. 232, LAB 60.2: This psalm, the most mystical passage in LAB, is centered on מעשה בראשית, "the work of creation." The primordial silence is also mentioned by the Syriac Apocalypse of 2 Baruch 3.7. Philonenko, p. 48, suggests that speculations such as these about silence were favored among the Essene circles, since, as Josephus, *BJ* 2.133, notes, the Essenes were particularly addicted to silence, which to outsiders took on the air of some awful mystery; but there is no evidence that their silence led to speculations about silence. The primordial syzygy of Darkness and Silence is to be found in Gnostic speculation. In Valentinian Gnosticism (Irenaeus, *Adversus Haereses,* 1.1.1) we read of   βυθός (the depth) and σιγή (silence) as partners. The antithesis that from silence came speech (λόγος) is found in Ignatius of Antioch, *Magnesians*, 8.2, *Evangelium Veritatis*, 27.10-12, and Mark the Magician (*ap.* Irenaeus, *Adversus Haereses*, 1.14.3), cited by Philonenko, pp. 49-50. The *Evangelium Veritatis*, 137. 10 ff., attributed by some to Valentinus, similarly speaks of "the mind which pronounces the unique word in silent grace." LAB's doctrine of the complementary nature of light and darkness is in opposition to that of the Manual of Discipline (1 QS 3.13-4.26), which speaks of light and darkness as antithetical. It is also in opposition to the midrashic statement (Shemoth Rabbah, 15.22), according to which darkness is born from water, and light from fire.

P. 232, LAB 60.2: "Then was thy name created": Philonenko, p. 50, interprets this to refer to God's name, but it is clear that in this psalm David addresses the evil spirit, and that "the tribe of spirits" at the end of this section refers to demons; moreover, David would hardly say (60.3) that God walks in Hell or that the Messiah born of David's loins would subdue God.

P. 232, line 32 (margin), on LAB 60.2: Add Cf. Gen. $1^{11,12}$.

P. 232, LAB 60.2: "man that should be made [*homini qui factus est*]": James, p. 22, upholds this, the reading of the Admont, Vienna, Vatican, and Cambridge MSS., on the ground that the point of the invective is that the evil spirits are a creation secondary to man. Philonenko, p. 51, favors the reading of the *editio princeps, omnibus quae facta sunt*, "all things that were made," on the ground that this is the *lectio difficilior*. The fact that in LAB 3.2 a similar variant occurs (*omnibus* vs. *hominibus*) and that there *omnibus* is the superior reading hardly proves that *homini* is preferable here, since *omnibus* and *hominibus* are easily confused transcriptionally, whereas this is not true for *omnibus* and *homini*; with Philonenko, we prefer the *editio princeps*.

P. 232, LAB 60.3: Dietzfelbinger, pp. 87 and 308, n. 605, takes issue with James' note, p. 233, and argues that we are dealing here with the creation of the name (60.2), not the creation of the demons themselves. But the end of 60.2 speaks of "the tribe of your spirits," where "your" refers not to the name but to the demon himself.

P. 232, LAB 60.3: "a second creation": Jubilees 2.2 asserts that the spirits were created on the first day; II Enoch 29.1 indicates that they were created on the second day.

P. 233, LAB 60.3: "unto many" [*multis: editio princeps*; the reading of the Vatican, Vienna, Cambridge, Admont, and Melk MSS. is *in multis*, "in many ways" (Dietzfelbinger, p. 308, n. 615), "among many"]: Philonenko, pp. 51-52, thinks that the many are הרבים, as used in the Dead Sea Scrolls to denote the adherents of the sect (the expression is particularly prominent in the second of the five Syriac psalms of David), and that the scene is a séance of exorcism held in the midst of an Essene community. But there is no evidence that this is a séance; nor is Dietzfelbinger, p. 308, n. 615, justified in concluding that since the scene (60.1) is at night it could not take place before an audience. M. Wadsworth (*per litt.*), citing Psalm 138.1, suggests that *multi* stands for angels, but the passage in Psalms does not have the equivalent of *multi*, and the only parallel is in "I sing praise (*psallo*)." In the Dead Sea Scrolls angels are referred to as "hosts," not as "the many."

P. 233, LAB 60.3: "echo": Philonenko, p. 52, notes that the distinction between the Echo and the Logos is typical of Valentinian Gnosticism.

P. 233, LAB 60.3: "new womb": Cf. 1 QH 3.9-10: "For now, amid throes of death, new life is coming to birth."

P. 233, LAB 60.3: "he that shall subdue you": James, p. 60, and Dietzfelbinger, p. 152, identify this as Solomon the master of demons (*Wisdom of Solomon*, 7.17-22, Josephus, *AJ* 8.45-49); but Riessler, p. 1318, and Philonenko, p. 52, identify him as the Messiah, who, according to the Testament of Levi 18, will at the end of time bind Belial and trample under foot the evil spirits. The phrase "after a time" points to the latter interpretation.

P. 233, LAB 61.1: The incident of David's encounter with the Midianites is unique with LAB.

P. 233, LAB 61.2: "Art not thou Saul": James does not indicate that "Saul" is his emendation, since all the MSS. read "Israel." Dietzfelbinger, p. 310, n. 625, follows James; in view of "And now that thou reignest" one expects "Saul" here. If James' emendation is correct, LAB is unique in having Goliath challenge Saul directly.

P. 233, line 23 (margin), on LAB 61.2: Add 1 Sam. 17⁹.

P. 234, LAB 61.2: "serve our gods": In the Bible (1 Samuel 17.9) the Israelites are told that if they lose to Goliath they will serve "us," i.e. the Philistines (not, as here, the Philistine gods).

P. 234, LAB 61.2: "40 days": So also Sotah 42b makes the same comparison in commenting on 1 Samuel 17.16: " 'And presented himself forty days.' R. Johanan said: [The period] corresponds to the forty days in which the Torah was given."

P. 234 (margin) on LAB 61.3: Add 17²².

P. 234, line 10 (margin), on LAB 61.3: For 17²³ read 17¹⁶,²⁸,²².

P. 234, line 16 (margin), on LAB 61.4: Add 1 Sam. 17³²,³⁶(LXX).

P. 234, LAB 61.4: For *eam* (James: "I will go"), which is grammatically and stemmatically impossible, read *iam* ("presently").

P. 234, LAB 61.5: LAB is unique in asserting that there were seven stones, and not five, as found in the Bible (1 Sam. 17.40).

P. 234, LAB 61.5: "Cervihel": Spiro, *Manners,* pp. 221-226, wonders why LAB chooses to detract from David's achievements by introducing an angel to assist him. He conjectures that LAB did so because there is a discrepancy in the Bible as to who slew Goliath, David (1 Samuel 17.20-58) or Elhanan (2 Samuel 21.19 and 1 Chronicles 20.5). Spiro theorizes that Goliath claimed that an angel (Elhanan is a theophoric name such as angels customarily bore) killed him; hence LAB's version. But the midrashic tradition reconciles the Biblical discrepancy by assigning many names to David (see Ginzberg, 6.260, n. 78), and, in any case, if LAB wished to suggest that Elhanan was an angel it should have given him that name instead of the name Cervihel, which is apparently another spelling for Zeruel (27.10), since both angels are set over strength.

P. 234, LAB 61.6: On the blood-relationship of David and Goliath see Sotah 42b, Tanhuma (Buber) 1.208, Ruth Rabbah 1.14, Ruth Zuta 4.20, Midrash Shemuel 20.106-108, cited by Ginzberg, 6.250, n. 27. "Thy mother (*mater tua*)" presumably means "thy ancestress," since Ruth must thus be taken.

P. 234, James' note on LAB 61.6: The *Quaestiones Hebraicae* is ascribed to Jerome.

P. 235, line 8 (margin), on LAB 61.6: Add Cf. 2 Sam. 21¹⁵⁻²².

P. 235, LAB 61.6: "thy three brethren": In 2 Samuel 21.15-22 there are four giants, they are not brethren, and they are slain not by David but by his men; Midrash Tehillim 18.5 agrees with LAB in declaring that it was David himself who slew these giants.

P. 235 (margin) on LAB 61.7: For 1 Sam. 17⁴⁹ read 1 Sam. 17⁴⁹⁻⁵¹.

P. 235 (margin) on LAB 61.9: Add 17⁵⁵⁻⁵⁸.

P. 235, LAB 61.9: Ginzberg, 6.252, n. 44, plausibly suggests that for "lifted up" the original Hebrew read [ה=א] נשא ("changed"), which was misread as נשא ("lifted up").

P. 235 (margin) on LAB 62.1: Add 18¹ ˢqq·.

P. 235, line 30 (margin), on LAB 62.1: Add 1 Sam. 19¹⁸.

P. 235, LAB 62.2: LAB gives the content of Saul's prophecy, whereas the Bible (1 Sam. 19.23) does not do so.

P. 235, line 36 (margin), on LAB 62.2: Add Cf 1 Sam. 31⁶.

P. 235, LAB 62.2: "thy son [*filius tuus*]": Ginzberg, 6.269, n. 113, emends to *filios tuos*, "your sons," which is the wrong case: grammar requires *filii tui*, which, as an emendation, is transcriptionally less probable than *filios tuos*. He made this emendation presumably because in 1 Samuel 31.6, we read that Saul died together with his three sons. But the context has just spoken (62.1) and will speak further (62.3 ff.) of the covenant between David and Saul's son Jonathan; and Saul is undoubtedly preoccupied with this son of his above all.

P. 236 (margin) on LAB 62.3: Add 1 Sam. 18³.

P. 236, line 8 (margin), on LAB 62.3: Add 1 Sam. 20³.

P. 236, LAB 62.4: "that the multitude of the prudent might hear the sentence [*ut audiant determinationem multitudo prudentium*]": James is here translating the *editio princeps*. The Admont and Vatican MSS. read: "so that he [Saul] may hear the resolutions of the assembled wise men" (*ut audiat determinationes congregatorum prudentium*).

P. 236, LAB 62.5: The concept of *ius talionis* here, namely, that if Saul kills David Saul too will die is not found in 1 Samuel 20.

P. 236, line 23 (margin), on LAB 62.5: Add Ps. 151¹(LXX).

P. 236, LAB 62.5: "For I was least among my brethren, feeding the sheep": The opening phrases of the Dead Sea Psalm 151 A are very similar, though not verbatim as claimed by J. A. Sanders, *The Dead Sea Psalms Scroll* (Ithaca, N.Y., 1967), p. 96, n. 2: "Smaller was I than my brothers, and the youngest of the sons of my father, so he made me shepherd of his flock."

P. 236, LAB 62.5: "the righteousness of my father": LAB here alludes to the tradition that Jesse, the father of David, was one of four who died because the serpent caused Adam and Eve to sin, rather than because of their own sin. Ginzberg, 6.245, n. 7, suggests that the Hebrew original may have read צדקת אבו', where אבו' is the abbreviation for אבות, "fathers," but which the translator read as אבי, "my father." But there is an obvious contrast between "thy father" of the previous question (and "thy father's" of the second half of this sentence) and "my father," and hence there is no need for the emendation.

P. 236, LAB 62.6: "flesh and blood": Cf. Matthew 16.17: "For flesh and blood has not revealed this to you" (Philonenko, *per litt.*).

P. 236, LAB 62.6: "harp": Though the context favors such a translation, there is no basis for it in the text, which reads *lancea*, "lance."

P. 237, line 11 (margin), on LAB 62.8: Add 1 Sam. 20⁸.

P. 237, line 18 (margin), on LAB 62.9: Add Cf. 1 Sam. 20¹⁷.

P. 237, line 26 (margin), on LAB 62.10: Add 20²³.

P. 238, line 12 (margin), on LAB 62.11: For 1 Sam. 20⁴² read 1 Sam. 20⁴¹, 21¹ (20⁴² LXX).

P. 238 (margin) on LAB 63.1: Add 22¹⁸,¹⁹.

P. 238, LAB 63.1: There is, as Ginzberg, 6.238, n. 78, remarks, a direct contrast between LAB's unfavorable opinion of the priests of Nob and the rabbinic tradition (Tanhuma [Buber] 3.45, Palestinian Sanhedrin 10.29a, Targum 1 Samuel 22.18) that the eighty-five priests of Nob whom Saul slew were worthy to be high priests. Josephus, *AJ* 6.260, we may add, bridges the difference between the two traditions by connecting the fate of the priests of Nob with God's prediction that by reason of the iniquities of Eli's two sons his posterity would be destroyed.

P. 238 (margin) on LAB 63.2: Add 1 Sam. 22¹³.

P. 238, LAB 63.2: Doech the Syrian: LAB and Josephus, *AJ* 6.244, follow the LXX; according to the Hebrew text he was an Edomite. Dietzfelbinger, who has (p. 92) an excursus on Doeg, is thus wrong in stating that LAB is alone in presenting Doeg as a Syrian and in arguing that this supports the thesis (Dietzfelbinger, pp. 61-62) that LAB is struggling against the religion of Mithraism brought from Syria.

P. 238, line 23 (margin), on LAB 63.2: Add 22[10].

P. 238, line 27 (margin), on LAB 63.2: For 22[16] read 22[16-19].

P. 238, LAB 63.2: "And Saul slew Abimelec": According to the Hebrew text (1 Sam. 22.18), LXX, and Josephus (*AJ* 6.259), it was Doeg who carried out Saul's order, rather than Saul himself who killed Ahimelech and his kin.

P. 238, line 29 (margin), on LAB 63.2: Add 22[20,21].

P. 238, LAB 63.3: "And God said": The text reads merely: "And then he said to him," where the subject is David, as we might expect from the end of 63.2 (where David is addressed) and from 1 Samuel 22.22. But the rest of 63.3, especially the statement "I will deliver them into the hands of their enemies," sounds as if God is the speaker.

P. 238, line 34 (margin), on LAB 63.3: Add Cf. 1 Sam. 14[45].

P. 238, LAB 63.3: LAB gives the number of slain priests as 385 (the Admont MS. has 375); and Ginzberg, 6.238, n. 78, comments that this is the number found in the LXX, whereas the Hebrew (1 Samuel 22.18) has only 85. Actually the LXX has 305. The MSS. of Josephus, *AJ* 6.260, dealing with this incident, are a good control, but they contain four different readings—85 (obviously corrected to conform with the Hebrew text), 305 (the Latin translation, obviously corrected to conform with the LXX), 530 (the reading of the Greek epitome), and 385 (the reading of the three oldest, though admittedly not always the best, MSS. of Josephus). In 6.268 Josephus himself, recounting this incident, gives the number of those slain as 300, but this is clearly a round number. The fact that the reading of the Admont MS. is nowhere supported by any of the various readings of Josephus argues against it, and it is now clear from Harrington's collation, soon to be published, that the Admont reading is indeed stemmatically impossible. The fact that LAB agrees with MSS. MSP of Josephus in giving 385 as the number supports this reading of Josephus; Marcus' text in the Loeb Classical Library should consequently be corrected from 305 to 385. B. Heller, "Ginzberg's Legends of the Jews," *Jewish Quarterly Review*, 24 (1933-34), pp. 189-190, cites this passage as proof that LAB made use of the LXX, but he is relying upon Ginzberg's misreading of the LXX.

P. 239, line 3 (margin), on LAB 63.3: For 1 Sam. 31 read 1 Sam 31[1] sqq.

P. 239, LAB 63.3: "they shall fall down wounded": LAB is here following the reading of the LXX of 1 Samuel 31.1, which, when recounting the actual event, says that the Israelites fell down wounded. The Hebrew text, followed by Josephus (*AJ* 6.369), says that they fell slain.

P. 239, LAB 63.4: The Mishnah in Sanhedrin 90a (so also Bereshith Rabbah 32.1 and 38.1, Eliyahu Rabbah 18.107) states that Doeg is one of the four commoners who have no portion in the world to come. R. Johanan (Sanhedrin 106b) speaks of a destroying angel who burnt Doeg's soul. Dietzfelbinger, p. 92, is wrong in claiming that Sanhedrin 104b (his citation should be corrected) asserts that Doeg has a share in the future world. On being eaten by worms see LAB 44.9.

P. 239 (margin) on LAB 63.6: Add 25[1], 28[3].

P. 239, LAB 63.6: Kisch, following the division in the Admont MS., makes this section the beginning of 64.1, as is more logical.

P. 239, LAB 63.6: Italicize "Samuel died . . . buried him."

P. 239, LAB 64.1: LAB is unique, as Ginzberg, 6.235-236, n. 73, remarks, in assigning this selfish motive to Saul's action in expelling the sorcerers, though the Midrashim (e.g., Pirke di R. Eliezer 33) do note the inconsistency in Saul's behavior in first expelling the sorcerers and then seeking the advice of the witch of Endor. As for Saul's motive, I Macc. 5.57 has similar language: "Let us also get us a name."

P. 239, LAB 64.1: "So shall men remember me": This, the reading of the *editio princeps,* is stemmatically impossible. The reading of the Admont and other MSS. is: "So shall he [presumably God] remember me."

P. 240, LAB 64.3: "Sedecla": LAB is unique in giving the name Sedecla to the witch of Endor.

P. 240, line 6, LAB 64.3: "Which [*qui*]" refers to Debin (or Adod) since the reading *que* (*quae*) adopted by Kisch (which would refer to Sedecla) is stemmatically impossible.

P. 240, James' note on 64.3: The *Quaestiones Hebraicae* is ascribed to Jerome.

P. 240, LAB 64.5: "the woman saw Samuel coming up, and beheld Saul with him": LAB, as Dietzfelbinger in his commentary notes, is here combining the Hebrew text of 1 Samuel 28.12, which reads "Samuel," and the reading "Saul" of certain MSS. of the LXX.

P. 240, line 24 (margin), on LAB 64.5: 28^{13} should be one line below.

P. 240 (margin) on LAB 64.6: Add $28^{14,13}$.

P. 241, LAB 64.6: "mantle": LAB has transliterated the Greek word *diplois,* which is used by the LXX (1 Sam. 28.14) and by Josephus (*AJ* 6.333).

P. 241, LAB 64.6: The depiction of Samuel as clad in a white robe and with two angels accompanying him leads Goodenough (*By Light, Light* [New Haven, 1935], p. 266) to remark that it is very tempting to identify him with the Logos. In his *Jewish Symbols,* vol. 13, p. 228, thirty years later, the identification becomes definite. But the white robe is simply the white shroud in which every dead Israelite has been and is buried. According to Jewish tradition (see Thackeray, in Loeb edition of Josephus, *AJ* 6.333), Samuel's robe was the one in which he had been buried; indeed, it is the general view of rabbinic tradition that the dead will rise clothed as they were when they were buried (see Palestinian Talmud, Shebi'ith 9.32b and other citations in Ginzberg, 6.237, n. 77). To be sure, the witch of Endor does not understand this and thinks that the white robe signifies that Samuel is a god (like a God, according to Josephus, *AJ* 6.333). The attempt to identify Samuel as an angel by his dress through citing LAB 9.10 and Ezekiel 9.2 as parallels is hardly justified, since not only angels are clothed in white linen, but ordinary Israelites are buried in white linen shrouds. The depiction of Samuel in a white robe at Dura (Goodenough, *Jewish Symbols,* vol. 9, p. 170) is of no special significance, since the Jews there would know the meaning of a white robe; and even if one sees a parallel between the depiction of Samuel here in LAB and in Dura there is hardly any justification for identifying Samuel with the Logos in particular. The two angels are LAB's innovation, based presumably on the tradition that a man has two guardian angels who accompany him (Ginzberg, 5.76, n. 20), though rabbinic tradition (Hagigah 4b) interprets "godlike beings coming up out of the earth" (1 Samuel 28.13) as a reference to Samuel being accompanied by Moses.

P. 241, line 4 (margin), on LAB 64.6: For 1 Sam. 19^{27} read 1 Sam. 15^{27}.

P. 241, LAB 64.6: "And Saul remembered the mantle": The rabbis disagree as to whether Samuel's or Saul's garment was then torn; see Ruth Rabbah 41.8 and Midrash Shemuel 18.100, cited by Ginzberg, 6.237, n. 77.

P. 241, LAB 64.6: "while he lived": This is the reading of the *editio princeps.* The Admont MS. reads: "when Samuel slew him."

P. 241, LAB 64.6: "smote his hands together and cast himself": All the MSS. read: "smote his hand and cast it [i.e., the hand]."

P. 241, LAB 64.7: "to receive the reward of my deeds": i.e., as Ginzberg, 6.237, n. 77, notes, the day of judgment.

P. 241, James' note on 64.7: The word *traditio,* here rendered "precept," is found in Quintilian 3.1.2, 3.1.3, and 12.11.16, and in Lactantius 7.8.3 in the sense of "teaching" or "instruction."

P. 241, LAB 64.8: Cf. Ben Sira 46.20.

P. 241, line 19 (margin), on LAB 64.8: For 28[1] read 28[19].

P. 241, LAB 64.8: In rabbinic literature (Pirke di R. Eliezer 33; correct 23 in Ginzberg, 6.237, n. 73) Saul's death is also depicted as a repentance for his sins; in Josephus, *AJ* 6.349, on the other hand, Saul's motive in meeting death is the desire for sheer glory and renown after death, reminiscent of the motives of an Achilles or a Hector in Homer's *Iliad* or a Turnus in Virgil's *Aeneid*.

P. 241, LAB 64.8: Kisch, following the Admont MS., separates "And Saul heard ... departed thence" (James, p. 241, lines 23-28) from 64.8 and makes this a separate section, 64.9.

P. 241, line 27 (margin), on LAB 64.8: Add 1 Sam. 28[25].

P. 242, James' note on 65: The *Quaestiones Hebraicae* is ascribed to Jerome.

P. 242, line 11 (margin), on LAB 65.3: For 2 Sam. 1 read 2 Sam. 1[7,9].

P. 242, LAB 65.3: "Take my sword": Though in 65.2, in a similar phrase, "take thy sword," LAB uses the word *romphea* for sword, here he suddenly shifts to the word *machera*. The former is the transliteration of the Greek word found in the LXX on 1 Samuel 31.4, but the latter is not found in the LXX. Interestingly enough, Josephus, in recounting the story of Saul's death likewise uses these words in successive sentences (6.370,371), though the word μάχαιραν in 6.371 is found in only two MSS., S and P, which, to be sure, when unsupported, are seldom trustworthy, but which in this case are supported by the Latin version, which gives the reading considerably more value, especially when now supported by LAB.

P. 242, line 14 (margin), on LAB 65.4: Add 1[8].

P. 242 (margin) on LAB 65.5: Add 1[10].

P. 256, line 25: Transfer "6" (before *de mea petra conclusa*) to line 27 (before *immisi in eum somnum*).

P. 262, lines 10-11: *pressurae ... domine*: A has this entire passage.

P. 263, line 12: For AV(R) read V(R).

P. 263, line 14: For P read AP.

P. 264, line 17: For *Oportet* AP read *Oportet* P, *oporteret* A.

P. 264, line 18: For *constituens* read *constitueris*.

P. 264, line 25: A agrees with V and R in reading *in danaben in monte*.

P. 265, line 1: Delete *si*.

P. 270, line 8: For 4. *angelus* read 5. *angelus*.

CHAPTER XV

INDEX OF BIBLICAL CITATIONS
AND PARALLELS IN LAB

Since it is LAB's habit frequently to cite Biblical passages in retrospect and not merely consecutively, the following index may be useful. It may also be of interest to note which Biblical Books LAB knows and to note that he never refers directly or indirectly to the Books of Ezra, Proverbs, Ecclesiastes, Song of Songs, Lamentations, and the Minor Prophets (except for Zechariah and Malachi). Because of the nature and relative brevity of LAB, however, failure to allude to these Books may not be significant.

Genesis	LAB	Genesis	LAB
1.9	15.6	5.6	1.5
1.11	60.2	5.7	1.5
1.12	60.2	5.9	1.7
1.28	13.8	5.10	1.7
1.29	13.8	5.12	1.9
2.3	11.8	5.13	1.9
2.11	25.11, 26.1	5.15	1.11
2.21	32.15	5.16	1.11
2.22	32.15	5.18	1.13
3.3	13.8	5.19	1.13
3.12	13.8	5.21	1.15
3.13	13.8	5.22	1.15
3.18	37.3	5.24	1.16
3.19	37.3	5.25	1.18
4.1-16	16.2	5.26	1.18
4.1	1.1	5.28	1.20
4.2	1.1	5.29	1.20
4.12	2.1	5.30	1.21
4.14	2.1	5.32	1.22
4.16	2.1	6.1	3.1
4.17	2.2, 2.3	6.2	3.1
4.18	2.5	6.3	3.2, 9.8, 48.1
4.19	2.6	6.5	3.3
4.20	2.7	6.7	3.3
4.21	2.7	6.8	3.4
4.22	2.9	6.9	3.4
4.23	2.10	6.13-15	3.4
4.24	2.10	6.18	3.4
4.25	1.1	6.21	3.4
5.3	1.1	7.2-4	3.4
5.4	1.2	7.5	3.5

Genesis	LAB	Genesis	LAB
7.7	3.5	11.9	7.5
7.10	3.5	11.18	4.10
7.11	3.5	11.19	4.10
7.12	3.5	11.21	4.12
7.23	3.7	11.22	4.13
7.24	3.7	11.23	4.13
8.1	3.7	11.24	4.14
8.14-20	3.8	11.25	4.14
8.21	3.8	11.26	4.15
8.22	3.9	11.27	4.15, 23.4
9.1	3.11	11.29	4.11, 23.4
9.3	3.11	12.4	8.1
9.4	3.11	12.5	8.1
9.6	3.11	12.7	10.2, 12.4, 23.5
9.8	3.11	13.12	8.1, 8.2
9.9	3.11	13.13	8.2
9.11	3.11	13.15	8.3
9.12	3.11	15.2-5	23.5
9.13	19.11	15.9	23.6
9.14	3.11	15.10	23.6
9.15	19.11	15.12	23.6
9.16	3.11	15.13	9.3, 15.5
9.18	4.1	15.14	15.5
9.28	5.8	15.17	23.6
9.29	5.8	16.1	8.1
10.2-4	4.2	16.10	49.6
10.2	5.4	16.15	8.1
10.3	5.4	17.5	8.3
10.5	4.3, 4.17	17.7	8.3
10.6	4.6, 5.5	17.8	8.3
10.7	4.6, 5.5	17.15	8.3
10.8	4.7, 5.5	18.17	18.5
10.9	4.7	18.30	35.6
10.13	4.7	19.5	45.3
10.14	4.7	19.10	45.2
10.19	4.8	19.11	45.2
10.22-25	4.9	21.2	8.3
10.22	5.6	21.3	8.3
10.26-29	4.10	22.2 sqq.	32.3, 40.2
10.31	4.17	22.12	32.4
10.32	4.17	22.17	14.2, 18.5, 32.4
11.2-4	6.1	22.18	32.4
11.3	6.2	25.12	8.1
11.4	7.1	25.16	8.1
11.5	7.2	25.20-26	8.4
11.6	7.2, 12.3	25.21	32.5
11.7	7.3, 7.5, 32.1	26.34	8.5
11.8	7.5	28.9	8.5

Genesis	LAB	Exodus	LAB
29.31-35	8.6	1.6	9.1
30.1-24	8.6	1.7	9.1
30.37-39	17.3	1.8	9.1
32.25-27	18.6	1.9	9.1
34.1	8.7	1.10	9.1
34.2	8.7	1.22	9.1
34.25	8.7	2.1	9.9
34.26	8.7	2.2	9.12
35.18	8.6	2.3	9.12
35.22 sqq.	8.6	2.5	9.15
35.23-26	8.6	2.6	9.15
36	8.5	2.10	9.16
36.2	8.5	2.23	10.1
36.4	8.5	2.24	10.1
36.5	8.5	3.1-6	19.9
36.11	8.5	3.8	15.4
36.13	8.5	3.13	10.4
36.14	8.5	3.14	10.4
37.1	8.7, 8.9	6.20	9.9
37.11	8.9	7.14-12.36	10.1
37.36	8.9	10.21	10.1
38	9.5	12.29 sqq.	32.16
39	43.5	13.18	14.1
39.1	8.9	13.21	10.7
41.41	8.10	14-15	32.17
41.56	8.10	14.8 sqq.	10.2
42.1	8.10	14.8	11.10
42.3	8.10	14.12	10.3
42.5	8.10	14.15	10.5
42.8	8.10, 12.1	14.16	10.5
46.4	24.5	14.22	10.6
46.8	8.11	14.25	31.1
46.9	8.11	15.8	10.5
46.10	8.11	17.14	58.1
46.11	8.11	19	32.7
46.12	8.11	19.1	11.1
46.13	8.11	19.14	11.3
46.14	8.11	19.15	11.2, 11.3
46.15	8.11	19.16	11.4
46.16-18	8.13	19.17	11.4
46.20-22	8.14	20	44.6
46.23	8.12	20.1	11.6
46.24	8.12	20.2	11.6
46.25	8.12	20.4-6	11.6
46.27	8.11	20.7	11.7, 44.10
49.10	21.5	20.8-10	11.8
49.33	24.5	20.11	11.8

Exodus	LAB	Numbers	LAB
20.12	11.9	14.13-19	15.7
20.13	11.11	14.32	15.6
20.13 (14)	11.10	14.35	20.3
20.13 (16)	11.12	15.37-41	16.1
20.14 (17)	11.13, 44.10	16.1-3	16.1
20.15-17(18-20)	11.14	16.3	53.9
20.18 (21)	11.15	16.15	57.2
24.18	11.15	16.30	16.3
25-31	11.15	16.32	16.6
25.8	11.15	17	17.1
25.9	11.15	17.17	17.1
28.17 sqq.	26.10	17.19-20	17.1
32.1	12.2	17.22-23	17.2
32.2	12.2, 12.3	21	18.1
32.7	12.4	22.2	18.2
32.8	12.4	22.3	18.2
32.19	19.7	22.5	18.2
32.20	12.7	22.6	18.2
34-40	13.1	22.8	18.3
34.1	12.10	22.9	18.4
34.29-35	12.1	22.12	18.6
40.33	13.1	22.13 sqq.	18.7
40.34	13.1	22.17	18.2
		22.18	18.3
Leviticus	LAB	22.19-21	18.8
1.1	13.2	22.27	18.9
1.10	13.2	22.31	18.9
1.14	13.2	22.32	18.9
14.2-6	13.3	22.41	18.10
23.4-8	13.4	23.2	18.10
23.15-21	13.5	23.6	18.10
23.24-32	13.6	23.7	18.10
23.33-43	13.7	23.10	28.10
26.2-5	13.10	24.11	18.12
		24.25	18.14
Numbers	LAB	25.1 sqq.	18.13
1.1-3	14.1	25.1	30.1
1.46	14.3	25.2	30.1
1.47	14.3	25.6 sqq.	47.1
1.49	14.3	31.16	18.13
2.33	14.3	31.27	19.1
9.1	14.5	36	29.1
12.8	11.14		
13.1-3	15.1	Deuteronomy	LAB
13.25-29	15.1	4.26 sqq.	19.4, 24.1
13.32-33	15.1	5.8	44.10
14.3	15.4	5.11	44.10
14.10	15.5	5.27	19.4

Deuteronomy	LAB	Joshua	LAB
5.29 (32)	38.2	22.21 sqq.	22.3
6.4	23.2	23.1	21.1
11.9	21.9	23.2	23.1
17.15	56.1	23.14	33.2
22.6	53.10	24	23.1
25.19	58.1	24.1	23.2
28.14	25.3	24.2	23.2, 23.4
28.62	14.2	24.3	23.8
29.17 (18)	25.5	24.4 (+LXX)	23.9
31.16 sqq.	19.2	24.5	23.9
31.16	19.6, 21.1	24.13	23.11
31.23	20.1	24.15	24.1
32.1	19.4	24.17	23.14
32.49	19.8	24.18	23.14
32.52	19.7	24.28 (LXX)	24.3
34.1	19.10	24.30	24.6
34.3	19.7		
34.4	19.10	Judges	LAB
34.5	19.16	1.1	24.6
34.6	19.12, 19.16	2.1-3	30.2
		2.17	30.1
Joshua	LAB	4.2-3	30.3
1.1-3	20.2	4.6	31.1
1.6	20.5	4.9	31.7
1.7	25.3, 38.2	4.15	31.3
1.8	22.6, 38.2	4.17	31.3
1.9	20.5	4.18	31.3
2.1	20.6	4.19	31.4, 31.5, 31.6
5.12	20.8	4.21	31.7
6.24	20.7	4.22	31.9
7.1	21.3	5.1	32.1
7.11	21.3	5.7	33.6
8.30-35	21.7	5.14-18	10.3
8.31	21.8, 21.9	5.20	31.1, 31.2
10.11	30.5	5.24	32.12
10.12	30.5, 32.10	5.26	31.7
10.13	30.5	5.28	31.3, 31.8
12.7-24	20.9	5.31	33.6
13.1 sqq.	20.9	6.1-6	34.1
13.1	21.1	6.1	34.5
14.6 sqq.	20.6, 20.10	6.7-10	34.4
14.13	20.10	6.11	35.1
15.46	29.2	6.12	35.1
19.1	25.2	6.13	35.2
22.10-12	22.1	6.13 (LXX)	35.3
22.15 sqq.	22.2	6.14	35.4
22.19	23.2	6.15	35.5

Judges	LAB	Judges	LAB
6.16	35.5	12.11	41.2
6.17	35.6	12.12	41.2
6.20	35.6, 35.7	12.13	41.1
6.21	35.7, 42.9	12.14	41.1
6.25	36.4	12.15	41.1
6.34	36.2	13.1	41.3
7.8	27.5	13.2	42.1
7.9-18	27.6	13.3	42.3, 42.4
7.14	36.1	13.4	42.3
7.15	36.2	13.5	42.3
7.19	36.1	13.6	42.4
7.20	36.2	13.7	42.4
8.24-27	36.3	13.8	42.5, 42.10
8.32	36.4	13.9	42.6
9.5	37.1	13.10-12	42.7
9.7 sqq.	37.2	13.10	42.6
9.14	37.3	13.14	42.3
9.15	37.3, 37.4	13.15	42.8
9.18	37.1	13.16	42.8, 42.10
9.22	37.5	13.17	42.10
9.28-41	29.1	13.18	42.10
9.53	37.5	13.19	42.9
10.3	38.1	13.20	42.9
10.9	39.1	13.22	42.10
10.13	39.6	13.23	42.9
10.17	39.1	13.24	42.3, 43.1
10.18	39.1	14.1 sqq.	43.1
11.1	39.2	14.5	43.4
11.2	39.2	14.6	43.4
11.3	39.2	15.4-5	43.4
11.5	39.3	15.6	43.1
11.6	39.3	15.9-14	43.4
11.7	39.4	15.15	43.4
11.11	39.6	16.1-3	43.2
11.12	39.8	16.1	43.5
11.14	39.9	16.3	43.3
11.24	39.9	16.4	43.5
11.28	39.10	16.6	43.6
11.29	39.8	16.15	43.6
11.30	39.10	16.16	43.6
11.31	39.10	16.19	43.6
11.32 sqq.	40.1	16.23	43.7
11.36	40.2	16.25	43.7
11.37	40.3	16.28	43.5, 43.7
11.38	40.3, 40.4	16.29	43.8
11.39	40.8	16.30	43.7, 43.8
11.40	40.8	16.31	43.8
12.7	40.9	17.1-4	44.2

Judges	LAB	1 Samuel	LAB
17.5	44.5	1.13	50.5
17.6	44.1	1.17	50.7
19.1	45.1	1.20	51.1
19.2	45.3	1.23	51.1
19.13	45.1	1.24	51.1
19.15	45.1	1.25	51.2
19.16-20	45.2	1.26	51.2
19.17	35.1	2.1	51.3
19.22	45.3	2.3	51.4
19.23	45.3	2.5	51.4
19.25	45.3	2.6	51.5
19.27	45.4	2.9	51.5
19.28	45.4	2.10	51.6
19.29	45.4	2.10 (LXX)	50.2
20.1	45.5	2.11	51.7, 52.1
20.3	46.1	2.12	52.1
20.5	45.4	2.23	52.2
20.6	45.5	2.25	52.3, 52.4
20.12	46.2	2.34	52.1
20.13	46.1, 46.2	3.1	53.1
20.21	46.2	3.3	53.2
20.23	46.3	3.4	53.3
20.24	46.3	3.5	53.3
20.25	46.3	3.6	53.5
20.26	46.3, 46.4	3.7	53.1, 53.2
20.27	46.1, 46.4	3.8	53.5, 53.7
20.28	46.1, 46.3, 46.4	3.9	53.5, 53.6
20.30	47.9	3.11	53.6
20.31	47.9	3.15	53.11, 53.12,
20.32	47.9		53.13
20.34	47.9	3.17	53.12
20.36	47.9	3.18	53.13
20.37	47.9	3.20	51.2
20.41	47.10	4.1-3	54.1
20.42	47.10	4.5	54.2
20.47	47.10	4.10	54.3
20.48	47.10	4.11	54.3
21.16 sqq.	48.3	4.12	54.4
21.25	48.4	4.16	54.4
		4.17	54.4
1 Samuel	LAB	4.18	54.5
1.2	50.1	4.19	54.5, 54.6
1.3	50.2	4.20	54.6
1.6	50.1	4.21	54.6
1.8	49.8, 50.2, 50.3	5.2-4	55.3
1.9	50.3	5.3	55.4
1.10	50.2	5.4	55.4
1.12-15	50.6	5.7	55.4

1 Samuel	LAB	1 Samuel	LAB
5.10	55.4	17.32	61.4
6.4 (5)	55.2	17.34-37	59.5
6.7-12	55.6	17.36 (LXX)	61.4
6.21	55.9	17.40	61.5
7.17	55.1	17.49-51	61.7
8.4	56.1	17.55-58	61.9
8.5	56.1, 56.7, 57.4	18.1 sqq.	62.1
8.6	56.2	18.3	62.3
8.9	56.3	19.18	62.1
9.1-4	56.4	19.23	62.2
9.9	56.4	20	62.3
9.15	56.3	20.3	62.3
9.18	56.4	20.8	62.8
9.19	56.4, 59.2	20.17	62.9
9.21	56.6	20.23	62.10
9.24	56.5	20.41	62.11
10.1	56.5	21.1 (20.42 LXX)	62.11
10.6	20.2	22.9	63.2
10.9	56.7	22.10	63.2
12.1-3	57.1	22.13	63.2
12.5	57.3	22.16-19	63.2
13.9	57.4	22.18	63.1
14.45	63.3	22.19	30.4, **63.1**
15.3	30.4, **58.1**	22.20	63.2
15.7	58.2	22.21	63.2
15.8	58.2	25.1	63.6
15.9	58.2	28.3	63.6, **64.1**
15.12	58.4	28.6	64.3
15.13	58.4	28.7	64.3
15.27	64.6	28.8-11	64.4
15.33	58.4	28.12	64.5
15.34	58.4	28.13	64.5, **64.6**
16.1-3	59.1	28.14	64.6
16.4-7	59.2	28.15	64.7
16.11-13	59.3	28.19	64.8
16.11	59.2	28.20	64.8
16.12	59.2	28.25	64.8
16.14 sqq.	60.1	31.1 sqq.	63.3
16.19	60.1	31.1	65.1
16.23	60.1, **60.3**	31.3	65.1
17.4	61.2	31.4	65.2
17.9	61.2	31.6	62.2
17.11	61.2		
17.15	61.1	2 Samuel	LAB
17.16	61.3	1.7	65.3
17.22	61.3	1.8	65.4
17.28	61.3	1.9	65.3
17.31	61.4	1.10	65.5

1 Samuel	LAB
21.15-22	61.6
23.10	27.11

1 Kings	...LAB
3.9	21.2
8.46 sqq.	19.9
17.1	48.1
17.4	48.1
18.24	38.2

2 Kings	LAB
12.4 sqq.	29.3

Isaiah	LAB
7.14	43.1
29.16 sqq.	53.13
40.15 sqq.	12.4
40.15	7.3
51.1	23.4
51.2	23.4
51.4	51.4, 51.6 (bis)
53.7	30.5
60.19	26.13
60.20	26.13
64.3 (4)	26.13
65.17	26.13

Jeremiah	LAB
1.6	56.6 (bis)
1.17	51.6
2.8	30.4
7.9	44.6

Ezekiel	LAB
3.18	37.2
8.1	28.6
10.2	9.10
20.1	28.6

Zechariah	LAB
3.9	26.9

Malachi	LAB
3.24 (4.6)	23.13

Psalms	LAB
18.10 (9)	23.10
27.10	59.4
42.3	50.5

Psalms	LAB
42.13	50.5
61.2	59.4
78.25 (LXX)	19.5
99.6	51.6
107.32	11.8
128.3	50.1
150.3-5	21.8
151.1 (LXX)	62.5

Job	LAB
38.3	51.6
42.13	8.8
42.14	8.8

Ruth	LAB
1.14	61.6

Esther	LAB
4.14	39.3

Daniel	LAB
2.22	22.3
3.22	6.17
3.27	6.17

Nehemiah	LAB
9.12	10.7

1 Chronicles	LAB
1.36	8.5
1.37	8.5
8	47.11

2 Chronicles	LAB
24.8 sqq.	29.3

CHAPTER XVI

CORRECTIONS TO KISCH'S EDITION

(Includes and supplements Kisch's own list of 20 corrigenda in *HUCA*, 23, Part II (1950–51), p. 93; seven of these 20 were listed on a slip of errata inserted into each copy of Kisch's edition.)

P. 16, line 32: For *proenotatur* read *praenotatur*.

P. 16, line 38: For *Aggrippinae* read *Agrippinae*.

P. 22, line 4: For *De Ecclesiasticis Scriptoribus* read *Liber De Scriptoribus Ecclesiasticis*.

P. 22, n. 29: Add: The first edition appeared in Basle in 1494.

P. 25, line 2: For *parchment* read *paper*.

P. 25, line 15: For *chartaceus* read *membranaceus*.

P. 26, line 15: For *chartaceus* read *membranaceus*.

P. 26, line 25: For *parchment* read *paper*.

P. 27, line 18: For *generationis* read *generationum*.

P. 27, line 21: Omit "?" after *parchment*.

P. 28, line 7: For *parchment* read *paper*.

P. 53, line 33: For *Handscriften* read *Handschriften*.

P. 67, line 8: For *eleventh* read *eleventh-*.

P. 99, line 28: For *Non quid* read *Nunquid*.

P. 99, line 31: The ה of הלא is inverted.

P. 99, line 38: Add: Jewish Division of the New York Public Library, New York City.

P. 100, line 6: For *Antiqutatum* read *Antiquitatum*.

P. 102, line 27: For *Jan-Baptiste* read *Jean-Baptiste*.

P. 104, lines 41-42: For *p. 19, note* 1 read *pp.* 265-266.

P. 105, line 3: For 1949 read 1950, *pp.* 425-446.

P. 108, line 9: For *Phillips* read *Phillipps*.

P. 109, line 2: For *in katalogo* read *in katalogo* a. Then add to Apparatus: a = Cathalogo M.

P. 109, line 3: For *Phylo* read *Phlyo*aa. Then add to Apparatus: aa=Philo M.

P. 109, line 16: For *Cladium* read *Claudium*.

P. 110, line 12: For *librum* read *librum*gg. Then add to Apparatus: gg=librum Adm.; librorum M.

P. 110, line 29, note h: For ΤΕΩΡΤΙΜΚΟ read ΤΕΩΡΤΙΤΚΟ

P. 110, line 30: For τεωρτιμκο read τεωρτιυκο .

P. 111, line 16, on LAB 1.3: For *et Anath* read *Zanath*dd. Then add to Apparatus: dd=zanath Adm. m; et Anath A.

P. 112, line 10, on LAB 1.14: For *viorum* read *virorum*.

P. 113, line 25, on LAB 1.22: For 5,31 read 5,32.

P. 120, line 23, on LAB 4.5: Omit Cf. Gen. 10, 13.

P. 120, line 35, note h on LAB 4.7: For *Petrosonun* read *Petrosonum*.

P. 125, line 37, note x on LAB 5.6: For *lac* read *lac*. (add period).

P. 125, line 37, note x on LAB 5.6: For LXXIII read $\overline{\text{LXXIII}}$.

P. 130, line 16, on LAB 6.17: For LXXXIII read $\overline{\text{LXXXIII}}$.

P. 134, line 10, on LAB 8.8: For *six* read *sex*.

P. 135, line 10, on LAB 8.11: For *six* read *sex*.

P. 137, line 30, on LAB 9.5: For *Gen.* 1,38 read *Gen.* 38,1.

P. 139, line 13, on LAB 9.11: For *invalescebant* read *invalescebat*.

P. 141, line 22, on LAB 10.4: For *filius* read *filiis*.

P. 147, line 3, on LAB 12.2: Omit the second *iudicium,* which is stemmatically impossible.

P. 147, lines 17-18, on LAB 12.4: For *spondidi* read *spopondi*.

P. 150, line 13, on LAB 13.4: For *inmemoriale* read *in memoriale* or *memorialem*.

P. 152, line 26, note n on LAB 14.2: For *scribe RAP* read AP (the reading of R, *conscribes,* agrees with that of the Admont MS.).

P. 156, line 33, note l on LAB 16.3: For *om. A* read *om. AP.*

P. 159, line 2, on LAB 18.4: For *Et quid* read *Et.*

P. 159, line 29, note h on LAB 18.4: For *paciscar A* read *paciscar R.*

P. 159, line 11, on LAB 18.5: Place question mark after *holocaustum.*

P. 164, lines 10-11: *Quis . . . peccavit* should be italicized.

P. 164, line 27: For *III Reg.* 8,46 read *Cf. III Reg.* 8,46.

P. 175, line 4, on LAB 23.4: For *unt* read *una.*

P. 178, line 27, on LAB 24.5: For *Gen.* 49,32 read *Gen.* 49,33.

P. 183, line 9, on LAB 25.11: For *relucebant* (Admont, which is stemmatically and grammatically impossible) read *relucebat.*

P. 194, line 19, on LAB 28.3: Place question mark after *refulgens.*

P. 197, line 27, on LAB 29.4: For *abdormivit* read *obdormivit.*

P. 199, line 23, LAB 30.5: For *eciam* read *etiam.*

P. 200, line 27, note d on LAB 30.7: For *reconciliabitur A* read *reconciliabitur AP.*

P. 201, line 9, on LAB 31.2: For *viroroum* read *virorum.*

P. 206, line 19, on LAB 32.13: For *qui* read *quia.*

P. 214, line 30, note g on LAB 37.2: For *malum A* read *malum AP.*

P. 218, line 30, note o on LAB 39.4: For *p.* 262, 8 read *p.* 262, 10-11.

P. 229, line 11, on LAB 44.3: For *veniet* read *veniet*ta. Then add to Apparatus: ta= venient A.

P. 236, line 19, on LAB 47.3: For *is* read *si.*

P. 237, line 27, LAB 47.7: For *inversutia* read *in versutia.*

P. 238, line 4, on LAB 47.8: For *iniquia* read *iniqua.*

P. 241, line 34, note x on LAB 49.4: For *semper in A* read *semper in A (praeter* 55.1*).*

P. 257, line 3, on LAB 56.6: For *Qui* (grammatically and stemmatically impossible) read *Quis.*

P. 264, line 10, LAB 62.2: Place question mark after *moriemini.*

P. 264, line 25, LAB 62.5: Place question mark after *patitur.*

P. 265, line 1, LAB 62.5: Place question mark after *morte.*

P. 265, line 3, LAB 62.5: Place question mark after *odit me.*

P. 267, line 27, note i on LAB 63.3: For *Dominus* read *Deus.*

P. 274, col. 2 s.v. James, M. R.: Add: 97, 98, 102, 103, 104, 105, 106, 108.

P. 275, col. 2, s.v. *Marcus, S.*: Read *Mark (Marcus), St.*

CHAPTER XVII
BIBLIOGRAPHY
(James, pp. 8–9; Kisch, pp. 98–106)

(Every attempt has been made at completeness; items marked with an asterisk are of particular value for the study of LAB.)

1. Azariah dei Rossi, *Sefer Meor Einayim* (ed. David Cassel [Vilna, 1866]).
2. Bernard J. Bamberger, *Fallen Angels* (Philadelphia, 1952), pp. 44-45.
3. Salo W. Baron, *A Social and Religious History of the Jews*, 2nd ed., vol. 6: *Laws, Homilies, and the Bible* (New York, 1958), pp. 195-197, 421-422 [on Jerahmeel and LAB].
4. Renée Bloch,"Note Méthodologique pour l'Étude de la Littérature rabbinique," *Recherches de Science Religieuse*, 43 (1955), pp. 206, 218 n. 38.
5. Pierre Bogaert, *L'Apocalypse syriaque de Baruch*, 2 vols. (Paris, 1969), esp. vol. 1, pp. 242-258 (parallels with LAB and esp. the dating of LAB).
6. Wilhelm Bousset, review of Moses Gaster's *Chronicles of Jerahmeel*, in *Theologische Literaturzeitung*, 25 (1900), pp 262-266.
7. Wilhelm Bousset, *Die Religion des Judentums im späthellenistischen Zeitalter*, 3rd ed. (Tübingen, 1926), p. 44.
8. J. Bowker, *The Targums and Rabbinic Literature* (Cambridge, 1969), pp. 30-31, 301-314 [contains a new translation of those portions of LAB pertaining to Genesis].
9. Umberto Cassuto, "Jerachmeel," in *Encyclopaedia Judaica*, vol. 8 (Berlin, 1931), pp. 1083-1084.
10. Leopold Cohn, "Prolegomena," in Leopoldus Cohn et Paulus Wendland, *Philonis Alexandrini Opera quae supersunt*, vol. 1 (Berlin, 1896), pp. L-LII.
*11. Leopold Cohn, "An Apocryphal Work Ascribed to Philo of Alexandria," *Jewish Quarterly Review*, Old Series, 10 (1898), pp. 277-332.
12. Leopold Cohn, "Einteilung und Chronologie der Schriften Philos," *Philologus*, Supplementband 7 (1899), p. 426.
13. Leopold Cohn, "Pseudo-Philo und Jerachmeel," *Festschrift zum siebzigsten Geburtstage Jakob Guttmanns* (Leipzig, 1915), pp. 173-185.
14. Leopold Cohn, "Prolegomena I," in Leopoldus Cohn et Paulus Wendland, *Philonis Alexandrini Opera quae supersunt*, vol. 6 (Berlin, 1915), pp. XII-XVIII.
15. Frederick C. Conybeare, *Philo about the Contemplative Life* (Oxford, 1895), pp. 139-142, 144-145.
16. Gustav Davidson, *A Dictionary of Angels* (New York, 1967), s.v. Gethel (Ingethel), Zeruel (Cervihel), Nathaniel, Phadahel.
17. Roger le Déaut, *La Nuit Pascale* (Rome, 1963), esp. pp. 188-194.
18. Mathias Delcor, "Pentecôte (La Fête de la)," no. 4: "Le livre des Antiquités bibliques du Pseudo-Philon," Supplément 7 in *Dictionnaire de la Bible* (Paris, 1966), pp. 868-869.
*19. Mathias Delcor, "Philon (Pseudo-)," Supplément 7 in *Dictionnaire de la Bible* (Paris, 1966), pp. 1354-1375.
20. Mathias Delcor, "Le Testament de Job, la prière de Nabonide et les traditions targoumiques," *Bibel und Qumran* (*Festschrift Hans Bardtke*) (Leipzig, 1968), pp. 57-74, esp. 64-65.
21. Gerhard Delling, *Jüdische Lehre und Frömmigkeit in den Paralipomena Jeremiae* (Berlin, 1967), p. 51.
22. Gerhard Delling, *Bibliographie zur jüdisch-hellenistischen und intertestamentarischen Literatur* 1900-1965 (in Verbindung mit Gerhard Zachhuber und

Heinz Berthold; *Texte und Untersuchungen zur Geschichte der altchristlichen Literatur*, Bd. 106 [Berlin, 1969], pp. 110-111).[lists 17 items and 2 cross-references].

*23. Christian Dietzfelbinger, *Pseudo-Philo, Liber Antiquitatum Biblicarum* (Theol. Diss., Göttingen, 1964), (xiii, 343 pp.) (mimeographed).

24. Christian Dietzfelbinger, forthcoming translation of LAB into German, with brief commentary.

25. Otto Eissfeldt, "Zur Kompositionstechnik des Pseudo-Philonischen Liber Antiquitatum Biblicarum," *Norsk Teologisk Tidsskrift*, 56 (1955) = N. A. Dahl and A. S. Kapelrud, eds., *S. Mowinckel Festschrift* (Oslo, 1955), pp. 53-71; reprinted in his *Kleine Schriften*, vol. 3 (Berlin, 1966), pp. 340-353.

26. Otto Eissfeldt, *Einleitung in das Alte Testament*, 3rd ed. (Tübingen, 1964), p. 853.

27. Joannes A. Fabricius, *Bibliotheca Graeca sive notitia scriptorum veterum Graecorum* (ed. Gottlieb C. Harles), vol. 4 (Hamburg, 1795), p. 746.

28. Louis H. Feldman, *Scholarship on Philo and Josephus* (1937-1962) (*Yeshiva University Studies in Judaica*, vol. 1), (New York, 1963), pp. 10-11, 25 [critical bibliography, desiderata].

29. William J. Ferrar, *The Uncanonical Jewish Books: A Short Introduction to the Apocrypha and Other Jewish Writings* 200 B.C.-100 A.D. (London, 1918), pp. 105-109.

30. David Flusser, " 'Do Not Commit Adultery,' 'Do Not Murder,' " *Textus*, 4 (1964), pp. 222-223.

31. Siegmund Fraenkel, "Notiz zu Jerachmeel," *Theologische Literaturzeitung*, 25 (1900), p. 452.

32. Julius Furst, *Bibliotheca Judaica: Bibliographisches Handbuch umfassend die Druckwerke der jüdischen Literatur einschliesslich der über Juden und Judenthum veröffentlichten Schriften*, vol. 3 (Leipzig, 1863), p. 89.

33. Moses Gaster, *The Chronicles of Jerahmeel*, or, *The Hebrew Bible Historiale* (Oriental Translation Fund, New Series, vol. 4), (London, 1899), pp. XXX-C.

*34. Louis Ginzberg, *The Legends of the Jews*, references cited in index, vol. 7 (Philadelphia, 1938), pp. 537-539.

35. Erwin R. Goodenough, *By Light, Light* (New Haven, 1935), pp. 265-266.

36. Erwin R. Goodenough, *Jewish Symbols in the Greco-Roman Period* (New York and Princeton, 1958-68), vol. 8, pp. 43 n.; 44 n., 136 n.; vol. 9, pp. 170 n., 190, 191; vol. 10, p. 34 n.; vol. 13, p. 228.

37. Howard L. Goodhart and Erwin R. Goodenough, "A General Bibliography of Philo Judaeus," in Erwin R. Goodenough, *The Politics of Philo Judaeus* (New Haven, 1938), pp. 177-179, 198-200, 320-321.

38. J. van Goudoever, *Biblical Calendars*, 2nd ed. (Leiden, 1961), pp. 116-123 ("The Calendar in Pseudo-Philo's Biblical Antiquities").

39. L. Gry, "La date de la fin des temps, selon les révelations et les calculs du Pseudo-Philon et de Baruch," *Revue Biblique*, 48 (1939), pp. 337-356.

*40. Daniel J. Harrington, *Text and Biblical Text in Pseudo-Philo's Liber Antiquitatum Biblicarum* (forthcoming [1969] doctoral dissertation on LAB, at Harvard University, under supervision of Professor John Strugnell).

*41. Daniel J. Harrington, (forthcoming) text and textual critical introduction of LAB for *Sources chrétiennes* series; Dom Pierre Bogaert and Abbé Charles Perrot will do a French translation, introduction, and commentary.

42. A. S. Hartom, translation into Hebrew of LAB, in *Hasefarim Hahizonim*, vol. 7 (Tel Aviv, 1967).

43. Bernhard Heller, "Ginzberg's Legends of the Jews," *Jewish Quarterly Review*, 24 (1933-34), pp. 184-190 [on Ginzberg's use of Pseudo-Philo].

44. Montague Rhodes James, *Apocrypha Anecdota*, in *Texts and Studies: Contributions to Biblical and Patristic Literature*, vol. 2, no. 3 (Cambridge, 1893), pp. 164-185 [four fragments, the author of which James is unable to identify, from LAB, which James translates into Greek and comments upon].

45. Montague Rhodes James, *Apocrypha Anecdota, Second Series*, in *Texts and Studies: Contributions to Biblical and Patristic Literature*, vol. 5, no. 1 (Cambridge, 1897), pp. 142-143 (corrections and notes to First Series).

46. Montague Rhodes James, "Notes on Apocrypha," *Journal of Theological Studies*, 7 (1906), p. 565.

47. Montague Rhodes James, "Transmission of an Old Text (Pseudo-Philo *Antiquitatum Biblicarum Liber*)," *Cambridge Philological Society: Proceedings*, 101 (Cambridge, 1915), pp. 9-10.

48. Montague Rhodes James, "Notes on Apocrypha," *Journal of Theological Studies*, 16 (1915), pp. 403-405 ("Pseudo-Philo and Baruch").

*49. Montague Rhodes James, *The Biblical Antiquities of Philo, Now First Translated from the Old Latin Version* (London, 1917).
   Reviewed by A. E. B., *Cambridge Review*, 30 May 1918, p. 418; by R. G. Bury, *Classical Review*, 32 (1918), pp. 132-133; by D. D. D., *Revue Bénédictine*, 33 (1921), pp. 64-65; and by Paul Riessler, *Theologische Quartalschrift*, 102 (1921), pp. 219-221.

50. Annie Jaubert, *La Notion d'Alliance dans le Judaïsme aux abords de l'Ere Chrétienne* (*Patristica Sorbonensia*, vol. 6; Paris, 1963), pp. 285-286.

51. Joachim Jeremias, "Das spätjüdische Deboragrab," *Zeitschrift des Deutschen Palästina-Vereins*, 82 (1966), pp. 136-138 [on LAB 33.6].

*52. Guido Kisch, *Pseudo-Philo's Liber Antiquitatum Biblicarum* (*Publications in Mediaeval Studies*, The University of Notre Dame, vol. 10) (Notre Dame, Indiana, 1949); Kisch writes, 2 March 1969, that he is currently assembling further notes on LAB.
   Reviewed by R. M. Grant, *Anglican Theological Review*, 32 (1950), p. 243; A. Kleinhaus, *Antonianum*, 26 (1951), pp. 134-135; J. Bonsirven, *Biblica*, 34 (1953), p. 404; J. P. Weisengoff, *Catholic Historical Review*, 37 (1951), pp. 194-195; W. E. Garrison, *Christian Century*, 67 (1950), p. 792; G. E. McCracken, *Crozer Quarterly*, 27 (1950), pp. 173-175; G. D. Kilpatrick, *Historia Judaica*, 12 (1950), pp. 77-79; H. M. Orlinsky, *In Jewish Bookland* (Dec. 1950); R. Marcus, *Journal of Biblical Literature*, 69 (1950), pp. 297-298; J. Hammer, *Latomus*, 9 (1950), pp. 465-467; P. Delhaye, *Mélanges de Science Religieuse*, 7 (1950), p. 340; H. Faber, *New York Times* (April 2, 1950); C. Matagne, *Nouvelle Revue Théologique*, 73 (1951), p. 425; O. Eissfeldt, *Orientalistische Literaturzeitung*, 50 (1955), pp. 396-397; J. Daniélou, *Recherches de Science Religieuse*, 37 (1950), pp. 592 ff.; B. Botte, *Recherches de Théologie Ancienne et Médiévale*, 18 (1951), pp. 163-164; M. Hadas, *Review of Religion*, 16 (1951), pp. 43-44; F. M. Abel, *Revue Biblique*, 57 (1950), pp. 643-644; T. Camelot, *Revue des Sciences philosophiques et théologiques*, 35 (1951), p. 305; E. R. Goodenough, *Speculum*, 26 (1951), pp. 394-395.

53. Guido Kisch, "The Editio Princeps of Pseudo-Philo's *Liber Antiquitatum Biblicarum*," Alexander Marx Jubilee Volume, ed. S. Lieberman (New York, 1949), pp. 425-446.

54. Guido Kisch, "A Note on the New Edition of Pseudo-Philo's Biblical Antiquities," *Historia Judaica*, 12 (1950), pp. 153-158 [rejoinder to McCracken's review].

55. Guido Kisch, "Pseudo-Philo's Liber Antiquitatum Biblicarum, Postlegomena to the New Edition," *HUCA*, 23, Part II (1950-51), pp. 81-93 [contains Kisch's addenda and corrigenda to his edition].

56. Joseph Klausner, *The Messianic Idea in Israel from Its Beginning to the Completion of the Mishnah* (translated by W. F. Stinespring; New York, 1955), pp. 366-369.
57. Kaufmann Kohler, "Angelology," *Jewish Encyclopedia*, vol. 1 (New York, 1901), p. 593.
58. Samuel Krauss, "The Names of Moses," *Jewish Quarterly Review*, O.S., 10 (1898), p. 726.
59. Paul Lehmann, *Johannes Sichardus und die von ihm benutzten Bibliotheken und Handschriften* (*Quellen und Untersuchungen zur lateinischen Philologie des Mittelalters*, Band 4, Heft 1) (Munich, 1912), pp. 51-52, 76-84, 118-120, 154-155.
60. Saul Lieberman, *Hellenism in Jewish Palestine* (New York, 1950), pp. 80-81 [on LAB 12.10].
61. Samuel E. Loewenstamm, *The Exodus from Egypt: A Literary Study Based on Comparison between the Report of the Book of Exodus and the Parallel Reports of the Extra-Pentateuchal Sources* (diss. [in Hebrew], Hebrew University, Jerusalem, 1960).
62. Samuel E. Loewenstamm, *The Tradition of the Exodus in Its Development* [in Hebrew] (Jerusalem, 1965), p. 123.
63. C. C. McCown, *The Testament of Solomon* (Leipzig, 1922), p. 91.
64. Martin McNamara, *The New Testament and the Palestinian Targum to the Pentateuch* (Rome, 1966), pp. 26, 52, 76, 165, 171, 174, 175, 224, 235.
65. Ralph Marcus, "A Sixteenth-Century Hebrew Critique of Philo," *HUCA*, 21 (1948), pp. 42-44 [on Azariah dei Rossi].
66. George Foot Moore, *Judaism in the First Centuries of the Christian Era: the Age of the Tannaim*, vol. 2 (Cambridge, Mass., 1927), p. 285.
67. Dov Neuman (Noy), *Motif Index of Talmudic-Midrashic Literature* (diss., Indiana Univ., 1954) [cites LAB via Ginzberg].
68. J. Perles, "Die Berner Handschrift des kleinem Aruch," *Jubelschrift zum Siebzigsten Geburtstage des Prof. Dr. H. Graetz* (Breslau, 1887), pp. 1-38 [Jerahmeel as a translation from Latin].
69. Charles Perrot, "Les Récits d'Enfance dans la Haggada antérieure au IIe Siècle de Notre Ère," *Recherches de Science Religieuse*, 55 (1967), pp. 481-518.
70. Marc Philonenko, "Quod oculus non vidit, I Cor. 2,9," *Theologische .Zeitschrift*, 15 (1959), pp. 51-52 [on LAB 26.12-14].
71. Marc Philonenko, "Remarques sur un hymne essénien de caractère gnostique," *Semitica*, 11 (1961), pp. 43-54 [on LAB 60].
72. Marc Philonenko, "Une paraphrase du cantique d'Anne," *Revue d'Histoire et de Philosophie Religieuses*, 42 (1962) (=*Mélanges Clavier*), pp. 157-168 [on LAB 51].
73. Marc Philonenko, "Essénisme et gnose chez le Pseudo-Philon. Le symbolisme de la lumière dans le Liber Antiquitatum Biblicarum," *Studies in the History of Religions*, 12 (Leiden, 1967), pp. 401-410.
74. Marc Philonenko, *Joseph et Aséneth: Introduction, Texte Critique, Traduction et Notes* (Leiden, 1968), pp. 149, 151, 154, 157, 168, 207.
75. Marc Philonenko, article on the hymn of Jephthah's daughter [LAB 40, (in preparation)].
76. Jean-Baptiste Cardinal Pitra, *Spicilegium Solesmense complectens Sanctorum Patrum Scriptorumque Ecclesiasticorum Anecdota Hactenus Opera*, vol. 2 (Paris, 1855), pp. 334, 335 [on the Book of Cethel].
77. Jean-Baptiste Cardinal Pitra, *Analecta Sacra Spicilegio Solesmensi Parata*, vol. 2 (Paris, 1884), pp. 298, 314, 319-322.
78. G. von Rad, *Das erste Buch Mose* (Göttingen, 1949-53), vol. 2, pp. 57, 90 ff., 119 ff.

79. Jacob Reiner, *The Book of the Hasmonean Kings from the Chronicles of Jerahmeel* (diss., D.H.L., Yeshiva University, Bernard Revel Graduate School, 1966), vol. 1, p. 62, n. 36.
80. Harald Riesenfeld, *Jésus Transfiguré* (Copenhagen, 1947), p. 87, n. 30 [on LAB 32.1-4, 18.5].
81. Paul Riessler, *Altjüdisches Schrifttum ausserhalb der Bibel, übersetzt und erläutert* (Augsburg, 1928), pp. 735-861, 1315-1318.
82. Samuel Sandmel, *Philo's Place in Judaism: A Study of Conceptions of Abraham in Jewish Literature* (Cincinnati, 1956), p. 50.
83. Wilhelm Schmid and Otto Stählin, *Geschichte der Griechischen Litteratur*, vol. 2.1 (Munich, 1920), p. 586.
84. J. Schmitt, "L'Organisation de l'Église primitive et Qumrân," in J. van der Ploeg, et al., *La Secte de Qumrân et les Origines du Christianisme* (Louvain, 1959), pp. 225-226.
85. Emil Schürer, *Geschichte des jüdischen Volkes im Zeitalter Jesu Christi*, vol. 3, 4th ed. (Leipzig, 1909), pp. 384-386.
86. Sixtus Senensis, *Bibliotheca Sancta* ([first edition, Venice, 1566]; Cologne, 1576), p. 314.
87. Alexander Souter, *A Glossary of Later Latin to 600 A.D.*, corrected ed. (Oxford, 1964).
88. Abram Spiro, "Samaritans, Tobiads, and Judahites in Pseudo-Philo; Use and Abuse of the Bible by Polemicists and Doctrinaires," *PAAJR*, 20 (1951), pp. 279-355.
89. Abram Spiro, "Pseudo-Philo's Saul and the Rabbis' Messiah ben Ephraim," *PAAJR*, 21 (1952), pp. 119-137.
90. Abram Spiro, "The Ascension of Phinehas," *PAAJR*, 22 (1953), pp. 91-114.
91. Abram Spiro, *Manners of Rewriting Biblical History from Chronicles to Pseudo-Philo* (diss., Columbia University, microfilm, 1953), pp. 173-248 [on Pseudo-Philo].
92. Abram Spiro, *The Anti-Schismatic Document of Ps.-Philo* (incomplete; parts are to be found among the late Prof. Spiro's papers at Wayne State University, Detroit, Michigan).
93. Odil Hannes Steck, *Israel und das Gewaltsame Geschick der Propheten* (= *Wissenschaftliche Monographien zum alten und neuen Testament*, vol. 23) (Neukirchen, 1967), pp. 173-176.
94. Fridericus Stegmüller, *Repertorium Biblicum Medii Aevi*, vol. 4 (Barcelona, 1954), p. 462 [lists 4 MSS. of LAB: Berlin, Munich 4569, Rein (hitherto unnoticed), and Würzburg (now Univ. of Mich. Fol. 276)].
95. Moritz Steinschneider, "Literarische Beilage: Lapidarien," *Hebräische Bibliographie*, 16 (1876), pp. 104-106.
96. Moritz Steinschneider, *Die Hebräische Uebersetzungen des Mittelalters und die Juden als Dolmetscher* (Berlin, 1893), pp. 237, n. 922; 603, n. 53; 963, n. 105.
97. Moritz Steinschneider, *Die Geschichtsliteratur der Juden in Druckwerken und Handschriften* (Frankfurt, 1905), pp. 41-43, 175-176 [on Jerahmeel and LAB].
98. Kenneth R. Stow, "Pseudo-Philo, an Essene Work" (unpublished essay, available from the author, 160 West 97 St., New York, N. Y. 10025; written under supervision of Prof. Gerson Cohen, Columbia University, 1968), 26 pp.
99. A. Strobel, "Eine Katechon-Parallele in Pseudo-Philo? Zur Interpretation von Cp. 51,5," in *Untersuchungen zum Eschatologischen Verzögerungsproblem auf Grund der Spätjüdischurchristlichen Geschichte von Habakuk 2.2 ff.* (Leiden, 1961), pp. 74-77.

100. John Strugnell, "More Psalms of David," *Catholic Biblical Quarterly*, 27 1965), pp. 207-216 [on LAB 59].
101. John Strugnell, "Philo (Pseudo-), Liber Antiquitatum Biblicarum," forthcoming in *Encyclopaedia Judaica* (Jerusalem), approximately 800 words.
102. H. St. John Thackeray, *The Relation of St. Paul to Contemporary Jewish Thought* (London, 1900), pp. 19-20, 124, 142, 209, 243-244.
103. Geza Vermès, "Deux traditions sur Balaam: Nombres XXII.2-21 et ses interprétations midrashiques," *Cahiers Sioniens*, 9 (1955), pp. 289-302 [pp. 292-299 have been translated into English in Vermès' *Scripture and Tradition*, pp. 128-135].
104. Geza Vermès, "La Figure de Moïse au tournant des deux Testaments," in H. Cazelles et al., *Moïse l'Homme de l'Alliance* (Paris, 1955), pp. 88-92.
105. Geza Vermès, "'The Torah Is a Light,'" *Vetus Testamentum*, 8 (1958), pp. 436-438.
106. Geza Vermès, *Scripture and Tradition in Judaism: Haggadic Studies* (Leiden, 1961), pp. 5-6 and 31 citations in index, p. 237.
107. Geza Vermès, "The Decalogue and the Minim," in Matthew Black and Georg Fohrer, eds., *In Memoriam Paul Kahle* (Berlin, 1968), pp. 232-240.
108. Bruno Violet, *Die Apokalypsen des Esra und des Baruch in deutscher Gestalt* (=*Die Griechischen Christlichen Schriftsteller der ersten [drei] Jahrhunderte*, vol. 32), pp. xlvii-xlix ("Die Quellen der Baruch-Apokalypse, besonders die Antiquitates biblicae des Ps.-Philo").
109. Michael Wadsworth, doctoral thesis on Apocalypse and Haggadah in Pseudo-Philo, in progress under Prof. Geza Vermès at the University of Oxford.
110. Meyer Waxman, *A History of Jewish Literature from the Close of the Bible to Our Own Days*, vol. 1, 2nd ed. (New York, 1938), pp. 529-530 [on Jerahmeel and LAB].
111. Paul Wilpert, "Philon bei Nikolaus von Kues," in P. Wilpert, ed., *Miscellanea Mediaevalia*, vol. 1: *Antike und Orient im Mittelalter* (Berlin, 1962), pp. 69-79 [on influence of LAB in Middle Ages].
112. Paul Winter, "*Monogenēs Para Patros*," *Zeitschrift für Religions- und Geistesgeschichte*, 5 (1953), pp. 335-365.
113. Paul Winter, "Jewish Folklore in the Matthaean Birth Story," *Hibbert Journal*, 53 (1954-55), pp. 34-42 [on LAB 9.10].
114. Paul Winter, "The Proto-Source of Luke I," *Novum Testamentum*, 1 (1956), pp. 184-199.
115. Paul Winter, "Note on Salem-Jerusalem," *Novum Testamentum*, 2 (1957), pp. 151-152.
116. Paul Winter, "Der gegenwärtige Stand der Erforschung der in Palästina neu gefundenen hebräischen Handschriften," *Theologische Literaturzeitung*, 82 (1957), p. 260 [suggests comparison of LAB and Genesis Apocryphon].
117. Paul Winter, "The Main Literary Problem of Luke I-II," *Anglican Theological Review*, 40 (1958), pp. 257-264.
118. Paul Winter, "The Holy Messiah," *Zeitschrift für die neutestamentliche Wissenschaft*, 50 (1959), p. 275 [on LAB 59.2].
119. Paul Winter, "Philo, Biblical Antiquities of," in *The Interpreter's Dictionary of the Bible*, vol. 3 (New York and Nashville, 1962), pp. 795-796.
120. Addison G. Wright, *An Investigation of the Literary Form, Haggadic Midrash, in the Old Testament and Intertestamental Literature* (diss., Catholic Univ., Washington, D.C., 1965), p. 175.
121. Addison G. Wright, *The Literary Genre Midrash* (Staten Island, N. Y., 1967), pp. 87-89.

Chapter XVIII
LIFE OF M. R. JAMES

Montague Rhodes James (1862–1936), the author of this work, was provost of King's College, Cambridge, from 1905 to 1918 and of Eton College from 1918 until his death. He was a distinguished and prolific scholar in the fields of Apocrypha and Pseudepigrapha, as seen in his editions of the Psalms of Solomon, the Testament of Abraham, the Revelation of Peter, the Fourth Book of Esdras, 2 Peter, and Jude. The other field in which he distinguished himself was in the cataloguing of manuscripts. The present work happily combines these two interests. He also wrote extensively in the field of the art and literature of the Middle Ages and contributed chapters to the *Cambridge Mediaeval History,* the *Cambridge Modern History,* and the *Cambridge History of English Literature.* Finally, and perhaps most remarkable of all, he composed a number of ghost stories which are still much read.

A. F. Scholfield, the author of a biographical memoir on James in the *Dictionary of National Biography* 1931–1940 (Oxford, 1949), pp. 471–473, notes that James was a rapid worker who realized that there were gaps in his work, and that he was a negligent proof-reader. There are a number of examples of these traits in the present work. Through the good offices of Mr. Patrick Strong of Eton College, the present writer was able to secure access to James' own corrections and comments, totaling twenty, mostly very short items and a few quite illegible, which he had written in the margin of the copy of his book which he bequeathed to the Eton College Library. A search by A. E. B. Owen of Cambridge of Dr. James' papers which he bequeathed to the Cambridge University Library yielded six items in his diary, none of significance.

There can be little doubt that in view of the fact that there was no critical edition of the text, let alone an English translation (though Cohn's article had given an extensive summary and many quotations), and that so little research had been done on LAB before James, his practically pioneer effort was of a high order of excellence. James' prodigious knowledge of the whole field of Apocrypha and Pseudepigrapha is manifested in the introduction, and the translation itself is in clear and vigorous English, though there is no attempt made to gloss over obscurities—which are many—in the Latin. But James himself acknowledged (p. 65) that his was not a critical edition, though it is the closest that we have to one to date, being based on three complete MSS., four extensive fragments, and the *editio princeps,* and without undue dependence upon any one manuscript. When it came to working with manuscripts James was very much at home and quite astute; as Arthur Darby Nock, who knew him personally, once said of him, he knew manuscripts better than he knew books. James' excellence becomes particularly evident when his work is compared with the German translation and commentary by Riessler, which is based solely on the *editio princeps,* which makes little attempt to explain most of the difficulties in the text, and which makes little attempt to give an objective and comprehensive survey of the relationship of the book to other works of the time. James realized (p. 65), however, that he had not exhausted the list of rabbinic parallels. One major gap in his work is his failure to realize the relationship of the Biblical paraphrase of Josephus' *Antiquities* to Pseudo-Philo's *Biblical Antiquities.* But his work, despite the proliferation of scholarship in the field, remains of primary importance for the student.

ADDENDA

Chapter II *g*: *Influence: The Middle Ages*

James, pp. 10-11, notes that in the catalogue of the Abbey of St. Riguier, dated 831, there is an entry "liber Philonis Iudaei unum volumen." Kisch, p. 20, refers to a twelfth-century letter requesting the loan of a "liber Philonis" and concludes that this must be a manuscript that contained LAB along with fragments of Philo's *Quaestiones in Genesin* and *De Vita Contemplativa*. But H. L. Goodhart and E. R. Goodenough in their "General Bibliography of Philo Judaeus," in E. R. Goodenough, *The Politics of Philo Judaeus* (New Haven, 1938), p. 178, list four Latin manuscripts, including one coming from the twelfth century, containing only the fragments of *Quaestiones in Genesin* and *De Vita Contemplativa*; they also list (p. 181) two manuscripts, one of the twelfth and the other of the thirteenth century, containing the Latin manuscript of the work *Interpretatio Hebraicorum Nominum*. There is no reason why the volume of Philo might not have been identical with one of these manuscripts and thus not have contained LAB.

Chapter III *f*: *Manuscripts: Relative merits of the Admont MS. and the* editio princeps

In the introduction to his forthcoming critical edition, Harrington shows conclusively that Sichardus, despite Kisch, is not, in general, responsible for emendations or for corrections in LAB's Biblical text so as to make it conform with the Vulgate; he was, Harrington concludes, a careful and faithful editor—even more careful and faithful than Kisch had suspected.

Chapter VII *e*: *Date: Quotations from the Bible as a criterion*

Harrington, in a forthcoming article, "The Biblical Text of Pseudo-Philo's *Liber Antiquitatum Biblicarum*," to appear in *Catholic Biblical Quarterly*, has systematically examined the Biblical quotations in LAB and concluded that LAB is witness to a stage in the history of the Hebrew text of the Bible, and that this text is the Palestinian text, in contrast to the Babylonian (Masoretic) text and the Egyptian (LXX) text. The Biblical documents from the Dead Sea suggest, according to F. M. Cross, "The History of the Biblical Text in the Light of Discoveries in the Judaean Desert," *Harvard Theological Review*, 57 (1964), pp. 287-288, that an authoritative text of the Hebrew Bible had been promulgated by the second century C.E. and perhaps, in view of the scrolls from Masada, even before 73. Since LAB used a variant Heberw text, he probably, theorizes Harrington, composed his work before 100 and most likely, because of the absence of any genuine reference to the fall of Jerusalem, before 70. But the fact that Josephus, who completed his *Antiquities* in 93 C.E. (*AJ* 20. 267), has Biblical texts which often disagree with our Hebrew text and is said to have used a proto-Lucianic text frequently agreeing with LAB, shows that after 70 variant texts had still not been suppressed. Most important of all, however, the Targumic and Midrashic traditions in Palestine, to judge from Biblical variants in the Talmud and Midrashim themselves, continued to permit considerable latitude in quoting, paraphrasing, and expounding the text.

Chapter XI *f*: *Relation to Other Books: Josephus*

Another instance where LAB and Josephus disagree is the following: According to LAB 63.2 it is Saul who killed Abimelech, whereas ,according to Josephus, *AJ* 6.259, following both the Hebrew text (1 Samuel 22.18) and the LXX, it was Doeg who carried out Saul's order.

Chapter XIV: *Commentary*

P. 87, LAB 5.4: "And first . . . all of them": Harrington, in his forthcoming critical edition, on the analogy with 5.6, emends to "And Phenech, the son of Japheth, looked upon all the sons of Gomer."

P. 98, LAB 8.9: That Joseph stayed with Potiphar for fourteen years is a detail apparently found only in LAB.

P. 98, LAB 8.11: Harrington, in his forthcoming edition, notes that LAB, in giving the name Namuhel, differs from both the Hebrew text and the LXX and all other versions of Genesis 46.10, and is in accord with only 1 Chronicles 4.24—another indication, we may note, to support the theory of those who think that LAB is following the tradition of the Chronicler (see Chapter VIII above).

P. 98 (bottom), LAB 8.11: That the number of Jacob's descendants who went down into Egypt was 72 is unique with LAB. The Hebrew text (Gen. 46.27) and Josephus (AJ 2.176) have 70, the LXX 75.

P. 108, line 11, LAB 11.8: "Keep the sabbath day": LAB here adopts the version of the Ten Commandments found in Deuteronomy 5.12, as against "remember," found in Exodus 20.8. In this, as Harrington, in his forthcoming article in Catholic Biblical Quarterly remarks, LAB agrees with the Samaritan Pentateuch on Exodus 20.8. The rabbis (Shebuoth 20b), in a famous comment, attempt to reconcile the two versions of this commandment by remarking that God uttered "keep" and "remember" as one word. Perhaps, we may suggest, LAB's adoption of "keep" is in line with the Deuteronomistic outlook (see above, Chapter IX a) that some have discerned in this work; but such a thesis seems highly doubtful.

P. 108, LAB 11.9: LAB is unique in prescribing that one should "love" or "cherish (dilige)" one's father and mother, whereas the Hebrew text (Ex. 20.12), the LXX, and Josephus (AJ 3.92) say that one should honor one's father and mother.

P. 113, LAB 13.1: There are considerable differences in the order of the items for the tabernacle in LAB, the Hebrew text, the LXX, and Josephus (AJ 3.102 ff.). See D. W. Gooding, The Account of the Tabernacle: Translation and Textual Problems of the Greek Exodus (Cambridge, 1959), which unfortunately makes no mention of the evidence of LAB on this point.

P. 114, LAB 13.2: One group of MSS. read "Then God cried to Moses and spake to him," in accordance with Leviticus 1.1.

P. 119, LAB 15.5: If Strugnell's emendation is accepted, in terram non suam should be in terra non sua, "in a land that is not their's."

P. 122, last line, note 1, on LAB 16.7: The MSS. read Syna, i.e., Sinai. James' translation is based on his emendation gyro, found on the next line of this section. Harrington suggests sinu; thus the meaning would be "in the bosom of this place." I should like to suggest taking Syna as an abbreviation for synagoga (as in 16.6), and the meaning would be "We cannot abide in the company of this place."

P. 127, line 21, LAB 19.3: In describing Moses as a shepherd of Israel, LAB parallels Philo, De Josepho 2 and De Vita Mosis 1.61, who, in speaking of Moses the shepherd, notes that this occupation prepared him well for his role as a statesman, since kings are called "shepherds of their people." This description of Moses becomes a commonplace in rabbinic tradition; see Targum Ecclesiastes 12.11, etc., cited by Ginzberg, 5.414, n. 109. See also R. Bloch, "Quelque aspects de la figure de Moïse," in H. Cazelles et al., Moïse l'Homme de l'Alliance (Paris, 1955), pp. 138-139.

P. 128, line 3, LAB 19.4: "Remember, ye wicked": B. J. Malina, The Palestinian Manna Tradition (Leiden, 1968), p. 72, notes that LAB is here in accord with the rabbinic interpretation of Deuteronomy 1.1 that Moses' words are words of reproof. Malina is wrong, however, in citing Josephus, AJ 4.194-195, as a parallel, since Moses in this passage has words not of reproach but of consolation for the Israelites. Indeed, in 4.189, in an extra-Biblical addition that indicates his intent, Josephus, in his paraphrase of Moses' discourse in Deuteronomy, has Moses declare, "I say this with no intent to reproach you."

P. 129, LAB 19.10: "the land of Egypt": Harrington, in his forthcoming commentary, notes that only LAB and the Samaritan text, in their version of Deuteronomy 34.1, add the land of Egypt to the list of lands shown to Moses by God.

P. 130, line 21, LAB 19.13: "heaven (*celum*)": Though the manuscripts are unanimous in this reading, Harrington, on the basis of the phrase *dies hesternus,* "yesterday," in the following line, plausibly emends to *seculum,* "generation."

P. 133, LAB 20.1-8: Malina, *The Palestinian Manna Tradition* (Leiden, 1968), p. 82, notes that Josephus, *AJ* 5.20, agrees with LAB in omitting the incident of the circumcision at Gilgal (Joshua 5.2-9).

P. 135, LAB 20.8: "the manna for the sake of Moses": Josephus, *AJ* 3.31, similarly remarks that the manna was sent by God as a favor to Moses.

P. 136, line 2, LAB 21.2: "mind (*sensum*)": In view of the context, which speaks of numbering the stars, Harrington plausibly suggests emending *sensum* to *censum,* "numbering."

P. 138, LAB 22.1: For "had built them [*sibi*] an altar" Harrington plausibly suggests, on the basis of the Hebrew text of Joshua 22.10, "had built there [*ibi*] an altar."

P. 144, line 15, LAB 23.13: "you (*vos*)": It is clear from the context that *vos* must be emended, as Harrington does, to *hos,* "them," referring to the fathers.

P. 169, line 18, LAB 30.2: "enemies": The Hebrew text has לְצִדִּים, "sides," but apparently LAB, like the LXX, understood it as לְצָרִים, though, as Harrington notes in his forthcoming article in *Catholic Biblical Quarterly,* the LXX rendered it as "narrow places," hence "distress," whereas LAB understood it, just as legitimately, as "enemies." This again would confirm Harrington's thesis that underlying LAB's Scriptural quotations is a Hebrew Biblical text rather than an inserted Greek text, as Cohn had assumed.

P. 170, line 24, LAB 30.5: "hailstones": LAB follows the LXX here; the Hebrew text (Joshua 10.11) speaks of "great stones from heaven."

P. 174, line 18, LAB 32.1: Evidence that LAB is here translating from a Hebrew text can be seen in *filius Abino et omnis populus,* "the son of Abino and all the people." Harrington, in his forthcoming article in *Catholic Biblical Quarterly,* plausibly suggests that LAB is here translating אֲבִינֹעַם as two words, *Abino* and עַם, "people." Perhaps, we may add, LAB was influenced by his desire to make the song of Deborah parallel to the song of Moses upon crossing the Red Sea, just as the rabbis did in selecting this passage as the Haphtarah for the weekly portion of the Torah containing the Song of Moses. In Moses' song (Exodus 15.1) we are told that the children of Israel joined in.

P. 184, lines 22-23, LAB 36.2: For "the sword of the Lord is upon us" the reading of the Admont and other MSS., following the Hebrew and LXX texts, is preferable, "a sword for the Lord and for Gideon!"

P. 185, line 11, LAB 36.4: "in a good old age and was buried in his own city": Here LAB, paraphrasing Judges 8.32, follows the Hebrew text in the phrase "in a good old age" and the LXX in "in his own city."

P. 185, line 14, LAB 37.1: "all": Harrington has noted that only LAB and the Lucianic text have "all."

P. 188, LAB 39.2: "Because he was jealous of his brothers": Harrington correctly points out, in accordance with Judges 11.2, that it is clear that Jephthah's brothers were jealous of him rather than vice versa. In the process of translation, a subjective genitive was, as he suggests, taken as an objective genitive.

P. 197, LAB 42.10: Phadahel: Harrington plausibly explains the name of the angel by noting that in Judges 13.18 the name is פֶּלִאי, which in Greek might be Phalalel; then Λ was confused with Δ to give Phadahel.

P. 198, LAB 43.2: In this picture and in that of LAB 43.7 of Samson the man of faith, LAB is closer to the New Testament (Hebrews 11.32) than to Josephus.

P. 204, line 28, LAB 45.3: "cast them forth": The MSS. read *eum*, and hence the translation should be "cast him forth." In Judges 19.25, the Levite puts the concubine out to the men; here, as the following clause, "they let the man go," shows, the men seized both the Levite and the concubine and then cast out the man.

P. 205, line 5, LAB 45.4: "throughout the twelve tribes": The Hebrew text of Judges 19.29 has "throughout all the territory (גְּבוּל, lit. "boundary"); the LXX agrees in having "to every boundary (ὁρίῳ). The Lucianic text, Josephus *AJ* 5.149, and LAB here agree in reading "tribes," but this may reflect merely a common Targumic tradition.

P. 207, line 15 (margin), on LAB 47.1: Add Num. 25⁶ sqq..

P. 207, LAB 47.1: For Jambri the Melk MS. correctly reads Zambri, in accordance with Numbers 25.14, where he is called Zimri.

P. 207, LAB 47.1: "I verily entered in": The Admont MS. has (unnecessarily) incorporated the gloss, *ad Madianitam,* "to the Midianite woman."

P. 207, LAB 47.1: "24,000": Dietzfelbinger, in his commentary, notes that this is one of the few instances where LAB agrees in numbers with the Biblical account. Strangely enough, though in other places Josephus agrees with LAB in deviating from the Bible (Num. 25.9), here (*AJ* 4.155) he diverges from both and reads "no less than 14,000 men" (one MS. to be sure, does read 24,000).

P. 207, LAB 47.2: "the declarations of thy truth (*manifestationes veritatis tue*)": Harrington, noting that this is the apparent rendering of *urim vetumim,* emends to "the declarations and thy truths (*manifestationes et veritates tue*).

P. 207, LAB 47.2: "are lying": i.e., are telling lies.

P. 207, LAB 47.3: "had I not sworn": This is the reading of the *editio princeps.* The Admont MS. reads "had you not sworn." But there is no mention previously of an oath by either God or Phinehas.

Pp. 207-208, LAB 47.4-6: Dan Ben-Amos and Haim Schwarzbaum (*per litt.*) have noted that the individual elements of LAB's fable are traditional: thus the lion as a ruler is found in the fable of the lion and the crane told by Rabbi Joshua ben Hananiah (Genesis Rabbah 64 end). The fable as a whole illustrates the motif (U-11) listed by Stith Thompson in his *Motif-Index of Folk Literature* (6 vols., 2nd ed., Copenhagen, 1955-1958), "small trespasses punished, large crimes condoned," on which see H. Schwarzbaum, *Studies in Jewish and World Folklore* (Berlin, 1968), pp. 353-354, who cites a story in modern Jewish folklore of how a lion acquitted a wolf, bear, and fox who had confessed to having devoured smaller and weaker creatures but condemned to death a sheep whose only crime was that she had eaten some hay from her owner's wooden shoes. The motif, however, does not appear in Talmudic or midrashic literature.

Pp. 207-208, LAB 47.4-6: An exhaustive search by the present editor leads him to conclude that this remarkable fable of the lion and the other beasts has no parallel in the Jewish tradition.

P. 208, line 18, LAB 47.6: Remove the comma after "unto it."

P. 215, line 32, LAB 50.5: "lest perchance I be not worthy": Better "Indeed, perhaps, I am not worthy," as the preferable reading *sum*, which is indicative, shows.

P. 221, line 19, LAB 53.6: "refrain (*taceat*)": Harrington, in his forthcoming edition, notes that the word *taceat,* "be silent," is inappropriate for an ear. The mistake has occurred in the translation of the Hebrew חֵרֵשׁ, which refers to someone who is both deaf and dumb. The meaning which the translator should have chosen is "be deaf." This would confirm the thesis that our text goes back to a Hebrew original.

P. 225, line 17, LAB 55.2: "scorpions": LAB, as Harrington notes, has read עֲקְרָב, "scorpion," for עַכְבָר, "mouse."

P. 232, LAB 59.5: "bulls": Harrington, in his forthcoming edition, notes that the combination וְרֹן of שׁוֹר is easily confused with ה of שֶׂה.

P. 233, line 16, LAB 61.2: "out of the camp": Here LAB agrees with the Hebrew text of 1 Samuel 17.4 and Josephus, *AJ* 6.171, against the LXX, which reads "out of the army."

P. 237, LAB 62.9: "that we should be parted from one another": This is the reading of the *editio princeps*. The Admont MS. reads: "that we should not be sated with one another." Harrington, in his forthcoming edition, suggests that the author of LAB or perhaps the Greek translator understood the Hebrew לְהַשְׂבִּיעַ of 1 Samuel 20.17 as coming from שָׂבַע, "to sate," rather than from שָׁבַע, "to swear."

P. 238, line 21, LAB 63.2: LAB also agrees with Josephus, *AJ* 6.244, in following the LXX on 1 Samuel 22.9 in the description of Doeg as being in charge of Saul's mules; the Hebrew text, on the other hand, speaks of Doeg as standing by Saul's servants.

P. 238, line 23, LAB 63.2: LAB agrees with Josephus, *AJ* 6.254, in following the LXX in giving the name Abimelech, whereas the Hebrew text of 1 Samuel 22.9 and 16 gives the name as Ahimelech.

Chapter XVII: *Bibliography*

Bonifatius Fischer, ed., *Vetus Latina: Die Reste der altlateinischen Bibel nach Petrus Sabatier neu gesammelt und herausgegeben von der Erzabtei Beuron*, vol. 2: *Genesis* (Freiburg, 1954), introduction, p. 21, and *passim* [systematically collates LAB with the Vetus Latina].

Daniel J. Harrington, "The Biblical Text of Pseudo-Philo's *Liber Antiquitatum Biblicarum*," to be published in *Catholic Biblical Quarterly*, 33 (1971), pp. 1-17.

Daniel J. Harrington, "The Original Language of Pseudo-Philo's *Liber Antiquitatum Biblicarum*," to be published in *Harvard Theological Review*, 63 (1970), pp. 503-514.

Bruce J. Malina, *The Palestinian Manna Tradition: The Manna Tradition in the Palestinian Targums and Its Relationship to the New Testament Writings* (Leiden, 1968), pp. 72, 81, 82, 85, 87, 90.

Addison G. Wright, "The Literary Genre Midrash," *Catholic Biblical Quarterly*, 28 (1966), pp. 423-424 [classifies LAB as a narrative midrash].

Acknowledgments

Dan Ben-Amos, George D. Kilpatrick, Haim Schwarzbaum.

6 November 1970.

ACKNOWLEDGMENTS

The present writer wishes to thank the following for their assistance: Arthur E. Barker, Paul E. Beichner, Jay Braverman, LeRoy A. Campbell, Henry Chadwick, Gerson D. Cohen, Shaye J. Cohen, Mathias Delcor, Gerhard Delling, Otto Eissfeldt, Juliette Ernst, Henry A. Fischel, Meir Havazelet, Alan Huffman, Johannes Irmscher, George Kennedy, Paul Oskar Kristeller, Hugo Mantel, A. E. B. Owen, Julian G. Plante, Alexander Scheiber, Menachem Schmelzer, Heinz Schreckenberg, Anthony J. Shelton, R. J. H. Shutt, Beryl Smalley, Morton Smith, Odil Hannes Steck, Kenneth R. Stow, Patrick Strong, Geza Vermès, Michael Wadsworth, and E. J. Wiesenberg. He owes a special debt of gratitude to Christian Dietzfelbinger, Daniel J. Harrington, Guido Kisch, Marc Philonenko, John Strugnell, and the late Paul Winter (died 9 October 1969). Finally he wishes to express his sincere thanks to Professor Harry M. Orlinsky, the general editor of this series, for inviting him to write the prolegomenon and for many helpful suggestions.

INTRODUCTION

1. THE book now presented to English readers has never been translated before: not only is this so, but the very existence of it has remained unknown to the great mass of students for over three hundred years, although it was printed no less than five times in the course of the sixteenth century.

What is it, and why is it worth reviving after so long a period of oblivion? It is a Bible history, reaching, in its present imperfect form, from Adam to the death of Saul. It has come to us only in a Latin translation (made from Greek, and that again from a Hebrew original), and by an accident the name of the great Jewish philosopher of the first century, Philo, has been attached to it. Let me say at once that the attribution of it to him is wholly unfounded, and quite ridiculous: nevertheless I shall use his name in italics (*Philo*) as a convenient short title.

Its importance lies in this, that it is a genuine and unadulterated Jewish book of the first century —a product of the same school as the *Fourth Book of Esdras* and the *Apocalypse of Baruch*, and written, like them, in the years which followed the destruction of Jerusalem in A.D. 70. It is thus contemporary with some of the New Testament writings, and throws light upon them as well as upon the religious thought of the Jews of its time.

7

2. (*a*) The HISTORY OF THE BOOK, as known to us, can be shortly told. It was printed by Adam Petri in 1527, at Basle, in a small folio volume, along with the genuine Philo's *Quaestiones et Solutiones in Genesim*[1] and a fragment of the *De Vita contemplativa* (called *De Essaeis*). These were followed by the *Onomasticon* (*de Nominibus Hebraicis*) ascribed in Philo, in Jerome's version, and a Latin rendering of the *De Mundo* by Guillaume Budé. The whole volume is in Latin, and was edited by Joannes Sichardus: for the first three tracts he used two manuscripts, from Fulda and Lorsch, of which more hereafter. In 1538 Henricus Petri (son of Adam) reprinted this collection in a quarto volume, which I have not seen, and in 1550 included it all in a larger collection of patristic writings called *Micropresbyticon*. In 1552 our book (without the accompanying tracts) was printed from Sichardus' text in a small volume issued by Gryphius at Lyons, under the title *Antiquitatum diversi auctores*, and in 1599 in a similar collection *Historia antiqua*, by Commelin, at Heidelberg, edited by Juda Bonutius.

During the sixteenth and seventeenth centuries *Philo* was read and occasionally quoted, *e. g.* by Sixtus Senensis in the *Bibliotheca Sancta*, and by Pineda in his treatise on Solomon: but the greatest critics and scholars of the eighteenth and nineteenth centuries seem never to have seen it. J. A. Fabricius would certainly have accorded it a place in his *Codex pseudepigraphus Veteris Testamenti* if he had read it: and very little escaped his notice. He does speak of it in his *Bibliotheca Graeca* (ed. Harles, IV. 743, 746), but only from the

---

[1] A volume issued by Ascensius at Paris in 1520, edited by Aug. Justiniani, contained only the *Quaestiones et Sol. in Genesim.*

point of view of the editions. It is not too much to say that the chance which kept it from him has kept it also from the flock of scholars who have followed him like sheep for two hundred years. The first investigator to pay any attention to it seems to have been Cardinal J. B. Pitra. In the *Spicilegium Solesmense* (1855, II. 345 note, III. 335 note, etc.) there are allusions to it: in the later *Analecta Sacra* (II. 321; 1884) he printed the Lament of Jephthah's daughter from a Vatican MS. of it, treating it as a known work, and referring to the printed edition.

In 1893 I came upon four detached fragments in a manuscript at Cheltenham, in the Phillipps collection, and printed them as a new discovery in a volume of *Apocrypha Anecdota* (1st series, *Texts and Studies*, II. 3). No one who reviewed the book in England or abroad recognized that they were taken from a text already in print. At length, in 1898, the late Dr. L. Cohn, who was engaged for many years upon an edition of Philo's works, published in the *Jewish Quarterly Review* an article in which the source of my fragments was pointed out and a very full account given of the whole book, with copious quotations. This article of Dr. Cohn's is at present our standard source of information. Nothing to supersede it has, so far as I know, appeared since. A few scholars, but on the whole surprisingly few, have used *Philo* in recent years, notably Mr. H. St. John Thackeray in his book, *The Relation of St. Paul to Contemporary Jewish Thought.*

(*b*) Can we trace the history of *Philo* further back than the printed edition of 1527 by means of quotations or allusions to it? The whole body of evidence is remarkably small. At the very end of the fifteenth century Joannes Trithemius, Abbot

of Sponheim, writes a book, *De Scriptoribus ecclesiasticis*, printed at Paris in 1512. On f. 18*b* is a
notice of Philo, derived principally from Jerome,
and a list of his writings. Among these he includes
De generationum successu, lib. I. (which is our book),
and adds the opening words: *Adam genuit tres
filios*, which shows that he had seen the text. It
is the *only* item so distinguished in all his list.
Then, going back and setting aside certain extracts
from the text (of which we shall speak under the
head of authorities), we find, in the twelfth century,
Petrus Comestor of Troyes, in his *Historia Scholastica* (one of the famous text-books of the Middle
Ages), making a single incorrect quotation from
our book (V. 8). He calls his source ' Philo the
Jew, or, as some say, a heathen philosopher, in his
book of questions upon Genesis ': the words show
that he was quoting a manuscript which contained that work as well as our text. His
quotation is borrowed by several later mediæval
chroniclers.

In the catalogues of monastic libraries *Philo* is
of rare occurrence. The Fulda catalogue of the
sixteenth century [1] has " Repertorii noni ordo
primus, liber Philonis antiquitatum 36." The
number 36 is the older library number, perhaps
as old as the thirteenth century, which was written
on the cover of the volume. This was one of the
two manuscripts used by Sichardus: we shall return
to it.

In the twelfth century a monk writes to the
Abbot of Tegernsee for the loan of the " liber
Philonis." In 831 the abbey of St. Riquier, near
Abbeville, has in its catalogue " liber Philonis Judaei

---

[1] C. Scherer, *Der Fuldaer Handschriften-Katalog aus
dem 16 Jahrh. (Centralblatt f. Bibliothekswesen* XXVI.
p. 105 ; 1902),

unum volumen." Both these references may be found in Becker's *Catalogi*.[1]

One possible hint, and one only, of the existence of *Philo* in the Eastern Church is known to me. The *Taktikon* of Nicon, cap. 13, in the Slavonic version, as quoted by Berendts (*Zacharias-Apokryphen*, p. 5, note 3), reckons among the canonical books of the Old Testament "the *Palaea* (the Eastern text-book of Bible history comparable to the *Historia Scholastica* in the West) and *Philo*."

The *Decretum Gelasianum* of the fifth or sixth century condemns, among many other apocryphal books, "liber de filiabus Adae Leptogeneseos." The natural and usual interpretation of the words is that they refer to the *Book of Jubilees*, which the Greeks called ἡ λεπτὴ γένεσισ, but it is worth noting that *Philo* mentions the daughters of Adam in the first few lines, whereas in *Jubilees* they do not occur before the fourth chapter.

I know of nothing in earlier centuries which looks like an allusion to *Philo*, unless it be a passage in Origen on John (Tom. VI. 14) in which he says[2]: "I know not what is the motive of the Jewish tradition that Phinees the son of Eleazar, who admittedly lived through the days of many of the Judges, is the same as Elias, and that immortality was promised to him in Numbers

---

[1] The Abbey of St. Bertin and that of Corbie in Picardy in their twelfth-century catalogues (Becker, nos. 77, 247, 79, 263) both have an entry of *Questiones in Genesim*; seemingly not those of St. Jerome, which occur elsewhere in the catalogues.

[2] καὶ περὶ μετωνυμίασ γάρ, ὡσ ἐν ἀποκρύφοισ, οὐκ οἶδα πόθεν κινούμενοι οἱ ἐβραῖοι παραδιδόασι Φινεέσ, τὸν Ἐλεαζάρου υἱόν, ὁμολογουμένωσ παρατείναντα τὴν ζωὴν ἕωσ πολλῶν κριτῶν· ὡσ ἐν τοῖσ κριταῖσ ἀνέγνωμεν, αὐτὸν εἶναι Ἠλίαν, καὶ τὸ ἀθάνατον ἐν τοῖσ Ἀριθμοῖσ αὐτῷ, διὰ τῆσ ὀνομαζομένησ εἰρήνησ ἐπηγγέλθαι, ἀνθ᾽ ὧν ζηλώσασ . . . ἐξεκέντησε τὴν Μαδιανῖτιν, κ.τ.λ.

(xxv. 12)," with more to the same effect. He refers to no book, but to a tradition which is, in fact, preserved in several Midrashim. The identification is found in *Philo*, c. XLVIII. See the note *in loc.*

3. The next business is to describe the AUTHORITIES FOR THE TEXT of *Philo*.

(*a*) We will take the printed edition of 1527 first (of which the four others of 1538–50–53–99 are mere reprints). Its symbol shall be A. In his preface, addressed to the monks of Fulda, Sichardus, like many editors of the Renaissance period, tells us but little of the manuscripts he used. The substance of what he says is as follows. At one time he had hoped to be able to remedy the many corruptions of the manuscripts, of which he had two; but he gradually came to despair of doing so, and resolved to give the text as he found it. His two manuscripts were as like each other as two eggs, so that he could not doubt that one was a copy of the other, though they were preserved in libraries far apart. He employed the Fulda copy, and had previously obtained the use of one from Lorsch Abbey, which was very old, and had expected that these would provide the materials for a satisfactory edition; moreover, he had got wind of the existence of another copy. But his manuscripts proved disappointing, and he is well aware that the present edition is inadequate. In preparing it he has aimed at following his manuscripts as closely as possible, and in issuing it now has judged that the evils of delay are greater than those of haste; especially as he looks forward to putting forth a greatly improved text in the future.[1]

---

[1] The important sentences in the original are: ut sensimus . . . exemplaria, quorum duo habuimus, tam constanter

(*b*) We have seen that the Fulda MS. is traceable in the library catalogues late in the sixteenth century. Until lately it was thought to have been lost, along with the bulk of the Fulda MSS.: but it has been identified, first by Dr. Cohn, and then, independently, by Dr. P. Lehmann, with a MS. at Cassel (*Theol.* 4° 3) of the eleventh century. The Lorsch MS. still remains undiscovered.

The identity of the Cassel MS. with that used by Sichardus is not doubtful. In its cover is an inscription by him stating that he had it rebound in 1527. It also retains the old label, of the fourteenth century, with the title *Liber Philonis Antiquitatum*, and the old Fulda press-mark.

The book which furnishes this information is a special study, published by Dr. Lehmann in 1912, of the libraries and manuscripts used by Sichardus for the purpose of his various editions of ancient authors. Dr. Lehmann has collected, *à propos* of Sichardus's *Philo*, notices of all the MSS. of the Latin *Philo* known to exist, and has succeeded in increasing the number, from three which were known to Dr. Cohn in 1898, to sixteen, eleven of

---

tamque ex composito mendos suos tueri, consilium, quod mutandorum quorundam coeperamus, plane abiecimus, imitati id quod utrumque exemplar haberet, quae tamen ita erant inter se similia, ut nec ouum diceres ouo magis, ut dubium mihi non esset, quin ex altero esset alterum descriptum, utcunque magno loci intervallo dissita. Quippe attuleramus commodum illud Fuldense uestrum, cum antea ex Laurissensi coenobio impetrassemus pervetustum quidem illud, et quod nobis felicissimae editionis magnam spem fecerat : sed progressos paululum non modo foede destituit, sed et fecit ut praeproperae nos editionis plurimum poeniteret . . . dedimus operam ut ab exemplaribus quam minimum discederemus, ut sicubi fortasse extaret aliud exemplar, id quod tum inaudieramus, eius collatione nostra . . . absolverentur.

which contain the text of the *Antiquities*. They are as follows—

Admont (an abbey in Austria) 359, of cent. xi., containing *Ant.* and *Quaest. in Gen.*

Cassel, theol. 4° 3, of cent. xi. (the Fulda MS.), containing *Ant.* and *Quaest.*

Cheltenham, Phillipps 461, of cent. xii, from Trèves, containing *Ant.*

Cues (near Trèves), 16 (or H. 11), of 1451, paper, containing *Ant.* and *Quaest.*

Munich, lat. 4569, of cent. xii., from Benedictbeuren, containing *Ant.* and *Quaest.*

Munich, lat. 17,133, of cent. xii., from Schäftlarn, containing *Ant.* and *Quaest.*

Munich, lat. 18,481, of cent. xi., from Tegernsee, containing *Ant.* and *Quaest.*

Rome, Vatican, lat. 488, of cent. xv., containing *Ant.* and *Quaest.*

Vienna, lat. 446, of cent. xiii., containing *Ant.*

Würzburg, M. ch. f. 210, of cent. xv. (paper), containing *Ant.*

Würzburg, M. ch. f. 276, of cent. xv. (paper), containing *Ant.* and *Quaest.*

Besides these, there are at Augsburg, Florence, Rome, Trèves, MSS. containing *Quaest.* only, and at Coblenz one of which no particulars were forthcoming.

For the purposes of the present volume only four of the above authorities have been employed, namely, the Fulda-Cassel MS. as represented by Sichardus's edition (and with it we must allow for some use of the lost MS. from Lorsch), the Cheltenham, Vatican, and Vienna MSS. The fact that Dr. Cohn was known to have in contemplation a full critical edition precluded others from trying to cover the whole ground, and, even had it been otherwise desirable to do so, the investigation would have been very difficult for anyone outside Germany. There are, for instance, no printed catalogues of the Admont, Cassel, or Würzburg libraries.

However, the paucity of authorities here brought to bear is of little importance. What Dr. Lehmann tells us[1] is sufficient to show that none of the MSS. present a completer text than we already know. All must go back to an ancestor which was already mutilated when our first transcripts of it were made. Upon this point more will be said. At present we will take account of what Dr. Lehmann has to say of Sichardus's MSS., and proceed to the description of the MSS. actually used, and of some subsidiary authorities.

Of the Fulda MS. we now learn that it is the work of more than one scribe, of the eleventh century. The *Antiquities* occupy ff. 1–65a, and have a title in a late medieval hand: *Libri Philonis Iudei de initio mundi*, which, or the like, is " usual in the MSS." The *Quaestiones*, entitled (in the original hand): *Filonis Questionum in genisi et solutionum*, follow on ff. 65a–89a, and in them is a noteworthy feature. On f. 86, in the middle of the page the MS. omits, without any sign of a break, a long passage containing the end of the *Quaestiones* and the beginning of the *De Essaeis*, and corresponding to pp. 82, l. 40–84, l. 16 of Sichardus's edition. At this point Sichardus has a marginal note : " Here the copies differed, but we have followed that of Lorsch, as being the older." Now this same gap is found in most, if not in all, of the other MSS., and not all of these are copied directly from the Fulda MS. We may say, therefore, that all MSS. showing this gap are independent of the Lorsch MS., but not necessarily dependent on the Fulda MS.

[1] P. Lehmann : *Johannes Sichardus und die von ihm benutzten Bibliotheken und Handschriften (Quellen und Untersuchungen zur Lateinische Philologie des Mittelalters*, IV. 1. 1912).

It is clear from what has been said that Sichardus was wrong in regarding the Fulda MS. as a copy of that of Lorsch, and that the latter represented an old and valuable tradition : and, further, that he exaggerates greatly when he says that the two MSS. were as alike as two eggs.[1] Dr. Lehmann's final remark is that the disappearance of the Lorsch MS. is very much to be deplored, for, judged by the Greek fragments and the Armenian version of the *Quaestiones*, it represented a better tradition than all the extant Latin MSS.

Of the other MSS. in the list given above, it may be observed that the Cues MS. (written at Gottweih in 1451) and the two Würzburg MSS. are not likely to be of very much value : and that, of the three Munich MSS., that from Tegernsee (18481) is to all appearance the parent of the other two. Probably the monk who wrote to Tegernsee to borrow a Philo (see p. 10) was a member of Benedictbeuren or Schäftlarn. The Schäftlarn copy (17133) was written between 1160 and 1164.[2]

I now proceed to give a detailed account of the three complete MSS. which I have been able to use, and of certain subsidiary authorities. The three MSS. are those mentioned by Dr. Cohn in his article, and I have been led to examine them during recent years by my interest in the text, and without serious thought of using them for the purposes of an edition. They are the copies preserved at Cheltenham, Vienna, and Rome.

---

[1] Dr. Lehmann quotes a number of instances in which Sichardus has deviated from the MS. in spelling : he is also clear that conjecture was resorted to. This last statement applies especially, I think, to the *Quaestiones*.

[2] The printed catalogue gives the title of the *Antiquities* in 4569 and 18481 as *Historia ab initio mundi usque ad Dauid regem.* In 18481 it is preceded by Jerome's notice *of Philo.*

P. The Phillipps MS. 461 is a small vellum book (6⅝ × 4¾ in.) of 124 leaves, with 20 lines to a page; a few leaves palimpsest, over not much older writing. It is of cent. XII., clearly written : on f. 1*a* the provenance is stated, in this inscription : Codex SX (?) *Sc̄i Eucharii primi Trevirorum archiepi. siquis eum abstulerit anathema sit. Amen.* A hand of cent. XV. adds the word *Mathie.* Then follows the title, of cent. XV. : *Philo iudeus de successione generacionis veteris Testamenti.* On f. 1*b* is Jerome's account of Philo (*de virr. illustr.* c. XI.) : the text of the book begins on 3*a* : *Adam genuit,* and ends on 119*b* without colophon. It is followed by a few pieces of medieval Latin verse, of no great interest. The first begins ; *Carnis in ardore flagrans monialis amore.* Another is on Chess : *Qui cupit egregium scacorum noscere ludum Audiat. ut potui carmine composui.*

V. Vindobonensis lat. 446, a small folio of 53 leaves, with 31 lines to a page, in a tall, narrow, rather sloping hand, doubtless German, by more than one scribe : of cent. XII. late or XIII. early. There is an old press-mark of cent. XVI. : XI°. 68. The text is preceded by *Jeronimus de Phylone in catalogo uirorum illustrium.* It begins *Incip. Genesis.* INITIUM MUNDI. *Adam genuit,* and ends on 53*a* without colophon, occupying the whole volume.

R. Vaticanus lat. 488, of cent. XV., in a very pretty Roman hand, in double columns of 35 lines. The first 80 leaves contain tracts of Augustine, Prosper and Jerome. Our book, to which is prefixed the extract from Jerome, begins on f. 81. It is headed : *Genesis,* and begins : *Inicium mundi. Adam Genuit.* The colophon is : *Explicit ystoria philonis ab initio mundi usque ad David regem.* It is followed by the *Quaestiones et Solutiones in Genesim,* which occupy ff. 129–148 (end). The arms of Paul V. and of Cardinal Scipione Borghese the librarian are on the binding : there is no other mark of provenance.

P is thus the only one of the three manuscripts whose old home can be definitely fixed. It belonged to the abbey of St. Eucharius, otherwise called of St. Matthias (whose body lies there), just outside Trèves.

(*c*) Next come certain manuscripts which contain extracts from the text.

B

Ph. The Phillipps MS. 391, of 92 ff., of cent. XII. early, contains principally tracts of Jerome, notably *Quaestiones Hebraicae*. On ff. 87–8 it has the four extracts which I printed in 1893 (see above). It belonged to Leander van Ess, and has an old press-mark C 1 or C 7.

T. No. 117 in the Town Library at Trèves. A paper MS., dated 1459. It contains five of the same tracts as Ph and two of the extracts from *Philo*. It retains its old press-mark, B 11, and an inscription showing that it belonged to the abbey of S. Maria ad Martyres at Trèves. The contents of the book and the text of the extracts make it clear that T is a copy of Ph or of a sister-book, while the form of the press-mark shows that Ph and T belonged to the same library. Thus T is only important as helping to "place" Ph.

F. MS. McClean 31 in the Fitzwilliam Museum, Cambridge (fully described in my catalogue of the McClean MSS.), is a remarkable copy of the *Aurora*, or versified Bible, of Petrus de Riga. It is of cent. XIII., and is copiously annotated. Among the *marginalia* are many extracts (a complete list will be found at the beginning of the Appendix on various Readings) from *Philo*, uniformly introduced under that name, and for the most part abridged. The manuscript may have been written in the Rhine Provinces, or in Eastern France.

J. The Hebrew *Chronicle of Jerahmeel*, edited in an English translation by Dr. M. Gaster (*Oriental Translation Fund, New series* IV., 1899), was compiled early in cent. XIV. somewhere in the Rhineland. It contains large portions of *Philo*, some *in extenso*, some abridged. A list is given in the Appendix. Dr. Gaster will have it that the Hebrew is the original text; but Hebraists do not agree with him, and it is, in fact, possible to show that the Hebrew writer was translating from Latin, and from a manuscript which contained misreadings common to those we now have. See the Appendix of Readings on III. 10, VII. 3.

(*d*) Glancing back over the list, we see that for all but one of the items a German origin is established. The Vatican MS. is the exception, and even this presents certain indications of German origin. Near the beginning of the book (III. 3) is a speech beginning *Deleam*. R reads *Vel eam*.

Now it is a habit with German scribes of the twelfth and thirteenth centuries to write their capital D's with a sharply-pointed base, making the letter very like the outline of the conventional harp, and also very like a capital V ; nor do I know any other script in which the likeness between D and V is so striking. My guess is that the scribe of R, encountering the puzzling letter near the beginning of his work, made the mistake, which he does not repeat; and I regard it as an indication that his archetype was a German book of the same age as V (and, I may say by anticipation, presenting a remarkably similar text to that of V).

Thus the geographical distribution of the authorities combines with the evidence of the literature to show that in the Middle Ages *Philo* was circulated within very narrow limits, and practically confines those limits to Germany and Northern France.

(*e*) Of these authorities I have transcribed A, collated P (on the spot), and R (from a photograph) in full; have examined and partially collated V (on the spot), and have transcribed Ph, T, and F : J is in print, and I have collated that also.

The complete copies which are known to us are all ultimately derived from a single imperfect ancestor. All exhibit the same *lacunae*. The text, as we have it, ends abruptly in the midst of Saul's last dying speech : " Say to David : Thus saith Saul : Be not mindful of my hatred nor of my unrighteousness." How much further the story went we shall discuss later on. That it is imperfect is clear, and all our copies agree in the imperfection. Two other obvious *lacunae* occur about two-thirds of the way through the book, in the story of Abimelech. After the death of Gideon (XXXVII. 1) we read that " he had a son by a concubine who slew all his brethren, desiring to be ruler over the people. Then came together all the trees of the field to the fig-tree, and said: Come reign over us." Thus we pass from the first entry of Abimelech to a point somewhere in the Parable of Jotham. I think we must assume that at this place a leaf was missing in the ancestor of all our copies. None of them make any attempt to fill the gap. At the end of the story of Abimelech is another bad place (XXXVIII. 1): "After these things Abimelech ruled over the people for one year and six months,-and died (under a certain tower) when a woman let fall half a mill-stone upon him. (Then Jair judged Israel twenty and two years.) He built a sanctuary to Baal," etc. The words in parentheses represent the supple-ments of P. The text as read in A would imply that Abimelech built a sanctuary to Baal; but it was in fact Jair who did so. Here, then, is another gap, the extent of which is uncertain. The imme-diate successor of Abimelech in the Bible is Tola. Our historian may or may not have noticed him: he does, later on, omit one of the minor judges, Ibzan. At most, another leaf is wanting at this point : at least, a few lines have been lost by casual damage.

There are, further, indications that the imperfect archetype was an uncial MS. with undivided words. In the early pages of the book much space is occupied by lists of names, which, being invented by the author, could not be corrected by recourse to the Bible. The many disagreements as to the divisions of the names (*e.g.* Sifatecia Sifa. Tecia, Lodo. Otim Lodoothim, filii aram filiarum, etc.) point to a stage at which the scribe had no guidance in this matter. So do such variants as memoraret artari for memorare tartari, in chaoma tonata for in chaomate nata. Again, in XIX. 15 certain unin-

telligible words (istic mel apex magnus) are written
in capitals in V, which I interpret as an attempt
on the part of the scribe to represent exactly the
ductus litterarum of an ancestor.

A minuscule stage is evidenced by frequent con-
fusions (in proper names) of *f* and *s*, of *c* and *z*, of
ch and *di*, and an occasional *r* for *n* or the converse.
This last error, were it more frequent, might point
to an "insular" ancestor somewhere in the pedigree.
There is an *a priori* likelihood that a rare text
current in the Rhenish district would have attracted
the notice of Irish monks and have been preserved
by them. A closer study of the variants may
perhaps confirm this notion.[1]

External and internal evidence combined lead
me to the conclusion that our text was preserved
in a single imperfect copy written in uncials, and
containing the *Antiquities*, the *Quaestiones in Genesim*, and *De Essaeis*, which had survived at some
centre of ancient culture in the Rhenish district,
most likely in or near Trèves.

(*f*) The authorities used in this book fall into
three groups : (1) Lorsch and Fulda, represented
by the printed text, which I call A ; (2) The Trèves
group P, Ph, T ; (3) VRFJ. This is a rough division.
Sichardus gives us no means of distinguishing
readings peculiar to either of his MSS. and, as we
have seen, is probably wrong in saying that they
were very closely allied. The Trèves MSS. are in
more frequent agreement with A than VR. V and
R, if not parent and child (and probably they are
not) are at least uncle and nephew. Generally
speaking I am of opinion that, though manifestly
wrong in a number of small points, A is preferable
to any one of the complete MSS. that I have
seen.

[1] In XVI. 7 *in syna* seems to be a mistake for *in gyro*.

It will be readily understood that, in an edition like this, a complete exposition of the evidence for the text is impossible : but by way of illustration we will take a short passage for which all our authorities except J are available, and in which the grouping is (if imperfectly) shown. The Song of David before Saul (LX. 2 *sqq.*) runs thus in APPhTVRF. A is taken as the basis.

Tenebrae et silentium erant (erat RF) antequam fieret seculum, et locutum est silentium et apparuerunt tenebrae.

Et factum est tunc (*om.* tunc RF) nomen tuum in compaginatione extensionis quod appellatum (+ est VRFPhT) superius coelum, inferius vocatum (invocatum V) est terra.

Et praeceptum est superiori ut plueret secundum tempus eius (suum F) et inferiori praeceptum est (praec. est inf. F : *om.* praec. est R) ut crearet escam omnibus quae facta sunt (homini qui factus est VRF).

Et post haec facta est tribus spiritum uestrorum (nostrorum F).

Et nunc molesta esse noli tanquam secunda creatura (factura VRF).

Si comminus memoraret artari in quo ambulas A.

Si comminus memorarer artare, etc. PPhT (artare rather obscure in T).

Si quominus memorare tartari (tractari R) in quo ambulabas VRF.

Aut non audire tibi sufficit quoniam per ea quae consonant in conspectu tuo multis (in multis VRF) psallo?

Aut immemor es quoniam de resultatione in chaoma tonata (in chaomate nata VRF) est uestra creatura?

Arguet autem tempora noua (te metra noua VRF) unde natus sum, de quo nascitur (de qua nascetur VRF) post tempus de lateribus meis qui uos donauit (domauit P, domabit PhTVRF).

VRF here show themselves the best in some important readings. The first (*homini* for *omnibus*) is the least obvious : but it will be quickly seen that the point of the invective is that evil spirits are a secondary creation, and particularly that they are inferior to man. If not actually created after man, at least they came into being after the earth, which was to supply food to him. Moreover, a similar variant occurs early in the book (III. 2), non diiudicabit spiritus meus in omnibus (AVR : hominibus P) istis. The

LXX of Gen. 6³, ἐν τοῖσ ἀνθρώποισ τούτοισ, shows that P is right.

But VR (F is rarely available) are not uniformly successful. They sometimes shirk difficulties. In IX. 13 Moses "natus est in testamento dei et in testamento carnis eius" (*i. e.* was born circumcised). Here VR read "in testamentum carnis," which makes nonsense: and a few lines later, where it is said of Pharaoh's daughter: "et dum uidisset in Zaticon (sc. διαθήκην) hoc est in testamento carnis," the whole clause is omitted by VR.

In III. 10 we have "et reddet infernus debitum suum, et perditio restituet *paratecem suam.*" This is the obviously right reading of AP: VR read *partem suam*, and J betrays itself not only as a version from Latin, but as dependent on a Latin MS. allied to VR, by saying "and Abaddon shall return its portion."

When Pharaoh has determined to destroy the Hebrew children, the people say (IX. 2): "ὠμοτοκείαν (ometocean cett.) passa sunt viscera mulierum nostrarum." All the authorities, including F, keep the strange word, but V writes "Ometocean id est passa sunt," showing that at some stage there was an intention to insert a Latin equivalent. Still, the word has survived.

The shirking of difficulties is not confined to VR. The priestly vestments, *epomis* (XI. 15) and *cidaris* (XIII. 1), become *ebdomas* and *cithara* in AP, but not in VR. In a list of the plagues of Egypt (X. 1), one, *pammixia*, is omitted by AP and retained by VR. This word *pammixia* (panimixia in the MSS.) deserves a passing note, for it does not seem to have made its way into dictionaries or concordances. It is intended to mean the plague of all manner of flies, for which the LXX and Vulgate equivalent is κυνόμυια, *coenomyia.* Jerome, writing on this, says it ought to be κοινόμυια, signifying a mixture of all manner of flies, and adds that Aquila's word for it was πάμμικτον. Older editors read πάμμυιαν for πάμμικτον, but Field, or some one before him, corrected it, and our text confirms the correction.

VR do not always go together: R, as being later, has corruptions of its own. *Psalphinga*, a trumpet, is a favourite word with our author: R at first writes this as *psalmigraphus;* later, when he has realised that this is nonsense, he reproduces *psalphinga* as he should.

We have not yet cited examples in which the Trèves MSS. stand apart. I will give two specimens, one of a few words, the other longer, in which this is the case.

i. XXIII. 4. Una petra erat unde effodi patrem uestrum ; et genuit *uir scopuli illius* duos uiros A. P has : incisco petre illius, which is nearly right : VRF have "incisio petre illius," which is quite right.

ii. In the *Lament of Jephthah's Daughter* (XL. 6 *seq.*) all our authorities are available except F. J is very loose and paraphrastic, and its evidence will be given after the rest.

The first clause has no important variants. After that, taking A as the basis, we have—

(*a*) Ego autem non sum saturata thalamo meo, nec repleta sum coronis nuptiarum mearum.

(*b*) Non enim uestita sum splendore sedens in genua mea.

Non enim uestita sum splendore sedens in uirginitate mea P.

Non enim uestita sum splendore sedens in ingenuitate mea PhT.

Non enim uestita sum splendore secundum ingenuam meam VR.

(*c*) Non sum usa Mosi odoris mei.

      „   „   preciosi odoramenti mei PPhT.

      „   „   moysi odoris mei VR (*om.* usa R).

(Sichardus conjectured Moscho for Mosi : Pitra prints non sunt thymia odoris.)

(*d*) Nec froniuit (fronduit V) anima mea oleo unctionis quod (quibus R) praeparatum est mihi AVR.

Nec froniuit animam meam oleum unctionis quod praeparatum est mihi PPhT.

(*e*) O mater, in uano (uanum V) peperisti unigenitam tuam AVR.

O mater, in uano peperisti unigenitam tuam et genuisti eam super terram PPhT (see below, (*g*)).

(*f*) Quoniam factus est infernus thalamus meus.

(*g*) et genuam meam super terram A.

et genua mea super terram VR (*om.* mea R).

PPhT have the equivalent above in (*e*).

(*h*) et confectio omnis olei quod praeparasti mihi effundatur.

(*om.* et) confectio omnis olei quam preparauit mihi mater mea eff. PPhT.

et confectio omnis olei quam preparasti mihi effundetur VR.

(*i*) et alba quam neuit mater mea tinea comedat eam.

et albam (alba Ph) quam neuit tinea comedat PPhT.

et albam quam neuit mater mea tinea comedet eam VR.

(*k*) et corona quam intexuit nutrix mea in tempore marcescat.

et corona quam intexuit mea nutrix in tempore marcescat PPhT.

et flores corone quam intexuit nutrix mea in tempore marcescant (marcescet R) VR.

(*l*) et stratoria quae texuit in genuam meam de Hyacinthino.   et purpura uermis ea corrumpet.

et stratoria quae texuit mihi de iacincto et purpura uermis ea corrumpat PPhT (corrumpet P).

et stratoria quae texuit ingenium meum de iacinctino et purpuram meam uermes corrumpant V.

et stratoriam quae texuit ingenium meum de iacinctino et purpuram meam uermis corrumpat R.

(*m*) et referentes de me conuirgines meae in gemitu per dies plangant me.

et referentes de me conuirgines meae cum gemitu per dies plangant me PPhT.

et referentes me conuirgines meae in gemitum per dies plangant me VR.

The passage reads thus in J, p. 178 (*a*) : "I have not beheld my bridal canopy, nor has the crown of my betrothal been completed.   (*b*) I have not been decked with the lovely ornaments of the bride who sits in her virginity.   (*c*) nor have I been perfumed with the myrrh and the sweet smelling aloe.

(*d*) I have not been anointed with the oil of anointment that was prepared for me.

(*e*) Alas, O my mother, it was in vain that thou didst give me birth.

Behold thine only one (*f*) is destined for the bridal chamber of the grave.

(*g*) Thou hast wearied thyself for me to no purpose.

(*h*) The oil with which I was anointed will be wasted.

(*i*) And the white garments with which I was clothed the moths will eat.

(*k*) The garlands of my crown with which thou hast exalted me will wither and dry up.

(*l*) And my garments of fine needlework in blue and purple the worm shall destroy.

(*m*) And now my friends will lament all the days of my mourning."

It will be seen that J has some equivalent for every clause (though in (*g*) he has wandered far from the text).

In (*b*) he read *sedens in uirginitate* or *ingenuitate* with the Trèves MSS. : in (*k*) "garlands of my crown" seems nearer to *flores corone* of VR. For the rest he is too paraphrastic to be followed closely.

It is very odd that three times over in this short passage the words *in genua mea, genuam meam, in genuam meam* should occur in one of the groups, each time disturbing the sense, while another group somehow avoids the difficulty. It looks suspicious for the group which does so. But the evidence of the Trèves group is not to be lightly dismissed. It would justify a theory that where the words first occur they are corrupt for *ingenuitate*, that on the second occasion an obscurity of a few letters genu . . . eam, present in the ancestor of the other MSS., was not in that of the Trèves group : and that in the third case the words are merely intrusive—perhaps wrongly inserted from a margin. Another blurring of a few letters would account for the differences between *moysi* and *preciosi*, and between *odoris* and *odoramenti*. But I do not regard this as a really satisfactory explanation.

4. The TITLE of the book is somewhat of a puzzle. Sichardus calls it *Philonis Judaei antiquitatum Biblicarum liber*, the Fulda catalogue (and the label on the Fulda MS.) *Philonis antiquitatum liber;* a late title in the same MS. is: *libri Philonis iudei de initio mundi;* P has a title of cent. XV.: *Philo iudeus de successione generationum veteris testamenti;* R, in the colophon: "*ystoria Philonis ab initio mundi usque ad David regem*" (so also two at least of the Munich MSS.); Trithemius has *De generationis successu*. Sixtus Senensis has two notices of the book: in the first, which is drawn from Sichardus, he calls it *Biblicarum antiquitatum liber;* in the second, which depends on some MS., his words are: "In Gen. Cap. 5 *de successione generis humani* liber unus, continens enarrationem genealogiae seu posteritatis Adae. Liber incipit : Ἀδὰμ ἐγέννησε *Adam genuit*

tres filios." The two Greek words I take to be no more than a re-translation from Latin. The MS. V has no title at all.

Thus we have authority for three names. The first, *Biblicarum antiquitatum*, I think, must be in part due to Sichardus; the epithet "Biblicarum" savours to my mind of the Renaissance, and has no certain MS. attestation. "Antiquitatum" (which is as old as cent. XIV.) is probably due to a recollection of Josephus's great work, the *Jewish Antiquities*. The other name, *de successione generationum* or the like, has rather better attestation, and: *Historia ab initio mundi*, etc. (if original in the Munich MSS.) the oldest of all. I can hardly believe, however, that any of them are original; it seems more probable that some Biblical name was prefixed to the book when it was first issued. Rather out of respect to the first editor than for any better reason I have retained the title *Biblical Antiquities*, under which the text was introduced to the modern world.

The ATTRIBUTION TO PHILO I regard as due to the accident that the text was transmitted in company with genuine Philonic writings.[1] Certainly, if the *Antiquities* had come down to us by themselves, no one in his senses could have thought of connecting them with Philo; unless, indeed, knowing of but two Jewish authors, Philo and Josephus, he assumed that, since one had written a history of the Jews, the other must needs have followed suit.

5. The ORIGINAL LANGUAGE of the book, its date, its form and its purpose, must now be discussed.

[1] Pitra thought that the Latin versions of these were by the same hand: I cannot confirm this idea, and indeed incline to question its correctness.

Original Language.—The Latin version, in which alone we possess the work, is quite obviously a translation from Greek. The forms of proper names, the occurrence of Greek words which puzzled the translator, *ometocea, pammixia, epomis,* etc., make this abundantly clear. It is hardly less plain that the Greek was a translation from Hebrew. As Dr. Cohn has pointed out, the whole complexion, and especially the connecting links of the narrative, are strongly Hebraic, and there is a marked absence of the Greek use of particles, or of any attempt to link sentences together save by the bald "et," which occurs an incredible number of times.

Some statistics may be given : *Et factum est* occurs at least 33 times ; *Et tum* (usually of the past) 37 ; *Tunc* 25 ; *Et nunc* (of present or future) 85 ; *In tempore illo* 18 ; *In diebus illis* (and the like) 10 ; *Et post haec*, or *postea* 30 ; *Ecce* 105 ; *Ecce nunc* 47 ; *Et ideo* 27 ; *Et erit cum,* or *si* 24. Other common links which I have not counted are *Et ut* (*uidit*, etc.), *Et cum, His dictis, Propterea.*

The leading Hebraisms are present : *adiicere*, or *apponere* with another verb, meaning "he did so yet again," 9 times at least ; the intensive participle and verb (*Illuminans illuminaui*) 15 times. We have *Si* introducing a question 4 times ; *a uiro usque ad mulierem* and the like (XXX. 4 ; XLVII. 10) ; *ad uictoriam, in uictoria* (= למנצח, "Utterly ") ; IX. 3 ; XII. 6 ; XLIX. 6.

Hebraists, among whom I cannot reckon myself, may probably detect the presence of plays upon words, passages written in poetical form (some of which are indeed obvious), and mistranslations.[1]

---

[1] Of mistranslations I can only point to one. In VIII. 13 Visui appears as a proper name. It seems clearly to be a mistake for "and Isui." The error implies a Hebrew original : it is not found in the LXX. See the Appendix on Readings *in loc.*

From what has just been said it will be rightly
gathered that the literary style of *Philo* is not its
strong point. Indeed, it is exceedingly monot-
onous, full of repetitions and catchwords. The
author's one device for obtaining an "effect" is
to string together a number of high-sounding
clauses, as he does, for example, in his repeated
descriptions of the giving of the Law. As a
narrator, he has another trick. An incident
is often compared to another in the past (or
future) history of Israel, and many times is an
episode from that history related in a speech or
prayer.

Some of the recurrent phrases are: *I spake of old saying*
about 25 times; *in vain,* or *not in vain* 14; *it is better for
us to do* this *than . . .* 7; *not for our sakes, but for . . .*
about 5 times; *who knoweth whether* 4; *dost thou not
remember* 3; *To thy seed will I give this land* (or the
like) 7–9; *the covenant which he made* 5–8; *I know that
the people will sin* 8–9; *God's anger will not endure for
ever* 10; *The Gentiles will say* 4–8; *I call heaven and earth
to witness* 4–5; *in the last days* 4; *make straight your
ways* 5–6; *corrupt* (your ways, etc.) 18; *remember* or *visit
the world* 6; *be for a testimony* 10. Of single words *accipere*
occurs 88 times in the first half of the text; *habitare, inhabi-
tare* about 80 times in the whole text; *iniquitas* 33; *dis-
ponere* 37; *testamentum* 47; *ambulare* 21; *uia, uiae* 25;
adducere 19; *seducere* 21; *saeculum* 27; *sempiternus* 15;
constituere 20; *expugnare* 27; *zelari* 14; *illuminare* 12;
renunciare 15.
Other lists are given in Appendix II.

6. As to the DATE of the book, a positive
indication of a *terminus a quo* has been detected
in the text by Dr. Cohn. He draws attention to
a speech of God to Moses (XIX. 7): "I will show
thee the place wherein the people shall serve me
850 (MSS. 740) years, and thereafter it shall be
delivered into the hands of the enemies, and they
shall destroy it, and strangers shall compass it

about; and it shall be on that day like as it was in the day when I brake the tables of the covenant which I made with thee in Horeb: and when they sinned, that which was written thereon vanished away. Now that day was the 17th day of the 4th month." Dr. Cohn's comment is: "These words are meant to signify that Jerusalem was taken on the 17th of Tamuz, on the same day on which the Tables of the Law were broken by Moses. The capture of Jerusalem by the Babylonians, however, took place on the 9th of Tamuz (Jer. 52[6]; cf. 2 Kings 25[3]). The . . . 17th of Tamuz can relate only to the second temple (*read* capture) as it is expressly mentioned in the Talmud (Taanith IV. 6, cf. *Seder Olam Rabbah*, cap. 6 and 30) that on that date the Tables of the Law were destroyed and Jerusalem was taken by Titus. Thus the author betrays himself by giving as the date of the capture of Jerusalem by the Babylonians what is really the date of the capture by Titus."

The point is so important that I have felt it only right to present the evidence in some detail. The Mishnah of *Taanith* IV. 6 says "Five calamities befell our fathers on the 17th of Tamuz and five on the 9th of Ab. On the 17th Tamuz the Tables of the Law were broken: the daily sacrifice ceased to be offered: the city of Jerusalem was broken into: Apostomos burnt the Law and set up an idol in the sanctuary. On the 9th of Ab our fathers were told that they should not enter the holy land (Num. xiv.). The first and the second temple were destroyed; Bethar was taken, and the plough passed over the soil of Jerusalem."

It must be borne in mind that the capture of Jerusalem, and not the destruction of the Temple, is the event of which the date is important. To establish Dr. Cohn's argument, it is necessary that the capture of the city by Titus, and not the capture by Nebuchadnezzar, should be assigned to the 17th Tamuz.

The Gemara of the Jerusalem Talmud on the Mishnah quoted above attempts to show that there is a confusion in the chronology, and that probably both captures took place on the 17th Tamuz. But that of the Babylonian Talmud, which Mr. I. Abrahams has kindly translated for me, makes the requisite distinction between the dates, in these terms—

The city was broken up on the 17th. Was it indeed so? Is it not written "in the 4th month, on the 9th of the month, the famine was sore" (Jer. 52⁶): and is it not written in the following verse: "then the city was broken up"? Raba replied: There is no difficulty: for the one refers to the first, the other to the second Temple. For there is a *baraitha* (teaching) which teaches: "On the first occasion the city was broken into on the 9th of Tamuz, and on the second occasion on the 17th."

This clearly justifies Dr. Cohn in taking the 17th of Tamuz as the date primarily associated with the capture by Titus. The attempt of the Jerusalem Talmud to place the Babylonian capture on the same date is of a later complexion, and is made, it seems, in the interests of a factitious symmetry. The *baraitha* quoted in the Babylonian Talmud is of the same age as the Mishnah (*i.e.* before A.D. 200).

Thus *Philo* is indeed referring to the capture by Titus, and is therefore writing at a date later than A.D. 70. But, apart from this piece of positive evidence, the general complexion of the book strongly supports Dr. Cohn when he holds that it was written after the destruction of the second Temple. There is a singular absence of interest in the Temple services and in the ceremonial Law, whereas the moral Law, and especially the Decalogue, is dwelt upon again and again. Of course we read of sacrifices and the like, and it was impossible for the author to avoid all mention of the Tabernacle and its vessels, and of the yearly feasts. But the space devoted to them is strikingly small. The Passover is twice mentioned by name, and its institution is once referred to, together with that of the Feasts of Weeks, of Trumpets, and of Tabernacles, but no stress is laid upon it. The prescriptions for the observance of the Sabbath mention only synagogal services. When we compare *Philo* with *Jubilees* (second cent. B. C.), where the constant effort is to antedate the ceremonial Law in every part, we feel that we are in a wholly different stage of Judaism. Further, the evidence derivable from the resemblances between *Philo* and other books certainly written after A.D. 70, which will be found collected in another part of this Introduction, points unequivocally in the same direction.

In the portion of the book which we have (and it is important to remember that it is but a fragment) the writer's anticipations of a restoration and his allusions to the desolation of Jerusalem are equally faint and dim. It is probable that as occasion served—*e.g.* when he came to treat of Solomon's temple—he would have spoken more plainly than he could well do when dealing with the earlier history. If an opinion based upon what we possess of his work is demanded, my own is that an appreciable interval must be placed between the destruction of the city and our

author's time.   I should assign him to the closing
years of the first Christian century.[1]

7. As to the FORM, I suggest that the chief
model which the author set before himself was the
Biblical *Book of Chronicles*.   He begins abruptly,
as that does, with genealogies and with Adam:
he introduces from time to time short pieces of
narrative, which rapidly increase in importance
until they occupy the whole field: he devotes
much space to speeches and prayers, and is fond
of statements of numbers.   His aim is to supplement existing narratives, and he wholly passes
over large tracts of the history, occasionally referring to the Biblical books in which further details
are to be found: and it is to be noted that he
seems to place his own work on a level with them.
" Are not these things written in the book of " the
Judges, or the Kings, is his formula, and it is that
of the Bible also.   In all these respects he follows
the Chronicler: only, as has been said, we miss
in him the liturgical and priestly interest of that
writer.   Like the Chronicler, too, he is, and I
believe was from the first, anonymous; I can find
no trace of an attempt to personate any individual
prophet, priest or scribe.

8. The PURPOSE of the author I read thus.   He
wishes to supplement existing narratives, as has
been said; and this he does by means of his fabulous genealogies (which, especially in the corrupt
state in which we have them, arouse but a faint

---

[1] It might even be said that the vagueness of his hopes
and aspirations points to an even later period, after the
crushing of the Bar-Cochba rising in A.D. 135.   However,
the fact of the acceptance of the book by the Christian
Church, which alone has preserved it, and the absence of
anti-Christian polemic, forbid us to assign to it a date at all
late in the second century.

interest) and also by his paraphrases[1] of Bible stories, (for example, those of Korah, Balaam, Jael, Micah) and by his fresh inventions, especially that of Kenaz, the first judge, which is on the whole his most successful effort. In this side of his work he seeks to interest rather than to instruct. On the religious side I detect a wish to infuse a more religious tone into certain episodes of the history, particularly into the period of the Judges, and to emphasize certain great truths, foremost among which I should place the indestructibility of Israel, and the duty of faithfulness to the one God. Lapse into idolatry and union with Gentiles are the dangers he most dreads for his people. I have collected the passages in which his positive teaching is most clear and prominent, and purpose in this place to digest them under several heads, usually in the order in which they occur in the text.

The Future State of Souls and the End of the World.

III. 10. When the years of the world (or age) are fulfilled, God will quicken the dead, and raise up from the earth them that sleep : Sheol will restore its debt, and Abaddon its deposit, and every man will be rewarded according to his works. There will be an end of death, Sheol will shut its mouth, the earth will be universally fertile. No one who is "justified in God" shall be defiled. There will be a new heaven and a new earth, an everlasting habitation.

XIX. 4. God will reveal the end of the world.

---

[1] Which in some cases rather deserve the name of perversions. Great liberties are taken with them : a notable fact

XIX. 7. Moses is not to enter into the promised land " in this age."

12. He is to be made to sleep with the fathers, and have rest, until God visits the earth, and raises him and the fathers from the earth in which they sleep, and they come together and dwell in an immortal habitation.

13. This heaven will pass away like a cloud, and the times and seasons be shortened when the end draws near, for God will hasten to raise up them that sleep, and all who are able to live will dwell in the holy place which he has shown to Moses.

XXI. 9. God told the fathers in the secret places of souls, how he had fulfilled his promises : cf. XXIV. 6 ; XXXII. 13.

XXIII. 6. He showed Abraham the place of fire in which evil deeds will be expiated, and the torches which will enlighten the righteous who have believed.

13. The lot of the righteous Israelites will be in eternal life : their souls will be taken and laid up in peace, until the time of the world is fulfilled, and God restores them to the fathers, and the fathers to them.

XXVI. 12. The precious stones of the temple will be hidden away until God remembers the world, and then will be brought out with others from the place which eye hath not seen nor ear heard, etc. The righteous will not need the light of the sun or moon, for these stones will give them light.

XXVIII. 10. The rest (*requies*) of the righteous when they are dead.

XXXII. 17. The renewal of the creation (cf. XVI. 3).

XXXIII. 2–5. There is no room for repentance

after death, nor can the fathers after their death intercede for Israel.

XXXVIII. 4. Jair's victims are quickened with "living fire" and are delivered. (This, however, does not seem strictly to apply to the future state : see the passage.)

XLVIII. 1. When God remembers the world Phinehas will taste of death. Until then he will dwell with those who have been "taken up" before him.

LI. 5. God quickens the righteous, but shuts up the wicked in darkness. When the bad die they perish : when the righteous sleep they are delivered.

LXII. 9. Jonathan is sure that souls will recognize each other after death.

The Lot of the Wicked.

XVI. 3. Korah and his company : their dwelling will be in darkness and perdition, and they will pine away until God remembers the world, and then they will die and not live, and their remembrance will perish like that of the Egyptians in the Red Sea and the men who perished in the Flood. 6. Korah and his company, when they were swallowed up, "sighed until the firmament should be restored to the earth."

XVIII. 12. Balaam will gnash his teeth because of his sins.

XXXI. 7. Sisera is to go and tell his father in hell that he has fallen by the hand of a woman.

XXXVIII. 4. Jair will have his dwelling-place in fire : so also Doeg, LXIII. 4.

XLIV. 10. Micah and his mother will die in torments, punished by the idols he has made. And this will be the rule for all men, that they shall suffer in such fashion as they have sinned.

Punishment, long deferred, for past sins, is much in our author's mind.

VI. 11. Abram says " I may be burned to death on account of my (former) sins. God's will be done."

XXVII. 7. If Kenaz falls in battle it will be because of his sins.

15. Certain men were punished, not for their present offence, but for a former one.

XLII. 2. Manoah's wife is barren because of sins.

XLV. 3. The Levite's concubine had sinned years before and is now punished.

XLIX. 5. Elkanah says : If my sins have over-taken me, I had better kill myself.

The greatness of Israel and of the Law.

VII. 4. The Holy Land was not touched by the Flood.

IX. 3. The world will come to naught sooner than Israel can be destroyed.

4. When Israel was not yet in being, God spoke of it.

XII. 9. If God destroys Israel there will be none left to glorify him.

XVIII. 13. Israel can only be defeated if it sins.

XXXII. 9, 14. The heavenly bodies are ministers to Israel, and will intercede with God if Israel is in a strait.

15. Israel was born of the rib of Adam.

XXXIX. 7. The habitable places of the world were made for Israel.

IX. 8. God thought of the Law in ancient days.

XI. 1. It is a light to Israel but a punishment to the wicked.

2, It is an everlasting Law by which God will

judge the world. Men shall not be able to say "we have not heard."

5. It is an eternal commandment which shall not pass away.

XXXII. 7. It was prepared from the birth of the world.

Of Union with Gentiles.

IX. 1. The worst feature of the Egyptian oppression was the proposal that the Hebrew girls should marry Egyptians.

5. Tamar sinned with Judah rather than mingle with Gentiles, and was justified.

XVIII. 13. The union with the daughters of Moab and Midian would be fatal to Israel.

XLIII. 5. Samson mingled with Gentiles, and was therefore punished. He was unlike Joseph.

Angelology.

The service of angels is fairly prominent, and several are named.

XI. 12. "Bear not false witness, lest thy guardians do so of thee." This, I think, refers to angels.

XV. 5. The angels will not intercede for the people if they sin. The angel of God's wrath will smite the people.

"I put angels under their feet." (Also XXX. 5.)

XVIII. 5. "I said to the angels that work subtilly (?)."

6. Jacob wrestled with the angel that is over the praises.

XIX. 16. The angels lament for Moses.

XXVII. 10. Gethel or Ingethel is the angel of hidden things; Zeruel the angel of strength. (Also LXI. 5.)

XXXII. 1, 2. The angels were jealous of Abraham.

XXXIV. 3. Certain angels were judged : those who were condemned had powers which were not given to others after them. They still assist men in sorceries.

XXXVIII. Nathaniel the angel of fire.

XLII. 10. The angel Phadahel.

LXIV. 6. When Samuel is raised up by the witch, two angels appear leading him.

Demons and Idols.

Of evil spirits hardly anything is said, but some space is devoted to descriptions of idols.

XIII. 8. Adam's wife was deceived by the serpent.

XXV. 9. " The demons of the idols."

9 *seq.* The idols and precious stones of the Amorites are dwelt upon.

XLIV. 5 *seq.* Micah's idols are described in terms which remind one slightly of the images in a sanctuary of Mithras. (See the note.)

XLV. 6. " The Lord said to the Adversary" (*anticiminus*, ὁ ἀντικείμενοσ). He is quite suddenly introduced, and without any explanation.

LIII. 3, 4. Eli wonders if an unclean spirit has deceived Samuel. If one hears two calls at night, it will be an evil spirit that is calling : three will mean an angel.

LXI. An evil spirit oppresses Saul.

Evil spirits were created after heaven and earth (on the Second Day) and are a secondary creation. They sprang from an echo in chaos : their abode was in " Tartarus."

A *holy spirit* is mentioned occasionally, but in rather vague terms.

XVIII. 3. Balaam says that the spirit (of prophecy) is given " for a time."

11. "Little is left of that holy spirit which is in me."

XXVIII. 6. The holy spirit leapt upon Kenaz.

XXXII. 14. (Deborah addressing herself.) "Let the grace of the holy spirit in thee awake."

The character of God and His dealings with men are, naturally, illustrated in many passages, in some of which there is a strange lack of perception of what is worthy and befitting.

XII. 9. Moses says, "Thou art all light."

XXII. 3. "Light dwells with him."

XVI. 5. The sons of Korah say that God, not Korah, is their true father: if they walk in his ways, they will be his sons.

XVIII. 4. God knew what was in the world before he made it.

XXI. 2. He knows the mind of all generations before they are born (cf. L. 4).

XXVIII. 4. He willed that the world should be made and that they who should inhabit it should glorify him.

XXX. 6. God is life.

XXXV. 3. He will have mercy on Israel "not for your sakes, but because of them that sleep" (cf. XXXIX. 11 *end*).

5. Men look on glory and fame, God on uprightness of heart.

XXXVI. 4. God will not punish Gideon in this life, lest men should say "It is Baal who punishes him": he will chastise him after death.

XXXIX. 4. (LXII. 6.) If God forgives, why should not mortal man?

God, being God, has time to cast away his anger.

11. He is angry with Jephthah for his vow. "If a dog were the first to meet him, should a dog be offered to me? It shall fall upon his only child."

XLV. 6. Israel took no notice of Micah's idols ;

but is horrified at the Benjamite outrage: therefore God will allow Benjamin to defeat them, and will deceive them (cf. LXIII. 3).

XLVI. He deceives Israel, telling them to attack Benjamin.

XLVII. 3. If God had not sworn an oath to Phinehas, he would not hear him now.

LII. 4. He will not allow Eli's sons to repent, because aforetime they had said "When we grow old we will repent."

LXIV. 1. Saul put away the wizards in order to gain renown: so he shall be driven to resort to them.

Man, especially in relation to sin.

XIII. 8. Man lost Paradise by sin.

XIX. 9. What man hath not sinned? Who will be born without sin? Thou wilt correct us for a time, and not in wrath.

XXXII. 5. Esau was hated because of his deeds.

XXXVI. 1. The Midianites say, "Our sins are fulfilled, as our gods told us, and we believed them not."

LII. 3. Eli says to his sons: "Those whom you have wronged will pray for you if you reform."

LXIV. 8. Saul thinks that perhaps his fall may be an atonement for his sins.

The Messiah.

Dr. Cohn speaks of the Messianic hope of the writer, but I am myself unable to find any anticipation of a Messiah in our text. It is always God, and no subordinate agency, that is to "visit the world" and put all things right.

The word *Christus* occurs in two chapters: in LI. 6, and LIX. 1, 4, which refer to Saul or David.

There are two other puzzling passages, of which

one inclines at first to say that the meaning is Messianic.

XXI. 6. Joshua says : "O Lord, lo, the days shall come when the house of Israel shall be likened to a brooding dove which setteth her young in the nest, and will not leave them or forget her place, like as also these, turning (*conuersi*) from their acts, shall fight against (*or* overcome) the salvation which shall be born of them (*or* is born to them)."

LI. 5. Hannah says : "But so doth all judgement endure, until he be revealed who holdeth *it* (*qui tenet*)." As, a few lines later, she says : "And these things remain so until they give a horn to his (*or* their) Anointed," which certainly refers to Saul ; it is probable that Saul or David is meant in the present passage also. Nevertheless the resemblance between *qui tenet* and ὁ κατέχων of St. Paul (2 Thess. ii. 6, 7) is noteworthy.

9. I have not raised the question of the UNITY of the book. No one has as yet suggested that it is composite, and I am content to wait until a theory is broached. That there are inconsistencies in it I do not deny (for instance, the story of Korah is told in two ways in XVI. and in LVII.), but they are not of a kind that suggest a plurality of writers. It may be that their presence here will furnish an argument against dissection of other books based on the existence of similar discrepancies.

As to the INTEGRITY of the text : We know that it is imperfect, and this matter will be discussed at a later stage.

The CONTENTS will be found summarized in a synopsis at the end of the Introduction.

10. THE RELATION OF PHILO TO OTHER BOOKS now comes up for consideration. The author's knowledge of the Old Testament literature is

apparent on every page. There are obvious bor-
rowings from all the books to the end of 2 Kings ;
of Chronicles he seems to be a definite imitator.
He knows the story of Job, and quotes a Psalm ;
he draws from Isaiah, Jeremiah, Ezekiel, Daniel.
With the Wisdom literature he has not much in
common, and traces of the use of the Minor
Prophets, of Ezra, Nehemiah, or Tobit, are hard
to find, though I will not deny their presence.[1]
If he lived, as I believe he did, near the end of
the first century, we should naturally credit him
with a knowledge of the whole Jewish canon.

It is more important to determine his relation
to the apocryphal books—the literature to which
he was himself a contributor. Four of these,
Enoch, *Jubilees*, the Syriac *Apocalypse of Baruch*,
and the *Fourth Book of Esdras*, afford interesting
material.

(*a*) Certain affinities with the *Book of Enoch* are
traceable in *Philo*. It is true that Enoch is not
one of his heroes ; in fact, he tells us no more of
him than is found in Genesis, but I believe that
the Book was known to him, though it is only in
the first part of it that I find any striking parallels.

In the first place, his view of the stars and other
heavenly bodies is like that of *Enoch*. They are
sentient beings, who receive commands from God
and move about to execute them. See the story
of Sisera, and the hymn of Deborah, and compare
in *Enoch* 6, etc., the punishment of the errant
stars.

Again, a passage in *Enoch* (14^8) seems to be the
model of some in *Philo*. "Behold, clouds called
me in my vision, and mists cried to me, and
runnings of stars and lightnings hastened me, and
in the vision winds gave me wings and lifted me

---

[1] Esther and Judith seem to be quoted, pp. 173, 188.

up." Compare *Philo* XI. 5: "The heavens were folded up, and the clouds drew up water . . . and the thunders and lightnings were multiplied, and the winds and tempests sounded; the stars were gathered together, and the angels ran before" (XIII. 7); "the winds shall sound and the lightnings run on," etc. (XV. 2); "the lightnings of the stars shone, and the thunders followed, sounding with them" (XXXII. 7); "the lightnings hasted to their courses, and the winds gave a sound out of their storehouses," etc. The phrase in *Enoch* 14⁸, ¹⁰, ¹⁷ is διαδρομαὶ ἀστέρων καὶ ἀστραπαί. In 16¹ we have ὁ αἰὼν ὁ μέγας, which may be the source of the *immensurabilis mundus* (*seculum tempus*) of *Philo* IX. 3, XXXII. 3, XXXIV. 2.

In *Enoch* 17³, τόξον πυρὸσ καὶ τὰ βέλη. *Philo* XIX. 16, *praecedebant eum fulgura et lampades et sagittae omnes unanimes.*

Enoch 18¹, Εἶδον τοὺσ θησαυροὺσ τῶν ἀνέμων; cf. *Philo* XXXII. 7, above. The winds gave a sound out of their storehouses (*promptuariis*).

In *Enoch* 18⁶ *seq.* we hear something of precious stones which reminds us of those of Kenaz in *Philo* XXVI. *seq.*

The words of 21²: "I saw neither heaven above nor earth founded, but a place imperfect and terrible" recall the vision of Kenaz in *Philo* XXVIII. 6 *seq.*

So also the description of the sweet plants of Paradise in *Enoch* 24 may have suggested the words of Moses in *Philo* XII. 9.

In *Enoch* 25² "to visit the earth" has more than one parallel in *Philo*, e.g. XIX. 12, 13, *visitare seculum, orbem :* and *Enoch* 25⁷ (Then I blessed the God of glory . . . who hath prepared such things for righteous men, etc.) is like *Philo* XXVI. 6: Blessed be God who hath wrought such signs for the sons of men, and 14 : Lo, how great good things God hath wrought for men.

(b) The *Book of Jubilees* is perhaps most nearly comparable to *Philo*, in that it follows the form of a chronicle of Bible history. Its spirit and plan are, to be sure, wholly different ; it is regulated by a strict system of chronology, and its chief interest is in the ceremonial law. It is also far earlier in date, belonging to the last years of the second century B.C.

Our author has read *Jubilees*, and to a certain extent supplements it in the portions which are common to both books. Thus *Jubilees* supplies us with the names of the wives of the early patriarchs : *Philo* omits these, but gives the names of their sons and daughters. It is true that he gives other names for the daughters of Adam, and that in the one case in which he supplies the name of a wife he also differs from *Jubilees* : with him Cain's wife is Themech, in *Jubilees* it is Awân (daughter of Adam and sister of Cain, which *Philo* may have wished to disguise). In the same way *Philo* devotes much space to the names and number of the grandsons of Noah and their families, which are wanting in *Jubilees* ; and whereas *Jubilees* gives full geographical details of the provinces which fell to Shem, Ham and Japhet, *Philo* indulges only in a series of bare names of places, now for the most part hopelessly corrupt. There is a small and seemingly intentional contradiction of *Jubilees* in this part of his history : *Jubilees* 11[8], says that Serug taught Nahor to divine, and worshipped idols. *Philo* agrees that divination began in the days of Terah and Nahor, but adds that Serug and his sons did *not* join in it, or in idolatry.

Then, whereas the bulk of *Jubilees* is occupied with the lives of Abraham, Isaac and Jacob, *Philo* tells in detail one episode—the rescue of Abram from the fire—which *Jubilees* omits, and passes over the rest of the period in a single page. Anything else that he has to say about Abraham and the rest is introduced into the speeches of later personages (Joshua, Deborah, etc.) by way of illustration. The two books agree in giving the names of the seventy souls who went down into Egypt.

All this seems to me to show a consciousness of *Jubilees*, and an intentional avoidance, in the main, of the ground traversed by that book. Very rarely is there any coincidence of thought, but two possible examples can be cited. *Philo* has surprisingly little to say about Satan or evil spirits, as we have seen: but suddenly (in XLV. 6) he says: *Et dixit Dominus ad anticiminum:* And the Lord said to *the Adversary*. This must surely be the equivalent of the "prince Mastema" whom we meet so frequently in *Jubilees*. There is also a difficult passage (XIII. 8) which may go back to *Jubilees*. God is speaking to Moses, and says: "And the nights shall yield their dew, as I spake after the flood of the earth, at that time when I commanded him (*or* Then he commanded him) concerning the year of the life of Noah, and said to him: These are the years which I ordained," etc. The words, which may be corrupt, at least remind me of the stress laid in *Jubilees* 6, upon the yearly feast that is to be kept by Noah after the Flood.

Upon the whole *Philo's* knowledge of *Jubilees* is to be inferred rather from what he does not say than from what he does.

(*c*) The Syriac APOCALYPSE OF BARUCH has, as I have elsewhere shown (JTS 1915, 403), certain very marked resemblances to *Philo*. It will be

right to repeat and expand the list of them here.
We will take the passages in the order in which
they appear in the Apocalypse, in Dr. R. H.
Charles's last translation (*Pseudepigrapha of O.T.*).

Bar. IV. 3. The building
now built in your midst is
not that which is revealed
with Me, that which was prepared beforehand here from
the time when I took counsel
to make Paradise and shewed
it to Adam before he sinned,
but when he transgressed
the commandment it was
removed from him, as also
Paradise.

IV. 4. And after these
things I shewed it to my
servant Abraham by night
among the portions of the
victims.

IV. 5. And again also I
shewed it to Moses on Mount
Sinai when I shewed to him
the likeness of the tabernacle
and all its vessels.

Ph. XIII. 8. And he said:
This is the place which I
showed the first-made man,
saying : If thou transgress
not that which I have commanded thee, all things shall
be subject unto thee. But he
transgressed my ways. . . .
And the Lord further shewed
him (Moses) the ways of
Paradise, and said to him :
These are the ways which
men have lost because they
walked not in them.

XXVI. 6. Kenaz says :
Blessed be God who hath
wrought such marvels for the
sons of men, and made the
protoplast Adam and shewed
him all things, that when
Adam had sinned therein,
then he should deprive him
of all things . . .

XXIII. 6. (of Abraham)
And sent a sleep upon him
and compassed him about
with fear, and set before him
the place of fire wherein the
deeds of them that work
wickedness against me shall
be expiated, etc.

XI. 15. (on Sinai) He
charged him concerning the
tabernacle and the ark . . .
and the candlesticks and the
laver and the base, and the
breastplate and the oracle
and the precious stones, and
shewed him the likeness of
them.

V. 5. Jabish, an unknown person, summoned with others by Baruch.

VI. 7. The forty-eight precious stones.

X. Baruch's lamentation generally resembles that of Jephthah's daughter.

X. 11. And do ye, O heavens, withhold your dew and open not the treasures of rain.

XI. 4. The righteous sleep in the earth in tranquillity.

XXI. 24. Abraham, etc., who sleep in the earth.

XIX. 10. (on Pisgah) He shewed him the place whence the manna rained upon the people, even up to the paths of paradise ; and he shewed him the manner of the sanctuary and the number of the offerings . . . (See also XIII. 8 above.)

XXVIII. 1. Kenaz summons the prophets Jabis and Phinees.

See below, p. 64.

XL. 5.

XLIV. 10. I will command the heaven, and it shall deny them rain.

XI. 9. I will command the heaven, and it shall give its rain.

XIII. 7. The nights shall yield their dew.

XXIII. 12. I will command the rain and the dew.

XXXII. 7. the storehouses of the wind.

XV. 5. the treasuries of darkness.

III. 10. I will raise up them that sleep from the earth.

XI. 6. I will recompense the sins of them that sleep.

XIX. 12. I will raise up thee and thy fathers from the earth (of Egypt *intrusive*) wherein ye shall sleep.

XXXV. 3. because of them that are fallen asleep.

LI. 5. when the righteous shall fall asleep, then shall they be delivered.

XI. 6, 7. That ye might go and announce in Sheol and say to the dead : Blessed are ye more than we who live.

XV. 5. Unless he had accepted my law.

XVII. 4. brought the law to the seed of Jacob and lighted a lamp for the nation of Israel (cf. LIX.).

LIX. 2. the lamp of the eternal law.

XIX. 1. (Moses) called heaven and earth to witness against them ; also LXXXIV. 2.

XX. 1. The times shall hasten more than the former, and the seasons shall speed on . . . the years shall pass more quickly.

LIV. 1. Thou dost hasten the beginnings of the times.

LXXXIII. 1. The most High will assuredly hasten his times and . . . bring on his hours.

XX. 2. That I may the more speedily visit the world in its season.

XXI. 23. Let Sheol be sealed, so that from this time forward it may not receive the dead, and let the treasu-

XXIV. 6. Who shall go and tell the righteous Moses (that Joshua is dead) ?

XXXI. 7. (To Sisera) Go and boast thyself to thy father in hell.

XXXII. 13. Go, ye angels, tell the fathers in the treasuries of souls.

LXI. 6. (To Goliath) then shall ye tell your mother (after death).

Emphasized in XLIV. 6 *seq.* (cf. XI. 2).

IX. 8. I will light for (Moses) my lamp.

XV. 6. I came down to light a lamp for my people.

XIX. 4. kindling among you an eternal lamp.

Besides repeated references to the Law as a light.

Occurs 4 times, of Moses (twice), Joshua, Jonathan.

XIX. 13. When I shall draw near to visit the world, I will command the times and they shall be shortened, and the stars shall be hastened, and the light of the sun shall make haste to set, etc.

XIX. 12. Until I visit the world.

(See also III. 10, XXVI. 12, XLVIII. 1.)

III. 10. Hell shall pay its debt and destruction restore its deposit . . . hell shall shut its mouth.

D

ries of souls restore those which are enclosed in them (cf. XXX. 2).

XLII. 7, 8. the dust shall be called, and there shall be said to it: Give back that which is not thine, and raise up all that thou hast kept until this time (cf. L. 2).

XXV. 4. The Mighty one doth no longer remember the earth.

XXVIII. 2. The measure and reckoning of that time are two parts a week of seven weeks.

XXIX. 8. the treasury of manna shall again descend from on high.

XXX. 4. the souls of the wicked . . . shall then waste away the more.

XLIV. 15. the dwelling of the rest who are many shall be in the fire.

LXIV. 7. (Manasseh) finally his abode was in the fire.

L. 3, 4. it will be necessary to show to the living that the dead have come to life again . . . and . . . when they have severally recog. nized those whom they now know.

XXXIII. 3. Death is now sealed up.

Hell will not restore its deposit unless it be required of him who gave it.

XXI. 9. our fathers in the hidden places of souls.

XXXII. 13. the fathers in the treasuries of their souls.

XXVI. 13. until I remember the world.

The phrase occurs at least five times.

(See the Note on *Ph.* XIX. 15.)

XIX. 10. the place whence the manna rained upon the people.

XVI. 3. Korah shall pine away until I remember the world.

XLIV. Micah's mother is to waste away in his sight. So also Doeg LXIII. 4.

XXXVIII. 4. (of Jair) in the fire wherein thou shalt die, therein shalt thou have thy dwelling-place.

LXIII. 4. (of Doeg) his dwelling shall be with Jair in unquenchable fire for ever.

XXIII. 13. until I restore you to the fathers and the fathers to you.

LXII. 9. (Jonathan) Even if death part us, I know that our souls will recognize each other.

LI. 11. the armies of the angels.

LIV. 1. the inhabitants of the earth.

5. thou breakest up the enclosure (of the ignorant).

9. What am I amongst men?

11. I will not be silent in praising.

LV. 3. Ramiel who presides over true visions.

LVI. 6. The list of disasters that followed the Fall is much in *Philo's* manner.

LIX. 2. The law which announced to them that believe the promise of their reward, and to them that deny, the torment of fire which is reserved for them.

3. but also the heavens at that time were shaken from their place.

4-11. He showed him the pattern of Zion and its measures, "the measures of the fire, the number of the drops of rain," etc., c.

militiae, of angels, occurs five times.

one of *Philo's* most frequent catchwords.

XXXIII. 6. Deborah closed up the hedge of her generation.

Cf. Gideon XXXV. 5, Saul LVI. 6.

Cf. Deborah and Hannah.

XVIII. 6. the angel who was over the praises.

XXVII. 10. Gethel set over hidden things. Zeruel, over strength (LXI. 5).

XXXIV. 2. angels are sorcerers.

XXXVIII. 3. Nathaniel who is over fire.

XXIII. 6. I set before (Abraham) the place of fire wherein the deeds of them that work wickedness against me shall be expiated, and showed him the torches of fire whereby the righteous that have believed in me shall be enlightened.

XI. 5. at Sinai. The heavens were folded up. I bared the heavens (XV. 6), XXIII. 10. I stopped the courses of the stars, etc. There are several lists of the portents which accompanied the giving of the law.

XIX. 10. He showed him the place whence the clouds draw up water, the place whence the river takes its watering . . . the place

4–11. The greatness of Paradise . . . the number of the offerings.

The splendour of the lightnings.

LX. 1. The works which the Amorites wrought and the spells of the incantations which they wrought, and the wickedness of their mysteries.[1]

whence the manna rained . . . up to the paths of Paradise . . . the measures of the sanctuary and the number of the offerings.
Very frequent in *Philo*.

XXV. 10. *seq.* The Amorites figure as great idolaters in the story of Kenaz the first Judge : their idols are called the holy Nymphs. The episode of Kenaz is almost the longest in *Philo*.
XXXIV. A wizard Aod came from Midian who sacrificed to fallen angels, and made the sun appear at night and seduced Israel.

2. But even Israel was then polluted by sins in the days of the Judges, though they saw many signs which were from Him who made them.
LXVI. 2. Josiah removed the magicians and enchanters and necromancers from the land.

LXXI. 1. The holy land will . . . protect its inhabiters at that time.

LXXVI. 2. Baruch is to be taken up (cf. XIII. 3 ; XXV. 1) and is to go up into a certain mountain, and the whole world will be shown to him. (See on LIX.)

LXIV. 1. Saul said : I will surely remove the wizards out of the land of Israel (though for unworthy motives).
Compare the statement (VII. 4) that the holy land was not touched by the Flood.
XLVIII. Phinehas is to go and live in a named mountain till he has fulfilled his destiny in the person of Elijah and then is to be taken up into the place where those before him have

---

[1] I see that this parallel is noticed by a writer in the *Jewish Encyclopædia*, s. v. *Amorites*. He quotes *Philo* through the medium of *Jerahmeel* only.

been taken up. These "*priores tui*" are the "others like thee" who are mentioned in *Bar.* II. 1; XIII. 5; (LVII. 1; LIX. 1); XXI. 24; LXVI. 7.

LXXVII. 6. if ye direct your ways.

    13. shepherds of Israel.

    20. he sends a letter by an eagle.

    25. Solomon's mastery over birds.

At least five times.

XIX. 3. of Moses.

XLVIII. An eagle is to feed Phinehas.

LX. 3. David predicts Solomon's mastery over evil spirits.

LXXXII. 3-5. The Gentiles will be like a vapour . . . like a drop . . . as spittle.

    9. as a passing cloud.

VII. 3; XII. 4. like a drop and like spittle.

XIX. 13. like a running cloud.

LXXXIV. 4. after Moses' death ye cast them (the precepts) away from you.

XXX. 5. Moses (and others) commanded you . . . while they lived ye shewed yourselves servants of God; but when they died, your heart died also.

At least nine times.

    7. (let this epistle) be for a testimony between me and you.

    10. that he may not reckon the multitude of your sins, but remember the rectitude of your fathers.

XXXV. 3. God will have mercy, not for your sakes, but because of those that have fallen asleep (cf. XXXIX. 11).

    11. for if He judge us not according to the multitude of His mercies, woe unto all us who are born.

XIX. 9. What man hath not sinned against thee? How shall thine heritage be stablished if thou have not compassion, etc.

XXVIII. 5. Is it not he that shall spare us according to the abundance of His mercy (cf. XXXIX. 7; LV. 2).

LXXXV. 9. That we may rest with our fathers.

XXVIII. 10. The rest of the righteous after they are dead.

12. There will be no place . . . for prayer . . . nor intercessions of the fathers, nor prayer of the prophets, nor help of the righteous.

XXXIII. 5. While a man yet liveth he can pray for himself and for his sons, but after the end he will not be able to pray . . . . Put not your trust therefore in your fathers.

It will be seen that these resemblances (not all of which, of course, are supposed by me to be equally strong) are scattered over the whole text of *Baruch*. To me they seem to constitute one among a good many weighty arguments against the hypothesis that *Baruch* is a composite work; but this is not the place to discuss that matter.

(*d*) We will examine 4 ESDRAS in the same fashion, only here it will be better to cite the Latin of both texts. We must keep in mind the difference between coincidences of vocabulary and parallels in matter. The versions of the two books are extraordinarily alike in their Latinity. One is tempted to say that they are by the same hand; but it will be safer to regard them as products of the same school and age.

4 *Esdr.* III. 13. Et factum est cum iniquitatem facerent coram te, elegisti ex his unum (Abraham) . . . et demonstrasti ei temporum finem solo secrete noctu et disposuisti ei testamentum aeternum et dixisti et ut non unquam derelinqueres semen eius.

Philo XXIII. 5. Et cum seducerentur habitantes terram singuli quique post praesumptiones suas credidit Abraham mihi . . . et dixi ei in uisu dicens : semini tuo dabo terram hanc.

VII. 4. Et ante omnes hos eligam puerum meum Abram . . . et disponam testamentum meum cum eo, etc.

17. Et adduxisti eos super montem Sina.

XV. 3. et adduxi eos sub montem Sina.

18. et inclinasti coelos.

et statuisti terram et com-
mouisti orbem et tremere
fecisti abyssos et conturbasti
saeculum.

22. permanens. 24. obla-
tiones. 27. tradidisti ciui-
tatem.
34. pondera in statera.

momentum puncti.

IV. 7. quantae uenae sunt
in principio abyssi.
exitus paradisi.

12. (and elsewhere) melius
erat nos . . . quam.
16. factus est in uano.
18. incipiebas (iustificare)
= μέλλειν.
35. animae iustorum in
promptuariis suis.

42. festinant reddere ea
quae commendata sunt.

44. si possibile est et si
idoneus sum,

XXIII. 10. et adduxi eos
in conspectu meo usque ad
montem Sina.
XXXII. 7. et duxit in
montem Sina.
XV. 3 ; XXIII. 10. et in-
clinaui coelos.
XXIII. 10. mouebantur in
descensu meo omnia . . .
obturaui uenas abyssi.
XXXII. 7. terra mota est
de firmamento suo et tremu-
erunt montes et rupes, etc.
All very common words
in *Philo*.

XL. 1. quis dabit cor
meum in statera et animam
meam in pondere.
XIX. 14. momenti pleni-
tudo.

uena five to six times ;
abyssus nine times.
uiae, semitae paradisi
XIII. 9 ; XIX. 10.
At least seven times.

Fourteen times.
Three times at least.

XXXII. 13. patribus in
promptuariis animarum
eorum.
III. 10. reddet infernus
debitum suum et perditio
restituet paratecem suam.
XXXIII. 3. mensura et
tempus et anni reddiderunt
depositum tuum . . . infernus accipiens sibi deposita
non restituet nisi reposcetur
ab eo qui deposuit ei.
LIII. 7. si possibilis sum.

si plus quam praeteriit habet uenire, etc.

IV. 50. superhabundauit quae transiuit mensura ; superauerunt autem guttae et fumus.

V. 4. relucescet sol noctu.

12. non dirigentur uiae eorum.

16. quare uultus tuus tristis.

18. pastor.

23. elegisti uineam unam also IX. 21).

26. columbam.

29. sponsionibus.

42. adsimilabo.

VI. 2. coruscuum.

3. militiae (angelorum).

8–10. manus Jacob tenebat calcaneum Esau, etc.

16. finem eorum oportet commutari.

VI. 18. quando adpropinquare incipio ut uisitem habitantes in terra.

IX. 2. uisitare saeculum.

VI. 26. qui recepti sunt homines qui mortem non gustauerunt.

39. tenebrae circumferebantur et silentium.

41. ut pars quidem sursum recederet, pars uero deorsum maneret.

XIX. 14. quanta quantitas temporis transiit, etc. ? . . . cyathi guttum, et omnia compleuit tempus. Quatuor enim semis transierunt et duae semis supersunt.

XXXIV. Nunquid aliquando uidistis solem noctu? . . . ostendit populis solem noctu.

Frequent.

L. 3. quare tristis es, etc.

XIX. 3. of Moses.

Israel as vine or vineyard occurs six times.

Israel as dove thrice.

Seven times.

Very common.

Six times in varying forms (coruscus -atio -ans).

Five times.

XIX. 13. apex ma(g)nus remains.

XXVIII. 9. cum completum fuerit tempus . . . pausabit uena et sic mutabuntur.

XIX. 13. cum appropinquauero uisitare orbem.

12. donec uisitem seculum.

XXVI. 13. et uisitabo habitantes terram.

XLVIII. eleuaberis . . . ubi eleuati sunt priores tui . . . et adducam uos et gustabitis quod est mortis.

LX. 2. Tenebrae et silentium erant antequam fieret seculum.

Both the song of David and the vision of Kenaz (XXVIII.) dwell on the division of the firmaments.

42. imperasti aquis con-
gregari, etc.

56. gentes saliuae adsimi-
latae sunt, et sicut stillicidium
de urceo.

VII. 32. terra reddet qui
in ea dormiunt.

74. non propter eos, sed.
75. creaturam renouare.

87. detabescent . . . mar-
cescent.

92. cum eis plasmatum
cogitamentum malum.
102. etc. Si iusti impios
excusare poterint, etc.

VIII. 15. tu magis scis.

53. Radix signata est a
uobis.
IX. 22. cum multo labore
perfeci haec.

XII. 20. anni citati.

XIII. 26. liberabit crea-
turam suam.
52. scire quid sit in pro-
fundo maris,

XV. 6. nihil simile factum
est uerbo huic ex qua die
dixi congregentur aquae sub
caelo, etc.
VII. 3. et tanquam stillicidium arbitrabor eos et in
scuto (sputo) approximabo
eos.
XII. 4. erit mihi hominum
genus tanquam stillicidium
urcei et tanquam sputum
aestimabitur.
III. 10. erigam dormientes
de terra.
XIX. 12. excitabo te et
patres tuos de terra [Aegypti]
in qua dormietis, etc.
About five times.
XVI. 3. ero innouans ter-
ram (cf. III. 10).
XXXII. 17. ut in innoua-
tione creaturae.
XVI. Korah, etc., tabes-
cent.
XLIV. Micah's mother,
erit marcescens.
XXXIII. 3. plasmatio ini-
qua perdet potestatem suam.
5. Adhuc uiuens homo po-
test orare . . . post finem
autem non poterit, etc.
tu plus scis, tu prae omnibus scis two or three times.
XXXIII. 3. signata est
iam mors.
XXVIII. 4. tu uidisti . . .
quantum laborauerim populo
meo : also XIX. 5.
XIX. 13. iubebo annis . . .
et breuiabuntur.
LI. 5. cum dormierint iusti
tunc liberabuntur.
XXI. 2. tu scis . . .
quid agat cor maris (cf.
XXIX. 4).

53. inluminatus es.
XIV. 3. Reuelans reuela- tus sum super rubum.
et locutus sum Moysi.

Twelve times in this sense.
LIII. 8. Illuminans illumi- naui domum Israel.
et elegi tunc mihi pro- phetam Mosen.

et adduxi eum super mon- tem Sina.

See above on III. 17.

et detinui eum apud me . . . et enarraui ei mirabilia et ostendi ei . . . temporum finem.

Cf. XIII. and XIX. quoted above on *Bar.* LIX. 4.

9. Tu enim recipieris ab hominibus et conuerteris . . . cum similibus tuis.

XLVIII. non descendes iam ad homines . . .
eleuaberis in locum ubi eleuati sunt priores tui.

In the later chapters of *Esdras*, which are taken up with visions, we—perhaps naturally—find fewer parallels than in the earlier.

Other instances of words and phrases common to the two books, which are stylistic rather than anything else, are—

Ecce dies uenient, qui inhabitant terram, sensus, delere orbis, sustinere, adinuentio, renuntiare, in nouissimis tem- poribus, odoramentum, in nihilum deputare, requietio, aera- mentum, corruptibilis, plasmare, uiuificare, mortificare, con- turbare, exterminare, humiliare, fructus uentris, apponere or *adicere* (*loqui*, etc.), *oblatio, pessimus* in the positive sense, *a minimo usque ad maximum, expugnare, scintilla.*

With the *Assumption of Moses* I find no com- munity of ideas. Moses' intercession for the people and Joshua's lament are rather like those of the people over Joshua and Deborah. But *Philo* dis- cards the story of the Assumption proper. Nor do I find illustrative matter in the *Testaments of the XII. Patriarchs.*

My general conclusion is that *Philo* is a product of the circle from which both *Baruch* and 4 *Esdras* emanated : and it seems to me clear that the writer of *Baruch* at least was acquainted with *Philo.* Let it be noted once more that a feature common to all three books is a remarkable want of interest in the subject of Satan and evil spirits : *Esdras* never mentions them, *Baruch* very seldom, *Philo* rather oftener, but not often, and always vaguely.

(*e*) What points of contact are there, it will be asked, between *Philo* and the NEW TESTAMENT ?

My answer is that there are not many direct resemblances. There are a few coincidences of language, and one or two illustrations of beliefs. That the author, living at the date to which I assign him, was conscious of the existence of Christianity, I do not doubt : whether he allows his consciousness to find expression in his book, I do doubt. He is not a speculative theologian or a controversialist ; he sticks very close to the language of the Old Testament, and steers clear of disputed questions. I see no veiled polemic in his stories of the idolatry under Kenaz, or of Aod the Magician and Micah. The persecution under Jair may very well be an imitation of the Maccabæan martyrdoms, or of the story of the Three Children. The stress laid on the eternity of the Law may as well be a prophylactic against heathenism as against Christianity. Paganism is, I think, a more formidable adversary in his eyes than heresy.

The tradition of the " rock that followed them " (X. 7, XI. 15 : see the notes) and of the identity of Phinehas with Elijah (XLVIII.) are the chief that bear on New Testament thought. With reference to the latter it should be noted that the words of St. Mark (ix. 13), " as it is written of him," are specially interesting, as showing that Elijah upon his return to earth was to suffer death (in which *Philo* agrees), and that there was written teaching to that effect.

Among coincidences of language I reckon : new heavens and earth, III. 10 ; they that sleep, *ibid.* and elsewhere ;

justified, *ibid.* ; fiat uoluntas dei, VI. 11 ; that which shall
be born of thee, IX. 10 ; I will judge all the world, XI. 2 ;
the law shall not pass away, XI. 5 ; Thou art all light,
XII. 9 ; we shall be the sons of God, XVI. 5 ; gnashing of
teeth, XVIII. 12 ; the end of the world, XIX. 4, etc. ;
uerbum (dei) uiuum, XXI. 4 ; God which knowest before
the hearts of all men, XXII. 7 (Acts i. 24) ; eye hath not
seen, etc., XXVI. 13 ; the righteous have no need of the
light of the sun, etc., XXVI. 13 ; qui tenet (cf. ὁ κατέχων,
2 Thess. ii. 6, 7), LI. 5 ; lumen genti huic, LI. 6.

11. A question remains to be discussed, for
answered it can hardly be unless fresh manuscript
evidence comes to hand. It is this : How far did
Philo carry on his narrative, and are there any
traces of the lost conclusion ?

There are certain anticipations in our text
which, it is reasonable to suppose, were fulfilled.
We can predict with confidence that Edab the son
of Agag, who appears in the last few lines as the
slayer of Saul, will be killed (as in 2 Sam. i.), with
appropriate denunciation. Again, there is a sensa-
tional story of the slaying of Ishbi-benob by David
and Abishai (Talmud, Tract *Sanhedr.*, f. 45, ap.
Eisenmenger, I. 413), in which Abishai kills Orpah
the mother of the giant, and eventually David says
to Ishbi, " Go, seek thy mother in the grave,"
whereat he falls. Now, in *Philo* (LXI. 6) David
reminds Goliath that Orpah was his mother, and
says to him, " After thy death thy three brethren
also will fall into my hands, and then shall ye say
unto your mother : He that was born of thy sister
(Ruth) did not spare us." I see a foreshadowing
here of another tale of giants slain by David.
Further, David in his song before Saul (LX.) predicts the mastery over evil spirits that will be
attained by Solomon ; and elsewhere the writer, in
his own person, names Solomon, and speaks of his
building the Temple (XXII. 9). The allusion to

Solomon and the demons, though unmistakable, is veiled, and, if I may judge from *Philo's* usual practice, would have received an explanation, accompanied by a reference back to David's song: *Nonne haec sunt uerba quae locutus est pater tuus*, etc. Another possible instance of foreshadowing is this: Phinehas (XLVIII.), when he has reached the term of 120 years, is commanded to go up into the Mount Danaben and dwell there. In years to come the heavens will be shut at his prayer, and opened again, and then he will be "taken up," and in a yet more remote future will taste of death. In other words, he will be Elijah. I do not think this obscure prediction would have been left hanging in the air: in some form it would have received interpretation. I imagine, therefore, that the story of Elijah (and Elisha) was told in the book. I hardly know if one can fairly adduce here the fact that in an old treatise called *Inuentiones Nominum* (printed by me in JTS, 1903) some names are given of personages belonging to that period who are anonymous in the Bible. Thus, Abisaac is the 'little maid" of 2 Kings v., Meneria is the Shunamite, and Phua the woman who devoured her child in the siege of Samaria. I lay no stress on this suggestion, for other names are given in the same document which disagree with those in *Philo*. Still, those I have cited did come from some written source of similar character.[1]

Here is another curious phenomenon. In the *Apostolic Constitutions* (II. 22, 23) the whole story of Manasseh is quoted in a text avowedly compounded fro.n 2 Kings and 2 Chronicles, with the addition of the Prayer and deliverance of Man-

[1] Another book which deserves consideration in this connexion is the *Lives of the Prophets*, attributed to Epiphanius.

asseh, which are non-Biblical, and after a short interval the story of Amon is given, with a spurious insertion to this effect: "Amon said, 'My father did very wickedly from his youth, and repented in his old age. Now therefore I will walk as my soul listeth, and afterward I will return to the Lord.'" Just so, in *Philo* LII. 4, when Eli said to Hophni and Phinehas, "Repent of your wicked ways," they said, "When we are grown old we will repent": and therefore God would not grant them repentance. The resemblance is arresting. The consideration of it suggests the question whether this of Amon and the Prayer of Manasseh and the story of his deliverance can be excerpts from *Philo*. So far as the Prayer is concerned I cannot think it likely, for that composition is not in our author's manner, and is not believed to be a translation from Hebrew. And, if the Prayer is not from *Philo*, we need not unnecessarily multiply the authorities used by *Const. Ap.*

For all that, the story of Manasseh and his deliverance may have been told in *Philo*: the form of it which appears in the *Apocalypse of Baruch* (64) rather suggests to me that it was. The Apocalyptist uses Philonic language when he says of Manasseh that "his abode was in the fire"; and, further, he does not account Manasseh's repentance to have been genuine or final, and in this — if I read my author rightly — he writes in the Philonic spirit: for *Philo*, if he is willing to dwell on the repentance and reform of Israel as a whole, seems to take pleasure in recording the apostasies and transgressions of individuals who do not repent — the sinners under Kenaz, Jair, Gideon, Micah, Doeg.

When Saul protests to Samuel that he is too obscure to be made King, Samuel says (LVI. 6):

"Your words will be like those of a prophet yet
to come who will be called Jeremiah." This odd
prediction is modelled, I suppose, upon the mention
of Josiah in 1 Kings 13², and is comparable to
Hannah's quotation of a psalm by Asaph (LI. 6).
That the fulfilment of it was mentioned is likely
enough, but by no means necessary.

Lastly, a phrase in the story of Kenaz demands
notice. When God gives him the new set of
twelve precious stones to replace certain others
that had been destroyed, He says (XXVI. 12) that
they are to be placed in the ark, and to be there
"until Jahel shall arise to build an house in my
name, and then he shall set them before me upon
the two cherubim . . . and when the sins of my
people are fulfilled, and their enemies begin to
prevail over their house, I will take those stones
and the former ones (*i.e.* those already in the
priest's breastplate) and put them back in the
place whence they were brought, and there shall
they be until I remember the world and visit them
that dwell on the earth. . . . And Kenaz placed
them in the ark . . . and they are there unto this
day."

Apart from the mention of Jahel (by whom
Solomon is meant, but why so called I know not)
this is rather a perplexing passage. Taken as it
stands, it ought to mean that the temple, or at
least the ark, was extant at the supposed date of
the writer, *i.e.* that the story was not carried down
as far as the destruction of Jerusalem by Nebuchadnezzar; which, on general grounds, one would
select as a likely point for the conclusion. We
must, however, remember the legend that the ark
and its contents were preserved and hidden by
Jeremiah or by an angel (2 *Macc.* 2. *Apoc. Bar.*
6⁴). Besides, *Philo* elsewhere says (XXII. 9)

that in the new sanctuary which was at Gilgal, "Joshua appointed unto this day (*usque in hodiernum diem*)" the yearly sacrifices of Israel, and that until the temple was built sacrifice at the other place was lawful. We cannot, then, press his use of the phrase "unto this day"; yet if it be insisted upon, there is a detail in *Baruch* (6⁷) which may throw some light on *Philo's* meaning. *Baruch* says that the angel took, among other things, "the forty-eight precious stones wherewith the priest was adorned" and committed them to the guardianship of the earth. No one offers any reason for the mention of forty-eight (instead of twelve) stones, and though only twelve more figure in the story of Kenaz, I think it not unreasonable to suggest that here as elsewhere the Apocalyptist has our text in his mind, and that a belief in the legend of the hidden ark was common to both.

The sketch of Israel's history contained in *Apoc. Bar.* 56–67 (a section which shows many resemblances to *Philo*), with its alternations of righteousness and sin, gives, to my mind, a very fair idea of what *Philo* may have comprised when it was complete. We begin with the sin of Adam and of the angels: both are alluded to more than once in *Philo*. Then we have Abraham (important in *Philo*), the wickedness of the Gentiles, and especially of the Egyptians (not emphasized in *Philo*), the ages of Moses and Joshua (treated at length), the sorceries of the Amorites under the Judges (dwelt on at great length), the age of David and Solomon (*Philo* breaks off in David), the times of Jeroboam and Jezebel and the captivity of the nine and a half tribes, the reign of Hezekiah, the wickedness of Manasseh, the reforms of Josiah, the destruction by Nebuchadnezzar. *Baruch* then continues the history to the Messianic kingdom and the final triumph of right, of which *Philo* speaks only in general terms, though it may have developed clearer views as it proceeded. For the present, my conjecture is that *Philo* ended with the Babylonian captivity, and not without an anticipation of the Return.[1]

12. I fear that we cannot regard the writer of *Philo* as a man of very lofty mind or of great literary talent. He has some imagination, and is sensible of the majesty of the Old Testament literature, but he has not the insight, the power, or the earnestness of the author of 4 *Esdras*, nor again the ethical perception of him who wrote the *Testaments of the Twelve Patriarchs*. From this point of view the obscurity which has hung over his book is not undeserved. Nevertheless it is a source by no means to be neglected by the student of Christian origins and of Jewish thought, and for that reason I have suggested that it should find a place in this series of translations.

I hope that the pretensions of this edition will not be misconceived. It is not a critical edition in the sense that it presents all the variants of all the authorities and lays the whole body of evidence before the reader. Such a presentation would only be possible if the text as well as the translation were included in this volume. (I do not myself, let me say in passing, believe that the result of a complete statement of various readings would differ very importantly from what the reader now has before him, seeing that the text depends upon a single thread of tradition.) Nor, again, will every available illustrative passage be found in such notes as I have written on the subject-matter: in Rabbinic literature especially it should be possible to find many more parallels. Notes of

---

[1] But see the Additional Note, p. 73.

E

a linguistic kind, too, are out of place where a translation only is in question. Neither has every Biblical allusion been marked : as a rule, the reader who knows his Bible will easily recognize the phrases which the author weaves together— often deftly enough. Besides these omissions, larger problems remain unsolved. There are not a few unhealed places in the text, and there are some whole episodes of which the bearing is very obscure.

On the other hand, I may claim that account has here been taken for the first time of a fairly representative selection of the authorities for the text, and that the relation of the book to some, at least, of its fellows has been elucidated ; and I hope that the translation, in which I have followed as closely as possible the language of the Authorised Version (though I have kept the Latin forms of the proper names), may be found readable.

I have, further, provided a means of referring to passages in the text by a division into chapters and verses, or sections, which I think must prove useful. Something of the kind was much needed, for it has hitherto only been possible to cite by the pages of one or other of the sixteenth-century editions. My division is of course applicable to any future edition.

The present volume is, then, a step in the direction of a critical edition, but only a step. Like the first editor, Sichardus, I recognize its defects (or some of them) and should welcome the opportunity, if it ever came, of producing an improved form of the original text. As it is the kindness of the Society under whose auspices the book appears allows me to include in it a selection of the most important readings and some particulars of the Latinity of the original. For this indulgence my readers, as well as myself, will assuredly be grateful.

13. SYNOPSIS OF THE CONTENTS.

CONTENTS 69

There is more than one plausible way of dividing
the book into episodes. The simplest is this—

A more elaborate subdivision would be—

Adam to Lamech, I.–II.
Noah and his descendants, III.–V.
Abraham to the death of Joseph, VI.–VIII.
The life of Moses, IX.–XIX.
Joshua, XX.–XXIV.
The Judges, the chief figures being—

> Kenaz, XXV.–XXVIII.
> Zebul, XXIX.
> Deborah, XXX.–XXXIII.
> Aod, XXXIV.
> Gideon, XXXV.–XXXVI.
> Jair, XXXVIII.
> Jephthah, XXXIX.–XL.
> Abdon, Elon, XLI.
> Samson, XLII.–XLIII.

The events of the last chapters of the Book of Judges, XLIV.–XLVIII.
Life of Samuel, to the return of the ark, XLIX.–LV.
Saul's career, LVI.–LXV., David entering upon the scene in LIX.

A third and more artificial method of division (which is followed to some extent by the MS. R) is into portions corresponding to the Biblical books, viz.—

Genesis, I.–VIII.
Exodus, IX.–XIII.
Leviticus, part of XIII.
Numbers, XIV.–XVIII.
Deuteronomy, XIX.
Joshua, XX.–XXIV.
Judges, XXV.–XLVIII.
I Samuel, XLIX.–LXV.

The space allotted to the period of the Judges emerges as the striking feature. It is rather greater than that given to the Pentateuch and Joshua, and more than double the share of 1 Samuel. And of it almost a third part is devoted to the doings of a person practically unknown to the Bible, namely, Kenaz.

ADDITIONAL NOTE

A passage in Origen *On Romans* (IV. 12, p. 646) deserves to be quoted as being very much in the manner of *Philo*. "We have found," he says, "in a certain apocryphal book (in quodam secretiore libello) mention of an angel of grace who takes his name from grace, being called Ananchel, *i.e.* the grace of God: and the writing in question says that this angel was sent by God to Esther to give her favour in the sight of the king." Just so in *Philo* appropriate angels are sent to Kenaz and to David and intervene to save the victims of Jair. I think it worth suggesting that the story of Esther found a place in *Philo*, and that this was the *secretior libellus* to which Origen refers.

NOTE

Phrases and sentences in *italics* mark quotations from the Old Testament : single words in *italics*, and short phrases to which no Biblical reference is attached in the margin, are supplements of the translator.

The following signs are also employed :

[ ] Words wrongly inserted into the text.
( ) Alternative readings of importance.
< > (As p. 151)⎱ Words that have fallen out, restored by
⟨ ⟩ (As p. 100)⎰ conjecture.
† † (As p. 89) Corrupt passages.

THE BIBLICAL
ANTIQUITIES OF PHILO

OR THE HISTORY OF PHILO FROM THE BEGINNING OF THE WORLD TO KING DAVID

I. The beginning of the world. Adam begat three sons and one daughter, Cain, Noaba, Abel and Seth. 2. And Adam *lived after he begat* Gen. 5⁴ *Seth* 700 *years, and begat* 12 *sons and* 8 *daughters.*

I. 1. *Initium mundi* appears to be the best reading. It is perhaps in the nature of a title : the proper LXX name for Genesis is γένεσισ κόσμου.

1., etc. It will be observed that almost all the names of sons and all those of daughters are imaginary. They do not agree with other legendary names, *e.g.* those of *Jubilees.* For the rest, the first three chapters are to a very large extent simply copied from Genesis iv–xi.

The spelling of the names is very uncertain in many cases. Where " ph " occurs, it is very often substituted by Sichardus for " f " in the MSS. ; but of course the " f " must represent a φ, seeing that the text has come to us through Greek. I have therefore allowed " ph " to stand.

The chronology, according to Dr. Cohn, was originally that of the Hebrew text, but has been to some extent modified by reference to the LXX. The Hebrew numbers (from Adam to the Flood) add up to 1656, those of the LXX to 2262, those of *Philo* to 2256 ; but *Philo* says (III. 6) that the Flood was in the 1652nd year of the world, which only requires the change of *secundus* to **sextus** to make it agree exactly with the Hebrew.

3. And these are the names of the males: Eli-
seel, Suris, Elamiel, Brabal, Naat, Zarama, Zasam,
Maathal, and Anath.

4. And these are his daughters: Phua, Iectas,
Arebica, Sifa, Tecia, Saba, Asin.

Gen. 5⁷
5. *And Seth lived* 105 *years and begat Enos.
And Seth lived after he begat Enos* 707 *years, and
begat* 3 *sons and* 2 *daughters.*

6. And these are the names of his sons: Elidia,
Phonna, and Matha: and of his daughters, Malida
and Thila.

5⁹, ¹⁰
7. *And Enos lived* 180 *years and begat Cainan.
And Enos lived after he begat Cainan* 715 *years,
and begat* 2 *sons and* a daughter.

8. And these are the names of his sons: Phoë
and Thaal; and of the daughter, Catennath.

5¹², ¹³
9. *And Cainan lived* 520 *years and begat Malalech. And Cainan lived after he begat Malalech*
730 *years, and begat* 3 *sons and* 2 *daughters.*

10. And these are the names of the males:
Athach, Socer, Lopha: and the names of the
daughters, Ana and Leua.

5¹⁵, ¹⁶
11. *And Malalech lived* 165 *years and begat Jareth.
And Malalech lived after he begat Jareth* 730 *years,
and begat* 7 *sons and* 5 *daughters.*

12. And these are the names of the males:
Leta, Matha, Cethar, Melie, Suriel, Lodo, Othim.
And these are the names of the daughters: Ada
and Noa, Iebal, Mada, Sella.

5¹⁸, ¹⁹
13. *And Jareth lived* 172 *years and begat Enoch.
And Jareth lived after he begat Enoch* 800 *years
and begat* 4 *sons and* 2 *daughters.* 14. And these
are the names of the males: Lead, Anac, Soboac
and Iectar: and of the daughters, Tetzeco, Lesse.

5²², ²³
15. *And Enoch lived* 165 *years and begat Matusalam. And Enoch lived after he begat Matusalam*
200 *years, and begat* 5 *sons and* 3 *daughters.*

16. But *Enoch pleased God* at that time *and was* Gen. 5²⁴
not found, for God translated him.

17. Now the names of his sons are : Anaz,
Zeum, Achaun, Pheledi, Elith ; and of the daughters, Theiz, Lefith, Leath.

18. *And Mathusalam lived* 187 *years and begat* 5²⁵,²⁶
Lamech. And Mathusalam lived after he begat
Lamech 782 *years, and begat* 2 *sons and* 2
daughters.

19. And these are the names of the males : Inab
and Rapho ; and of the daughters, Aluma and
Amuga.

20. *And Lamech lived* 182 *years and begat a son,* 5²⁸,²⁹
and called him according to his nativity *Noe, say-*
ing : This child will give rest to us and to the
earth from those who are therein, upon whom (*or*
in the day when) a visitation shall be made because
of the iniquity of their evil deeds.

21. *And Lamech lived after he begat Noe* 585 5³⁰
years.

22. *And Noe lived* 300 *years and begat* 3 *sons,* 5³²,6²⁰
Sem, Cham, and Japheth.

II. But Cain dwelt in the earth trembling, Cf. Gen.
according as God appointed unto him after he 4¹ᵃ
slew Abel his brother ; and the name of his wife
was Themech.

2. *And Cain knew* Themech *his wife and she* 4¹⁷
conceived and bare Enoch.

3. Now Cain was 15 years old when he did these
things ; and from that time he began to build cities,
until he had founded seven cities. And these are 4¹⁷
the names of the cities : The name of the first
city according to the name of his son Enoch.
The name of the second city Mauli, and of the
third Leeth, and the name of the fourth Teze,

II. 3. The names of Cain's cities, except the first, do not
occur elsewhere.

and the name of the fifth Iesca ; the name of
the sixth Celeth, and the name of the seventh
Iebbath.

4. And Cain lived after he begat Enoch 715
years and begat 3 sons and 2 daughters. And
these are the names of his sons : Olad, Lizaph,
Fosal; and of his daughters, Citha and Maac.
And all the days of Cain were 730 years, and he
died.

5. Then took Enoch a wife of the daughters
of Seth, which bare him Ciram and Cuuth and
Madab. But Ciram begat Matusael, and Matusael
begat Lamech.

Gen. 4¹⁹
6. *But Lamech took unto himself two wives : the
name of the one was Ada and the name of the other
Sella. 7. And Ada bare him* Iobab: *he was the
father of all that dwell in tents and feed flocks.*
And again she bare him *Iobal, which was the first
to teach all playing of instruments (lit.* every psalm
of organs). 8. And at that time, when they that
dwelt on the earth had begun to do evil, every
one with his neighbour's wife, defiling them, God
was angry. And he began to play upon the *lute
(kinnor) and the harp* and on every instrument of
sweet psalmody (*lit.* psaltery), and to corrupt the
earth.

4²¹

4²²
9. *But Sella bare Tubal* and Misa and Theffa,
and this is that Tubal which showed unto men
arts in lead and tin and iron and copper and silver
and gold : and then began the inhabiters of the
earth to make graven images and to worship
them.

10. *Now Lamech said unto his two wives Ada*

5. *Jerahmeel* says that Enoch, son of Cain, took Niba,
daughter of Shem, to wife.   His source is unknown to me.
8. See the Appendix on Readings.
10. *Jubilees* does not speak of this Lamech.   The turn

*and Sella : Hear my voice, ye wives of Lamech,
give heed to my precept :* for I have corrupted men
for myself, and *have taken away* sucklings from the
breasts, that I might show my sons how to work
evil, *and the inhabiters of the earth.* And now *shall
vengeance be taken seven times of Cain, but of
Lamech seventy times seven.*

III. *And it came to pass when men had begun* Gen. 6[1]
to multiply on the earth, that beautiful *daughters
were born unto them. And the sons of God saw the
daughters of men that they were* exceeding *fair, and
took them wives of all that they had chosen.* 2. *And
God said: My spirit shall not* judge *among these
men for ever, because they are of flesh; but their
years shall be* 120. Upon whom he laid (*or
wherein I have set*) the ends of the world, and in
their hands wickednesses were not put out (*or the   6[5]
law shall not be quenched*). 3. *And God saw that
in all the dwellers upon earth works of evil were
fulfilled : and inasmuch as their thought was upon
iniquity all their days,* God said : *I will blot
out man* and all things that have budded upon
the earth, *for it repenteth me that I have made
him.*

4. *But Noe found grace* and mercy *before the*

here given to his "song" suggests that his offence was
against morality ; this view is found elsewhere.

III. 2 *fin.* See the variants, which are difficult to explain. If the reading *et in manibus eorum scelera non
extinguebantur* is right, the clause would be better placed
after *opera malignitatum* in the next verse. "And God saw
that in all the inhabiters of the earth works of wickedness
were fulfilled, and in their hands," etc. I have preferred
the other reading : the whole sentence will then refer to the
new race who are to arise after the Flood, and especially to
Moses (see IX. 8 *fin.*) : the last preceding words ("their
years shall be 120") do certainly apply to them and to him.
The antediluvians are to perish utterly. See on XVI. 3.

Lord, and these are his generations. Noe, which was a righteous man and undefiled *in his generation,*

Gen. 6¹³ *pleased the Lord.* Unto whom *God said: The time of all men that dwell upon the earth is come, for their deeds are very evil. And now make thee an ark of* cedar wood, *and thus shalt thou make it.* 300 *cubits shall be the length thereof, and*

6¹⁸ 50 *cubits the breadth, and* 30 *cubits the height. And thou shalt enter into the ark, thou and thy wife and thy sons and thy sons' wives with thee. And I will make my covenant with thee,* to destroy all the

7²⁻⁴ dwellers upon earth. *Now of clean beasts and of the fowls of the heaven that are clean thou shalt take by sevens male and female, that their seed may be saved alive upon the earth. But of unclean beasts and fowls thou shalt take to thee by twos male and*

6²¹ *female, and shalt take provision for thee and for them also.*

7⁵, ⁷   5. *And Noe did that which God commanded him, and entered into the ark, he and all his sons with*

7¹⁰ *him. And it came to pass after* 7 *days that the*

7¹¹ *water of the flood began to be upon the earth. And in that day all the depths were opened* and the great spring *of water and the windows of heaven, and there was rain upon the earth* 40 *days and* 40 *nights.*

6. And it was then the 1652nd (1656th) year from the time when God had made the heaven and the earth in the day when the earth was corrupted with the inhabiters thereof by reason of the iniquity of their works.

7. And when the flood continued 140 days upon the earth, Noe only and they that were with him in the ark remained alive: and when God remembered Noe, he made the water to diminish.

8¹⁶   8. And it came to pass on the 90th day that God

dried the earth, and *said unto Noe: Go out of the ark, thou* and all that are with thee, *and grow and multiply upon the earth. And Noe went out of the ark, he and his sons and his sons' wives, and all the beasts and creeping things and fowls and cattle* brought he forth with him as God commanded him. *Then built Noe an altar unto the Lord, and took of all the cattle and of the clean fowls and offered burnt offerings on the altar:* and it was accepted of the Lord for a savour of rest.

Gen. 8²¹

9. *And God said: I will not again curse the earth for man's sake, for the guise of man's heart* hath left off *from his youth. And therefore I will not again destroy together all living as I have done.* But it shall be, when the dwellers upon earth have sinned, I will judge them by famine or by the sword or by fire or by pestilence (*lit.* death), and there shall be earthquakes, and they shall be scattered into places not inhabited (*or,* the places of *their* habitation shall be scattered). But I will not again spoil the earth with the water of a flood, and *in all the days of the earth seed time and harvest, cold and heat, summer and autumn, day and night shall not cease,* until I remember them that dwell on the earth, *even* until the times are fulfilled. 10. But when the years of the world shall be fulfilled, then shall the light cease and the darkness be quenched: and I will quicken the dead and raise up from the earth them that sleep: and Hell shall pay his debt and destruction give back that

8²²

9. *the guise of man's heart hath left off* (*figura cordis hominis desiit*: Cohn suggests *desipit*) "ὁ Ἑβραῖοσ"(ap. Euseb. Emis. in Catena : see Field's *Hexapla* in loc.) has τὸ πλάσμα τῆσ καρδίασ ἀνθρώπου.

10. This is the first really characteristic passage.
that hath been justified in me. The word occurs in XLIX. 4, "Is Armathem *iustificata* more than all the cities of Israel?" and in LI. 2.

F

which was committed unto him, that I may render unto every man according to his works and according to the fruit of their imaginations, *even* until I judge between the soul and the flesh. And the world shall rest, and death shall be quenched, and Hell shall shut his mouth. And the earth shall not be without birth, neither barren for them that dwell therein : and none shall be polluted that hath been justified in me. And there shall be another earth and another heaven, even an everlasting habitation.

Gen 9⁸   11. *And the Lord spake* further *unto Noe and to his sons saying : Behold I will make my covenant with you and with your seed after you, and will not* 9²   *again spoil the earth with the water of a flood. And all that liveth and moveth therein shall be to you for meat. Nevertheless the flesh with the blood of the soul shall ye not eat. For he that sheddeth man's blood, his blood shall be shed ; for in the image of God was man made. And ye, grow ye and multiply and fill the earth* as the multitude of fishes that 9¹²   multiply in the waters. And God said : This is the covenant that I have made betwixt me and you ; *and it shall be when I cover the heaven with clouds, that my bow shall appear in the cloud, and it shall be for a memorial of the covenant betwixt me and you, and all the dwellers upon earth.*

9¹⁸   IV. *And the sons of Noe which went forth of the ark were Sem, Cham, and Japheth.*

10²   2. *The sons of Japheth : Gomer, Magog, and Madai,* Nidiazech, *Tubal,* Mocteras, Cenez, *Riphath, and Thogorma, Elisa,* Dessin, Cethin, Tudant.

IV. The variants in the forms and divisions of the names are many. In the Appendix on Readings I have pointed out the Biblical equivalents. It is obvious that some names and words have dropped out of *Philo.* In the translation I have introduced very few corrections.

And the sons of Gomer : Thelez, Lud, Deberlet.

And the sons of Magog : Cesse, Thipha, Pharuta, Ammiel, Phimei, Goloza, Samanach.

And the sons of Duden : Sallus, Phelucta Phallita.

And the sons of Tubal : Phanatonova, Eteva.

And the sons of Tyras : Maac, Tabel, Ballana, Samplameac, Elaz.

And the sons of Mellech : Amboradat, Urach, Bosara.

And the sons of ⟨As⟩cenez : Jubal, Zaraddana, Anac.

And the sons of Heri : Phuddet, Doad, Dephadzeat, Enoc.

And the sons of Togorma : Abiud, Saphath, Asapli, Zepthir.

And the sons of Elisa : Etzaac, Zenez, Mastisa, Rira.

And the sons of Zepti : Macziel, Temna, Aela, Phinon.

And the sons of Tessis : Meccul, Loon, Zelataban.

And the sons of Duodennin : Itheb, Beath, Phenech.

3. And these are they that were scattered abroad, and dwelt in the earth with the Persians and Medes, and in the islands that are in the sea. And Phenech, the son of Dudeni, went up and commanded that ships of the sea should be made : and then was the third part of the earth divided.

4. Domereth and his sons took Ladech ; and Magog and his sons took Degal ; Madam and his sons took Besto ; Iuban (*sc.* Javan) and his sons took Ceel ; Tubal and his sons took Pheed ; Misech and his sons took Nepthi ; ⟨T⟩iras and his sons took ⟨Rôô⟩ ; Duodennut and his sons took

Goda; Riphath and his sons took Bosarra; Torgoma and his sons took Fud; Elisa and his sons took Thabola; Thesis (sc. Tarshish) and his sons took Marecham; Cethim and his sons took Thaan; Dudennin and his sons took Caruba.

5. And then began they to till the earth and to sow upon it: and when the earth was athirst, the dwellers therein cried unto the Lord and he heard them and gave rain abundantly, and it was so, when the rain descended upon the earth, that the bow appeared in the cloud, and the dwellers upon earth saw the memorial of the covenant and fell upon their faces and sacrificed, offering burnt offerings unto the Lord.

Gen. 10⁶   6. *Now the sons of Cham were Chus, Mestra, and Phuni, and Chanaan.*

And the sons of Chus: Saba, and . . . Tudan.

And the sons of Phuni: [Effuntenus], Zeleutelup, Geluc, Lephuc.

And the sons of Chanaan were Sydona, Endain, Racin, Simmin, Uruin, Nenugin, Amathin, Nephin, Telaz, Elat, Cusin.

10⁸   7. *And Chus begat Nembroth. He began to be proud before the Lord.*

10¹³, ¹⁴   *But Mestram begat Ludin* and Megimin and Labin and Latuin and Petrosonoin and Ceslun: *thence came forth the Philistines* and the Cappadocians.

8. And then did they also begin to build cities: and these are the cities which they built: Sydon, and the parts that lie about it, that is Resun, Beosa, Maza, Gerara, Ascalon, Dabir, Camo, Tellun, Lacis, Sodom and Gomorra, Adama and Seboim.

10²²   9. *And the sons of Sem: Elam, Assur, Arphaxa, Luzi, Aram.* And the sons of Aram: Gedrum, Ese. *And Arphaxa begat Sale, Sale begat Heber, and unto Heber were born two sons: the name of the one was Phalech, for in his days the earth was divided, and the name of his brother was Jectan.*

10. *And Jectan begat Helmadam and Salastra and Mazaam, Rea, Dura, Uzia, Deglabal, Mimoel, Sabthphin, Evilac, Iubab.*

And the sons of Phalech: Ragau, Rephuth, Zepheram, Aculon, Sachar, Siphaz, Nabi, Suri, Seciur, Phalacus, Rapho, Phalthia, Zaldephal, Zaphis, and Arteman, Heliphas. These are the sons of Phalech, and these are their names, and they took them wives of the daughters of Jectan and begat sons and daughters and filled the earth. Cf. Gen. 11[18]

11. But Ragau took him to wife Melcha the daughter of Ruth, and she begat him Seruch. And when the day of her delivery came she said: Of this *child* shall be born in the fourth generation one who shall set his dwelling on high, and shall be called perfect, and undefiled, and he shall be the father of nations, and his covenant shall not be broken, and his seed shall be multiplied for ever.

12. *And Ragau lived after he begat Seruch* 119 *years and begat 7 sons and 5 daughters.* And these are the names of his sons: Abiel, Obed, Salma, Dedasal, Zeneza, Accur, Nephes. And these are the names of his daughters: Cedema, Derisa, Seipha, Pherita, Theila. 11[21]

13. *And Seruch lived* 29 *years and begat Nachor. And Seruch lived after he begat Nachor* 67 *years and begat 4 sons and 3 daughters.* And these are the names of the males: Zela, Zoba, Dica and Phodde. And these are his daughters: Tephila, Oda, Selipha.

14. *And Nachor lived* 34 *years and begat Thara. And Nachor lived after he begat Thara* 200 *years and begat 8 sons and 5 daughters.* And these

are the names of the males: Recap, Dediap, Berechap, Iosac, Sithal, Nisab, Nadab, Camoel. And these are his daughters: Esca, Thipha, Bruna, Ceneta.

15. *And Thara lived 70 years and begat Abram, Nachor, and Aram. And Aram begat Loth.*

16. Then began they that dwelt on the earth to look upon the stars, and began to prognosticate by them and to make divination, and to make their sons and daughters pass through the fire. But Seruch and his sons walked not according to them.

17. And these are the generations of Noe upon the earth according to their languages and their tribes, out of whom the nations were divided upon the earth after the flood.

V. Then came the sons of Cham, and made Nembroth a. prince over themselves: but the sons of Japheth made Phenech their chief: *and* the sons of Sem gathered together and set over them Jectan to be their prince.

2. And when these three had met together they took counsel that they would look upon and take account of the people of their followers. And this was done while Noe was yet alive, *even* that all men should be gathered together: and they lived at one with each other, and the earth was at peace.

3. Now in the 340th year of the going forth of

IV. 16. As is noted in the Introduction, this verse contradicts *Jubilees* on the subject of Serug, and implicitly rejects the story that Terah, Abraham's father, was an idolater.

V. The numbers in this chapter are hopelessly incorrect. The separate items in the text add up to 704,000; the totals in the text to 734,500, omitting the evidently corrupt figure 9000 assigned to Shem and his descendants. The matter is of no importance,

Noe out of the ark, after that God dried up the flood, did the princes take account of their people.

4. And *first* Phenech the son of Japheth looked upon them.

The sons of Gomer all of them passing by according to the sceptres of their captaincies were in number 5,800.

But of the sons of Magog all of them passing by according to the sceptres of their leading the number was 6,200.

And of the sons of Madai all of them passing by according to the sceptres of their captaincies were in number 5,700.

And the sons of Tubal all of them passing by according to the sceptres of their captaincies were in number 9,400.

And the sons of Mesca all of them passing by according to the sceptres of their captaincies were in number 5,600.

The sons of Thiras all of them passing by according to the sceptres of their captaincies were in number 12,300.

And the sons of Ripha⟨th⟩ passing by according to the sceptres of their captaincies were in number 11,500.

And the sons of Thogorma passing by according to the sceptres of their captaincy were in number 14,400.

But the sons of Elisa passing by according to the sceptres of their captaincy were in number 14,900.

And the sons of Thersis all of them passing by according to the sceptres of their captaincy were in number 12,100.

The sons of Cethin all of them passing by according to the sceptres of their captaincy were in number 17,300.

And the sons of Doin passing by according to the sceptres of their captaincies were in number 17,700.

And the number of the camp of the sons of Japheth, all of them men of might and all girt with their armour, which were set in the sight of their captains was 140,202 besides women and children.

The account of Japheth in full was in number 142,000.

5. And Nembroth passed by, he and the son(s) of Cham, all of them passing by according to the sceptres of their captaincies were found in number 24,800.

The sons of Phua all of them passing by according to the sceptres of their captaincies were in number 27,700.

And the sons of Canaan all of them passing by according to the sceptres of their captaincies were found in number 32,800.

The sons of Soba all of them passing by according to the sceptres of their captaincies were found in number 4,300.

The sons of Lebilla all of them passing by according to the sceptres of their captaincies were found in number 22,300.

And the sons of Sata all of them passing by according to the sceptres of their captaincies were found in number 25,300.

And the sons of Remma all of them passing by according to the sceptres of their captaincies were found in number 30,600.

And the sons of Sabaca all of them passing by according to the sceptres of their captaincies were found in number 46,400.

And the number of the camp of the sons of Cham, all of them mighty men, and furnished with

armour, which were set in the sight of their captaincies was in number 244,900 besides women and
children.

6. And Jectan the son of Sem looked upon the
sons of Elam, and they were all of them passing
by according to the number of the sceptres of their
captaincies in number 47,000.

And the sons of Assur all of them passing by
according to the sceptres of their captaincies were
found in number 73,000.

And the sons of Aram all of them passing by
according to the sceptres of their captaincies were
found in number 87,300.

The sons of Lud all of them passing by according to the sceptres of their captaincies were found
in number 30,600.

[The number of the sons of Cham was 73,000.]

But the sons of Arfaxat all of them passing by
according to the sceptres of their captaincies were
in number 114,600.

And the whole number of them was 347,600.
7. The number of the camp of the sons of Sem,
all of them setting forth in valour and in the
commandment of war in the sight of their
captaincies was † ix † besides women and children.

8. And these are the generations of Noe set
forth separately, whereof the whole number together was 914,000. And all these were counted
while Noe was yet alive, and in the presence of
Noe 350 years after the flood. And all the days
of Noe were 950 years, and he died.

VI. Then all they that had been divided and

8. It is part of this verse which is quoted (and that not
accurately) by Petrus Comestor. See Introduction, p. 10.

VI. This particular legend of the rescue of Abram from
the fire is peculiar to *Philo*. Most of the stories make
Nimrod the principal actor. Various forms may be seen in

dwelt upon the earth gathered together there-after, and dwelt together ; *and they set forth from the East and found a plain in the land of Babylon : and there they dwelt, and they said every man to his neighbour :* Behold, it will come to pass that we shall be scattered every man from his brother, and in the latter days we shall be fighting one against another. *Now, therefore, come and let us build for ourselves a tower, the head whereof shall reach unto heaven, and we shall make us a name* and a renown upon the earth.

2. And they said everyone to his neighbour : Let us take bricks (*lit.* stones), and let us, each one, write our names upon the bricks and burn them with fire : and that which is thoroughly burned shall be for mortar and brick. (*Perhaps,* that which is not thoroughly burned shall be for mortar, and that which is, for brick.)

3. And they took every man their bricks, saving 12 men, which would not take them, and these are their names : Abraham, Nachor, Loth, Ruge, Tenute, Zaba, Armodath, Iobab, Esar, Abimahel, Saba, Auphin. 4. And the people of the land laid hands on them and brought them before their princes and said : These are the men that have trans-gressed our counsels and will not walk in our ways. And the princes said unto them : Where-fore would ye not set every man your bricks with the people of the land ? And they answered and said : We will not set bricks with you, neither will we be joined with your desire. One Lord know we, and him do we worship. And if ye should cast us into the fire with your bricks, we will not

Beer's *Leben Abrahams* or Baring-Gould's *Legends of O. T. Characters.*

3. Several of the names here are those of the sons of Jectan in IV. 10. Auphin is probably for Ophir.

consent to you. 5. And the princes were wroth
and said: As they have said, so do unto them,
and if they consent not to set bricks with you,
ye shall burn them with fire together with your
bricks. 6. Then answered Jectan which was the
first prince of the captains : Not so, but there shall
be given them a space of 7 days. And it shall
be, if they repent of their evil counsels, and will
set bricks along with us, they shall live; but if
not, let them be burned according to your word.
But he sought how he might save them out of
the hands of the people ; for he was of their tribe,
and he served God.

7. And when he had thus said he took them and
shut them up in the king's house : and when it
was evening the prince commanded 50 mighty
men of valour to be called unto him, and said unto
them : Go forth and take to-night these men that
are shut up in mine house, and put provision for
them from my house upon 10 beasts, and the men
bring ye to me, and their provision together with
the beasts take ye to the mountains and wait for
them there : and know this, that if any man shall
know what I have said unto you, I will burn you
with fire.

8. And the men set forth and did all that their
prince commanded them, and took the men from
his house by night ; and took provision and put it
upon beasts and took them to the hill country as
he commanded them.

9. And the prince called unto him those 12 men
and said to them : Be of good courage and fear
not, for ye shall not die. For God in whom ye
trust is mighty, and therefore be ye stablished in
him, for he will deliver you and save you. And
now lo, I have commanded 50 men to take [you
with] provision from my house, and go before you

into the hill country and wait for you in the valley :
and I will give you other 50 men which shall guide
you thither : go ye therefore and hide yourselves
there in the valley, having water to drink that
floweth down from the rocks : hold yourselves
there for 30 days, until the anger of the people of
the land be appeased and until God send his wrath
upon them and break them.   For I know that the
counsel of iniquity which they have agreed to
perform shall not stand, for their thought is vain.
And it shall be when 7 days are expired and they
shall seek for you, I will say unto them : They
have gone forth and have broken the door of the
prison wherein they were shut up and have fled
by night, and I have sent 100 men to seek them.
So will I turn them from their madness that is
upon them.

10. And there answered him 11 of the men
saying : Thy servants have found favour in thy
sight, in that we are set free out of the hands
of these proud men.   11. But Abram only kept
silence, and the prince said unto him : Wherefore answerest thou not me, Abram, servant of
God ? Abram answered and said : Lo, I flee
away to-day into the hill country, and if I
escape the fire, wild beasts will come out of the
mountains and devour us.   Or our victuals will
fail and we shall die of hunger ; and we shall be
found fleeing from the people of the land and shall
fall in our sins.   And now, as he liveth in whom I
trust, I will not remove from my place wherein
they have put me : and if there be any sin
of mine so that I be indeed burned, the will of
God be done.   And the prince said unto him :

9. *and go before you,* etc., *et praecedite uos in montana et
sustinete uos in ualle.* Some such change as I have made
in the translation appears necessary.

Thy blood be upon thy head, if thou refuse to go forth with these. But if thou consent, thou shall be delivered. Yet if thou wilt abide, abide as thou art. And Abram said : I will not go forth, but I will abide here.

12. And the prince took those 11 men and sent other 50 with them, and commanded them saying: Wait, ye also, in the hill country for 15 days with those 50 which were sent before you ; and after that ye shall return and say : " We have not found them," as I said to the former ones. And know that if any man transgress one of all these words that I have spoken unto you, he shall be burned with fire. So the men went forth, and he took Abram by himself and shut him up where he had been shut up aforetime.

13. And after 7 days were passed, the people were gathered together and spake unto their prince saying : Restore us the men which would not consent unto us, that we may burn them with fire. And they sent captains to bring them, and they found them not, save Abram only. And they gathered all of them to their prince saying : The men whom ye shut up are fled and have escaped that which we counselled. 14. And Phenech and Nemroth said unto Jectan : Where are the men whom thou didst shut up ? But he said : They have broken prison and fled by night : but I have sent 100 men to seek them, and commanded them if they find them that they should not only burn them with fire but give their bodies to the fowls of the heaven and so destroy them. 15. Then said they : This *fellow* which is found alone, let us burn him. And they took Abram and brought him before their princes and said to him : Where are they that were with thee ? And he said : Verily at night I slept, and when I awaked I found them not.

16. And they took him and built a furnace and kindled it with fire, and put bricks burned with fire into the furnace. Then Jectan the prince being amazed (*lit.* melted) in his mind took Abram and put him with the bricks into the furnace of fire.   17. But God stirred up a great earthquake, and the fire gushed forth of the furnace and brake out into flames and sparks of fire and consumed all them that stood round about in sight of the furnace; and all they that were burned in that day were 83,500.   But upon Abram was there not any the least hurt by the burning of the fire.

Dan. 3²²

3²⁷

18. And Abram arose out of the furnace, and the fiery furnace fell down, and Abram was saved. And he went unto the 11 men that were hid in the hill country and told them all that had befallen him, and they came down with him out of the hill country rejoicing in the name of the Lord, and no man met them to affright them that day.   And they called that place by the name of Abram, and in the tongue of the Chaldeans Deli, which is being interpreted, God.

VII. And it came to pass after these things, that the people of the land turned not from their evil thoughts: and they came together again unto their princes and said: The people shall not be overcome for ever: and now let us come together and build us a city and a tower which shall never be removed.

2. And when they had begun to build, God saw the city and the tower which the children of men were building, *and he said: Behold, this is one people and their speech is one*, and this which they have begun to build the earth will not sustain, neither will the heaven suffer it, beholding it: and it shall be, if they be not now hindered, that they shall dare all things that they shall take in mind to do.

Gen. 11⁶

3. *Therefore, lo, I will divide their speech,* and scatter them over all countries, that they may not know every man his brother, neither every man understand the speech of his neighbour. And I will deliver them to the rocks, and they shall build themselves tabernacles of stubble and straw, and shall dig themselves caves and shall live therein like beasts of the field, and thus shall they continue before my face for ever, that they may never devise such things. And I will esteem them as a drop of water, and liken them unto spittle : and unto some of them their end shall come by water, and other of them shall be dried up with thirst. 4. And before all of them will I choose my servant Abram, and I will bring him out from their land, and lead him into the land which mine eye hath looked upon from the beginning when all the dwellers upon earth sinned before my face, and I brought *on them* the water of the flood : and *then* I destroyed not *that land,* but preserved it. Therefore the fountains of my wrath did not break forth therein, neither did the water of my destruction come down upon it. For there will I make my servant Abram to dwell, and I will make my covenant with him, and bless his seed, and will be called his God for ever.

5. Howbeit when the people that dwelt in the land had begun to build the tower, God divided their speech, and changed their likeness. And

VII. 3. *I will liken them unto spittle* (also XII. 4). The source is Isa. 40^{15}; but this clause is not in our present Hebrew text. It occurs, however, in the LXX; it is also in 4 *Esdras* 6^{56}, *Apoc. Bar.* 82^{5}, both of which books are believed to have been written in Hebrew. We need not, therefore, count its occurrence in *Philo* as implying dependence on the LXX. Compare the combinations of phrases from Isaiah in XXVI. 13.

5. *changed their likeness.* J adds "into that of

they knew not every man his brother, neither did each understand the speech of his neighbour. So it came to pass that when the builders commanded their helpers to bring bricks they brought water, and if they asked for water, the others brought them straw. And so their counsel was broken and they ceased building the city: and *God scattered them thence over the face of all the earth. Therefore was the name of that place called Confusion, because there God confounded their speech, and scattered them thence over the face of all the earth.*

Gen. 12⁵

16¹

25¹²

VIII. *But Abram went forth thence and dwelt in the land of Chanaan, and took with him Loth his brother's son, and Sarai his wife.* And because Sarai was barren and had no offspring, then Abram took Agar her maid, and she bare him Ismahel. And Ismahel begat 12 sons.

13¹², ¹³   2. Then Loth departed from Abram and dwelt in Sodom [but Abram dwelt in the land of Cam]. And the men of Sodom were very evil and sinners exceedingly.

13¹⁴, 17³   3. And God appeared unto Abraham saying: Unto thy seed will I give this land; and thy

17¹⁵   name shall be called Abraham, and Sarai thy wife shall be called Sara. And I will give thee of her an eternal seed and make my covenant with

21², ³   thee. And Abraham knew Sara his wife, and she conceived and bare Isaac.

25²⁰ *sqq.*   4. And Isaac took him a wife of Mesopotamia,

monkeys," probably from the Book of Jashar (see Migne, *Dict. des Apocryphes* II. s. v. *Yaschar*). The Greek *Apocalypse of Baruch* describes the builders of the Tower as changed into bestial forms. The story of the workmen misunderstanding each other is in *Bereshith Rabbah, Jashar,* etc.

VIII. 2. [*But Abram dwelt in the land of Cam*] obviously intrusive, repeated from ver. 1, *Cam* being for *Canaan*.

the daughter of Bathuel, which conceived and bare
him Esau and Jacob.   5. And Esau took to him
for wives Judin the daughter of Bereu, and Base-
math the daughter of Elon, and Elibema the
daughter of Anan, and Manem the daughter of
Samahel.

Gen. 26³
36

And ⟨Basemath⟩ *bare him Adelifan,* and the *sons
of Adelifan were Temar, Omar, Seffor, Getan, Tenaz,
Amalec.*   And Judin bạre Tenacis, Ieruebemas,
Bassemen, Rugil: and the *sons of Rugil were Naizar,
Samaza; and Elibema bare Auz, Iollam, Coro.*

Gen. 36¹¹
1 Chron.
1³⁶
Gen. 36¹²
1 Chron.
1³⁷

Manem bare Tenetde, Thenatela.

6. And Jacob took to him for wives the daughters
of Laban the Syrian, Lia and Rachel, and two
concubines, Bala and Zelpha.   And Lia bare him
Ruben, Simeon, Levi, Juda, Isachar, Zabulon, and
Dina their sister.

Gen. 35²²
sqq.

But Rachel bare Joseph and Benjamin.

Bala bare Dan and Neptalim, and Zelpha bare
Gad and Aser.

These are the 12 sons of Jacob and one daughter.

7. And Jacob dwelt in the land of Chanaan, and
Sichem the son of Emor the Correan forced his
daughter Dina and humbled her.   And Simeon and
Levi the sons of Jacob went in and slew all their
city with the edge of the sword, and took Dina
their sister, and went out thence.   8. And thereafter Job took her to wife and begat of her 14 sons
and 6 daughters, even 7 sons and 3 daughters before
he was smitten with affliction, and thereafter when
he was made whole 7 sons and 3 daughters.   And
these are their names: Eliphac, Erinoe, Diasat,
Philias, Diffar, Zellud, Thelon: and his daughters

34

8. That Job married Dinah *after* his affliction is
told in the *Testament of Job* and the Targum on Job. etc.
Note that *Philo* disregards the Biblical names of Job's
daughters, though he accepts the Bible story of Job.

G

Meru, Litaz, Zeli. And such as had been the names of the former, so were they also of the latter.

Gen. 37

9. Now Jacob and his 12 sons dwelt in the land of Chanaan : and *his sons* hated their brother Joseph, whom also they delivered into Egypt, to Petephres the chief of the cooks of Pharao, and he abode with him 14 years.

41

10. And it came to pass after that the king of Egypt had seen a dream, that they told him of Joseph, and he declared him the dreams. And it was so after he declared his dreams, that Pharao made him prince over all the land of Egypt. At that time there was a famine in all the land, as

41, 42, etc.

Joseph had foreseen. And his brethren came down into Egypt to buy food, because in Egypt only was there food. And Joseph knew his brethren, and was made known to them, and dealt not evilly with them. And he sent and called his father out of the land of Chanaan, and he came down unto him.

46⁸ *sqq.*

11. *And these are the names of the sons of Israel which came down into Egypt with Jacob*, each one

46⁹, ¹⁰

with his house. *The sons of Reuben, Enoch and Phallud, Esrom and Carmin ; the sons of Simeon, Namuhel and Iamin and Dot and Iachin, and Saul the son of a Canaanitish woman.*

46¹¹, ¹²

The sons of Levi, Gerson, Caat and Merari : but *the sons of Juda, Auna, Selon, Phares, Zerami.*

46¹³, ¹⁴

The sons of Isachar, Tola and Phua, Iob and Sombram. The sons of Zabulon, Sarelon and Iaillil. And Dina their sister bare 14 sons and 6 daughters.

46¹⁵

And these are the generations *of Lia whom she bare to Jacob. All the souls of sons and daughters were 72.*

11 *seq.* On the names here see Appendix on Readings.

12. *Now the sons of Dan were Usinam.*[1] *The sons* Gen.
of Neptalim, Betaal, Neemmu, Surem, Optisariel. 46^{23, 2}
And these are the generations of Balla which she 46²⁵
bare to Jacob. All the souls were 8.

13. *But the sons of Gad: . . .* Sariel, Sua, Visui, 46^{16. 1}
Mophat *and Sar:*[2] *their sister* the daughter of
Seriebel, Melchiel. *These are the* generations *of
Zelpha* the wife of Jacob *which she bare to him.
And all the souls of sons and daughters were* in
number 10.

14. *And the sons of Joseph, Ephraim and Manas-* 46^{20, 21}
sen: and Benjamin begat Gela, *Esbel, Abocmephec,*
Utundeus. *And these were the souls which Rachel
bare to Jacob,* 14.
And they went down into Egypt and abode
there 210 years.

IX. And it came to pass after the departure of Ex. 1^{6 7}
Joseph, *the children of Israel were multiplied and
increased greatly. And there arose another king in* 1⁸
*Egypt which knew not Joseph: and he said to his
people: Lo, this people is multiplied more than we.* 1⁹
*Come let us take counsel against them that they
multiply not. And the king of Egypt commanded* 1²²
*all his people saying: Every son that shall be born
to the Hebrews, cast into the river, but keep the
females alive.* And the Egyptians answered their
king saying: Let us slay their males and keep
their females, to give them to our bondmen for

IX. 1. A Midrash quoted by Cohn (p. 317) agrees that
the Egyptians desired to marry the Hebrew girls. *Jashar*
and other authorities also say that Amram, in common with
others, put away his wife when the Egyptian decree was
promulgated.

---

[1] *Read:* Usin. But the sons of N.
[2] *Read:* But the sons of Gad (*gap, to Sariel: and the sons
of Aser*). . . . Mophat, and Sara their sister: and the sons
of Beria, Heber, Melchiel.

wives: and he that is born of them shall be a bondman and serve us. And this is that that did appear most evil before the Lord.

2. Then the elders of the people assembled the people with mourning and mourned and lamented saying: An untimely birth have the wombs of our wives suffered. Our fruit is delivered over to our enemies and now we are cut off. Yet let us appoint us an ordinance, that no man come near his wife, lest the fruit of their womb be defiled, and our bowels serve idols: for it is better to die childless, until we know what God will do.

3. And Amram answered and said: It will sooner come to pass that the age shall be utterly abolished and the immeasurable world fall, or the heart of the depths touch the stars, than that the race of the children of Israel should be diminished. And it shall be, when the covenant is fulfilled whereof God when he made it spake to Abraham saying: Surely thy sons shall dwell in a land that is not theirs, and shall be brought into bondage and afflicted 400 years.—And lo, since the word was passed which God spake to Abraham, there are 350 years. ⟨And⟩ since we have been in bondage in Egypt it is 130 years. 4. Now therefore I will not abide by that which ye ordain, but will go in and take my wife and beget sons, that we may be made many on the earth. For God will not continue in his anger, neither will he alway forget his people, nor cast forth the race of Israel to nought upon the earth, neither did he in vain make his covenant with our fathers: yea, when as yet we were not, God spake of these things. 5. Now therefore I will go and take my wife, neither will I consent to

3. *in uictoria minuatur seculum:* utterly, εἰσ νῖκοσ. The Hebraism (למנצח). occurs again, XII. 6, and perhaps in XLIX. 6.

the commandment of this king.   And if it be right
in your eyes, so let us do all of us, for it shall be,
when our wives conceive, they shall not be known
to be great with child until 3 months are fulfilled,
like as also our mother Thamar did, for her intent
was not to fornication, but because she would not
separate herself from the sons of Israel she took
thought and said : It is better for me to die for
sinning with my father-in-law than to be joined to
Gentiles.   And she hid the fruit of her womb till
the 3rd month, for then was it perceived.   And as
she went to be put to death she affirmed it saying :
The man whose is this staff and this ring and goatskin, of him have I conceived.   And her device
delivered her out of all peril.   6. Now therefore
let us also do thus.   And it shall be when the time
of bringing forth is come, if it be possible, we will
not cast forth the fruit of our womb.   And who
knoweth if thereby God will be provoked, to deliver
us from our humiliation ?

7. And the word which Amram had in his heart
was pleasing before God : and God said : Because
the thought of Amram is pleasing before me, and
he hath not set at nought the covenant made
between me and his fathers, therefore, lo now, that
which is begotten of him shall serve me for ever,
and by him will I do wonders in the house of
Jacob, and will do by him signs and wonders for
my people which I have done for none other, and
will perform in them my glory and declare unto
them my ways.   8. I the Lord will kindle for him
my lamp to dwell in him, and will show him my

---

5. *Tamar.*   Here the author first introduces a story from
the past history of Israel by way of illustration : it is his
constant practice later on.

Affirmed it : statuit hoc.   Perhaps "presented" the staff,
etc.

covenant which no man hath seen, and manifest to him my great excellency, and my justice and judgments and will shine for him a perpetual light. For in ancient days I thought of him, saying: My spirit shall not be a mediator among these men for ever, for they are flesh, and their days shall be 120 years.

9. And Amram of the tribe of Levi went forth and took a wife of his tribe, and it was so when he took her, that the residue did after him and took their wives. Now he had one son and one daughter, and their names were Aaron and Maria.

10. And the spirit of God came upon Maria by night, and she saw a dream, and told her parents in the morning saying: I saw this night, and behold a man in a linen garment stood and said to me: Go and tell thy parents: behold, that which shall be born of you shall be cast into the water, for by him water shall be dried up, and by him will I do signs, and I will save my people, and he shall have the captaincy thereof alway. And when Maria had told her dream her parents believed her not.

11. But the word of the king of Egypt prevailed against the children of Israel and they were humiliated and oppressed in the work of bricks.

12. But Jochabeth conceived of Amram and hid *the child* in her womb 3 months, for she could not hide it longer: because the king of Egypt had appointed overseers of the region, that when the Hebrew women brought forth they should cast the males into the river straightway. And she took her child and made him an ark of the bark of a

8. *fin.* The point of the quotation is that Moses was 120 years old when he died. Cf. III. 2.

10. Miriam's vision. In *Jashar* and elsewhere (*e. g.* Talmud Bab. *Megillah*, tr. Rodkinson, p. 36) Miriam prophesies the birth of Moses. Cf. Cohn, p. 318.

pine-tree and set the ark on the edge of the river. 13. Now the boy was born in the covenant of God and in the covenant of his flesh. 14. And it came to pass, when they cast him out, all the elders gathered together and chode with Amram saying: Are not these the words which we spake saying: "It is better for us to die childless than that our fruit should be cast into the water?" And when they said so, Amram hearkened not to them.

15. But the daughter of Pharao came down to wash in the river according as she had seen in a dream, and her maids saw the ark, and she sent one of them and took it and opened it. And when she saw the child and looked upon the covenant, that is, the testament in his flesh, she said: He is of the children of the Hebrews. 16. And she took him and nourished him and he became her son, and she called his name Moyses. But his mother called him Melchiel. And the child was nourished and became glorious above all men, and by him God delivered the children of Israel, as he had said.

X. Now when the king of Egypt was dead another king arose, and afflicted all the people of Israel. But they cried unto the Lord and he heard them, and sent Moses and delivered them out of the land of Egypt: and God sent also upon

15. *according as she had seen in a dream.* The usual story is that God sent a great heat upon Egypt, so that the people were constrained to bathe (*Jashar*, etc.).

covenant. Zaticon = διαθήκην. The Midrashim (Cohn, l. c.) agree that Moses was born circumcised.

16. Melchiel. Syncellus and Cedrenus say that he was called by his parents Melchias. Clement of Alexandria (*Strom.* I. 23) says they called him Ioacim, and he "had a third name after the assumption, as the initiated (μύσται) say, viz. Melchi." *Jashar* (and *Jerahmeel*) give a number of names, but Melchiel is not among them.

them 10 plagues and smote them. Now these
were the plagues, namely, blood, and frogs, and all
manner of flies, hail, and death of cattle, locusts
and gnats, and darkness that might be felt, and the
death of the firstborn.

Ex. 14⁸
sqq.

2. And when they had gone forth thence and
were journeying, the heart of the Egyptians was
yet again hardened, and they continued to pursue
them, and found them by the Red Sea. And the
children of Israel cried unto their God and spake
to Moyses saying: Lo, now is come the time of
our destruction, for the sea is before us and the
multitude of enemies behind us, and we in the
midst. Was it for this that God brought us out,
or are these the covenants which he made with our
fathers saying: To your seed will I give the land
wherein ye dwell? and now let him do with us
that which seemeth good in his sight. 3. Then did
the children of Israel sever their counsels into three
divisions of counsels, because of the fear of the
time. For the tribe of Ruben and of Isachar and
of Zabulon and of Symeon said: Come, let us cast
ourselves into the sea, for it is better for us to die
in the water than to be slain of our enemies. And
the tribe of Gad and of Aser and of Dan and
Neptalim said: Nay, but let us return with them,
and if they will give us our lives, we will serve
them. But the tribe of Levi and of Juda and
Joseph and the tribe of Benjamin said: Not so,
but let us take our weapons and fight them, and
God will be with us. 4. Moses also cried unto the
Lord and said: O Lord God of our fathers, didst

X. 1. *All manner of flies, pammixia.* See p. 23.
3. The idea of the divided counsels of the tribes comes
from Deborah's song (Judges 5¹⁵, ¹⁶): "for the divisions of
Reuben there were great searchings of heart." It appears
in *Jashar*, but there four divisions are given.

thou not say unto me: Go and tell the sons of
Lia, God hath sent me unto you? And now,
behold, thou hast brought thy people to the brink
of the sea, and the enemy follow after them: but
thou, Lord, remember thy name. 5. And God
said: Whereas thou hast cried unto me, take thy
rod and smite the sea, and it shall be dried up.
And when Moses did all this, God rebuked the
sea, and the sea was dried up: the seas of waters
stood still and the depths of the earth appeared,
and the foundations of the dwelling-place were laid
bare at the noise of the fear of God and at the
breath of the anger of my Lord.

6. And Israel passed over on dry land in the
midst of the sea. And the Egyptians saw and
went on to pursue after them, and God hardened
their mind, and they knew not that they were
entering into the sea. And so it was that while
the Egyptians were in the sea God commanded
the sea yet again, and said to Moses: Smite the
sea yet once again. And he did so. And the
Lord commanded the sea and it returned unto his
waves, and covered the Egyptians and their chariots
and their horsemen unto this day.

7. But as for his own people, he led them forth Ps. 78[52]
into the wilderness: forty years did he rain bread
from heaven for them, and he brought them quails
from the sea, and a well of water following them

5. *The breath of the anger of my Lord.* This sudden
adopting of the first person does not occur again. R omits
mei here.

7. *A well of water following them.* Cf. 1 Cor. 10[4] and
XI. 15 of our text, which agrees very closely with the wording of the Targum of Onkelos on Numbers. See Thackeray,
St. Paul and Contemporary Jewish Thought, p. 206, etc., on
the genesis of the legend. He shows that it arises from a
current interpretation of Num. 21[16] *seq.* The Bible has:
(16) And from thence (they journeyed) to Beer. . . . (18) And

brought he forth for them. And in a pillar of
cloud he led them by day and in a pillar of fire by
night did he give light unto them.

XI. *And in the 3rd month of the journeying of
the children of Israel out of the land of Egypt,
they came into the wilderness of Sinai*. And God
remembered his word and said: I will give light
unto the world, and lighten the habitable places,
and make my covenant with the children of men,
and glorify my people above all nations, for unto
them will I put forth an eternal exaltation which
shall be unto them a light, but unto the ungodly a
chastisement. 2. And he said unto Moses: Behold,
I will call thee to-morrow: be thou ready and tell
my people: "For three days let not a man come
near his wife," and on the 3rd day I will speak unto
thee and unto them, and after that thou shalt come
up unto me. And I will put my words in thy
mouth and thou shalt enlighten my people. For
I have given into thy hands an everlasting law
whereby I will judge all the world. For this shall
be for a testimony. For if men say: "We have
not known thee, and therefore we have not served

from the wilderness (they journeyed) to Mattanah, (19) And
from Mattanah to Nahaliel, and from Nahaliel to Bamoth.
The Targum of Onkelos has: (16) "And thence was given
them the well (Beer = well) . . . (18) It was given to them
from (in) the wilderness (Mattanah = gift). (19) And from
(the time) that it was given them, it descended with them to
the rivers, and from the rivers it went up with them to the
height (Nahaliel = rivers of God, Bamoth = height)." This
Targum represents first-century teaching: the later Targum
of Palestine amplifies the theme to some extent. See also
Driver in *Expositor*, 1889, I. 15.

XI. 1. *For upon them will I put forth an eternal exaltation*: in quem eliciam excelsa sempiterna, or *in whom I have
ordained high things eternal. In quo disposui excelsa sempiterna.* In either case the Law is meant.

2. *If men say, "we have not known thee,"* etc. Compare

thee," therefore will I take vengeance upon them, because they have not known my law.

3. And Moses did as God commanded him, and sanctified the people and said unto them : *Be ye ready on the 3rd day*, for after 3 days will God make his covenant with you. And the people were sanctified. 4. *And it came to pass on the 3rd day that, lo, there were voices of thunderings (lit. them that sounded) and brightness of lightnings and the voice of instruments sounding aloud. And there was fear upon all the people that were in the camp. And Moses put forth the people to meet God.* 5. And behold the mountains burned with fire and the earth shook and the hills were removed and the mountains overthrown : the depths boiled, and all the habitable places were shaken : and the heavens were folded up and the clouds drew up water. And flames of fire shone forth and thunderings and lightnings were multiplied and winds and tempests made a roaring : the stars were gathered together and the angels ran before, until God established the law of an everlasting covenant with the children of Israel, and gave unto them an eternal commandment which should not pass away.

6. *And at that time the Lord spake unto his people all these words, saying: I am the Lord thy God which brought thee out of the land of Egypt, out of the house of bondage. Thou shalt not make to thyself graven gods, neither* shalt thou make any abominable *image* of the sun or the moon or any of the ornaments of the heaven, nor the *likeness of all things that are upon the earth* nor of such as creep in the

Ex. 19[14]

19[16]

20[1]

20[4]

the injunction to the Apostles in a fragment of the *Preaching of Peter:* "After twelve years go forth into the world, lest any say, ' we did not hear.' "

5. Similar lists of the wonders which accompanied the giving of the Law are in XV. 6, XXIII. 10, XXXII. 7, 8.

waters or upon the earth. *I am the Lord thy God, a jealous God, requiting the sins* of them that sleep upon the living children of the ungodly, if they walk in the ways of their fathers, *unto the third and fourth generation, doing* (or *shewing*) *mercy unto* 1000 *generations to them that love me and keep my commandments.*

Ex. 20⁷

7. *Thou shalt not take the name of the Lord thy God in vain,* that my ways be not made vain. *For God* abominateth *him that taketh his name in vain.*

20⁸

8. *Keep the sabbath day to sanctify it. Six days do thy work, but the seventh day is the sabbath of the Lord. In it thou shalt do no work, thou and all* thy

Ps. 107³² labourers, saving that therein ye *praise the Lord in the congregation of the elders and glorify* the Mighty One *in the seat of the aged. For in six days the Lord made heaven and earth, the sea and all that are in them,* and all the world, the wilderness that is not inhabited, and all things that do labour, ·and all the order of the heaven, *and God rested*

Gen. 2³ *the seventh day. Therefore God sanctified the seventh day,* because he rested therein.

Ex. 20¹² 9. *Thou shalt love thy father and thy mother* and fear them : and then shall thy light rise, and I will command the heaven and it shall pay thee the rain thereof, and the earth shall hasten her fruit, and thy days shall be many, and thou shalt dwell in thy land, and shalt not be childless, for thy seed shall not fail, even that of them that dwell therein.

8. The gloss on the 4th Commandment, as Dr. Cohn says, shows that the writer has little interest in the Temple services, and is appropriate to a time when those services had ceased. It is rather the Synagogue and its ritual that occur to him as the obvious form of worship. The words are adapted from Ps. cvii. 32.

all things that do labour: quaecunque operantur.

10. *Thou shalt not commit adultery,* for thine Ex. 20¹⁴ enemies did not commit adultery with thee, but thou camest out with a high hand.

11. *Thou shalt not kill:* because thine enemies 20¹³ got not the mastery over thee to slay thee, but thou beheldest their death.

12. *Thou shalt not bear false witness against* 20¹⁶ *thy neighbour,* speaking falsely, lest thy watchmen speak falsely against thee.

13. *Thou shalt not covet thy neighbour's house, nor* 20¹⁷ *that which he hath,* lest others also covet thy land.

14. And when the Lord ceased speaking, the 20¹⁸ people feared with a great fear : and they saw the mountain burning with torches of fire, and they said to Moses : *Speak thou unto us, and let not God speak unto us, lest peradventure we die.* For, lo, to-day we know that God speaketh with man face to face, and man shall live. And now have we perceived of a truth how that the earth bare the voice of God with trembling. And Moses said unto them : Fear not, for for this cause came this voice unto you, that ye should not sin (*or,* for this cause, that he might prove you, God came unto you, that ye might receive the fear of him unto you, that ye sin not). 15. *And all the people* 20²¹ *stood afar off, but Moses drew near unto the cloud,* knowing that God was there. And then God spake unto him his justice and judgements, and kept him by him 40 days and 40 nights. And there did he command him many things, and showed him the tree of life, whereof he cut and

12. *thy watchmen : custodes.* I interpret this of angels.

15. The statement that the tree of life sweetened the waters of Marah, and that these were the waters that followed Israel, are both peculiar to this book. For Marah the MSS. seen by me read *myrrha,* but the Fulda MS. has *myrra;* it is Μεββα in the LXX.

took and put it into Mara, and the water of Mara was made sweet and followed them in the desert 40 years, and went up into the hills with them and came down into the plain. Also he commanded him concerning the tabernacle and the ark of the Lord, and the sacrifice of burnt offerings and of incense, and the ordinance of the table and of the candlestick and concerning the laver and the base thereof, and the shoulder-piece and the breastplate, and the very precious stones, that the children of Israel should make them so: and he shewed him the likeness of them to make them according to the pattern which he saw. And said unto him: Make for me a sanctuary and the tabernacle of my glory shall be among you.

XII. And Moses came down: and whereas he was covered with invisible light—for he had gone down into the place where is the light of the sun and moon,—the light of his face overcame the brightness of the sun and moon, and he knew it

Ex. 34²⁹,
etc.

not. And it was so, when he came down to the children of Israel, they saw him and knew him not. But when he spake, then they knew him. And this was like that which was done in Egypt

Gen. 42⁸

when *Joseph knew his brethren but they knew not him.* And it came to pass after that, when Moses knew that his face was become glorious, he made him a veil to cover his face.

Ex. 32

2. But while he was in the mount, the heart of the people was corrupted, and *they came together to Aaron saying: Make us gods* that we may serve them, as the other nations also have. *For this Moses* by whom the wonders were done before us,

XII. 1. *descended into the place where is the light of the sun and moon.* Compare with this the Revelation vouchsafed to Moses which is related in *Jerahmeel*, c. 52, as reported by R. Joshua ben Levi.

is taken from us. And Aaron said unto them :
Have patience, for Moses will come and bring
judgement near to us, and light up a law for us,
and set forth from his mouth the great excellency
of God, and appoint judgements unto our people.
3. And when he said this, they hearkened not unto
him, that the word might be fulfilled which was
spoken in the day when the people sinned in
building the tower, when God said : And now if
I forbid them not, *they will adventure all that they* Gen. 11⁶
take in mind to do, and worse.   But Aaron feared,
because the people was greatly strengthened, and
said to them : Bring us the earrings of your wives. Ex. 32²
And the men sought every one his wife, and they
gave them straightway, and they put them in the
fire and they were made into a figure, and there
came out a molten calf.

4. And the Lord said to Moses: Make haste 32⁷
hence, for the people is corrupted and hath dealt
deceitfully with my ways which I commanded
them.   What and if the promises are at an end
which I made to their fathers when I said : To your
seed will I give this land wherein ye dwell?   For
behold the people is not yet entered into the land,
even though they bear *my* judgements, *yet* have they
forsaken me.   And therefore I know that if they
enter the land they will do yet greater iniquities.
Now therefore I also will forsake them : and I will
turn again and make peace with them, that a house
may be built for me among them ; and that house
also shall be done away, because they will sin
against me, and the race of men shall be unto me
as a drop of a pitcher, and shall be counted as Isa. 40¹⁵,
spittle.   5. And Moses hasted and came down and etc.

4. *even though they bear my judgements: etiam portans
iudicium ;* i. e. even though they carry with them the law I
have given.

saw the calf, and he looked upon the tables and saw that they were not written: and he hasted and brake them; and his hands were opened and he became like a woman travailing of her firstborn, which when she is taken in her pangs her hands are upon her bosom, and she shall have no strength to help her to bring forth. 6. And it came to pass after an hour he said within *himself*: Bitterness prevaileth not for ever, neither hath evil the dominion alway. Now therefore will I arise, and strengthen my loins: for albeit they have sinned, *yet* shall not these things be in vain that were
Ex. 32[20] declared unto me above. 7. And he arose and brake the calf and cast it into the water, and made the people drink. And it was so, if any man's will in his mind were that the calf should be made, his tongue was cut off, but if any had been constrained thereto by fear, his face shone.

8. And then Moses went up into the mount and prayed the Lord, saying: Behold now, thou art God which hast planted this vineyard and set the roots thereof in the deep, and stretched out the shoots of it unto thy most high seat. Look upon it at this time, for the vineyard hath put forth her fruit and hath not known him that tilled her. And now if thou be wroth with thy vineyard and root it up out of the deep, and wither up the shoots from thy most high eternal seat, the deep will come no more to nourish it, neither thy throne to refresh that

5. *the writing vanishes from the tables.* Cf. XIX. 7. The *Pirke R. Eliezer*, c. 45 (tr. Friedlander), says, "the writing fled from off the tables," and Cohn quotes the same story from other Midrashim.

7. The common story is that the beards of those who had sinned appeared gilt (*Historia Scholastica*). This detail was occasionally embodied in mediæval pictures of the scene.

9. The house, which is described in terms somewhat resembling *Enoch* (see Introd., p. 44), is Paradise.

thy vineyard which thou hast burned. 9. For thou art he that art all light, and hast adorned thy house with precious stones and gold and perfumes and spices (*or* and jasper), and wood of balsam and cinnamon, and with roots of myrrh and costum hast thou strewed thine house, and with divers meats and sweetness of many drinks hast thou satisfied it. If therefore thou have not pity upon thy vineyard, all these things are done in vain, Lord, and thou wilt have none to glorify thee. For even if thou plant another vineyard, neither will that one trust in thee, because thou didst destroy the former. For if verily thou forsake the world, who will do for thee that that thou hast spoken as God? And now let thy wrath be restrained from thy vineyard the more ⟨because of⟩ that thou hast said and that which remaineth to be spoken, and let not thy labour be in vain, neither let thine heritage be torn asunder in humiliation. 10. And God said to him: Behold I am become merciful according to thy words. Hew thee out therefore two tables of stone from the place whence thou hewedst the former, and write upon them again my judgements which were on the first.

XIII. And Moses hasted and did all that God commanded him, and came down and made the tables ⟨and the tabernacle⟩, and the vessels thereof, and the ark and the lamps and the table and the altar of burnt offerings and the altar of incense and the shoulderpiece and the breastplate and the precious stones and the laver and the bases and all things that were shewn him. And he ordered all the vestures of the priests, the girdles and the *rest*, the mitre, the golden plate and the holy crown: he made also the anointing oil for the

Ex. 34

9. *costum*, for which there is no English equivalent, occurs in *Jub.* 16^{24}, and fairly often in Latin literature.

H

priests, and the priests themselves he sanctified. And when all things were finished the cloud covered all of them. 2. Then Moses cried unto the Lord, and God spake to him from the tabernacle saying : This is the law of the altar, whereby ye shall sacrifice unto me and pray for your souls. But as concerning that which ye shall offer me, offer ye of cattle the calf, the sheep and the she goat : but of fowls the turtle and the dove. 3. And

Lev. 14 if there be leprosy in your land, and it so be that the leper is cleansed, let them take for the Lord two live young birds, and wood of cedar and hyssop and scarlet ; and he shall come to the priest, and he shall kill one, and keep the other. And he shall order the leper according to all that I have commanded in my law. 4. And it shall be when the times come round to you, ye shall sanctify me with a feast-day and rejoice before me at the feast

23 of the unleavened bread, and set bread before me, keeping a feast of remembrance because on that day ye came forth of the land of Egypt. 5. And

XIII. 1, 2. *altar: thuribulum* (*lit.* censer).

2–7. This short section contains practically all that is said of the ceremonial law. It is remarkably "scrappy" and unsystematic.

4–7. This passage is well illustrated by one in the Talmud. *Tract. Rosh ha-Shana* (tr. Schwab, p. 63) : A 4 époques différentes de l'année, le monde est jugé par Dieu : à Pâques pour la récolte ; à Pentecôte pour les produits des arbres ; à la fête du nouvel-an tous les êtres de la terre passent devant l'Éternel comme les troupeaux devant le berger, puisqu'il est dit (Ps. xxxiii. 15) : *Celui qui a créé tous les cœurs, qui connaît toutes leurs actions* (il sait et scrute tout). Enfin, aux Tabernacles, la question des eaux sera résolue.

This corresponds fairly well with our text. The same four feasts are spoken of in connexion with the Passover. The harvest is not mentioned ; it is only said *constituetis in conspectu meo panem*. At Pentecost (the Feast of Weeks) we have *facietis mihi oblationem pro fructibus vestris*. At the Feast of Trumpets (the New Year feast) the words are no in the feast of weeks ye shall set bread before me and make me an offering for your fruits. 6. But the feast of trumpets shall be for an offering for your watchers, because therein I oversaw *my* creation, that ye may be mindful of the whole world. In the beginning of the year, when ye show them me, I will acknowledge the number of the dead and of them that are born, and the fast of mercy. For ye shall fast unto me for your souls, that the promises of your fathers may be fulfilled. 7. Also the feast of tabernacles bring ye to me: ye shall take for me the pleasant fruit of the tree, and boughs of palm-tree and willows and cedars, and branches of myrrh: and I will remember the whole earth in rain, and the measure of the seasons shall be established, and I will order the stars and command the clouds, and the winds shall sound and

doubt obscure, but they contain mention of a review of the whole creation. "But the Feast of Trumpets shall be for an offering to (or for) your watchers (*prospeculatoribus vestris:* or *pro spec.* I suppose angelic guardians to be meant), inasmuch as I reviewed (*praespexi, perspexi*) the whole creation, that ye may be mindful of the whole world" (the connexion of this clause is obscure): "and at the beginning of the year I will acknowledge, when ye show them, the number of your dead, and of them that are born, and the fast of mercy. For ye shall fast unto me for your souls," etc. This represents the sense of the text as I understand it. Lastly, of the Feast of Tabernacles it is said: "I will remember the whole earth in rain." The comment on this passage of the Talmud makes it clear that this is the meaning of the "question des eaux": prayer for rain was offered at the Feast of Tabernacles (cf. *Taanith* I.).

7. *fin.*, 8. "*As I spake after the flood of the earth, at what time I gave commandment concerning the year of the life of Noah, and said unto him: These are the years which I ordained after that I visited the city of men* (*i.e.* at the flood) *at the time when I showed them* (? him) *the place of generation and the colour, and said: This is the place whereof I taught the first-formed man,*" etc. This is the text of VR,

the lightnings run abroad, and there shall be a storm of thunder, and this shall be for a perpetual sign. Also the nights shall yield dew, as I spake after the flood of the earth 8. when I (*or* Then he) gave him precept as concerning the year of the life of Noe, and said to him : These are the years which I ordained after the weeks wherein I visited the city of men, at what time I shewed them (*or* him) the place of birth and the colour (*or* and the serpent), and I (*or* he) said : This is the place of which I taught the first man saying : If thou transgress not that I bade thee, all things shall be subject unto thee. But he transgressed my ways and was persuaded of his wife, and she was deceived by the serpent. And then was death ordained unto the generations of men. 9. And furthermore the Lord shewed (*or*, And the Lord said further : I shewed) him the ways of paradise and said unto him : These are the ways which men have lost by not walking in them, because they have sinned against me.

10. And the Lord commanded him concerning the salvation of the souls of the people and said : If they shall walk in my ways I will not forsake them, but will alway be merciful unto them, and will bless their seed, and the earth shall haste to yield her fruit, and there shall be rain for them to

and on the whole it seems the best, but it is not at all clear. As is remarked in the Introduction, there may be a reference to a passage in *Jubilees*. It seems to be implied that God showed Paradise to Noah. The words, "*and the colour : et colorem*" are particularly puzzling. Ought we to read *et colubrum* "and the serpent"? Two lines below we have *de colubro*. Or is there a reference to what we find in the Revelation of Moses in *Jerahmeel* 92[10]? God showed him the heavenly temple, and the four different hues in which the tabernacle was made, by means of angels clothed in blue, white, scarlet, and purple.

9. Here God seems certainly to show Paradise to Moses.

increase their gains, and the earth shall not be barren. Yet verily I know that they will corrupt their ways, and I shall forsake them, and they will forget the covenants which I made with their fathers. Yet will I not forget them for ever : for in the last days they shall know that because of their sins their seed was forsaken ; for I am faithful in my ways.

XIV. *At that time God said unto him : Begin to* Num. 1² *number my people from* 20 *years and upwards* unto 40 years, that I may show your tribes all that I declared unto their fathers in a strange land. For by the 50th part *of them* did I raise them up out of the land of Egypt, but 40 and 9 parts of them died in the land of Egypt. 2. When thou hast ordered them and numbered them (*or*, while ye abode there. And when thou hast numbered them, etc.), write the tale of them, till I fulfil all that I spake unto their fathers, and set them firmly in their own land : for I will not diminish any word of those I have spoken unto their fathers, even of those which I said to them : Your seed shall be as the stars of heaven for multitude. By number shall they enter into the land, and in a short time shall they become without number. 3. Then Moses went down and numbered them, and the number of the people was 604,550. *But the* 1¹⁶ *tribe of Levi numbered he not among them, for so was it commanded him;* only he numbered them that were upwards of 50 years, of whom the number was 47,300. Also he numbered them that were below 20 years, and the number of them was 850,850. And he looked over the tribe of Levi and the whole number of them was CXX. CCXD. DCXX. CC. DCCC.

XIV. 3. The number at the end of this verse is hopelessly corrupt.

4. And Moses declared the number of them to God ; and God said to him : These are the words which I spake to their fathers in the land of Egypt, and appointed a number, even 210 years, unto all that saw my wonders. Now the number of them all was 9000 times 10,000, 200 times 95,000 men, besides women, and I put to death the whole multitude of them because they believed me not, and the 50th part of them[1] was left and I sanctified them unto me. Therefore do I command the generation of my people to give me tithes of their fruits, to be before me for a memorial of how great oppression I have removed from them. 5. And when Moses came down and declared these things to the people, they mourned and lamented and abode in the desert two years.

Num. 13   XV. And Moses sent spies to spy out the land, even 12 men, for so was it commanded him. And when they had gone up and seen the land, they returned to him bringing of the fruits of the land, and troubled the heart of the people, saying : Ye will not be able to inherit the land, for it is shut up with iron bars by their mighty men. 2. But two men out of the 12 spake not so, but said : Like as hard iron can overcome the stars, or as weapons can conquer the lightnings, or the fowls of the air put out the thunder, so can these men resist the Lord. For they saw how that as they went up the lightnings of the stars shone and the thunders followed, sounding with them. 3. And these are the names of the men : Chaleb the son of

4. The number 2,180,000 seems as if it ought to bear a relation to the 210 years spent in Egypt : *qu.* 2,100,000?

XV. 3. The names in the pedigrees of Caleb and Joshua are not easily reconciled with those in 1 Chron. 2, 7[23 *sqq.*].

---

[1] *i.e.* 2,180,000.

Jephone, the son of Beri, the son of Batuel, the
son of Galipha, the son of Zenen, the son of
Selimun, the son of Selon, the son of Juda. The
other, Jesus the son of Naue, the son of Eliphat,
the son of Gal, the son of Nephelien, the son of
Emon, the son of Saul, the son of Dabra, the son
of Effrem, the son of Joseph. 4. But the people
would not hear the voice of the twain, but were
greatly troubled, and spake saying: Be these the
words which God spake to us saying: I will bring
you into a land flowing with milk and honey?
And how now doth he bring us up that we may
fall on the sword, and our women shall go into
captivity? 5. And when they said thus, the glory
of God appeared suddenly, and he said to Moses:
Doth this people thus persevere to hearken unto
me not at all? Lo now the counsel which hath
gone forth from me shall not be in vain. I will
send the angel of mine anger upon them to break
up their bodies with fire in the wilderness. And I
will give commandment to mine angels which
watch over them that they pray not for them, for I
will shut up their souls in the treasuries of darkness, and I will say to my servants their fathers:
Behold, this is the seed unto which I spake saying:
Your seed shall come into a land that is not theirs, Gen.
and the nation whom they shall serve I will judge. 15$^{13, 14}$
And I fulfilled my words and made their enemies
to melt away, and subjected angels under their
feet, and put a cloud for a covering of their heads,
and commanded the sea, and the depths were
broken before their face and walls of water stood
up. 6. And there hath not been the like of this
word since the day when I said: Let the waters
under the heaven be gathered into one place, unto
this day. And I brought them out, and slew their
enemies and led them before me unto the Mount

Sina. And I bowed the heavens and came down to kindle a lamp for my people, and to set bounds to all creatures. And I taught them to make me a sanctuary that I might dwell among them. But they have forsaken me and become faithless in my words, and their mind hath fainted, and now behold the days shall come when I will do unto them as they have desired and I will cast forth their bodies in the wilderness. 7. And Moses said: Before thou didst take seed wherewith to make man upon the earth, did I order his ways? therefore now let thy mercy suffer us unto the end, and thy pity for the length of days.

Num. 16

XVI. At that time did he give him commandment concerning the fringes: and then did Choreb rebel and 200 men with him and spake saying: What if a law which we cannot bear is ordained for us? 2. And God was wroth and said: I commanded the earth and it gave me man, and unto him were born at the first two sons. And the elder arose and slew the younger, and the earth hasted and swallowed his blood. But I drove forth Cain, and cursed the earth and spake unto Sion saying: Thou shalt not any more swallow up blood. And

---

XVI. 1. In Num. 15³⁷ the ordinance of fringes immediately precedes the story of Korah; and the two are brought into connexion by the Targum on Numbers and by others: *Jerahmeel* 55 connects them in this fashion: "and when God commanded Moses to tell the children of Israel to make themselves fringes, Korah arose in the night, and, weaving 400 garments of blue, put them on 400 men. Then, standing before Moses, he said to him: "Do these garments require fringes, as they are now made wholly of this blue?" Moses replied: "Korah, does a house full of holy books require a Mezuzah?" "Yes," said Korah. "So also do these garments require fringes." This encounter of Korah with Moses is the last of several which are told at some length in *Jerahmeel*.

now are the thoughts of men greatly polluted.
3. Lo, I will command the earth, and it shall
swallow up body and soul together, and their dwelling shall be in darkness and in destruction, and
they shall not die but shall pine away until I
remember the world and renew the earth.   And
then shall they die and not live, and their life shall
be taken away out of the number of all men:
neither shall Hell vomit them forth again, and
destruction shall not remember them, and their
departure shall be as that of the tribe of the nations
of whom I said, " I will not remember them," that
is, the camp of the Egyptians, and the people
whom I destroyed with the water of the flood.
And the earth shall swallow them, and I will not
do any more *unto them.*

4. And when Moses spake all these words unto
the people, Choreb, and his men were yet unbeliev-
ing.   And Choreb sent to call his seven sons
which were not of counsel with him.   5. But they
sent to him in answer saying: As the painter
showeth not forth an image made by his art unless
he be first instructed, so we also when we received
the law of the Most Mighty which teacheth us his
ways, did not enter therein save that we might
walk therein.   Our father begat us [not], but the
Most Mighty formed us, and now if we walk in his
ways we shall be his children.   But if thou believe
not, go thine own way.   And they came not up
unto him.

6. And it came to pass after this that the earth

---

3. It appears that Korah and his company are to be annihilated at the final judgement.   *The people of whom I said:
I will not remember them.*   Compare *Pirke R. Eliezer* 33.
" All the dead will rise at the resurrection of the dead, except
the generation of the Flood."   Christianity (1 Peter 3) did
not recognize this exception.

opened before them, and his sons sent unto him saying: If thy madness be still upon thee, who shall help thee in the day of thy destruction? and he hearkened not unto them. And the earth opened her mouth and swallowed them up, and their houses, and four times was the foundation of the earth moved to swallow up the men, as it was commanded her. And thereafter Choreb and his company groaned, until the firmament of the earth should be delivered back. 7. But the assemblies of the people said unto Moses: We cannot abide round about[1] this place where Choreb and his men have been swallowed up. And he said to them: Take up your tents from round about them, neither be ye joined to their sins. And they did so.

Num. 17 XVII. Then was the lineage of the priests of God declared by the choosing of a tribe, and it was said unto Moses: *Take throughout every tribe one rod and put them in the tabernacle, and then shall the rod of him* to whomsoever my glory shall speak, *flourish, and I will take away the murmuring from my people.* 2. And Moses did so and set 12 rods, and the rod of Aaron came out, and put forth *blossom and yielded seed of almonds.* 3. And this likeness which was born there was like unto the work which Israel wrought while he was in Meso-. potamia with Laban the Syrian, when he took rods of almond, and put them at the gathering of waters, and the cattle came to drink and were divided among the peeled rods, and brought forth [kids] white and speckled and parti-coloured. 4. There-

6. *until the firmament* (AP) or *foundation* (VR) *of the earth should be restored: quousque redderetur firmamentum terrae.* Probably to be understood in the same sense as the words of 3: *ero innouans terram.*

---

[1] The MSS. have: in Sina of this place.

fore was the synagogue of the people made like
unto a flock of sheep, and as the cattle brought
forth according to the almond rods, so was the
priesthood established by means of the almond
rods.

XVIII. At that time Moses slew Seon and Og, the kings of the Amorites, and divided all their land unto his people, and they dwelt therein. 2. But Balac was the king of Moab, that lived over against them, and he was greatly afraid, and sent to Balaam the son of Beor the interpreter of dreams, which dwelt in Mesopotamia, and charged him saying : Behold I know how that in the reign of my father Sefor, when the Amorites fought against him, thou didst curse them and they were delivered up before him. And *now come and curse this people, for they are many, more than we, and I will do thee great honour.* 3. And Balaam said : Lo, this is good in the sight of Balac, but he knoweth not that the counsel of God is not as man's counsel. And he knoweth not that the spirit which is given unto us is given for a time, and our ways are not guided except God will. *Now therefore abide ye here, and I will see what the Lord will say to me this night.* 4. And in the night *God said unto him : Who are the men that are come unto thee?* And Balaam said : Wherefore, Lord, dost thou tempt the race of man ? They therefore cannot sustain it, for thou knewest more than they, all that was in the world, before thou foundedst it. And now enlighten thy servant if it be right that I go with them. 5. And God said to him : Was it not concerning this people that I spake unto Abraham in a vision saying : *Thy seed shall be as the stars of heaven,* when I raised him up above the firmament and showed him all the orderings of the stars, and required of him his son for a burnt offering ? and

Num. 21

22

22⁶

22¹⁷

22⁸, ⁹

Gen. 22¹⁷

he brought him to be laid upon the altar, but I restored him to his father. And because he resisted not, his offering was acceptable in my sight, and for the blood of him did I choose this people. And then I said unto the angels that work subtilly :

Gen. 18¹⁵ Said I not of him : *To Abraham will I reveal all that I do?*

6. Jacob also, when he wrestled in the dust with the angel that was over the praises, did not let him go until he blessed him. And now, behold, thou thinkest to go with these, and curse them whom I have chosen. But if thou curse them, who is he

Num. 22¹³ *sqq.* that shall bless thee? 7. *And Balaam arose in the morning and said: Go your way, for God will not have me to come with you. And they went and told Balac* all that was said of Balaam. And *Balac sent yet again other men to Balaam* saying : Behold, I know that when thou offerest burnt offerings to God, God will be reconciled with man, and now ask yet again of thy Lord, and entreat by burnt offerings, as many as he will. For if peradventure he will be propitiated in my necessity, thou shalt have thy reward, if so be God accept thy offerings. 8. And Balaam said to them : Lo, the son of Sephor is foolish, and knoweth not that he

22¹⁹ dwelleth hard by (*lit.* round about) the dead : *And*

XVIII. 5. *And then I said unto the angels that work subtilly.* The clause has dropped out of AP, but must be genuine. *Angelis minute operantibus* is a curious expression. *Minute* should be λεπτῶσ. Is the reference to evil angels (as in XXXIV.), or to angels set over small things, or to the angels who envied Abraham, as in XXXII. 1, 2?

Probably we ought to follow R in the next words also, and read : "Unto Abraham will I reveal all that I do, and unto Jacob his son's son whom he (I) called (my) first born. Who when he wrestled," etc.

8. *nescit quoniam inhabitat in gyro mortuorum.* Are the "mortui" anything more than Balak's idols?

now tarry here this night and I will see what God will say unto me. And God said to him : Go with them, and thy journey shall be an offence, and Balac himself shall go unto destruction. And he arose and went with them. 9. And his she-ass came by the way of the desert and saw the angel, and he opened the eyes of Balaam and he saw the angel and worshipped him on the earth. And the angel said to him : Haste and go on, for what thou sayest shall come to pass with him.

10. And he came unto the land of Moab and built an altar and offered sacrifices : and when he had seen a part of the people, the spirit of God abode not in him, and he took up his parable and said : Lo, Balac hath brought me hither unto the mount, saying : Come, run into the fire of these men. ⟨Lo⟩ I cannot abide that ⟨fire⟩ which waters quench, but that fire which consumeth water who shall endure? And he said to him : It is easier to take away the foundations and all the topmost part of them, and to quench the light of the sun and darken the shining of the moon, than for him who will to root up the planting of the Most Mighty or spoil his vineyard. And *Balac* himself hath not known it, because his mind is puffed up, to the intent his destruction may come swiftly. 11. For behold, I see the heritage which the Most Mighty showed me in the night, and lo the days come when Moab shall be amazed at that which befalleth her, for Balac desired to persuade the Most Mighty with gifts and to purchase decision with money. Oughtest thou not to have asked what he sent upon Pharao and upon his land because he would bring them into bondage? Behold an overshadowing vine, desirable exceedingly, and who shall be

Num. 23, 24

11. *decision : dogma.*

jealous against it, for it withereth not? But if any say in his counsel that the Most Mighty hath laboured in vain or chosen them to no purpose, lo now I see the salvation of deliverance which is to come unto them. I am restrained in the speech of my voice and I cannot express that which I see with mine eyes, for but a little is left to me of the holy spirit which abideth in me, since I know that in that I was persuaded of Balac I have lost the days of my life: 12. Lo, again I see the heritage of the abode of this people, and the light of it shineth above the brightness of lightning, and the running of it is swifter than arrows. And the time shall come when Moab shall groan, and they that serve Cham (Chemosh?) shall be weak, even such as took this counsel against them. But I shall gnash my teeth because I was deceived and did transgress that which was said to me in the night. Yet my prophecy shall remain manifest, and my words shall live, and the wise and prudent shall re-member my words, for when I cursed I perished, and though I blessed I was not blessed. And when he had so said he held his peace. And Num. 24[11] Balac said: Thy God hath defrauded thee of many gifts from me.

31[16] 13. Then Balaam said unto him: Come and let us advise what thou shalt do to them. Choose out the most comely women that are among you and that are in Midian and set them before them naked, and adorned with gold and jewels, and it shall be when they shall see them and lie with them, they will sin against their Lord and fall into your hands,

12. *the heritage of the abode of this people: haereditatem dissolutionis.* I take *dissolutionis* to be a wrong rendering of κατάλυσισ, which means "abode" in Jer. 49[19] (LXX).

13. *Pirke R. Eliezer* 47: Balaam said: "You will not be able to prevail against this people, unless they have

for otherwise thou canst not subdue them. 14. And
so saying Balaam turned away and returned to
his place. And thereafter the people were led
astray after the daughters of Moab, for Balac did
all that Balaam had showed him.

XIX. At that time Moses slew the nations, and
gave half of the spoils to the people, and he began
to declare to them the words of the law which God
spake to them in Oreb. 2. And he spake to them,
saying : Lo, I sleep with my fathers, and shall go   Dt. 31²⁷
unto my people. But I know that ye will arise   etc.
and forsake the words that were ordained unto you
by me, and God will be wroth with you and forsake
you and depart out of your land, and bring against
you them that hate you, and they shall have dominion over you, but not unto the end, for he will
remember the covenant which he made with your
fathers. 3. But then both ye and your sons and   Asc. Mos.
all your generations after you will arise and seek   11⁹ *sqq.*
the day of my death and will say in their heart :
Who will give us a shepherd like unto Moses, or
such another judge to the children of Israel, to pray
for our sins at all times, and to be heard for our   Dt. 4²⁶,
iniquities ? 4. Howbeit, *this day I call heaven and*   etc.
earth to witness against you, for the heaven shall
hear this and the earth shall take it in with her
ears, that God hath revealed the end of the world,

sinned before their Creator." *peccabunt domino suo* . . .
aliter expugnare eos non poteris.

   XIX. 3. *to pray for our sins at all times.* cf. *Assumption
of Moses*, 11¹¹, ¹⁷ ; 12³.

   4. DCCXL. years of the MSS. should, as Dr. Cohn
suggests, be changed to DCCCL. From the death of Moses
to the building of the first temple 440 years are reckoned,
and from thence to its destruction 410. The *Seder Olam
Rabbah* XI. reckons seventeen Jubilees (850 years) from the
entrance into the Holy Land to the Captivity (Cohn, p. 327,
note).

that he might covenant with you upon his high
places, and hath kindled an everlasting lamp among
you. Remember, ye wicked, how that when I
spake unto you, ye answered saying : All that
God hath said unto us we will hear and do. But
if we transgress or corrupt our ways, he shall call
a witness against us and cut us off. 5. But know
ye that ye did eat the bread of angels 40 years.
And now behold I do bless your tribes, before my
end come. But ye, know ye my labour wherein I
have laboured with you since the day ye came up
out of the land of Egypt.

6. And when he had so said, God spake unto
him the third time, saying : Behold, thou goest to
sleep with thy fathers, and this people will arise
and seek me, and will forget my law wherewith I
have enlightened them, and I shall forsake their
seed for a season. 7. But unto thee will I show
the land before thou die, but thou shall not enter
therein in this age, lest thou see the graven images
whereby this people will be deceived and led out of
the way. I will show thee the place wherein they
shall serve me 740 (*l.* 850) years. And thereafter it
shall be delivered into the hand of their enemies,
and they shall destroy it, and strangers shall
compass it about, and it shall be in that day as it
was in the day when I brake the tables of the
covenant which I made with thee in Oreb : and
when they sinned, that which was written therein
vanished away. Now that day was the 17th day
of the 4th month.

8. And Moses went up into Mount Oreb, as God
had bidden him, and prayed, saying : Behold, I
have fulfilled the time of my life, even 120 years.
And now I pray thee let thy mercy be with thy
people and let thy compassion be continued upon
thine heritage, Lord, and thy long-suffering in thy

Dt. 32⁵², 34⁴

place upon the race of thy choosing, for thou hast
loved them more than all.   9. And thou knowest
that I was a shepherd of sheep, and when I fed the
flock in the desert, I brought them unto thy Mount
Oreb, and then first saw I thine angel in fire out of
the bush ; but thou calledst me out of the bush, and
I feared and turned away my face, and thou sentest
me unto them, and didst deliver them out of Egypt,
and their enemies thou didst sink in the water.
And thou gavest them a law and judgements where-
by they should live. *For what man is he that hath*   1 K. 8⁴⁶
not sinned against thee ?   How shall thine heritage   etc.
be established except thou have mercy on them ?
Or who shall yet be born without sin ?   Yet wilt
thou correct them for a season, but not in anger.

10. Then the Lord shewed him the land and
all that is therein and said : This is the land which   Dt. 34¹
I will give to my people.   And he shewed him the
place from whence the clouds draw up water to
water all the earth, and the place whence the river
receiveth his water, and the land of Egypt, and
the place of the firmament, from whence the holy
land only drinketh.   He shewed him also the
place from whence it rained manna for the people,
and even unto the paths of paradise.   And he
shewed him the measures of the sanctuary, and
the number of the offerings, and the sign whereby
men shall interpret (*lit.* begin to look upon) the
heaven, and said : These are the things which
were forbidden to the sons of men because they
sinned.   11. And now, thy rod wherewith the

10. *the place of the firmament from whence the holy land only
drinketh.* cf. Babylonian Talmud *Taanith* 1 (tr. Rodkinson,
p. 24). "The land of Israel is watered by the Lord himself,
while the rest of the world is watered by a messenger . . .
The land of Israel is watered by rain, while the rest of the
world is watered by the residue remaining in the clouds."

J

signs were wrought shall be for a witness between me and my people. And when they sin I shall be wroth with them and remember my rod, and spare them according to my mercy, and thy rod shall be in my sight for a remembrance all the days, and shall be like unto the bow wherein I made a covenant with Noe when he came out of the ark, saying: I will set my bow in the cloud, and it shall be a sign between me and men that the water of a flood be no more upon the earth. 12. But thee will I take hence and give thee sleep with thy fathers and give thee rest in thy slumber, and bury thee in peace, and all the angels shall lament for thee, and the hosts *of heaven* shall be sorrowful. But there shall not any, of angels or men, know thy sepulchre wherein thou art to be buried, but thou shalt rest therein until I visit the world, and raise thee up and thy fathers out of the earth [of Egypt] wherein ye shall sleep, and ye shall come together and dwell in an immortal habitation that is not subject unto time. 13. But this heaven shall be in my sight as a fleeting cloud, and like yesterday when it is past, and it shall be when I draw near to visit the world, I will command the years and charge the times, and they shall be shortened, and the stars shall be hastened, and the light of

---

11. The rod of Moses is to be transported to heaven and to become a sign like the rainbow. Perhaps the Milky Way is meant. No such tradition is cited in Mr. I. Abrahams' interesting paper on "The Rod of Moses," in *Papers read before the Jews' College Literary Society* (1887, p. 28), nor in Daehnhardt's *Natursagen*, nor in other sources which I have consulted.

12. *give thee sleep.* Dormificabo R., which must be preferred, I think, to *glorificabo* of AP.

the earth [*of Egypt*]. The word *Aegypti* is certainly intrusive, written mechanically after *excitabo te*, etc., *de terra*.

the sun make speed to set, neither shall the light
of the moon endure, because I will hasten to raise
up you that sleep, that in the place of sanctification which I shewed thee, all they that can
live may dwell therein.

14. And Moses said : If I may ask yet one
thing of thee, O Lord, according to the multitude
of thy mercy, be not wroth with me. And shew
me what measure of time hath passed by and what
remaineth. 15. And the Lord said to him : An
instant, the topmost part of a hand,[1] the fulness of
a moment, and the drop of a cup. And time hath
fulfilled all. For 4½ have passed by, and 2½ remain.

---

15. The corrupt words *istic mel apex magnus* I emend into
stigma et apex manus, cf. 4 Esdr. 4[48-50] ; 6[9, 10]. *The fulness
of a moment : momenti plenitudo.* Perhaps this renders
ῥοπῆσ πλήρωμα, that which fills the scale of the balance and
causes it to sink.

four and a half have passed and two and a half remain
(cf. 4 Esdr. 14[11]). The total, seven, agrees with that in the
Vision of Kenaz (XXVIII. 8), "men shall dwell in the world
VII. (*i.e.* 7000) years." The calculation in the present
passage ought to mean that 4500 years are past and 2500
remain : but no other authority seems to place the death of
Moses so late as A.M. 4500. The *Assumption of Moses*
puts it in 2500, the Hebrew in 2706, the LXX in 3859,
Jubilees in 2450.

There is a certain plausibility in the following view : 4½
stands for 45, and 2½ for 25 : the 45 and 25 consist of weeks
of years. Then 45 = 3150, and 25 = 1750 : total 4900, or
7 × 700, a good mystical number. Only it disagrees with
the 7000 of XXVIII. 8. With that passage in view, I think
we must take it that 4½ = 4500, and 2½ 2500, the unit being
100 years.

The *Assumption of Moses* (10[11]) says that from the death
of Moses "to the advent of Messiah there will be 250
times," which is superficially like 2½. The "times" here
are commonly taken to mean weeks of years, making 1750.
But if we could take each "time" to be ten years, then 250

---

[1] *Lit.* : Here *is* honey, a great summit.

16. And Moses when he heard was filled with understanding, and his likeness was changed gloriously : *and he died* in glory according *to the mouth of the Lord, and he buried him* as he had promised him, and the angels lamented at his death, and lightnings and torches and arrows went before him with one accord. And on that day the hymn of the hosts was not said because of the departure of Moses. Neither was there any day like unto it since the Lord made man upon earth, neither shall there be any such for ever, that he should make the hymn of the angels to cease because of a man ; for he loved him greatly ; and he buried him with his own hands on an high place of the earth, and in the light of the whole world.

times would be 2500 years or fifty jubilees, and we should *only* have to alter *bis millesimus et quingentesimus* (I^2) to *quater* (*IIII.*) *millesimus*, etc., to bring it into exact agreement with *Philo!* Perhaps this method of dealing with authorities may find more favour with others than it does with me.

I think it quite possible that the unexplained verse in *Apoc. Bar.* 28^2, "and the measure and reckoning of that time are two parts weeks (or two parts a week), of seven weeks" may contain the same calculation, the week being 1000 years, and "two parts a week" being corrupt for $2\frac{1}{2}$ weeks. But if so we should have to assume that the writer of *Apoc. Bar.* had not allowed for the difference in date between Moses and Baruch—some 850 years. I do not think that such an inadvertence is quite out of the question.

Another possibility is that our author, in making his calculation, has in mind not so much the date of Moses, as that at which he is himself writing.

Taking the texts as they stand, the calculation, and the whole account of the death of Moses, show that *Philo* quite disregards the *Assumption*, though he may very likely have read it. When I came across the passage as a separate extract in a MS. and published it, in 1893, I spent much space in trying to prove that it was actually part of the *Assumption*. The view neither was nor deserved to be accepted.

XX. And at that time God made his covenant
with Jesus the son of Naue which remained of the
men that spied out the land : for the lot had fallen
upon them that they should not see the land because they spake evil of it, and for this cause that
generation died. 2. Then said God unto Jesus
the son of Naue : Wherefore mournest thou, and
wherefore hopest thou in vain, thinking that Moses
shall yet live? Now therefore thou waitest to no
purpose, for Moses is dead. Take the garments
of his wisdom and put them on thee, and gird thy
loins with the girdle of his knowledge, and thou
shalt be changed and become another man. Did
I not speak for thee unto Moses my servant,
saying : " He shall lead my people after thee, and
into his hand will I deliver the kings of the
Amorites " ? 3. And Jesus took the garments of
wisdom and put them on, and girded his loins with
the girdle of understanding. And it came to pass
when he put it on, that his mind was kindled
and his spirit stirred up, and he said to the people :
Lo, the former generation died in the wilderness
because they spake against their God. And,
behold now, know, all ye captains, this day that
if ye go forth in the ways of your God, your paths
shall be made straight. 4. But if ye obey not his
voice, and are like your fathers, your works shall
be spoiled, and ye yourselves broken, and your
name shall perish out of the land, and then where
shall be the words which God spake unto your
fathers? For even if the heathen say : It may be
God hath failed, because he hath not delivered his
people, yet whereas they perceive that he hath
chosen to himself other peoples, working for them
great wonders, they shall understand that the
Most Mighty accepteth not persons. But because
ye sinned through vanity, therefore he took his

power from you and subdued you. And now arise and set your heart to walk in the ways of your Lord and he shall direct you.

5. And the people said unto him : Lo, this day see we that which Eldad and Modat prophesied in the days of Moses, saying : After that Moses resteth, the captainship of Moses shall be given unto Jesus the son of Naue. And Moses was not envious, but rejoiced when he heard them ; and thenceforth all the people believed that thou shouldest lead them, and divide the land unto them in peace : and now also if there be conflict, be strong and do valiantly, for thou only shalt be leader in Israel. 6. And when he heard that, Jesus thought to send spies into Jericho. And he called Cenez and Seenamias his brother, the two sons of Caleph, and spake to them, saying : I and your father were sent of Moses in the wilderness and went up with other ten men : and they returned and spake evil of the lands and melted the heart of the people, and they were scattered and the heart of the people with them. But I and your father only fulfilled the word of the Lord, and lo, we are alive this day. And now will I send you to spy out the land of Jericho. Do like unto your father and ye also shall live. 7. And they went up and spied out the city. And when they brought back word, the people went up and besieged the city and burned it with fire.

8. And after that Moses was dead, the manna ceased to come down for the children of Israel, and then began they to eat the fruits of the land. And these are the three things which God gave his people

Jos. 2

14⁶ *sqq.*

5¹²

XX. 5. The Targum, and a Midrash quoted by Cohn, p. 320, say that Eldad and Medad, according to some, prophesied that Moses should die and Joshua should lead Israel into the Promised Land.

for the sake of three persons, that is, the well of the
water of Mara for Maria's sake, and the pillar of
cloud for Aaron's sake, and the manna for the
sake of Moses.   And when these three came to an
end, those three gifts were taken away from them.

9. Now the people and Jesus fought against the
Amorites, and when the battle waxed strong
against their enemies throughout all the days of
Jesus, 30 and 9 kings which dwelt in the land were
cut off.   And Jesus gave the land by lot to the
people, to every tribe according to the lots, according as he had received commandment.   10. Then
came Caleph unto him and said: Thou knowest   Jos. 14⁶ ˢᵠᵠ·
how that we two were sent by lot by Moses to go
with the spies, and because we fulfilled the word
of the Lord, behold we are alive at this day: and
now if it be well-pleasing in thy sight, let there be
given unto my son Cenez for a portion the territory of the three (*or* the tribe of the) towers.   And
Jesus blessed him, and did so.

XXI. And when Jesus was become old and   23
well-stricken in years, God said to him: Behold,
thou waxest old and well-stricken in days, and the
land is become very great, and there is none to
divide it (*or* take it by lot), and it shall be after
thy departure this people will mingle with the
inhabitants of the land and go astray after other
gods, and I shall forsake them as I testified in my
word unto Moses; but do thou testify unto them
before thou diest.   2. And Jesus said: Thou
knowest more than all, O Lord, what moveth
the heart of the sea before it rageth, and thou hast
tracked out the constellations and numbered the

8. In the same way Cohn cites Midrashim (*Seder Olam
Rabbah*, etc.) which agree exactly with *Philo* as to the
withdrawal of the three heavenly gifts.   The Babylonian
Talmud (*Taanith* 1, Rodkinson, p. 22) has the same story.

stars, and ordered the rain. Thou knowest the mind of all generations before they be born. And now, Lord, give unto thy people an heart of wisdom and a mind of prudence, and it shall be when thou givest these ordinances unto thine heritage, they shall not sin before thee and thou shall not be wroth with them. 3. Are not these the words which I spake before thee, Lord, when Achar stole of the curse, and the people were delivered up before thee, and I prayed in thy sight and said : Were it not better for us, O Lord, if we had died in the Red Sea, wherein thou drownedst our enemies? or if we had died in the wilderness, like our fathers, than to be delivered into the hand of the Amorites that we should be blotted out for ever ? 4. Yet if thy word be about us, no evil shall befall us : for even though our end be removed unto death, thou livest which art before the world and after the world ; and whereas a man cannot devise how to put one generation before another, he saith " God hath destroyed his people whom he chose" : and, behold, we shall be in Hell : yet thou wilt make thy word alive. And now let the fulness of thy mercies have patience with thy people, and choose for thine heritage a man which shall rule over thy people, he and his generation. 5. Was it not for this that our father Jacob spake, saying : *A prince shall not* Gen. 49¹⁰ *depart from Juda, nor a leader from his loins.* And now confirm the words spoken aforetime, that the nations of the earth and tribes of the world may learn that thou art everlasting. 6. And he said furthermore : O Lord, behold the days shall come

XXI. 4. *And whereas a man cannot devise*, etc. There is an antithesis between the short sight of man and the eternal knowledge of God : but either the text is unsound or I fail to understand it, for it seems to me inconsequent as it stands.

and the house of Israel shall be like unto a brooding
dove which setteth her young *in the nest* and will not
forsake them nor forget her place.   So, also, these
shall turn from their deeds and fight against the
salvation that shall be born unto them.

7. And Jesus went down from Galgala and Jos. 8³⁰
built an altar of very great stones, and brought
no iron upon them, as Moses had commanded,
and set up great stones on mount Gebal, and
whitened them and wrote on them the words of
the law very plainly : and gathered all the people
together and read in their ears all the words of
the law.   8. And he came down with them and
offered upon the altar peace-offerings, and they
sang many praises, and lifted up the ark of the
covenant of the Lord out of the tabernacle with
timbrels and dances and lutes and harps and
psalteries and all instruments of sweet sound.
9. And the priests and Levites were going up
before the ark and rejoicing with psalms, and
they set the ark before the altar, and lifted up on
it yet again peace-offerings very many, and the
whole house of Israel sang together with a loud
voice saying : Behold, our Lord hath fulfilled that
which he spake with our fathers saying : To your
seed will I give a land wherein to dwell, a
land flowing with milk and honey.   And lo, he
hath brought us· into the land of our enemies
and hath delivered them broken in heart before
us, and he is the God which sent to our fathers
in the secret places of souls, saying : Behold, the
Lord hath done all that he spake unto us.   And
now know we of a truth that God hath confirmed
all the words of the law which he spake to us in
Oreb ; and if our heart keep his ways it will be
well with us, and with our sons after us.   10. And
Jesus blessed them and said : The Lord grant

your heart to continue therein (*or* in him) all the days, and if ye depart not from his name, the covenant of the Lord shall endure with you. And *he grant* that it be not corrupted, but that the dwelling-place of God be builded among you, as he spake when he sent you into his inheritance with mirth and gladness.

Jos. 22

XXII. And it came to pass after these things, when Jesus and all Israel had heard that the children of Ruben and the children of Gad and the half tribe of Manasse which dwelt about Jordan had built them an altar and did offer sacrifices thereon and had made priests for the sanctuary, all the people were troubled above measure and came unto them to Silon. 2. And Jesus and all the elders spake to them saying: What be these works which are done among you, while as yet we are not settled in our land? Are not these the words which Moses spake to you in the wilderness saying: See that when ye enter into the land ye spoil not your doings, and corrupt all the people? And now wherefore is it that our enemies have so much abounded, save because ye do corrupt your ways and have made all this trouble, and therefore will they assemble against us and overcome us.

22²¹ *sqq.*

3. And the children of Ruben and the children of Gad and the half tribe of Manasse said unto Jesus and all the people of Israel: Lo now hath God enlarged the fruit of the womb of men, and hath set up a light that that which is in darkness may see, for he knoweth what is in the secret places of the deep, and with him light abideth. Now the Lord God of our fathers knoweth if any of us or if we ourselves have done this thing in the way of iniquity, but only for our posterity's sake, that their heart be not separated from the

Lord our God lest they say to us: Behold now, our brethren which be beyond Jordan have an altar, to make offerings upon it, but we in this place that have no altar, let us depart from the Lord our Gôd, because our God hath set us afar off from his ways, that we should not serve him. 4. And then verily spake we among ourselves: Let us make us an altar, that they may have a zeal to seek the Lord. And verily there be some of us that stand by and know that we are your brothers and stand guiltless before your face. Do ye therefore that which is pleasing in the sight of the Lord. 5. And Jesus said: Is not the Lord our king mightier than 1000 sacrifices? And wherefore taught ye not your sons the words of the Lord which ye heard of us? For if your sons had been *occupied* in the meditation of the law of the Lord, their mind would not have been led aside after a sanctuary made with hands. Or know ye not that when the people were forsaken for a moment in the wilderness when Moses went up to receive the tables, their mind was led astray, and they made themselves idols? And except the mercy of the God of your fathers had kept *us*, all the synagogues should have become a byword, and all the sins of the people should have been blazed abroad because of your foolishness. 6. Therefore now go and dig down the sanctuaries that ye have builded you, and teach your sons the law, and they shall be meditating therein day and night, that the Lord may be with them for a witness and a judge unto them all the days of their life. And God shall be witness and judge between me and you, and between my heart and your heart, that if ye have done this thing in subtlety it shall be avenged upon you, because you would destroy your brothers: but if ye have done it ignorantly as ye say, God will be merciful unto you for your sons' sake. And all the people answered: Amen, Amen.

7. And Jesus and all the people of Israel offered for them 1,000 rams for a sin-offering (*lit.* the word of excusing), and prayed for them and sent them away in peace: and they went and destroyed the sanctuary, and fasted and wept, both they and their sons, and prayed and said:

Acts 1[24] O God of our fathers, that knowest before the heart of all men, thou knowest that our ways were not wrought in iniquity in thy sight, neither have we swerved from thy ways, but have served thee all of us, for we are the work of thy hands: now *therefore* remember thy covenant with the sons of thy servants.

8. And after that Jesus went up unto Galgala, and reared up the tabernacle of the Lord, and the ark of the covenant and all the vessels thereof, and set it up in Silo, and put there the Demonstration and the Truth (*i. e.* the Urim and Thummim). And at that time Eleazar the priest which served the altar did teach by the Demonstration all them of the people that came to inquire of the Lord, for thereby it was shown unto them, but in the new sanctuary that was in Galgala, Jesus appointed even unto this day the burnt offerings that were offered by the children of Israel every year. 9. For until the house of the Lord was builded in Jerusalem, and so long as the offerings were made in the new sanctuary, the people were not forbidden to offer therein, because the Truth and the Demonstration revealed all things in Silo. And until the ark was set by Solomon in the sanctuary of the Lord they went on sacrificing there unto that day. But Eleazar the son of Aaron the priest of the Lord ministered in Silo.

XXIII. And Jesus the son of Naue ordered Jos. 24
the people and divided unto them the land, being
a mighty man of valour. And while yet the
adversaries of Israel were in the land, the days
of Jesus drew near that he should die, and he
sent and called all Israel throughout all their land
with their wives and their children, and said unto
them : Gather yourselves together before the ark
of the covenant of the Lord in Silo and I will
make a covenant with you before I die. 2. And
when all the people were gathered together on
the 16th day of the 3rd month before the face
of the Lord in Silo with their wives and their
children, Jesus said unto them : Hear, O Israel,
behold I make with you the covenant of this law
which the Lord ordained with our fathers in Oreb,
and therefore tarry ye here this night and see Num. 22¹⁹
what God will say unto me concerning you. 3.
And as the people waited there that night, the
Lord appeared unto Jesus in a vision and spake
saying : According to all these words will I speak
unto this people. 4. And Jesus came in the morning and assembled all the people and said unto
them : Thus saith the Lord : One rock was there Isa. 51¹, ²
from whence I digged out your father, and the
cutting of that rock brought forth two men, whose
names were Abraham and Nachor, and out of the
chiselling of that place were born two women
whose names were Sara and Melcha. And they
dwelled together beyond the river. And Abraham
took Sara *to wife* and Nachor took Melcha.
5. And when the people of the land were led
astray, every man after his own devices, Abraham
believed in me and was not led aside after them.
And I saved him out of the fire and took him and
brought him over into all the land of Chanaan.
And I spake unto him in a vision saying : Unto

thy seed will I give this land. And he said unto
me: Behold now thou hast given me a wife and
she is barren. And how shall I have *seed* of that
womb that is shut up? 6. And I said unto him:

15⁹
Take for me a calf of three years old and a she-goat
of three years and a ram of three years, a turtle-
dove and a pigeon. And he took them as I com-

15¹²
manded him. And *I sent a sleep upon him* and
compassed him about with fear, and *I set* before

15¹⁷
him the place of fire wherein the works of them
that commit iniquity against me shall be avenged,
and I showed him the torches of fire whereby the
righteous which have believed in me shall be enlightened. 7. And I said unto him: These shall be
for a witness between me and thee that I will give
thee seed of the womb that is shut up. And I
will liken thee unto the dove, because thou hast
received for me the city which thy sons shall
(begin to) build in my sight. But the turtle-dove
I will liken unto the prophets which shall be born
of thee. And the ram will I liken unto the wise
men which shall be born of thee and enlighten
thy sons. But the calf I will liken unto the multitude of the peoples which shall be multiplied
through thee. And the she-goat I will liken unto
the women whose wombs I will open and they
shall bring forth. These things shall be for a
witness betwixt us that I will not transgress my
words.

8. And I gave him Isaac and formed him in
the womb of her that bare him, and commanded
it that it should restore him quickly and render
him unto me in the 7th month. And for this

XXIII. 6. The vision in Gen. 15 is here the occasion of
Abraham's receiving revelations of a future state. Compare
the Slavonic *Apocalypse of Abraham*, in which future *history*
is revealed to him at this time.

cause every woman that bringeth forth in the
7th month, her child shall live: because upon
him did I call my glory, and showed forth the
new age. 9. And I gave unto Isaac Jacob and
Esau, and unto Esau I gave the land of Seir for
an heritage. And Jacob and his sons went down
into Egypt. And the Egyptians brought your
fathers low, as ye know, and I remembered your
fathers, and sent Moses my friend and delivered
them from thence and smote their enemies.

10. And I brought them out with a high hand
and led them through the Red Sea, and laid the
cloud under their feet, and brought them out
through the depth, and brought them beneath the
mount Sina, and I *bowed the heavens and came* Ps. 18⁹
down, and I congealed the flame of the fire, and
stopped up the springs of the deep, and im-
peded the course of the stars, and tamed the
sound of the thunder, and quenched the fulness
of the wind, and rebuked the multitude of the
clouds, and stayed their motions, and interrupted
the storm of the hosts, that I should not break
my covenant, for all things were moved at my
coming down, and all things were quickened at
my advent, and I suffered not my people to be
scattered, but gave unto them my law, and enlightened them, that if they did these things they
may live and have length of days and not die.
11. And I have brought you into this land and
given you vineyards. Ye dwell in cities which ye
built not. And I have fulfilled the covenant which
I spake unto your fathers.

12. And now if ye obey your fathers, I will set
my heart upon you for ever, and will overshadow
you, and your enemies shall no more fight against
you, and your land shall be renowned throughout
all the world and your seed be elect in the midst

of the peoples, which shall say: Behold the faithful
people; because they believed the Lord, therefore
hath the Lord delivered them and planted them.
And therefore will I plant you as a desirable
vineyard and will rule you as a beloved flock, and
I will charge the rain and the dew, and they shall
satisfy you all the days of your life. 13. And it
shall be at the end that the lot of every one of
you shall be in eternal life, both for you and
your seed, and I will receive your souls and lay
them up in peace, until the time of the age is
fulfilled, and I restore you unto your fathers and
your fathers unto you, and they shall know at
your hand that it is not in vain that I have chosen
you. These are the words that the Lord hath
spoken unto me this night. 14. And all the
people answered and said: The Lord is our God,
and him only will we serve. And all the people
made a great feast that day and a renewal thereof
for 28 days.

XXIV. And after these days Jesus the son
of Naue assembled all the people yet again, and
said unto them: Behold now the Lord hath testified unto you this day: I have called heaven and
earth to witness to you that if ye will continue to
serve the Lord ye shall be unto him a peculiar
people. But if ye will not serve him and will obey
the gods of the Amorites in whose land ye dwell,
say so this day before the Lord and go forth.
But I and my house will serve the Lord. 2. And
all the people lifted up their voice and wept
saying: Peradventure the Lord will account us
worthy, and it is better for us to die in the fear
of him, than to be destroyed out of the land.

Dt. 4²⁶, etc.

Jos. 24¹⁵

14. *a renewal: innouationem. qu.* ἐγκαινισμόν: cf. 2 Chron.
30²³.

3. And Jesus the son of Naue blessed the
people and kissed them and said unto them : Let
your words be for mercy before our Lord, and let
him send his angel, and preserve you : Remember
me after my death, and *remember ye* Moses the
friend of the Lord.   And let not the words of the
covenant which he hath made with you depart
from you all the days of your life.   And he sent
them away and they departed every man to his
inheritance.

4. But Jesus laid himself upon his bed, and sent
and called Phineës the son of Eleazar the priest
and said unto him : Behold now I see with mine
eyes the transgression of this people wherein they
will begin to deceive : but thou, strengthen thy
hands in the time that thou art with them.   And
he kissed him and his father and his sons and
blessed him and said : The Lord God of your
fathers direct your ways and *the ways* of this
people.   5. And when he ceased speaking unto
them, *he drew up his feet into the bed* and slept   Gen. 49³³
with his fathers.   And his sons *laid their hands*   46⁴
upon his eyes.

6. And then all Israel gathered together to
bury him, and they lamented him with a great
lamentation, and thus said they in their lamenta-
tation : Weep ye for the wing of this swift eagle,
for he hath flown away from us.   And weep ye
for the strength of this lion's whelp, for he is
hidden from us.   Who now will go and report
unto Moses the righteous, that we have had forty
years a leader like unto him ?   And they fulfilled
their mourning and *buried him* with their own   Jos. 24³⁰
hands *in the mount Effraim* and returned every
man unto his tent.   And after the death of Jesus
the land of Israel was at rest.

XXV. And the Philistines sought to fight with
K

the men of Israel: and they inquired of the Lord
and said: Shall we go up and fight against the

XXV. Up to this point *Philo* has followed the Bible
story faithfully enough. He now draws freely on his own
imagination, and presents us with an entirely new history
of the beginning of the period of the Judges.

Kenaz is the first Judge. He and Seenamias, as we read
in XX. 6, were the sons of Caleb, and were the two spies
sent by Joshua to Jericho (who in the Bible are nameless):
at Caleb's request (XX. 10) Joshua gave Kenaz the territory
of the three towers (or the tribe of the towers). The context in which this is told is copied from Josh. 14[6] (cf. 15[16 *sqq.*]).
In that place, and in Num. 32[12], Caleb is called the Kenezite.
In Josh. 15, Othniel, son of Kenaz, the (younger) brother of
Caleb (but another view makes Othniel brother of Caleb),
takes Kirjath-sepher and marries Caleb's daughter. This is
repeated in Judges 1[13]. In Judges 3[10, 11] Othniel figures as
the first of the Judges proper: but all that is said of him is
that the Spirit of the Lord came upon him, and he judged
Israel and conquered Chushan-rishathaim.

Thus in the Bible Kenaz is a mere name: he is a younger
brother (or other relative) of Caleb, and father of Othniel
the first judge: and his is an ancestral or clan-name in the
family of Caleb. In *Philo* he completely ousts Othniel, and
there is no pretence of assimilating his story to that of any
one who appears in the Bible. He figures as a divinely
appointed ruler, a detecter of crime, a mediator, it may be
said, between God and Israel, and the recipient of God's
own instructions: then as a mighty man of valour, and
lastly as a seer. In respect of the amount of space devoted
to him he is second only to Moses. It may be merely the
author's desire to strike out a new line, or perhaps to import
a fresh religious interest into the history of the Judges
(though this he could do in other ways, and much of the
story of Kenaz has no religious value) that has prompted
this sudden burst of inventiveness; or there may have been
another motive at work and a hidden meaning in the tale,
which I cannot penetrate. I do not find any hint in other
writings that tradition clustered round the name of Kenaz:
but it is noticeable that the best text of Josephus (Ant. V.
33) substitutes his name (Κενιαζοσ) for that of Othniel: and
that in the Pseudo-Epiphanian *Lives of the Prophets* it is
said that Jonah was buried " in the cave of Kainezias, who
was judge of one tribe in the days of the anarchy," a sen-

Philistines? and God said to them: If ye go up with a pure heart, fight; but if your heart is defiled, go not up. And they inquired yet again saying: How shall we know if all the heart of the people be alike? and God said to them: Cast lots among your tribes, and it shall be unto every tribe that cometh under the lot, that it shall be set apart into one lot, and then shall ye know whose heart is clean and whose is defiled. 2. And the people said: Let us first appoint over us a prince, and so cast lots. And the angel of the Lord said to them: Appoint. And the people said: Whom shall we appoint that is worthy, Lord? And the angel of the Lord said to them: Cast the lot upon the tribe of Caleb, and he that is shown by the lot, even he shall

tence which neither suggests a knowledge of *Philo* nor explains itself. All that it, and the passage of Josephus, do suggest is that *Philo* may be following a current fashion in discarding the name of Othniel, and that he has taken as his text the words in Judges: " the Spirit of the Lord came upon " Othniel, and has written a variation upon that theme.

The next judge is Zebul. The name is taken, no doubt, from the story of Abimelech in Judges 9²⁸, etc. Otherwise he is a completely imaginary figure. From him we pass to Deborah; she is followed by Aod (= Ehud), who is here not a judge, but a Midianitish wizard. As in the case of Zebul, *Philo* has borrowed a Biblical name from another part of Judges, and affixed it to a totally different personality. The remainder of his judges follow the Biblical order fairly well: Gideon, Abimelech (Tola may have disappeared in a *lacuna*), Jair (whose character is gratuitously blackened), Jephtha (Ibzan is then omitted), Addo (= Abdon), Elon (these two being transposed from the Biblical order), Samson. Then follow, as in the Bible, the stories of Micah's idolatry (the migration of the Danites being wholly passed over) and of the Benjamite outrage, which is located at Nob, the priestly city, instead of Gibeah. Thus the narrative in Judges is represented with approximate faithfulness, save in the case of the first judges, where *Philo* substitutes Kenaz and Zebul for Othniel, Ehud, and Shamgar.

be your prince. And they cast the lot for the tribe of Caleb and it came out upon Cenez, and they made him ruler over Israel. 3. And Cenez said to the people: Bring your tribes unto me and hear ye the word of the Lord. And the people gathered together and Cenez said to them: Ye know that which Moses the friend of the Lord charged you, that ye should not transgress the law to the right hand or to the left. And Jesus also who was after him gave you the same char e. And now, lo, we have heard of the mouth of the Lord that your heart is defiled. And the Lord hath charged us to cast lots among your tribes to know whose heart hath departed from the Lord our God. Shall not the fury of anger come upon the people? But I promise you this day that even if a man of mine own house come out in the lot of sin, he shall not be saved alive, but shall be burned with fire. And the people said: Thou hast spoken a good counsel, to perform it.

4. And the tribes were brought before him, and there were found of the tribe of Juda 345 men, and of the tribe of Ruben 560, and of the tribe of Simeon 775, and of the tribe of Levi 150, and of the tribe of Zabulon 655 (*or* 645), and of the tribe of Isachar 665, and of the tribe of Gad 380. Of the tribe of Aser 665, and of the tribe of Manasse 480, and of the tribe of Effraim 468, and of the tribe of Benjamin 267. And all the number of them that were found by the lot of sin was 6110. And Cenez took them all and shut them up in prison, till it should be known what should be done with them.

XXV. 4. In the enumeration of the sinners among the tribes Dan has accidentally dropped out, though it appears in 9. The separate numbers in the text add up to 5410 or 5400, so that 700 or 710 is the number to be assigned to Dan in order to make up the total of 6110.

5. And Cenez said: Was it not of this that Moses the friend of the Lord spake saying: *There is a* Dt. 29[18] *strong root among you bringing forth gall and bitterness?* Now blessed be the Lord who hath revealed all the devices of these men, neither hath he suffered them to corrupt his people by their evil works. Bring hither therefore the Demonstration and the Truth and call forth Eleazar the priest, and let us inquire of the Lord by him. 6. Then Cenez and Eleazar and all the elders and the whole synagogue prayed with one accord saying: Lord God of our fathers, reveal unto thy servants the truth, for we are found not believing in the wonders which thou didst for our fathers since thou broughtest them out of the land of Egypt unto this day. And the Lord answered and said: First ask them that were found, and let them confess their deeds which they did subtilly, and afterwards they shall be burned with fire. 7. And Cenez brought them forth and said to them: Behold now ye know how that Achiar confessed when the lot fell on him, and declared all that he had done. And now declare unto me all your wickedness and your inventions: who knoweth, if ye tell us the truth, even though ye die now, yet God will have mercy upon you when he shall quicken the dead? 8. And one of them named Elas said unto him: Shall not death come now upon us, that we shall die by fire? Nevertheless I tell thee, my Lord, there are none inventions like unto these which we have made wickedly. But if thou wilt search out the truth plainly, ask severally the men of every tribe, and so shall some one of them that stand by perceive the difference of their sins. 9. And Cenez asked them of his own tribe and they told him: We desired to imitate and make the calf that they made in the wilderness. And after that he asked the men

of the tribe of Ruben, which said: We desired to sacrifice unto the gods of them that dwell in the land. And he asked the men of the tribe of Levi, which said: We would prove the tabernacle, whether it were holy. And he asked the remnant of the tribe of Isachar, which said: We would inquire by the evil spirits of the idols, *to see* whether they revealed plainly: and he asked the men of the tribe of Zabulon, which said: We desired to eat the flesh of our children and to learn whether God hath care for them. And he asked the remnant of the tribe of Dan, which said: The Amorites taught us that which they did, that we might teach our children. And lo, they are hid under the tent of Elas, who told thee to inquire of us. Send therefore and thou shall find them. And Cenez sent and found them. 10. And thereafter asked he them that were left over of the tribe of Gad, and they said: We committed adultery with each other's wives. And he asked next the men of the tribe of Aser,which said: We found seven golden images which the Amorites called the holy Nymphs, and we took them with the precious stones that were set upon them, and hid them: and lo, now

9. *under the tent of Elas, who told thee to inquire of us.* R. has : under the mount of Abraham, and laid up under a mound of earth. J has : under the mount of Abarim.

10 *seq.* The Amorites are described in *Jubilees* 29[11] as being particularly wicked. A special section in the Talmud treating of superstitious practices is called "the ways of the Amorites" (see *Jewish Encycl.*, s.v. *Amorites*).

The idols are too vaguely described to enable us to form an idea of them : *Philo* does not seem to have had any special heathen deities in mind. Of the seven sinners who made them we recognize the names of Canaan, Phuth, Nimrod, Elath, who are mentioned in IV. 6, 7, as descendants of Ham. The land of Euilat (Havilah) is described in Gen. 2[11, 12] as the home of gold, bdellium, and onyx.

they are laid up under the top of the mount
Sychem. Send therefore and thou shalt find them.
And Cenez sent men and removed them thence.
11. Now these are the Nymphs which when they
were called upon did show unto the Amorites their
works in every hour. For these are they which were
devised by seven evil men after the flood, whose
names are these: <? Cham> Chanaan, Phuth,
Selath, Nembroth, Elath, Desuath. Neither shall
there be again any like similitude in the world
graven by the hand of the artificer and adorned
with variety of painting, but they were set up
and fixed for the consecration (*i. e.* the holy place?)
of idols. *Now* the stones were precious, brought
from the land of Euilath, among which was a crystal
and a prase (*or* one crystalline and one green), and
they shewed their fashion, being carved after the
manner of a stone pierced with open-work, and
another of them was graven on the top, and another
as it were marked with spots (*or* like a spotted chrysoprase) so shone with its graving as if it shewed
the water of the deep lying beneath.

12. And these are the precious stones which the
Amorites had in their holy places, and the price

10. *the mount Sychem :* possibly a malicious allusion to the
Samaritans.
11. *stone pierced with open-work: uelut in diatrium
sculpti.* Here, and a few lines below, where we have *in
modum diatridis* or *diatriti sculptus*, I think *diatretos* must
be restored. The word is used by Martial and in the
Digest.
as it were marked with spots. The variants are
caraxatus stigminis and *chrysoprassus stigmatus.* I prefer
the first, because it seems clearly right in XXVI. 10.
There we have: "The 6th stone was as if it had been
{a chrysoprase *chrysoprassus*} . . . and was like a jasper,"
{marked (*in*) *caraxatus*}
and there the chrysoprase is plainly superfluous. *Caraxatus*
is also the harder word.

of them was above reckoning. For when any entered in by night, he needed not the light of a lantern, so much did the natural light of the stones shine forth. Wherein that one gave the greatest light which was cut after the form of a stone pierced with open-work, and was cleansed with bristles; for if any of the Amorites were blind, he went and put his eyes thereupon and recovered his sight. Now when Cenez found them, he set them apart and laid them up till he should know what should become of them.

13. And after that he asked them that were left of the tribe of Manasse, and they said: We did only defile the Lord's sabbaths. And he asked the forsaken of the tribe of Effraim, which said: We desired to pass our sons and our daughters through the fire, that we might know if that which was said were manifest. And he asked the forsaken of the tribe of Benjamin, which said: We desired at this time to examine the book of the law, whether God had plainly written that which was therein, or whether Moses had taught it of himself.

XXVI. And when Cenez had taken all these words and written them in a book and read them before the Lord, God said to him: Take the men

---

12. "*was cleansed with bristles*": *de setis emundabatur* (*-bitur* VR). This looks as if it must be wrong, but I find in Damigeron, *de lapidibus*, 47 (ap. Pitra, *Spicil. Solesm* III. 335), that the chrysolite "*pertusus et transiectus cum setis†* *aseminis* † (? *asininis*") and worn on the left arm, puts demons to flight. This suggests that, though *emundabatur* is not very clear, *de setis* is probably correct.

I may remark in passing that the old Latin version of Epiphanius, *de XII. lapidibus* (ed. Dindorf, *Opp.* IV. 1), has phrases recalling our text, *e.g.* p. 193 : *flauum ostentat colorem;* p. 198 : *hyacinthus tranquilli maris similitudinem refert.*

and that which was found with them and all their
goods and put them in the bed of the river Phison,
and burn them with fire that mine anger may
cease from them. 2. And Cenez said : Shall we
burn these precious stones also with fire, or sanctify them unto thee, for among us there are none
like unto them? And God said to him : If God
should receive in his own name any of the accursed
thing, what should man do ? Therefore now take
these precious stones and all that was found, both
books and men : and when thou dealest so with the
men, set apart these stones with the books, for fire
will not avail to burn them, and afterwards I will
shew thee how thou must destroy them. But the
men and all that was found thou shalt burn with
fire. And thou shalt assemble all the people, and
say to them : Thus shall it be done unto every
man whose heart turneth away from his God.
3. And when the fire hath consumed those men,
then the books and the precious stones which cannot be burned with fire, neither cut with iron, nor
blotted out with water, lay them upon the top of
the mount beside the new altar ; and I will command a cloud, and it shall go and take up dew
and shed it upon the books, and shall blot out
that which is written therein, for they cannot be
blotted out with any other water than such as
hath never served men. And thereafter I will
send my lightning, and it shall burn up the books
themselves.

4. But as concerning the precious stones, I will
command mine angel and he shall take them and
go and cast them into the depths of the sea, and
I will charge the deep and it shall swallow them
up, for they may not continue in the world because
they have been polluted by the idols of the Amorites. And I will command another angel, and he

shall take for me twelve stones out of the place
whence these seven were taken; and thou, when
thou findest them in the top of the mount where
he shall lay them, take and put them on the
shoulder-piece over against the twelve stones which
Moses set therein in the wilderness, and sanctify
them in the breastplate (*lit.* oracle) according to
the twelve tribes: and say not, How shall I know
which stone I shall set for which tribe? Lo, I will
tell thee the name of the tribe answering unto the
name of the stone, and thou shall find both one
and other graven. 5. And Cenez went and took
all that had been found and the men with it,
and assembled all the people again, and said to
them: Behold, ye have seen all the wonders which
God hath shewed us unto this day, and lo, when
we sought out all that had subtilly devised evil
against the Lord and against Israel, God hath
revealed them according to their works, and now
cursed be every man that deviseth to do the like
among you, brethren. And all the people answered Amen, Amen. And when he had so said,
he burned all the men with fire, and all that was
found with them, saving the precious stones.

6. And after that Cenez desired to prove
whether the stones could be burned with fire,
and cast them into the fire. And it was so,
that when they fell therein, forthwith the fire was
quenched. And Cenez took iron to break them,
and when the sword touched them the iron thereof
was melted; and thereafter he would at the least blot
out the books with water; but it came to pass that
the water when it fell upon them was congealed.
And when he saw that, he said: Blessed be God
who hath done so great wonders for the children
of men, and made Adam the first-created and
shewed him all things; that when Adam had

sinned thereby, then he should deny him all these things, lest if he shewed them unto the race of men they should have the mastery over them.

7. And when he had so said, he took the books and the stones and laid them on the top of the mount by the new altar as the Lord had commanded him, and took a peace-offering and burnt-offerings, and offered upon the new altar 2000, offering them all for a burnt sacrifice. And on that day they kept a great feast, he and all the people together. 8. And God did that night as he spake unto Cenez, for he commanded a cloud, and it went and took dew from the ice of paradise and shed it upon the books and blotted them out. And after that an angel came and burned them up, and another angel took the precious stones and cast them into the heart of the sea, and he charged the depth of the sea, and it swallowed them up. And another angel went and brought twelve stones and laid them hard by the place whence he had taken those seven. And he graved thereon the names of the twelve tribes.

9. And Cenez arose on the morrow and found those twelve stones on the top of the mount where himself had laid those seven. And the graving of them was so as if the form of eyes was portrayed upon them. _{Cf. Zech. 3⁹}

Cf. Zech. 3^9

10. And the first stone, whereon was written the name of the tribe of Ruben, was like a sardine

See Ex. 28^{17} *sqq.*

XXVI. 7. *superponens (ea in holocaustum)*. This is the word used in the old Latin of Lev. iv., etc , in the Würzburg palimpsest. The Lyons Pentateuch has *inponens*.

10 *seq.* The order of the stones agrees with that of Exod. 28^{17} *sqq.*, except that agate and amethyst are here transposed, and in the Hebrew carbuncle precedes emerald. The principle of the list seems to be that each of the new stones is "likened to" (should we render "placed opposite

stone. The second stone was graven with a tooth
(*or* ivory), and therein was graven the name of the
tribe of Simeon, and the likeness of a topaz was
seen in it; and on the third stone was graven the
name of the tribe of Levi, and it was like unto
an emerald. But the fourth stone was called a
crystal, wherein was graven the name of the tribe
of Juda, and it was likened to a carbuncle. The
fifth stone was green, and upon it was graven the
name of the tribe of Isachar, and the colour of
a sapphire stone was therein. And of the sixth
stone the graving was as if it had been inscribed,
(*or* as a chrysoprase) speckled with diverse markings,
and thereon was written the tribe of Zabulon, and
the jasper stone was likened unto it.

11. Of the seventh stone the graving shone and
shewed within itself, as it were, *enclosed* the water
of the deep, and therein was written the name of
the tribe of Dan, which stone was like a ligure.
But the eighth stone was cut out with adamant,
and therein was written the name of the tribe
of Neptalim, and it was like an amethyst. And
of the ninth stone the graving was pierced, *and*
it was from Mount Ophir, and therein was written
the tribe of Gad, and an agate stone was likened
unto it. And of the tenth stone the graving
was hollowed, and gave the likeness of a stone
of Theman, and there was written the tribe of
Aser, and a chrysolite was likened unto it. And
the eleventh stone was an elect stone from Libanus,
and thereon was written the name of the tribe of
Joseph, and a beryl was likened to it. And the

to" or "corresponds to"?) a stone already in the breastplate;
but the new stones, being supernatural, have as a rule no
names of their own.

11. (The 9th stone) *pierced.* I read *terebrata*, with R, for
tenebrata.

twelfth stone was cut out of the height of Sion (*or the quarry*), and upon it was written the tribe of Benjamin ; and the onyx stone was likened unto it.

12. And God said to Cenez : Take these stones and put them in the ark of the covenant of the Lord with the tables of the covenant which I gave unto Moses in Oreb, and they shall be there with them until Jahel arise to build an house in my name, and then he shall set them before me upon the two cherubim, and they shall be in my sight for a memorial of the house of Israel. 13. And it shall be when the sins of my people are filled up, and their enemies have the mastery over their house, that I will take these stones and the former together with the tables, and lay them up in the place whence they were brought forth in the beginning, and they shall be there until I remember the world, and visit the dwellers upon earth. And then will I take them and many other better than they, from that *place* which *eye hath not seen nor ear heard neither hath it come up into* Isa. 64⁴,ᵉᵗᶜ. *the heart of man*, until the like cometh to pass

11. (The 12th stone) *cut out of the height of Sion.* Again I prefer R's reading, *de excelso Syon*, to *de excisione* of AP.

12. *until Jahel* (*Jabel* R) shall arise. J substitutes *Solomon* in its paraphrase of the passage, and no doubt Solomon is meant; but I cannot find any other instance of this name being applied to him, or any reason for it. The Jael of Judges iv. means a gazelle : Jael is also found as a name of God (Jah El) in the Greek *Apoc. of Moses :* neither helps us here. It can hardly be a corruption of Ἰεδδεδί, the Greek form of Jedidiah (2 Sam. 12 ²⁵).

13. *from that place which eye hath not seen, nor ear heard, neither hath it come up into the heart of man.* This is a combination of phrases from Isa. 64⁴; 65¹⁶,¹⁷. It is quoted in this form by St. Paul in 1 Cor. 2⁹. Mr. Thackeray, in *St. Paul and Contemporary Jewish Thought*, p. 240 *seq.*, discusses the source in the light of this passage, and concludes, I believe rightly, that the combination was already

Isa. 60¹⁹, ²⁰ unto the world, and the just shall *have no need of the light of the sun nor of the shining of the moon,* for the light of the precious stones shall be their light. 14. And Cenez arose and said: Behold what good things God hath done for men, and because of their sins have they been deprived of them all. And now know I this day that the race of men is weak, and their life shall be accounted as nothing. 15. And so saying, he took the stones from the place where they were laid, and as he took them there was as it were the light of the sun poured out upon them, and the earth shone with their light. And Cenez put them in the ark of the covenant of the Lord with the tables as it was commanded him, and there they are unto this day.

XXVII. And after this he armed of the people 300,000 men and went up to fight against the Amorites, and slew on the first day 800,000 men, and on the second day he slew about 500,000. 2. And when the third day came, certain men of the people spake evil against Cenez, saying: Lo, now, Cenez alone lieth in his house with his wife and his concubines, and sendeth us to battle, that we may be destroyed before our enemies. 3. And when the servants of Cenez heard, they brought him word. And he commanded a captain of fifty, and he brought of them thirty-seven men

current in Jewish circles when Paul wrote. The early commentators on the Epistle assigned to the *Secreta Eliae* (Origen), *Apocalypse of Elias,* or *Ascension of Isaiah.*

15. *there they are unto this day.* See p. 63.

XXVII. 1. *The Amorites.* In XXV. 1, the enemy were the Philistines, *Allophyli.* But the Amorites, of whose idols so much has been said in the interim, seem to have absorbed *Philo's* attention.

3. I can only make thirty-six names from the manuscripts unless Eliesor is divided into two.

who spake against him and shut them up in
ward.   4. And their names are these : Le and
Uz, Betul, Ephal, Dealma, Anaph, Desac, Besac,
Gethel, Anael, Anazim, Noac, Cehec, Boac, Obal,
Iabal, Enath, Beath, Zelut, Ephor, Ezeth, Desaph,
Abidan, Esar, Moab, Duzal, Azath, Phelac, Igat,
Zophal, Eliesor, Ecar, Zebath, Sebath, Nesach and
Zere.   And when the captain of fifty had shut
them up as Cenez commanded, Cenez said : When
the Lord hath wrought salvation for his people by
my hand, then will I punish these men.   5. And
so saying, Cenez commanded the captain of fifty,
saying : Go and choose of my servants 300 men,
and as many horses, and let no man of the people
know of the hour when I shall go forth to battle ;
but only in what hour I shall tell thee, prepare
the men that they be ready this night.   6. And
Cenez sent messengers, spies, to see where was the
multitude of the camp of the Amorites.   And the
messengers went and spied, and saw that the multitude of the camp of the Amorites was moving
among the rocks devising to come and fight
against Israel.   And the messengers returned and
told him according to this word.   And Cenez
arose by night, he and 300 horsemen with him,
and took a trumpet in his hand and began to go
down with the 300 men.   And it came to pass,
when he was near to the camp of the Amorites,
that he said to his servants : Abide here and I
will go down alone and view the camp of the
Amorites.   And it shall be, if I blow with the
trumpet ye shall come down, but if not, wait for
me here.

7. And Cenez went down alone, and before he
went down he prayed, and said : O Lord God of
our fathers, thou hast shewn unto thy servant the
marvellous things which thou hast prepared to do

by thy covenant in the last days: and now, send unto thy servant one of thy wonders, and I will overcome thine adversaries, that they and all the nations and thy people may know that the Lord delivereth not by the multitude of an host, neither by the strength of horsemen, when they shall perceive the sign of deliverance which thou shalt work for me this day (*or* horsemen, and that thou, Lord, wilt perform a sign of salvation with me this day). Behold, I will draw my sword out of the scabbard and it shall glitter in the camp of the Amorites: and it shall be, if the Amorites perceive that it is I, Cenez, *then* I *shall* know that thou hast delivered them into mine hand. But if they perceive not that it is I, and think that it is another, *then* I *shall* know that thou hast not hearkened unto me, but hast delivered me unto mine enemies. But and if I be indeed delivered unto death, I *shall* know that because of mine iniquities the Lord hath not heard me, and hath delivered me unto mine enemies; but he will not destroy his inheritance by my death.

8. And he set forth after he had prayed, and heard the multitude of the Amorites saying: Let us arise and fight against Israel: for we know that our holy Nymphs are there among them and will deliver them into our hands. 9. And Cenez arose, for the spirit of the Lord clothed him *as a garment,* and he drew his sword, and when the light of it shone upon the Amorites like sharp lightning, they saw it, and said: Is not this the sword of Cenez which hath made our wounded many? Now is the word justified which we spake, saying that our holy Nymphs have delivered them into our hands. Lo, now, this day shall there be feasting for the Amorites, when our enemy is

delivered unto us. Now, therefore, arise and let everyone gird on his sword and begin the battle.

10. And it came to pass when Cenez heard their words, he was clothed with the spirit of might and changed into another man, and went down into the camp of the Amorites and began to smite them. And the Lord sent before his face the angel Ingethel (*or* Gethel), who is set over the hidden things, and worketh unseen, (and another) angel of might helping with him: and Ingethel smote the Amorites with blindness, so that every man that saw his neighbour counted them his adversaries, and they slew one another. And the angel Zeruel, who is set over strength, bare up the arms of Cenez lest they should perceive him; and Cenez smote of the Amorites forty and five thousand men, and they themselves smote one another, and fell forty and five thousand men. 11. And when Cenez had smitten a great multitude, he would have loosened his hand from his sword, for the handle of the sword clave, that it could not be loosed, and his right hand had taken into it the strength of the sword.

Then they that were left of the Amorites fled into the mountains; but Cenez sought how he might loose his hand: and he looked with his eyes and saw a man of the Amorites fleeing, and he caught him and said to him: I know that the Amorites are cunning: now therefore shew me how I may loose my hand from this sword, and I will let thee go. And the Amorite said: Go and take a man of the Hebrews and kill him, and while his blood is yet warm hold thine hand beneath and receive his blood, so shall thine hand be loosed. And Cenez said: As the Lord

11. Kenaz's hand cleaves to his sword like that of Eleazar, the mighty man in 2 Sam. 23^{10}.

L

liveth, if thou hadst said, Take a man of the Amorites, I would have taken one of them and saved thee alive: but forasmuch as thou saidest "of the Hebrews" that thou mightest show thine hatred, thy mouth shall be against thyself, and according as thou hast said, so will I do unto thee. And when he had thus said Cenez slew him, and while his blood was yet warm, he held his hand beneath and received it therein, and it was loosed.

12. And Cenez departed and put off his garments, and cast himself into the river and washed, and came up again and changed his garments, and returned to his young men. Now the Lord cast upon them a heavy sleep in the night, and they slept and knew not any thing of all that Cenez had done. And Cenez came and awaked them out of sleep; and they looked [upon him] with their eyes and saw, and behold, the field was full of dead bodies: and they were astonished in their mind, and looked every man on his neighbour. And Cenez said unto them: Why marvel ye? Are the ways of the Lord as the way of men? For with men a multitude prevaileth, but with God that which he appointeth. And therefore if God hath willed to work deliverance for this people by my hands, wherefore marvel ye? Arise and gird on every man your swords, and we will go home to our brethren.

13. And when all Israel heard the deliverance that was wrought by the hands of Cenez, all the people came out with one accord to meet him, and said: Blessed be the Lord which hath made thee ruler over his people, and hath shown that those things are sure which he spake unto thee: that which we heard by speech we see now with our eyes, for the work of the word of God is manifest.

14. And Cenez said unto them: Ask *now* your

brethren, and let them tell you how greatly they laboured with me in the battle. And the men that were with him said: As the Lord liveth, we fought not, neither knew we *anything*, save only when we awaked, we saw the field full of dead bodies. And the people answered: Now know we that when the Lord appointeth to work deliverance for his people, he hath no need of a multitude, but only of sanctification.

15. And Cenez said to the captain of fifty which had shut up those men in prison: Bring forth those men that we may hear their words. And when he had brought them forth, Cenez said to them: Tell me, what saw ye in me that ye murmured among the people? And they said: Why askest thou us? Why askest thou us? Now therefore command that we be burned with fire, for we die not for this sin that we have now spoken, but for that former one wherein those men were taken which were burned in their sins; for then we did consent unto their sin, saying: Peradventure the people will not perceive us; and then we did escape the people. But now have we been (rightly) made a public example by our sins in that we fell into slandering of thee. And Cenez said: If ye yourselves therefore witness against yourselves, how shall I have compassion upon you? And Cenez commanded them to be burned with fire, and cast their ashes into the place where they had burned the multitude of the sinners, even into the brook Phison.

16. And Cenez ruled over his people fifty and seven years, and there was fear upon all his enemies all his days.

XXVIII. And when the days of Cenez drew

15. *made a public example: transducti.* In the old Latin Bible versions *transduco* renders παραδειγματίζω, ἐλέγχω.

nigh that he should die, he sent and called all men (*or* all the elders), and the two prophets Jabis and Phinees, and Phinees the son of Eleazar the priest, and said to them : Behold now, the Lord hath showed me all his marvellous works which he hath prepared to do for his people in the last days.

2. And now will I make my covenant with you this day, that ye forsake not the Lord your God after my departing. For ye have seen all the marvels *which came* upon them that sinned, and all that they declared, confessing their sins of their own accord, and how the Lord our God made an end of them for that they transgressed his covenant. Wherefore now spare ye them of your house and your sons, and abide in the ways of the Lord your God, that the Lord destroy not his inheritance.

3. And Phinees, the son of Eleazar the priest, said : If Cenez the ruler bid me, and the prophets and the people and the elders, I will speak a word which I heard of my father when he was a-dying, and will not keep silence concerning the commandment which he commanded me when his soul was being received. And Cenez the ruler and the prophets said : Let Phinees say on. Shall any other speak before the priest which keepeth the commandments of the Lord our God, and that, seeing that truth proceedeth out of his mouth, and out of his heart a shining light ?

4. Then said Phinees : My father, when he was a-dying, commanded me saying : Thus shalt thou

XXVIII. 1. The *"two prophets Jabis and Phinees, and Phinees the son of Eleazar"* are suspicious. I should not wonder if originally there had been but one prophet, Jabis, and Phinees the son of Eleazar. The plural *prophetae*, which occurs again in 3, might be a consequential change.

say unto the children of Israel when they are gathered together unto the assembly : The Lord appeared unto me the third day before this in a dream in the night, and said unto me : Behold, thou hast seen, and thy father before thee, how greatly I have laboured for my people ; and it shall be after thy death that this people shall arise and corrupt their ways, departing from my commandments, and I shall be exceeding wroth with them. Yet will I remember the time which was before the ages, *even* in the time when there was not a man, and therein was no iniquity, when I said that the world should be, and they that should come should praise me therein, and I will plant a great vineyard, and out of it will I choose a plant, and order it and call it by my name, and it shall be mine for ever. But when I have done all that I have spoken, nevertheless my planting, which is called after me, will not know me, the planter thereof, but will corrupt his fruit, and will not yield me his fruit. These are the things which my father commanded me to speak unto this people.

5. And Cenez lifted up his voice, and the elders, and all the people with one accord, and wept with a great lamentation until the evening and said : Shall the shepherd destroy his flock to no purpose, except it continue in sin against him ? And shall it not be he that shall spare according to the abundance of his mercy, seeing he hath spent great labour upon us ?

6. Now while they were set, the holy spirit that Ezek. 8[1] dwelt in Cenez leapt upon him and took away from

6 *seq.* There are several resemblances in this section to the diction of Ezekiel. The Spirit comes upon Kenaz as he sits among the elders : so in Ezek. 8[1] (20[1],[2]). *fundamentum* may be compared with στερέωμα (Ezek. 1[22]); *subdiuum* with

him his *bodily* sense, and he began to prophesy,
saying : Behold now I see that which I looked not
for, and perceive that I knew not.   Hearken now, ye
that dwell on the earth, even as they that sojourned
therein prophesied before me, when they saw this
hour, *even* before the earth was corrupted, that .
ye may know the prophecies appointed aforetime,
all ye that dwell therein. 7. Behold now I see flames
that burn not, and I hear springs of water awaked
out of sleep, and they have no foundation, neither
do I behold the tops of the mountains, nor the
canopy of the firmament, but all things unappear-
ing and invisible, which have no place whatsoever,
and although mine eye knoweth not what it seeth,
mine heart shall discover that which it may learn
(*or* say).   8. Now out of the flame which I saw,
and it burned not, I beheld, and lo a spark came
up and as it were builded for itself a floor under
heaven, and the likeness of the floor thereof was
as a spider spinneth, in the fashion of a shield.
And when the foundation was laid, I beheld, and
from that spring there was stirred up as it were a
boiling froth, and behold, it changed itself as it were
into another foundation ; and between the two
foundations, even the upper and the lower, there
drew near out of the light of the invisible place
as it were forms of men, and they walked to and
fro : and behold, a voice saying : These shall be for
a foundation unto men and they shall dwell therein
7000 years.   9. And the lower foundation was a
pavement and the upper was of froth, and they
that came forth out of the light of the invisible
place, they are those that shall dwell therein, and

αἴθριον (9³, 10⁴); *imagines hominum* with ὁμοίωμα ἀνθρώπου
(1⁹); *similitudo* with ὁμοίωσισ (1¹⁰); *ecce uox dicens* with ἰδοὺ
φωνὴ ὑπεράνωθεν τοῦ στερεώματοσ (1²⁵).

9. *they are those that shall dwell therein, and the name of*

the name of that man is <Adam>. And it shall
be, when he hath (*or* they have) sinned against
me and the time is fulfilled, that the spark shall be
quenched and the spring shall cease, and so they
shall be changed.

10. And it came to pass after Cenez had spoken
these words that he awaked and his sense returned
unto him: but he knew not that which he had
spoken neither that which he had seen, but this
only he said to the people: If the rest of the Cf. Num.
righteous be such after they are dead, it is better 23^{10}
for them to die to the corruptible world, that they
see not sin. And when Cenez had so said, he died
and slept with his fathers, and the people mourned
for him 30 days.

XXIX. And after these things the people appointed Zebul ruler over them, and at that time he
gathered the people together and said unto them:
Behold now, we know all the labour wherewith Cf. Num.
Cenez laboured with us in the days of his life. 36
Now if he had had sons, they should have been
princes over the people, but inasmuch as his
daughters are yet alive, let them receive a greater
inheritance among the people, because their father
in his life refused to give it unto them, lest he

that man is *. A puts an asterisk after "dwell therein" as
well as at the end of the sentence. VR read: *these are they
which shall have the name of that man: qui habebunt nomen
eius hominis.* J says "and the light which is between them
and illumines the path of man is Jerusalem, and there the
men will dwell."

I do not think that any mystical name filled the blank,
or that there was any mention of a definite place, such as
Jerusalem: the lines on which the vision is drawn are too
broad to admit of this. "Adam" is the most likely supplement, if we consider the words which come next: "and it
shall be when he hath sinned against me, and the time is
fulfilled."

should be called covetous and greedy of gain.
And the people said : Do all that is right in thine
eyes. 2. Now Cenez had three daughters whose
names are these : Ethema the firstborn, the second
Pheila, the third Zelpha. And Zebul gave to the
firstborn all that was round about the land of the
Phœnicians, and to the second he gave the oliveyard of Accaron, and to the third all the tilled
land that was about Azotus. And he gave them
husbands, namely to the firstborn Elisephan, to
the second Odiel, and to the third Doel.

Cf. 2 Chr.
24⁸

3. Now in those days Zebul set up a treasury
for the Lord and said unto the people : Behold, if
any man will sanctify unto the Lord gold and
silver, let him bring it to the Lord's treasury in
Sylo : only let not any that hath stuff belonging
to idols think to sanctify it to the Lord's treasures,
for the Lord desireth not the abominations of the
accursed things, lest ye disturb the synagogue of
the Lord, for the wrath that is passed by sufficeth.
And all the people brought that which their heart
moved them *to bring*, both men and women, *even*
gold and silver. And all that was brought was
weighed, *and it was* 20 talents of gold, and 250
talents of silver. 4. And Zebul judged the people
twenty and five years. And when he had accomplished his time, he sent and called all the people
and said : Lo, now I depart to die. Look ye to the
testimonies which they that went before us testified,
and let not your heart be like unto the waves of
the sea, but like as the wave of the sea understandeth not save only those things which are in
the sea, so let your heart also think upon nothing

XXIX. 2. The giving of an inheritance to the daughters
of Kenaz is modelled on Num. 36 : the sacred treasury,
perhaps, was suggested by 2 Kings 12 ; 2 Chron. 24.

save only those things which belong unto the law. And Zebul slept with his fathers, and was buried in the sepulchre of his father.

XXX. Then had the children of Israel no man whom they might appoint as judge over them: and their heart fell away, and they forgot the promise, and transgressed the ways which Moses and Jesus the servants of the Lord had commanded them, and were led away after the daughters of the Amorites, and served their gods. 2. And the Lord was wroth with them, and sent his angel and said: Behold, I chose me one people out of all the tribes of the earth, and I said that my glory should abide with them in this world, and I sent unto them Moses my servant, to declare unto them my great majesty and my judgements, and they have transgressed my ways. Now therefore behold I will stir up their enemies and they shall rule over them, and then shall all *the* people[s] say: Because we have transgressed the ways of God and of our fathers, therefore are these things come upon us. Yet there shall a woman rule over them which shall give them light 40 years. Jud. 2¹

3. And after these things the Lord stirred up against them Jabin king of Asor, and he began to fight against them, and he had as captain of his might Sisara, who had 8000 chariots of iron. And he came unto the mount Effrem and fought against the people, and Israel feared him greatly, and the people could not stand all the days of Sisara. 4˙

4. And when Israel was brought very low, all the children of Israel gathered together with one accord unto the mount of Juda and said: We did call ourselves blessed more than *all* people, and now, lo, we are brought so low, more than all nations, that we cannot dwell in our land, and our enemies bear rule over us. And now who hath done all this

unto us? Is it not our iniquities, because we have
forsaken the Lord God of our fathers, and have
walked in those things which could not profit us?
Now therefore come let us fast seven days, both
men and women, and from the least (*sic*) even to the
sucking child. Who knoweth whether God will be
reconciled unto his inheritance, that he destroy not
the planting of his vineyard?

5. And after the people had fasted 7 days,
sitting in sackcloth, the Lord sent unto them
on the 7th day Debbora, who said unto them : Can
the sheep that is appointed to the slaughter answer
before him that slayeth it, when both he that
slayeth <. . .> and he that is slain keepeth
silence, when he is sometimes provoked against it?
Now ye were born to be a flock before our Lord.
And he led you into the height of the clouds, and
subdued angels beneath your feet, and appointed
unto you a law, and gave you commandments by
prophets, and chastised you by rulers, and shewed
you wonders not a few, and for your sake commanded the luminaries and they stood still in the
places where they were bidden, and when your
enemies came upon you he rained hailstones upon
them and destroyed them, and Moses and Jesus
and Cenez and Zebul gave you commandments.
And ye have not obeyed them. 6. For while they
lived, ye shewed yourselves as it were obedient
unto your God, but when they died, your heart
died also. And ye became like unto iron that is
thrust into the fire, which when it is melted by the
flame becometh as water, but when it is come out
of the fire returneth unto its hardness. So ye also,
while they that admonish you burn you, do show

XXX. 5. *Can the sheep*, etc. Something is wrong with
this sentence. I suggest that words are wanting after
occidit. See the App. on Readings.

the effect, and when they are dead ye forget all things. 7. And now, behold, the Lord will have compassion upon you this day, not for your sakes, but for his covenant's sake which he made with your fathers and for his oath's sake which he sware, that he would not forsake you for ever. But know ye that after my decease ye will begin to sin in your latter days. Wherefore the Lord will perform marvellous things among you, and will deliver your enemies into your hands. For your fathers are dead, but God, which made a covenant with them, is life.

XXXI. And Debbora sent and called Barach and said to him: Arise and gird up thy loins as a man, and go down and fight against Sisara. For I see the constellations greatly moved in their ranks and preparing to fight for you. I see also Jud. 5²⁰ the lightnings unmoveable in their courses, and setting forth to stay the wheels of the chariots of them that boast in the might of Sisara, who saith: I will surely go down in the arm of my might to fight against Israel, and will divide the spoil of them among my servants, and their fair women will I take unto me for concubines. Therefore hath the Lord spoken concerning him that the arm of a weak woman shall overcome him, and maidens shall take his spoil, and he also himself shall fall into the hands of a woman.

2. And when Debbora and the people and Barach went down to meet their enemies, immediately the Lord disturbed the goings of his stars, and spake unto them saying: Hasten and go ye, for our (*or* your) enemies fall upon you: confound their arms and break the strength of their

XXXI. 1, etc. *The stars fighting.* Cf. *Pirke R. Eliezer* 52: Joshua, when fighting, saw the magicians of Egypt compelling the constellations to come against Israel.

hearts, for I am come that my people may prevail. For though it be that my people have sinned, yet will I have mercy on them. And when this was said, the stars went forth as it was commanded them and burned up their enemies. And the number of them that were gathered (*or* burned) and slain in one hour was 90 times 97,000 men. But Sisara they destroyed not, for so it was commanded them.

Jud. 4¹⁷

3. And when Sisara had fled on his horse to deliver his soul, Jahel the wife of Aber the Cinean decked herself with her ornaments and came out to meet him : now the woman was very fair : and when she saw him she said : Come in and take food, and sleep : and in the evening I will send my servants with thee, for I know that thou wilt remember me and recompense me. And Sisara came in, and when he saw roses scattered upon the bed he said : If I be delivered, O Jahel, I will go unto my mother and thou shalt (*or* Jahel shall) be my wife. 4. And thereafter was Sisara athirst and he said to Jahel : Give me a little water, for I am faint and my soul burneth by reason of the flame which I beheld in the stars. And Jahel said unto him : Rest a little while and then thou shalt drink. 5. And when Sisara was fallen asleep, Jahel went to the flock and milked milk therefrom. And as she milked she said : Behold now, remember, O Lord, when thou didst divide every tribe and nation upon the earth, didst thou not choose out Israel only, and didst not liken him to any beast save only unto the ram that goeth before the flock and leadeth it ? Behold therefore and see how Sisara hath thought *in his heart* saying : I will go and punish the flock of the Most Mighty. And lo, I will take of the milk of the beasts whereunto thou didst liken thy people, and will go and

give him to drink, and when he hath drunk he shall become weak, and after that I will kill him. And this shall be the sign that thou shalt give me, O Lord, that, whereas Sisara sleepeth, when I go in, if he wake and ask me forthwith, saying : Give me water to drink, *then* I *shall* know that my prayer hath been heard.

6. So Jahel returned and entered in, and Sisara awaked and said to her : Give me to drink, for I burn mightily and my soul is inflamed. And Jahel took wine and mingled it with the milk and gave him to drink, and he drank and fell asleep. Jud. 4¹⁹

7. But Jahel took a stake in her left hand and drew near unto him saying : If the Lord give me this sign I *shall* know that Sisara shall fall into my hands. Behold I will cast him upon the ground from off the bed whereon he sleepeth, and it shall be, if he perceive it not, that I shall know that he is delivered up. And Jahel took Sisara and pushed him from off the bed upon the earth, but he perceived it not, for he was exceeding faint. And Jahel said : Strengthen in me, O Lord, mine arm this day for thy sake and thy people's sake, and for them that put their trust in thee. And Jahel took the stake and set it upon his temple and smote with the hammer. And as he died Sisara said to Jahel : Lo, pain hath come upon me, Jahel, and I die like a woman. And Jahel said unto him : Go boast thyself before thy father in hell, and tell him that thou hast fallen into (*or* say, I have been delivered into) the hands of a woman. And she made an end and slew him and laid his body *there* until Barach should return. Judith 13⁹ · 13⁷ · Jud. 4²¹

8. Now the mother of Sisara was called Themech, and she sent unto her friends saying : Come, let us 5²⁸

go forth together to meet my son, and ye shall see the daughters of the Hebrews whom my son will bring hither to be his concubines.

Jud 4²²
9. But Barach returned from following after Sisara and was greatly vexed because he found him not, and Jahel came forth to meet him, and said: Come, enter in, thou blessed of God, and I will deliver thee thine enemy whom thou followedst after and hast not found. And Barach went in and found Sisara dead, and said: Blessed be the Lord which sent his spirit and said: Into the hands of a woman shall Sisara be delivered. And when he had so said he cut off the head of Sisara and sent it unto his mother, and gave her a message saying: Receive thy son whom thou didst look for to come with spoil.

5¹
XXXII. *Then Debbora and Barach the son of Abino* and all the people together *sang* an hymn unto the Lord *in that day, saying:* Behold, from on high hath the Lord shewn unto us his glory, even as he did aforetime when he sent forth his voice to confound the tongues of men. And he chose out our nation, and took Abraham our father out of the fire, and chose him before all his brethren, and kept him from the fire and delivered him from the bricks of the building of the tower, and gave him a son in the latter days of his old age, and brought him out of the barren womb, and all the angels were jealous against him, and the orderers of the hosts envied him. 2. And it came to pass, when they were jealous against him, God said unto him: Slay for me the fruit of thy belly and offer for my

XXXII. 1, 2. The angels were jealous of Abraham. In *Jubilees* it is the adversary Mastema who suggests the sacrifice of Isaac: in *Pirke R. Eliezer* the ministering angels intercede for Isaac. I have not found the statement of our text elsewhere.

sake that which I gave thee. And Abraham did not gainsay him and set forth immediately. And as he went forth he said to his son: Lo, now, my son, I offer thee for a burnt offering and deliver thee into his hands who gave thee unto me. 3. And the son said to his father: Hear me, father. If a lamb of the flock is accepted for an offering to the Lord for an odour of sweetness, and if for the iniquities of men sheep are appointed to the slaughter, but man is set to inherit the world, how then sayest thou now unto me: Come and inherit a life secure, and a time that cannot be measured? What and if I had not been born in the world to be offered a sacrifice unto him that made me? And it shall be my blessedness beyond all men, for there shall be no other *such thing;* and in me shall the generations be instructed, and by me the peoples shall understand that the Lord hath accounted the soul of a man worthy to be a sacrifice unto him. 4. And when his father had offered him upon the altar and had bound his feet to slay him, the Most Mighty hasted and sent forth his voice from on high saying: Kill not thy son, Gen. 22^{12} neither destroy the fruit of thy body: for now have I showed forth *myself* that I might appear to them that know me not, and have shut the mouths of them that always speak evil against thee. And thy memorial shall be before me for ever, and thy name and the name of this *thy son* from one generation to another.

5. And to Isaac he gave two sons, which also were from a womb shut up, for at that time their mother was in the third year of her marriage. And it shall not be so with any other woman, neither shall any wife boast herself so, that cometh near to her husband in the third year. And there were born to him two sons, even Jacob and Esau. And

God loved Jacob, but Esau he hated because of his deeds.

6. And it came to pass in the old age of their father, that Isaac blessed Jacob and sent him into Mesopotamia, and there he begat 12 sons, and they went down into Egypt and dwelled there.

7. And when their enemies dealt evilly with them, the people cried unto the Lord, and their prayer was heard, and he brought them out thence, and led them unto the mount Sina, and brought forth unto them the foundation of understanding which he had prepared from the birth of the world ; and then the foundation was moved, the hosts sped forth the lightnings upon their courses, and the winds sounded out of their storehouses, and the earth was stirred from her foundation, and the mountains and the rocks trembled in their fastenings, and the clouds lifted up their waves against the flame of the fire that it should not consume the world. 8. Then did the depth awake from his springs, and all the waves of the sea came together. Then did Paradise give forth the breath of her fruits, and the cedars of Libanus were moved from their roots. And the beasts of the field were terrified in the dwellings of the forests, and all his works gathered together to behold the Lord when he ordained a covenant with the children of Israel. And all things that the Most Mighty said, these hath he observed, having for witness Moses his beloved.

9. And when he was dying *God* appointed unto him the firmament, and shewed him these witnesses whom now we have, saying : Let the heaven where-

---

9. *appointed unto him the firmament: Disposuit ei firmamentum.* Perhaps the meaning is "displayed the firmament arranged in its order."

into thou hast entered and the earth wherein thou hast walked until now be a witness between me and thee and my people. For the sun and the moon and the stars shall be ministers unto us (*or* you).

10. And when Jesus arose to rule over the people, it came to pass in the day wherein he fought against the enemies, that the evening drew near, while yet the battle was strong, and Jesus said to the sun and the moon : O ye ministers that were appointed between the Most Mighty and his sons, lo now, the battle goeth on still, and do ye forsake your office? Stand still therefore to-day and give light unto his sons, and put darkness upon our enemies. And they did so.

11. And now in these days Sisara arose to make us *his* bondmen, and we cried unto the Lord our God, and he commanded the stars and said: Depart out of your ranks, and burn mine enemies, that they may know my might. And the stars came down and overthrew their camp and kept us safe without any labour.

12. Therefore will we not cease to sing praises, neither shall our mouths keep silence from telling of his marvellous works : for he hath remembered his promises both new and old, and hath shown us his deliverance : and therefore doth Jahel boast herself among women, because she alone hath brought this good way to success, in that with her own Judith 13[20] hands she slew Sisara.

13. O earth, go thou, go, ye heavens and lightnings, go, ye angels and hosts, [go ye] and tell the fathers in the treasure-houses of their souls, and say : The Most Mighty hath not forgotten the least of all the promises which he made with us, saying : Many wonders will I perform for your sons. And now from this day forth it shall be

M

known that whatsoever God hath said unto men that he will perform, he will perform it, even though man die. 14. Sing praises, sing praises, O Debbora (*or*, if man delay to sing praises to God, yet sing thou, O Debbora), and let the grace of an holy spirit awake in thee, and begin to praise the works of the Lord : for there shall not again arise such a day, wherein the stars shall bear tidings and overcome the enemies of Israel, as it was commanded them. From this time forth if Israel fall into a strait, let him call upon these his witnesses together with their ministers, and they shall go upon an embassy to the most High, and he will remember this day, and will send a deliverance to his covenant. 15. And thou, Debbora, begin to speak of that thou sawest in the field : how that the people walked and went forth safely, and the stars fought on their part (*or*, how that, like peoples walking, so went forth the stars and fought). Rejoice, O land, over them that dwell in thee, for in thee is the knowledge of the Lord which buildeth his stronghold in thee. For it was of right that God took out of thee the rib of him that was first formed, knowing that out of his rib Israel should be born. And thy forming shall be for a testimony of what the Lord hath done for his people.

16. Tarry, O ye hours of the day, and hasten not onward, that we may declare that which our understanding can bring forth, for night will come upon us. And it shall be like the night when God smote the firstborn of the Egyptians for the sake of his firstborn. 17. And then shall I cease from my hymn because the time will be hastened (*or* prepared) for his righteous ones. For I will sing unto him as in the renewing of the creation, and the people shall remember this deliverance, and it

shall be for a testimony unto them. Let the sea also bear witness, with the deeps thereof, for not only did God dry it up before the face of our fathers, but he did also overthrow the camp from its setting and overcame our enemies.

18. And when Debbora made an end of her words she went up with the people together unto Silo, and they offered sacrifices and burnt offerings and sounded upon the broad trumpets. And when they sounded and had offered the sacrifices, Debbora said: This shall be for a testimony of the trumpets between the stars and the Lord of them.

XXXIII. And Debbora went down thence, and judged Israel 40 years. And it came to pass when the day of her death drew near, that she sent and gathered all the people and said unto them: Hearken now, my people. Behold, I admonish you as a woman of God, and give you light as one of the race of women; obey me now as your mother, and give ear to my words, as men that shall yourselves die. 2. Behold, I depart to die by the way of all flesh, whereby ye also shall go: only direct your heart unto the Lord your God in the time of your life, for after your death ye will not be able to repent of those things wherein ye live. 3. For death is now sealed up, and accomplished, and the measure and the time and the years have restored that which was committed to them. For even if ye seek to do evil in hell after your death, ye will not be able, because the desire of sin shall cease, and the evil creation shall lose its power, and hell,

18. *on the broad trumpets: de latis psalphingis.* Can this be meant to render ἐν σάλπιγξιν ἐλαταῖσ (Ps. 97⁷)?

XXXIII. 3. *the evil creation: plasmatio iniqua.* The equivalent of the *yetzer hara'*, the evil tendency, of Rabbinic theology.

which receiveth that that is committed to it, will not restore it unless it be demanded by him that committed it. Now, therefore, my sons, obey ye my voice while ye have the time of life and the light of the law, *and* direct your ways. 4. And when Debbora spake these words, all the people lifted up their voice together and wept, saying: Behold now, mother, thou diest and forsakest thy sons; and to whom dost thou commit them? Pray thou, therefore, for us, and after thy departure thy soul shall be mindful of us for ever. 5. And Debbora answered and said to the people : While a man yet liveth he can pray for himself and for his sons; but after his end he will not be able to entreat nor to remember any man. Therefore, hope not in your fathers, for they will not profit you unless ye be found like unto them. But then your likeness shall be as the stars of the heaven, which have been manifested unto you at this time.

4 Esd. 7
102-4

6. And Debbora died and slept with her fathers and was buried in the city of her fathers, and the people mourned for her 70 days. And as they bewailed her, thus they spake a lamentation, saying : Behold, a mother is perished out of Israel, and an holy one that bare rule in the house of Jacob, which made fast the fence about her generation, and her generation shall seek after her. And after her death the land had rest seven years.

XXXIV. And at that time there came up a certain Aod of the priests of Madian, and he was a wizard, and he spake unto Israel, saying : Wherefore give ye ear to your law ? Come and I

XXXIV. Aod reminds us of the traditional Antichrist, one of whose great feats will be to make the sun appear at night : *Ascension of Isaiah* (4[5]) : " and at his word the sun will shine at night."

will shew you such a thing as your law is not. And the people said : What canst thou shew us that our law hath not ? And he said to the people : Have ye ever seen the sun by night ? And they said : Nay. And he said : Whensoever ye will, I will shew it unto you, that ye may know that our gods have power, and will not deceive them that serve them. And they said : Shew us. 2. And he departed and wrought with his magic, commanding the angels that were set over sorceries, because for a long time he did sacrifice unto them. 3. *⟨For this was formerly in the power of the angels and was⟩ performed by* the angels before they were judged, and they would have destroyed the unmeasurable world; and because they transgressed, it came to pass that the angels had no longer the power. For when they were judged, then the power was not committed unto the rest : and by these *signs* (or *powers*) do they work who minister unto men in sorceries, until the unmeasurable age shall come. 4. And at that time Aod by art magic shewed unto the people the sun by night. And the people were astonished and said : Behold, what great things can the gods of the Madianites do, and we knew it not ! 5. And God, willing to try Israel whether they were yet in iniquity, suffered *the angels*, and their work had good success, and the people of Israel were deceived and began to serve the gods of the Madianites. And God said : I will deliver them into the hands of the Madianites, inasmuch as by them are they

3. The sentences about the angels who preside over sorceries are somewhat obscure. They depend upon the story, told at such length in *Enoch*, of the fallen angels who made known secret arts to mankind. The powers possessed by these were not conferred upon those who replaced them.

deceived. And he delivered them into their hands, and the Madianites began to bring Israel into bondage.

XXXV. Now Gedeon was the son of Joath, the most mighty man among all his brethren. And when it was the time of summer, he came to the

Jud. 6¹¹

mountain, having sheaves with him, to thresh them there, and escape from the Madianites that pressed upon him. And the angel of the Lord met him, and said unto him: Whence comest thou and where is thine entering in? 2. He said to him: Why askest thou me whence I come? for straitness encompasseth me, for Israel is fallen into affliction, and they are verily delivered into the hands of the Madianites. And where are the wonders which our fathers have told us, saying: The Lord chose Israel alone before all the peoples of the earth? Lo, now he hath delivered us up, and hath forgotten the promises which he made to our fathers. For we should have chosen rather to be delivered unto death once for all, than that his people should be punished thus time after time. 3. And the angel of the Lord said unto him: It is not for nothing that ye are delivered up, but your own inventions have brought these things upon you, for like as ye have forsaken the promises which ye received of the Lord, these evils are come upon you, and ye have not been mindful of the commandments of God, which they commanded you that were before you. Therefore are ye come into the displeasure of your God. But he will have mercy upon you, as no man hath mercy, *even* upon the race of Israel, and that not for your sakes, but because of them that are fallen asleep. 4. And now come, I will send thee, and thou shalt deliver Israel out of the hand of the Madianites. For thus saith the Lord: Though Israel be not righteous, yet because the Madianites are sinners, therefore, knowing the iniquity of my people, I will forgive them, and after that I will rebuke them for that they have done evil, but upon the Madianites I will be avenged presently. 5. And Gedeon said : Who Jud. 6¹⁵ am I and what is my father's house, that I should go against the Madianites to battle? And the angel said unto him : Peradventure thou thinkest that as is man's way so is the way of God. For men look upon the glory of the world and upon riches, but God looketh upon that which is upright *and* good, and upon meekness. Now therefore go, gird up thy loins, and the Lord shall be with thee, for thee hath he chosen to take vengeance of his enemies, like as, behold, he hath bidden thee. 6. And Gedeon said to him : *Let not my Lord be* Gen. 18³⁰ *wroth if I speak* a word. Behold, Moses, the first of all the prophets, besought the Lord for a sign, and it was given him. But who am I, except the Lord that hath chosen me give me a sign that I may know that I go aright. And the angel of the Lord said unto him : Run and take for me water out of the pit yonder and pour it upon this rock, and I will give thee a sign. And he went and took it as he commanded him. 7. And the angel said unto him : Before thou pour the water upon the rock, ask what thou Jud. 6²¹ wouldst have it to become, either blood, or fire, or that it appear not at all. And Gedeon said : Let it become half of it blood and half fire. And Gedeon poured out the water upon the rock, and it came to pass when he had poured it out, that the half part became flame, and the half part blood, and they were mingled together, that is, the fire and the blood, yet the blood did not quench the fire, neither did the fire consume the blood. And when Gedeon saw that, he asked for yet other signs, and they were given him. Are not these written in the book of the Judges?

XXXVI. And Gedeon took 300 men and departed and came unto the uttermost part of the camp of Madian, and he heard every man speaking to his neighbour and saying: Ye shall see a confusion above reckoning, of the sword of Gedeon, coming upon us, for God hath delivered into his hands the camp of the Madianites, and he will begin to make an end of us, even the mother with the children, because our sins are filled up, even as also our gods have shewed us and we believed them not. And now arise, let us succour our souls and fly. 2. And when Gedeon heard these words, immediately he was clothed with the spirit of the Lord, and, being endued with power, he said unto the 300 men : Arise and let every one of you gird on his sword, for the Madianites are delivered into our hands. And the men went down with him, and he drew near and began to fight. And they blew the trumpet and cried out together and said : The sword of the Lord is upon us. And they slew of the Madianites about 120,000 men, and the residue of the Madianites fled.

3. And after these things Gedeon came and gathered the people of Israel together and said unto them : Behold, the Lord 'sent me to fight your battle, and I went according as he commanded me. And now I ask one petition of you : turn not away your face ; and let every man of you give me the golden armlets which ye have on your hands. And Gedeon spread out a coat, and every man cast upon it their armlets, and they were all weighed, and the weight of them was found to be 12 talents (*or* 12,000 shekels). And Gedeon took them, and of them he made idols and worshipped them. 4. And God said : One way is *verily* ap-

Jud. 7[11]

7[20]

8[24]

pointed, that I should not rebuke Gedeon in his life-
time, even because when he destroyed the sanctuary of Baal, then all men said : Let Baal avenge
himself.   Now, therefore, if I chastise him for that
he hath done evil against me, ye will say : It was
not God that chastised him, but Baal, because he
sinned aforetime against him.   Therefore now shall
Gedeon die in a good old age, that they may not
have whereof to speak.   But after that Gedeon is
dead I will punish him once, because he hath transgressed against me.   And Gedeon died in a good
old age and was buried in his own city.

XXXVII. And he had a son by a concubine
whose name was Abimelech ; the same slew all his
brethren, desiring to be ruler over the people.   Jud. 9⁵

[*A leaf gone.*]

2. Then all the trees of the field came together 9⁷ *sqq.*
unto the fig-tree and said : Come, reign over us.
And the fig-tree said : Was I indeed born in the
kingdom or in the rulership over the trees? or was
I planted to that end that I should reign over you?
And therefore even as I cannot reign over you,
neither shall Abimelech obtain continuance in his
rulership.   After that the trees came together unto
the vine and said : Come, reign over us.   And the

XXXVI. 4. *One way is verily appointed : Una uia posita
est, ut.* I understand this to mean : " This at least is clear,"
but others may be able to suggest a better interpretation.

XXXVII. 2 *seq.* This adaptation of the parable of
Jotham is singularly inept as it stands : possibly the lost
beginning of it may have made it more plausible : possibly
it may contain plays upon Hebrew words which I do not
detect. Two sentences in it are particularly obscure : (1)
Nascente spina, ueritas in specie praelucebat. Can there be
here an allusion to Ps. 84 (85)¹², ἀλήθεια ἐκ τῆσ γῆσ ἀνέτειλε ?
(2) *quia malus facta est in castigatores, et ficus facta est in
populum, et uinea facta est in praecessores.* Ought we to
render *facta est* by " stands for " or " represents "?

vine said: I was planted to give unto men the
sweetness of wine, and I am preserved by rendering
unto them my fruit. But like as I cannot reign over
you, so shall the blood of Abimelech be required
at your hand. And after that the trees came unto
the apple and said: Come, reign over us. And he
said: It was commanded me to yield unto men
a fruit of sweet savour. Therefore I cannot reign
over you, and Abimelech shall die by stones.
3. Then came the trees unto the bramble and
said: Come, reign over us. And the bramble
said: When the thorn was born, truth did shine
forth in the semblance of a thorn. And when our
first father was condemned to death, the earth
was condemned to bring forth thorns and thistles.
And when the truth enlightened Moses, it was by
a thorn bush that it enlightened him. Now therefore it shall be that by me the truth shall be heard
of you. Now if ye have spoken in sincerity unto
the bramble that it should in truth reign over you,
sit ye under the shadow of it: but if with dis-
sembling, then let fire go forth and devour and
consume the trees of the field. For the apple-tree
was made for the chastisers, and the fig-tree was
made for the people, and the vine[yard] was made
for them that were before us.

4. And now shall *the bramble* be unto you
even as Abimelech, which slew his brethren with
wrong, and desireth to rule over you. If Abimelech
be worthy of them (*or* Let Abimelech be a fire
unto them) whom he desireth to rule, let him be
as the bramble which was made to rebuke the
foolish among the people. And there went forth
fire out of the bramble and devoured the trees that
are in the field.

5. After that Abimelech ruled over the people
for one year and six months, and he died hard by

a certain tower, whence a woman cast down upon Jud. 9¹⁰ˢᵟᵟ.
him the half of a millstone.

[A gap of uncertain length in the text.]

XXXVIII. (Then did Jair judge Israel 22 years.)   10³
The same built a sanctuary to Baal, and led the
people astray saying : Every man that sacrificeth
not unto Baal shall die.   And when all the people
sacrificed, seven men only would not sacrifice
whose names are these : Dephal, Abiesdrel, Geta-
libal, Selumi, Assur, Jonadali, Memihel.   2. The
same answered and said unto Jair : Behold, we
remember the precepts which they that were before
us commanded us, and Debbora our mother, saying :
Take heed that ye turn not away your heart to the
right hand or to the left, but attend unto the law of
the Lord day and night.   Now therefore why dost
thou corrupt the people of the Lord and deceive
them, saying : Baal is God, let us worship him ?   And
now if he be God as thou sayest, let him speak as a
God, and then we will sacrifice unto him.   3. And
Jair said : Burn them with fire, for they have blas-
phemed Baal.   And his servants took them to burn
them with fire.   And when they cast them upon
the fire there went forth Nathaniel, the angel which
is over fire, and quenched the fire and burned up
the servants of Jair : but the seven men he made
to escape, so that no man of the people saw them,
for he had smitten the people with blindness.
4. And when Jair came to the place (*or* it came
to the place of Jair) he also was burned.   But
before he burned him, the angel of the Lord said
unto him : Hear the word of the Lord before thou
diest.   Thus saith the Lord : I raised thee up out

XXXVIII.   It is not clear why Jair is selected for the
part of an apostate and idolatrous judge.   The story of
the Three Children (Dan. 3), and perhaps also those of
the Maccabæan martyrs, have been in the writer's mind.

of the land of Egypt, and appointed thee ruler over my peoples. But thou hast risen and corrupted my covenant, and hast led them astray, and hast sought to burn my servants in the flame, because they reproved thee, which though they be burned with corruptible fire, yet now are they quickened with living fire and are delivered. But thou shalt die, saith the Lord, and in the fire wherein thou shalt die, therein shalt thou have thy dwelling. And thereafter he burned him, and came even unto the pillar of Baal and overthrew it, and burned up Baal with the people that stood by, even 1000 men.

XXXIX. And after these things came the children of Ammon and began to fight against Israel and took many of their cities. And when the people were greatly straitened, they gathered together in Masphath, saying every man to his neighbours: Behold now, we see the strait which encompasseth us, and the Lord is departed from us, and is no more with us, and our enemies have taken our cities, and there is no leader to go in and out before our face. Now therefore let us see whom we may set over us to fight our battle.

2. *Now Jepthan the Galaadite was a mighty man of valour,* and because he was jealous of his brothers, they had cast him out of his land, and he went and *dwelt in the land of Tobi. And vagrant men gathered themselves unto him* and abode with him.

3. And it came to pass when Israel was overcome in battle, that they came into the land of Tobi to Jepthan and said unto him: Come, rule over the people. For who knoweth whether thou wast therefore preserved to this day or wast therefore delivered out of the hands of thy brethren that thou mightest at this time bear rule over thy people? 4. And Jepthan said unto them: Doth love so return after hatred, or doth time overcome

Jud. 10$^{17, 18}$

11^1

11^3

11^5

Esther 4^{14}

all things? For ye did cast me out of my land and out of my father's house; and now are ye come unto me when ye are in a strait? And they said unto him: If the God of our fathers remembered not our sins, but delivered us when we had sinned against him and he had given us over before the face of our enemies, and we were oppressed by them, why wilt thou that art a mortal man remember the iniquities which happened unto us, in the time of our affliction? Therefore be it not so before thee, lord. 5. And Jepthan said: God indeed is able to be unmindful of our sins, seeing he hath time and place to repose himself of his long-suffering, for he is God; but I am mortal, made of the earth: whereunto I shall return, and where shall I cast away mine anger, and the wrong wherewith ye have injured me? And the people said unto him: Let the dove instruct thee, whereunto Israel was likened, for though her young be taken away from her, yet departeth she not out of her place, but spurneth away her wrong and forgetteth it as it were in the bottom of the deep.

6. And Jepthan arose and went with them and gathered all the people, and said unto them: Ye know how that when our princes were alive, they admonished us to follow our law. And Ammon and his sons turned away the people from their way wherein they walked, to serve other gods which should destroy them. Now therefore set your hearts in the law of the Lord your God, and let us entreat him with one accord. And so will we fight against our adversaries, and trust and hope in the Lord that he will not deliver us up for ever. *For* although our sins do overabound, nevertheless his mercy filleth *all* the earth.

7. And the whole people prayed with one accord, both men and women, boys and sucklings. And

when they prayed they said : Look, O Lord, upon the people whom thou hast chosen, and spoil not the vine which thy right hand hath planted ; that this people may be before thee for an inheritance, whom thou hast possessed from the beginning, and whom thou hast preferred alway, and for whose sake thou hast made the habitable places, and brought them into the land which thou swarest unto them ; deliver us not up before them that hate thee, O Lord. 8. And God repented him of his anger and strengthened the spirit of Jepthan.

Jud. 11¹⁴ And he sent a message unto Getal the king of the children of Ammon and said : Wherefore vexest thou our land and hast taken my cities, or wherefore afflictest thou us? Thou hast not been commanded of the God of Israel to destroy them that dwell in the land. Now therefore restore unto me my cities, and mine anger shall cease from thee. But if not, know that I will come up unto thee and repay thee for the former things, and recompense thy wickedness upon thine head : rememberest thou not how thou didst deal deceitfully with the people of Israel in the wilderness? And the messengers of Jepthan spake these words unto the king of the children of Ammon. 9. And Getal said : Did Israel take thought when he took the land of the Amorites? Say therefore : Know ye that now I will take from thee the remnant of thy cities and will repay thee thy wickedness and will take vengeance for the Amorites whom thou hast wronged. And Jepthan sent yet again to the king of the children of Ammon saying : Of a truth I perceive that God hath brought thee hither that I may destroy thee, unless thou rest from thine iniquity wherewith thou wilt vex Israel. And therefore I will come unto thee and show myself unto thee. For they are not, as ye say, gods which have given

you the inheritance that ye possess. But because
ye have been led astray after stones, fire shall follow
after you unto vengeance.

10. And because the king of the children of
Ammon would not hear the voice of Jepthan,
Jepthan arose and armed all the people to go forth
and fight in the borders saying : When the children   Jud. 11³¹
of Ammon are delivered into my hands and I am
returned, any that first meeteth with me shall be
for a burnt offering unto the Lord.

11. And the Lord was very wroth and said:
Behold, Jepthan hath vowed that he will offer unto
me that which meeteth with him first. Now therefore if a dog meet with Jepthan first, shall a dog
be offered unto me? And now let the vow of
Jepthan be upon his firstborn, even upon the fruit
of his body, and his prayer upon his only begotten
daughter. But I will verily deliver my people at
this time, not for his sake, but for the prayer which
Israel hath prayed.

XL. And Jepthan came and fought against the
children of Ammon, and the Lord delivered them
into his hand, and he smote threescore of their
cities. And Jepthan returned in peace. And the   11³⁴
women came out to meet him with dances. And
he had an only begotten daughter ; the same came
out first in the dances to meet her father. And
when Jepthan saw her he fainted and said : Rightly
is thy name called Seila, that thou shouldest be
offered for a sacrifice. And now who will put my
heart in the balance and weigh my soul? and I
will stand and see whether one will outweigh *the
other*, the rejoicing that is come or the affliction
which cometh upon me? for in that I have opened
my mouth unto my Lord in the song of *my* vows,

XL. 1. *Seila.* The name, according to Dr. Cohn, may
mean "she who was demanded."

I cannot call it back again. 2. And Seila his daughter said unto him : And who is it that can be sorrowful in their death when they see the people delivered? Rememberest thou not that which was in the days of our fathers, when the father set his son for a burnt offering and he gainsaid him not, but consented unto him rejoicing? And he that was offered was ready, and he that offered was glad. 3. Now therefore annul not anything of that thou hast vowed, but grant unto me one prayer. I ask of thee before I die a small request : I beseech thee that before I give up my soul, I may go into the mountains and wander (*or* abide) among the hills and walk about among the rocks, I and the virgins that are my fellows, and pour out my tears there and tell the affliction of my youth ; and the trees of the field shall bewail me and the beasts of the field shall lament for me ; for I am not sorrowful for that I die, neither doth it grieve me that I give up my soul : but whereas my father was overtaken in his vow, [and] if I offer not myself willingly for a sacrifice, I fear lest my death be not acceptable, and that I shall lose my life to no purpose. These things will I tell unto the mountains, and after that I will return. And her father said : Go. 4. And Seila the daughter of Jepthan went forth, she and the virgins that were her fellows, and came and told it to the wise men of the people. And no man could answer her words. And after that she went into the mount Stelac, and by night the Lord thought upon her, and said : Lo, now have I shut up the tongue of the wise among my people before this generation,

Jul. 11[37]

11[36]

4 *end*. The addition in R, "and when she departeth, she shall fall into the bosom of her mothers," may be genuine. "Her mothers," an unusual phrase, would correspond to the ordinary one " her (your, their) fathers."

that they could not answer the word of the daughter of Jepthan, that my word might be fulfilled, and my counsel not destroyed which I had devised : and I have seen that she is more wise than her father, and a maiden of understanding more than all the wise which are here.   And now let her life be given her at her request, and her death shall be precious in my sight at all times.

5. And when the daughter of Jepthan came unto the mount Stelac, she began to lament.   And this is her lamentation wherewith she mourned and bewailed herself before she departed, and she said : Hearken, O mountains, to my lamentation, and look, O hills, upon the tears of mine eyes, and be witness, O rocks, in the bewailing of my soul. Behold how I am accused, but my soul shall not be taken away in vain.   Let my words go forth into the heavens, and let my tears be written before the face of the firmament, that the father overcome not (*or* fight not against) his daughter whom he hath vowed to offer up, that her ruler may hear that his only begotten daughter is promised for a sacrifice.
6. Yet I have not been satisfied with my bed of marriage, neither filled with the garlands of my wedding.   For I have not been arrayed with brightness, sitting in my maidenhood ; I have not used my precious ointment, neither hath my soul enjoyed the oil of anointing which was prepared for me. O my mother, to no purpose hast thou borne thine only begotten, and begotten her upon the earth, for hell is become my marriage-chamber.   Let all the mingling of oil which thou hast prepared for me be poured out, and the white robe which my mother wove for me, let the moth eat it, and the crown of flowers which my nurse plaited for me aforetime, let it wither, and the coverlet which she wove of violet and purple for my virginity, let the

N

worm spoil it; and when the virgins, my fellows, tell of me, let them bewail me with groaning for *many* days. 7. Bow down your branches, O ye trees, and lament my youth. Come, ye beasts of the forest, and trample upon my virginity. For my years are cut off, and the days of my life are waxen old in darkness.

Jud. 11³⁹

8. And when she had so said, Seila returned unto her father, and he did all that he had vowed, and offered burnt offerings. Then all the maidens of Israel gathered together and buried the daughter of Jepthan and bewailed her. And the children

11⁴⁰

of Israel made a great lamentation and appointed in that month, on the 14th day of the month, that they should come together every year and lament for the daughter of Jepthan four days. And they called the name of her sepulchre according to her own name Seila.

12⁷

9. And Jepthan judged the children of Israel ten years, and died, and was buried with his fathers.

12¹²

XLI. And after him there arose a judge in Israel, Addo the son of Elech of Praton, and he also judged the children of Israel eight years. In his days the king of Moab sent messengers unto him saying: Behold now, thou knowest that Israel hath taken my cities: now therefore restore them in recompense. And Addo said: Are ye not yet instructed by that which hath befallen the children of Ammon, unless peradventure the sins of Moab be filled up? And Addo sent and took of the people 20,000 men and came against Moab, and fought against them and slew of them 45,000 men. And the remnant fled before him. And Addo returned in peace and offered burnt offerings and sacrifices unto his Lord, and died, and was buried in Ephrata his city.

2. And at that time the people chose Elon and Jud. 12¹¹ made him judge over them, and he judged Israel twenty years. In those days they fought against the Philistines and took of them twelve cities. And Elon died and was buried in his city.

3. But the children of Israel forgat the Lord their God and served the gods of the dwellers in the land. Therefore were they delivered unto the Philistines and served them forty years.

XLII. Now there was a man of the tribe of 13⁹ Dan, whose name was Manue, the son of Edoc, the son of Odo, the son of Eriden, the son of Phadesur, the son of Dema, the son of Susi, the son of Dan. And he had a wife whose name was Eluma, the daughter of Remac. And she was barren and bare him no child. And when Manue her husband said to her day by day: Lo, the Lord hath shut up thy womb, that thou shouldest not bear; set me free, therefore, that I may take another wife lest I die without issue. And she said: The Lord hath not shut up me from bearing, but thee, that I should bear no fruit. And he said to her: Let the law make plain our trial. 2. And as they contended day by day and both of them were sore grieved because they lacked fruit, upon a certain night the woman went up into the upper chamber and prayed saying: Do thou, O Lord God of all flesh, reveal unto me whether unto my husband or unto me it is not given to beget children, or to whom it is forbidden or to whom allowed to bear fruit, that to whom it is forbidden, the same may mourn for his sins, because he continueth without fruit. Or if both of us be deprived, reveal this also unto us, that we may bear our sin and keep silence before thee. 3. And

XLII. 1. *Let the law make plain our trial: Experimentum nostrum manifestat (-et* P. *-abit* R) *lex.*

the Lord hearkened to her voice and sent her his angel in the morning, and said unto her: Thou art the barren one that bringeth not forth, and thou art the womb which is forbidden to bear fruit. But now hath the Lord heard thy voice and looked Jud. 13⁴,⁷ upon thy tears and opened thy womb. And behold thou shalt conceive and bear a son and shall call his name Samson, for he shall be holy unto thy Lord. But take heed that he taste not of any fruit of the vine, neither eat any unclean thing, for as himself hath said, he shall deliver Israel from the hand of the Philistines. And when the angel of the Lord had spoken these words he departed from her. 4. And she came unto her husband into the house and said unto him: Lo, I lay mine hand upon my mouth and will keep silence before thee all my days, because it was in vain that I boasted myself, and believed not thy words. For the angel of the Lord came unto me to-day, and showed me, saying: Eluma, thou art barren, but thou shalt conceive and bear a son. 5. And Manue believed not his wife. And he was ashamed and grieved and went up, he also, into the upper chamber and prayed saying: Lo, I am not worthy to hear the signs and wonders which God hath wrought in us, or to see the face of his messenger. 6. And it came to pass while he thus spake, the angel of the Lord came yet again unto his wife. Now she was in the field and Manue was in his house. And the angel said unto her: Run and call unto thine husband, for God hath accounted him worthy to hear my voice. 7. And the woman ran and called to her husband, and he hasted and came unto the angel in the field in Ammo (?), which said unto him: Go in unto thy wife and do quickly all these things. But he said to him: Yet see thou to

it, Lord, that thy word be accomplished upon thy
servant. And he said: It shall be so. 8. And   Jud. 13^{15}
Manue said unto him: If I were able, I would
persuade thee to enter into mine house and eat
bread with me, and know that when thou goest away
I would give thee gifts to take with thee that thou
mightest offer a sacrifice unto the Lord thy God.
And the angel said unto him: I will not go in
with thee into thine house, neither eat thy bread,
neither will I receive thy gifts. For if thou
offerest a sacrifice of that which is not thine, I cannot show favour unto thee. 9. And Manue built
an altar upon the rock, and offered sacrifices and
burnt offerings. And it came to pass when he   13^{19}
had cut up the flesh and laid it upon the holy
place, the angel put forth *his hand* and touched it
with the end of his sceptre. And there came forth
fire out of the rock and consumed the burnt
offerings and sacrifices. And the angel went up   13^{20}
from him with the flame of the fire. 10. But
Manue and his wife when they saw that, fell upon
their faces and said: We shall surely die, because   13^{22}
we have seen the Lord face to face. And it
sufficed *me* not that I saw him, but I did also ask
his name, knowing not that he was the minister
of God. Now the angel that came was called
Phadahel.

XLIII. And it came to pass in the time of   13^{24}
those days, that Eluma conceived and bare a son
and called his name Samson. And the Lord was
with him. And when he was begun to grow up,
and sought to fight against the Philistines, he took   15^{6}
him a wife of the Philistines. And the Philistines
burned her with fire, for they were brought very
low by Samson.

2. And after that Samson entered into (*or* was   16^{1}
enraged against) Azotus. And they shut him in

and compassed the city about and said: Behold, now is our adversary delivered into our hands. Now therefore let us gather ourselves together and succour the souls one of another. And when Samson was arisen in the night and saw the city closed in he said: Lo, now, these fleas have shut me up in their city. And now shall the Lord be with me, and I will go forth by their gates and fight against them. 3. And he went and set his left hand under the bar of the gate and shook it and threw down the gate of the wall. One of the gates he held in his right hand for a shield, and the other he laid upon his shoulders and bare it away, and because he had no sword he pursued after the Philistines with it, and killed therewith 25,000 men. And he lifted up all the purtenances of the gate and set them up on a mountain.

Jud. 15

4. Now concerning the lion which he slew, and the jawbone of the ass wherewith he smote the Philistines, and the bands which he brake off from his arms as it were of themselves, and the foxes which he caught, are not these things written in the book of the Judges?

16⁴

5. Then Samson went down unto Gerara, a city of the Philistines, and saw there an harlot whose name was Dalila, and was led away after her, and took her to him to wife. And God said: Behold, now Samson is led astray by his eyes and hath forgotten the mighty works which I have wrought with him, and is mingled with the daughters of the Philistines, and hath not considered my servant Joseph which was in a strange land and became a crown unto his brethren because he would not afflict his seed. Now therefore shall his concupiscence be a stumbling-block unto Samson, and his mingling shall be his destruction, and I will deliver him to his enemies and they

shall blind him. Yet in the hour of his death will I remember him, and will avenge him yet once upon the Philistines.

6. And after these things his wife was im- Jud. 16⁶
portunate unto him, saying unto him: Show me thy strength, and wherein is thy might. So shall I know that thou lovest me. And when Samson had deceived her three times, and she continued importunate unto him every day, the fourth time he showed her his heart. But she made him 16¹⁶ drunk, and when he slumbered she called a barber, and he shaved the seven locks of his head, and his might departed from him, for so had himself revealed unto her. And she called the Philistines, 16¹⁹ and they smote Samson, and blinded him, and put him in prison.

7. And it came to pass in the day of their 16²³ banqueting, that they called for Samson that they might mock him. And he being bound between two pillars prayed saying: O Lord God of my 16²⁶ fathers, hear me yet this once and strengthen me that I may die with these Philistines: for this sight of the eyes which they have taken from me was freely given unto me by thee. And Samson added saying: Go forth, O my soul, and be not grieved. Die, O my body, and weep not for thyself. 8. And 16²⁹ he took hold upon the two pillars of the house and shook them. And the house fell and all that was in it and slew all them that were round about it, and the number of them was 40,000 men and women. And the brethren of Samson came down 16¹³ and all his father's house, and took him and buried him in the sepulchre of his father. And he judged Israel twenty years.

XLIV. And in those days there was no 17⁶ prince in Israel: but every man did that which was pleasing in his sight.

Jud. 17²

Jos. 7²¹

2. At that time Michas arose, the son of Dedila the mother of Heliu, and he had 1000 drachms of gold and four wedges of molten gold, and 40 didrachms of silver. And his mother Dedila said unto him: My son, hear my voice and thou shalt make thee a name before thy death: take thou that gold and melt it, and thou shalt make thee idols, and they shall be to thee gods, and thou shalt become a priest to them. 3. And it shall be that whoso will inquire by them, they shall come to thee and thou shalt answer them. And there shall be in thine house an altar and a pillar built, and of that gold thou hast, thou shalt buy thee incense for burning and sheep for sacrifices. And it shall be that whoso will offer sacrifice, he shall give for sheep 7 didrachms, and for incense, if he will burn it, he shall give one didrachm of silver of *full* weight. And thy name shall be Priest, and thou shalt be called a worshipper of the gods. 4. And Michas said unto her: Thou hast well counselled me, my mother, how I may live: and now shall thy name be greater than my name, and in the last days these things shall be required of thee. 5. And Michas went and did all that his mother had commanded him. And he carved out and made for himself three images of boys, and of calves, and a lion and an eagle and a dragon and a dove. And it was so that all that were led astray came to him, and if any would ask for wives, they

XLIV. 4, 5. Images of boys, calves, lion, eagle, dragon, dove. This recalls the furniture of a sanctuary of Mithras, in which two torch-bearing youths, Mithras slaying a bull, a lion, a serpent, and a bird (not, I think, an eagle) commonly appeared.

The words *ask for* are my rendering of *interrogare pro :* perhaps *inquire concerning* would be better.

inquired of him by the dove; and if for sons, by the image of the boys: but he that would ask for riches took counsel by the likeness of the eagle, and he that asked for strength by the image of the lion: again, if they asked for men and maidens they inquired by the images of calves, but if for length of days, they inquired by the image of the dragon. And his iniquity was of many shapes, and his impiety was full of guile. 6. Therefore then, when the children of Israel departed from the Lord, the Lord said: Behold I will root out the earth and destroy all the race of men, because when I appointed great things upon mount Sina, I showed myself unto the children of Israel in the tempest and I said that they should not make idols, and they consented that they should not carve the likeness of gods. And I appointed to them they should not take my name in vain, and they chose this, even not to take my name in vain. And I commanded them to keep the sabbath day, and they consented unto me to sanctify themselves. And I said to them that they should honour their father and mother: and they promised that they would so do. And I appointed unto them not to steal, and they consented. And I bade them do no murder, and they received it, that they should not. And I commanded them not to commit adultery, and they refused not. And I appointed unto them to bear no false witness, and not to covet every man his neighbour's wife or his house or anything that is his: and they accepted it. 7. And now, whereas I spake unto them that they should not make idols, they have made the works of *all* those gods that are born of corruption by the name of *a* graven *image*. And also of them through whom all things have been corrupted. For mortal men made them, and the fire served in the melting of them: the act of men brought them forth, and hands have wrought them, and understanding contrived them. And whereas they have received them, they have taken my name in vain, and have given my name to graven images, and upon the sabbath day which they accepted, to keep it, they have wrought abominations therefrom. Because I said unto them that they should love their father and mother, they have dishonoured me their maker. And for that I said to them they should not steal, they have dealt thievishly in their understanding with graven images. And whereas I said they should not kill, they do kill them when they deceive. And when I had commanded them not to commit adultery, they have played the adulterer with their jealousy. And where they did choose not to bear false witness, they have received false witness from them whom they cast out, and have lusted after strange women. 8. Therefore, behold, I abhor the race of men, and to the end I may root out my creation, they that die shall be multiplied above the number of them that are born. For the house of Jacob is defiled with iniquities and the impieties of Israel are multiplied and I cannot [*some words lost*] wholly destroy the tribe of Benjamin, because that they first were led away after Michas. And the people of Israel also shall not be unpunished, but it shall be to them an offence for ever to the memory of all generations. 9. But Michas will I deliver unto the fire. And his mother shall pine away in his sight, living upon the earth, and worms shall issue forth out of her body. And when they shall speak one to the other, she shall say as it were a mother rebuking her son: Behold what a sin hast thou committed. And he shall answer as it were a son obedient to his mother and dealing craftily: And thou hast wrought yet greater iniquity. And the likeness of the dove which he made shall be to put out his eyes, and the likeness of the eagle shall be to shed fire from the wings of it, and the images of the boys he made shall be to scrape his sides, and for the image of the lion which he made, it shall be unto him as mighty ones tormenting him. 10. And thus will I do not only unto Michas but to all them also that sin against me. And now let the race of men know that they shall not provoke me by their own inventions. Neither unto them only that make idols shall this chastisement come, but it shall be to every man, that with what sin he hath sinned therewith shall he be judged. Therefore if they shall speak lies before me, I will command the heaven and it shall defraud them of rain. And if any will covet the goods of his neighbour, I will command death and it shall deny them the fruit of their body. And if they swear by my name falsely I will not hear their prayer. And when the soul parteth from the body, then they shall say: Let us not mourn for the things which we have suffered, but because whatsoever we have devised, that shall we also receive.

XLV. And it came to pass at that time that a certain man of the tribe of Levi came to Gabaon, and when he desired to abide there, the sun set. *Jud. 19¹*

10. The doctrine that the punishment shall be suited to the offence is perhaps first enunciated in a crude form in *Jubilees* 4³². It is a recurrent thought in the *Wisdom of Solomon*, and runs through many of the Apocalypses that describe hell. It grows out of the *lex talionis*.

Philo's treatment of the story of Micah is a noteworthy example of his freedom in dealing with the Biblical narrative. Evidently Micah is here represented as remaining in possession of his idols until his death ; there is no hint that he was deprived of them by the Danites.

And when he would enter in there, they that dwelt there suffered him not. And he said to his lad: Go on, lead the mule, and we will go to the city of Noba, peradventure they will suffer us to enter in there. And he came thither and sat in the street of the city. And no man said unto him: Come into my house. 2. But there was there a certain Levite whose name was Bethac. The same saw him and said unto him: Art thou Beel of my tribe? And he said: I am. And he said to him: Knowest thou not the wickedness of them that dwell in this city? Who counselled thee to enter in hither? Haste and go out hence, and come into my house wherein I dwell, and abide there to-day, and the Lord shall shut up their heart before us, as he shut up the men of Sodom before the face of Lot. And he entered into the city and abode there that night. 3. And all the dwellers in the city came together and said unto Bethac: Bring forth them that came unto thee this day, and if not we will burn them and thee with fire. And he went out unto them and said to them: Are not they our brethren? Let us not deal evilly with them, lest our sins be multiplied against us. And they answered: It was never so, that strangers should give commands to the indwellers. And they entered in with violence and took out him and his concubine and cast them forth, and they let the man go, but they abused his concubine until she died; for she had transgressed against her husband at one time by sinning with the Amalekites, and therefore did the Lord God deliver her into the hands of sinners.

Jud. 19¹⁵ (margin)
19²² (margin)
19²⁵ (margin)

XLV. 1, 2. As noted above, the Benjamites' crime is transferred from Gibeah to Nob.

The name Bethac occurs again in LII. 1. Hophni and Phinehas lived near the house of Bethac,

4. And when it was day Beel went out and
found his concubine dead. And he laid her upon
the mule and hasted and went out and came to
Gades. And he took her body and divided it and
sent it into *all* parts (*or* by portions) throughout
the twelve tribes, saying : These things were done
unto me in the city of Noba, for the dwellers
therein rose up against me to slay me and took
my concubine and shut me up and slew her.
And if this is pleasing before your face, keep ye
silence, and let the Lord be judge : but if ye will
avenge it, the Lord shall help you. 5. And all
the men, even the twelve tribes, were confounded.
And they gathered together unto Silo and said
every man to his neighbour : Hath such iniquity
been done in Israel ?

6. And the Lord said unto the Adversary : Seest
thou how this foolish people is disturbed ? In the
hour when they should have died, even when
Michas dealt craftily to deceive the people with
these, *that is*, with the dove and the eagle and
with the image of men and calves and of a lion and
of a dragon, then were they not moved. And
therefore because they were not provoked to anger,
let their counsel *now* be vain and their heart
moved, that they who allow evil may be consumed
as well as the sinners.

XLVI. And when it was day the people of
Israel were greatly moved and said : Let us go up
and search out the sin that is done, that the iniquity
may be taken away from us. And they spake
thus, and said : Let us inquire first of the Lord
and learn whether he will deliver our brethren into

6. *The adversary, Anticiminus.* This sudden introduction of a personage nowhere else named in the book is very
curious. That Satan (probably called Mastema in the
original, as in *Jubilees*) is meant, I do not doubt.

our hands. And if not, let us forbear. And Phinees
said unto them: Let us offer the Demonstration
and the Truth. And the Lord answered them
and said: Go up, for I will deliver them into
your hands. But he deceived them, that he might
accomplish his word.

Jud. 20[13] 2. And they went up to battle and came to the
city of Benjamin and sent messengers saying:
Send us the men that have done this wickedness
and we will spare you, but requite to every man
his evil doing. And the people of Benjamin
hardened their heart and said unto the people of
Israel: Wherefore should we deliver our brethren
unto you? If ye spare *them* not, we will even fight
20[21] against you. And the people of Benjamin came
out against the children of Israel and pursued after
them, and the children of Israel fell before them
and they smote of them 45,000 men. 3. And the
heart of the people was very sore vexed, and they
came weeping and mourning unto Silo and said:
Behold, the Lord hath delivered us up before the
dwellers in Noba. Now let us inquire of the Lord
which among us hath sinned. And they inquired
of the Lord and he said unto them: If ye will, go
up and fight, and they shall be delivered into your
hands; and then it shall be told you wherefore
ye fell before them. And they went up the
20[24] second day to fight against them. And the children of Benjamin came out and pursued after
Israel and smote of them 46,000 men. 4. And the
heart of the people was altogether melted and they
said: Hath God willed to deceive his people? or
hath he so ordained because of the evil that is
done that as well the innocent should fall as they
20[26, 28] that do evil? And when they spake thus they fell
down before the ark of the covenant of the Lord
and rent their clothes and put ashes upon their

heads, both they and Phinees the son of Eleazar the priest, which prayed and said: What is this deceit wherewith thou hast deceived us, O Lord? If it be righteous before thy face which the children of Benjamin have done, wherefore didst thou not tell us, that we might consider it? But if it was not pleasing in thy sight, wherefore didst thou suffer us to fall before them?

XLVII. And Phinees added and said: O God of our fathers, hear my voice, and tell thy servant this day if it is well done in thy sight, or if peradventure the people have sinned and thou wouldest destroy their evil, that thou mightest correct among us also them that have sinned against thee. For I remember in my youth when Jambri sinned in the days of Moses thy servant, and I verily entered in, and was zealous in my soul and lifted up both of them upon my sword, and the remnant would have risen against me to put me to death, and thou sentest thine angel and didst smite of them 24,000 men and deliver me out of their hands. 2. And now thou hast sent the eleven tribes and brought them hither saying: Go and smite them. And when they went they were delivered up. And now they say that the declarations of thy truth are lying before thee. And now, O Lord God of our fathers, hide it not from thy servant, but tell us wherefore thou hast done this iniquity against us. 3. And when the Lord saw that Phinees prayed earnestly before him, he said to him: By myself have I sworn, saith the Lord, that had I not sworn, I would not have remembered thee in that thou hast spoken, neither would I have answered you this day. And now say unto the people: Stand up and hear the word of the Lord. 4. Thus saith the Lord: There was a certain mighty lion in the midst of the forest, and unto him all the beasts committed the forest that he should guard it by his power, lest perchance other beasts should come and lay it waste. And while the lion guarded it there came beasts of the field from another forest and devoured all the young of the beasts and laid waste the fruit of their body, and the lion saw it and held his peace. Now the beasts were at peace, because they had entrusted the forest unto the lion, and perceived not that their young were destroyed. 5. And after a time there arose a very small beast of those that had committed the forest unto the lion, and devoured the least of the whelps of another very evil beast. And lo the lion cried out and stirred up all the beasts of the forest, and they fought among themselves, and every one fought against his neighbour. 6. And when many beasts were destroyed, another whelp out of another forest like unto it, saw *it*, and said : Hast thou not destroyed as many beasts? What iniquity is this, that in the beginning when many beasts and their young were destroyed unjustly by other evil beasts, and when all the beasts should have been moved to avenge themselves, seeing the fruit of their body was despoiled to no purpose, then thou didst keep silence and spakest not, but now one whelp of an evil beast hath perished, and thou hast stirred up the whole forest that all the beasts should devour one another without cause, and the forest be diminished. Now therefore thou oughtest first to be destroyed, and so the remnant be established. And when the young of the beasts heard that, they slew the lion first, and put over them the whelp in his stead, and so the rest of the beasts were subject together.

7. Michas arose and made you rich by that which he committed, both he and his mother. And there were evil things and wicked, which none devised

before them, but in his subtlety he made graven
images, which had not been made unto that day,
and no man was provoked, but ye were all led
astray, and did see the fruit of your body spoiled,
and held your peace even as that evil lion. 8. And
now when ye saw how that this man's concubine
which suffered evil, died, ye were moved all of you
and came unto me saying : Wilt thou deliver the
children of Benjamin into our hands ? Therefore
did I deceive you and said : I will deliver them
unto you. And now I have destroyed them which
then held their peace, and so will I take vengeance
on all that have done wickedly against me. But
you, go ye up now, for I will deliver them unto
you.

9. And all the people arose with one accord and
went. And the children of Benjamin came out
against them and thought that they would overcome them as heretofore. And they knew not that
their wickedness was fulfilled upon them. And
when they had come on as at first, and were pursuing after them, the people fled from the face of them
to give them place, and then they arose out of their
ambushes, and the children of Benjamin were in
the midst of them. 10. Then they which were
fleeing turned back, and the men of the city of
Noba were slain, both men and women, even 85,000
men, and the children of Israel burned the city and
took the spoils and destroyed all things with the
edge of the sword. And no man was left of the
children of Benjamin save only 600 men which fled
and were not found in the battle. And all the
people returned unto Silo and Phinees the son of
Eleazar the priest with them.

11. Now these are they that were left of the

Jud. 20^{30}

20$^{32, 36}$

20^{33}

20^{48}

XLVII. 8. *which suffered evil: iniqua gerens:* perhaps
allowed the evil, as above, XLV. 6.

O

race of Benjamin, the princes of the tribe, of ten
families whose names are these : of the 1st family :
Ezbaile, Zieb, Balac, Reindebac, Belloch ; and of the
2nd family : Nethac, Zenip, Phenoch, Demech,
Geresaraz ; and of the 3rd family : Jerimuth,
Veloth, Amibel, Genuth, Nephuth, Phienna ; and
of the 4th city : Gemuph, Eliel, Gemoth, Soleph,
Raphaph, and Doffo ; and of the 5th family :
Anuel, Code, Fretan, Remmon, Peccan, Nabath ;
and of the 6th family : Rephaz, Sephet, Araphaz,
Metach, Adhoc, Balinoc ; and of the 7th family :
Benin, Mephiz, Araph, Ruimel, Belon, Iaal, Abac ;
and (of) the (8th, 9th and) 10th family : Enophlasa,
Melec, Meturia, Meac ; and the rest of the princes
of the tribe which were left, in number threescore.

12. And at that time did the Lord requite unto
Michas and unto his mother all the things that he
had spoken. And Michas was melted with fire
and his mother was pining away, even as the Lord
had spoken concerning them.

XLVIII. At that time also Phinees laid himself down to die, and the Lord said unto him :
Behold thou hast overpassed the 120 years that
were ordained unto all men. And now arise and
go hence and dwell in the mount Danaben and
abide there many years, and I will command mine

11. The names of the Benjamite chiefs are drawn, in part
at least, from the list of the descendants of Benjamin in
1 Chron. 8, but they are so disfigured as to defy complete
identification. The divisions and the orthography are alike
incapable of being settled by the evidence before me.

XLVIII. Phinehas identified with Elijah. See the passage quoted from Origen in the Introd., p. 11. In *Pirke R.
Eliezer* the belief is stated twice : c. 29, when Elijah says :
"I have been very zealous" (1 Kings 19[10]), God says : Thou
art always zealous. Thou wast zealous in Shittim . . .
because it is said : Phinehas . . . turned my wrath away,
etc. Here also art thou zealous. c. 47. *R. Eliezer* said—

eagle and he shall feed thee there, and thou shalt 1 Kings 17¹
not come down any more unto men until the time
come and thou be proved in the time. And then 17¹
shalt thou shut the heaven, and at thy word it
shall be opened. And after that thou shalt be
lifted up into the place whither they that were
before thee were lifted up, and shalt be there until
I remember the world. And then will I bring you
and ye shall taste what is death. 2. And Phinees
went up and did all that the Lord commanded
him. Now in the days when he appointed him to
be priest, he anointed him in Silo.

3. And at that time, when he went up, then it Jud. 21¹⁶,
came to pass that the children of Israel when they etc.
kept the passover commanded the children of
Benjamin saying : Go up and take wives for yourselves by force, because we cannot give you our
daughters, for we sware in the time of our anger :
and it cannot be that a tribe perish out of Israel.
And the children of Benjamin went up and seized
for themselves wives and built Gabaon for themselves and began to dwell there.

4. And whereas in the meanwhile the children 21²⁵
of Israel were at rest, they had no prince in those
days, and every man did that which was right in
his own eyes.

5. These are the commandments and the judgments and the testimonies and the manifestations
that were in the days of the judges of Israel, before
a king reigned over them.

XLIX. And at that time the children of Israel

He called the name of Phinehas by the name of Elijah . . .
He gave him the life of this world and the life of the world
to come. In the *Quaest. Hebr. in libros Regum* it is said of
the man of God who came to Eli (1 Sam. 2) : *Hunc uirum
Dei Iudaei Phinees dicunt : quem et Eliam autumant.*
   Ye shall taste what is death : gustabitis quod est mortis.

began to inquire of the Lord, and said: Let us
all cast lots, that we may see who there is that
can rule over us like Cenez, for peradventure we
shall find a man that can deliver us from our afflic-
tions, for it is not expedient that the people should
be without a prince. 2. And they cast the lot
and found no man; and the people were greatly
grieved and said: The people is not worthy to be
heard by the Lord, for he hath not answered us.
Now therefore let us cast lots even by tribes, if
perchance God will be appeased by a multitude,
for we know that he will be reconciled unto them
that are worthy *of him*. And they cast lots by
tribes, and upon no tribe did the lot come forth.
And Israel said: Let us choose one of ourselves,
for we are in a strait, for we perceive that God
abhorreth his people, and that his soul is displeased
at us. 3. And one answered and said unto the
people, whose name was Nethez: It is not he that
hateth us, but we ourselves have made ourselves to
be hated, that God should forsake us. And therefore, even though we die, let us not forsake him,
but let us flee unto him *for refuge;* for we have
walked in our evil ways and have not known him
that made us, and therefore will our device be vain.
For I know that God will not cast us off for ever,
neither will he hate his people unto all generations:
therefore now be ye strong and let us pray yet
again and cast lots by cities, for although our sins
be enlarged, yet will his long-suffering not fail.
4. And they cast lots by cities, and the lot came
upon Armathem. And the people said: Is Armathem accounted righteous beyond all the cities of
Israel, that he hath chosen her thus before all the
cities? And every man said to his neighbour:
In that same city which hath come forth by lot
let us cast the lot by men, and let us see whom

the Lord hath chosen out of her. 5. And they cast the lot by men, and it took no man save Elchana, for upon him the lot leapt out, and the people took him and said : Come and be ruler over us. And Elchana said unto the people : I cannot be a prince over this people, neither can I judge who can be a prince over you. But if my sins have found me out, that the lot should leap upon me, I will slay myself, that ye defile me not ; for it is just that I should die for my *own* sins only and not have to bear the weight of the people.

6. And when the people saw that it was not the will of Elchana to take the leadership over them, they prayed again unto the Lord saying : O Lord God of Israel, wherefore hast thou forsaken thy people in the victory of the enemy and neglected thine heritage in the time of trouble? Behold even he that was taken by the lot hath not accomplished thy commandment; but only this *hath come about*, that the lot leapt out upon him, and we believed that we had a prince. And lo, he also contendeth against the lot. Whom shall we yet require, or unto whom shall we flee, and where is the place of our rest? For if the ordinances are true which thou madest with our fathers, saying : I will enlarge your

XLIX. 5, etc. *the lot leapt out : superuolauit.* The word, which occurs several times in these verses, indicates, I suppose, that the lot which fell upon Elkanah came out of the receptacle for lots in some unusual way. At least it does not occur in the other passages which mention the casting of lots.

6. *in the victory of the enemy : (quare) in uictoria inimicorum (dereliquisti).* It is natural to think that *in uictoria* is the Hebraism for "utterly," εἰσ νῖκοσ, and that *inimicorum* should be omitted as a gloss : but the phrase is balanced in the next clause by *et in tempore angustiae neglexisti.*

but only this hath come about, etc. : *sed solum hoc est, quod superuolauit super illum sors.*

seed, and they shall know of this, then it were better that thou saidst to us, I will cut off your seed, than that thou shouldest have no regard to our root. 7. And God said unto them: If indeed I recompensed you according to your evil deeds, I ought not to give ear unto your people; but what shall I do, because my name cometh to be called upon you? And now know ye that Elchana upon whom the lot hath fallen cannot rule over you, but it is rather his son that shall be born of him; he shall be prince over you and shall prophesy; and from henceforth there shall not be wanting unto you a prince for many years. 8. And the people said: Behold, Lord, Elchana hath ten sons, and which of them shall be a prince or shall prophesy? And God said: Not any of the sons of Phenenna can be a prince over the people, but he that is born of the barren woman whom I have given him to wife, he shall be a prophet before me, and I will love him even as I loved Isaac, and his name shall be before me for ever. And the people said: Behold now, it may be that God hath remembered us, to deliver us from the hand of them that hate us. And in that day they offered peace offerings and feasted in their orders.

L. Now [whereas] Elchana had two wives, the name of the one was Anna and the name of the other Phenenna. And because Phenenna had sons, and Anna had none, Phenenna reproached her, saying: What profiteth it thee that Elchana thine husband loveth thee? but thou art a dry tree. I know moreover that he will love me, because he delighteth to see my sons standing about him like the planting of an oliveyard. 2. And so it was, when she reproached her every day, and Anna was very sore at heart, and she feared God from her youth, it came to pass when the good day of the pass-

1 Sam. 1[2]

1[6]

Isa. 56[3]

Ps. 128[3]

over drew on, and her husband went up to do sacrifice, that Phenenna reviled Anna saying: A woman is not *indeed* beloved even if her husband love her or her beauty. Let not Anna therefore boast herself of her beauty, but he that boasteth let him boast when he seeth his seed before his face ; and when it is not so among women, even the fruit of their womb, then shall love become of no account. For what profit was it unto Rachel that Jacob loved her ? except there had been given her the fruit of her womb, *surely* his love would have been to no purpose ? And when Anna heard that, her soul was melted within her and *her eyes ran* down with tears. 3. And her husband saw ^{I Sam. I⁸} her and said: *Wherefore art thou sad, and eatest not, and why is thy heart within thee cast down ?* Is not thy behaviour better than the ten sons of Phenenna ? And Anna hearkened to him and arose after she had eaten, and came unto Silo to the house of the Lord where Heli the priest abode, whom Phinees the son of Eleazar the priest had presented as it was commanded him. 4. And Anna prayed and said: Hast not thou, O Lord, examined the heart of all generations before thou formedst the world? But what is the womb that is born open, or what one that is shut up dieth, except thou will it ? And now let my prayer go up before thee this day, lest I go down hence empty, for thou knowest my heart, how I have walked before thee from the days of my youth. 5. And Anna would not pray aloud as do all men, for she took thought at that time saying: Lest perchance I be not worthy to be heard, and it shall be that Phenenna will envy me yet more and reproach me as she daily saith: Where is thy God in whom thou trustest ? And I know that it is not she that hath

L. 3. *thy behaviour: mores tui.*

many sons that is enriched, neither she that lacketh them is poor, but whoso aboundeth in the will of God, she is enriched. For they that know for what I have prayed, if they perceive that I am not heard in my prayer, will blaspheme. And I shall not only have a witness in mine own soul, for my tears also are handmaidens of my prayers. 6. And as she prayed, Heli the priest, seeing that she was afflicted in her mind and carried herself like one drunken, said unto her: Go, put away thy wine from thee. And she said: Is my prayer so heard that I am called drunken? *Verily* I am drunken with sorrow and have drunk the cup of my weeping. 7. And Heli the priest said unto her: Tell me thy reproach. And she said unto him: I am the wife of Elchana, and because God hath surely shut up my womb, therefore I prayed before him that I might not depart out of this world unto him without fruit, neither die without leaving mine own image. And Heli the priest said unto her: Go, for I know wherefore thou hast prayed, and thy prayer is heard. 8. But Heli the priest would not tell her that a prophet was foreordained to be born of her: for he had heard when the Lord spake concerning him. And Anna came unto her house, and was consoled of her sorrow, *yet* she told no man of that for which she had prayed.

LI. And in the time of those days she conceived and bare a son and called his name Samuel, which is interpreted Mighty, according as God called his name when he prophesied of him. And Anna sat and gave suck to the child until he was two years old, and when she had weaned him, she went up with him bearing gifts in her hands, and the child was very fair and the Lord was with him. 2. And Anna set the child before the face of Heli and said unto him: This is the desire which I

1 Sam. 1¹³

1¹⁷

1²⁰

1²³

1²⁶

desired, and this is the request which I sought.
And Heli said unto her : Not thou only didst seek
it, but the people *also* prayed for this.   It is not
thy request alone, but it was promised aforetime
unto the tribes; and by this child is thy womb
justified, that thou shouldest set up prophecy before
the people, and appoint the milk of thy breasts for
a fountain unto the twelve tribes.

3. And when Anna heard that, she prayed and
said : Come ye at my voice, all ye peoples, and give
ear unto my speech, all ye kingdoms, for my mouth
is opened that I may speak, and my lips are commanded that I may sing praises unto the Lord.
Drop, O my breasts, and give forth your testimonies, for it is appointed to you to give suck.
For he shall be set up that is suckled by you, and
by his words shall the people be enlightened, and
he shall shew unto the nations their boundaries,
and his horn shall be greatly exalted. 4. And
therefore will I utter my words openly, for out of
me shall arise the ordinance of the Lord, and all
men shall find the truth.   Haste ye not to talk
proudly, neither to utter high words out of your
mouth, but delight yourselves in boasting when
the light shall come forth out of which wisdom
shall be born, that they be not called rich which
have most possessions, neither they that have
borne abundantly be termed mothers : for the
barren hath been satisfied, and she that was multiplied in sons is become empty ; 5. For the Lord
killeth with judgement, and quickeneth in mercy :
for the ungodly are in this world : therefore quickeneth he the righteous when he will, but the ungodly he will shut up in darkness.   But unto
the righteous he preserveth their light, and when
the ungodly are dead, then shall they perish, and
when the righteous are fallen asleep, then shall

1 Sam. 2¹

2³

they be delivered. And so shall all judgement endure until he be revealed which holdeth *it*. 6. Speak thou, speak thou, O Anna, and keep not silence: sing praises, O daughter of Bathuel, because of thy wonders which God hath wrought with thee. Who is Anna, that a prophet should come out of her? or who is the daughter of Bathuel, that she should bring forth a light for the peoples? Arise thou also, Elchana, and gird up thy loins. Sing praises for the signs of the Lord : For of thy son did Asaph prophesy in the wilderness saying : *Moses and Aaron among his priests and Samuel among them.* Behold the word is accomplished and the prophecy come to pass. And these things endure thus, until they give an horn unto his anointed, and power cleaveth unto the throne of his king. Yet let my son stand here and minister, until there arise a light unto this people.

Ps. 99[6]

7. And they departed thence and set forth with mirth, rejoicing and exulting in heart for all the glory that God had wrought with them. But the people went down with one accord unto Silo with timbrels and dances, with lutes and harps, and came unto Heli the priest and offered Samuel unto him, whom they set before the face of the Lord and anointed him and said : Let the prophet live among the people, and let him be long a light unto this nation.

LII. But Samuel was a very young child and knew nothing of all these things. And whilst he served before the Lord, the two sons of Heli, which walked not in the ways of their fathers, began to do wickedly unto the people and multiplied their iniquities. And they dwelt hard by the house of Bethac, and when the people came together to

1 Sam. 2[11,12]

LI. 6. The quotation of Ps. 99[6] is a curious phenomenon, comparable to the mention of Jeremiah in LVI. 6.

sacrifice, Ophni and Phinees came and provoked
the people to anger, seizing the oblations before
the holy things were offered unto the Lord.
2. And this thing pleased not the Lord, neither
the people, nor their father. And their father
spake thus unto them: What is this report 1 Sam. 2²³
that I hear of you? Know ye not that I have
received the place that Phinees committed unto
me? And if we waste that we have received,
what shall we say if he that committed it require
it again, and vex us for that which he committed
unto us? Now therefore make straight your ways,
and walk in good paths, and your deeds shall
endure. But if ye gainsay *me* and refrain not from
your evil devices, ye will destroy yourselves, and
the priesthood will be in vain, and that which was
sanctified will come to nought. And then will
they say: To no purpose did the rod of Aaron
spring up, and the flower that was born of it is
come to nothing. 3. Therefore while ye are yet   2²⁵
able, my sons, correct that ye have done ill, and
the men against whom ye have sinned will pray
for you. But if ye will not, but persist in your
iniquities, I shall be guiltless, and I shall not only
sorrow lest (*or* and now I shall not blot out these
great evils in you, lest) I hear of the day of your
death before I die, but also if this befall (*or* but
even if this befall not) I shall be clear of blame:
and though I be afflicted, ye shall nevertheless
perish. 4. And his sons obeyed him not, for the   2²⁵
Lord had given sentence concerning them that
they should die, because they had sinned: for
when *their father* said to them: Repent you of
your evil way, they said: When we grow old, then
will we repent. And for this cause it was not

LII. 4. *When we grow old we will repent.* Cf. Amon in
Apostolic Constitutions, (See Introd., p. 61.)

given unto them that they should repent when they were rebuked of their father, because they had always been rebellious, and had wrought very unjustly in despoiling Israel. But the Lord was angry with Heli.

1 Sam. 3¹,⁷ LIII. But Samuel was ministering before the Lord and knew not as yet what were the oracles of the Lord : for he had not yet heard the oracles of the Lord, for he was 8 years old. 2. But when God remembered Israel, he would reveal his words unto Samuel, and Samuel did sleep in the temple of the Lord. And it came to pass when God called unto him, that he considered first, and said : Behold now, Samuel is young that he should be (*or* though he be) beloved in my sight ; nevertheless because he hath not yet heard the voice of the Lord, neither is he confirmed unto the voice of the Most Highest, yet is he like unto Moses my servant : but unto Moses I spake when he was 80 years old, but Samuel is 8 years old. And Moses saw the fire first and his heart was afraid. And if Samuel shall see the fire now, how shall he abide it ? Therefore now shall there come unto him a voice as of a man, and not as of God. And when he understandeth, then I will speak unto him as God. 3.

3⁴,⁵ And at midnight a voice out of heaven called him : and Samuel awoke and perceived as it were the voice of Heli, and ran unto him and spake saying : Wherefore hast thou awaked me, father ? For I was afraid, because thou didst never call me in the night. And Heli said : Woe is me, can it be that an unclean spirit hath deceived my son Samuel ? And he said to him : Go and sleep, for I called thee not. Nevertheless, tell me if thou remember, how often he that called thee cried. And he said : Twice. And Heli said unto him : Say now, of whose voice wast thou aware, my son ? And he

said : Of thine, therefore ran I unto thee. 4.
And Heli said : In thee do I behold the sign that
men shall have from this day forward for ever,
that if one call unto another twice in the night or
at noonday, they shall know that it is an evil
spirit. But if he call a third time, they shall know
that it is an angel. And Samuel went away and
slept.

5. And he heard the second time a voice from 1 Sam. 3⁸
heaven, and he arose and ran unto Heli and said
unto him : Wherefore called he me, for I heard the
voice of Elchana my father? Then did Heli understand that God did begin to call him. And Heli
said : In those two voices wherewith God hath
called unto thee, he likened himself to thy father
and to thy master, but now the third time *he will
speak as* God.

6. And he said unto him : With thy right ear
attend and with thy left refrain. For Phinees the
priest commanded us, saying : The right ear
heareth the Lord by night, and the left ear an
angel. Therefore, if thou hear with thy right ear,
say thus : Speak what thou wilt, for I hear thee,   3⁹
for thou hast formed me ; but if thou hear with the
left ear, come and tell me. And Samuel went
away and slept as Heli had commanded him.

7. And the Lord added and spake yet a third   3¹⁰
time, and the right ear of Samuel was filled *with
the voice.* And when he perceived that the speech
of his father had come down unto him, Samuel
turned upon his other side, and said : If I be able,
speak, for thou hast formed me (*or* knowest well
concerning me).

8. And God said unto him : Verily I enlightened
the house of Israel in Egypt and chose unto me
at that time Moses my servant for a prophet, and
by him I wrought wonders for my people, and

avenged them of mine enemies as I would, and I took my people into the wilderness, and enlightened them as they beheld. 9. And when one tribe rose up against another tribe, saying: Wherefore are the priests alone holy? I would not destroy them, but I said unto them : Give ye every one his rod, and it shall be that he whose rod flourisheth I have chosen him for the priesthood. And when they had all given their rods as I commanded, then did I command the earth of the tabernacle that the rod of Aaron should flourish, that his line might be manifested for many days. And now they which did flourish have abhorred my holy things. 10. Therefore, lo, the days shall come that I will cut off (*lit.* stop) the flower that came forth at that time, and I will go forth against them because they do transgress the word which I spake unto my

Deut. 22²⁶ servant Moses, saying : *If thou meet with a nest, thou shalt not take the mother with the young*, therefore it shall befall them that the mothers shall die with the children, and the fathers perish with the sons.

1 Sam. 3¹⁵ 11. And when Samuel heard these words his heart was melted, and he said : Hath it thus come against me in my youth that I should prophesy unto the destruction of him that fostered me? and how then was I granted at the request of my mother? and who is he that brought me up? how hath he charged me to bear evil tidings? 12. And Samuel arose in the morning and would not tell

3¹⁷ it unto Heli. And Heli said unto him : Hear now, my son. Behold, before thou wast born God promised Israel that he would send thee unto them to prophesy. And now, when thy mother came hither and prayed, for she knew not that which had been done, I said unto her : Go forth, for that which shall be born of thee shall be a son unto me. Thus spake I unto thy mother, and thus hath the Lord directed thy way. And even if thou chasten thy nursing-father, as the Lord liveth, hide thou not from me the things that thou hast heard. 13. Then Samuel was afraid, and told him all the words that he had heard. And he said: *Can the thing formed answer him that formed it?* So also can I not answer when he will take away that which he hath given, even the faithful giver, the holy one which hath prophesied, for I am subject unto his power.

LIV. And in those days the Philistines assembled their camp to fight against Israel, and the children of Israel went out to fight with them. And when the people of Israel had been put to flight in the first battle, they said: Let us bring up the ark of the covenant of the Lord, peradventure it will fight with us, because in it are the testimonies of the Lord which he ordained unto our fathers in Oreb. 2. And as the ark went up with them, when it was come into the camp, the Lord thundered and said: This time shall be likened unto that which was in the wilderness, when they took the ark without my commandment, and destruction befel them. So also, at this time, shall the people fall, and the ark shall be taken, that I may punish the adversaries of my people because of the ark, and rebuke my people because they have sinned.

3. And when the ark was come into the battle, the Philistines went forth to meet the children of Israel, and smote them. And there was there a certain Golia, a Philistine, which came even unto the ark, and Ophni and Phinees the sons of Heli

1 Sam. 3¹⁸

Isa. 29¹⁶, etc.

1 Sam. 4¹⁻³

4⁵, ⁶

4¹⁰

LIV. 3. That Goliath was the slayer of Eli's sons, and that Saul brought the tidings to Eli, is also said in the Targum on Samuel and in the *Midrash Samuel* (Cohn).

and Saul the son of Cis held the ark. And Golia took *it* with his left hand and slew Ophni and Phinees. 4. But Saul, because he was light on his feet, fled from before him ; and he rent his clothes, and put ashes on his head, and came unto Heli the priest. And Heli said unto him : Tell me what hath befallen in the camp? And Saul said unto him : Why askest thou me these things? for the people is overcome, and God hath forsaken Israel. Yea, and the priests also are slain with the sword, and the ark is delivered unto the Philistines. 5. And when Heli heard of the taking of the ark, he said : Behold, Samuel prophesied of me and my sons that we should die together, but the ark he named not unto me. And now the testimonies are delivered up unto the enemy, and what can I more say? Behold, Israel is perished from the truth, for the judgements are taken away from him. And because Heli despaired wholly, he fell off from his seat. And they died in one day, even Heli and Ophni and Phinees his sons.

6. And Heli's son's wife sat and travailed ; and when she heard these things, all her bowels were melted. And the midwife said unto her : Be of good cheer, neither let thy soul faint, for a son is born to thee. And she said to her : Lo now is one soul born and we four die, that is, my father and his two sons and his daughter-in-law. And she called his name, Where is the glory? saying : The glory of God is perished in Israel because the ark of the Lord is taken captive. And when she had thus said she gave up the ghost.

LV. But Samuel knew nothing of all these things, because three days before the battle God sent him *away*, saying unto him : Go and look upon the place of Arimatha, there shall be thy dwelling. And when Samuel heard what had

I Sam. 4¹³
4¹⁶
4¹⁷
4¹⁸
4¹⁹
4²⁰
4²¹

befallen Israel, he came and prayed unto the Lord,
saying: Behold, now, in vain is understanding
denied unto me that I might see the destruction
of my people. And now I fear lest my days grow
old in evil and my years be ended in sorrow, for
whereas the ark of the Lord is not with me, why
should I yet live? 2. And the Lord said unto
him: Be not grieved, Samuel, that the ark is
taken away. I will bring it again, and them that
have taken it will I overthrow, and will avenge
my people of their enemies. And Samuel said:
Lo, even if thou avenge them in time, according to
thy longsuffering, yet what shall we do which die
now? And God said to him: Before thou diest
thou shalt see the end which I will bring upon
mine enemies, whereby the Philistines shall perish
and shall be slain by scorpions and by all manner
of noisome creeping things.

3. And when the Philistines had set the ark of 1 Sam. 5²⁻⁴
the Lord that was taken in the temple of Dagon
their god, and were come to enquire of Dagon
concerning their going forth, they found him fallen
on his face and his hands and feet laid before the
ark. And they went forth on the first morning,
having crucified his priests. And on the second
day they came and found as on the day before,
and the destruction was greatly multiplied among
them. 4. Therefore the Philistines gathered to- 5⁶
gether in Accaron, and said every man to his
neighbour: Behold now, we see that the destruc-

LV. The plagues that afflicted the Philistines are only
obscurely indicated. They appear to have consisted of
noxious reptiles which particularly attacked the children and
the mothers. In 9 it is said that *sedilia aurea* (ἕδρας LXX)
were offered *pro reptilibus pessimis quae exterminauerunt
eos*, whereas in the Bible these objects represented the
bubones characteristic of the plague—the "emerods" of A.V.

P

tion is enlarged among us, and the fruit of our body perisheth, for the creeping things that are sent upon us destroy them that are with child and the sucklings and them also that give suck. And they said: Let us see wherefore the hand of the Lord is strong against us. Is it for the ark's sake? for every day is our god found fallen upon his face before the ark, and we have slain our priests to no purpose once and again. 5. And the wise men of the Philistines said: Lo, now by this may we know if the Lord have sent destruction upon us for his ark's sake or if a chance affliction is come upon us for a season? 6. And now, whereas all that are with child and give suck die, and they that give suck are made childless, and they that are suckled perish, we also will take kine that give suck and yoke them to a new cart, and set the ark upon it, and shut up the young of the kine. And it shall be, if the kine indeed go forth, and turn not back to their young, we shall know that we have suffered these things for the ark's sake; but if they refuse to go, yearning after their young, we shall know that the time of our fall is come upon us. 7. And certain of the wise men and diviners answered: Assay ye not only this, but let us set the kine at the head of the three ways that are about Accaron. For the middle way leadeth to Accaron, and the way on the right hand to

5. The phrase *et* (*aut* R) *conueniens* (+ *temporarie* R) *dominatio* is unusual. *temporarie*, which seems likely to be genuine, would represent πρόσκαιροσ. I adopt the *aut* of R, and take *conueniens* to be a mistranslation of some word meaning fortuitous (from συμβαίνω or συντυγχάνω or the like): in 1 Sam. 6⁷ LXX the word used is σύμπτωμα ("it was a chance that happened to us").

7. The passage about the three roads in 7 is confused in the MSS. I have made a smooth conflate text which probably conveys the original writer's meaning.

Judæa, and the way on the left hand to Samaria. And direct ye the kine that bear the ark in the middle way. And if they set forth by the right-hand way straight unto Judæa, we shall know that of a truth the God of the Jews hath laid us waste; but if they go by those other ways, we shall know that an evil (*lit.* mighty) time hath befallen us, for now have we denied our gods. 8. And the Philistines took milch kine and yoked them to a new cart and set the ark thereon, and set them at the head of the three ways, and their young they shut up at home. And the kine, albeit they lowed and yearned for their young, went forward nevertheless by the right-hand way that leadeth to Judæa. And then they knew that for the ark's sake they were laid waste. 9. And all the Philistines assembled and brought the ark again unto Silo with timbrels and pipes and dances. And because of the noisome creeping things that laid them waste, they made seats of gold and sanctified the ark. 10. And in that plaguing of the Philistines, the number was of them that died being with child 75,000, and of the sucking children 65,000, and of them that gave suck 55,000, and of men 25,000. And the land had rest seven years.

LVI. And at that time the children of Israel required a king in their lust. And they gathered together unto Samuel, and said: Behold, now, thou art grown old, and thy sons walk not in the ways of the Lord; now, therefore, appoint a king over us to judge betwixt us, for the word is fulfilled which Moses spake unto our fathers in the wilderness, saying: Thou shalt surely appoint over thee a prince of your brethren. 2. And when Samuel heard mention of the kingdom, he was sore

1 Sam. 84, 5

Deut. 17^{15}

7. *an evil* (*lit.* mighty) *time : ualidum tempus.*

grieved in his heart, and said: Behold now I see
that there is no more (*or* not yet) for us a time of
a perpetual kingdom, neither of building the house
of the Lord our God, inasmuch as these desire a
king before the time. And now, if the Lord refuse
it altogether (*or* But even if the Lord so will), it
seemeth unto me that a king cannot be established. 3. And the Lord said unto him in the
night: Be not grieved, for I will send them a
1 Sam. 9¹⁵ king which shall lay them waste, and he himse'f
shall be laid waste thereafter. Now he that shall
come unto thee to-morrow at the sixth hour, he
it is that shall reign over them.

9¹⁻⁴ 4. And on the next day, Saul, the son of Cis, was
coming from Mount Effrem, seeking the asses of
his father; and when he was come to Armathem,
he entered in to inquire of Samuel for the asses.
Now he was walking hard by Baam, and Saul
9⁹ said unto him: Where is he that seeth? For at
that time a prophet was called Seer.· And Samuel
9¹⁶ said unto him: I am he that seeth. And he said:
Canst thou tell me of the asses of my father? for
they are lost. 5. And Samuel said unto him:
Refresh thyself with me this day, and in the
morning I will tell thee that whereof thou camest
to inquire. And Samuel said unto the Lord: Direct,
O Lord, thy people, and reveal unto me what
thou hast determined concerning them. And Saul
refreshed himself with Samuel that day and rose
in the morning. And Samuel said unto him:
Behold, know thou that the Lord hath chosen thee
to be prince over his people at this time, and hath
raised up thy ways, and thy time shall be directed.
9²¹ 6. And Saul said to Samuel: Who am I, and
what is my father's house, that my lord should
speak thus unto me? For I understand not what
thou sayest, because I am a youth. And Samuel

said to Saul: Who will grant that thy word should
come even unto accomplishment of itself, that thou
mayest live many days? but consider this, that thy
words shall be likened unto the words of a prophet,
whose name shall be Hieremias. 7. And as Saul Jer. 1⁶
went away that day, the people came unto Samuel,
saying: Give us a king as thou didst promise us.
And he said to them: Behold, the king shall come
unto you after three days. And lo, Saul came.
And there befell him all the signs which Samuel
had told him. Are not these things written in
the book of the Kings?

LVII. And Samuel sent and gathered all the 1 Sam.
people, and said unto them: Lo, ye and your king 12¹⁻⁴
are here, and I am betwixt you, as the Lord commanded me. 2. And therefore I say unto you,
before the face of your king, even as my lord Moses,
the servant of God, said unto your fathers in the
wilderness, when the synagogue of Core arose
against him: Ye know that I have not taken
aught of you, neither have I wronged any of you;
and because certain lied at that time and said, Thou
didst take, the earth swallowed them up. 3. Now,
therefore, do ye whom the Lord hath not punished
answer before the Lord and before his anointed,
if it be for this cause that ye have required a
king, because I have evil entreated you, and the
Lord shall be your witness. But if now the word
of the Lord is fulfilled, I am free, and my father's
house. 4. And the people answered: We are thy
servants and our king with us; because we are
unworthy to be judged by a prophet, therefore
said we: Appoint a king over us to judge us.

LVI. 6. *Who will grant*, etc.: *quis dabit uerbum tuum
per se uenire usque ad finem ut longaeuus sis?*
LVII. 2. A wrong turn is here given to the story of
Korah, and one inconsistent with that in XVI.

And all the people and the king wept with a great lamentation, and said: Let Samuel the prophet live. And when the king was appointed they offered sacrifices unto the Lord.

5. And after that Saul fought with the Philistines one year, and the battle prospered greatly.

I Sam. 15³ LVIII. And at that time the Lord said unto Samuel: Go and say unto Saul: Thou art sent to destroy Amalech, that the words may be fulfilled Ex. 17¹⁴ which Moses my servant spake saying: I will destroy the name of Amalech out of the land whereof I spake in mine anger. And forget not to destroy every soul of them as it is commanded thee. 2. And Saul departed and fought against Amalech, and 15⁸ saved alive Agag the king of Amalech because he said to him: I will shew thee hidden treasures. Therefore he spared him and saved him alive and brought him unto Armathem. 3. And God said unto Samuel: Hast thou seen how the king is corrupted with money even in a moment, and hath saved alive Agag king of Amalech and his wife? Now therefore suffer Agag and his wife to come together this night, and to-morrow thou shalt slay him; but his wife they shall preserve till she bring forth a male child, and then she also shall die, and he that is born of her shall be an offence unto Saul. But thou, arise on the morrow and slay Agag: for the sin of Saul is written before my face alway. 15¹³ 4. And when Samuel was risen on the morrow, Saul came forth to meet him and said unto him: The Lord hath delivered our enemies into our hands as he said. And Samuel said to Saul: Whom hath Israel wronged? for before the time was come that a king should rule over him, he demanded thee for his king, and thou, when thou wast sent to do the will of the Lord, hast transgressed it. Therefore

5. *and the battle prospered greatly: pugna expedientissima.*

he that was saved alive by thee shall die now, and
those hidden treasures whereof he spake he shall
not show thee, and he that is born of him shall be
an offence unto thee. And Samuel came unto
Agag with a sword and slew him, and returned   1 Sam.15 [3]
unto his house.

LIX. And the Lord said unto him : Go, anoint
him whom I shall tell thee, for the time is fulfilled
wherein his kingdom shall come. And Samuel
said : Lo, wilt thou now blot out the kingdom of
Saul ? And he said : I will blot it out. 2. And
Samuel went forth unto Bethel, and sanctified the   16[1-7]
elders, and Jesse, and his sons. And Eliab the
firstborn of Jesse came. And Samuel said : Behold
now the holy one, the anointed of the Lord. And
the Lord said unto him : Where is thy vision which
thine heart hath seen ? Art not thou he that saidst
unto Saul : I am he that seeth? And how knowest
thou not whom thou must anoint? And now let
this rebuke suffice thee, and seek out the shepherd,
the least of them all, and anoint him. 3. And
Samuel said unto Jesse : Hearken, Jesse, send and   16[11]
bring hither thy son from the flock, for him hath
God chosen. And Jesse sent and brought David,
and Samuel anointed him in the midst of his
brethren. And the Lord was with him from that
day *forward*.

4. Then David began to sing this psalm, and   Ps. 61[2]
said : In the ends of the earth will I begin to
glorify *him*, and unto everlasting days will I sing
praises. Abel at the first when he fed the sheep,
his sacrifice was acceptable rather than his brother's.
And his brother envied him and slew him. But it
is not so with me, for God hath kept me, and hath
delivered me unto his angels and his watchers to
keep me, for my brethren envied me, and my father
and my mother made me of no account, and when

the prophet came they called not for me, and when the Lord's anointed was proclaimed they forgat me. But God came near unto me with his right hand, and with his mercy: therefore will I not cease to sing praises all the days of my life.

1 Sam. 17³⁴ 5. And as David yet spake, behold a fierce lion out of the wood and a she-bear out of the mountain took the bulls of David. And David said: Lo, this shall be a sign unto me for a mighty beginning of my victory in the battle. I will go out after them and deliver that which is carried off and will slay them. And David went out after them and took stones out of the wood and slew them. And God said unto him: Lo, by stones have I delivered thee these beasts in thy sight. And this shall be a sign unto thee that hereafter thou shalt slay with stones the adversary of my people.

16¹⁴ LX. And at that time the spirit of the Lord was taken away from Saul, and an evil spirit oppressed (*lit.* choked) him. And Saul sent and fetched David, and he played a psalm upon his harp in the night. And this is the psalm which he sang unto Saul that the evil spirit might depart from him.

2. There were darkness and silence before the world was, and the silence spake, and the darkness became visible. And then was thy name created, even at the drawing together of that which was stretched out, whereof the upper was called heaven and the lower was called earth. And it was commanded to the upper that it should rain according to its season, and to the lower that it should bring forth food for man that *should be* made. And after that was the tribe of your spirits made. 3. Now therefore, be not injurious, whereas thou art a second creation, but if not, then remember Hell (*lit.* be mindful of Tartarus) wherein thou walkedst. Or is it not enough for thee to hear

that by that which resoundeth before thee I sing unto many? Or forgettest thou that out of a rebounding echo in the abyss (*or* chaos) thy creation was born? But that new womb shall rebuke thee, whereof I am born, of whom shall be born after a time of my loins he that shall subdue you.

And when David sung praises, the spirit spared Saul.   1 Sam. 16²³

LXI. And after these things the Philistines came to fight against Israel. And David was returned   17¹⁵
to the wilderness to feed his sheep, and the Madianites came and would have taken his sheep, and he came down unto them and fought against them and slew of them 15,000 men. This is the first battle that David fought, being in the wilderness.

2. And there came a man out of the camp of   17⁴
the Philistines by name Golia, and he looked upon Saul and upon Israel and said: Art not thou Saul which fleddest before me when I took the ark from you and slew your priests? And now that thou reignest, wilt thou come down unto me like a man and a king and fight against us? If not, I will come unto thee, and will cause thee to be taken

LX. 3. *evil spirits born of an echo in chaos: de resultatione in chaomate.* In the *Testament of Solomon* a female demon, Onoskelis, says that she was born ἀπὸ φωνῆσ ἀκαίρου τῆσ καλουμένησ ἤχου οὐρανοῦ † μολύβδου † φωνὴν ἀφέντοσ ἐν ὔλη. Again, in a text on the Creation in the Leyden magical papyrus, of which Dieterich gives an edition in *Abraxas*, p. 17 *seq.*, are several such phrases as this: God laughed seven times, and when he laughed seven gods were born . . . He laughed the second time . . . and the earth heard the echo (ἤχουσ) . . . and a god appeared: p. 19, καὶ ἐγεννήθη ἐκ τοῦ ἤχουσ μέγασ θεὸσ κ.τ.λ.

That evil spirits (*Mazzikin*) were created on the second day (as our text states) is the view expressed in some texts of *Pirke R. Eliezer* 3, and in *Jerahmeel* I. 3: c. 18 of *Pirke R. E.* and later books say they were created on the eve of the first Sabbath day.

I ᶜam. 17¹¹

17²⁸

17³¹

17⁴⁰

captive, and thy people to serve our gods. And
when Saul and Israel heard that, they feared
greatly. And the Philistine said: According to
the number of the days wherein Israel feasted
when they received the law in the wilderness, even
40 days, I will reproach them, and after that I will
fight with them. 3. And it came to pass when
the 40 days were fulfilled, and David was come to
see the battle of his brethren, that he heard the
words which the Philistine spake, and said: Is this
peradventure the time whereof God said unto me:
I will deliver the adversary of my people into thy
hand by stones? 4. And Saul heard these words
and sent and took him and said: What was the
speech which thou spakest unto the people? And
David said: Fear not, O king, for I will go and
fight against the Philistine, and God will take away
the hatred and reproach from Israel. 5. And David
went forth and took 7 stones and wrote upon them
the names of his fathers, Abraham, Isaac, and Jacob,
Moses and Aaron, and his own name, and the
name of the Most Mighty. And God sent Cervihel,
the angel that is over strength. 6. And David
went forth unto Golia and said unto him: Hear a
word before thou diest. Were not the two women
of whom thou and I were born sisters? and thy
mother was Orpha and my mother was Ruth.

LXI. 5. The *Midrash Samuel,* quoted by Cohn, says:
The five stones which David chose, he took in the name of
God, in the name of Aaron the priest, and in the names of
Abraham, Isaac, and Jacob.

6. Orpah is identified in the Midrashim of Ruth and of
Samuel (Cohn) with Harapha (2 Sam. 21¹⁸ margin) who was
thought to be the mother of giants there mentioned So,
too, in the *Quaest. Hebr. in Paral.* She also figures as the
mother of Ishbi-benob in a tale in the Talmud (*Sanhedrin,*
95) quoted by Eisenmenger, *Entdecktes Judenthum,* i. 413.
See Introd., p. 60.)

And Orpha chose for herself the gods of the Philistines and went after them, but Ruth chose Ruth 1^{14}
for herself the ways of the Most Mighty and walked in them.   And now thou and thy brethren are born of Orpha, and as thou art arisen this day and come to lay Israel waste, behold, I also that am born of thy kindred am come to avenge my people.   For thy three brethren also shall fall into my hands after thy death.   And then shall ye say unto your mother: He that was born of thy sister hath not spared us.   7. And David put a stone in 1 Sam. 17^{49}
his sling and smote the Philistine in his forehead, and ran upon him and drew his sword out of the sheath and took his head from him.   And Golia said unto him while his life was yet in him : Hasten and slay me and rejoice.   8. And David said unto him : Before thou diest, open thine eyes and behold thy slayer which hath killed thee.   And the Philistine looked and saw the angel and said : Thou hast not killed me by thyself, but he that was with thee, whose form is not as the form of a man.   And then David took his head from him.   9. And the angel of the Lord lifted up the face of David and no man knew him.   And when Saul saw David he asked him who he was, and there was no man that knew him who he was.

LXII. And after these things Saul envied David and sought to kill him.   But David and Jonathan, Saul's son, made a covenant together.   And when David saw that Saul sought to kill him, he fled unto Armathem ; and *Saul* went out after him.

2. And the spirit abode in Saul, and he prophe- 19^{23}
sied, saying : Why art thou deceived, O Saul, or whom dost thou persecute in vain ?   The time of thy kingdom is fulfilled.   Go unto thy place, for thou shalt die and David shall reign.   Shalt not thou and thy son die together ?   And then shall

the kingdom of David appear. And the spirit departed from Saul, and he knew not what he had prophesied.

I Sam. 20 3. But David came unto Jonathan and said unto him : Come and let us make a covenant before we be parted one from the other. For Saul, thy father, seeketh to slay me without cause. And since he hath perceived that thou lovest me he telleth thee not what he deviseth concerning me. 4. But for this cause he hateth me, because thou lovest me, and lest I should reign in his stead. And whereas I have done him good he requiteth me with evil. And whereas I slew Golia by the word of the Most Mighty, see thou what an end he purposeth for me. For he hath determined concerning my father's house, to destroy it. And would that the judgement of truth might be put in the balance, that the multitude of the prudent might hear the sentence. 5. And now I fear lest he kill me and lose his own life for my sake. For he shall never shed innocent blood without punishment. Wherefore should my soul suffer persecution ? For I was the least among my brethren, feeding the sheep, and wherefore am I in peril of death ? For I am righteous and have none iniquity. And wherefore doth thy father hate me ? Yet the righteousness of my father shall help me that I fall not into thy father's hands. And seeing I am young and tender of age, it is to no purpose that Saul envieth me. 6. If I had wronged him, I would pray him to forgive me the sin. For if God forgiveth iniquity, how much more thy father who is flesh and blood ? I have walked in his house with a perfect heart, yea, I grew up before his face like a swift eagle. I put mine hands unto the harp and blessed him in songs, and he hath devised to slay me, and

like a sparrow that fleeth before the face of the
hawk, so have I fled before his face. 7. Unto
whom have I spoken this, or unto whom have I
told the things that I have suffered save unto thee
and Melchol thy sister? For as for both of us, let
us go together in truth. 8. And it were better, my
brother, that I should be slain in battle than that
I should fall into the hands of thy father: for in
the battle mine eyes were looking on every side
that I might defend him from his enemies. O
my brother Jonathan, hear my words, and if there
be iniquity in me, reprove me.

9. And Jonathan answered and said: Come
unto me, my brother David, and I will tell thee
thy righteousness. My soul pineth away sore at
thy sadness because now we are parted one from
another. And this have our sins compelled, that
we should be parted from one another. But let
us remember one another day and night while we
live. And even if death part us, yet I know that
our souls will know one another. For thine is the
kingdom in this world, and of thee shall be the
beginning of the kingdom, and it cometh in its
time. 10. And now, like a child that is weaned
from its mother, even so shall be our separation.
Let the heaven be witness and let the earth be-
witness of those things which we have spoken
together. And let us weep each with the other
and lay up our tears in one vessel and commit the
vessel to the earth, and it shall be a testimony
unto us. 11. And they bewailed each one the   1 Sam. 20⁴¹
other sore, and kissed one another. But Jonathan
feared and said unto David: Let us remember, O
my brother, the covenant that is made betwixt us,
and the oath which is set in our heart. And if
I die before thee and thou indeed reign, as the
Lord hath spoken, be not mindful of the anger

of my father, but of the covenant which is made betwixt me and thee. Neither think upon the hatred wherewith my father hateth thee in vain but upon my love wherewith I have loved thee. Neither think upon that wherein my father was unthankful unto thee, but remember the table whereat we have eaten together. Neither keep in mind the envy wherewith my father envied thee evilly, but the faith which I and thou keep. Neither care thou for the lie wherewith Saul hath lied, but for the oaths that we have sworn one to 1 Sam. 20⁴² another. And they kissed one another. And after that David departed into the wilderness, and Jonathan went into the city.

LXIII. At that time the priests that dwelt in Noba were polluting the holy things of the Lord and making the firstfruits a reproach unto the people. And God was wroth and said: Behold, I will wipe out the priests that dwell in Noba, because they walk in the ways of the sons of Heli. 22⁹ 2. And at that time came Doech the Syrian, which was over Saul's mules, unto Saul and said unto him: Knowest thou not that Abimelec the priest taketh counsel with David and hath given him a sword and sent him away in peace? And Saul sent and called Abimelec and said unto him: 22¹⁶ Thou shalt surely die, because thou hast taken counsel with mine enemy. And Saul slew Abimelec and all his father's house, and there was not so much as one of his tribe delivered save only Abiathar his son. The same came to David and told him all that had befallen him. 3. And God said: Behold, in the year when Saul began to ~reign, when Jonathan had sinned and he would have put him to death, this people rose up and suffered him not, and now when the priests were slain, even 385 men, they kept silence and said nothing. Therefore, lo, the days shall come quickly that I will deliver them into the hands of their enemies and they shall fall down wounded, they and their king. 4. And unto Doech the Syrian thus said the Lord : Behold, the days shall come quickly that the worm shall come up upon his tongue and shall cause him to pine away, and his dwelling shall be with Jair for ever in the fire that is not quenched.

1 Sam. 31

5. Now all that Saul did, and the rest of his words, and how he pursued after David, are they not written in the book of the kings of Israel ?

6. And after these things Samuel died, and all Israel gathered together and mourned him, and buried him.

LXIV. Then Saul took thought, saying : I will surely take away the sorcerers out of the land of Israel. So shall men remember me after my departure. And Saul scattered all the sorcerers out of the land. And God said : Behold, Saul hath taken away the sorcerers out of the land, not because of the fear of me, but that he might make himself a name. Behold, whom he hath scattered, unto them let him resort, and get divination from them, because he hath no prophets.

28^3

2. At that time the Philistines said every man to his neighbour : Behold, Samuel the prophet is dead and there is none that prayeth for Israel. David, also, which fought for them, is become Saul's adversary and is not with them. Now, therefore, let us arise and fight mightily against them, and avenge the blood of our fathers. And the Philistines assembled themselves and came *up* to battle. 3. And when Saul saw that Samuel was dead and David was not with him, his hands were loosened. And he inquired of the Lord, and he hearkened not unto him. And he sought

28^6

I Sam. 28⁷ prophets, and none appeared unto him. And Saul said unto the people: Let us seek out a diviner and inquire of him that which I have in mind. And the people answered him: Behold, now there is a woman named Sedecla, the daughter of Debin (*or* Adod) the Madianite, which deceived the people of Israel with sorceries: and lo she 28⁸⁻¹¹ dwelleth in Endor. 4. And Saul put on vile raiment and went unto her, he and two men with him, by night and said unto her: Raise up unto me Samuel. And she said: I am afraid of the king Saul. And Saul said unto her: Thou shalt not be harmed of Saul in this matter. And Saul said within himself: When I was king in Israel, even though the Gentiles saw me not, yet knew they that I was Saul. And Saul asked the woman, saying: Hast thou seen Saul at any time? And she said: Oftentimes. And Saul went out and wept and said: Lo, now I know that my beauty is changed, and that the glory of my kingdom is passed from me.

28¹²   5. And it came to pass, when the woman saw Samuel coming up, and beheld Saul with him, 28¹³ that she cried out and said: Behold, *thou art Saul, wherefore hast thou deceived me?* And he said unto her: *Fear not, but tell me what thou sawest.* And she said: Lo, these 40 years have I raised up the dead for the Philistines, but this appearance hath not been seen, neither shall it be seen hereafter. 6. And Saul said unto her: What is his form? And she said: Thou inquirest of me

LXIV. 3. The witch of Endor, here called Sedecla, daughter of Debin or of Adod (doubtless Aod of XXXIV.), is in *Pirke R. Eliezer* 33 " the wife of Zephaniah, the mother of Abner." Kimchi *in loc.*, it seems, calls her Zephaniah. The *Quaest. Hebr.* agree that she was Abner's mother. Perhaps " the wife of " in *Pirke* should go out.

concerning the gods. For, behold, his form is not the form of a man. For he is arrayed in a white robe and hath a mantle upon it, and two angels leading him. And Saul remembered the mantle which Samuel had rent while he lived, and he smote his hands together and cast himself upon the earth.

I Sam. 19²⁷

7. *And Samuel said unto him : Why hast thou disquieted me to bring me up?* I thought that the time was come for me to receive the reward of my deeds. Therefore boast not thyself, O king, neither thou, O woman. For it is not ye that have brought me up, but the precept which God spake unto me while I yet lived, that I should come and tell thee that thou hadst sinned yet the second time in neglecting God. For this cause are my bones disturbed after that I had rendered up my soul, that I should speak unto thee, and that being dead I should be heard as one living. 8. Now therefore *to-morrow shalt thou and thy sons be with me*, when the people are delivered into the hands of the Philistines. And because thy bowels have been moved with jealousy, therefore that that is thine shall be taken from thee. And Saul heard the words of Samuel, and his soul melted and he said : Behold, I depart to die with my sons, if perchance my destruction may be an atonement for mine iniquities. And Saul arose and departed thence.

28¹⁵

28¹

28²ᵘ

LXV. *And the Philistines fought against Israel.* And Saul went out to battle. *And Israel fled*

31¹

6. *Two angels leading him.* Compare the *Gospel of Peter*, where two angels lead Christ out of the sepulchre.

7. The word which I render *precept* is *traditio.* I cannot cite a parallel to this curious use of it.

8. *if my destruction may be an atonement (exoratio) for mine iniquities.* In *Pirke R. Eliezer* 33, Samuel says to Saul : If thou wilt hearken to my advice, to fall by the sword, then shall thy death be an atonement for thee.

Q

before the Philistines : and when Saul saw that the
1 Sam. 31³ battle waxed hard exceedingly, he said in his
heart : Wherefore strengthenest thou thyself to
live, seeing Samuel hath proclaimed death unto
31⁴ thee and to thy sons ? 2. *And Saul said to him
that bare his armour : Take thy sword and slay me
before the Philistines come and abuse me. And he
that bare his armour would not lay hands upon him.*
3. *And he himself bowed upon his sword,* and he
could not die. *And he looked behind him and saw*
2 Sam. 1⁷ a man running and called unto him and said :
Take my sword and slay me. *For my life is yet
in me.* 4. And he came to slay him. And Saul
said unto him : Before thou kill me, tell me, who
art thou ? And he said unto him : I am Edab, the
son of Agag king of the Amalechites. And Saul
said : Behold, now the words of Samuel are come
upon me even as he said : He that shall be born
of Agag shall be an offence unto thee. 5. But go
thou and say unto David : I have slain thine
enemy. And thou shalt say unto him : Thus
saith Saul : Be not mindful of my hatred, neither
of mine unrighteousness. . . .

LXV. According to the *Quaest. Hebr. in loc.*, the armour-
bearer of Saul was Doeg, and the man who killed Saul the
son of Doeg.

APPENDIX I

ON VARIOUS READINGS AND CORRUPT PASSAGES

THE portions of text contained in our several authorities are as follows:

A (the printed text), P (Phillipps 461), V (Vienna lat. 446), R (Vatican lat. 488), contain the whole text.

Ph (Phillipps 391) has: XIX. 14–16, XXVIII. 6–10, XL. 5–8, LX. 2, 3.

T (Trèves 117) has the last two of the above four extracts.

F (Fitzwilliam Museum McClean 31) has, usually in an abridged form, the following portions: I., II., III. 5–11, IV. 5, 11–15, 16, V. 2 (3), VI., VII. 5, most of VIII., IX., XX. 6, 7, XXIII. 4–8 (om. 5), XXV.–XXVII. (the substance), XXIX. 1, XXX., XXXI., XLVIII. 1, 2, LX., LXI.

J (*Chronicles of Jerahmeel*, tr. Gaster) has, also abridged to some extent: I., II., III. 9, 10, IV.–VII., IX., XXV.–XXVIII., XXXI. 2 to end, XXXV. 6, 7, XXXVIII., XXXIX., XL., XLIV. 5, XLVI. 3–XLVII. 2, XLVII. 7–10, XLVIII. 1, 2,

In the following selection of various readings (which is only to be regarded as illustrative) I confine myself to giving such readings as materially affect the sense or throw light upon the relation between our authorities, neglecting differences in spelling, in order of words, and the like.

The numerous variants in the spelling and division of the fabulous proper names in I.–V. will not be recorded in full.

I. 1. A is the only authority for Initio Mundi. P omits the words. VR have Initium mundi.

II. 8. The first part of the verse seems intrusive. I suggest the omission of the words "indignatus est deus et." But the text is just tolerable as it stands, though awkward.

III. 2. (Non diiudicabit spiritus meus in) omnibus (istis) AVRF hominibus P (rightly): LXX. ἐν τοῖσ ἀνθρώποισ τούτοισ.

> in quos posuit (terminos seculi) AP.
> in quo posuit VR.
> in quo posui F.
> (in manibus eorum) scelera non extinguebantur AP.
>   lex non extinguetur VRF.

4. et procreatio eius AP et he procreationes eius VR.

9. Cum autem peccauerint AP. Erit autem cum pecc. VR.
   dispergentur in inhabitabilia AVR.
   dispergentur inhabitabilia P.
   dispergentur inhabitantes in terra F. I shall scatter them hither and thither J.

10. perditio restituet paratecem (-n) suam AP.
    perditum restituet partem suam VR.
    Abaddon shall return its portion J (betraying its origin from Latin).

11. (in sanguine animae) editis A. non edetis PV.
    non edatis R.
    (qui enim effundet) sanguinem hominis, sanguis eius effundetur, quoniam ad imaginem dei factus est homo AP.
    Sanguinem hominis in manu dei sanguis eius eff. (fund. R.) quoniam ad ymag. suam fecit deus (dei R.) hominem VR.

IV. The names here can be checked to some extent by the text of the Bible.

2. *Read:* Filii Iapheth ⟨Gomer⟩ Magog Madai † Nidiazec † Tubal M⟨os⟩oc Tiras ⟨et filii Gomer⟩ Ascenez, etc.

Nidiazec stands in place of Javan. J has the correct text.

After Thogorma *read* ⟨et filii Iauan⟩ Elisa ⟨Tharsis⟩ Cethin Dudanim.

    Et filii Gomer—Deberlet *seems intrusive.*

    (Et filii) Duden *should be* Madai.

Javan should follow here, but has in reality been given already.

For Mellech we expect Mosoc : but if so, he should precede Diras (= Tiras).

    Cenez is for Ascenez.

    Heri = Riphath.

    Zepti, Tessis correspond to Cethin, Tharsis.

  3. Monadas A. Monidos P (V) R. Media J.

  4. Domereth = Gomer.

    Madam = Madai.

    Iuban = Iauan.

    Iras = Tiras.

    Duodennut = Ascenez !

    Thesis = Tharsis.

At the beginning of this verse J reads : At that time a third part of the land of Romidath was flooded, and his sons subdued Yedid.

    P omits part of the verse, from Tiras to Elisa.

On Riphath J has : and Riphath without his sons conquered Godo, and the sons of R. conquered Bosrah.

  6. Phuni = Phuth.

  6. Filii Ethii (Ethu P) Chus Saba et Tudan AP.

    Et hi filii Chus, etc. R (J).

Read: Et hi filii Chus, Saba ⟨Heuila Sabatha Regma Sabatacha. Et filii Regma Saba⟩ et Tudan. A line had fallen out by homoeoteleuton in the archetype.

    Et filii Effuntenus Zeleutelup, etc. AP.

    Et filii Funi Zeleu. Telup R.

    Vabni Maipon Tinos Silio Tiluf J.

    Et filii Chanaan Sidona RJ. AP omit Chanaan.

  8. In the names of the cities I follow Genesis and J. The MSS. have—

    Resun Beosamaza Gerras Calon (Scalon P).

      Dabircaino (·camo P) Tellun lacis . . . Segom

      (Seboim R).

9. Aram : et filiarum Assum Gedrummese APR.
Aran and the sons of Ashur, Gezron, Ishai J.
filii Aram Us Hul Gether Mes Gen 10^{22} Vulg.
Οὐζ Οὐλ Γατερ Μοσοχ LXX.
Read : et filii Aram As Hul Geder Mes, or something like it.

10. The sons of Jectan. I have followed the Latin text, which is—

Elimodan (Helmadan P) Salastra Mazaam Rea Dura Uzia Deglabal Mimoel Sabthphin Euilac Iubab APR.

The Bible text (LXX and Vulgate) is—

Elmodad Saleph Asarmoth Iare (Ἰαραδ) Aduram (Ὀδορρα) Uzal (Αἰζηλ) Decla Ebal (Γεβαλ) Abimael Saba (Σαβευ) Ophir Hevila Iobab.

Hence we get something like :

Elmodan Salath Sarmaz (??) Iare Adura Uza Decla Ebal Abimael Saba Ophir (Θ and O confused) Euilac Iubab.

J has not corrected his text by that of Genesis, but preserves the worst of the corruptions, *e.g.* Diqalbel, Shabethfin, etc.

V. 4. The names of the sons of Japhet are fairly correct, but Doin should be Dudanim.

5. The list for Ham is corrupt : Phua = Phuth, Soba = Saba, Lebilla = Heuila, Sata = Sabatha, Remma = Regma.

6. In the list for Shem A omits the name of Aram, leaving a blank.
After the sons of Lud is a line which I take to be intrusive, viz.—

Factus est numerus filiorum Cam * A.

Factus est numerus filiorum Cham LXXIII P.

Et hic uniuersus (*l* numerus) filiorum Sem (V). R.

7. The number IX in the last words of the verse is corrupt.

VI. 2. et erit quod perustum fuerit in luto et in latere MSS. P leaves a small blank space after *latere*, which falls at the end of a page. Something is wanting : I suggest an emendation in the translation.

4. nec coniungimur uoluptati (uoluntati P) uestrae AP.
nec coniungimus uoluntatem nostram uobiscum R.

14. frangentes fregerunt noctu A. fr. carcerem
fugierunt P. fr. freg. vincula VR.

15. congregemus eum A. concrememus igni P.
concrememus *only* VR.

17. non est quidem modica facta laesura concrematione
ignis A.

non est nec modica facta laesura in concrematione
ignis PV.

non est modica les facta in concrematione ignis R.

VII. 3. in scuto approximabo eos. MSS.

I will fight (*or* draw near unto) them with shields J,
implying the same text.

Of course scuto is wrong for sputo. The Latin origin
of J is here betrayed.

VIII. 5. Esau's wives and children. The Bible
sources are Gen. 26³⁴, 28⁹, 36² *seq.*, 1 Chr. 1³⁵.

Six persons are mentioned in Genesis as wives of
Esau : Judith ('Ιουδιν) daughter of Beeri, Bashemath
daughter of Elon, Mahalath daughter of Ishmael, Adah
daughter of Elon, Aholibamah daughter of Anah, Bashemath daughter of Ishmael. It is evident that confusion
is present.

In *Philo* we have Judin daughter of Bereu, Bassemech
daughter of Elon, Elibema, daughter of Anan, Massem
daughter of Samael. The last is meant for Mahalath
daughter of Ishmael. Adah is not mentioned as a wife,
but we should probably read (et genuit ei) Ada Eliphan
for Adeliphan.

In the next line read : Et Iudin genuit † Tenacis
Ieruebemas † et Basseman genuit ei Rugil (with RF).

For Tenacis Ieruebemas (AP) R has tenach · isier ·
ubemas, F Thenach Isier Vebemas. Perhaps the last
may be a corruption of "and Bashemath" in the original
Hebrew.

Of the last line (Manem genuit Tenetde Thenatela
(AP) teneth · chenatela R) I do not know the source.

The names, except those of the sons of Judin and
Manem, are sufficiently recognizable.

11. The names here are in great confusion. The writer is reproducing Gen. 46⁸ *seq.* The list in *Jubilees* does not help.

Sons of Simeon: Namuel et Ianunetdot et Iacim Esaul fil. Canan⟨i⟩tidis A.

> Namuhel et Iamin et dot et iachim esaul fil. Cananitidis P.

> Namuhel et Iamin et doth et iachim et Saul fil. Chan. R.

R is most nearly right. Namuel represents Ἰεμουηλ, Dot = Ἀωδ (Δ for Λ). One son Σααρ is omitted.

Judah: Er has fallen out.

Issachar: Iob agrees with Heb. and Josephus. LXX. has Ἰασουφ.

Zebulun: We should read, for Sarelon, Sared, Elon. Iaillil is nearer to Jahleel (Heb.) than to Ἀλοηλ (LXX).

> Et haec sunt generationes filiorum quas peperit Iacob A.

> Et haec sunt generationes filiorum quos peperit Iacob P.

> Et haec (*om* sunt) generationes filiorum quos genuit Iacob R.

Supply Liae *after* filiorum.

Here *Philo* inserts the sons of Bilhah, who stand last of all in the Bible.

12. *Dan:* Filii autem Dan Usinam AP.

> Filii autem Dan Us . inam R.

> *Read:* Usin (= Hushim, Ἀσομ). Nam. (filii Nept., etc.).

Naphtali: Filii Neptalim Betaal Neemmu Surem Optisarielet AP.

> Filii autem Neptalim Betaal Neemmu Surem Opti . sarielech VR.

The final et (ech) belongs to the next clause.

Read Sariel. Et hae generationes, etc.

The names are very corrupt. Heb. Jahzeel Guni Jezer Shillem. LXX. Ἀσιηλ Γωννι Ἰσσααρ Συλλημ.

13. *Gad* (*Asher*): Nam filii Gad Sariel Sua Visui Mophat (Mofar) et Sar soror eorum filia Seriebel Melchiel AP.

Nam filii Gad Sariel Sua Visui Mofar et Sar soror eorum. Filii autem asser iebel et Melchiel R.

Heb. (Gad) Ziphion Haggi Shuni Ezbon Ezi Arodi Areli.

LXX. Σαφων ῾Αγγεισ Σαυνισ Θασοβαν ᾿Αηδισ ᾿Αροηδισ ᾿Αροηλεισ.

Heb. (Asher) Jimnah and Ishuah and Isui and Beriah and Serah their sister : and the sons of Beriah, Heber and Melchiel.

LXX. ᾿Ιεμνα κ. ᾿Ιεσσαι κ. ᾿Ιεουλ κ. Βαρια κ. Σααρ ἀδελφὴ αὐτῶγ ·υἱοὶ δὲ Βαρια, Χοβορ κ. Μελχιηλ.

Thus we see that most of Gad's sons and the beginning of Asher's have dropped out. R has seen that Asher was missing, and has supplied him in the wrong place.

Read probably : Nam filii Gad . . . Areli ⟨filii autem Asser Iemna Ie⟩sua Visui † Mophat † et Sar(a) soror eorum. Filii Berie Ebel (Eber) Melchiel.

Note *Visui*, which seems to be a mistranslation of the Hebrew *and Isui*.

   Mophat I cannot account for.

14. *Benjamin :* Gela Esbel Nanubal Abocinephec Utundeus A.

   Gela Esbel Nanubal Ahocmefec Utundeus P.

   Gela Esbel hamibal · aboch · mefach (*om* Utundeus) V.

   Gela Esbel nanubal aboch mefech (*om* Utundeus) R.

Heb. : Belah Becher Ashbel Gera Naaman Ehi Rosh Muppim Huppim Ard.

LXX. Βαλα Χοβωρ ᾿Ασβηλ (*sons of Bala*) Γηρα Νοεμαν ᾿Αγχεισ ῾Ρωσ Μαμφειν ᾿Οφιμιν (*son of Gera*) ; ᾿Αραδ.

   Nanubal a (boc) may conceal Nam filii Bala.

   boc mephec surely conceals Ros (῾ΡΩC) Mephin (or the like).

   Utundeus remains hopeless.

IX. 2. ὠμοτοκείαν A. ometoceam (-an) *cett.* V adds : id est.

   3, etc. A reads Anra or Anram throughout ; not so the others.

immensurabilis AP.   in inmensurabile R.

minoretur A.   minuatur PR.

7. testamentum inter me et patres ejus dispositum AP.

testamentum inter me et placuit eius disposit(i)o R.

9. accepit uxorem de tribu sua AP.   acc. mulierem stirpis sue nomine iocobe (iacobe R.) VR.

12. Iacob A.   Iochabeth P.   Iacobe VR.

concepit : + masculum VR.

13. et in testamento carnis AP.   et in testamentum c. VR.

15. et dum uidisset in Zaticon hoc est in testamentum (-oP) carnis AP : *om* VR.

X. 1. ranae : + et panimixia V.   et pammixia R.

intractabiles AP.   tractabiles VR.

5. Domini mei : *om* mei R.

6. cooperuit A.   ceperunt P *om* R.

et equites eorum AP.   et equos eorum usque in hodiernum diem R.

et submersit Egyptios et currus et equites eorum usque in hod. diem V.

XI. 1. in quem eiiciam excelsa sempiterna AP.

in quo disposui excelsa sempiterna VR.

4. uox organorum AP.   uox psalphingarum V.

uox psalmigrafi R.

(angeli) praecurrebant AP.   procurrebant V.

percurrebant R.

6. ornamentorum celi : + et militie eius R.

quae repunt in aquis uel super terram AP.

quae natant in aquis uel repunt sub terra R.

8. sanctifica A.   sanctificate P.   et sanctifica VR.

operatio AP.   cooperatio VR.

in ea laudes AP.   in eo laudetis VR.   *also* glorificetis VR.

14. propterea enim ut probaret uos uenit deus ut recipiatis timorem eius in uos ut (et R). non peccetis A VR.

propterea enim hec uox uenit in uos ut non
  peccetis P.
15. et de obseruatione mensis et candelabro A.
    et de obseruatione mense et candelabri P.
    et obseruationem mense et candelabri VR.
    et uasis (eius) AP. et uase VR : *read* base.
    (et de) hebdomade A. eptomade P. eppo-
    mede VR.
XII. 1. descendit in locum (ubi lumen) . . . . uicit
    lumen faciei A.
    descendit in locum (ubi lumen) . . . uicit
    enim lumen faciei P.
    ut descenderat in locum (ubi lumen) . . .
    uicit lumine faciei VR.
    We should probably read : descendit enim.
  2. Et dum esset in monte APR. Et dum deus,
    etc. V.
    Fac nobis deos quibus seruiamus quemado-
    dum AP.
    Fac nobis deos et da nobis quibus seruiamus
    sicut onortet quemadmodum VR.
    Coram nos AP. coram nobis VR.
    appropiabit AVR. apportabit P.
    iudicium : + manus (!) V. maius R.
  4. concordabor eis AP. reconciliabor R.
  6. quomodo si (peccauerint) A. quoniam (?) si
    peccauerint P. quoniam etiam si R.
  8. (uinea) ista emisit (fructum) AP. illa amisit R.
    si irasceris AP. si non irascaris (!) R.
  9. et iaspide AP. eciam spicis R.
    (saturasti) eam AP. tuam creaturam R.
  9. maius (quod a te praedictum est) A. magis
    PVR.
XIII. 1. *After* tabulas, et tabernaculum *must be added.*
    thuribulum holocaustomatum AP : + et
    thuribulum incensorum VR.
(bases) omniaque quae A. et omnia que PVR.
et caeteras et citharam et lamina aurea A.
et cetera et cytharam et laminam auream P.
et cetera et cidarim et laminam auream VR.

et oleum AP. et composuit ol. VR.

2. Exclamauit Moses ad dominum et locutus est ei deus AP.

Exclamauit ad Moysen deus, etc. VR.

festiuitatem memorialem A. festiuitatem maiorem P. festiuitatem in memoriale V. festiuitatem immemoriale R.

6. psalphingarum APV. psalmigraphi R.

praespexi (creaturam) A. prospexi P. perspexi VR.

memores sitis AP. ut memores sitis VR.

per initia (ostendentibus uobis, etc.) AP. et in (R om. in) initium annorum ostend VR.

per ieiunium misericordiae. Ieiunabitis enim mihi AP.

Et ieiunium misericordie ieiunabitis michi VR.

7. et salicum et cedrum et ramos myrrhae AP.

et salicum et myrti ramos VR.

8. Tunc precepit ei de anno . . . et dixit AP.

Tunc cum precepi de anno . . . et dixi VR.

(ostendi) eis. *qu.* ei?

et colorem. *qu.* et colubrum?

9. Et adiecit dominus adhuc ostendere uias paradisi et dixit AP.

Et adiecit adhuc dominus : Ostendi uias paradisi et dixi VR (dixit R).

Haec sunt quae (perdiderunt) A. haec sunt uiae quas PVR.

10. erit eis in lucrificationem et non sterilizabit AP.

erit eis et lucrificationes et terra non ster VR.

non in sempiterno A. non in sempiternum PR.

in sempiternum (*om.* non) V.

XIV. 2. in terra Aegypti. Dum insisteris et cum (*om.* cum P) inspexeris scribe AP.

in terra Aegypti dum ibi staretis. Et erit cum inspexeris scribe R.

confidenter : + et non in corde suo R.

minueram ex his quae dixi eis. Semen uestrum . . . erit AP.

minuerunt. Et dixi eis. Erit semen uestrum, etc. R.

4. ut dent mihi decimationes AP. ut demant mihi demptiones R.

in memoriam quantos labores abstuli ab eis AP.

in memoriam omnibus diebus patrum uestrorum quantos abstuli ab eis R.

XV. 1. deposuerunt (fructus) A. deportantes P. deportauerunt R.

3. (filii) Ride AP. iude R.

5. (nubes) in tabernaculum AP. in umbraculum R.

7. *fin.*: + quoniam nisi tua miserearis quis procreabitur? R.

XVI. 1. (lex) insufferibilis A. insufferabilis P. intollerabilis R.

3. *fin.*: non adiciam amplius A. non adiciam ultra amplius P. non adiciam amplius super eis R.

5. non intrabimus (intrauimus P). in eas nisi ut in eis ambulemus AP.

non intramus legitime in eas (*om.* in eas R) nisi in eis ambulemus VR.

Pater nos non genuit sed fortissimus non (*om.* P : *l.* nos) plasmauit AP.

Pater nos genuit sed fortissimus nos (*om.* R) plasmauit VR.

et nunc si ambulauerimus in uiis eius (tuis VR) erimus filii sui (tui VR).

6. Si (adhuc instat): Sic V.

firmamentum. *In* P firmamentum *is corrected from* fundamentum.

7. non possumus manere in syna loci huius. *Read* in gyro loci.

XVII. 3. albos hoedos . . . et uarios AP. albidos . . . cenarios R (*for* cinerarios?).

(The *Lyons Pentateuch* has: exalbidi et uarii et cinericii et sparsi (Gen. 31^{10}).)

4. similis facta est synagoga populi gregi ouium A.

      „   „   „   „   grege hominum P.

similis est synagoga populorum gregibus ouium R.

XVIII. 4. (si rectum est ut) proficiscar (cum eis) AP. paciscar R.

5. pro sanguine eius elegi istos : + Et dixi tunc angelis minute operantibus (Nonne, etc.) R.
6. Et Iacob : + filio eius tertio. quem uocauit (? *l.* uocaui) primogenitum.   Qui cum luctaretur R.
9. uidit angelum : + et subsedit sub eo R.
10. irrue in ignem hominum istorum, quem aquae non extinguent non sustineo, ignem uero, etc. AP.

   irrue in ignem hominum quem aqua extinguere non poterit.   Ignem uero R.

   read istorum.   Ignem quem, etc. *as* AP.

   intenebriscare A.   intenebrescere PR : *read* intenebrificare *as* XXXIII. 10.
11. quae futura est.   Et continens eos retineo A.

   quae futura est et continget eis.   Retineor P.

   quae futura est contingens eis.   Retineor R.
12. ecce adhuc uideo haereditatem dissolutionis AP.

   et ecce hora mea que superest, ecce adhuc uideo haereditatem et dissolutionem R.

   Cham MSS. *qu.* Chamos?

   pro eo quod deductus sum et transgressus sum AP.

   pro eo quod seductus sum et quia transgressus sum R.
13. quae sunt in Mazia MSS. : *sc.* Madian.

XIX. 4. et incendens in uobis sempiternam lucernam et recordabimini iniqui.   Cum autem locutus sum AP.

   incendit in uobis sempiternalem lucernam Recordamini iniqui cum locutus sum R.

8. in montem Oreb AP.   in montem Abarim R.

   peto misericordia tua cum populo tuo et miseratio tua cum hereditate tua solidetur domine et longanimitas tua in loco tuo super electionis genus A.

   peto ut misericordia tua sit cum, etc. P.

   peto misericordiam tuam cum populo tuo et miserationem tuam cum hereditate tua solidetur domine longanimitas tua in locum tuum et suplectionis genus R.

9. in quibus uiuent.   Quis est autem homo AP (enim *for* autem P).

in quibus uiuerent et intrarent sicud filii hominum,
  quis est enim homo R.
peccauit? Quomodo constabilietur haereditas tua
  AP.
peccauit? Et nisi permaneat longanimitas tua
  quomodo stabilietur, etc. R.
10. R *transposes the sentences* Et ostendit ei locum—
  paradisi *and* Et ostendit ei . . . mensuras.
12. glorificabo AP. dormificabo VR.
  militiae: + celi VR.
  in quo incipies sepeliri: + sed in eo requiesces
  VR.
  uenietis simul APR. inueniens simul V.
13. (dies) . . . externus A. hesternus PVR.
15. Istic. MEL . APEX . MAGNUS V.
  ciathi (cyati, ciati) gutum APPh. ciati gutta VR.
16. pro recessu Moysi A. processu PPh. pro
  decessu VR.
  ut humilietur . . . hymnus AVR. humiliet . . .
  ymnum PPh.
XX. 1. 2. (Male locuti fuerant) de ea et propter hoc
defuncta est generatio illa. Tunc dixit, etc. AP.
  de ea propter hoc defuncta generatione illa dixit
  dominus deus ad Iesum. Ut quid, etc. R.
2. (Iste) ducet AP. ducabit R.
6. *and elsewhere* P *writes* Zenez. 10. R *has* Zenec.
XXI. 4. Et si circa nos verbum est A : cett *om.* si.
  ut proponat generationem unam, uni dicit : cor-
  rumpit deus A.
  ut proponat generationem unam. uni dicit corrupit deus P.
  ut preponat generationem unam uni dicit corrupit
  deus VR.
4. (eligat) haereditas tua uerum quia ipse AP.
      haereditati tue uirum qui et ipse VR.
6. sicut et isti (conuersi) AP. sic et isti VR.
  (Salutem quae) nascitur eis AP. nascetur ex eis
  VR.
8. et nablis et cum citharis AP. et nablis et cinaris
  (-eris R) VR.

9. (iubilantes in) psalmis AP. psalphingis VR.

terram fluentem lac AP. terram in qua inhabitatis terram fluentem, etc. VR.

in occultis (animarum) AP. de occultis an R.

quae locutus est ad nos in Oreb, et si custodiat A.

quae locutus est ad nos (uos R). Et uere modo cognouimus quoniam statuit deus omne uerbum legis sue quod locutus est ad nos in Oreb. Et erit si custodiat PVR.

XXII. 3. ecce deus amputauit fructum MSS. *I read* ampliavit.

4. aliqui ex nobis adstantes : + gessimus R.

5. non seducerentur A. non seducebantur PR.

7. *for* miserere (testamenti tui) : *qu.* memorare?

XXIII. 1. Eleazar uero filius Nauae A. Eleazar uero filius Aaron sacerdotis deseruiebat in Sylon (Sylo VR). Iesus autem filius Naue PVR.

3. in aromate A. in åromate P. in oromate VR.

4. uir scopuli illius A. incisco petre illius P. incisio petre illius VRF.

5. et superduxi eum in omnem terram Chanaan A. *om.* et superduxi eum P. et perduxi eum in terra Chanaan VR.

6. de mea petra conclusa AV. de ea metra conclusa P. de mea conclusa R.

inmisi in eum somnum, etc. locum ignis in quo expientur AVR.

inmisi his   in quo expientur P.

7. de conclusa (dabo) AP. de conclusa metra R.

sapientibus qui de te nascentur illuminantibus filios tuos APR.

sapientibus et legis peritis qui de te procedent regentes filios tuos F.

et parient. Haec erunt in testimonium AP.

et parient. Et ipsi prophete et uox hec erunt testim RF.

10. cessaui (sonos tonitruum) AP. mansuetaui R.

XXIV. 1. si sustinetis seruire domino : + eritis ei populus peculiaris R.

XXV. 1. (si omne cor populi) aequale sit AP.   equale
    scitur R.

9. sub tabernaculo Elas AP.   sub monte abrahe et
    sub mole terre deposita sunt Mitte R.
    under the mount Ebarim J.

10. de tribu Gad et illi dixerunt.   Nos inuenimus vii,
    etc. *om. cet.* R.

11. Hae sunt (+ sancte VR) nymphae.
    confixa : + clauis R.   in consecrationem AP.   in
    considerationem R.
    in diatrium AR.   indiatrium P.
    uelut chrysopassus (crisoprassus P) stigmatus
    (stigminis P) ita relucebat sculptura AP.
    uelut caraxatus stigminis ita lucebat sculpturis VR.

12. (in modum) diatridis A.   diatris P.   diatriti V.
    diatri R.
    emundabatur AP.   -bitur VR.

XXVI. 2. quae inuenta sunt in libro et cum homines
    sic dispones AP.
    quae inuenta sunt tam libros quam homines et sic
    dispones R.

4. (in) logio A.   longitudine P.   logice*n* R.

6. ut cum peccasset in ipsis Adam tunc haec uniuersa
    adnegaret (abn- P) ne ostendens haec generi
    hominum dominarentur eis AP.
    ut cum peccasset in ipsis abnegaret hec uniuersa os-
    tendens generi hominum nec hec dominarentur
    eis R.

10. tanquam Chrysoprassus esset . . . stigmatus (-um
    P) AP.
    tamquam incaraxatus (carax- V) esset . . . stig-
    matum VR.

11. (9th *stone*) tenebrata AP.   terebrata R.
    (12th *stone*) de excisione AP.   de excelso syon R.

12. Iahel AP.   Iabel R.

14. Scio . . . quoniam genus hominum A : + fragile
    P, + instabile R.

XXVII. 10. Angelum in Gethel (ingethel P) super-
    positum occultis . . . angelum uirtutis AP.
    angelum Gethel super oculis et alium angelum VR.

R

(percussit) in Gethel AP.   angelus R.

Et Zeruel (+ angelus P) qui praeerat AP.   et angelus qui praeerat VR.

11. (assumpserat) uirtutem gladii AVR.   uirtute gladium P.

15. (in illo priori de (in P) quo) comprehensi sumus. Confessi sunt uiri qui AP.

   . . . comprehensi sunt uiri qui R.

XXVIII. 3. (dixerunt Cenez dux et) prophetae AP. seniores populi R.

  4. (plantatio mea) quae a me (nominata est) AVR. que fe ame P.

  6. super terram.   sicut commorantes AP, Ph. super terram commemorantes R.

  7. (non sciat) quod uideat . . . quae dicat AR.

             q°de non uideat . . . que discat P.

             quid uideat . . . que dicat V.

  8. (scintilla) ascendit AP, Ph.   descendit R. subdium Ph.

ortiens AP, Ph.   Ordiens VR.

spuma ebulliens AR.   Spumam ebullientem P, Ph.   dum mutauit AP, Ph.   demutauit R.

inuisibilis loci AP, Ph.   inuisibili R (*and* V *in verse* 9).

Hec pro fundamento (erunt) A.   hec fundamenta P, Ph.   profundamenta R.

et habitantibus in eis annis vii AP, Ph.   et in eis annis iiii°ʳ milia R (V).

  9. despumauerat AP, Ph.   de spuma erat firmamentum VR.

(hi erunt) qui habitabunt, et nomen homınıs illius* AP, Ph.   (*blank at end:* P *has in margin* ℞.)

qui habebunt nomen eius hominis VR.

XXIX. 3. (thesaurum domini in) Silon praeterea ne A.   Sylo preter ne PR.

  4. (sunt) praecessores (nostri) A.   predecessores P. uobis predecessores R.

XXX. 2. Ecce unum populum A : + elegeram PR.

5. Si (Sic P) potest occidenda ouis respondere in conspectu occidentis eam, cum et qui occidit et qui occiditur taceat, cum aliquoties contristetur in eam APR (*om.* occidit et qui R).

6. Nam uiuentibus illis ostendistis . . . mortuis autem his AP.

Nam cum uiuentibus his ostendissetis . . . tamen mortuis illis R.

Dum uos urunt hi qui uos monent AP.   dum urgent hi qui uos mouent, uos (demonstratis) R.

reconciliabitur AP.   inuiscerabitur RF.

XXXI. 1. ad impedienda (-um P). curruum AP. ad imp. uasa currum R.

2. conteremini uirtutem A.   conterite uirtutem P. conteratur uirtus R.

(numerus) congregatorum : *qu.* concrematorum. cf. VI. 15.

3. Iahel uxor : + Aber P.

et sume cibum et dormiens (-es P) ad uesperum AP.   et resume te et dormies et ad uesp. R.

(ibo ad matrem) meam Iahel et erit mihi mulier A.
                     meam O Iahel et eris michi
                     mulier P.
                     meam et Iahel erit michi mulier
                     R.

9. (persequens) non inuenisti AP.   laborasti R.

XXXII. 1. turrificationis A.   thurif- P.   turif- R.

cultores militiarum.   *Should we read* custodes ?

2. zelarent ei A.   zelaretur eum P.   zelarent eum R.

offeres pro me sacrificium quod donatum a me tibi A.

offer pro me sacr. quod tibi donatum est a me P.

offer mihi in sacrificium quod donatum est tibi a me R.

Ecce nunc fili offero te holocaustomata et in (+ eius P) manus te trado qui te donauit mihi (t.m.d.P) AP.

Ecce nunc offero te (+ in R) holocaustum deo, in manus te trado (+ ei R) qui te m.d. VR.

(Positus est) in hereditatem seculi AP.   ad
inhereditandum sec. R.

5. quaecumque foemina.   In tertio autem anno
appropinquans nati sunt ei AP.   quaec.
sic ffem. tert. anno appropinquans uiro et nati
sunt R.

11. dixit : discedite AP.   dixit adiciens : descendite
R.

12. (memoratus est et) iuuenum . . . (sponsionum)
AP.   nouarum R.

(Iahel) sola (direxit) AP.   soror R.

13. sponsionum minima quas disposuit nobis dicens :
Multa faciam miracula (mirabilia P) cum filiis
uestris AP.

sponsionum quas disposuit uobis.   Minima enim
uobis dicens multa fecit filiis uestris R.

(si) moratur (homo) AP.   moriatur R.

hymnizare deo, hymniza uel tu Debbora et euigilet sancti spiritus gratia in te et incipe laudare
opera domini AP.

Ymniza ymniza Debbora euigilet spiritus sanctus
uite (*or* in te) et incipe enunciare opera
fortissimi R.

15. quoniam populi securi ambulantes profecti sunt,
astra pugnabant (et astra pugnant VR) AVR.

quoniam sicuti populi ambulantes profecta sunt
astra et pugnabant P.

16. Erit similis A.   Erit autem similis P.   Eritque
similis R.

17. (tempus) praeparabitur AP.   properabitur R.

sed et castra de dispositionibus suis euertit et
expugnauit inimicos nostros AP.

sed et astra de dispositione sua ei expugnauerunt
inimicos nostros R.

18. de latis psalpingis psallauerunt.   Et cum psalle-
rent oblatisque sacrificiis dixit Debbora : Erit
hoc in testimonium psalpingum AP.

de latis psalphingis (psalf. R.) ut psalphidiarent
cum sacrificiis dixit (*om.* V) Debbora : Erit hoc
in testimonium psalphingarum VR.

XXXIII. 6. haec uerba dixerunt AP. in hec uerba
    dixerunt trenon dicentes R.
    (Sancta) quae rebat (ducatum) A. querebat P.
    que gerebat R.
    (obdurauit) septem A. sepem PR.
XXXIV. 2, 3. immolabat eis multo tempore * in hoc
    enim quod monstrabatur APR. (A *alone has the*
    asterisk.)
    multo tempore immolabat eis. In hoc enim
    demonstrabatur V.
  3. factum est ut angeli in potestate non essent AP.
    factum est in potestatem non essent R.
XXXV. 1. (ut excuteret) eos in montem et fugeret
    imminentes Madianitas AP.
                eos et in monte abscondens
  se imminentes Madianitas effugeret R.
XXXVI. 3. talenta XII AR. $\overline{\text{XII}}$ sicli P.
  4. ut quod loquantur A. + mentiantur P. unde
    habeant quid loquantur R.
XXXVII. 1. Et filium de concubina habens occidit
    fratres suos omnes uolens esse dux populi.
    Tunc conuenerunt A.
  Et filium nomine Abimelech de concubina habebat
  qui occidit, etc. P.
  Et filium de concubina habens qui occidit omnes
  fratres suos, etc. VR.
  2. suauitatem · uenite et sustinete ortus (hortus P)
    mei fructum AP.
    suauitatem uini et sustineor eis meum reddens
    fructum R.
    ad malum AP. ad mirtum R.
  3. per senticetum A. senticem PR.
  4. si dignus est Abimelech eorum quorum uult
    principatum sit AP.
    sit ignis Abimelech eorum qui uolunt principari
    sibi et sit R.
    et exiuit (ignis) AP. Et sicut ex. R.
  5. et mortuus est. Et dimittente muliere super eum
    medium fragmentum molae aedificauit sacrarium
    Baal A.

et mortuus est sub quadam turre muliere inde super eum demittente medium fragmentum mole. Deinde iudicauit israel iair uiginti duos annos qui edificauit, etc. P.

et mortuus est demittente muliere super eum de muro medium fragmentum mole. Ipse edificauit, etc. VR.

XXXVIII. 4. ut uenit usque (*om*. R) ad locum iair AR. ut uenit iair usque ad locum P.

XXXIX. 4. *fin.* praessurae nostrae A + Et ideo non sit ita coram te PVR + domine PR.

   8. aut contristaris? quare tibi non praecepit Israel ut disperderes AV.

aut cur contristas nos? Tibi non precepit deus isr. ut disp. P.

(*om*.) Quare non prec tibi isr. ut disp. R.

(Si) quod minus A. quominus PR.

   9. Putabat Israel in quantum acceperat terram Amorrhaeorum? AP.

Putabat Israel quoniam in quantum acceperat terram amorrhaeorum possideatur R.

adduxit te deus ut disperdam te nisi requiescas AP.

adduxit deus regem filiorum ammon ut disperdat eum nisi quiescat R.

  10. (et in) praecinctu (pugnaret) A. procinctu PR. oratio (Iepthae) AR. iuratio P.

XL. 1. uidebo utrum epulatio AR. uidebo quis preponderabit, etc. R.

   3. permeem (in collibus) A. permaneam P. maneam R.

   4. *fin.* omni tempore: + et abiens decidet in synum matrum suarum R.

   6. *seq. The variants of the Lament have been set forth in the Introduction, pp. 24 sqq.*

XLII. 1., etc. Manuc A. Manue PR. (P *always*, R *usually*.)

   2. immescat (in peccatis suis) A. ingemiscat PR.

   7. uenit (ad angelum) in agro in animo A. in agro in ammo P. *om.* in animo R.

facie ad faciem : + et dixit manuc R

XLIII. 7. quoniam uisus quem isti sustulerunt mihi
gratis mihi datus est a te AP.

quoniam hec ab his edificata sunt, uisum autem
quem sustulerunt mihi datus mihi est R.

morere corpus (+ meum VR) et AVR. mori
corpore ac P.

XLIV. 2. dragmas (auri) AP. didragmata VR.

quatuor tegulas A. ligulas PVR.

5. (effigies) tres (puerorum) A(V)R. sex P.

6. (Et) nunc A. tunc PVR.

acceptauerunt ut non facerent idola nec opera
deorum omnium qui AV(R).

acc. Et nunc quod dixi eis ut non facerent idola.

fecerunt opera deorum eorum qui P.

7. Sed eos per quae facta sunt omnia corrupta A.

et eorum per quos sunt omnia corrupta P.

Sed per eos per quos facta sunt omnia corrupta VR.

8. hominum, et ut eradicem plasmata (-os P) AP.

hominum eorum et succidam radicem plasmatis R.

10. in adinuentionibus quae (quas P) faciunt, sed
omni homini erit illa punitio ut in quo peccato
peccauerit in eo adiudicabitur (diiud- P) AP.

in adinuentionibus suis. Nec solum his qui
faciunt ydola erit prima punitio sed omnis homo
in quo, etc., in eo et iudicabitur R.

XLV. 5. Seron A. Sylon PR. Si facta est talis
iniquitas (+ in P) Israel AP + pausabit Israel R.

6. Anteciminum A (R). anticiminum P. anteci^{i}mu^{nu}
V.

In terra in qua. *Read:* In hora?

quam (uersute) A. cum PR.

et draconis : + non conturbatus est P.

ut eum peccatores consumant quam iniqua
gerentes A.

ut eos peccatores consumant et iniqua gerentes P.

ut cum peccatoribus consumentur iniqua gerentes R.

Read: ut tam peccatores consumantur quam, etc.

XLVI. 2. Et si parcitis non pugnabimus contra uos
AP.

Si non parcitis etiam pugnabimus contra uos R.

4. ut aequaliter cadant qui faciunt iniqua AP.

ut eq. cadant iam (*l.* tam) innoxii quam hi qui . . . R.

(quare non renuntiasti nobis) ut incenderemus A.

ut non ascenderemus P.   ut intenderemus R.

XLVII. 1. et ingressus intraui ego et zelatus sum animae meae AP.

et ingressus intrauit ad Madianitam, et ego zelatus sum zelum animae R.

6. uidit alius catulus leonem de alia sylua tanta et dixit A.

uidit unus catulus de alia silua magna leonem et dixit P.

uidit unus catulus leonem de alia silua tanta mala et dixit R.

minoretur A.   aretur PR.

Oportet AP.   opportuerat R.

et sic constituens residua A.   ne sic constituam residua P.   et sic constitui residua R.

8. Propterea vos fefelli -illos *om.* P.

fin. gesserunt : + in me.   Sed uos ascendite nunc quia tradam illos uobis P.

11. Et decima patria Enophlasa, etc. A.   Et de Octaua p. P.   De VIII^a VIIII^a et X^{ma} patria R.

XLVIII. 1. (habita) Danaben in monte A.   in monte danaben P.

in danaben in monte VR.   in danaben monte F.

2. Et ascendit Phinees et fecit omnia quae praecepit ei dominus.   In diebus autem quibus constituit AR.

Et ascendit Fin.   Ipse enim fecit omnia quae praecepit ei dominus omnibus diebus quibus constituit P.

XLIX. 2. de domino quia non respondit nobis.   Et nunc sortiamur uel per tribus si uel per multitudinem AP.

a domino propter quod nobis respondebit—tribus et uideamus si per multitudinem R.

4. sortitus est Armathen A.   sortiata est Arm. P.

sortita est Armathes R.

6. (factus est) in sorte si non repugnaret AP.   In
   sorte repugnans R.
   locus (pausationis et R) requietionis.

7. *fin.* plurimis annis usque ad annos multos.   *Ap-*
   parently a doublet.

8. (de manu odientium.)   Et in illa die fecerunt
   sacrificia AP.   Et dixit dominus̄ in illa die ut
   facerent sacrificia R.

L. 2. non est dilectus mulieris si diligat AP.   Non
   est dilecta mulier etiam si diligat R.
   confusa (est) A.   perfusa PR.

  5. et erit ut plus me zelans improperet Phenenna A.
   et fiat plus me z. inproperet mihi Fenenna P.
   et plus me z. fenenna improperet mihi R.

  6. (aufer uinum tuum) arae A.   a te PR.
   si siti (sit P) in me exaudita est oratio mea ut
   ebrie audiam (*small blank in* P) AP.
   sic est exaudita est oratio mea ut ebria audiam R.

  7. (quoniam) scis (pro quibus oraueris) AP.   scio R.

LI. 2. (ut statuas) prophetiam A.   profectum P.
   proficuum R.

  3. (populus illuminabitur) aceruus eius A.
   a uerbis eius PR.

  6. (Et haec) si (manent) A.   sic PR.

LII. 3. et non tantummodo delebo A.   et tanta mala
   in uobis modo non delebo P.   et tantummodo
   dolebo (delebo R) VR.
   et si hoc factum fuerit uocabo culpam A.   et si
   hoc ṇoṇ fuerit factum uocabo f̣ạc̣ṭụṃ culpam P.
   et si hoc factum fuerit uacabo culpa VR.

  4. non datum est ut peniterentur AP.   non datum
   est cor ut penitentiam agerent R.

LIII. 2. similis est Mosi famulo meo octogenario.
   Locutus sum Samuel octo annorum est A.
   similis est Mosi famulo meo octogenario locuturus
   sum Samuel octo annorum enim est P.
   similis, etc., meo.   Octogenario (-us V).   Moysi
   locutus sum.   Samuel, etc. VR.

  4. *init. blank in* A.   Et ait heli P.   Et dixit heli
   VR.

sciam (quia angelus) A.   scient P.   scio R.

7. tu plus de me nosti MSS.   *qu.* tu me plasmasti?
   as just above.

9. (praecepi) tertiae tabernaculi A.   terre tabernaculi
   P.   *om.* R.

13. Si respondebit plasma ei qui eum (plasmauit) AP.
    Sicut non respondebit ei plasma qui ipsum R.

LIV. 4. recepit (Israel) A.   reliquid P.   reiecit R.

6. mulier Heli A.   mulier filii heli P.   mulier finees
   R.

LV. 1. (inspice locum) Aromathae ubi   erit AP.
    (Aromate P) Arimathe ubi erat R.

4. Acharon A.   in accaron PR.
   periet (periit P) fructus uentris nostri (+ et P)
      quoniam repentia quae missa sunt in nos AP.
   disperdet fructus nostri quoniam reptantia que
      misit in nos R.
   sugentes: + mammas R.   (eas) qui lactant AP.
      que lactabunt R.

5. et conueniens dominatio AP.   aut conu. tempor
   arie dominatio R.

7. (Non hoc tantum) tempus AR.   temptetis P.
   initio trium uiarum quae sunt circa Acharon
      ponamus uaccas.   Media enim uia dirigite
      Acharon et dextera in Iudaeam.   Et si sinis-
      tram uiam proficiscentes in Iudaeam sciemus
      A.
   initio trium uiarum quae sunt circa accaron.   et
      dextra in iudeam.   media uia dirigite uaccas
      archam portantes.   Eſ si sinistram uiam profi-
      ciscantur in iudeam sciemus P.
   initio trium uiarum quae sunt circa accaron.
      Media enim uia accaron dirigit (dirigite R) et
      dextra in iudeam et sinistra in samariam.   Et
      si dextra uia proficiscentes dirigant in iudeam,
      sciemus VR.
   ut nunc deos nostros negauimus AP.   et nunc de
      hoc deos nostros negabimus VR.

LVI. 2. Quod si totum (ita P) uoluerit dominus AP.
    quod si in totum noluerit dominus R.

4, 5. (Et dixit ad eum Samuel) : Resume te mecum A. Ego sum qui uideo. Resume, etc., P.

Ego sum qui uideo. Et ille dixit : Si poteris mihi adnuntiare de asinis patris sui quoniam perierunt ? Et dixit ad eum Samuel. Resume tecum hic R.

6. (uerbum tuum) per se uenire AP. perseuerare R.

LVII. 4. Nunc statue super nos regem qui nos iudicet AP. Tunc diximus constitue super nos regem qui iudicet nos per omnia R.

(Viuat) propheta Samuel. Et constituente (constituto P) rege AP. propheta Samuel consistente rege R.

attulerunt AP. Et attulerunt R.

LVIII. 3. (mulierem eius) consuluerunt (quousque pariat) A. consolatur P. conseruabunt R.

4. quem nocuit Israel quoniam A. quoniam nocuit Israeli quod P. quam uocauit Israel quoniam R.

LIX. 3. mitte adhuc filium AP. mitte et adduc filium R.

LX. *Song of David. For the variants see p. 22.*

LXI. 2. captiuare (-ri P) te faciam et populum tuum seruire AP.

captiuabo te et faciam te et populum tuum seruire R.

5. Ceruihel A. Ceruiel P. Zervihel VF. R *omits the clause.*

6. exurgens hodie uenisti deuastare Israel natus de cognatione tua ecce ueni (uenio P) et ego uindicare populum meum AP.

exurgis hodie deuorare (deuotare F) israel sicut natus de cognatione tua et ecce ego ueni uindicare populum tuum R.

et tunc dicitis (matri uestrae) AP. et abibitis et gloriantes dicetis R.

LXII. 2. Et abiit Saul AP. Et abiit spiritus a saul R.

4. ut audiant determinationem multitudo prudentium (-tum P) AP.

ut audiat determinationes congregatorum prudentium R.

5. nunquam (+ impune P) effundet AP.   nunquam
    effugiet R.
9. ut separemur ab inuicem AP.   ut non saturemur
    in alterutrum R.
LXIII. 2. Doech (Dohec R) Syrus : + qui super
    mulas erat Saul R.
    Tune scis A.   Tu nescis P.   Tu scis R.
4. Et ad Adoch (Doech P) Syrum haec dixit AP.
    Et addo hec syrum dixit R.
5. in libro regum Israel AP.   in libro uerborum
    regum israel R.
LXIV. 3. (Sedecla) nomine et haec filia Debicum
                    dianitae A.
            nomine et haec filia Debin Madi-
            anite P.
            nomine filia Adod madianite VR.
LXV. 4. Edab A.   Edabus P.   Eduabus R.

APPENDIX II

ON THE VOCABULARY, ETC. OF THE LATIN VERSION

SOMETHING has been said of the language of our Latin version of *Philo* in the Introduction. The limits of this edition do not permit of my supplementing those observations by a full study of the version from a linguistic point of view. Naturally its nearest congeners will be found in the Old Latin versions of the historical books of the Old Testament and of such books as *Jubilees*, *Assumption of Moses*, and *Ascension of Isaiah*. The marked resemblance to the Latin of 4 *Esdras* has been illustrated to some extent on pp. 54–58. It is perhaps nearest to our book of any. Our Latin *Esdras* is quoted copiously by Ambrose in the fourth century, and he is the first writer who certainly quotes it. We do not know how long before his time the version was made. That this of *Philo* belongs to the same school, and is therefore not later than the fourth century, seems obvious. I know of no evidence which should lead us to date it earlier than the third.

For the convenience of students I have put together in this Appendix lists of (*a*) the Greek words, (*b*) the more remarkable Latin words, (*c*) some frequently recurring words, in *Philo*. The last is supplementary to one in the Introduction (p. 29).

(*a*) Greek words in *Philo*, in the order of their first occurrence in the text.

II. 7. psalmus, organum; 8. cynera, cithara, psalterium.

III. 4. cedrinus; 5. abyssus, cataracta; 7. cataclysmus; 8. holocaustoma; 10. paratece.

V. 4. sceptrum.

VI. 9. petra ; 16. caminus.

VII. 3. calamus.

IX. 2. omotocea, idolum ; 5. melotis ; 6 zelari ; 10. byssinus ; 12. tybis ; 14. presbyter ; 15. zaticon (διαθήκην).

X. 1. pammixia, cynifes ; 7. ortigometra.

XI. 1. eremus ; 4. angelus ; 8. sabbatum, ecclesia, cathedra, pausare ; 10. moechari ; 14. lampas ; 15. myrrha (Mara, LXX Μερρα), basis (= xiii. i), epomis, logion.

XII. 8. thronus ; 9. aroma (iaspis *wrongly*) balsamum, cinnamomum, myrrha, costum.

XIII. 1. cidaris ; 3. lepra -osus, hyssopus, coccinum, azyma ; 5. hebdomas ; 6. psalphinga ; 7. scenopegia ; 8. protoplastus ; 9. paradisus.

XV. 4. romphaea.

XVI. 5. plasmare ; 6. synagoga.

XVII. 2, 3. amygdalus, -inus.

XVIII. 7. holocaustum ; 8. in gyro, scandalum ; 10. parabola ; 11. dogma ; 12. prophetia.

XIX. 7. inplanari ; 15. stigma, *conj.*, cyathus ; 16. hymnus.

XX. 2. zona ; 5. prophetare.

XXI. 3. anathema ; 8. hymnizare, tympanum, chorus, nabla ; 9. psallere.

XXIII. 3. oroma (ὅραμα) ; 5. metra ; 7. propheta.

XXV. 1. allophili ; 9. daemon ; 10. nympha ; 11. crystallinus, prasinus, caraxatus (*v. l.*), stigmatus.

XXVI. 10, 11. *names of gems.*

XXVII. 6. psalpingare ; 7. theca.

XXVIII. 6. prophetatio.

XXIX. 3 talentum.

XXX. 5. cilicium.

XXXII. 15. plasmatio ; 18. psalphidiare, *v. l.*

XXXIII. 6. trenus *v. l.*

XXXIV. 2. magica.

XXXVII. 3. hypocrisis.

XL. 1. statera ; 5. trenus ; 6. thalamus, hyacinthinus.

XLIII. 3. plectrum.

XLIV. 2. dragma, didragma ; 4. draco ; 7. zelus ; 8. plasma.

XLV. 6. anticiminus.

XLVII. 11. patria = *family.*

XLVII. 3. pascha.

L. 5. blasphemare.

LI. 6. Christus.

LIII. 11. prophetizare, evangelizare (*and* LXV. 1., *both times of bad news*).

LX. 3. Tartarus, chaoma.

LXIV. 6. stola, diploïs.

LXV. 3. machaera.

(*b*) Notable Latin words in *Philo* in the order of their first occurrence in the text.

I. 20. natiuitas.

II. 7, 8. initiare ; 9. aeramentum χαλκόσ obseruatio = *speech.*

III. 3. malignitas, procreatio, uiuificare, *here* = ζωο-ποιεῖν *elsewhere* ζωογονεῖν *keep alive ;* 8. requietio, ἀνά- *or* κατά-παυσισ ; 10. adinuentio ἐπιτήδευμα iustificare ; 11. innubilare συννεφεῖν.

IV. 5. ampliare ; 16. imaginari.

V. 2, 4. considerare, consideratio, *review ;* 4. ducatus -atio ἡγεμονία uirtutificare ἐνδυναμοῦν.

VI. 7. stipendia, *provisions ;* 9. animositas, *wrath* (XXI. 4, *eagerness*) ; 16. liquefactus sensu ; 17. laesura.

VII. 4. eiicere ἐξάγειν.

VIII. 1. conceptus *subst. ;* 8. passio πληγή ; 10. malignari πονηρεύεσθαι.

IX. 3. Celerius est ut, inmensurabilis, minorare ἐλαττοῦν ; 4. amplificare ; 5. recogitare ; 8. super-excellentia, mediator.

X. 1. (in) tractabilis primitiuus πρωτότοκοσ.

XI. inhabitabilia ; 4. coruscantes ἀστραπαί *elsewhere* coruscus- atio, frequentare ; 6. abominamentum βδέ-λυγμα ; 8. operatio *workpeople.*

XII. 2. appropiare *trans.* effigiare, conflatilis ; 4. praeuaricari, sponsio ; 6. ad uictoriam εἰσ νῖκοσ, amaritudo ; 8. sarmentum, refrigerare.

XIII. 1. praecinctoria ; 4. iocundari, memorialis ;

6. prospeculator ;   10. saluatio, lucrificatio, sterilizare *intrans*.

XIV. 4. mortificare, decimatio (*v. l.* demptio).

XV. 1. contribulare συντρίβειν ; 5. tabefacere umbraculum *v. l.*, sanctimonium ; 7. pietas.

XVI. 1. insufferibilis ; 3. tabescere, rememorari ; 4. diffidens.

XVII. 3. decoriatus albidus *v. l.*, cinerarius σποδοειδής *conj.*

XVIII. 1. haereditare *trans.* ; 2. honorificare, 5. sacrarium, componi in sacrario, acceptabilis ; 7. propitiari ;   10.   intenebriscare   (-bricare)   -brificare XXXII. 10. plantago ; 11. in desiderio (XXIII. 2), superflue ; 12. dissolutio, fraudare.

XIX. 8. solidare (XXIII. 10 : solidari LIII. 2) ; 9. constabilire ;   10. irrigatio, sanctuarium ;   11. similare (assimilare *often*) ; 12. dormificare *v. l.* ; 13. breuiare ; 14. momentum (LVIII. 4), unanimis, recessus *death* (XXXIII. 4).

XX. 3. intelligentia ; 4. extollentia μετεωρισμόσ ; 5. principari, beneplacitum.

XXI. 1. processior (dierum) ; 6. foetans.

XXII. 3. amputare, prolongare ; 7. excusatio, praescius.

XXIII. 4. dolatura ; 5. praesumptio, superducere ἐπάγειν ; 6. trimus, expiare ; 10. obturare, mansuetari ἡμεροῦν animari ; 14. innouatio, epulatio *feast* (XL. 1. epulatio *joy* epulans *joyful*).

XXV. 6. astute agere ; 11. picturae, varietas, consecratio, ostentare ; 12. inaestimabilis, explendere (splendere), sequestrare ; 13. perscrutari.

XXVI. 5. recongregare uersute ; 7. superponere (*techn.*) ; 8. ros *neuter* (flos *neuter* LII. 7) ; 10. consimilari, distinctio, terebratus *v. l.* ; 13. potentari.

XXVII. 2. conterere ; 3. quinquagenarius ; 6. conuersari ; 7. euaginare ; 11. indissolubiliter ; 15. transducere παραδειγματίζειν, ἐλέγχειν.

XXVIII. 4. plantatio -ator ; 5. perpeccare διαμαρτάνειν ; 6. praedestinatus ; 7. suspensorium, inapparens ; 8. substernere-stratum, subdiuum, ordiri ; 10. corruptibilis.

XXIX. 1. audire *be called* (L. 6.) ; 2. cultiua *neut. pl.; 3.* praeter (-ea) ne ; 4. praecessor XXXVII. 3, XXXVIII. 2.

XXX. 4. replacari ; 6. inuiscerari σπλαγχνίζεσθαι *v. l.*

XXXI. 5. ducator ; 7. percussit de malleo ; 9. persecutio *pursuit.*

XXXII. 1. turrificatio (15. turrificare) ; 3. beatitudo, dignificare ; 7. promptuarium (XXXII. 13), compago ; 12. iuuenis *adj.;* 14. pressura θλῖψισ ; 17. iustificatio.

XXXIII. 3. depositum ; 6. sepes.

XXXIV. 1. maleficus -ficium.

XXXV. 2. singularis ; 4. arguere ἐλέγχειν ; 5. directum bonum.

XXXVI. 2. tubare, ululare ; 3. dextrale (-is), pensare ; 4. redarguere.

XXXVII. 2. perseverantia, deinceps, praelucere, senticetum, castigator.

XXXIX. 1. coangustari ; 8. importunus, subdolus ; 10. procinctus *subst. v. l.*

XL. 1. resolutus est (LIV. 6) in cantico uotorum ; 3. postulatio, permeare, campestris, praeoccupare, spontanea ; conuirginales (-gines) sensatus συνετόσ ; 5. recedere *die,* fronire (= frui), nere, stratoria, ingenuitas *v. 1.;* 7. inueterare.

XL. 1. remissio.

XLII. 1. experimentum ; 2. altercari, solarium ὑπερῷον ingemiscere *v. l.;* 8. gratificari tibi.

XLIII. 5. fornicaria, commixtio ; 6. soporatus ; 8. iactare *shake.*

XLIV. 2. ligula *v. l.;* 4. multiformis, irreligiositas ; 6. eradicare, acceptare, corruptela ; 7. conflatio, inhonorificare, creator ; 8. exhorresco, impunis ; 10. mentiri *trans.* discernere *separate.*

XLVI. 2. indurare.

XLVII. 3. attente orare ; 6. exagitare.

XLIX. 1. inconueniens ; 3. cogitatus *subst.;* 5. superuolare (sors).

L. 1. improperare (-ium 7) ; 2. perfundi *v. l.;* 3. es = edis, inspeculari ; 6. anxiari ; 8. praenumerare, mitificare.

LI. 3. alloquutio ; 4. gloriatio.

s

LII. 2. exterere ; 4. aduersantes.

LIII. 7. possibilis ; 12. nutritor.

LIV. 2. intonare ; 6. resumere se, captiuare.

LV. 1. ueterascere παλαιοῦσθαι; 3. crucifigere ; 5. conueniens (temporarie *v. l.*) dominatio ; 6. filii uaccarum ; 7. ualidum tempus ; 6. sedilia.

LVII. 5. expedientissimus.

LIX. 2. exprobratio.

LX. 1. praefocare πνίγειν; 2. compaginatio, extensio ; 3. resultatio.

LXI. 6. deuastare (deuotare *v. l.*); 8. interfector.

LII. 5. mollis dierum.

LIII. 1. exprobrantes primitiua ; 4. inextinguibilis.

LXIV. 7. inquietare παρενοχλεῖν traditio, red(d)itio ; 8. exoratio.

(*c*) Words of common occurrence in *Philo*, with the number of times they occur—

cogitare, 19	militiae (*of angels*), 5
complere, 25	mittere *to put*, 10
contaminare, 9	multiplicare, 17
delere, 7	obaudire, 10
disperdere, 15	operari, 12
dissipare, 6	peccare -ator -atum, 63
eiicere, 8	permanere, 14
exstinguere, 7	pessimus, 9
firmamentum, 6	salus, 7
fortissimus (*of God*) 9	sensus, 8
fundamentum, 11	sponsio, 7
intendere, 14	uisitare, 5
liberare, 24	

INDEX

NOTE.—I have not included in this Index the numerous proper names which occur in the genealogies or in other groups of names invented by the author (at pp. 90, 151, 159, 187, 210) nor the very corrupt place-names on pp. 78, 83, 84. Also, reference to the several tribes of Israel must be sought under *Patriarchs and Tribes*.

Benjamin, war with, 206 sqq. ;
survivors, 210
Bethac, 204, 218
Bethel (mistake for Bethlehem),
231
Bonutius, J., 8

Cain, 75, 77, 120
Caleb, 118, 135
Calf, Golden, 111 sq., 149
Cambridge, MS. at, 18, 243
Cappadocians, 84
Cassel, MS. at, 13, 14, 15
Cedrenus, Georgius, 103 n.
Cenez. *See* Kenaz
Census of descendants of Noah,
86–9
Cervihel (Zeruel), angel, 161,
234
Chaleb. *See* Caleb
Cham. *See* Ham
Cheltenham, MS. at. *See*
Phillipps
Chemosh, 126
Choreb. *See* Korah
Christus, 41
Chronicles, Book of, 33
Chronology, 75 n.
Cities founded, 78, 84
Clement of Alexandria, 103 n.
Cohn, L., 9, 29–31, notes *passim*
Commandments, Ten. *See*
Decalogue
Commelin, 8
Corbie, MS. at, 11 n.
Core. *See* Korah
Costum, 113
Cues, MS. at, 14, 16

Dagon, 225
Dalila, 198
Damigeron, 152 n.
Danaber, Mount, 210
Date of *Philo*, 29 sqq.
David, text of his Song, 22, 60 ;
story of, 231–42
Debin, 240
Deborah (Debbora), 170 ; song
of, 174 sqq. ; death of, 179

Decalogue, 107 sqq., 201 sqq.
Dedila, mother of Micah, 200,
210
Deli (place), 94
Delilah, 198
Demonology, 39
Demonstration and Truth. *See*
Urim and Thummim.
Diatretos, 151 n.
Dinah, 97
Divination, origin of, 86
Divisions of *Philo*, 71
Doech, Doeg, 237, 242 n.
Dove, simile of, 137, 189

Ebal. *See* Gebal
Edab, son of Agag, 60, 242
Effrem. *See* Ephraim
Egypt, Israel in, 100 sqq.
Ehud. *See* Aod
Elas, 149, 150
Elchana. *See* Elkanah
Eldad and Medad, 134
Eleazar the priest, 140, 149,
164 ; mighty man, 161 n.
Eli, 215, 218 sqq. ; death, 224
Eliab, 231
Elias, Elijah, 59, 61 ; Apoca-
lypse of, 158 n. *See* Phineas
Elkanah, 213 sqq., 218, 221
Elon, judge, 195
Eluma, mother of Samson, 195
sqq.
Endor, witch of, 240
Enoch, 77 ; Book of, and *Philo*,
43 ; 181 n.
Ephraim, Mount, 145, 169, 228
Ephrata, 194
Epiphanius, *Vit. Proph.*, 61 n.,
146 n. ; *de lapid.*, 152 n.
Esau, wives and sons of, 97,
143, 176, 247
Eschatology of *Philo*, 34 sqq.
Esdras (4) and *Philo*, 54 sqq.,
95 n., 131 n., 269
Esther, 73
Euilath. *See* Havilah.
Eye hath not seen, etc., 157 n.
Ezekiel, 165 n.